# A Critical
# Handbook
# of Japanese
# Film Directors

# A Critical Handbook of Japanese Film Directors

## From the Silent Era to the Present Day

Alexander Jacoby

Foreword by Donald Richie

Stone Bridge Press • Berkeley, California

*Published by*
Stone Bridge Press
P.O. Box 8208
Berkeley, CA 94707
TEL 510-524-8732 • sbp@stonebridge.com • www.stonebridge.com

Text © 2008 Alexander Jacoby.

Cover design by Linda Ronan.

The author gratefully acknowledges the support of the Daiwa Anglo-Japanese Foundation.

Printed in the United States of America.

2013 2012 2011 2010 2009 2008     10 9 8 7 6 5 4 3 2 1

LIBRARY OF CONGRESS CATALOGING-IN-PUBLICATION DATA
Jacoby, Alexander.
  A critical handbook of Japanese film directors : from the silent era to the present day / Alexander Jacoby ; foreword by Donald Richie.
    p. cm.
  Includes bibliographical references and index.
  ISBN 978-1-933330-53-2 (pbk.)
  1. Motion picture producers and directors—Japan—Biography—Dictionaries. 2. Motion picture producers and directors—Japan—Credits. 3. Motion pictures—Japan. I. Title.
  PN1998.2.J29 2008
  791.43023'3092252—dc22
  [B]
                    2008007836

*To D.R. and D.R.*

# Contents

# Foreword

This is a book for which there is a need. Not only does it list almost all important Japanese film directors and their works, it is also the first recent volume to give a description of the director's work, to indicate the nature of his or her accomplishment.

Back in the mid-1950s when Joseph Anderson and I were writing *The Japanese Film: Art and Industry*, the first book in English on Japanese cinema, we initially spent much of our time making lists and sketching profiles. These lists were all concerned with chronology, with genre, and with who did what. The most difficult yet most necessary of these listings were those given over to film directors and their work.

The necessity was that each director's work offered a dimension to the Japanese cinema as a whole and we could not describe this until we had examined everything he had done. The difficulty was that there were few sources.

Naturally, we used Japanese-language resources in this research, but these besides being few were often incomplete, particularly for earlier directors. I remember our trying to find out about early works by such directors as Shōzō Makino, or attempting to identify all of the films by such a prolific director as Hiroshi Inagaki. Even a director as well-known as Kenji Mizoguchi did not then have a complete filmography that we could use.

Fortunately we had the assistance of the late Tokutarō Osawa, then editor of the film magazine, *Eiga Hyron*, who remembered things everyone else had forgotten. And, just as providential for us, Jun'ichirō Tanaka was, as we wrote, publishing his monumental history of the Japanese film and we could check our lists against his.

Such directories of directors are extremely helpful. They indicate the shape of the career, give examples of its contours. They help trace development, or lack of it and offer a full account of a life's work. They record and they register.

Nonetheless such a full accounting in English of the complete works of those who made the Japanese film has been long in coming. The first appeared as late as 1971 when Arne Svenson wrote his *Screen Series Guide: Japan*. Though useful (not only directors but also actors and technicians were listed), it did not pretend to be complete and was further limited by being a volume in a series which designated how long the manuscript. should be. For present purposes it is also restricted in that its cut-off date for inclusion was 1969.

Then, in 1996, came *The Japanese Filmography: 1900–1994* by Stuart Galbraith IV. It included more complete entries on directors, actors, and others contributing to the film. In addition it gave full cast and credits for 1,300 Japanese films, a feat yet to be equalled.

In 1998 appeared (to subscribers) Stephen Cremin's *The Asian Film Library Reference to Japanese Film*. This was a large loose-leaved, two-volume work: the first of which listed the films, with basic credits; the second listed directors, actors, photographers, producers, etc. Here was the most complete director-listings yet.

Useful as these volumes were, however, they were never marketed in a manner which made them available to all. Also it appears that they have not been regularly updated which leaves a decade's worth of film and film directors unaccounted for.

There is thus a real need for Alexander Jacoby's new comprehensive register of Japanese film directors and their works. He lists everything and gives succinct descriptions of each director included. The reader is thus provided not only with a record but also with an indication of the director's accomplishments and the critical opinion which has followed these.

There has never been in English a more comprehensive compilation than this, and even many Japanese sources are not this complete. This is the book which, had Joe and I had it back in the Fifties, would have been enormously useful to us. It would have helped us as it will now help all scholars, researchers, students, and fans of the Japanese film.

*Donald Richie*

# Introduction

In the first decade of the twenty-first century, the Japanese cinema found itself with at least two separate audiences in the West. There was the audience that had made an overwhelming success of international touring retrospectives devoted to such classical directors as Kenji Mizoguchi, Yasujirō Ozu, and Akira Kurosawa, whose work, some fifty years earlier, had first brought Japanese films to international attention. At the same time, another set of viewers was enjoying a different mode of Japanese filmmaking, typified by the eerie "J-horror" of Hideo Nakata or the gangster films of Takeshi Kitano. When this audience looked back into the history of Japanese film, it was to the gritty *yakuza* movies of Kinji Fukasaku or the flamboyant samurai films of Kenji Misumi. The two audiences rarely met, the former inhabiting art houses and *cinémathèques*, the latter exploring the expanding DVD market.

That the cinema of one nation can sustain two international audiences with such different interests, concerns, and priorities is a mark of its abiding richness and variety. The Japanese cinema cannot easily be defined, any more than can the country that produced it. The neon and concrete city is as "typically Japanese" as the forested mountain; the *zen* garden as the *pachinko* parlor; the Noh theater as the comic strip. It is unsurprising that this contradictory country has produced a cinema of great range and scope. Japanese films can be among the world's most tender or the world's most violent; they can be understated or melodramatic, leisurely or hectic; in subject matter they span more than a thousand years of history and every genre. There is certainly enough variety in the Japanese cinema to satisfy a good deal more than two audiences.

Inevitably, then, this book is intended for more than one group of readers; and its focus is the common factor which links the various international audiences for Japanese films. This is an awareness of the people who made the films. When the first English-language history of the Japanese cinema, Joseph Anderson and Donald Richie's *The Japanese Film: Art and Industry*, was published in 1959, it was dedicated to "that little band of men who have tried to make the Japanese film industry what every film industry should be: a director's cinema." Viewers of both classical and modern Japanese films are likely to second that sentiment. Applied to the Japanese cinema, the *auteur* theory has never been controversial. In the days when the theory was in its infancy, and when the arbiters of critical opinion in the West still refused to endorse the attention being extended to Hitchcock and Hawks in the pages of *Cahiers du Cinéma*, no one doubted that Kurosawa and Mizoguchi were the authors of their own films. It would have come as a shock to many in the West to discover that Japan, as much as California, had a flourishing studio system, with its own codes, genres, and hierarchy of stars; it was easier to think of films such as *Rashomon* (*Rashōmon*, 1950) and *Ugetsu* (*Ugetsu monogatari*, 1953) as the lofty products of individual genius. In fact, the genius of the system was to allow a significant measure of freedom to individual directors, while providing the backing of substantial capital and resources. Artists such as Mizoguchi, Ozu, Keisuke Kinoshita, Kōzaburō Yoshimura, and (in the earlier part of his career) Kurosawa flourished not despite but because of this system. Their films would mostly °have been inconceivable without the technical resources of the big studios, which enabled their imaginative visions to become concrete reality. Yet until the 1960s, studio bosses were wise enough to know that the creativity of individual artists was their greatest asset.

In due course, the studio system declined. The major production companies still made films; but their work became increasingly repetitive and derivative. As the products of the major studios grew more routine, a growing number of talented directors, including Nagisa Ōshima, Shōhei Imamura, Yoshishige Yoshida, and Masahiro Shinoda, found that it was more profitable, in creative if not in financial terms, to operate outside the system. This made funding very much harder to obtain. From the mid-sixties onwards, those filmmakers who wished to work creatively often found that they had no choice but to establish independent production companies. Today, many of these directors have become cult figures, admired for their determination as well as for their achievement.

The 1970s and 1980s are often considered a low point in the quality of the Japanese film. To a degree, this is true. The studios produced more pedestrian work and opportunities to make films outside the studio system diminished. However, the growing availability of 8mm film stock enabled a younger generation of directors to begin to make films for private exhibition. Others trained in television or in the straight-to-video market, and initiatives such as the PIA film festival gave support to promising younger talents. The result was a minor Renaissance in the nineties, when a number of new directors in generic and art house cinema began to stamp their material with personal concerns and individual styles.

The Japanese cinema, then, in phases both of industrial and independent production, has been a director's cinema—which is to say that it is a cinema in which individual artists have been able to sustain their creativity and to explore personal concerns. And this creativity has been remarkably robust. Outstanding filmmakers have been at work in Japan from the twenties to the present day; there are periods of more and less consistent achievement, but Japanese directors have succeeded in producing distinguished films in every decade, despite social changes and varying political and economic pressures. Since the majority of this book will consist of profiles of these directors and accounts of their work, it is worth examining the context here. No one imagines that even the greatest artists conjure their work out of thin air; film production can be successfully undertaken only under favorable circumstances. In order to discuss the circumstances that have allowed Japanese filmmakers to produce work of so consistently high a standard, I want to provide a brief history of the development of the Japanese film.

### Film Before the Pacific War: The Birth of a System

The vitality of the studio system in the period from the 1920s to the early 1960s has already been mentioned, but the existence of such a system was not inevitable. It presupposes that there is capital to make films, a means to distribute them, and an audience to watch them. Japan, from the start, had all three. As early as 1909, the establishment of what was to become the Japan Cinematograph Corporation (Nippon Katsudō Shashin—later shortened to Nikkatsu) gave Japan a production company that owned both studios and theaters; it was thus possible to make and distribute films efficiently. By 1920 Nikkatsu had a major competitor, Shochiku, which entered the film production market after starting out as a Kabuki production company. Like Nikkatsu, Shochiku owned theaters; it also had the advantage of starting with substantial capital to produce and distribute films. In the decade from 1925 to 1935, the number of theaters in Japan doubled from just over eight hundred to well over fifteen hundred; at the same time, audiences steadily increased. The arrival of sound came a little later than in the U.S.A. or Europe, being widely accepted only from about 1935. This perhaps contributed to the smooth transition; sound equipment was by then sophisticated enough to avoid the problems that had beset talkies elsewhere in the world around 1930. Indeed, the early years of sound in Japan, from 1935 to about 1939, were among the richest periods of Japanese film production.

One of the favorable circumstances, both in the silent and early sound period, was that a ready audience existed for locally made films. In contrast to many countries, where imported films were more popular than domestic productions, the mass audience in Japan favored Japanese films from the start. This meant that the Japanese film industry, which scarcely exported any films in the prewar period, could remain profitable solely on the basis of domestic takings. It also meant that Japanese directors were able to develop a distinct style of filmmaking, different from the styles of the West. It is true that Western culture and Western aesthetics were fashionable in the late Meiji period (up to 1912) and the Taisho period (1912–26) when the Japanese cinema gradually achieved artistic maturity. Foreign productions were appreciated in sophisticated circles; and in the twenties, many critically admired Japanese films, such as Minoru Murata's classic *Souls on the Road* (*Rojō no reikon*, 1921) made for Shochiku, were consciously inspired by foreign literature (Gorky, Ibsen) and foreign cinema (D.W. Griffith). However, this fashionable Westernization was always an elite phenomenon, confined largely to a wealthy, urban milieu. The majority of filmgoers preferred *chanbara*—period films based on traditional Japanese narratives or historical events, the central attraction of which was slickly choreographed scenes of combat. In general, these films were less advanced technically than the Western-influenced cinema of the period, which tended to use more modern editing techniques and a greater variety of camera positions. But the existence of two traditions—a technically sophisticated, Westernized school of filmmaking and a technically primitive school which drew on native subject matter—paved the way for developments in the last years of the silent era, when techniques initially borrowed from the West were applied to specifically Japanese narratives. By the early thirties, directors such as Ozu, Mizoguchi, Daisuke Itō, and Shigeyoshi Suzuki were making films that were as technically advanced as any in the West, yet which adopted a style and subject matter that were unique to Japan.

Those years also saw the increasing emergence of different house styles at the major studios: for instance, the home drama or *shomin-geki* became the specialty of Shochiku, while Nikkatsu became notable for realistic period films (*jidai-geki*), producing some of the best films of Itō and of *wunderkind* Sadao Yamanaka. With the coming of sound, Nikkatsu also began to specialize in the *junbungaku* or "pure literature" film—drama based on respected novels—which was the favored genre of such directors as Tomu Uchida and Tomotaka Tasaka. In 1933, a new studio, P.C.L. (later renamed Toho) was founded specifically to take advantage of sound technology. It also specialized in literary adaptation, generally favoring modern novels, and allowing directors like Mikio Naruse and Sotoji Kimura to direct inventive and experimental films such as Naruse's early masterpiece, *Wife, Be Like a Rose* (*Tsuma yo bara no yōni*, 1935).

The coming of sound also furthered the evolution of a uniquely Japanese style. In the immediate prewar period, it may be admitted, the development of a particularly Japanese cinema was assisted by the country's growing political isolation. The general excellence of Japanese films in the late thirties is in sharp contrast to the gradual decline in quality of the cinemas of Germany and Russia, both countries which had produced outstanding films through the late twenties and early thirties. In fairness, the early films of Douglas

Sirk (Detlef Sierk, as he then was) in Nazi Germany, or the Soviet trilogy about the childhood and youth of Maxim Gorky, made by Mark Donskoi from 1938 to 1940, are evidence that talented directors could continue to produce films that were both stylish and not wholly consonant with the values of totalitarianism. In both these countries, however, creative cinema was increasingly scarce by the late thirties. Japanese directors, by contrast, continued to produce a considerable number of distinguished films. Moreover, the Japanese cinema of the late thirties is, in both style and subject matter, unlike any other national cinema. Noel Burch, in his fascinating but tendentious account of prewar cinema in Japan, has argued that "the social pressure to adopt Western modes undoubtedly abated during those dark years," and it may be that nationalist sentiment encouraged the development of a style of cinema influenced by Japanese traditions. Directors such as Mizoguchi in *The Story of the Late Chrysanthemums* (*Zangiku monogatari*, 1939) and Hiroshi Shimizu in his children's films perfected the use of long shots to situate characters in their environment, a technique owing much to the aesthetics of traditional Japanese painting. But those directors, along with others such as Mansaku Itami and, until his conscription and death, Yamanaka, continued through the thirties to make films with a strong element of social criticism. Moreover, some of the most individual aspects of Japanese films at this time actually incurred the disapproval of the authorities. The quotidian banality of Ozu's narratives, and those of other directors specializing in the realist genre of *shomin-geki*, had no parallel in Western popular cinema of the time. Yet this genre was specifically discouraged by the military government, since its slice-of-life method seemed to serve no purpose in furthering the militarist agenda. It is heartening that, at a time when a Japanese government inspired by nationalist ideals was perverting native traditions and leading the country to disaster, Japanese filmmakers were continuing to produce works of art founded in the more humane aspects of their cultural inheritance.

### Imperial Screen, Colonial Screen: Japanese Film in War and Occupation

Japan had pursued a full-scale war with China from 1937, and by the time the Pacific War broke out in 1941, the militarists had succeeded, more or less, in establishing a stranglehold over film production. The active companies were consolidated into three large concerns: Shochiku and Toho absorbed some smaller studios, while the new Daiei was founded from the rest. Scripts were vetted before production and individual talent was repressed: willingly or not, directors were obliged to produce work which furthered the war effort. With a few notable exceptions—for example, *The Life of Matsu the Untamed* (*Muhō Matsu no isshō*, 1943), a humane and moving period film, scripted by Mansaku Itami, directed by Hiroshi Inagaki—the films of the wartime period were too constrained by the ideology of the time to achieve the aesthetic distinction of their forebears. Nevertheless, the war provided an impetus to the careers of some younger directors. With many filmmakers drafted or otherwise engaged, assistants such as Kurosawa and Kinoshita found themselves abruptly promoted into the director's chair. Their careers would flower in the postwar era.

After Japan's surrender, the industry and its individual talents became subject to other controls. Many prewar and wartime films were deliberately destroyed by the Occupation authorities, further reducing an archive already depleted by aerial bombing, natural disasters, and plain indifference. Other films were released or re-released in censored prints. Meanwhile, the production of new films was subject to stringent criteria: scripts were censored, period films in general were discouraged, and directors were expected to promote democratic ideals. At times this led to rather heavy-handed social commentary: films such as Kinoshita's *Morning for the Osone Family* (*Ōsone-ke no asa*, 1946) were less concerned to create characters than to manufacture mouthpieces for political positions. But Allied dictates gave some directors the scope to explore personal interests which a purely commercial cinema might not have permitted. Mizoguchi's most uncompromisingly feminist films were produced in response to American demands that films show the emancipation of women, a theme that Mizoguchi pushed far further than MacArthur's regime can have intended; *My Love Has Been Burning* (*Waga koi wa moenu*, 1949), in particular, was more radical in its conclusions than any commercial Hollywood film dared to be either then or since. At around the same time, Kōzaburō Yoshimura made *The Ball at the Anjo House* (*Anjō-ke no butōkai*, 1947), the subject of which was the decline of the prewar aristocracy; with this film, the director initiated an intelligent analysis of social change in Japan which was to prove his abiding concern, lasting throughout the 1950s.

## The 1950s: The Genius of the System

Nevertheless, it was the departure of the occupying authorities in 1952 that heralded a Golden Age for the Japanese cinema. Censorship no longer promoted certain topics or prohibited others; indeed, the only regulation of content came from a voluntary body known as *Eirin*, which gave the industry and its artists a remarkable freedom to depict matters political, social, and personal. The studios did not, in general, provoke the wrath of the Moral Majority: fearing the re-imposition of government censorship, they eschewed the depiction of explicit sex or violence through the early and mid-fifties. Yet anyone comparing Japanese cinema of this period with Hollywood productions of the same era will notice the generally greater frankness of Japanese films. Shirō Toyoda's *Marital Relations* (*Meoto zenzai*, 1955), to take one example, attempts no explicit treatment of sexuality, yet it remains as emotionally perceptive and as adult an account of a love affair as any film produced anywhere in the world at that time.

At the same time, Japanese audiences remained avid consumers of Japanese films. By now the major studios had fully developed their distinctive house styles, appealing to different segments of the viewing public. Shochiku continued to be celebrated for the bittersweet "Ōfuna flavor"—named after the location of its studios outside Tokyo —of its home dramas, comedies, and melodramas, which directors such as Ozu and Kinoshita raised to its highest level. Toho's prestige director was Kurosawa, who made almost all his films there; otherwise, the studio made white-collar comedies

©Nikkatsu Corporation

Jochūkko / The Maid's Kid *(1955)*: *Director Tomotaka Tasaka's masterpiece, about a country girl in the big city, exemplified the richness of Japanese cinema in the 1950s.*

and monster movies, including the world-famous *Godzilla* (*Gojira*), directed by Ishirō Honda. Daiei made some prestigious adaptations of classic and contemporary literature, often focusing on female protagonists; Mizoguchi, Yoshimura, and Toyoda made some of their finest films there. Later in the decade, Daiei moved downmarket, making *chanbara* which profited from the flair of such expert younger artisans as Kenji Misumi. These established outfits were joined by the resurgent Nikkatsu, which had resumed production in 1954. Nikkatsu spent several years casting around for a style; this period of uncertainty produced at least one masterpiece, Tomotaka Tasaka's *The Maid's Kid* (*Jochūkko*, 1955), before the studio eventually decided to court the youth market. Two younger companies, Toei and ShinToho (the latter originally an offshoot of Toho), made more generic films: the former concentrated almost exclusively on *chanbara*, while the latter produced numerous thrillers and horror films. Among many relatively undistinguished films, Toei produced some superior *jidai-geki* and some of the major works of socially conscious filmmaker Tadashi Imai, while ShinToho was responsible for the striking ghost stories of Nobuo Nakagawa.

The balance of popular and prestige projects is notable, illustrating how, with a loyal audience and decent profit margins, the major studios were able to take risks, offering their best directors the freedom to pursue their own concerns. Of course, this freedom was never absolute; for instance, the plot of Mizoguchi's masterpiece, *Ugetsu*, was altered at studio insistence to provide a more commercially acceptable ending. Still, the cinema—a medium more than any other dependent on financial support—has always had to make such compromises. A film like *Ugetsu*, with its visual grandeur and dramatic scope, could not have been created outside the commercial system. That system gave directors such as Mizoguchi, Kurosawa, and Uchida the resources to produce meticulously detailed and richly atmospheric films, often on an epic scale. Yet the distinction of these films lay in the individuality of their attitude to people: the pessimistic humanism of Mizoguchi, the heroic humanism of Kurosawa, the satiric irony of Uchida. At the same time, the Japanese studio system produced the delicate family dramas of Ozu, the romantic tragedies of Naruse, Kinoshita's sentimental melodramas, and Heinosuke Gosho's varied, complex accounts of the emotional lives of men, women, and children. Compared to the historical epics of the period, these films were made on a small scale. Yet their visual beauty and outstanding acting continued to demonstrate the technical professionalism guaranteed by the studio system, while illustrating, at the same time, the personal concerns of their directors. Moreover, these personal concerns included a marked degree of social criticism, no less barbed for being subtly inflected.

For the studio system and its major artists, however, this Golden Age was also an autumnal one. In the late fifties, Japanese productions took three quarters of the domestic market share, and more than five hundred films were made annually. Yet within a decade the industry had virtually collapsed: its most creative established talents had either retired or were producing second-rate films, while the most creative artists of a younger generation were able to work only outside the studio system. When were the danger signs visible? Perhaps, even in the period of the Japanese cinema's outstanding achievement, there were some. In the first place, while the fifties produced some of the Japanese cinema's finest and more complex achievements, it also offered an increasing number of remakes: Hiroshi Inagaki's *Musashi Miyamoto* trilogy (1954–55), admired in the West, was a new version of a wartime production; Ozu, in *Floating Weeds* (*Ukigusa*, 1959) and *Good Morning* (*Ohayo*, 1959), reworked prewar successes. Yet this was not a new phenomenon: the Japanese cinema has always been accustomed to retelling old stories. Filmed accounts of the perennial *Chūshingura* story of the loyal 47 ronin had numbered in the dozens during the silent era alone.

Perhaps it was less that the classical tradition of Japanese cinema was exhausted than that it was doomed because the society that produced it was changing. The films realized by the major directors of the fifties drew substantially on the nation's cultural traditions: distinguished authors both classical (Saikaku, Sōseki Natsume) and contemporary (Jun'ichirō Tanizaki, Yasunari Kawabata, Yukio Mishima) furnished their plots; their styles often drew on the pictorial traditions of screen paintings and woodblock prints; their thematic concerns derived from a set of cultural assumptions which, increasingly, were being challenged. Ozu's subtle, moving family dramas were really, at this period, accounts of the disintegration of the traditional family system; meanwhile, younger directors such as Yūzō Kawashima and Kon Ichikawa satirized the new, commercially oriented, increasingly Westernized Japan. At this time, the classical, delicate, understated dramas of directors such as Toyoda, Naruse, and Gosho must have seemed quaint to a generation of viewers who had grown up after the war, and who desired a more direct confrontation with social realities. Their attitudes were not dissimilar to those of the Young Turk critics of *Cahiers du cinéma* magazine in Paris, who condemned the literary methods of directors such as Jean Delannoy and Claude Autant-Lara. While the Japanese cinema of the fifties was substantially richer than the French cinema of those years, one can understand the impatience of a younger generation who must have looked on their admired elders as a conservative establishment.

## Iconoclasts and Innovators: The Sun Tribe and the New Wave

The first signs of rebellion came from within the industry. In the mid-fifties, the genre of *taiyōzoku* (sun tribe) films was inaugurated by *Season of the Sun* (*Taiyō no kisetsu*, 1956), a Nikkatsu production based on a novel by Shintarō Ishihara, then an *enfant terrible*, now a conservative politician. The commercial success of this film ensured that it spearheaded a series of works with similar themes, about the alienation and irresponsibility of Japanese youth. Established directors such as Kon Ichikawa, who made *Punishment Room* (*Shokei no heya*, 1956), and newcomers like Yasuzō Masumura with his debut, *Kisses* (*Kuchizuke*, 1957), contributed to the genre, but these rebellious films were nevertheless made within the studio system; their profitability guaranteed that the major production companies would cash in on the craze. Although the *taiyōzoku* genre did display a new explicitness in its depiction of sex and violence, its products were not immune to melodramatic sensationalism. This rising sun, in any case, proved something of a false dawn; public outrage soon led to an informal agreement on the part of the studios to cease production of the genre.

For a few years, therefore, the Japanese cinema continued to produce films that were traditional in style and content. But the face of the industry was radically transformed between 1960 and 1965. Social change, as the modernization of the country accelerated, may have made this inevitable, but the catalyst, as in France at the same period, was the emergence of a younger generation of directors, pre-eminently Ōshima, Imamura, Shinoda and Yoshida. The control exerted by studios over distribution made the path of independent production, favored by their French contemporaries, much more difficult for Japanese filmmakers. Most of the filmmakers of the Japanese New Wave started out working for the majors, especially Shochiku, whose formidable head of production, Shirō Kido, hoped that cheaply made, innovative pictures could emulate the success of the *Nouvelle Vague* in Europe. He was disappointed; but his decision made it briefly possible for a younger generation of directors to work within the studio system while exploring modern themes and essaying stylistic experimentation. The commercial failure of these films spelled the end of studio support for the Japanese New Wave, but Kido's policy had given the careers of several young directors an impetus. By the mid-sixties, many of the most creative had found it possible to obtain funds for independent production. This meant, inevitably, working on low budgets, but the new Art Theater Guild (ATG) provided an alternative distribution network to that of the majors, and independence offered a degree of aesthetic freedom which the studios could not. The best films of the New Wave directors were characterized by a stylistic modernism which drew eclectically on European influences from Godard to Antonioni, but their true focus was the realities, sometimes uncomfortable, of contemporary Japanese society, examined with an uncompromising eye. Ōshima, in particular, touched on controversial subjects such as capital punishment and the circumstances of Korean immigrants in Japan in films such as *Death by Hanging* (*Kōshikei*, 1968). Imamura's films, in his own words, explored "the connection between the lower half of the human body and the lower half of the social structure." These artists examined their society with none of the restraint and delicacy of the older generation, and made the mid-to-late sixties the Golden Age of independent filmmaking in Japan.

This was also the period in which a number of remarkable documentary directors, pre-eminently Shinsuke Ogawa, came to the fore; some had cut their teeth on PR and educational films at Iwanami Productions, which also trained such notably individualistic directors as Susumu Hani and Kazuo Kuroki, whose fiction features displayed the influence of both documentary and the New Wave. Regrettably, this fertile period of independent filmmaking did not last. By the seventies, though ATG continued to finance creative films, it had again become increasingly difficult to obtain funding for production outside the studio system. Of the major New Wave figures, Imamura spent the decade working on experimental documentaries; Ōshima became reliant on foreign capital to realize a diminishing number of films; Yoshida, too, worked less and less frequently; and Shinoda renounced experimentation for the careful, academic adaptation of classic literature.

## *The Studios after 1960: The Decline of a System*

The studios, meanwhile, had found the content of their pictures increasingly dictated by commercial priorities. ShinToho went bankrupt in 1961; Daiei would ultimately follow in the early seventies. The steady audience which had sustained production through the thirties, forties, and fifties had disappeared as television began to keep once-devoted filmgoers at home. In particular, the conventional period film—so long the staple moneymaker for Japanese studios—was taken up by television. Nikkatsu and Toei responded by shifting focus to films about the *yakuza* (in both its incarnations: the professional gamblers of the past and the gangsters of the present). Certain talented directors, such as Seijun Suzuki and Tai Katō, worked in this increasingly popular genre, and the latter especially achieved considerable individuality by using its tortuous plots as a vehicle for formal experimentation. In general, however, and even though "Nikkatsu action" became a trademark, its products showed neither the complexity and richness of the best genre films of the past nor the originality of the major independent productions of the time. Nevertheless, *yakuza* films continued to make up a substantial proportion of Japanese film production throughout the seventies, when directors such as Toei-based Kinji Fukasaku moved away from the romanticized portrayal of chivalrous gangsters in the so-called *ninkyō-eiga* towards an allegedly more realistic style, known as *jitsuroku* ("true record") *eiga* and characterized by extreme violence and a pseudo-documentary style involving the use of a handheld camera. Shochiku, after struggling through the sixties as its traditional format became unfashionable, hit on a surefire commercial success with Yōji Yamada's Tora-san (*Otoko wa tsurai yo*) series; these repetitive but warm and funny accounts of life in an old-fashioned Tokyo community gave the studio a hit twice a year, and kept it solvent until the nineties.

The other commercial success story during this period was pornography. During the 1960s, a number of directors had begun to make so-called "pink" films—sexually explicit (though softcore) low-budget movies made and distributed outside the studio system. Some directors, notably Kōji Wakamatsu, took advantage of the relative freedom of this milieu to make occasionally trenchant political commentary; this was presumably not what the audience went to see, but pornography soon seemed the safest commercial bet for studios facing difficult times. By the early seventies, Nikkatsu, on the verge of bankruptcy, had decided to switch production almost exclusively to a slightly more decorous form of sex film, often based on respected novels, known as Roman Porno. A handful of interesting directors, notably Noboru Tanaka, worked in this sector, although most of its products did little more than fulfill their intended function. By the seventies, too, "pink" cinema was beginning to lose any political impetus, though, in fairness, a number of the more critically and commercially successful directors of the eighties and nineties, such as Kazuyuki Izutsu and Shun Nakahara, started out in "pink."

### *Film in the Bubble Era: Endings and New Beginnings*

A paradox of the era of Japan's booming "bubble economy" was that the nation's growing prosperity did not translate into money for film production. Consequently, the seventies and eighties marked a low point in the Japanese cinema's international reputation, at least as far as new films were concerned. While touring retrospectives introduced appreciative audiences to a wider range of classics, including the films of Naruse, Gosho, Kinoshita, and Shimizu, the number of recent Japanese films exported had plummeted. Those which did obtain foreign distribution were made by older, established figures: the later works of Kurosawa and Imamura were respectfully received, but international exposure of films by younger directors was restricted to the isolated success of specific titles, one example being Mitsuo Yanagimachi's much-feted *Fire Festival* (*Himatsuri*, 1985). The only younger filmmaker to establish a truly international reputation at this time was Jūzō Itami, whose witty satires of Japanese life and society earned him wide praise. While his films were uncompromisingly modern and engaged directly with the peculiarities of society at the time of the bubble economy, Itami was also the standard bearer of a family tradition, doing for the eighties what his father Mansaku had done for the thirties. By this time, however, the traditions of the Japanese cinema must have seemed on the verge of extinction to foreign viewers.

Inside Japan, however, the picture was not entirely bleak. During the 1970s, a number of younger filmmakers, frustrated with the difficulty of entering an industry which no longer operated the traditional apprenticeship system, took matters into their own hands, and made independent films on 8mm. Some of these, like Yoshimitsu Morita and Kazuki Ōmori, became successful commercial filmmakers in the eighties. At that time, independent directors like Yanagimachi and Kōhei Oguri generally struggled to find funding, but intermittently made works of outstanding distinction. In the mainstream, publisher Haruki Kadokawa had entered the market, and produced a series of big-budget, glossy genre films; these included some rather individual works, such as Nobuhiko Ōbayashi's silly but engaging fantasies set in his native Onomichi. Among the most important directors to work for Kadokawa was Shinji Sōmai: initially making youth films, he developed an imaginative style using long takes and long shot, which somewhat paralleled the classical styles of directors such as Mizoguchi and Shimizu. Ultimately crossing into the art house market, Sōmai became one of the era's most distinguished filmmakers. At the same time, a theoretical impetus came from Rikkyō University, where the influence of scholar Shigehiko Hasumi

©PIA Film Festival

Hatachi no binetsu / A Touch of Fever *(1993): In the 1990s, PIA funding enabled talented directors like Ryōsuke Hashiguchi to explore unusual or uncommercial themes.*

encouraged such students as Kiyoshi Kurosawa and Shinji Aoyama to experiment, like Sōmai, with austere long takes. These directors were to become some of the most interesting artists of the 1990s. Another significant development was the success of the PIA Film Festival, set up to discover talented young directors. From 1984, winners were awarded scholarships to direct their own features, and PIA thus kick-started the careers of several of the most interesting newer talents, such as Ryōsuke Hashiguchi, Akihiko Shiota, and Tomoyuki Furumaya.

### Genre and Art: Japanese Film in the 1990s and Beyond

The last decade or so has seen an improvement both in the quality of work produced and in its international stature. The Japanese cinema of the 1990s and the first years of the twenty-first century has been varied enough to defy summary. On the one hand there are the genre filmmakers, such as Takeshi Kitano and Hideo Nakata, who have specialized in gangster and horror movies and who have gained the Japanese cinema an appreciative new audience, both at home and abroad. Their approach was unashamedly commercial, but was also personal—the melancholy fatalism of Kitano's *yakuza* pictures is as recognizable as was the delicate realism of Ozu. On the other hand, there are those directors who have tried to uphold the established traditions of Japanese filmmaking, looking back to old masters such as Ozu and Mizoguchi or to modernists like Ōshima for inspiration, while forging individual styles and examining modern concerns. They include such artists as Hirokazu Koreeda, whose affecting studies of loss and isolation have been among the most moving of modern Japanese films, and Jun Ichikawa, whose best films, such as *Tokyo Marigold* (*Tōkyō marīgōrudo*, 2001), have subtly conveyed the emotional dislocation of contemporary life. Such films are more clearly aimed at the art house market, and their commercial success has been limited; nevertheless, they have achieved critical esteem both at home and abroad, and testify to the continuing vitality of a tradition. There are also directors who have struck a balance between the two approaches: Kiyoshi Kurosawa, to my mind the most distinguished modern director of horror, makes genre films that look like art movies, and states that he works in genres "in order better to distance myself from them." This fusion of art house and genre traditions also testifies to the fact that the distinction between studio and independent production is becoming less clear-cut.

One of the most basic signs of the continuing richness of the Japanese cinema is that films are still made and shown in decent numbers. This is no longer a given anywhere apart from the United States: Hollywood films constitute the majority of films exhibited in most countries today. Some take this as a symptom of American cultural imperialism, but it is also a fact that international audiences choose to support Hollywood productions instead of local ones. Those national cinemas which maintain a healthy level of production and continue to produce work of aesthetic distinction have usually legislated to counter the operation of the free market. The Korean cinema, one of the most fertile in the world today, has relied on government quotas guaranteeing that 40% of screen time is devoted to domestic product. In Iran, purveyor of some of the world's most individual contemporary films, strict censorship ensures that many foreign films are never released; meanwhile, art films are produced with an eye on the export market. Japan, by contrast, now neither restricts the importation of foreign films nor legislates to support her own film industry. And yet, in 2004, 247 out of 622 films released in Japan were domestic productions, and Japanese films commanded about a third of the total market share in their native country. These are totals that would be envied by any other country in the world, except India and the United States. The relative commercial success of new Japanese films goes hand in hand with a continuing niche interest in the classics of Japanese cinema. Admittedly this is sustained in large part by an older generation of viewers, but Tokyo still has several repertory cinemas devoted solely or mainly to the revival of old Japanese films. It is difficult to imagine the equivalent in London. At the same time, the growth of the DVD market has begun to make the classics available to a wider audience.

In the West, too, Japanese films old and new continue to inspire interest and admiration. Among their admirers, *auteur*ism, unfashionable in academic circles, still lives: which is to say that interest continues to be focused on the work of certain directors. Almost every recent major international retrospective of classic Japanese cinema has been a tribute to an individual director, whether already in the pantheon (Mizoguchi, Ozu, Kurosawa) or hitherto little-known (Masumura, Uchida). Interest in modern Japanese films, commercial or art house, also focuses on individual talents: the release of new films by directors such as Nakata, Kitano, Koreeda, and Shin'ya Tsukamoto is as eagerly anticipated in some quarters as the appearance at festivals of the latest Kurosawa was in the fifties. Donald Richie has spoken disparagingly of the way in which directors such as Ozu have become "brand names"; the problem is not that Ozu does not deserve plaudits, but that, for many viewers his films are the Japanese domestic drama, just as, in the modern era, Kitano is the *yakuza* thriller. In reality, Japan has produced dozens of directors who remain barely known in the West, yet whose work is richly deserving of wider distribution. I would cite, of the classical generation, Yoshimura, who has still never had the major international retrospective he deserves, or, of the younger, Furumaya, responsible for some of the most humane and unassuming dramas of recent years.

For many of these artists, the difficulty of seeing their films is exacerbated by the difficulty, for the non-Japanese-speaking reader, of learning about them in the first place; it can be almost impossible to locate factual information in English about all but the most famous directors. In recent years, the Internet has made things a little better, but its resources are often flawed: dates are mistaken or absent; filmographies are incomplete or untranslated. Likewise, critical information about the films is often scanty, or scattered in various books and journals.

With this book, therefore, I have set out to do two things. My first aim is to provide accurate factual information: names, dates, and filmographies. The filmographies are intended to list all films made for cinema release by each director, and in practice are as complete as available information allows. Films are included that were released or screened in festivals up to the end of 2007, when the final draft of this book was submitted for editing. The dates given are those of the first public screenings, in so far as I can trace them. The titles have been transliterated from original Japanese sources and translated into English with the aid of native speakers. My second aim is to provide a concise description of the themes and style of each director. While excellent histories of the Japanese cinema do exist, and while a handful of the most famous directors have enjoyed detailed book-length studies of their work, there is still no book which attempts to offer a comprehensive introduction to the work of the major directors from every period of the Japanese cinema. This book, I hope, will fill that niche. In doing so, I want to show that the acknowledged masters of Japanese cinema were not isolated figures of genius, but were the leaders of a large group of individual artists—some of them still unknown to most in the West—who, from the silent era to the present day, have shaped the unique contours of a national cinema.

This book, therefore, includes profiles and filmographies for more than 150 Japanese filmmakers at work in live-action cinema between the silent era and the present day. I have focused mainly on directors of feature-length narrative film, which I believe is likely to be the main interest of most readers. I have, however, included the most important directors of documentary films. Directos notable for experimental or short films have been included if they have also made distinguished features. Thus, Nobuhiko Ōbayashi and Toshio Matsumoto have made experimental shorts and narrative features; Torajirō Saitō is best-known for his comedy shorts, but made feature-length films too. The majority of directors represented here, however, have worked or are working in the medium of the narrative fiction film, whether active in the studio system or independently.

There are two conscious omissions. For reasons of space, I have chosen to confine my focus to directors making films for theatrical release. Directors working exclusively for television have been excluded. Where directors have made films for both the big and the small screen, I have discussed important television projects in the profiles, but I have not generally listed television work in the filmographies. Films made for straight-to-video release have likewise generally been excluded. However, this distinction has become less meaningful in recent years since films made primarily for television or video sometimes receive limited cinema releases as well, or are shown on cinema screens at foreign festivals and retrospectives. In such cases, I have listed the titles. I have also listed amateur films made on 8mm and 16mm formats, generally for private screenings; although, in many cases, these films are not readily available, they have been important in forming the style of many directors since the seventies, and thus merit inclusion.

The other conscious exclusion, perhaps more controversial, is *anime*. Without disputing the vitality and commercial success of Japanese animated film, I would argue that the distinction between animated and live-action cinema is roughly analogous to that between painting and photography; essentially, the two are different media, and merit separate books. This is particularly the case where direction is concerned, since the role of a director in recording a series of drawings is qualitatively different from that of a director working with live actors in real settings. This exclusion does not convey any relative valuation of the two, merely a recognition of their essential difference. There are, of course, a few filmmakers who have worked in both live-action and animated film; these artists are included if the quality of their work in live-action alone justifies it.

It is more difficult to offer a coherent set of criteria for inclusion. I have based my decisions on my sense of each director's importance in Japanese cinema, and to an extent on my own evaluation of their talent. I have not excluded directors simply because I dislike their work; if they are generally considered significant, they are here. However, I have made space for little-known directors who do not command a wide reputation if I am personally enthusiastic about their work. Other things being equal, I have been more inclined to include directors whose work is accessible in some form to non-Japanese-speaking viewers, whether available on DVD or video, or in distribution in subtitled prints, or where subtitled copies are not in general distribution but are available for festival or retrospective screenings. This does not always mean that the work of the directors I have covered is *readily* available; subtitled prints may exist in archives, but emerge infrequently in the context of touring retrospectives which visit only major cities. This frustrating situation is a familiar misery for lovers of the Japanese cinema. At the time of writing, however, things are definitely improving. Hitherto inaccessible films by Naruse and Yamanaka have been released on DVD in Britain and the United States; it is becoming more common for releases in Japan to carry the option of English subtitles; and a wide range of subtitled films is now available in Hong Kong and accessible via specialist importers. There are still many gaps; but today's reader is perhaps in a better position to test my judgments than ever before.

To examine and discuss so many Japanese filmmakers, even briefly, is an enormous task. In the course of my research I have watched over a thousand films, and I have tried wherever possible to see a representative sample of the work of each director under consideration. However, there have inevitably been occasions where important films have proved elusive, or, indeed, where they are believed to be lost. Thus, my descriptions are based on a mixture of first-hand experience and secondary reading. Lest there be any misunderstanding, the mere mention of a film in the text, a summary of its plot, or a description of its subject matter and concerns should not be taken as proof that I have seen it. Of course, where I have advanced an opinion on a film, or given a detailed description of its tone or stylistic features, this is based on my own viewing.

This book is intended as a source of both factual information and critical discussion. I have endeavored to make the facts as accurate as possible. Critical opinions, of course, are always a matter for debate. I hope that this book will lead its readers back to the films, so that they can form their own.

# A Note on Translation

The Japanese writing system is arguably the most complex in the world, and transliterating it into Roman letters is itself a difficult task, while producing readable translations is even more so. Since the same character can have multiple readings, and the correct reading is not always clear from the context, even Japanese readers sometimes stumble. In order to establish the correct readings I have worked with two native speakers, Maiko Miyoshi and Etsuko Takagi, to transliterate titles from original Japanese sources, and wherever possible have tried to confirm our readings by consulting sources which give a phonetic reading, whether in Japanese *kana* or in Roman script. The sources I have consulted are listed in the Bibliography. However, I have avoided relying wholly on previously published filmographies, as mistakes have sometimes been made by one writer and then perpetuated. Also, most published filmographies in Roman script do not indicate the lengths of most vowels. Because of this, I have transliterated wherever possible from scratch, and then compared my readings with other published sources.

I have transliterated according to the Revised Hepburn system, which is the most widely used system of Romanization. Thus, in native Japanese or Chinese-derived words, long vowels 'a', 'o' and 'u' are indicated by a macron, long 'i' by 'ii', and long 'e' by 'ei' (as in 'geisha'). In words taken from foreign languages other than Chinese, and thus written in Japanese in *katakana*, I have followed the convention of using macrons to lengthen all vowels (so Yoshimitsu Morita's *Family Game* is "*Kazoku gēmu*," not "*Kazoku geimu*"). I have made an exception for a few titles where the original *katakana* depart from this convention. Syllabic 'n' is always represented as 'n'; thus, I depart from some previous scholars of the Japanese cinema in referring to swordplay films as *chanbara* rather than *chambara*. Where a vowel or 'y' follows a syllabic 'n', I use an apostrophe to avoid confusion; thus, the author of *The Makioka Sisters* is Jun'ichirō Tanizaki and the director of *Tetsuo* is Shin'ya Tsukamoto. I have transliterated titles using loan words exactly as spelled in *kana*: thus, the Japanese language title of Kinji Fukasaku's *Battle Royale* is given as *Batoru Rowaiaru*. Where the original credits of the film give the title in Roman script (an increasingly common practice nowadays), I have of course reproduced it as spelled.

In listing Japanese-language titles in the filmographies I have adhered to the Revised Hepburn system strictly, so that they are transliterated as accurately as possible. In the body of the text, however, and in supplying English translations of the titles, I have departed from Hepburn in the case of naturalised English words or names. Thus, I write Tokyo not Tōkyō and refer to Noh theater not Nō theater. I have considered the names of production companies and historical periods to be naturalized words for this purpose. Where personal names or place names occur in film titles, I dispense with macrons in the English translation, since official English-language release titles never supply them; thus, for instance, I give *Rashōmon* (with macron) as the Japanese-language film title, and *Rashomon* (without macron) as the English-language one.

I have endeavored to supply a translation for all titles, except where the title is the name of a person or a place, or an untranslatable set phrase. Where films have been released abroad, I have used the official release title; if a film has been written about elsewhere and thus has a semi-official title, I have used that unless I judge it to be in error. If the film is widely known under more than one title, I have supplied two or several, although where alternative titles are basically variations on the same idea, I have not listed every possible permutation. I have usually listed the most frequently used translation first, except where I consider it misleading. If the most commonly used translation is not the most literal one, I have indicated which title is most literal. Where the only previously used titles are not literal, I have where possible supplied a literal translation in parentheses, particularly where the literal title suggests aspects of the film which standard translations do not.

Where the title of a film has not previously been translated into English, I have devised my own. In general, these titles have been kept at literal as possible, even at the risk of sounding ungainly in English. However, where titles use descriptive words such as *maki* ("reel") to indicate different episodes, I have dropped these in translation if the result sounds impossibly convoluted. In a few cases, too, I have opted for a translation which seems truer to Japanese usage—for instance, where an idiomatic phrase has a direct parallel in a different English idiom. Where a title might have several possible meanings, I have tried to choose the most accurate translation by seeking information about the film's content. Sometimes, however, particularly in the case of lost films, information about content is not readily available, and in these cases I have had to make an educated guess.

The issue of name order is a thorny one. When the Japanese write their name in their own language, they put surname first, as do the Chinese, Koreans, and Hungarians. Scholars of Chinese almost invariably preserve Chinese name order: thus, the maker of *Farewell My Concubine* is Chen Kaige, not Kaige Chen. On the other hand, writers on the Hungarian cinema do not usually talk about Jancsó Miklós. In the field of Japanese studies, convention is somewhat divided; most scholarly books favor the Japanese name order; books aimed at the general reader generally give Western name order. I have decided to opt for Western name order because when films are distributed abroad, the credits invariably follow Western name order. I have made an exception if a film has been distributed abroad under a title which includes a personal name and preserves Japanese name order: thus, I translate Noboru Tanaka's *Jitsuroku Abe Sada* as *The True Story of Abe Sada* and *A Woman Called Abe Sada* because these are titles which have been used in foreign screenings and DVD releases. Another exception is the name of the writer Edogawa Ranpo, because it is a pseudonym which derives from a pun on the name of American author Edgar Allen Poe. Naturally, in the heading of each entry, I also put surname first, as this is the usual convention of encyclopedias in Western languages. This has the advantage that the Romanized name in the heading appears in the same order as the Japanese name in *kanji*, which is supplied along with it.

# Acknowledgments

A book such as this naturally incurs so many debts that I hardly know where to begin. I do not have space to list the many friends and family members whose affection and encouragement has helped me to find the energy to finish it; they know who they are, and I am grateful to them all. I must however mention my parents, Michael Jacoby and Ann Jacoby, and my stepfather Gus Baker, who tolerated my sometimes obsessive passion for Japanese cinema, supported my initial decision to live and work in Japan, and assisted financially with the expenses involved in writing this book. Beyond that, I want to thank them for their immeasurable emotional support, encouragement, and love.

My heartfelt thanks go to Beth Cary for her tireless editorial work, which has saved me from more than a few errors (needless to say, in the old phrase, any that remain are entirely my own responsibility). I thank, too, everyone at Stone Bridge Press, especially Peter Goodman for his patience with a project that has taken rather longer to complete than I anticipated. I should also acknowledge the patience of Alastair Phillips, my Ph.D. supervisor at the University of Warwick, who has displayed a supreme tolerance and understanding as time that should have been devoted to my studies was absorbed instead by this book.

The completion of this project was made possible by a generous grant from the Daiwa Anglo-Japanese Foundation, which enabled me to fund a vital research trip to Japan in the summer of 2006. I thank Marie Conte-Helm and all her colleagues at Daiwa for their faith in my abilities and their support for my work.

Much of the research for this book was done at the Tokyo office of the Japan Foundation, whose staff displayed a generosity beyond the call of duty in allowing me extensive access to their collection of subtitled prints over a lengthy period, at some inconvenience to themselves. I am grateful especially to Yūko Murata, Marie Suzuki, Aiko Yatsuhashi, Mirai Itsutsuji, and Kiyo Seike. I was able to conduct supplementary research at the Kawakita Memorial Film Institute and at the Film Center of the Museum of Modern Art, Tokyo. At the former institution, my thanks are due to Masayo Okada and Atsuko Fukuda; at the latter, to Akira Tochigi and Hisashi Okajima.

The production of filmographies in Romanized Japanese and English would have been impossible without the dedication of my two teachers, Etsuko Takagi and Maiko Miyoshi, to both of whom I am deeply grateful. Hiroshi Komatsu of Waseda University made me the beneficiary of his formidable knowledge of Japanese film and his unerring accuracy in factual matters, and was especially helpful in providing correct readings for some of the most obscure titles. With his wife, Ritsuko, he was also a welcoming host while I conducted my research in Tokyo in 2006. For their hospitality during that trip, I also thank Jonathan Cant, Ben Rowlett and Kazuhito Yamada, Richard Smart, Shōtarō Yamauchi and family, Mitsukazu Yoshida, and especially Cathy Lambshead, who was my host for longer than I had any right to ask.

I owe a particular debt to Richard Chatten, who as a film historian sadly has yet to achieve the recognition he deserves. He made me a generous loan to cover the cost of photographs included in the book, and read the entire manuscript in draft, offering many useful suggestions, spotting various errors, and sharpening numerous turns of phrase. Michael Walker, a model teacher, also read the whole book in draft and commented perceptively on matters both factual and critical. Others who read and commented on portions of the manuscript include Aaron Gerow, Mark LeFanu, Arthur Nolletti, Bob Quaif, and James Quandt. Jasper Sharp gave generously of his considerable expertise and knowledge of the byways of Japanese film, and put his extensive collection of DVDs at my disposal. Johan Nordström shared the pleasure of viewing a good few of the films discussed in this book, helped to shape my thoughts on them, and was a constant source of enthusiasm. Stephen Wan assisted with the transliteration of Cantonese in the titles of Hong Kong–made films. For their help, advice, and encouragement, I should also thank Kevin Brownlow, Michael Campi, Michelle Carey, Roland Domenig, Mika Kō, Michael McCaskey, Abe Mark Nornes, Steve Pickles, and especially Glynford Hatfield and Franco Picollo, whose assistance to this project was invaluable.

For giving me permission to reproduce and supplying the many beautiful still photographs which illustrate this book, I must thank the following: At Shochiku, Junko Kawaguchi and Shin'ya Watanabe; at Nikkatsu, Shinako Matsuda and Noritoshi Nakano; at Kadokawa Pictures, Yukka Seki and Akiko Takahashi; Ikkō Kawamura at Toei; Osamu Minakawa at Kokusai Hōei; Kumi Kamimura at Bitters End; Shōko Kimizuka at Wowow; Naomi Osada at Nippon Eiga Shinsha; and Kijū (Yoshishige) Yoshida for supplying a still from one of his own films as director. A double thankyou for permission to use stills without charge is due to Miyuki Fukuma at TV Man Union;

Gō Hirasawa at Wakamatsu Pro; Shintaro Horikawa at Altamira Pictures; Toshimi Kawasaki at Opus; Kiyo Joo and Ryō Ikeuchi at Goldview; Mutsuko Kumagai at Argo Pictures; Jōji Nishiyama at Hitachi; Yūko Nomura and Akira Yamashita at Pony Canyon, Inc.; Miki Ōi at PIA; Mikako Otani at Athenée Français; Kazunao Sakaguchi at Stance Company; Hanayasu Shizuka at Kindai Eiga Kyokai; Sakiko Yamagami of Siglo; Yoshio Yasui at Planet Bibliothèque de Cinéma; Hayao Yamamoto at Dokuritsu Pro; and Katsumasa Morita of Seido Productions. Some stills no longer in copyright were supplied by the Kawakita Memorial Film Institute, and I thank the staff of that institution again here.

Lastly, I must acknowledge two men whose combined involvement in film culture stretches over more than a century. David Robinson, one of the world's most thorough and knowledgeable film historians, commissioned my first piece of published writing on film, and, since I met him in 2001 at the Pordenone Festival of Silent Film, has been an unfailing source of wise advice and encouragement in all my projects. Donald Richie, pioneer and pathfinder in the Western appreciation of Japanese film, encouraged me to write this book, submitted it to Stone Bridge Press on my behalf, smoothed my way at the Japan Foundation, Kawakita Institute and Film Center, read and commented in detail on successive drafts, and kindly consented to write the Foreword. I owe these two gentlemen more than I can repay. I dedicate this book, with love, to them both.

# A Critical
# Handbook
# of Japanese
# Film Directors

## ABE Yutaka
### (February 2, 1895–January 3, 1977)
阿部豊

A director from the mid-twenties, Abe had trained in Hollywood, where he played bit parts in films starring his compatriot, Sessue Hayakawa. After returning home, he became known as the Lubitsch of Japan, a reputation founded on his witty and polished social satires. *A Mermaid on Land* (*Riku no ningyo*, 1926) traced the romantic rivalry between two young women, one spoilt and rich, the other poor but sincere. *Five Women around Him* (*Kare o meguru gonin no onna*, 1927) focused on a bachelor and his several girlfriends. Most famous was *The Woman Who Touched the Legs* (*Ashi ni sawatta onna*, 1926), a twice-remade ironic comedy about a writer's encounter with a female thief. These films, along with most of Abe's prewar work, are now lost, but among his prewar sound films, *Children of the Sun* (*Taiyō no ko*, 1938) remains extant. This interesting story about a home for delinquent children in Hokkaido revealed his eye for landscape and confirmed his capability in a more serious vein.

The vague liberalism of that film was soon abandoned as Abe, with blockbusters such as *Flaming Sky* (*Moyuru ōzora*, 1940) and *Fire on That Flag* (*Ano hata o ute*, 1944), became one of the leading producers of nationalistic propaganda before and during the Pacific War. Even in the fifties, *Battleship Yamato* (*Senkan Yamato*, 1953) and *I Was a Siberian POW* (*Watashi wa Shiberiya no horyo datta*, 1952) exposed his continuing admiration for Japanese militarism. Much of Abe's postwar work consisted of undistinguished genre films such as *Desert in Ginza* (*Ginza no sabaku*, 1958), a brutal and silly crime thriller set against the backdrop of Tokyo's fashionable yet seedy Ginza district. However, he achieved a commercial success with the first film adaptation of Jun'ichirō Tanizaki's novel about life among Osaka's prewar upper middle class, *The Makioka Sisters* (*Sasameyuki*, 1950). Later, the freewheeling comedy *Season of Affairs* (*Uwaki no kisetsu*, 1959) carried some of his old satirical feeling in its amused take on contemporary social mores. It is unfortunate that the films which earned Abe his fame as a satirist in the silent era are not preserved today.

**1925**  **Bokō no tameni** / For the Alma Mater

  **Hasha no kokoro** / Heart of a Champion

Shōhin eigashū / Collection of
Short Stories on Film (*co-director*)
1926 Shinsei no aikō / New Life through
the Light of Love
Nyōbō kawaiya / Loving Wife
Setsujoku no hi / Day of
Vindication
Kyōko to Shizuko / Kyoko and
Shizuko
Sekai no chiemono / The World's
Wisest Man
Riku no ningyo / A Mermaid on
Land
Ashi ni sawatta onna / The
Woman Who Touched the Legs
Shin Nihontō / New Japanese
Island
1927 Kare o meguru gonin no onna /
Five Women around Him
Tabi geinin / Traveling Players
Ningyō no ie / A Doll's House
Shikabane wa katarazu / The
Dead Don't Talk
1928 Hanayome hanamuko saikonki
/ Record of the Bride and Groom's
Remarriage
Chikyū wa mawaru: Dainibu:
Gendai hen / The World Turns:
Part 2: Modern Chapter
Haha izuko / Where Is Mother?
1929 Kyōen onna samazama / Women
in Competition
Karatachi no hana / Trifoliate
Orange Blossom
Aojiroki bara / Pale Blue Rose
Hijō keikai / Caution: Emergency
1930 Josei homare / Woman's
Reputation
Nihonbare / Fair Weather
Haha sannin / Three Mothers
Nikkatsu onparēdo / Nikkatsu on
Parade
1931 Nikkatsu aramōdo / Nikkatsu à la
Mode
Gōruin / Success
1932 Tengoku no hatoba / Heaven's
Pier
Modan seisho: Tosei risshi

tokuhon kan'ichi / Modern Bible:
Model for Success in Modern
Times, Volume One
1933 Hikari: Tsumi to tomo ni / Light:
With a Sin
Suma no adanami / Ebb and Flow
at Suma
Atarashiki ten (Zenpen; Kōhen) /
The New Heaven (Parts 1 and 2)
1934 Kokoro no hatoba / The Heart's
Pier
Tetsu no machi / Town of Iron
Wakafūfu shiken bekkyo / Trial
Separation of a Young Couple
Tajō busshin / Fickle but Not
Unfeeling
1935 Nichizō getsuzō / Keepers of the
Sun and Moon
Kaikoku Dainippon / Greater
Japan, Maritime Nation
Midori no chiheisen (Zenpen;
Kōhen) / The Green Horizon
(Parts 1 and 2)
1936 Hakui no kajin / Beautiful Women
in White
Ren'ai to kekkon no sho: Ren'ai
hen / Book of Love and Marriage:
Love Volume
Ren'ai to kekkon no sho: Kekkon
hen / Book of Love and Marriage:
Marriage Volume
1937 Jūji hōka / Crossfire
1938 Taiyō no ko / Children of the
Sun
1939 Waremokō: Zenpen / The Great
Burnet: Part 1
Waremokō: Kōhen: Sen'ya ni
saku / The Great Burnet: Part 2:
Blooming on the Battlefield
Roppa no Hōjiro-sensei / Roppa
as Mr. Hojiro the Teacher
Onna no kyōshitsu: Gakkō no
maki: Nanatsu no omogake /
Women's Classroom: School Reel:
Memories of Seven
Kodomo to heitai / Children and
Soldiers
Onna no kyōshitsu: Kōhen /
Women's Classroom: Part 2

1940 **Moyuru ōzora** / Flaming Sky / Burning Sky
1942 **Nankai no hanataba** / Bouquet of the South Seas
1944 **Ano hata o ute** / Fire on That Flag / Dawn of Freedom
1945 **Uta e! Taiyō** / Sing! The Sun!
1946 **Boku no ojisan** / My Uncle
1947 **Ai yo hoshi to tomo ni** / Love, Live with the Stars!
1948 **Ten no yūgao** / Heaven's Evening Glory
1949 **Ryūsei** / Shooting Star
**Daitokai no kao** / Face of the Big City
1950 **Sasameyuki** / The Makioka Sisters (lit. A Light Snowfall)
**Aizenka** / Scent of Enlightenment
1951 **Nozokareta ashi** / The Leg That Was Peeped At
**Tsuki yori no haha** / Mother from the Moon
1952 **Ōzora no chikai** / Oath of Heaven
**Watashi wa Shiberiya no horyo datta** / I Was a Siberian POW
**Otome no honnō: Bōto hachinin musume** / Young Woman's Instinct: 8 Girls and a Boat
1953 **Onna to iu shiro: Mari no maki** / A Castle Called Woman: Mari's Reel
**Onna to iu shiro: Yūko no maki** / A Castle Called Woman: Yuko's Reel
**Koibito no iru machi** / Town of Lovers
**Senkan Yamato** / Battleship Yamato
1954 **Shunshuku Oden no kata: Edo-jō enjō** / The Desirable Lady Oden: Great Fire of Edo Castle
**Nihon yaburezu** / Japan Undefeated / Immortal Japan
1955 **Seishun kaidan** / Ghost Story of Youth
**Hana shinju** / Flower Pearl
**Hanran** / Rebellion
1956 **Daihachi kanbō** / Cell No. 8
**Iro zange** / Penitence for Lust
**Nikutai no mitsuyu** / People Smuggling

1957 **Saigo no totsugeki** / The Last Charge
**Madamu** / Madame
**Suashi no musume** / The Barefoot Girl
**Mebana** / The Awakening (lit. Female Flower)
1958 **Shundeini** / The Story of a Nun
**Unga** / The Flow / The Canal (lit.)
**Ginza no sabaku** / Desert in Ginza / Wasteland of a Metropolis
**Ōsaka no kaze** / Wind of Osaka
1959 **Kamen no onna** / Masked Woman
**Nirenjū no Tetsu** / "Double-Barreled" Tetsu
**Uwaki no kisetsu** / Season of Affairs
1960 **Kizudarake no okite** / Tarnished Rule
**Shizukana datsugokusha** / The Quiet Fugitive
1961 **Daishusse monogatari** / Story of Great Success
**Inochi no asa** / Morning of Life / Dawn of a Canvas

## ADACHI Masao
**(b. May 5, 1939)**
足立正生

Adachi's career testifies to the opportunities which "pink" cinema provided for the expression of dissident attitudes. He had achieved notice as a student filmmaker collaborating on such creative experimental films as *The Lacquered Bowl* (*Wan*, 1961), a tragedy set in an isolated village. From 1966 to 1971, he worked for Kōji Wakamatsu's production company, scripting some of Wakamatsu's own works, and directing a sequence of "pink" films in which sexual titillation was secondary to political commentary advanced from a far-left perspective. *Sex Play* (*Seiyūgi*, 1968) charted the personal and ideological entanglements of two groups of leftist students, drawing imprecise parallels between sexual and political liberation. *Female Student Guerrillas* (*Jogakusei gerira*, 1969) took this theme to an extreme in its account of the violent revolutionary activities of a group of students in the mountains. The film's portrayal of their brutalities was unenlightening, but there were suggestive moments; the opening and closing shots of Mount Fuji—the Shochiku logo—seemed not only to demolish a national symbol, but also to mock the studio system.

Although rough-and-ready in execution, these films were visually inventive, revealing the influence of Jean-Luc Godard in their use of such distancing devices as onscreen text and switches from black and white to color. More mature in theme and somewhat more professional in style was *Prayer of Ejaculation: 15-Year-Old Prostitute* (*Funshutsu kigan: 15-sai no baishunfu*, 1971), an austere, affecting examination of the tragic life and suicide of a teenage prostitute, in which Adachi's political concerns seemed more directly anchored in the realities of individual experience. The hypocrisy of the adult world was suggested by the character of the middle-aged teacher who begins an affair with the heroine, while images of tanks in the streets hinted at a wider context. Outside the "pink" arena, Adachi made *AKA Serial Killer* (*Rakushō: Renzoku shasatsuma*, 1969), an admired documentary, which recorded the locations that must have been visited by teenage serial killer Norio Nagayama before he committed his crimes.

In 1971, Adachi journeyed with Wakamatsu to the Middle East, visiting territory disputed between Israel and her Arab neighbors. Their encounters with a group of Palestinian guerrillas and interviews conducted in Beirut with artists, refugees, hijackers, and others, formed the basis of a documentary, *Red Army–PFLP–Declaration of World War* (*Sekigun–PFLP–Sekai sensō sengen*, 1971), screenings of which were restricted by pressure from the Japanese police. Adachi returned in 1975 to Beirut, where he lived for more than two decades, acting as a spokesman for the Japanese Red Army in Lebanon. In 1997, he was arrested and deported on the orders of the Lebanese government and, on returning to Japan, spent two years in prison. After his release, he documented his life in an autobiographical book, *Film/Revolution* (*Eiga/Kakumei*, 2003), and took steps to restart his directorical career. *Prisoner/Terrorist* (*Yūheisha: Terorisuto*, 2007) controversially charted the ill-treatment in Israeli captivity of Kōzō Okamoto, one of the perpetrators of the 1972 Lod Airport Massacre. This lengthy, repetitious, and rather amateurish work was not a particularly distinguished comeback: a fact that is doubly regrettable, since Adachi's own experiences would certainly offer fascinating material for drama or documentary.

1961  **Wan** / The Lacquered Bowl (*16mm short; co-director*)
1963  **Sa'in** / The Sealed Vagina (*co-director*)
1966  **Datai** / Abortion
    **Hinin kakumei** / The Birth Control Revolution
1967  **Gingake** / The Galaxy
1968  **Sei chitai** / Sex Zone
    **Seiyūgi** / Sex Play
1969  **Jogakusei gerira** / Female Student Guerrillas / The High School Girls' Revolt
    **Ryakushō: Renzoku shasatsuma** / AKA Serial Killer

**1970 Sakarame: Mugen jigoku /** Woman in Revolt: Phantasmagoric Hell

**1971 Funshutsu kigan: 15-sai no baishunfu /** Prayer of Ejaculation: 15-Year-Old Prostitute

**Sekigun–PFLP–Sekai sensō sengen /** Red Army–PFLP–Declaration of World War (*co-director*)

**2007 Yūheisha: Terorisuto /** Prisoner / Terrorist

## AOYAMA Shinji
## (b. July 13, 1964)
## 青山真治

Aoyama's work resembles that of Kiyoshi Kurosawa (also a former student at Rikkyō University of film theorist Shigehiko Hasumi) in its offbeat approach to generic motifs. The gulf between his nineties exploitation films and his twenty-first-century art movies is more apparent than real: his recent, more rarefied work has drawn inspiration, at several removes, from thrillers and science fiction, while his early genre films borrowed the stylistic attributes of art movies. In such offbeat gangster films as *Helpless* (1996) and *Wild Life* (*Wild Life: Jump into the Dark*, 1997) he used extended sequence shots and slow, meditative camera movements to record not only violent action, but also the dead spots in between: snacks in cafes and restaurants, morning showers, journeys, time spent waiting and doing nothing. The individuality of these films lay in their unglamorous concentration on the mundane realities of criminal life. *An Obsession* (*Tsumetai chi*, 1997), another crime thriller, reworked Akira Kurosawa's *Stray Dog* (*Nora inu*, 1949) in its story of a police detective whose stolen gun is used in a series of murders. This film's setting in an alternative present-day Tokyo, peopled by executioners in anti-radiation suits, foreshadowed the apocalyptic tone of Aoyama's later work.

In the late nineties, Aoyama also worked in genres other than the crime film. *Embalming* (*EM Enbāmingu*, 1999) was a silly horror movie pastiche, notable mainly for a slyly self-mocking performance from director Seijun Suzuki. *Shady Grove* (1999), loosely inspired by a Sōseki Natsume short story, was a melancholy romantic comedy about a young woman trying to come to terms with rejection. Around this time, Aoyama also made a documentary, *To the Alley* (*Roji e: Nakagami Kenji no nokoshita firumu*, 2000): in part an examination of the plight of the *burakumin* underclass, this was more centrally an investigation of the role of cinema itself in preserving history.

Aoyama gained an international reputation with *Eureka* (2000), about the gradual recovery of three survivors from the trauma of a bus hijack. Over three hours long, virtually plotless, and shot in sepia-tinted monochrome, this extraordinary, haunting film took its director's style to a new extreme; its slow, sinuous camera movements, sometimes following the characters, sometimes moving independently, conveyed the sense of a world indifferent to individual suffering. Even closer to abstraction was *Eli, Eli, Lama Sabachthani* (*Eri eri rama sabakutani*, 2005), a Werner Herzog-like vision of apocalypse set in a dystopian future where an infectious disease is inducing mass suicides. Though lacking the narrative control of *Eureka*, it contained passages of breathtaking visual beauty. *Desert Moon* (*Tsuki no sabaku*, 2001) was a more socially critical film, focusing on a selfish businessman whose obsession with

*Eureka (2000): This brooding epic about trauma and recovery took its director's style to a new extreme.*

work threatens to destroy his marriage. While thematically intriguing, it was somewhat ponderous in execution.

Aoyama's films have often focused on the tension between free will and determinism. He has seemed sometimes to view human actions as wholly governed by external factors: in *Embalming*, for instance, the human brain can be mechanically reset like a computer. *Eli, Eli, Lama Sabachthani*, albeit more ambiguously, traced suicidal actions to the influence of a virus, and even *Eureka*, though more psychological in emphasis, saw violence as a kind of infection, the trauma of the original hijack leading one victim to commit murder in turn. *Sad Vacation (Saddo vakeishon,* 2007), about a man scarred by his mother's desertion, also examined the way in which past events determine human behavior,

a theme given a metacinematic dimension by the presence of characters from Aoyama's own earlier work. Nevertheless, Aoyama's recent films have generally been therapeutic in theme, charting a process of recovery. Often a change of environment permits a cure: if *Eureka* portrayed a countryside contaminated by urban phenomena such as crime, *Desert Moon* found tentative hope in the protagonists' rejection of urban for rural life, while the suicidal heroine of *Eli, Eli, Lama Sabachthani* is cured in a remote field. In these films, the affection between individuals was also seen as grounds for hope, and it may be that Aoyama is moving towards a genuine humanism.

The tension between freedom and determinism is reflected in Aoyama's technique, which allows his collaborators a certain latitude to improvise: thus, he apparently often permits his regular cameraman, Masaki Tamura, to make his own choices about where and how to move the camera. This improvisional aspect relates also to Aoyama's interest in the spontaneity of music (which cures the disease victims in *Eli, Eli, Lama Sabachthani*). Significantly, in addition to fiction features, he has directed concert films, and collaborated with students at the Film School of Tokyo on an epic documentary about music critic Akira Aida, who introduced free jazz to Japan in the 1970s. The variety and eccentricity of his work make it difficult to predict future developments, but Aoyama will likely remain an original and suggestive filmmaker.

**1996**  **Helpless**
  **Chinpira** / Two Punks
**1997**  **Wild Life: Jump into the Dark** / Wild Life
  **Tsumetai chi** / An Obsession (lit. Cold Blood)
**1998**  **Kaosu no fuchi** / June 12, 1998: The Edge of Chaos
**1999**  **Shady Grove**
  **EM Embāmingu** / Embalming
**2000**  **Eureka**
  **Roji e: Nakagami Kenji no nokoshita firumu** / To the Alley (lit. To the Alley: The Film Left by Kenji Nakagami)
**2001**  **Tsuki no sabaku** / Desert Moon
**2002**  **Sude ni oita kanojo no subete ni tsuite wa kataranu tameni** / So as Not to Say Everything about Her Already Aged Self (*video*)
  **Shiritsu tantei Hama Maiku: Namae no nai mori** / A Forest with No Name
**2003**  **Deka matsuri** / Cop Festival (*co-director*)
  **Ajimā no uta: Uehara Tomoko tenjō no utagoe** / Song of Ajima: Tomoko Uehara, Voice of Heaven

**Nokishita no narazumono mitai ni** / Like a Desperado under the Eaves (*short*)
  **Shūsei tabi nikki** / Days in the Shade (*short*)
**2004**  **Reikusaido mādā kēsu** / Lakeside Murder Case
**2005**  **Eri eri rama sabakutani** / Eli, Eli, Lama Sabachthani / My God, My God, Why Hast Thou Forsaken Me?
**2006**  **Kōrogi** / Crickets
  **AA**
**2007**  **Saddo vakeishon** / Sad Vacation

## CHIBA Yasuki
**(June 24, 1910–September 18, 1985)**
千葉泰樹

Though remembered largely for his inventive postwar *shomin-geki*, Chiba specialized initially in period films before achieving commercial success with such popular romances as *Hideko the Cheerleader* (*Hideko no ōendanchō*, 1940), a vehicle for the teenage Hideko Takamine. Among his wartime films, *Women's Brick Factory* (*Renga jokō*, 1940; released 1946), a story about female factory workers, was banned for its proletarian sentiments, while *The White Mural* (*Shiroi hekiga*, 1942), shot on location in Okinawa, was a humanist account of a doctor from the mainland treating blackwater fever among the indigenous population.

Chiba's reputation for love stories led him to be assigned after the war to *A Certain Night's Kiss* (*Aru yo no seppun*, 1946), in which the Japanese cinema's much-anticipated first kissing scene was infamously obscured by an umbrella. However, Chiba's work in the fifties displayed a new individuality, combining personal drama with social commentary. In *Sunflower Girl* (*Himawari musume*, 1953) a woman's affection for her boss causes conflict with her more class-conscious coworkers, while in *Death Fire* (*Onibi*, 1956) a gas company employee demands sexual favors from a poor woman in lieu of payment. Chiba was also admired for his creative use of period settings: *The Happy Pilgrimage* (*Yajikita dōchūki*, 1958) was an offbeat *jidai-geki* about a pair of samurai who embark on a pilgrimage to Ise in order to escape their wives. More often, however, Chiba set his films in the recent past. *Downtown* (*Shitamachi*, 1957), based on a novel by Mikio Naruse's favorite writer, Fumiko Hayashi, conveyed the despondent mentality of the Occupation era through its depiction of a doomed romance. *Crazy Guy* (*Okashina yatsu*, 1956) recounted the life story of a *rakugo* performer from the twenties to the Occupation, and was remarkable for its sudden shifts from comedy to tragedy; like *Downtown*, it ended with an unexpected fatal accident. Chiba's most significant work is usually considered to be the *Large Size* (*Ōban*, 1957–58) series, described by Donald Richie as "a Balzac-like chronicle of [the] various falls and rises" of an ambitious young man in the early Showa period.

In the sixties, Chiba worked on such international co-productions as *A Night in Hong Kong* (*Honkon no yoru*, 1961) and *A Star of Hong Kong* (*Honkon no hoshi*, 1962), both sentimental stories of love affairs between Japanese men and Chinese women. With *Different Sons* (*Futari no musuko*, 1961) and *The Daphne* (*Chinchōge*, 1966), he directed melodramatic family sagas depicting difficult relationships between parents and children. Although several of his films secured foreign distribution at the time, Chiba is now neglected even in Ja-

pan. The breadth of his subject matter and his high reputation in his day suggest that he merits reappraisal.

1930 **Surōnin shōbai ōrai** / Trade and Traffic of a Humble Ronin
**Kunisada Chūji: Kantō daisatsu hen** / Chuji Kunisada: The Great Kanto Murder
**Tenpō yogarasuden** / Chronicle of a Night Crow in the Tenpo Era
**Yūkyō shiranami hanashi** / Story of Debauchery and White Waves
**Osaraba Denji** / Farewell, Denji

1931 **Oshiroigumo** / Spider with a Powdered Face
**Jinsei Hizakurige** / Life and Shank's Mare
**Hakone arashi otoko no tabi** / Travels of a Stormy Man in Hakone
**Ada shamisen** / Shamisen of Revenge
**Kyōkotsu date kurabe** / Chivalry Competition
**Usuisansai hiwa: Matsuyama Onami** / Secret Story of the Fortress on Mt. Usui: Onami of Matsuyama
**Matsuyama Onami: Gojitsudan** / Onami of Matsuyama: Sequel
**Kekka** / River of Blood
**Tenka no bushi** / The Shogun's Warrior
**Shunjū nagadosu** / Spring and Autumn with a Long Sword
**Tsubanari Kōshūji** / Ringing Swords on the Koshu Road
**Kagokaki kenpō** / Fighting Style of a Palanquin Bearer
**Tsubakuro no Otaki** / Otaki the Swallow
**Mujun** / Contradiction
**Matatabi jingi** / Wanderers' Code
**Inaka musume shuren no hayawaza** / Sleight of Hand of a Country Girl

1932 **Kinkanban Jinkurō** / Jinkuro of the Golden Sign
**Mito Kōmon** / Mito Komon

**Byakko** / The White Fox
**Datezakura** / Cherry Blossom of Date
**Ansei taigoku** / The Ansei Incident
**Gijin Guhō** / The Story of Wu Pong (lit. The Righteous Man Wu Pong) (*Taiwan; co-director*)
1933 **Kaishinshi** / Mysterious Gentleman (*Taiwan*)
**Koi no odoriko** / Dancing Girl of Love
**Boku no seishun** / My Youth
1934 **Hiren no honoo** / Flames of Tragic Love
**Jūdō senshu no koi** / The Love of a Judo Player
**Ureshii musume** / Happy Girl
**Nihon koko ni ari** / Here Is Japan
**Geisha sandaiki** / Record of Three Generations of Geisha
1935 **Akachan to daigakusei** / The Baby and the Student
**Jakku kenkachō** / Jack's Fighting Notebooks
**Makaze koikaze** / Wind of Seduction, Wind of Love
**Koi nyōbō** / My Beloved Wife
**Tanoshiki wakaremichi** / The Happy Road of Separation
1936 **Anata to yobeba** / If I Call You
**Koi wa ame ni nurete** / It Rains on Our Love
**Shōkyū sake gassen** / Advancement by Drinking Competition
**Onna no kaikyū** / Woman's Rank
**Uchi no nyōbō nya hige ga aru** / My Wife Has a Beard
1937 **Ren'ai bekarazu tokuhon** / Textbook against Love
**A, sore na no ni** / Ah, Even Though...
**Bokō no hanagata** / Star of the Alma Mater
**Takarajima sōdōki** / Record of Trouble on Treasure Island
**Kokkyō no fūun** / Border Situation
**Gunshin Nogi-san** / Nogi, God of the Army

**Utsukushiki taka** / Beautiful Hawk
**Atashi kōfuku yo** / I Am Happy
1938 **Magokoro banzai** / Viva Sincerity
**Hito wa wakamono** / People Are Young
**Jinsei gekijō: Zankyō hen** / Theater of Life: Chivalry Chapter
**Sugikyō no saiminjutsu** / Sugikyo's Hypnotism
**Josei kōro** / Women's Journey
1939 **Chijō tengoku** / Heaven on Earth
**Dōke no machi** / Town of Folly
**Hanazono no tenshi** / Angel in the Flower Garden
**Nēsan no oyomeiri** / Older Sister's Marriage
**Kūsō buraku** / Fantasy Village
1940 **Hideko no ōendanchō** / Hideko the Cheerleader
**Hikoroku naguraru** / Hikoroku Is Beaten
**Hanzuiin Chōbei** / Chobei Hanzuiin
1941 **Josei shinsō** / Women's New Clothes
1942 **Shiroi hekiga** / The White Mural
**Umineko no minato** / Seagull Harbor
1943 **Aozora kōkyōgaku** / Symphony of the Blue Sky
1944 **Chi no tsumemoji** / Letters Scratched in Blood / Words the Bloody Fingernails Wrote
1945 **Sugata naki teki** / Invisible Enemy
1946 **Hyōtan kara deta koma** / Unexpected Dividend (lit. Spinning Top from a Gourd)
**Renga jokō** / Women's Brick Factory (*made in 1940*)
**Aru yo no seppun** / A Certain Night's Kiss
1947 **Hana saku kazoku** / Blossoming Family
**Kōfuku e no shōtai** / Invitation to Happiness
1948 **Utsukushiki hyō** / Beautiful Leopard
**Ikiteiru gazō** / The Living Portrait

1949 **Niizuma kaigi** / New Wives'
Conference
**Onna no tatakai** / Woman's Struggle
**Kamen butōkai** / Masked Ball

1950 **Tōkyō mushuku** / Tokyo
Wanderer
**Tsuma to onna kisha** / Wife and
Woman Journalist
**Yama no kanata e: Daiichibu:
Ringo no hoo** / Beyond the
Mountains: Part One: Applecheek
**Yama no kanata e: Dainibu:
Sakana no seppun** / Beyond the
Mountains: Part Two: Fish's Kiss
**Yoru no hibotan** / Red Peony of
Night

1951 **Wakai musumetachi** / Young Girls
**Nakinureta ningyō** / Weeping Doll
**Wakōdo no uta** / Song of a Young
Person

1952 **Keian hichō** / Secret Notes of the
Keian Period
**Kin no tamago** / The Golden Egg
**Tōkyō no koibito** / Tokyo
Sweetheart / Jewels in Our Hearts
**Oka wa hanazakari** / Hill in Bloom

1953 **Himawari musume** / Sunflower
Girl / Love in a Teacup
**Aijō ni tsuite** / About Love
**Kōfuku-san** / Mr. Happiness

1954 **Koyoi hito yoru o** / Tonight's the
Night
**Kakute yume ari** / Thus I Dreamed
**Aku no tanoshisa** / Temptation of
Pleasure / Happy to Be Bad

1955 **Magokoro no hana hiraku: Jokyū**
/ Blossoming Flowers of Sincerity:
Hostess
**Sararīman** / Salaryman
**Atsukama-shi to Oyakama-shi** /
Mr. Impudent and Mr. Noisy
**Zoku sararīman** / Salaryman 2

1956 **Hesokuri shachō** / The President's
Boss (lit. The Boss' Nest Egg)
**Zoku hesokuri shachō** / The
President's Boss 2
**Onibi** / Death Fire / Will o'the
Wisp (lit.)

**Kōjinbutsu no fūfu** / Loving
Couple
**Okashina yatsu** / Crazy Guy

1957 **Ōban** / Large Size / Mr. Fortune
Maker
**Zoku ōban: Fūun hen** / Large Size
2: Sinister Chapter / Mr. Fortune
Maker 2: Sinister Chapter
**Shitamachi** / Downtown
**Zoku zoku ōban: Dotō hen** /
Large Size 3: Angry Waves Chapter
/ Mr. Fortune Maker 3: Angry
Waves Chapter

1958 **Yajikita dōchūki** / The Happy
Pilgrimage / Yaji and Kita on the
Road (lit.)
**Ōban: Kanketsu hen** / Large Size:
Concluding Part / Mr. Fortune
Maker: Concluding Part
**Yajikita dōchūki: Sugoroku** / The
Happy Pilgrimage: Backgammon
/ Yaji and Kita on the Road:
Backgammon (lit.)

1959 **Kitsune to tanuki** / Fox and
Raccoon Dog
**Wakai koibitotachi** / Young Lovers

1960 **Haori no taishō** / The Happicoat
Comedian / General in a Cloak (lit.)
**Gametsui yatsu** / Greedy Guy /
This Greedy Old Skin

1961 **Ginza no koibitotachi** / Lovers of
Ginza
**Honkon no yoru** / A Night in
Hong Kong
**Futari no musuko** / Different Sons
/ Two Sons (lit.)

1962 **Honkon no hoshi** / A Star of Hong
Kong
**Kawa no hotori de** / By the River's
Edge / Born in Sin

1963 **Onna ni tsuyoku naru kufū no
kazukazu** / Many Ways to Attract
Women
**Ōban: Sōshū hen** / Large Size:
Complete Version / Mr. Fortune
Maker: Complete Version
**Honoruru Tōkyō Honkon** /
Honolulu-Tokyo-Hong Kong
**Miren** / Lingering Affection

1964 **Hadaka no jūyaku** / The Naked
Executive
**Danchi nanatsu no taizai** / Seven
Deadly Sins in a Housing Complex
1966 **Bankokku no yoru** / A Night in
Bangkok
**Chinchōge** / The Daphne
1968 **Haruranman** / Spring Abundance /
Devils-in-Law
**Kawachi fūtenzoku** / The Carefree
Tribe of Kawachi / Hippies of
Kawachi
**Wakamono yo chōsen seyo** /
Young Challengers
1969 **Mito Kōmon man'yūki** / Record of
Mito Komon's Pleasure Trip

## FUJITA Toshiya
**(January 16, 1932–August 29, 1997)**
藤田敏八

Fujita is ironically best-known in the
West for one of his least personal films,
the overblown, ultra-violent action
movie *Lady Snowblood* (*Shurayuki hime*,
1973), which charted a young woman's
quest for revenge on the men who murdered her father and raped her mother.
Though featuring a memorably icy star
performance from Meiko Kaji and filled
with striking color effects, the film was
distinctly heavy-handed in approach
and barely questioned the eye-for-an-
eye morality espoused by its heroine. Its
sequel, *Lady Snowblood 2: Love Song of
Vengeance* (*Shurayuki hime: Urami renka*,
1974), displayed a certain political edge
in its examination of class conflicts during the Meiji era, but its analysis was
compromised by the crudities of its exploitation format.

Fujita had begun his career working with similar exploitation material
at Nikkatsu, where he contributed two
installments to the *Stray Cat Rock* (*Nora

neko rokku*) series. His first major critical
success was *Wet Sand in August* (*Hachigatsu no nureta suna*, 1971), a melodrama,
set on the Shōnan Coast southwest of
Tokyo, about the friendships and romances of a group of young people with
few hopes for the future. This earned
him a reputation for dealing with youthful subjects; after a short period working
on Nikkatsu Roman Porno, he returned
to the experiences of the young with a
series of films in a realist mode. *Virgin
Blues* (*Bājin Burūsu*, 1974) and *Did The
Red Bird Escape?* (*Akai tori nigeta?*, 1973)
dramatized the generation gap through
stories of teenagers who turn to crime
and are rejected by their parents. *The Red
Lantern* (*Aka chōchin*, 1974) depicted a
young couple's fruitless search for a room
in Tokyo; Gregory Barrett has argued
that the story expressed the younger
generation's "futile attempt to escape
from a restrictive society." *Days That
Have Passed* (*Kaerazaru hibi*, 1978), an account of the life of a high school boy who
returns from Tokyo to his native Nagano
after his father's death, topped the annual
Kinema Junpō critics' poll. Fujita also directed *Temptation Angel* (*Tenshi o yūwaku*,
1979), perhaps the best of the several star
vehicles for the popular romantic pairing
of Momoe Yamaguchi and Tomokazu
Miura. Despite occasional stylistic indul-
gences, it was a warmly observed account
of the everyday problems of a young sub-
urban couple, and contained some of the
first indications of Miura's talent as a serious actor.

During the eighties, Fujita made
*Do the Slow Boogie with Me* (*Surōna bugi
ni shite kure*, 1981) for Kadokawa; this
was another romantic drama, about
the relationship between a girl and a
middle-aged man. *The Miracle of Joe the
Petrel* (*Umitsubame Jō no kiseki*, 1984)
melded aspects of the youth film with

elements of the crime thriller; it was set among the Manila underworld, and its hero was a half-Okinawan, half-Filipino yakuza. Fujita's last film as director, *Revolver* (*Riborubā*, 1988), charted the lives of various characters connected by a single gun. By this time, Fujita was established as an actor, appearing notably for Seijun Suzuki in *Zigeunerweisen* (*Tsigoineruwaizen*, 1980). He continued to act until his death, and, with the exception of *Lady Snowblood*, is now perhaps best known in the West for his performances. Nevertheless, his realist films of the seventies were well-regarded in their time, and might benefit from wider distribution abroad.

1967  **Hikō shōnen: Hinode no sakebi** / Bad Boy: Crying at Sunrise
1968  **Nippon zeronen** / Japan, Year Zero (*released in 2002*)
1970  **Hikō shōnen: Wakamono no toride** / Bad Boy: A Young Man's Stronghold
**Nora neko rokku: Wairudo janbo** / Stray Cat Rock: Wild Jumbo
**Shinjuku autorō: Buttobase** / Shinjuku Outlaw: Send It Flying
1971  **Nora neko rokku: Bōsōshūdan '71** / Stray Cat Rock: Motorcycle Gang '71
**Hachigatsu no nureta suna** / Wet Sand in August
1972  **Hachigatsu wa Erosu no nioi** / The Summer Affair / Scent of Eros in August (lit.)
**Erosu no yūwaku** / Seduction of Eros
1973  **Akai tori nigeta?** / Did the Red Bird Escape?
**Erosu wa amaki kaori** / Eros Smells Sweet
**Shurayuki hime** / Lady Snowblood
1974  **Aka chōchin** / The Red Lantern
**Shurayuki hime: Urami renka** / Lady Snowblood 2: Love Song of Vengeance

**Imōto** / Younger Sister
**Bājin burūsu** / Virgin Blues
**Honoo no shōzō** / Portrait of Flame
1975  **Hadashi no burūjin** / Barefoot in Blue Jeans
1977  **Yokosuka otokogari: Shōjo: Etsuraku** / Yokosuka Manhunt: Young Girl: Pleasure
**Jitsuroku furyō shōjo** / Confessions of a Teenage Mother (lit. True Record of a Delinquent Girl)
1978  **Kikenna kankei** / Dangerous Liaisons
**Kaerazaru hibi** / Days That Have Passed / Bittersweet
1979  **Motto shinayaka ni, motto shitataka ni** / Smoother and Harder
**Jūhassai, umi e** / 18-Year-Old, To the Sea
**Tenshi o yūwaku** / Temptation Angel
1981  **Surōna bugi ni shite kure** / Do the Slow Boogie with Me
1982  **Daiamondo wa kizu tsukanai** / Diamonds Don't Scratch
1983  **Daburu beddo** / Double Bed
1984  **Umitsubame Jō no kiseki** / The Miracle of Joe the Petrel / The Stormy Petrel
1986  **Hakkō kirameku hate** / Beyond the Shining Sea
1988  **Riborubā** / Revolver

## FUKASAKU Kinji
**(July 3, 1930–January 12, 2003)**
深作欣二

A specialist in action cinema from the early sixties onwards, Fukasaku had acquired an international profile within the industry as early as 1970, having taken charge of the Japanese half of the Pearl Harbor saga *Tora! Tora! Tora!* (a

Jingi naki tatakai / Battles without Honor and Humanity *(1973): This seminal work exemplified Fukasaku's style and the hyperrealist violence of the* jitsuroku-eiga *genre.*

Toei-20th Century Fox co-production) after Akira Kurosawa was removed from the project. Despite this and two later science fiction co-productions—*Message from Space* (Uchū kara no messēji, 1978) and *Virus* (Fukkatsu no hi, 1980) —with international casts, he ironically achieved a reputation among foreign audiences only at the end of his life. A retrospective at Rotterdam in 2000 was followed by the wide distribution of his last completed feature, *Battle Royale* (Batoru rowaiaru, 2000), which had courted controversy in Japan with its story of a class of teenagers compelled to fight to the death in a radical government measure to deal with youth crime. In fact, this savage satire was atypically elaborate in concept compared to the genre pieces which constituted the bulk of Fukasaku's work. Based largely at Toei during the sixties and seventies,

he worked primarily on yakuza films, distinguished by their postwar settings (in contrast to the Edo- or Meiji-era yakuza films of Toei colleagues such as Tai Katō) and by the stylistic immediacy which would typify Toei's seventies specialty, the *jitsuroku-eiga*.

Fukasaku acknowledged the influence of the French New Wave, an influence most obviously visible in *Blackmail Is My Life* (Kyōkatsu koso ga waga jinsei, 1968), with its use of jump cuts and switches from black and white to color, and in the bold stylization of *The Black Lizard* (Kurotokage, 1968) and *Black Rose Mansion* (Kurobara no yakata, 1969), high camp vehicles for transvestite star Akihiro Miwa. Generally, however, Fukasaku opted for a hyperrealist style, using a handheld camera and the zoom lens to give his work the immediacy of newsreel footage. This style reached its apogee in his most famous gangster film, *Battles without Honor and Humanity* (*Jingi naki tatakai*, 1973), the first in a long-running series of which Fukasaku directed all but one installment. Here, a meticulous recreation of Occupation-era Hiroshima captured the post-apocalypse *zeitgeist* and showed how crime flourished in the political near-vacuum of immediate postwar Japan.

The trauma of World War II, generally a backdrop to Fukasaku's work, was the subject of his best film, *Under the Flag of the Rising Sun* (*Gunki hatameku moto ni*, 1972), a *Rashomon*-like investigation into the circumstances of a military execution, revealed in flashback through the differing accounts of four witnesses. Free from the conventions of genre filmmaking, Fukasaku produced a subversive examination of a taboo subject, and an acknowledgement that the historical record, shaped by partial personal testimony, is inevitably unreliable. Another politically conscious non-genre film was *If You Were Young: Rage* (*Kimi ga wakamono nara*, 1970), in which the bleak experiences of five working-class men in Tokyo were used with some intelligence and plausibility as a microcosm of the problems of the Japanese proletariat as a whole.

Nevertheless, Fukasaku's champions have tended to place undue emphasis on elements of social criticism in his genre pieces, from the depiction of life in the slums in such early films as *Greed in Broad Daylight* (*Hakuchū no buraikan*, 1961) and *Wolves, Pigs and Men* (*Ōkami to buta to ningen*, 1964), to the exposure of political corruption in *Blackmail Is My Life*, to the implied association of the yakuza with the pro-militarist far right in *Japan Organized Crime Boss* (*Nihon bōryokudan: Kumichō*, 1969), and the explicit links between the mob and the police in *Cops vs. Thugs* (*Kenkei tai soshiki bōryoku*, 1975) and *Yakuza Graveyard* (*Yakuza no hakaba: Kuchinashi no hana*, 1976). Jasper Sharp and Tom Mes have praised the way in which Fukasaku's yakuza films explored the dark underside of Japan's postwar reconstruction, but the presentation of petty criminals as heroic rebels against the establishment merely suggested a preference for anarchic violence over authoritarian violence. Even in his most interesting films, Fukasaku's effects were calculated to place sadistic emphasis on the physical details of bloodshed. In *Under the Flag of the Rising Sun*, monochrome flashbacks dissolve into color to display killings more graphically; freeze frames hold severed limbs in lingering close up in *Battles without Honor and Humanity*; and onscreen text tallies the death toll in *Battle Royale*. The limitation of Fukasaku's work was not so much that his characters lacked honor and humanity as that the director himself rarely adopted a compensating moral perspective on their brutality.

Though he continued intermittently to make crime thrillers, such as *The Triple Cross* (*Itsu ka giragira suru hi*, 1992), until the end of his career, Fukasaku also made *jidai-geki* in his later years. Some were purely commercial: *Legend of the Eight Samurai* (*Satomi hakkenden*, 1983) consisted almost solely of special effects and action thrills, paying scant regard to narrative plausibility or historical reality. Nevertheless, Fukasaku's characteristic anti-authoritarianism was visible in such works as *Shogun's Samurai* (*Yagyū ichizoku no inbō*, 1978), which iconoclastically rewrote history by depicting the fictitious murder of Shogun Iemitsu, and *Sure Death: Revenge* (*Hissatsu 4: Urami harashimasu*, 1987), which portrayed the ill-treatment of Edo-period slum dwellers by samurai. Though these films were more style than substance, they earned Fukasaku a reputation as a reliable commercial director, which gave him the freedom to mount such offbeat projects as *Fall Guy* (*Kamata kōshinkyoku*, 1982), a satire on the film industry depicting the relationship between an arrogant star and his devoted stunt double, and later *Battle Royale*. He died while directing the sequel to that film; completed by his son Kenta, it was poorly received. After years of neglect, however, Fukasaku's own reputation is now higher than it deserves to be.

1961 **Fūraibō tantei: Akai tani no sangeki** / The Drifting Detective: Tragedy of the Red Valley

**Fūraibō tantei: Misaki o wataru kuroi kaze** / The Drifting Detective: Black Wind across the Cape

**Fankī hatto no kaidanji** / Vigilante in the Funky Hat

**Fankī hatto no kaidanji: Nisen-man-en no ude** / Vigilante in the Funky Hat: The 20 Million Yen Arm

**Hakuchū no buraikan** / Greed in Broad Daylight / High Noon for Gangsters

1962 **Hokori takaki chōsen** / The Proud Challenge

**Gyangu tai G-men** / Gang vs. G-Men

1963 **Gyangu dōmei** / Gang Alliance

1964 **Jakoman to Tetsu** / Jakoman and Tetsu

**Ōkami to buta to ningen** / Wolves, Pigs and Men

1966 **Odoshi** / Threat

**Kamikaze yarō: Mahiru no kettō** / The Kamikaze Guy: Duel at High Noon

**Hokkai no abareryū** / Exploding Dragon of the North Sea

1967 **Kaisanshiki** / Dissolution Ceremony / The Breakup

1968 **Bakuto kaisanshiki** / Gamblers' Dissolution Ceremony

**Kurotokage** / The Black Lizard

**Kyōkatsu koso ga waga jinsei** / Blackmail is My Life / Call Me Blackmail

**Ganma 3-gō: Uchū daisakusen** / The Green Slime / Battle Beyond the Stars (lit. Gamma 3: Big Operation in Space)

1969 **Kurobara no yakata** / Black Rose Mansion

**Nihon bōryokudan: Kumichō** / Japan Organized Crime Boss

1970 **Chizome no daimon** / Bloody Coat of Arms

**Kimi ga wakamono nara** / If You Were Young: Rage / Our Dear Buddies

**Tora! Tora! Tora!** (*co-director*)

1971 **Bakuto gaijin butai** / Gambler: Foreign Opposition / Gamblers in Okinawa / Sympathy for the Underdog

1972 **Gunki hatameku moto ni** / Under the Flag of the Rising Sun

**Gendai yakuza: Hitokiri yota** / Street Mobster / The Code of the Killer / Modern Yakuza: Outlaw Killer (lit.)

**Hitokiri yota: Kyōken sankyōdai** / The Code of the Killer: Three Mad Dog Brothers

1973 **Jingi naki tatakai** / Battles without Honor and Humanity / The Yakuza Papers

**Jingi naki tatakai: Hiroshima shitō hen** / Battles without Honor and Humanity: Fight to the Death in Hiroshima

**Jingi naki tatakai: Dairi sensō** / Battles without Honor and Humanity: Proxy War

1974 **Jingi naki tatakai: Chōjō sakusen** / Battles without Honor and Humanity: Police Tactics / Battles without Honor and Humanity: Summit Maneuvers

**Jingi naki tatakai: Kanketsu hen** / Battles without Honor and Humanity: Final Episode

**Shin jingi naki tatakai** / New

Battles without Honor and
Humanity
1975 **Jingi no hakaba** / Graveyard of
Honor
**Kenkei tai soshiki bōryoku** / Cops
vs. Thugs / Prefectural Police vs.
Organized Crime (lit.)
**Shikingen gōdatsu** / Theft of
Capital
**Shin jingi naki tatakai: Kumichō
no kubi** / New Battles without
Honor and Humanity: It's Time to
Kill the Boss
1976 **Bōsō panikku: Daigekitotsu** /
Violent Panic: The Big Crash
**Shin jingi naki tatakai: Kumichō
saigo no hi** / New Battles without
Honor and Humanity: The Boss's
Final Day
**Yakuza no hakaba: Kuchinashi no
hana** / Yakuza Graveyard
1977 **Hokuriku dairi sensō** / Hokuriku
Proxy War
**Dōberuman deka** / Detective
Doberman
1978 **Yagyū ichizoku no inbō** / Shogun's
Samurai / The Yagyu Conspiracy (lit.)
**Uchū kara no messēji** / Message
from Space
**Akō-jō danzetsu** / The Fall of Ako
Castle
1980 **Fukkatsu no hi** / Virus / Day of
Resurrection (lit.)
1981 **Seishun no mon** / The Gate of
Youth (*co-director*)
**Makai tenshō** / Samurai
Resurrection
1982 **Dōtonborigawa** / Lovers Lost /
The River Dotonbori (lit.)
**Kamata kōshinkyoku** / Fall Guy
(lit. Kamata March)
1983 **Jinsei gekijō** / Theater of Life (*co-director*)
**Satomi hakkenden** / Legend of
Eight Samurai
1984 **Shanhai Bansu Kingu** / Shanghai
Rhapsody (lit. Shanghai Vance
King)
1986 **Kataku no hito** / House on Fire

1987 **Hissatsu IV: Urami harashimasu** /
Sure Death 4 / Sure Death: Revenge
1988 **Hana no ran** / Rage of Love / A
Chaos of Flowers (lit.)
1992 **Itsu ka giragira suru hi** / The
Triple Cross
1994 **Chūshingura gaiden: Yotsuya
kaidan** / Crest of Betrayal (lit.
Supplement to Chushingura:
Yotsuya Ghost Story)
1999 **Omocha** / The Geisha House (lit.
Plaything)
2000 **Batoru Rowaiaru** / Battle Royale
2003 **Batoru Rowaiaru II: Chinkonka**
/ Battle Royale II: Requiem (*co-director*)

## FURUHATA Yasuo
(b. August 19, 1934)
降旗康男

A proficient commercial director, Furuhata made his debut with the youth film *Bad Girl Yoko* (*Hikō shōjo Yōko*, 1966), about a girl who, along with her boyfriend, escapes Japan by boarding a boat to San Tropez. He truly cut his teeth, however, on two popular series of Toei action pictures: *Modern Yakuza* (*Gendai yakuza*), of which he directed two episodes, and *Abashiri Prison* (*Abashiri bangaichi*), to which he contributed six. The latter series cemented a productive working relationship with tough-guy star Ken Takakura, and, with its Hokkaido settings, established the director's penchant for snowbound locations.

Furuhata worked again with Takakura on *Winter Flower* (*Fuyu no hana*, 1978), about a former yakuza looking after the teenage daughter of a fellow gangster for whose death he was responsible. The film's mood earned comparisons with French crime pictures. Takakura also starred in *Station* (*Eki*, 1981), following twelve years in the life and career of a policeman who also competes as an Olympic sharpshooter, and *Demon* (*Yasha*, 1985), about an ex-criminal who has left the gangster life to marry and work as a fisherman in a coastal village. Both films centered more on personal drama than on action: *Demon* was a mature character study, rich in local color and commenting intelligently on the reaction of small communities to such ostensibly urban phenomena as alcohol abuse, gambling, and crime. Though this film included action scenes more typical of a crime thriller, Furuhata also made more straightforwardly dramatic films, often with romantic themes. *Love* (*Izakaya Chōji*, 1983) charted the enduring passion between former lovers. *Buddies* (*A un*, 1989) was an account of a friendship destroyed by the unspoken love of one friend for the wife of the other; it was set against the backdrop of prewar society and politics, as was *Winter Camellia* (*Kantsubaki*, 1992), a story about rival politicians and the yakuza who work for them competing for the favor of a geisha in the provincial city of Kōchi. *Time of Wickedness* (*Ma no toki*, 1985), considered by Japanese critics to be Furuhata's masterpiece, was a study of an incestuous relationship between mother and son.

Furuhata's biggest hit, however, was *The Railroad Man* (*Poppoya*, 1999), a sentimental melodrama again starring Takakura as the ageing stationmaster of a declining former mining town in Hokkaido. While expertly made, the film was, in Raymond Durgnat's phrase, a "male weepie," idolizing a hero who puts work before family even when his wife and child are dying. Another hit was *The Firefly* (*Hotaru*, 2001), a film about the survivors of the kamikaze corps, which examined the role of servicemen from colonized Korea in the war effort. The melodramatic *Red Moon* (*Akai tsuki*, 2004) also evoked the war, dramatizing the loves and sufferings of colonists in Manchuria at the time of the Soviet invasion. It was criticized in some quarters for ignoring the cruelties the Japanese inflicted on the local population; Mark Schilling hinted that Furuhata's implicitly nationalist attitudes have denied him an international reputation. Nevertheless, his consistent commercial and intermittent critical success within Japan suggest that his oeuvre might merit further exploration.

**1966** **Hikō shōjo Yōko** / Bad Girl Yoko
**Jigoku no okite ni asu wa nai** / The Law of Hell Has No Tomorrow
**1967** **Gyangu no teiō** / The Sovereign of All Gangsters / Gang 11
**Chōeki jūhachinen: Karishutsugoku** / Parole (lit. 18 Years' Penal Servitude: Parole)
**1968** **Gokuchū no kaoyaku** / The Boss in Jail
**Uragiri no ankokugai** / Treacherous Underworld
**1969** **Gendai yakuza: Yotamono no okite** / Modern Yakuza: Gangster Code
**Gendai yakuza: Yotamono jingi** / Modern Yakuza: Honor among Gangsters
**Shin Abashiri bangaichi: Runin misaki no kettō** / New Abashiri Prison: Bloody Battle of Exile Cape
**1970** **Nihon jokyōden: Makkana dokyōbana** / Chronicle of Strong Women of Japan: Bright Red Flower of Courage
**Ninkyō kōbō shi: Kumichō to daigashi** / History of the Rise and Fall of Chivalry: The Boss and the Moneylender's Agent
**Sutemi no narazumono** / Desperate Outlaw
**Shin Abashiri bangaichi: Daishinrin no kettō** / New Abashiri Prison: Bloody Battle of the Great Forest

Shin Abashiri bangaichi: Fubuki no hagure ōkami / New Abashiri Prison: Stray Wolf in a Snowstorm

1971 Gorotsuki mushuku / Wandering Rogue

Shin Abashiri bangaichi: Arashi o yobu Shiretoko misaki / New Abashiri Prison: Stormy Cape Shiretoko

Shin Abashiri bangaichi: Fubuki no daidassō / New Abashiri Prison: Great Escape in a Snowstorm

1972 Nihon bōryokudan: Koroshi no sakazuki / Japan's Violent Gangs: Killers' Cup

Shin Abashiri bangaichi: Arashi yobu danpu jingi / New Abashiri Prison: Stormy Dump Truck Honor

1973 Shikima ōkami / Sex-Crazed Wolf

1974 Yoru no enka: Shinobigoi / Night Ballad: Hidden Love

1978 Fuyu no hana / Winter Flower

1979 Honjitsu tadaima tanjō / Just Born Today

Waga seishun no irebun / Our Youth's Eleven

Nihon no fikusā / Japanese Fixer

1981 Shikakenin Baian / Baian the Assassin

Eki / Station

1983 Izakaya Chōji / Love (lit. Bar Choji)

1985 Ma no toki / Time of Wickedness

Yasha / Demon

1987 Wakarenu riyū / Reason for Not Divorcing

1989 Shōgun Iemitsu no ranshin: Gekitotsu / Shogun's Shadow / Gekitotsu: The Insanity of Shogun Iemitsu (lit.)

Gokudō no onnatachi: Sandaime anego / Yakuza Wives: Third Generation Female Boss

A un / Buddies (lit. Alpha and Omega)

1990 Tasumania monogatari / Tasmania Story

Isan sōzoku / Inheritance

1991 Don ni natta otoko / The Man Who Became a Don

1992 Kantsubaki / Winter Camellia

1994 Shin gokudō no onnatachi: Horetara jigoku / New Yakuza Wives: Hell If You Fall in Love

1995 Kura / Kura (lit. Storehouse)

1997 Gendai ninkyōden / A Story of Modern Chivalry

1999 Poppoya / The Railroad Man

2001 Hotaru / The Firefly

2004 Akai tsuki / Red Moon

2007 Tsukigami / The Haunted Samurai

## FURUMAYA Tomoyuki
(b. November 14, 1968)
古厩智之

One of the most promising of younger Japanese directors, Furumaya made short films in 8 and 16mm formats before winning the PIA Film Festival scholarship to realize his first feature, *This Window Is Yours* (*Kono mado wa kimi no mono*, 1995). This story of a teenage romance won praise for its sensitivity to the nuances of adolescent behavior, its way of keeping emotions implicit, and its careful evocation of the details of life in provincial Japan. These qualities were also visible in Furumaya's semi-autobiographical second film, *Bad Company* (*Mabudachi*, 2001), about a trio of delinquents at junior high school. Virtually without major incident, apart from one tragic event, this subtly affecting film captured the beauty of rural Nagano without subsiding into mere prettiness and employed meditative long takes that faintly recalled the work of Hiroshi Shimizu in their way of observing, rather than passing judgment on, the characters.

Furumaya's next film, *Robocon* (*Ro-*

*bokon*, 2003), also focused on alienated youth: its central character was a disenchanted girl at vocational school who becomes determined to win a robotics competition. In *Goodbye, Midori* (*Sayonara Midori-chan*, 2005), Furumaya shifted his focus for the first time to adult relationships, examining the dilemma of a female office worker attracted, despite herself, to an unworthy man. Visually more austere than *Bad Company*, the film was distinguished by its intelligent awareness of the way in which posture and facial expression reveal subtleties of character. With his detached yet compassionate style, Furumaya may succeed in sustaining a classical Japanese tradition of film drama based in realistic detail and behavioral nuance through the coming decades.

1991 **Sutego no Sutekichi** / Sutekichi the Abandoned Child (*8mm short*)
**Shakunetsu no dojjibōru** / Scorching Hot (lit. Red-Hot Dodgeball) (*16mm short*)

1992 **Hashiruze** / Running / Run! (*16mm short*)

1994 **Tetsu to hagane** / Steel Blue (lit. Iron and Steel) (*short*)

1995 **Kono mado wa kimi no mono** / This Window Is Yours (*16mm*)

1999 **Indies B: Bokusā to tako** / Indies B: The Boxer and the Kite (*short*)

2001 **Mabudachi** / Bad Company

2003 **Robokon** / Robocon / Robot Competition

2005 **Sayonara Midori-chan** / Goodbye Midori

**FUTAGAWA Buntarō**
**(June 18, 1899–March 28, 1966)**
二川文太郎

A specialist in *jidai-geki*, Futagawa is re-

©PIA Film Festival

Kono mado wa kimi no mono / This Window Is Yours *(1995): Furumaya's first feature revealed his gift for the nuances of behavior and subtleties of film technique.*

membered largely for the silent films he made at Makino Productions in collaboration with popular action hero Tsumasaburō Bandō. Several of these survive: *Kageboshi* (*Edo Kaizokuden: Kagebōshi*, 1925) is admired for having introduced a greater psychological depth into a genre hitherto concerned largely with action, while the most famous, *Orochi* (1925), is considered of importance in establishing the anti-heroic persona of the "nihilist hero" in revolt against society, which would be developed by Daisuke Itō. The film's melancholy mood was genuinely affecting, though it lacked Itō's depth of political implication, the hero's sufferings being the result more of hard luck than of social injustice.

Noel Burch has called Futagawa "the epitome of the academic neo-Western director"; however, while his style had a certain classical economy, his preference for staging action scenes in long shot was as characteristically Japanese as were his thematic concerns. It seems, moreover, that he made occasional films in a deliberately experimental mode: the lost *When the Gravestone Snores* (*Boseki ga ibikisuru koro*, 1925) was apparently influenced by the then fashionable expressionism of *The Cabinet of Dr. Caligari* (1920, Robert Wiene).

In the thirties, Futagawa worked at Shochiku, where he continued to specialize in period films, often starring the dashing Chōjūrō Hayashi (later renamed Kazuo Hasegawa). However, his sound films were not widely admired, and he retired from direction in 1939. An attempted comeback in the fifties was unsuccessful. Futagawa's younger brother, Eisuke Takizawa, also worked as a director.

1923 **Shinkirō** / Mirage
1924 **Kaiketsu taka** / The Mighty Hawk
**Buaku no men** / The Devil's Mask
**Kekkon subekarazu** / Don't Get Married
**Gekkyūbi no yoru no dekigoto (Kyūryōbi no yoru)** / Incidents on the Night After Payday (Payday Night)
**Shisen ni tateba** / Standing Between Life and Death
**Jōnetsu no hi** / Fires of Passion
**Bonnō jigoku** / Hell of Desire
**Maen no kiyuru koro** / When the Devil-Fire Is Quenched
**Koi no ryōnin** / Love Hunter
**Natsuyoimachi shinjū** / Double Suicide at Natsuyoimachi
**Kunisada Chūji Shinshū miyako ochi** / Chuji Kunisada Leaves the Capital for Shinshu
**Gyakuryū** / Retaliation

1925 **Kunisada Chūji** / Chuji Kunisada
**Edo kaizokuden: Kagebōshi** / Kageboshi (lit. Legend of the Phantom Thief in Edo: The Shadow)
**Boseki ga ibikisuru koro** / When the Gravestone Snores
**Aru tonosama no hanashi** / A Certain Lord's Story
**Rantō** / Swordfight
**Zoku rantō** / Swordfight 2
**Orochi** / Orochi / The Serpent
1926 **Enpō kibun: Bijōfu** / Strange Story of the Enpo Period: A Handsome Young Man
**Shura hakkō (Daiippen; Dainihen; Dansanpen)** / The Pains of Hell (Parts 1, 2, and 3)
**Guren no chimata: Buke katagi** / Neighborhood of Foolish Love: Nature of a Samurai Household
**Dondorobori** / Muddy Moat
**Teru hi kumoru hi (Daiippen; Dainihen)** / Bright Day, Cloudy Day (Parts 1 and 2)
**Kagebōshi torimonochō: Zenpen** / Casebooks of the Shadow: Part 1
1927 **Kagebōshi torimonochō: Kōhen** / Casebooks of the Shadow: Part 2
**Akuma no hoshi no moto ni** / Under the Devil's Stars
**Miyokichi goroshi** / The Killing of Miyokichi
1928 **Dokuhebi** / Poisonous Snake
**Madara hebi** / Spotted Snake
**Shinpan Ōoka seidan (Zenpen; Chūhen)** / Ooka's Trial: New Version (Parts 1 and 2)
**Hi no warai** / Red Smile
**Kotsuniku** / Flesh and Bone
1929 **Taika shinsei** / New Dispensation of the Taika Era (*co-director*)
**Isetsu: Shimizu Ikkaku** / Heterodoxy: Ikkaku Shimizu
**Hatamoto Kobushinshū** / Carpenter Retainers of the Shogun
**Kunisada Chūji no iji** / The Son of the Late Chuji Kunisada

**Katana o nuite** / Drawing the Sword

**Araki Mataemon** / Mataemon Araki

**Aisuru mono no michi** / Way of a Lover

**Zoku kagebōshi: Kyōsō hen** / Kageboshi 2: Thirst-Crazed Chapter

1930 **Donfuku dairensen** / Fortunate Great Love

**Mōmoku no otōto** / Blind Younger Brother

**Kaidan Kasanegafuchi** / The Ghost of Kasane Swamp

**Harenchi gaidō** / Shameless Heresy

1931 **Kagoya dainagon** / Palanquin Bearer and Minister

**Ryakudatsu yomego** / Abduction of the Bride

**Nagebushi Yanosuke: Michinoku no maki** / Bawdy Song of Yanosuke: Michinoku Reel

**Nagebushi Yanosuke: Edo no maki** / Bawdy Song of Yanosuke: Edo Reel

1932 **Yajikita: Bijin sōdōki** / Yaji and Kita: Trouble About a Beauty

**Nawanuke Jihei: Shiranami zaifu** / Jihei Nawanuke: The Wallet of Shiranami

**Kurama Tengu: Taifū no maki** / Kurama Tengu: Typhoon Reel

**Kamiyui Shinzō** / Shinzo the Hairdresser

**Tenbare Hisaroku** / Hisaroku under Clear Skies

**Adauchi kyōdai kagami** / Model Avenging Brothers

1933 **Kōsetsu: Nuretsubame** / Rumor: Wet Swallow

**Yatō to seishun** / The Night Thief and Youth

**Matagorō kyōdai** / The Brothers Matagoro

**Unka no kyōteki** / Rivals in Cloud and Mist

**Tenmei hatamotogasa: Kōrui no maki** / A Retainer's Helmet of the Tenmei Era: A Beautiful Woman's Tears

1934 **Tenmei hatamotogasa: Hareru hi no maki** / A Retainer's Helmet of the Tenmei Era: Brightening Days

**Yarisabi renbo** / Love of a Rusted Spear

**Rinzō shusse tabi** / Rinzo's Journey to Success

**Tsujigiri zange** / Penitence for the Killing at the Crossroads

1935 **Jingi wa kagayaku** / Glory of Honor

**Umon torimonochō: Hanayome jigoku hen** / The Casebooks of Detective Umon: A Bride's Hell

1936 **Iseya koban** / Iseya's Gold

1937 **Ruten: Daiichibu: Honoo** / Vicissitudes of Life: Part 1: The Flame

**Ruten: Dainibu: Hoshi** / Vicissitudes of Life: Part 2: The Star

1938 **Shunpū Ise monogatari** / Tale of the Spring Breeze at Ise

**Isetsu: Hatamoto gonin otoko** / Heterodoxy: Five Retainers

**Nagadosu jiai** / Competition of Long Swords

**Kimen mikazukitō** / Demon-Masked Group of the Crescent Moon

1939 **Chūji tabi nikki** / Chuji's Travel Diary

**Nijibare kaidō** / Road under a Rainbow

1955 **Fukushū Jōrurizaka: Onibuse tōge no shūgeki** / Revenge at Jorurizaka: Attack at Onibuse Pass

**Fukushū Jōrurizaka: Akatsuki no kessen** / Revenge of Jorurizaka: Bloody Battle at Dawn

## GOSHA Hideo
### (February 16, 1929–August 30, 1992)
五社英雄

The work of Hideo Gosha inhabits a middle ground between the historical detail and physical realism of *jidai-geki* and the pure action of *chanbara*. Initially employed as a television director at Fuji Television, he learned to convey essential plot points economically and to stage sudden climaxes effectively. The success of his most famous TV series, *Three Outlaw Samurai (Sanbiki no samurai)*, earned him an invitation to adapt it as a feature film for Shochiku in 1964. Influenced in style and content by Kurosawa, Gosha's big screen debut was arguably his best work, combining razor-sharp black and white cinematography with narrative drive and incorporating some trenchant social commentary in its depiction of the ill treatment of farmers by a callous chamberlain.

This sympathy for the underdog was a recurrent feature of Gosha's work. In *Official Gold (Goyōkin*, 1969), the inhabitants of a fishing village are murdered on the orders of a provincial aristocrat to prevent them from bearing witness to the theft of a shipload of the Shogunate's gold, while the mad dog warrior protagonist of *Tenchu (Hitokiri*, 1969) is a pawn in a political game, first used, then discarded by his master. These were among Gosha's most politically acute films, but here as elsewhere, the tone of his work was ultimately nihilistic. In *Three Outlaw Samurai*, despite the protection of the samurai, the farmers are too fearful to present their petition for better treatment to their lord, while in *Tenchu*, the anti-hero willingly sacrifices his own life in order to exact revenge on his betrayer.

Among Gosha's other sixties films, *Samurai Wolf (Kiba Ōkaminosuke*, 1966) was a paradoxically terse yet overblown account of the conflict between a hired bodyguard and a hired killer. With its outlandish characterizations and exaggerated imagery, it was more reminscent of a spaghetti Western than an orthodox samurai picture. *Secret of the Urn (Tange Sazen: Hien iaigiri*, 1966) was an uncharacteristically lighthearted film about the one-eyed, one-armed samurai Sazen Tange; actually a remake of Sadao Yamanaka's *The Pot Worth a Million Ryo (Tange Sazen yowa: Hyakuman-ryō no tsubo*, 1935), it lacked the original's delicate blend of humor and pathos. *Cash Calls Hell (Gohiki no shinshi*, 1966), a rare *gendai-geki*, was a superior thriller about a convict on parole who agrees to commit murder at the request of a fellow prisoner. Its New Wave stylistic tics were often overemphatic, but it boasted superb monochrome photography and an impressively brooding lead performance from Tatsuya Nakadai.

In the seventies, Gosha's approach became more conventionally generic. *The Wolves (Shussho iwai*, 1971), set against the historical backdrop of an amnesty granted to criminals at the time of the Showa Emperor's accession, was an ordinary yakuza story, albeit with a visually striking festival climax. *Bandits vs. Samurai Squadron (Kumakiri Nizaemon*, 1978) was a bland *chanbara*. *Hunter in the Dark (Yami no kariudo*, 1979) was somewhat more individual, with the amnesiac ronin a quintessential Gosha "little man" protagonist, threatened by machinations that he does not understand. Nevertheless, the film's narrative was excessively convoluted and the characterizations shallow.

Despite the machismo of these films, Gosha in the eighties acquired something of a reputation as a specialist in stories with strong women as protagonists. *Gate of Flesh* (*Nikutai no mon*, 1988) was the fifth adaptation of Taijirō Tamura's novel about the lives of prostitutes during the Occupation, while *Heat Haze* (*Kagerō*, 1991) was a Showa-era revenge saga about a female professional gambler. Also notable among Gosha's later work were *Four Days of Snow and Blood* (*226*, 1989), an account of the attempted military coup of February 26, 1936, and his last film, *Oil Hell Murder* (*Onnagoroshi abura jigoku*, 1992), a revenge tragedy derived from Chikamatsu.

Gosha has a high reputation among devotees of Japanese action genres; Alain Silver has cited *Tenchu* as "one of the most accomplished examples of the samurai genre since World War II." Certainly, Gosha had a flair for orchestrating grisly, shocking moments: witness the image, in *Hunter in the Dark*, of a sword suspended from the ceiling, clutched by a severed hand. His sword-fights had a brutal realism, placing much emphasis on spurting blood and the sound of metal penetrating flesh. Regrettably, he did not extend a comparable realism to his characters who rarely expanded beyond the confines of generic stereotyping. Gosha's stylistic limitations exacerbated this flaw; adept at choreographing action, he was less skilled at handling the camera. His direction, with its frequent resort to zooms, close-ups, and slow motion, was content to rest on the surface, with the consequence that the impact of his films was generally more physical than emotional.

**1964** **Sanbiki no samurai** / Three Outlaw Samurai

**1965** **Kedamono no ken** / Sword of the Beast

**1966** **Gohiki no shinshi** / Cash Calls Hell (lit. Five Violent Gentlemen)

**Tange Sazen: Hien iaigiri** / Secret of the Urn

**Kiba Ōkaminosuke** / Samurai Wolf

**1967** **Kiba Ōkaminosuke: Jigokugiri** / Samurai Wolf: Hell Cut / Samurai Wolf 2

**1969** **Goyōkin** / Official Gold / Goyokin / Steel Edge of Vengeance

**Hitokiri** / Tenchu! / Heaven's Punishment / The Killer

**1971** **Shussho iwai** / The Wolves / Prison Release Celebration (lit.)

**1974** **Bōryokugai** / Street of Violence / Violent City

**1978** **Kumokiri Nizaemon** / Bandits vs. Samurai Squadron (lit. Nizaemon Kumokiri)

**1979** **Yami no kariudo** / Hunter in the Dark

**1982** **Kirūin Hanako no shōgai** / Onimasa (lit. The Life of Hanako Kiruin )

**1983** **Yōkirō** / The Geisha

**1984** **Kita no hotaru** / Fireflies in the North

**1985** **Kai** / The Oar

**Usugeshō** / Tracked / Light Makeup (lit.)

**1986** **Jittemai** / Death Shadows (lit. Truncheon Dance)

**Gokudō no onnatachi** / Yakuza Wives

**1987** **Yoshiwara enjō** / Tokyo Bordello / Yoshiwara Conflagration (lit.)

**1988** **Nikutai no mon** / Gate of Flesh / Carmen 1945

**1989** **226** / Four Days of Snow and Blood

**1991** **Kagerō** / Heat Haze

**1992** **Onnagoroshi abura jigoku** / Oil Hell Murder

## GOSHO Heinosuke
### (February 1, 1902–May 1, 1981)
五所平之助

One of the outstanding practitioners of *shomin-geki*, Gosho specialized in the genre after serving as assistant at Shochiku to its pioneer, Yasujirō Shimazu. His twenties films are all lost, but melodramas such as *The Village Bride* (*Mura no hanayome*, 1928) and *Tricky Girl* (*Karakuri musume*, 1927) apparently focused on themes of illness and physical and mental disability; this concern, rooted in Gosho's own, and his family's, experience of poor health, would be carried over into his postwar work. A similar pathos was apparent in some of his thirties films. *The Izu Dancer* (*Izu no odoriko*, 1933) was a low-key silent romance based on a Kawabata novella about the love affair between a student and an itinerant actress, which climaxed in a moving scene of separation. Gosho also made realist dramas such as *Burden of Life* (*Jinsei no onimotsu*, 1935), in which the most affecting scenes focused on the sadness of a boy neglected by his father.

However, much of the director's work early in the sound era was more cheerful in tone. *The Neighbor's Wife and Mine* (*Madamu to nyōbō*, 1931), Japan's first full sound-on-film film, was a diverting comedy about a writer distracted by various noises, a slim plot that nevertheless allowed Gosho to exploit the new medium with creativity and wit. This and the later pair of comedies *The Bride Talks in Her Sleep* (*Hanayome no negoto*, 1933) and *The Groom Talks in His Sleep* (*Hanamuko no negoto*, 1935) balanced slapstick with satire on contemporary mores. Gosho soon became celebrated for the tension in his work between humor and sadness, and for the expressive editing patterns that earned him a reputation as "the director who uses three shots where others use one."

Gosho sought to minimize militarist content in his wartime films, and after the war, in *Once More* (*Ima hitotabi no*, 1947), produced a melodramatic account of the plight of liberals during the thirties. His postwar films combined social criticism with affecting personal drama. His most famous work, *Where Chimneys Are Seen* (*Entotsu no mieru basho*, 1953), though marred slightly by over-explicit symbolism, was an exemplary depiction of the balance between aspiration and despair in a country recovering from war. *Dispersing Clouds* (*Wakaregumo*, 1951), a very touching film, studied a selfish woman's growth into maturity during a holiday in rural Nagano, where she witnesses the sufferings of the poor and sick. Also most affecting was *The Yellow Crow* (*Kiiroi karasu*, 1957), shot beautifully in color on location in Kamakura, and recounting a bittersweet story about a boy's troubled relationship with his father, lately repatriated from China.

Despite the frequent pathos of his stories, Gosho's worldview in his films from the thirties well into the fifties was a relatively optimistic one. Whereas Ozu's family dramas tended to conclude with the disintegration of families, *Burden of Life*, *Where Chimneys Are Seen*, and *The Yellow Crow* ended with family reunions, while couples who have been divided by quarrels or political circumstances are reconciled or reunited in *The Neighbor's Wife and Mine*, *Once More*, and *Twice on a Certain Night* (*Aru yo futatabi*, 1956). In *Where Chimneys Are Seen* and *The Cock Crows Twice* (*Niwatori wa futatabi naku*, 1954), characters attempt or contemplate suicide, but resolve finally to live on. Gosho's ideals

*Niwatori wa futatabi naku / The Cock Crows Twice (1954): Compassion, tolerance, and human sympathy were the distinguishing features of Gosho's art.*

were tolerance, compromise, and rationality, and his films usually manifested a faith in progress. It is significant that the protagonists of *Once More* and *Dispersing Clouds* were doctors; Gosho associated their work with the regeneration of postwar Japanese society, and in both films, the heroines achieve moral integrity through nursing.

From the mid-fifties, however, Gosho's films began to grow darker in tone. *An Inn at Osaka* (*Ōsaka no yado*, 1954), which used an inn in Japan's commercial capital as a microcosm of society, attacked the materialist values and growing inequality of postwar Japan. Though nominally set in the Meiji period, *Growing Up* (*Takekurabe*, 1955) was also a social critique, condemning a purely commercial outlook which overpowers humane feelings. Both films fea-

tured women who have no option but to become prostitutes. *Twice on a Certain Night*, final reconciliation notwithstanding, showed the corruption of family relationships by financial priorities: a wife, believing that she cannot afford to raise a child, has an abortion. *The Cock Crows Twice*, a bleakly quirky black comedy set in a small coastal town, touched on the unfair lot of the working class as workers drilling for oil strike a hot spring instead, but receive scant payment for a discovery which will bring prosperity to the town.

Elsewhere, Gosho examined unhappy love affairs. *Elegy of the North* (*Banka*, 1957), a study in angst set atmospherically against the bleak backdrop of a Hokkaido port town in early spring, and *Hunting Rifle* (*Ryōjū*, 1961), a melodrama which in tone and imagery anticipated Chabrol or Fassbinder, were accounts of the misery and suspicion caused by infidelity; both culminated in suicide. *An Innocent Witch* (*Osorezan no onna*, 1965) showed the flip side of Gosho's faith in rationality: a prostitute is believed to be cursed and dies while undergoing a Shinto ceremony of exorcism. Here, Gosho associated superstition with the wider irrationality that fueled militarism in the thirties. Militarist fanaticism, along with its corrosive effect on human relationships, was also the subject of his last major film, *Rebellion of Japan* (*Utage*, 1967).

Gosho was both an enquiring dramatist and an intelligent visual stylist, with a subtle montage-based technique designed to highlight significant details and elucidate the nuances of character and the particularities of milieu. His work was distinguished, in Arthur Nolletti's words, by its "compassion and affection for character" and its "unerring sense of life's injustices, contradictions, and complexities." This sense of complexity, and the complementary avoidance of easy answers, gave Gosho's work its remarkable richness and depth. Its poignancy derived from the humanism that he espoused, believing that "only if we love our fellow human beings can we create."

1925 **Sora wa haretari** / The Sky Is Clear
**Otokogokoro** / Man's Heart
**Seishun** / Youth
**Tōsei tamatebako** / The Magnificent Pearl Box
1926 **Machi no hitobito** / Town People
**Hatsukoi** / First Love
**Honryū** / Rapid Stream
**Haha yo koishi** / Mother, I Miss You
**Musume** / Daughter
**Kaeranu sasabue** / Bamboo Grass Flute of No Return

**Itoshi no wagako** / My Beloved Child
**Kanojo** / Girlfriend
1927 **Sabishiki ranbōmono** / The Lonely Roughneck
**Hazukashii yume** / Shameful Dream
**Karakuri musume** / Tricky Girl
**Shojo no shi** / Death of a Virgin
**Okame** / Moon-Faced / A Plain Woman
**Tōkyō kōshinkyoku** / Tokyo March
1928 **Suki nareba koso** / Because I Love You So
**Mura no hanayome** / The Village Bride
**Dōraku goshinan** / Guidance for the Indulgent
**Kami e no michi** / The Way to God
**Hito no yo no sugata** / A Daughter of Two Fathers / Appearance of the Human World (lit.)
**Gaitō no kishi** / Knight of the Street
**Haha yo kimi no na o kegasu nakare** / Mother, Don't Sully Your Name
1929 **Yoru no mesuneko** / Cat of the Night
**Shinjoseikan** / A New Kind of Woman
**Oyaji to sono ko** / A Father and His Child
**Ukiyoburo** / Bath of the Floating World
**Jōnetsu no ichiya** / One Night of Passion
1930 **Dokushinsha goyōjin** / Bachelors Beware
**Dai Tōkyō no ikkaku** / A Corner of Greater Tokyo
**Hohoemu jinsei** / A Smiling Life
**Onna yo kimi no na o kegasu nakare** / Woman, Don't Sully Your Name
**Shojo nyūyō** / Virgin Wanted

Kinuyo monogatari / Story of Kinuyo

Aiyoku no ki / Record of Love and Desire

1931 Jokyū aishi / Sad Story of a Barmaid

Yoru hiraku / Blooming at Night

Madamu to nyōbō / The Neighbor's Wife and Mine

Shima no ratai jiken / Island of Naked Scandal

Gutei kenkei / Silly Younger Brother and Clever Older Brother

Wakaki hi no kangeki / Memories of Youthful Days

1932 Nīsan no baka / My Stupid Brother

Ginza no yanagi / Willows of Ginza

Tengoku ni musubu koi / Love Requited in Heaven

Satsueijo romansu: Ren'ai annai / A Studio Romance: Guidance for Love

Hototogisu / The Cuckoo

Koi no Tōkyō / Love in Tokyo

1933 Hanayome no negoto / The Bride Talks in Her Sleep

Izu no odoriko / The Izu Dancer / The Dancing Girls of Izu

Jūkyū no haru / Nineteenth Spring

Shojo yo sayonara / Goodbye, Virgin

Ramūru / L'Amour / Caresses

1934 Onna to umareta kara nya / Since I Was Born a Woman

Sakura ondo / Cherry Blossom Chorus

Ikitoshi ikerumono / Everything that Lives

1935 Hanamuko no negoto / The Groom Talks in His Sleep

Hidari uchiwa / The Easy Life (lit. Left-Handed Fan)

Fukeyo koikaze / Breezes of Love

Akogare / Yearning

Jinsei no onimotsu / Burden of Life

1936 Okusama shakuyōsho / A Married Lady Borrows Money

Oboroyo no onna / Woman of the Mist / Woman of a Misty Night (lit.)

Shindō (Zenpen; Kōhen) / The New Road (Parts 1 and 2)

1937 Hanakago no uta / Song of the Flower Basket

1940 Bokuseki / Wooden Head / Wood and Stone

1942 Shinsetsu / Fresh Snow / New Snow

1944 Gojū no tō / The Five-Storied Pagoda

1945 Izu no musumetachi / The Girls of Izu

1947 Ima hitotabi no / Once More

1948 Omokage / A Face to Remember

1951 Wakaregumo / Dispersing Clouds

1952 Asa no hamon / Morning Conflicts

1953 Entotsu no mieru basho / Where Chimneys Are Seen / Four Chimneys

1954 Ōsaka no yado / An Inn at Osaka

Ai to shi no tanima / The Valley between Love and Death

Niwatori wa futatabi naku / The Cock Crows Twice

1955 Takekurabe / Growing Up

1956 Aru yo futatabi / Twice on a Certain Night

1957 Kiiroi karasu / The Yellow Crow / Behold Thy Son

Banka / Elegy of the North / Dirge

1958 Hotarubi / The Fireflies / Firefly Light (lit.)

Yoku / Avarice

Ari no machi no Maria / Maria of the Ant Village

1959 Karatachi nikki / Journal of the Orange Flower

1960 Waga ai / When a Woman Loves / My Love (lit.)

Shiroi kiba / White Fangs

1961 Ryōjū / Hunting Rifle

Kumo ga chigireru toki / As the Clouds Scatter

Aijō no keifu / Love's Family Tree

1962 Kāchan kekkon shiroyo / Mother, Get Married

1963 **Hyakumannin no musumetachi /**
A Million Girls
1965 **Osorezan no onna** / An Innocent
Witch / A Woman of Osore-zan
(lit.)
1966 **Kāchan to jūichinin no kodomo /**
Our Wonderful Years / Mother and
Eleven Children (lit.)
1967 **Utage** / Rebellion of Japan /
Banquet (lit.)
1968 **Onna to misoshiru** / Woman and
Miso Soup
**Meiji haru aki** / Four Seasons of
the Meiji Period
1977 **Waga machi Mishima** / My Town
Mishima (*short*)

## HANEDA Sumiko
(b. January 3, 1926)
羽田澄子

Haneda has sustained a half-century-long career in documentary film-making, realizing numerous films on cultural, socially critical, and feminist themes. She worked initially at Iwanami Productions, where she served as assistant to Susumu Hani before making her debut with *Women's College in the Village* (*Mura no fujin gakkyū*, 1957), which earned praise for its realism. Her next film, *Ancient Beauty* (*Kodai no bi*, 1958), became the first in a trilogy of documentaries depicting works of art and artifacts in the possession of the Tokyo National Museum. Meanwhile, in films such as *Cabbage Butterflies* (*Monshirochō: Kōdō no jikkenteki kansatsu*, 1968), she applied innovative techniques to the depiction of the natural world.

Haneda made her first independent film with the acclaimed *The Cherry Tree with Gray Blossoms* (*Usuzumi no sakura*, 1977); this, in Eric Cazdyn's words, was "a gorgeously haunting representation of a famous cherry tree's seasonal transformations, punctuated by the coming-of-age changes of a teenage girl." Shortly thereafter, Haneda left Iwanami Productions permanently to work freelance. Among her most important later films were two works documenting the problems of the elderly: *How to Care for the Senile* (*Chihōsei rōjin no sekai*, 1985) and *Getting Old with a Sense of Security* (*Anshin shite oiru tameni*, 1990). On a related topic, *All's Well That Ends Well* (*Owari yokereba subete yoshi*, 2007) was a study of terminal medical care, posing the question of whether it is possible to achieve a "good death."

Elsewhere, Haneda has examined the place of women in Japanese society, particularly with a historical focus. *Women's Testimony: Pioneering Women in the Labor Movement* (*Onnatachi no shōgen: Rōdō undō no naka no senkuteki joseitachi*, 1996) depicted the role of women in labor unions during an oppressive era, while *Woman Was the Sun: The Life of Raicho Hiratsuka* (*Hiratsuka Raichō no shōgai: Genshi, josei wa taiyō de atta*, 2002) related the life story of the noted early twentieth-century Japanese writer, peace activist, and feminist. Haneda has also realized a sequence of films, initiated by *Welfare as Chosen by Our Town's Citizens* (*Jūmin ga sentaku shita machi no fukushi*, 1997), about local politics in modern Japan; these charted the efforts of a reforming mayor in a northern town to improve the lot of senior citizens and to boost local participation in politics.

Haneda's most consistent focus, however, has been the cultural traditions of Japan, particularly in the performing arts. *Ode to Mount Hayachine* (*Hayachine no fu*, 1982) recorded a devotional dance performed in northern Iwate Prefecture and juxtaposed this tradition, unaltered since the medieval era, with the changes reaching the mountainous region in a time of modernization. It won widespread commercial distribution in Japan, an achievement rare for a documentary. By contrast, *Akiko: Portrait of a Dancer* (*Akiko: Aru dansā no shōzō*, 1985) charted the work and life of one of the country's most important modern dancers. Haneda has also made several films about Kabuki, including a series of documentaries charting the final years of actor Nizaemon Kataoka. More recently, *Into the Picture Scroll: The Tale of Yamanaka Tokiwa* (*Yamanaka Tokiwa*, 2004) used a famous picture scroll to retell the tragic legend of folk hero Yoshitsune's quest to avenge his mother's murder.

Haneda has not only tackled a broad range of subjects but has also revealed a determination to explore them exhaustively, often making sequences of films in which each episode touches on a new facet of her theme. That her work remains almost unknown in the West probably says more about audience attitudes towards the documentary medium than anything else.

1957 **Mura no fujin gakkyū** / Women's College in the Village

1958 **Kodai no bi** / Ancient Beauty

1967 **Fūzokuga: Kinsei shoki** / Genre Pictures in the Late 16th Century

1968 **Monshirochō: Kōdō no jikkenteki kansatsu** / Cabbage Butterflies (lit. Cabbage Butterflies: Experimental Observation of Their Activity)

1969 **Kyōgen** / Kyogen

1971 **Hōryū-ji kennō hōmotsu** / Treasures Donated to Horyu-ji

1972 **Gendai rinshō igaku taikei** / The System of Modern Clinical Medicine

1973 **Fuyu ni saku hana wa dō naru ka** / What Will Become of the Flowers That Blossom in Winter?

**Ōta-ku ni tsutawaru mukei bunkazai** / Intangible Cultural Assets of Ota-ku

1974 **Ki to ie** / Wood and Houses

1975 **Bamboo**

1976 **Tenkoku: Kokuji** / Writing Carved in Stone

1977 **Usuzumi no sakura** / The Cherry Tree with Gray Blossoms

1979 **Karei: Hada no henka to sono shikumi** / Ageing: The Change of the Skin and its Mechanics

1980 **Uemachi : Ima mukashi** / Uemachi: Now the Past

1981 **Hayachine: Kagura no sato** / Hayachine: Village of Kagura

1982 **Hayachine no fu** / Ode to Mount Hayachine

**Kabuki no miryoku: Kanshōjō Kataoka Nizaemon** / The Appeal of Kabuki: Nizaemon Kataoka as Sugawara no Michizane

1983 **Tsukuba 1983**

1985 **Kabuki no miryoku: Ongaku: Osan Mohei daikeishi mukashi koyomi ni miru** / The Appeal of Kabuki: Osan and Mohei the Great Fortune Tellers: Looking in an Old Almanac

**Akiko: Aru dansā no shōzō** / Akiko: Portrait of a Dancer

**Chihōsei rōjin no sekai** / How to Care for the Senile

1987 **Kabuki no miryoku: Shin kabuki** / The Appeal of Kabuki: New Kabuki

1990 **Anshin shite oiru tameni** / Getting Old with a Sense of Security

1992 **Kabuki yakusha: Kataoka Nizaemon** / Kabuki Actor: Nizaemon Kataoka

1994 **Kabuki yakusha: Kataoka Nizaemon: Tōsen no maki** / Kabuki Actor: Nizaemon Kataoka: Chapter of Tosen

1995 **Kadoya Shichirōbei no monogatari: Betonamu no Nihonjin machi** / Tale of Shichirobei Kadoya: A Japanese Town in Vietnam

1996  **Onnatachi no shōgen: Rōdō undō no naka no senkuteki joseitachi** / Women's Testimony: Pioneering Women in the Labor Movement

1997  **Jūmin ga sentaku shita machi no fukushi** / Welfare as Chosen by Our Town's Citizens

2000  **Zoku jūmin ga sentaku shita machi no fukushi: Mondai wa kore kara desu** / Welfare as Chosen by Our Town's Citizens, Part 2: Questions Yet Remain

2002  **Hiratsuka Raichō no shōgai: Genshi, josei wa taiyō de atta** / Woman Was the Sun: The Life of Raicho Hiratsuka

2004  **Yamanaka Tokiwa** / Into the Picture Scroll: The Tale of Yamanaka Tokiwa

2006  **Ano Takanosumachi no sono go** / Takanosumachi Thereafter

   **Ano Takanosumachi no sono go: Zokuhen** / Takanosumachi Thereafter: Sequel

2007  **Owari yokereba subete yoshi** / All's Well That Ends Well

## HANI Susumu
**(b. October 10, 1928)**
羽仁進

If Imamura was the anthropologist of the Japanese New Wave, then Hani was its sociologist. During the nineteen-sixties, his subtle, probing films explored many of the social issues confronting postwar Japan, including the gap between rich and poor, the role of women in society, the alienation of youth, and the country's relations with the outside world. His early documentaries, made for Iwanami Productions, focused particularly on children and paved the way for his first feature, *Bad Boys* (*Furyō shōnen*, 1960), a low-key study of the lives of juvenile delinquents in a reformatory. With its use of amateur actors and location shooting in a real reformatory, it seemed as much neo-realist as New Wave. Its non-judgmental approach would prove typical of Hani, who was to return to the theme of life in a community of children in *Children Hand in Hand* (*Te o tsunagu kora*, 1964), an engaging remake of a 1948 Hiroshi Inagaki film which observed teaching methods and the relations between schoolfellows in a progressive school.

Meanwhile, in *A Full Life* (*Mitasareta seikatsu*, 1962) and *She and He* (*Kanojo to kare*, 1963), Hani crafted intricate miniatures of Japanese society, focused through the attempts of independent women to find meaning in life. The former linked its heroine's struggle for personal emancipation with the political campaign against the U.S.-Japan security treaty. The latter examined the growing disparity between rich and poor through its portrait of the relationship between a middle-class woman, her husband, and a local ragpicker living in the slums adjacent to their modern apartment block. A detailed examination of the attitudes of the prosperous towards the poor and the gulf between bourgeois and working class morality, this was also a penetrating psychological study of the motivation behind one woman's compulsive desire to do good. Hani's most famous film abroad, the powerful *Inferno of First Love* (*Hatsukoi: Jigoku hen*, 1968), was more purely psychological in its concerns, tracing the roots of an adolescent boy's impotence to the trauma of childhood sexual abuse. Adolescent psychology was likewise the subject of *Morning Schedule* (*Gozenchū no jikanwari*, 1972), an incoherent experimental film whose failure

Furyō shōnen / Bad Boys *(1960): Hani's first feature combined elements of documentary, neo-realism, and New Wave.*

marked the end of Hani's regular feature film production.

Hani is a rare case of a Japanese director who has worked successfully abroad: *Bride of the Andes (Andesu no hanayome*, 1966) was shot in Peru, *Mio (Yōsei no uta*, 1971) in Sardinia, and *The Song of Bwana Toshi (Buwana Toshi no uta*, 1965) and *Africa Story (Afurika monogatari*, 1980) in Kenya. Of these, *Bwana Toshi* and *Bride of the Andes* were intriguing studies of culture clash: in the former, the Japanese hero, posted to Africa, learns gradually to cooperate with the locals in building a house, while the latter was about a mail-order bride who goes to marry an archaeologist stationed in a tribal village. Both films explored the way in which the experience of being an expatriate impels people to self-definition and also implicitly criticized Japan's insular mentality.

Although *Inferno of First Love* expressed its hero's psychological traumas through visual pyrotechnics typical of the New Wave, Hani's style was generally more restrained than those of such contemporaries as Nagisa Ōshima, Shōhei Imamura, and Masahiro Shinoda. His gently probing, often hand-held camera observed his characters with sympathetic detachment: *Bad Boys* neither condemned, nor approved of, the actions of its juvenile delinquents, while *The Song of Bwana Toshi* extended the same placid curiosity to the Japanese hero, his African colleagues, and the animals of the savannah. Often, Hani's actors improvised scenes, a method taken to its extreme in *Morning Schedule*, where the actors themselves collaborated on shooting 8mm footage which was incorporated into the final film. With his semi-documentary approach, it was not surprising that Hani eventually came to specialize in wildlife documentaries for television. The curtailment of his career in feature filmmaking is to be regretted, for his sixties films rank among the most humanly engaging products of the Japanese New Wave.

1952 **Seikatsu to mizu** / Life and Water (*short*)

1953 **Yuki matsuri** / Snow Festival (*short*)
     **Machi to gesui** / The Town and Its Drains (*short*)

1955 **Kyōshitsu no kodomotachi** / Children in Class (*short*)

1956 **E o kaku kodomotachi** / Children Who Draw (*short*)
     **Sōseiji gakkyū** / Twin School (*short*)

1957 **Dōbutsuen nikki** / Zoo Diary (*short*)

1958 **Umi wa ikiteiru** / The Sea Is Alive (*short*)
     **Hōryū-ji** / Horyu-ji (*short*)

1960 **Furyō shōnen** / Bad Boys

1962 **Mitasareta seikatsu** / A Full Life

1963 **Kanojo to kare** / She and He

1964 **Te o tsunagu kora** / Children Hand in Hand

1965 **Bwana Toshi no uta** / The Song of Bwana Toshi

1966 **Andesu no hanayome** / Bride of the Andes

1968 **Hatsukoi: Jigoku hen** / Inferno of First Love / Nanami: First Love

1969 **Aido** / Aido: Slave of Love

1970 **Koi no daibōken** / Love's Great Adventure

1971 **Yōsei no uta** / Mio (lit. The Fairy's Song)

1972 **Gozenchū no jikanwari** / Morning Schedule

1980 **Afurika monogatari** / Africa Story

1982 **Yogen** / Prophecy

1983 **Rekishi = Kakukyōran no jidai** / History: Age of Nuclear Madness

## HARA Kazuo
## (b. June 8, 1945)
## 原一男

Hara's small body of work—six features in thirty-five years—has earned him a reputation as one of the most creative and challenging Japanese documentarists. From the beginning, he tackled controversial subject matter. His remarkable debut, *Goodbye CP* (*Sayōnara CP*, 1972), focused on sufferers of cerebral palsy at a time when people with disabilities were virtually ostracized from Japanese society. Moreover, Hara probed aspects of the lives of the disabled, such as their sexuality, which even today are not often publicly acknowledged. His credo, stated in interview, is that "a documentary should explore things that people don't want explored, bring things out of the closet, to examine why people want to hide certain things [....] These personal taboos and limitations reflect societal taboos and limitations. I want to get at just the things they don't want to talk about, their privacy." His second film, *Extreme Private Eros: Love Song 1974* (*Kyokushiteki Erosu: Renka 1974*, 1974), was a frank examination of Hara's own personal life: depicting his relationships with two women, it explored alternatives to traditional family structures and, obliquely, examined U.S.-Japan relations through its setting on Okinawa, the site of a considerable American military presence.

The goal of investigating taboos acquired more explicitly political dimensions in Hara's most famous film, *The Emperor's Naked Army Marches On* (*Yuki yukite shingun*, 1987), an account of the one-man crusade by war veteran Kenzō Okuzaki to expose the responsibility of the Emperor and the Japanese people for wartime atrocities. Here, Hara probed a national taboo, and showed how history is shaped or concealed by personal testimony with personal motivations. *A Dedicated Life* (*Zenshin shōsetsuka*, 1994) combined a study of a man facing death with another investigation of the fallibility of individual testimony: its subject was the cancer-stricken writer Mitsuharu Inoue, who had not only created fictions, but also fictionalized his personal history.

Despite the individuality of Hara's style, his approach is necessarily collaborative: he has consistently allowed his subjects considerable input into the content of his documentaries, and the power of his work depends on the responses of people to the act of being filmed. He has stated that "when one is in front of the camera, one cannot help being conscious of the camera"; indeed, the sophistication of his films lies in their awareness that a situation is changed by the act of recording it. Consequently, his work seems to call into question the morality of the documentary form: the viewer watches the birth of a child in *Extreme Private Eros: Love Song 1974* wanting the filmmaker to assist, or an assault by Okuzaki on an elderly man unwilling to admit his guilt in *The Emperor's Naked Army Marches On* feeling that he should intervene.

Given Hara's collaborative method, it was appropriate that he should make *My Mishima* (*Watashi no Mishima*, 1999), a study of the daily life and customs in a remote island off Western Japan, in cooperation with the members of Cinema Juku, a discussion group for young aspiring filmmakers. Hara's most recent film, *Days of Chika* (*Mata no hi no Chika*, 2005), examined four stages in the life of a woman as seen through the eyes of four men. Though, as his first fiction feature, it marked a new departure in

his work, it nevertheless sustained his abiding concern with the inescapable interrelation of the personal and the political.

1972  **Sayōnara CP** / Goodbye CP
1974  **Kyokushiteki Erosu: Renka 1974** / Extreme Private Eros: Love Song 1974
1987  **Yuki yukite shingun** / The Emperor's Naked Army Marches On
1994  **Zenshin shōsetsuka** / A Dedicated Life
1999  **Watashi no Mishima** / My Mishima (*co-director*)
2005  **Mata no hi no Chika** / Days of Chika / The Many Faces of Chika

## HARADA Masato
(b. July 3, 1949)
原田真人

If Ozu has sometimes been called "the most Japanese of Japanese directors," then Harada, by common consent, is the most American. During the seventies, he reported from Hollywood for Japanese publications and while there met veteran director Howard Hawks, whose work significantly influenced his own. Harada has set several of his own films in America and elsewhere outside Japan; some have been co-productions, including the German-Japanese *Windy* (*Uindī*, 1984), about a racing driver. The U.S.-Japanese co-production *Painted Desert* (1993) was a curious story set in a Nevada cafe run by a Japanese-American woman, charting her relationship with a local mobster. Also set in America, though filmed in Canada, was *Rowing Through* (*Eikō to kyōki*, 1996), about a Harvard rower whose hopes of an Olympic medal are dashed when the U.S. boycotts the 1980 Moscow Games. More recently, Harada played the villainous Omura in Hollywood's take on the end of the samurai era, *The Last Samurai* (2003, Ed Zwick).

Like another avowed Hawksian, John Carpenter, Harada appears to have been inspired more by his mentor's able handling of genre than by his talent for exploring group dynamics. His debut, *Goodbye Flickmania* (*Saraba eiga no tomoyo: Indian samā*, 1979), recalled Hawks' *A Girl in Every Port* (1928) and was intended as a homage. However, its theme of a film buff unable to tell celluloid from reality set the tone for much of Harada's later career. The dystopian science fiction film *Gunhed* (*Ganheddo*, 1988) was not unlike Carpenter's 1982 *The Thing* (itself a remake of a film Hawks produced) in stressing set design, action, and noise at the expense of nuanced characterization and emotional reality. Harada achieved a rare balance of tension and characterization in *Kamikaze Taxi* (1994), a moving, well-acted account of the relationship between a small-time hood, on the run after robbing his colleagues, and his Peruvian-Japanese taxi driver. Filmed with intelligent restraint, it tackled the prejudices faced by foreigners even of Japanese extraction and the racist and belligerent attitudes of many mainstream Japanese politicians; it also caught a genuinely Hawksian mood of stoicism in the face of death.

Subsequently, however, Harada has tended to take on controversial themes in safe ways. *Bounce KoGals* (*Baunsu ko-GALS*, 1997), about the phenomenon of *enjo kōsai* ("compensation dating," or less euphemistically, teenage prostitution) made its heroines so charming as to come close to endorsing their behavior. Certainly, its hyperactive cam-

erawork lacked the discipline needed to comment constructively on their actions. *Spellbound* (*Kin'yū fushoku rettō: Jubaku*, 1999) was an entertaining but meretricious account of a bank scandal, with Kōji Yakusho's air of irreproachable honesty used to imply that a mere change of personnel will suffice to root out institutional corruption. *Inugami* (2001), a fantasy about a family in remote Shikoku possessed by malevolent spirits, addressed incestuous themes and was apparently intended by Harada as a metaphor for the origins of the Imperial Family; however, these implications were obscured by the general tone of hysteria. *The Choice of Hercules* (*Totsunyūseyo! Asama Sansō jiken*, 2002) was criticized for avoiding political engagement by telling the story of the 1972 Asama Sansō Red Army hostage incident entirely from the point of view of the police.

The limitations of these films were those of Harada's approach, which echoes the shallow facility of modern Hollywood: frenetic cutting is preferred to expressive composition, gloss supplants style. Nevertheless, with *Bluestockings* (*Jiyū ren'ai*, 2005), Harada won praise for combining intelligent dramaturgy with a trenchant account of the difficulties facing independent women during the Taisho period, an era torn between tradition and modernity. It is unfortunate that, *Kamikaze Taxi* aside, he has rarely integrated personal and political themes so successfully with generic material. Indeed with his recent horror films, *The Suicide Song* (*Densen uta*, 2007) and *The Box of Evil Spirits* (*Mōryō no hako*, 2007), Harada would appear to have made some of his most conventional work to date.

**1979 Saraba eiga no tomoyo: Indian samā** / Goodbye Flickmania

1984 **Uindī** / Windy / Races
1985 **Tōsha: 250-ppun no 1-byō** /
Indecent Exposure / Out of Focus
1986 **Paris-Dakar 15000: Eikō e no
chōsen** / Paris-Dakar 15000:
Challenge for Glory
**Onyanko za mūbī: Kiki ippatsu** /
Onyanko the Movie
1987 **Saraba itoshiki hito yo** / The
Heartbreak Yakuza
1988 **Ganheddo** / Gunhed
1993 **Painted Desert**
1994 **Kamikaze Taxi** (*2-part TV version
released as* "Fukushū no tenshi," lit.
"Angel of Revenge")
1995 **Toraburushūtā** / Troubleshooters /
Trouble With Nango
1996 **Eikō to kyōki** / Rowing Through
(lit. Glory and Madness)
1997 **Baunsu koGALS** / Bounce KoGals
/ Bounce / Leaving
1999 **Kin'yū fushoku rettō: Jubaku** /
Spellbound / Jubaku
2001 **Inugami**
2002 **Totsunyūseyo! Asama Sansō jiken**
/ The Choice of Hercules (lit. Break
in! Asama Sanso Incident)
2005 **Jiyū ren'ai** / Bluestockings (lit. Free
Love)
2007 **Densen uta** / The Suicide Song /
Gloomy Sunday
**Mōryō no hako** / The Box of Evil
Spirits / Kyogokudo 2

# HASEBE Yasuharu
(b. April 4, 1932)
長谷部安春

Hasebe's films are high on camp and low in intelligence, a combination that has earned him a cult reputation in some quarters. Having trained at Nikkatsu with Seijun Suzuki, he took the elder director's fondness for absurd plots and stylized visuals to a disreputable extreme

in films such as his debut, *Black Tight Killers* (*Ore ni sawaru to abunai ze*, 1966). This crazy pastiche of action movie conventions was admirable mainly for Akiyoshi Satani's inventive art direction, but it established the director's working relationship with tough/tender leading man Akira Kobayashi, who also starred in such serious yakuza films as *Turf War* (*Shima wa moratta*, 1968), *Roughneck* (*Arakure*, 1969) and *Bloody Territories* (*Kōiki bōryoku: Ryūketsu no shima*, 1969). The last of these, about a classically honorable yakuza clan being edged out by unscrupulous successors, achieved moments of elegiac power among its scenes of nihilistic violence. Hasebe also worked with a more macho action star, Jō Shishido, on *Massacre Gun* (*Minagoroshi no kenjū*, 1967), filmed in black and white and considered a companion piece to Seijun Suzuki's contemporary *Branded to Kill* (*Koroshi no rakuin*, 1967).

In the early seventies, Hasebe realized three out of five entries in the Nikkatsu *Stray Cat Rock* (*Nora neko rokku*) series, starring Meiko Kaji as a gang girl; fans generally consider *Stray Cat Rock: Sex Hunter* (*Nora neko rokku: Sekkusu hantā*, 1970) to be the best. With its day-glo colors and stylized sets it was certainly visually striking, and its focus on Japanese concerns with racial purity—a gang leader sets out to clear a town of its mixed-race inhabitants—was intriguing. However, these virtues were overwhelmed by sadism, incoherence, and the limitations of the exploitation format. Hasebe was one of the few established Nikkatsu directors to remain at the studio after it switched to producing Roman Porno in the early seventies, apparently making some of the nastiest of this subgenre. Among these was *Assault: Jack the Ripper* (*Bōkō: Kirisaki Jakku*, 1976), a notorious film about a couple who become serial killers after being sexually aroused when they accidentally kill a hitchhiker.

In later years, Hasebe returned to mainstream production. *Fossil Plain* (*Kaseki no kōya*, 1982) was a big-budget action film; *Dangerous Detectives* (*Abunai deka*, 1987) was a slick but silly thriller about two cops with unorthodox methods; and *Lesson* (*Ressun*, 1994) was an uncharacteristically romantic story about a journalist who falls for an older widow. Alongside these occasional cinema features, Hasebe worked prolifically in television and on films made for straight-to-video release. Overall, the impressive style of his films has never sufficiently compensated for the shallowness and cruelty of their content.

1966  Ore ni sawaru to abunai ze / Black Tight Killers (lit. It's Dangerous to Touch Me)

1967  Bakudan otoko to iwareru aitsu / The Singing Gunman (lit. The Guy Called the Bomb Man)
      Minagoroshi no kenjū / Massacre Gun

1968  Shima wa moratta / Turf War / Territorial Dispute / Retaliation

1969  Yajū o kese / Savage Wolf Pack / Exterminate the Wild Beasts (lit.)
      Arakure / Roughneck / Coarse Violence
      Kōiki bōryoku: Ryūketsu no shima / Bloody Territories / District of Violence

1970  Sakariba jingi / Pleasure Resort Gambling Code / A Gangster's Morals
      Onna banchō: Nora neko rokku / Girl Boss: Stray Cat Rock
      Ashita no Jō / Tomorrow's Joe
      Nora neko rokku: Sekkusu hantā / Stray Cat Rock: Sex Hunter
      Nora neko rokku: Mashin animaru / Stray Cat Rock: Machine Animal

1971  Otoko no sekai / A Man's World
      Soshiki bōryoku: Ryūketsu no kōsō / Bloody Feud

1972  Sengoku rokku: Hayate no onnatachi / Sengoku Rock: Female Warriors / The Naked Seven

1973  Joshū sasori: 701-gō uramibushi / Female Convict Scorpion: Number 701's Song of Hate

1974  Sukeban Deka: Dāti Marī / Girl Boss Detective: Dirty Mary

1976  Okasu! / Rape!
      Bōkō: Kirisaki Jakku / Assault! Jack the Ripper

1977  Reipu 25-ji: Bōkan / Rape: 25 Hours of Sexual Assault
      Maruhi hanemūn: Bōkō ressha / Secret Honeymoon: Assault Train

1978  Osou!! / Attack!!
      Erochikkuna kankei / Erotic Liaisons
      Yaru! / Rampage! / Outrage! / Do It!
      Kawajan hankōzoku / Leather Jacket Rebellious Tribe

1982  Kaseki no kōya / Fossil Plain / Petrified Wilderness

1987  Abunai deka / Dangerous Detectives

1994  Ressun / Lesson

## HASEGAWA Kazuhiko
(b. January 5, 1946)
長谷川和彦

Hasegawa's two features rank among the most provocative Japanese films to have emerged during the seventies. After some years spent at Nikkatsu as an assistant director and scriptwriter to Roman Porno directors such as Tatsumi Kumashiro, he made his debut, the ATG-produced *Youth to Kill* (*Seishun no satsujinsha*, 1976), an explosive account of a young man who murders his parents. Filming in a mixture of icy long takes and edgy montage, eliciting performances of devastating intensity from his actors, Hasegawa crafted a piercing study of alienation, fixed in the context of the disintegration of traditional Japanese family structures as the country modernized.

Three years later, at Toho, Hasegawa directed *The Man Who Stole the Sun* (*Taiyō o nusunda otoko*, 1979), about an eccentric science teacher who holds Tokyo to ransom with a nuclear bomb constructed in his flat. Although in its later scenes the film became a relatively conventional action movie, with car chases and implausible climactic twists, the early sequences, with their skillful balance of suspense and black comedy, were remarkable. Moreover, though some of the more gimmicky aspects of Hasegawa's style now feel very much of their particular time, the theme of a lone individual armed with weapons of mass destruction seems unnervingly contemporary.

Hasegawa's vision was extremely dark: his work focused on characters totally alienated from society. At the end of both his films, his anti-heroes have cheated death and eluded justice, but have no plausible future. Hasegawa hoped to continue his examination of people rebelling violently against conventional society with a project about the 1972 Asama Sansō Red Army hostage crisis; regrettably, this was never realized. Since the seventies, Hasegawa has devoted himself mainly to encouraging younger directors through his foundation of the Directors' Company, though he also acted for Seijun Suzuki in *Yumeji* (1991). The power of his work, coupled with his subsequent unexpected retirement from cinema, has earned Hasegawa something of the cult

status enjoyed in America by Terrence Malick, also the maker of two distinctive films during the seventies. Indeed, *Youth to Kill* had certain similarities in plot to Malick's own debut, *Badlands* (1973). Sadly, Hasegawa, unlike Malick, has never subsequently returned to direction.

1976 **Seishun no satsujinsha** / Youth to Kill / Young Murderer
1979 **Taiyō o nusunda otoko** / The Man Who Stole the Sun

## HASHIGUCHI Ryōsuke
(b. July 13, 1962)
橋口亮輔

A subtle dramatist and chronicler of gay subculture in Japan, Hashiguchi won the PIA Film Festival scholarship for his short film, *A Secret Evening* (*Yūbe no himitsu*, 1989), and thus was able to fund his first low-budget feature, *A Touch of Fever* (*Hatachi no binetsu*, 1993). This bleak yet compassionate story of the lives of teenage hustlers in Tokyo was followed by *Like Grains of Sand* (*Nagisa no Shindobaddo*, 1995), an appealingly quirky rites-of-passage movie about a high school boy's crush on his best friend. Both films were intelligent examinations of the fluidity of youthful sexual identity. Hashiguchi's next work was *Hush* (*Hasshu*, 2001), a melancholy comedy about the triangular relationship between a closeted, thirty-something gay man, his partner, and the unhappy woman who wants him to father her child. Looser and freer in style than his earlier films, it hinted that homosexuality might be liberating in the context of Japan's restrictive family structures.

Hashiguchi's work has proved ad-

*Hasshu / Hush (2001): Gay subculture provides an escape route from Japan's restrictive family structures.*

mirable for its depth of characterization and delicacy of approach. He elicits subtle performances from his actors, using an austere technique which employs long takes, often without camera movement, to record details of gesture, posture, and intonation, thereby suggesting depths of feeling and motivation which are not verbally expressed. In consequence, his films paradoxically seem both dispassionate and intimate. His impartial, observant method respects the ambiguities of human behavior, acknowledging the gulfs between people and the impossibility of complete understanding. The viewer's first impressions of his characters are often misleading: thus, in *A Touch of Fever* and *Like Grains of Sand*, the people who initially seem the most assured turn out ultimately to be the most insecure, while *Hush* deftly charted the shifting balance of power between lovers, friends, and family members.

Hashiguchi's stories have striven to avoid pat dramatic effects, preferring to mirror the untidiness of real life. The endings of his first two features were remarkably inconclusive, and much of the power of *Hush* lay in its unpredictable switches between humor and tragedy (as in the sudden death of the protagonist's brother). Hashiguchi's non-judgmental sympathy for flawed individuals has made him one of the most engaging Japanese directors of recent years. It is a matter of regret that he has not been more prolific, especially as he seems intent on exploring new territory: at the time of writing, he had just completed his fourth feature, the first to focus primarily on heterosexual characters.

1982 **Reberu 7 +** $\alpha$ / Level Seven +
Alpha (*8mm short*)
**Sansetto** / Sunset (*8mm short*)
1983 **Rara . . . 1981–1983** (*8mm shorts*)
**Fa** (*8mm short*)
1984 **Shōnen no kuchibue** / A Boy's
Whistle (*8mm short*)
1985 **Hyururu** (*8mm*)
1986 **Mirāman hakusho 1986** /
Mirrorman's White Paper 1986
(*8mm short*)
1989 **Yūbe no himitsu** / A Secret
Evening / The Secret of Last Night
(*8mm short*)
1993 **Hatachi no binetsu** / A Touch of
Fever / Slight Fever of a 19-Year-
Old (*16mm*)
1995 **Nagisa no Shindobaddo** / Like
Grains of Sand
2001 **Hasshu!** / Hush!

## HATANAKA Ryōha
**(b. May 21, 1877; d. 1963, precise date unknown)**
畑中蓼坡

Primarily associated with the stage, Hatanaka trained as an actor in New York before returning to Japan in 1918, where he joined the theatrical company of actress Sumako Matsui, a pioneer of Western-style *shingeki* theater in Japan. After her suicide, he continued to work in *shingeki*, appearing in such plays as Chekhov's *Uncle Vanya*. His output as a filmmaker was limited, comprising only four films. Of these the most famous today is *Winter Camellias* (*Kantsubaki*, 1921), a melodrama, extremely well-acted by Masao Inoue and Yaeko Mizutani, about an elderly miller who kills his daughter's disreputable suitor when he plans to rob her employers. In this film, Hatanaka combined Western and Japanese elements: the lyrical landscape

shots were indebted to the American cinema of the teens, but the plot was rooted in the native traditions of *shinpa*, while long, static dialogue scenes were clearly conceived for the *benshi* to explain.

Hatanaka's next film as director, *Children of the Street* (*Chimata no ko*, 1924), was a socially conscious account of urban child poverty; though also extant, it lacks the fame of its predecessor. After co-directing *Easygoing Dad* (*Nonkina tōsan*, 1925) with Tokuji Ozawa, Hatanaka returned to the theater. His postwar career included acting roles in some noteworthy Nikkatsu films, such as Tomotaka Tasaka's *The Pram* (*Ubaguruma*, 1955) and Tadashi Imai's *Darkness at Noon* (*Mahiru no ankoku*, 1956).

1921 **Kantsubaki** / Winter Camellias
1924 **Chimata no ko** / Children of the
Street
1925 **Nakayama Yasubei** / Yasubei
Nakayama
**Nonkina tōsan** / Easygoing Dad
(*co-director*)

## HAYASHI Kaizō
**(b. July 15, 1957)**
林海象

Hayashi is the movie brat of modern Japanese directors: his films, often shot nostalgically in black and white, have essayed postmodern reworkings of classical genres. Before directing, he worked with Shūji Terayama's Tenjōsajiki theatrical troupe, a background faintly visible in the carnivalesque elements and surreal touches of *To Sleep So as to Dream* (*Yume miru yōni nemuritai*, 1986) and *Circus Boys* (*Nijūseiki shōnen dokuhon*, 1989). Both these early films showed definite promise. The former was a film buff's joke: a silent film, shot in lustrous monochrome, in which two private detectives discover a kidnapping victim trapped in a fragment of an old *chanbara*. Though something of an exercise, the film played wittily with the way in which a star's filmed image ultimately supplants the real, mortal self. More emotionally affecting was *Circus Boys*, a bittersweet account of the different paths taken in life by two brothers brought up in a traveling circus. Here the black and white visual poetry spoke for a human rather than an aesthetic nostalgia, creating a low-key poignancy in its sense of the difficulties and disappointments of adult life compared to the simplicity of childhood dreams.

In *The Most Terrible Time in My Life* (*Waga jinsei saiaku no toki*, 1994), Hayashi again opted for black and white, turning modern Yokohama into a moody backdrop to a marvelously well-judged pastiche of *film noir*. Though admittedly a little too reminiscent of a minor Truffaut twenty-five years too late, it was given human depth by Masatoshi Nagase's superb performance as inept private eye Maiku Hama, and the ending was genuinely cathartic. Hayashi made two more films featuring the same character, but these, relatively blandly shot in color, suffered from the diminishing returns characteristic of most sequels. Nevertheless, Hayashi later revived the character for a television series in which each episode was directed by a filmmaker of note; Shinji Aoyama's contribution, *The Forest with No Name* (*Shiritsu tantei Hama Maiku: Namae no nai mori*, 2002), later received a cinema release in its own right.

Hayashi's attempts to parody other genres have proved less successful. *Zipang* (1990), was a wild *jidai-geki* set in a stylized medieval Japan vaguely in-spired by Marco Polo's misapprehensions; spectacular art direction did not compensate for its overall vacuity. Even sillier was *Cat's Eye* (1997), a paper-thin, crudely characterized and clumsily plotted adaptation of a manga about a trio of female cat burglars. Nevertheless, Hayashi has remained willing to experiment with new approaches, even attempting a hyperrealist style in *The Breath* (*Umihōzuki*, 1996), which used only ambient light to film a story about a washed-up detective investigating a disappearance in Taiwan. With his first American film *Lost Angeles* (2000), Hayashi brought his penchant for pastiche to a realist genre, producing a spoof documentary about the experiences of a Japanese rock band in the United States. However, this was rather poorly received, and Hayashi has not since realized a theatrical feature. Even his best films clearly owed much to his collaborators, particularly art director Takeo Kimura and cinematographer Yūichi Nagata (significantly, his monochrome films have proved much better than his color ones). But the directorial flair and wit of *Circus Boys* and *The Most Terrible Time in My Life* should not be discounted.

**1986  Yume miru yōni nemuritai** / To Sleep So as to Dream

**1988  Idea** (*short*)

**1989  Nijūseiki shōnen dokuhon** / Circus Boys / The Boy's Own Book of the 20th Century (lit.)

**1990  Zipang** / Zipang / The Legend of Zipang

**1991  Figaro Stories** (*co-director*)

**1994  Waga jinsei saiaku no toki** / The Most Terrible Time in My Life

**1995  Harukana jidai no kaidan o** / Stairway to the Distant Past

**1996  Wana** / The Trap

**Umihōzuki** / The Breath

1997 **Romance** (*short*)
　　 **Cat's Eye**
　　 **Chinnanē** / Born to be Baby (*short*)
1998 **Otome no inori** / A Maiden's
　　 Prayer (*short; unreleased*)
2000 **Lost Angeles**


## HIGASHI Yōichi
**(b. November 14, 1934)**
東陽一
───────────────────

Known in the West mainly for one film, *Village of Dreams* (*E no naka no boku no mura*, 1996), Higashi has in fact produced an oeuvre of consistent intelligence and unobtrusive political commitment along liberal and progressive lines. His feature debut, *People of the Okinawa Islands* (*Okinawa rettō*, 1969), was hailed by Joan Mellen as "aesthetically the single finest example of the new documentary [then] emerging in Japan." Using a hidden camera to record forbidden footage of American installations, Higashi produced a critical examination of the continuing U.S. military presence on Okinawa at the time of its reversion to Japanese rule. His next film and first fiction feature, *Gentle Japanese* (*Yasashii Nipponjin*, 1971), also dealt with the legacy of the Okinawan experience in World War II; it recounted the political awakening of a young man who, as a baby at the time of the defeat, had survived a mass suicide on the island. In *Satori* (*Nihon yōkaiden: Satori*, 1973), Higashi used a supernatural story to examine the anxieties of modern Japanese.

Higashi's most critically acclaimed film in Japan was *Third* (*Sādo*, 1978), a powerful semi-documentary study of the life of a juvenile murderer in a reformatory, scripted by Shūji Terayama.

The extreme understatement of Toshiyuki Nagashima's lead performance, and the precision with which the camera picked out details in the bare prison environment, gave some scenes a near-Bressonian austerity. After this, Higashi switched his focus to women protagonists in a sequence of subtly feminist films. *No More Easy Going* (*Mō hōzue wa tsukanai*, 1979) was a melodrama about a college student who, torn between two unsatisfactory lovers, finally learns that she must live without them both. *Natsuko* (*Shiki: Natsuko*, 1980) subtly chronicled a 20-year-old woman's quest for personal and professional fulfilment, while *Manon* (1981), vaguely inspired by the Abbé Prévost's novel, followed the protagonist's relationships with numerous men. *Second Love* (*Sekando rabu*, 1983) was about a woman trying to deal with the unmotivated jealousy of her insecure, younger second husband. These films were noted for their unusually strong heroines. In contrast, *The Rape* (*Za reipu*, 1982) and *Metamorphosis* (*Keshin*, 1986) dealt with the oppression of women in a patriarchal society.

During the nineties, Higashi adapted Sue Sumii's epic novel, *The River without a Bridge* (*Hashi no nai kawa*, 1992), set in the Meiji and Taisho periods, about discrimination against the *burakumin* underclass. The same theme was touched on obliquely in *Village of Dreams*, a delicate account of the childhood of twin brothers in rural Shikoku during the late forties. Despite its hints of social criticism, the ultra-picturesque settings and elements of magic realism (the group of witches perching in the trees to comment on events) slightly over-sweetened the tone, but the film was atmospheric and affecting. In *The Crying Wind* (*Fūon*, 2004), Higashi used the same magical realist approach in

Fūon / The Crying Wind *(2004): In this film, Higashi again revealed his ability to dramatize the emotions of the young with subtlety and sensitivity.*

©Siglo Company Ltd.

a return to the Okinawa setting of his earliest features. The adult stories, in which now elderly protagonists come to terms with their memories of wartime traumas, were somewhat glib, but Higashi again showed his skill at dramatizing the intense emotional lives of children. *My Grandpa* (*Watashi no guranpa*, 2003) focused on a slightly older child, tracing the experiences of a 14-year-old girl ostracized at school after the discovery that her grandfather is a murderer. Again, this film revealed Higashi's consistent sympathy for the outsider. Although his work is arguably more interesting in subject matter than in style, he commands respect for his intelligence and integrity.

1963  **A Face** (*short*)
1964  **Higashi-Murayama-shi** / Higashi-Murayama City (*short*)
1967  **Jōdō** / Motion-Emotion (*short*)

1969  **Okinawa rettō** / People of the Okinawa Islands (lit. Okinawa Archipelago)
1971  **Yasashii Nipponjin** / Gentle Japanese
1973  **Nippon yōkaiden: Satori** / Satori / A Japanese Demon / Spiritual Awakening
1978  **Sādo** / Third / Third Base / A Boy Called Third Base
1979  **Mō hōzue wa tsukanai** / No More Easy Going
1980  **Shiki: Natsuko** / Natsuko / The Four Seasons of Natsuko (lit.)
      **Rabu retā** / Love Letter
1981  **Manon**
1982  **Za reipu** / The Rape
      **Jerashī gēmu** / Jealousy Game
1983  **Sekando rabu** / Second Love
1984  **Wangan dōro** / Coastal Road
1986  **Keshin** / Metamorphosis
1988  **Ureshi hazukashi monogatari** / A Tale of Happiness and Shame

## HIRAYAMA Hideyuki
### (b. September 18, 1950)
平山秀幸

Hirayama has sustained parallel careers as a proficient craftsman of big-budget commercial entertainments and as an artist realizing small-scale, offbeat, and imaginative projects. After a long freelance apprenticeship to such directors as Jūzō Itami and Kichitarō Negishi, he made his debut, a comic horror film, for the Directors' Company. Lighthearted horror continued to occupy him through much of the nineties, as he directed three installments of the popular *Haunted School* (*Gakkō no kaidan*) series, a sub-Spielberg exercise in thrills and spills for kids, with endearingly inept special effects. By this time, however, he had achieved critical notice with *The Games Teachers Play* (*Za chūgakkō kyōshi*, 1992), about a junior high school teacher trying to deal with delinquency by encouraging his charges to dispense their own justice. Mark Schilling praised the film's "clear-eyed view of [the] teenage world, minus adult romanticizing, caricaturing, and demonizing." Also well-received during the nineties was *Begging for Love* (*Ai o kou hito*, 1998), an account of a girl suffering abuse at the hands of her mother, which fixed its story in the context of the social instability of Japan after World War II.

Since the millennium, Hirayama has won further acclaim for two remarkable black comedies. *The Laughing Frog* (*Warau kaeru*, 2002) was a droll, dry satire with a faintly Bunuelian touch to its cynical portrait of bourgeois life, the black sheep husband ultimately proving the most sympathetic figure among the venal and selfish, if respectable, characters who surround him. Hirayama's precise framing, using a mainly static camera, observed the unfolding comedy with neither indulgence nor contempt, and the performances were superb. *Out* (2002) focused on a middle-aged woman who murders her husband and conspires with her colleagues at a boxed lunch factory to dispose of the body. Despite the melodramatic premise, its theme was the ordinary frustrations of female experience in a patriarchal society.

Hirayama has continued to work in a variety of genres. *Turn* (*Tān*, 2001) was an engaging fantasy in which a woman finds herself doomed, after a car crash, to relive endlessly the same 24 hours in a parallel universe of which she appears to be the only inhabitant. Especially in the early stages, Hirayama intelligently dramatized the reactions of his heroine to her isolation, and the film was rather touching. *Lady Joker* (*Redī Jōkā*, 2004) used a thriller plot about a plan to kidnap a company president to launch an investigation into corruption in Japanese society. *Samurai Resurrection* (*Makai tenshō*, 2003), however, was a more purely commercial work: a large, dumb action movie which submerged story and characterization under a barrage of special effects. Still, while Hirayama remains an uneven director, he has been responsible for some of the more original and diverting Japanese films of recent years. In 2007, two films inspired by the style and tradition of *rakugo* comic storytelling confirmed his versatility: *Talk, Talk, Talk* (*Shaberedomo shaberedomo*) was a story about a modern practitioner of this old-fashioned art form training three reluctant recruits for a performance, while *Three for the Road* (*Yajikita dōchū: Teresuko*) was a lighthearted road movie reworking the oft-filmed eighteenth-century novel *Shank's Mare* (*Hizakurige*).

1990 **Maria no ibukuro** / Maria's Stomach

1992 **Za chūgaku kyōshi** / The Games Teachers Play (lit. The Junior High School Teacher)

1993 **Ningen kōsaten: Ame** / Human Crossroads: Rain

1994 **Yoi ko to asobō** / Let's Play with the Good Children

1995 **Gakkō no kaidan** / Haunted School

1996 **Gakkō no kaidan 2** / Haunted School 2

1998 **Ai o kou hito** / Begging for Love

1999 **Gakkō no kaidan 4** / Haunted School 4

2001 **Tān** / Turn

2002 **Warau kaeru** / The Laughing Frog Out

2003 **Makai tenshō** / Samurai Resurrection

2004 **Redī Jōkā** / Lady Joker

2007 **Shaberedomo shaberedomo** / Talk, Talk, Talk

**Yajikita dōchū: Teresuko** / Three for the Road

**HIROKI Ryūichi**

**(b. January 1, 1954)**

廣木隆一

Of the directors who have graduated from "pink film" to the mainstream,

Hiroki has remained perhaps the most faithful to his origins: he continues to make films on sexual themes, though titillation has given was to analysis. In the eighties, after serving as assistant to prolific "pink" director Genji Nakamura, he made pornographic films for both straight and gay audiences; likewise, his first mainstream feature, *800 Two Lap Runners* (1994), explored both hetero- and homosexual feeling in its account of the awkward relationship between a teenage runner and the former girlfriend of the dead trackmate with whom he once had a sexual experience.

Hiroki's next film, *Midori* (*Monogatari kara ashibyōshi yori: Midori*, 1996), was another drama about adolescent emotions, focusing on a disaffected high school girl who feigns illness to spend time with her boyfriend. Female protagonists continued to be central to Hiroki's most interesting work, which dealt with young adults and with their sexual conduct in the fragmented society of modern urban Japan. *Tokyo Trash Baby* (*Tōkyō gomi onna*, 2000), *Vibrator* (*Vaiburēta*, 2003), and *Girlfriend: Someone Please Stop the World* (*Gārufurendo*, 2004) were all moving, understated films about lonely, alienated women seeking solace in romantic fantasy and transient attachments. The heroine of *Tokyo Trash Baby*, obsessed with her neighbor, rifles through his garbage for mementos of his life; this rubbish, and the well-stocked but soulless convenience store where *Vibrator* begins, seemed metaphors for today's prosperous yet rootless society, in which consumer goods fail to satisfy emotional needs. Hiroki shot these films on digital video, and his informal style, with its loose compositions and low-key performances, effectively dramatized the haphazard lives of his protagonists, insecure both in work and

©Argo Pictures Inc.

800 Two Lap Runners *(1994): This is the youth film that marked Hiroki's transition from pornography to the mainstream.*

relationships. Darker and more melodramatic in plot was *L'Amant* (2004), a coolly observed account of a teenage schoolgirl who sells herself for a year as a sex slave to three brothers. By refusing to pass judgment on the perverse actions it depicted, Hiroki's detached style forced the viewer to confront his own taboos. The director again explored the extremes of sexual behavior in *M* (2006); described by Jasper Sharp as "a *Belle de Jour* for the internet age," it charted the experiences of a housewife who begins to work as a prostitute after receiving an email from a dating website.

Beside these troubling and emotionally complex films, *The Silent Big Man* (*Kikansha-sensei*, 2004) was an unexpectedly chaste, academic work, set safely in the past, and prettily photographed against the scenic backdrops of the Inland Sea. Recalling Keisuke

Kinoshita in its story of a mute teacher assigned to an island school, it lacked Kinoshita's skill for melodrama, and though Hiroki's dry style restrained its sentimentality somewhat, he seemed ill suited to the material. Happily, with *It's Only Talk* (*Yawarakai seikatsu*, 2005), a subtly compelling chronicle of the life of an unemployed thirty-something woman suffering from manic depression, Hiroki returned to his more fruitful preoccupation with the problems of contemporary urban life. Here his use of locations in Tokyo's down-at-heel Kamata district was especially well judged, anchoring the drama in a near-documentary record of a specific place. *Love on Sunday* (*Koi suru nichiyōbi*, 2006), meanwhile, revisited the territory of the director's earliest mainstream features, exploring adolescent emotions as it charted a teenage girl's last 24 hours in her country home. In his recent work, Hiroki has proved himself one of the modern Japanese cinema's most intelligent students of character, as well as one of the most precise analysts of Tokyo's twenty-first-century *zeitgeist* and Japan's twenty-first-century malaise.

1982 **Seigyaku! Onna o abaku** / Sexual Abuse! Exposed Woman / Urban Style

1983 **Kimata Saburō-kun no koto: Bokura no jidai** / Our Generation

**Bokura no kisetsu** / Our Season

1984 **Nishikawa Serina: Nozokibeya no onna** / Serina Nishikawa: A Woman Peeps into the Room

**Hakuchū joshi kōsei o okasu** / Raping a High School Girl in Broad Daylight

**Chikan to sukāto** / Pervert and Skirt

**Sensei, watashi no karada ni hi o tsukenaide** / Teacher, Don't Turn Me On

**Mitsu ni nureru onna** / Woman with Wet Juice

1985 **Yarinko Chie: Ichijiku shinsatsudai** / Chie the Tart: Couch of Figs

**Bokura no shunkan** / Our Moment

1986 **Hakui chōkyō** / Training in a White Coat

**Kindan: Ikenie no onna** / Forbidden: Sacrificed Woman

**SM kyōshitsu: Shikkin** / SM Classroom: Toilet in the Wrong Place

**Tōsatsu mania: Furaidē no onna** / Secret Filming Mania: Friday's Woman

**Hatsujō musume: Guriguri asobi** / Girl in Heat: Rubbing Play

**Romanko kurabu: Ecchi ga ippai** / Club Romanko: Highly Sexed

1987 **Kobayashi Hitomi no honshō** / The True Self of Hitomi Kobayashi

1988 **Kikuchi Eri: Kyonyūzeme** / Eri Kikuchi: Huge Breasts

**Seijuku onna** / Holy Mature Woman

1989 **Dōtei monogatari 4: Boku mo sukī ni tsuretette** / Story of a Male Virgin: Take Me Skiing Too

1990 **Sawako no koi: Jōzuna uso no ren'ai kōza** / A Love Affair with Sawako (lit. Sawako's Love: Lecture on Convincing Lies in Love)

1991 **Ji go ro: Āban naito sutōrī** / Gigolo: Urban Night Story

1993 **Maōgai: Sadisuchikku shitī** / Sadistic City (*video*)

1994 **Muma** / Evil Dream

**800 Two Lap Runners**

1995 **Kimi to itsu made mo** / Forever with You

**Gerende ga tokeru hodo koi shitai** / I Want to Make Love Until the Ski Slopes Melt

1996 **"Monogatari kara ashibyōshi" yori: Midori** / Midori

1999 **Tenshi no misuterareta yoru** / The Night the Angel Turned Away

2000 **Futei no kisetsu** / I Am an S and M Writer (lit. Season of Adultery)

**Tōkyō gomi onna** / Tokyo Trash Baby

2001 **Bikyaku meiro** / Labyrinth of Leg Fetishism

2002 **Rihatsu tenshu no kanashimi** / The Barber's Sadness

2003 **Deka matsuri** / Cop Festival (*co-director*)

**Vaiburēta** / Vibrator

2004 **Kikansha-sensei** / The Silent Big Man (lit. Mr. Locomotive)

**Gārufurendo** / Girlfriend: Someone Please Stop the World

**L'Amant**

2005 **Female** (*co-director*)

**Yawarakai seikatsu** / It's Only Talk

2006 **Koi suru nichiyōbi** / Love on Sunday

**Yokan** / Premonition (*short*)

**M**

2007 **Koi suru nichiyōbi: Watashi: Koi shita** / Love on Sunday: I Did Love

# HONDA Ishirō
## (May 7, 1911–February 28, 1993)
## 本多猪四郎

The most famous director of Japanese monster movies or *kaijū-eiga*, Honda served as assistant at Toho to several directors, most notably Kajirō Yamamoto on *Horse* (*Uma*, 1941), *Kato's Falcon Fighters* (*Katō hayabusa sentōtai*, 1944), and numerous comedies starring the clown Enoken (Ken'ichi Enomoto). After war service, he assisted Akira Kurosawa on *Stray Dog* (1949) before returning to Toho to become a director in his own right, working at first on documentaries. His fiction debut, *The Blue Pearl* (*Aoi shinju*, 1951), already revealed an interest in special effects as Honda used an underwater camera to record scenes of women diving for pearls. *Eagle of the Pacific* (*Taiheiyō no washi*, 1953) was a spectacular war film, but the course of Honda's career was fixed by *Godzilla* (*Gojira*, 1954), a famous science fiction movie about an attack on Tokyo by a giant lizard, which achieved international distribution in a cut, dubbed version incorporating new footage starring Raymond Burr.

Honda continued to specialize in science fiction for the rest of his career, realizing numerous sequels to *Godzilla*, including some in which the monster encountered such figures from Western fantasy as Frankenstein and King Kong. Among his other notable monsters was the eponymous giant moth of *Mothra* (*Mosura*, 1961). These films retain a considerable sociological fascination: Godzilla's rampages expressed Japanese anxieties about natural disasters and recalled the wartime devastation of the nation's cities. Radiation was also a preoccupation: Godzilla was originally woken by nuclear tests, while, in *The Mysterians* (*Chikyū bōeigun*, 1957) about an invasion from space, the aliens have suffered genetic damage through nuclear war. Admittedly, these concerns were expressed in the scripts rather than through any directorial subtleties: Honda's style was generally anonymous and pedestrian. His audiences were doubtless more interested in spectacle than in *mise-en-scène*, and his technique was likely restricted by the need to showcase Eiji Tsuburaya's special effects. As evidence, one may note that *Matango* (1963), which used effects sparingly and was mainly a claustrophobic study of tensions among the marooned survivors of a shipwreck, was rather efficiently directed. Even so, Honda is remembered more because his name happens to be attached to some famous titles than because of any personal distinction. After retiring from direction, he collaborated again with his old friend and colleague Akira Kurosawa, working as an assistant and second-unit director on *Kagemusha* (1980), *Ran* (1985), *Dreams* (*Yume*, 1990), and *Madadayo* (*Mādadayo*, 1993).

1949 **Kyōdō kumiai no hanashi** / A Story of a Co-Op
1950 **Iseshima** / Ise Island
1951 **Aoi shinju** / The Blue Pearl
1952 **Nangoku no hada** / Skin of the South
   **Minato e kita otoko** / The Man Who Came to Port
1953 **Zoku shishunki** / Adolescence 2
   **Taiheiyō no washi** / Eagle of the Pacific
1954 **Saraba Rabauru** / Farewell Rabaul
   **Gojira** / Godzilla
1955 **Koi geshō** / Love Makeup
   **Oen-san** / Oen-san / Cry Baby
   **Jūjin yukiotoko** / Beast Man, Snow Man / Half Human: The Story of the Abominable Snowman
1956 **Wakai ki** / Young Tree

Yakan chūgaku / Night School

Tōkyō no hito sayōnara / People of Tokyo, Goodbye

Sora no daikaijū: Radon / Radon, Monster from the Sky / Radon / Rodan

1957 Kono futari ni sachi are / Good Luck to These Two

Wakare no chatsumiuta / A Teapicker's Song of Goodbye

Waga mune ni niji wa kiezu / A Rainbow Plays in My Heart

Wakare no chatsumiuta: Shimai hen: Onēsan to yonda hito / A Teapicker's Song of Goodbye: Sisters Chapter: The Person I Called Sister

Chikyū bōeigun / The Mysterians / Earth Defense Force (lit.)

1958 Hanayome sanjūsō / Song for a Bride (lit. Trio for a Bride)

Bijo to ekitai ningen / The H-Man / Beauty and the Liquid Man (lit.)

Daikaijū Baran / Baran, Monster from the East / The Great Monster Baran (lit.)

1959 Kodama wa yondeiru / An Echo Calls You

Tetsuwan tōshu: Inao monogatari / Inao: Story of an Iron Arm

Uwayaku, shitayaku, godōyaku / Seniors, Juniors, Co-Workers

Uchū daisensō / The Great Space War / Battle in Outer Space

1960 Gasu ningen daiichigō / The First Gas Human / The Human Vapor

1961 Mosura / Mothra

Shinku no otoko / The Crimson Man

1962 Yōsei Gorasu / Gorath, the Mysterious Star / Gorath / Astronaut 1980

Kingu Kongu tai Gojira / King Kong vs. Godzilla

1963 Matango / Matango / Matango: Fungus of Terror

Kaitei gunkan / Atragon: Flying Supersub / Undersea Battleship (lit.)

1964 Mosura tai Gojira / Mothra vs. Godzilla / Godzilla Fights the Giant Moth / Godzilla vs. the Thing

Uchū daikaijū Dogora / Dogora / Dagora the Space Monster

Sandaikaijū: Chikyū saidai no kessen / Ghidrah, the Three-Headed Monster / Monster of Monsters / The Greatest Battle on Earth

1965 Furankenshutain tai chitei kaijū / Frankenstein vs. Baragon / Frankenstein vs. the Giant Devil Fish / Frankenstein Conquers the World

Kaijū daisensō / War of the Monsters / Godzilla vs. Monster Zero / Invasion of the Astros

1966 Furankenshutain no kaijū: Sanda tai Gaira / Frankenstein's Monsters: Sanda vs. Gaira / Duel of the Gargantuas

Oyome ni oide / Come Marry Me

1967 Kingu Kongu no gyakushū / King Kong Strikes Back / King Kong Escapes

1968 Kaijū sōshingeki / Destroy All Monsters! / Monster Invasion (lit.) / All Monsters Attack

1969 Ido zero daisakusen / Latitude Zero / Atragon 2

Gojira, Minira, Gabara: Ōru kaijū daishingeki / All Monsters Attack / Godzilla's Revenge / Minya: Son of Godzilla

1970 Kessen! Nankai no daikaijū / The Space Amoeba / Yog: Monster from Space (lit. Decisive Battle: Great Monster of the South Seas)

1972 Mirāman / Mirrorman

1975 Mekagojira no gyakushū / The Terror of Mechagodzilla / Revenge of Mechagodzilla (lit.) / Mechagodzilla vs. Godzilla

## HORIKAWA Hiromichi
## (b. December 28, 1916)
## 堀川弘通

Akira Kurosawa's assistant on numerous films including *Ikiru* (1952) and *Seven Samurai* (*Shichinin no samurai*, 1954), Horikawa has never achieved his mentor's fame. Kurosawa himself scripted his directorial debut, *A Story of Fast-Growing Weeds* (*Asunaro monogatari*, 1955), about an adolescent and the first three women in his life. A concern with youthful experience was also visible in Horikawa's second and third films, *Summer Eclipse* (*Nisshoku no natsu*, 1956), a *taiyōzoku* ("sun tribe") film based on a Shintarō Ishihara novel, and *The Last Day of Oishi* ("*Genroku Chūshingura: Ōishi saigo no ichinichi*" *yori: Koto no tsume*, 1957), a reworking of the *Chūshingura* story that focused particularly on the youngest of the participating ronin and his fiancée. Another retelling of a classical Japanese story was the Chikamatsu adaptation *Oil Hell Murder* (*Onnagoroshi abura jigoku*, 1957), but Horikawa returned to contemporary subject matter with *The Naked General* (*Hadaka no taishō*, 1958), a portrait of mentally handicapped collage artist Kiyoshi Yamashita. In this darkly humorous account of a stubborn non-conformist, Horikawa touched for the first time on the subject of World War II, ironically showing how the artist's apparent madness enabled him to escape the draft. The melodrama *Eternity of Love* (*Wakarete ikiru toki mo*, 1961), tracing a woman's unhappy marriages and affairs, also unfolded against a wartime backdrop.

During the sixties, Horikawa made several thrillers: the socially conscious aspects of these films suggest the continuing influence of Kurosawa while also evoking Masaki Kobayashi, whose regular actor Tatsuya Nakadai appeared in *The Blue Beast* (*Aoi yajū*, 1960) and *Pressure of Guilt* (*Shiro to kuro*, 1963). The former charted the rise and fall of a low-ranking executive who exploits both labor and management, while the latter was a tangled psychological thriller about an attorney who, having strangled his lover, faces a moral dilemma when another man confesses. Later, *Goodbye Moscow* (*Saraba Mosukuwa gurentai*, 1968) used the relationship between a Japanese jazz pianist, an American soldier on leave from Vietnam, and a group of young Russian dissidents as a metaphor for Japan's situation in the Cold War era. *The Militarist* (*Gekidō no Shōwashi: Gunbatsu*, 1970) was a critical biopic of General Tōjō, which dramatized the military coup of February 26, 1936, while *Sun Above, Death Below* (*Sogeki*, 1968) was a conventional if snappily edited thriller about a doomed hitman.

By this time, Horikawa was considered Toho's most reliable director of prestige material, but his seventies work was less noteworthy. He continued to deal with youthful experience in *Have Wings on Your Heart* (*Tsubasa wa kokoro ni tsukete*, 1978) and *Song of Mutsuko* (*Mutchan no uta*, 1985), both tragedies about terminally ill children. The latter again had a wartime backdrop, as did Horikawa's last films: *War and Flowers* (*Hana monogatari*, 1989) was another account of female experience during the war years, while *Asian Blue* (*Eijian Burū: Ukishima Maru sakon*, 1995) focused on the sufferings of Korean forced laborers, in particular those killed in the sinking of a ship carrying them home after Japan's surrender. Though Horikawa worked consistently with interesting subject matter, his films seem to have been imperfectly realized: Anderson and Richie condemned *A Story of Fast-Growing Weeds* for not fully developing Kurosawa's script, Tadao Satō found *Goodbye Moscow* sentimental despite its political interest, and Joan Mellen criticized *The Militarist* for political naivety. Nevertheless, some of Horikawa's films were considered worthy of foreign distribution in the sixties, and they may still merit revival.

1955　**Asunaro monogatari** / A Story of Fast-Growing Weeds / Growing Up

1956　**Nisshoku no natsu** / Summer Eclipse

1957　**"Genroku Chūshingura: Ōishi saigo no ichinichi" yori: Koto no tsume** / The Last Day of Oishi / Last Day of Samurai
　　　**Onnagoroshi abura jigoku** / Oil Hell Murder / The Prodigal Son

1958　**Hadaka no taishō** / The Naked General

1959　**Suzukake no sanpomichi** / The Path under the Plantanes

1960　**Kuroi gashū: Aru sararīman no shōgen** / The Lost Alibi / Black Book of Paintings: Testimony of a Salaryman (lit.)
　　　**Aoi yajū** / The Blue Beast

1961　**Wakarete ikiru toki mo** / Eternity of Love (lit. Even When We Live Apart)
　　　**Neko to katsuobushi: Aru sawashi no monogatari** / Cat and Fish Flakes: Story of a Swindler

1962　**Musume to watashi** / My Daughter and I

1963　**Shiro to kuro** / Pressure of Guilt (lit. Black and White)

1964　**Aku no monshō** / Brand of Evil
　　　**Les Plus Belles Escroqueries du Monde** / The World's Greatest Swindles (*co-director; international co-production released in Japan as* Sekai sagi monogatari)

1965　**Saigo no shinpan** / Last Judgement

　　　**Ore ni tsuite koi** / You Can If You Try / Follow Me

1968　**Saraba Mosukuwa gurentai** / Goodbye Moscow / Farewell to the Gang in Moscow (lit.)
　　　**Sogeki** / Sun Above, Death Below (lit. Sniper)

1969　**Haha to musuko no taiwa** / Dialogue between Mother and Son (*short*)

1970　**Gekidō no Shōwa shi: Gunbatsu** / The Militarist (lit. History of Showa-Era Turbulence: Military Clique)
　　　**Gakuensai no yoru: Amai keiken** / Night of the School Fete: Sweet Experience

1972　**Anata wa kikijōzu?** / Are You a Good Listener? (*short*)

1973　**Ōshō** / The Chess Master / The King

1975　**Kokuso sezu** / Not Accusing
　　　**Shin hakkenden** / New Legend of Eight Samurai (*co-director*)

1976　**Shōnen to sei** / Elementary School Students and Sex (*short*)

1977　**Arasuka monogatari** / Alaska Story

1978　**Tsubasa wa kokoro ni tsukete** / Have Wings on Your Heart

1979　**Kodomo wa jisatsu o yokoku suru** / Warning Signs of Suicide in Children (*short*)

1981　**Toshi wa tottemo…** / Even Though We're Getting Older (*short*)

1985　**Mutchan no uta** / Song of Mutsuko

1989　**Hana monogatari** / War and Flowers

1995　**Eijian Burū: Ukishima maru sakon** / Asian Blue

## ICHIKAWA Jun
(b. November 25, 1948)
市川準

Though Ichikawa (no relation to his namesake Kon) has had a successful career as a director of commercials, his fiction features could scarcely be further from the techniques of advertising. He has opted for a slow pace and a style of delicate restraint, characterized by critics and sometimes by Ichikawa himself, as *"jimi"* (unspectacular). He has acknowledged the influence of Yasujirō Ozu: the title of *Tokyo Siblings* (*Tōkyō kyōdai*, 1995) was a tribute to Ozu, its understated acting and austere compositions echoed Ozu's technique, and its plot—the relationship between a cohabiting brother and sister, the effect of that relationship on their romantic liaisons, and vice versa—was a loose paraphrase of *Late Spring* (*Banshun*, 1949). The early *Story of a Company* (*Kaisha monogatari: Memories of You*, 1988), like many of Ozu's prewar comedies, examined the situation of white-collar workers, concentrating on a company man depressed by the prospect of retirement. Stylistically, the mostly still camera in *The Manga Apartment* (*Tokiwasō no seishun*, 1996) and *Dying in a Hospital* (*Byōin de shinu to iu koto*, 1993), and the use of pillow shots—background images, empty of human activity, that punctuate the drama—in *Tokyo Lullaby* (*Tōkyō yakyoku*, 1997), also revealed a debt to Ozu's example.

By comparison with Ozu, however, Ichikawa has tended to concentrate on characters who fit less comfortably into ordinary social and familial structures. *Tokyo Lullaby* was a purposely fragmented, indirect account of the emotional dislocation caused by a failed love affair: its theme was the corrosive effect of these passions on family life. More recently, *How to Become Myself* (*Ashita no watashi no tsukurikata*, 2007) focused on two schoolgirls dealing, via the medium of pseudonymous text messages, with their respective problems at home and at school. Often, Ichikawa's characters have been disabled or ailing. *Tsugumi* (1990) was an affecting low-key melodrama describing the tragic life of a physically and intellectually challenged young woman. *Gratitude* (*Aogeba tōtoshi*, 2006) dealt with the responses of a schoolteacher and one of his pupils to the deaths of their respective fathers. *Dying in a Hospital* focused on six terminally ill patients; Donald Richie has commented that the use of camera distance reflects how hard it is for the healthy to get close to the dying. In other films, Ichikawa's protagonists were unsuccessful artists. *Osaka Story* (*Ōsaka monogatari*, 1999) was about a poor couple—stand-up comedians in the Osaka *manzai* tradition—and their daughter. *The Manga Apartment* dealt with a kind of surrogate family: a community of manga artists struggling to make a name for themselves and to make ends meet. Perhaps Ichikawa's most precisely pitched film, this was immaculately shot in muted, brown-gray color schemes, which created a tone of melancholy nostalgia, celebrating the camaraderie of the early 1960s while never sentimentalizing its hardships.

In some of his more recent work, Ichikawa's manner has become more stylized. *Tokyo Marigold* (*Tōkyō marīgōrudo*, 2001) was a non-judgmental account of the year-long romance between a naive woman and a cynical man who has another girlfriend in New York; the backgrounds of Tokyo and Yokohama at night formed almost abstract patterns of light and color, visually suggesting the atomization of modern society. *Tony Takitani* (*Tonī Takitani*, 2004), based on a Haruki Murakami story, was a brief yet devastating study of emotionally empty lives. Narrated in a series of short scenes, with more voiceover than dialogue, it was a telling examination of the emptiness at the heart of modern materialist values and, despite its distancing effects, very moving.

Though the tone of Ichikawa's films is generally downbeat, his films have rarely felt depressing, perhaps because the personal tragedies he chronicles seem too modest to be making a generalized statement about "the human condition." Rather, his concern is to illuminate the large and small sorrows of individual lives in specific circumstances, a task he carries out with perceptiveness and humanity.

1987  BU•SU
1988  Kaisha monogatari: Memories of You / Story of a Company
1989  Nō raifu kingu / No Life King
1990  Tsugumi
1991  Goaisatsu / Greetings (co-director)
1993  Kin-chan no Shinemajakku / Kin-chan's Cinema-jack
       Byōin de shinu to iu koto / Dying in a Hospital
       Kurēpu / Crèpe
1995  Tōkyō kyōdai / Tokyo Siblings
1996  Tokiwasō no seishun / The Manga Apartment (lit. Youth in the Tokiwa Apartment)
1997  Tōkyō yakyoku / Tokyo Lullaby
1998  Tadon to chikuwa / Tadon and Chikuwa
1999  Ōsaka monogatari / Osaka Story
2000  Zawa zawa Shimokitazawa
2001  Tōkyō marīgōrudo / Tokyo Marigold
2002  Ryōma no tsuma to sono otto to aijin / Ryoma's Wife, Her Husband and Her Lover
2004  Tōni Takitani / Tony Takitani
2006  Aogeba tōtoshi / Gratitude
2007  Ashita no watashi no tsukurikata / How to Become Myself

# ICHIKAWA Kon
## (November 20, 1915–February 13, 2008)
## 市川崑

One of the first Japanese directors to acquire an international reputation, Ichikawa is now somewhat underrated, partly because much of his later work was disappointing, but more because his apparent eclecticism of theme and style defied auteurist notions of consistency. He himself divided his films into "light" and "dark," but the two categories were united by his wry attitude towards experience: in the words of one-time pupil and fellow director, Yasuzō Masumura, he "does not present us with the humor, anger, sadness, and joy of humanity in all its rawness, but instead observes it with an ironic and detached gaze."

Detachment notwithstanding, Ichikawa's work demonstrably reflected his life history. His birth and upbringing in the Kansai region were recalled in the many films, such as The Key (Kagi, 1959), Conflagration (Enjō, 1958), Bonchi (1960), The Old Capital (Koto, 1980), and The Makioka Sisters (Sasameyuki, 1983), which he set in its major cities of Osaka and Kyoto; he also made Kyoto the subject of a short 1969 documentary. Likewise, his early interest in painting and his training as an animator continued to shape his visual style. Thus, Mr. Pu (Pū-san, 1953) was a wild social satire adapted from a popular comic strip; Ten Dark Women (Kuroi jūnin no onna, 1961), about a wife conspiring with her husband's nine mistresses to kill him, exaggerated the stylistic tropes of film noir into cartoon-like pastiche; and An Actor's Revenge (Yukinojō henge, 1963), an eccentric Edo-period melodrama about a Kabuki female impersonator seeking to destroy the men responsible for the deaths of his parents, iconoclas-

©Kadokawa Pictures

Bonchi *(1960): Ichikawa observed human passions and human foibles with "an ironic and detached gaze."*

tically blended the imagery of animation, *ukiyo-e*, and traditional theater.

Ichikawa's oeuvre was also united by his abiding concern with the recent history of his country. He often set films between the late Meiji period and the Second World War; novels of those years furnished the plots of *The Heart* (*Kokoro*, 1955), *The Outcast* (*Hakai*, 1962), and *Nihonbashi* (1956), while *The Woman Who Touched the Legs* (*Ashi ni sawatta onna*, 1952) and *An Actor's Revenge* were remakes of famous prewar films. Indeed, Ichikawa's taste for satiric ironies and absurdism can be traced to his early admiration for such prewar directors as Sadao Yamanaka and Mansaku Itami. His accounts of prewar life, however, focused on its less attractive realities: the oppressiveness of traditional family structures in *Bonchi*, a wry

and witty account of matriarchy among the Osaka merchant class; the persecution of the *burakumin* underclass in *The Outcast*, a somewhat stolid adaptation of a Tōson Shimazaki novel; the impotence and hypocrisy of the liberal middle class in his solo feature debut, *A Flower Blooms* (*Hana hiraku*, 1948). In *The Heart*, a faithful adaptation of Sōseki Natsume's novel about a student idolizing a guilt-ridden teacher, a drama of loneliness and betrayal was set against the backdrop of the death of the Meiji Emperor.

Ichikawa's films about the war itself, though perhaps his most famous in the West, were not among his finest work; both the sentimental *The Burmese Harp* (*Biruma no tategoto*, 1956), about a Buddhist monk searching for the bodies of Japanese war dead, and the visceral *Fires on the Plain* (*Nobi*, 1959), detailing the hellish experiences of a soldier lost in the Philippines at the end of the war, largely avoided tackling the political context of the conflict. By contrast, Ichikawa's fifties *gendai-geki* were scathing critiques of the pillars of postwar Japanese society: the family, big business, government, and the education system. The melodrama of teenage alienation, *Punishment Room* (*Shokei no heya*, 1956), and the caustic satire on the rat race, *A Full-Up Train* (*Man'in densha*, 1957), starred the same young actor, Hiroshi Kawaguchi, and formed a diptych examining rebellion and conformity, both paths leading to the protagonist's defeat. Ichikawa's endings tended towards despair: for instance, Mr. Pu remarking "How simple to go mad," or the mass poisonings which concluded his blackest comedies, *A Billionaire* (*Okuman chōja*, 1954) and *The Key*.

Ichikawa's heroes were often "little men," like the tax collector striving and failing to combat official corruption in *A Billionaire*, or outsiders—individuals, in Max Tessier's words, "pursuing an absurd goal, often alone." Examples include the soldier turned monk in *The Burmese Harp*; the monk turned arsonist, destroying the temple he loves to preserve its purity, in the Mishima adaptation *Conflagration*; the lonely African athlete in the documentary record of the 1964 Olympics, *Tokyo Olympiad* (*Tōkyō Orinpikku*, 1965); and the 23-year-old Ken'ichi Horie, sailing single-handedly from Nishinomiya in western Japan to San Francisco, in *Alone on the Pacific* (*Taiheiyō hitoribotchi*, 1963). This last film, with its subtle, sympathetic analysis of its protagonist's motives, actions, and emotions during his voyage, was arguably Ichikawa's masterpiece. Its focus, like that of most of the above

films, was the alienation of the young. Similarly, *Her Brother* (*Otōto*, 1960), a moving yet acerbic family drama about a delinquent brother ill with tuberculosis, centered on the irony that only when the boy is dying can his family bear to live with him. Later, *The Wanderers* (*Matatabi*, 1973) was a bitterly satiric *chanbara* in which the yakuza code of honor compels one of the protagonists to kill his father.

Ichikawa's films were distinguished by their dramatic efficacy, intelligence of characterization, and, during his period at Daiei in the late fifties and early sixties, by a masterly use of the Cinemascope frame; *An Actor's Revenge* and *Alone on the Pacific*, in particular, were magnificent exercises in film style. Credit for this was due partly to such collaborators as cinematographers Kazuo Miyagawa and Setsuo Kobayashi and especially his wife and regular screenwriter, Natto Wada. Certainly, the quality of Ichikawa's work declined with their departure and with the collapse of the old studio system. After a flirtation with independent production (*The Wanderers*, for instance, was made for ATG), he returned to studio filmmaking with *The Inugami Family* (*Inugami-ke no ichizoku*, 1976), a convoluted murder mystery, and the commercial success that allowed him to continue working through the eighties and nineties. His later films lacked the relevance of his best work; indeed, Ichikawa settled self-consciously into his role as a veteran, recreating the old-time Japanese film industry in *Actress* (*Eiga joyū*, 1987), a biopic of Kinuyo Tanaka; realizing a 30-year-old script, co-written with Akira Kurosawa, Masaki Kobayashi, and Keisuke Kinoshita, in the comic period film *Dora-Heita* (2000); and remaking a past success in *The Burmese Harp*

*(Biruma no tategoto*, 1985). He remained active into his nineties, directing a new version of *The Inugami Family (Inugami-ke no ichizoku)* in 2006. His death severed one of the last remaining links to the Japanese cinema's Golden Age.

1945 **Musume Dōjō-ji** / A Girl at Dojo Temple (*short*)
1947 **Tōhō sen'ichiya** / A Thousand and One Nights of Toho (*co-director*)
1948 **Hana hiraku** / A Flower Blooms
 **Sanbyakurokujūgoya: Tōkyō hen** / 365 Nights: Tokyo Chapter
 **Sanbyakurokujūgoya: Ōsaka hen** / 365 Nights: Osaka Chapter
1949 **Ningen moyō** / Human Patterns
 **Hateshi naki jōnetsu** / Passion without End
1950 **Ginza Sanshirō** / Sanshiro of Ginza
 **Netsudeichi** / Heat and Mud
 **Akatsuki no tsuiseki** / Pursuit at Dawn
1951 **Ieraishan** / Nightshade Flower
 **Koibito** / The Lover
 **Mukokusekisha** / The Man without a Nationality
 **Nusumareta koi** / Stolen Love
 **Bungawan Soro** / Bengawan Solo
 **Kekkon kōshinkyoku** / Wedding March
1952 **Rakkī-san** / Mr. Lucky
 **Wakai hito** / Young People
 **Ashi ni sawatta onna** / The Woman Who Touched the Legs
 **Ano te kono te** / This Way, That Way
1953 **Pū-san** / Mr. Pu
 **Aoiro kakumei** / The Blue Revolution
 **Appare ichiban tegara: Seishun Zenigata Heiji** / The Youth of Heiji Zenigata (lit. Bravo, First Exploit: Young Heiji Zenigata)
 **Aijin** / The Lovers
1954 **Watashi no subete o** / All of Myself
 **Okuman chōja** / A Billionaire

**Josei ni kansuru jūnishō** / Twelve Chapters on Women
1955 **Seishun kaidan** / Ghost Story of Youth
 **Kokoro** / The Heart
1956 **Biruma no tategoto** / The Burmese Harp / Harp of Burma
 **Shokei no heya** / Punishment Room
 **Nihonbashi** / Nihonbashi / Bridge of Japan
1957 **Man'in densha** / A Full-Up Train / The Crowded Streetcar
 **Tōhoku no zummutachi** / The Men from Tohoku
 **Ana** / The Pit
1958 **Enjō** / Conflagration
1959 **Anata to watashi no aikotoba: Sayonara konnichi wa** / Goodbye, Hello (lit. Your Words of Love and Mine: Goodbye, Hello)
 **Kagi** / The Key / Odd Obsession
 **Nobi** / Fires on the Plain
1960 **Jokyō** / A Woman's Testament (*co-director*)
 **Bonchi** / Bonchi / The Son
 **Otōto** / Her Brother
1961 **Kuroi jūnin no onna** / Ten Dark Women
1962 **Hakai** / The Outcast / The Sin / The Broken Commandment
 **Watashi wa nisai** / I Am Two / Being Two Isn't Easy
1963 **Yukinojō henge** / An Actor's Revenge / The Revenge of Yukinojo (lit. The Avenging Ghost of Yukinojo)
 **Taiheiyō hitoribotchi** / Alone on the Pacific
1964 **Dokonjō monogatari: Zeni no odori** / Money Talks / The Money Dance
1965 **Tōkyō Orinpikku** / Tokyo Olympiad
1967 **Toppo Jījo no botan sensō** / Topo Gigio and the Missile War
1968 **Seishun** / Youth (*co-director*)
 **Kyō** / Kyoto (*short*)
1970 **Tsuru** / Crane (*short*)

**Panpa no katsuyaku** / Activity on the Pampas (*short*)

**Nihon to Nihonjin** / Japan and the Japanese (*short*)

1971 **Ai futatabi** / To Love Again

1973 **Matatabi** / The Wanderers

**Visions of Eight** (*co-director*)

1975 **Wagahai wa neko de aru** / I Am a Cat

1976 **Tsuma to onna no aida** / Between Wife and Woman

**Inugami-ke no ichizoku** / The Inugami Family

1977 **Akuma no temariuta** / The Devil's Bouncing-Ball Song / A Rhyme of Vengeance

**Gokumontō** / Island of Horrors

1978 **Joōbachi** / Queen Bee

**Hinotori** / The Phoenix

1979 **Byōinzaka no kubi kukuri no ie** / The House of Hanging

1980 **Koto** / The Old Capital / Ancient City

1981 **Kōfuku** / Lonely Heart

1983 **Sasameyuki** / The Makioka Sisters (lit. A Light Snowfall)

1984 **Ohan**

1985 **Biruma no tategoto** / The Burmese Harp

1986 **Koneko monogatari** / Story of a Kitten (*co-director*)

**Rokumeikan** / The Hall of the Crying Deer / High Society of Meiji

1987 **Eiga joyū** / Actress (lit. Film Actress)

**Taketori monogatari** / Princess from the Moon

1988 **Tsuru** / Crane

1991 **Tenkawa densetsu satsujin jiken** / Noh Mask Murders

1993 **Kaette kita Kogarashi Monjirō** / Fusa / The Return of Monjiro Kogarashi (lit.)

1994 **Shijūshichinin no shikyaku** / The 47 Ronin

1996 **Yatsuhakamura** / Village of Eight Gravestones

2000 **Shinsengumi**

**Dora Heita** / Dora-Heita / Alley Cat

2001 **Kāchan** / Big Mama

2006 **Yume jūya** / Ten Nights of Dreams (*co-director*)

**Inugami-ke no ichizoku** / The Inugami Family

## IEKI Miyoji
## (September 10, 1911–February 22, 1976)
## 家城巳代治

Though he has never acquired a reputation abroad, Ieki was a distinguished exponent of domestic drama whose films deserve admiration for their intelligence and humanity. He worked initially at Shochiku as assistant to Heinosuke Gosho and Minoru Shibuya, and his debut, *Torrent* (*Gekiryū*, 1944), made to encourage increased productivity in the mines, was a project that he took over when Shibuya was drafted. After the war, he directed youth films and romances such as *Sad Whistle* (*Kanashiki kuchibue*, 1949), a sentimental vehicle for child *enka* singer Hibari Misora, before being expelled from Shochiku in its 1950 purge of suspected Communist sympathizers.

During the fifties, working for independent production companies, Ieki produced his most notable films. *Beyond the Clouds* (*Kumo nagaruru hate ni*, 1953) was a sombre account of the training and last days of kamikaze pilots, stressing their indoctrination and the waste of young lives. *Tomoshibi* (1954), a study of schoolchildren in a poor farming community, voiced a subtle anger at the conservatism of traditional education methods and the extent of rural poverty. *Sisters* (*Shimai*, 1955) was a richly

©Dokuritsu Pro

*Tomoshibi (1954): Actress Kyōko Kagawa gave a typically touching performance in this richly textured, politically incisive drama of rural life.*

textured family drama, well acted and capturing the atmosphere of provincial Japan early in the Showa period. Perhaps Ieki's best film was *Half Brothers* (*Ibō kyōdai*, 1957), in which the domestic cruelties within an army officer's family became a microcosm of the wider tyranny of prewar militarism. Superbly acted by Kinuyo Tanaka as the family's maid and Rentarō Mikuni as the army officer forced to marry her after raping her, it was a film of both political sophistication and emotional intensity.

Ieki returned to studio production, at Toei, with *The Naked Sun* (*Hadaka no taiyō*, 1958); this was an account of life among poor railway workers. Like his earlier films, it showed a sensitivity to the problems of the young. Ieki continued to direct films about children and young people through the six-

ties. Among them were *A Pebble by the Wayside* (*Robō no ishi*, 1964), a remake of Tomotaka Tasaka's 1938 adaptation of a Yūzō Yamamoto novel set in the Meiji era, about the four hundred blows suffered by an unhappy child, and *The Only Child* (*Hitorikko*, 1969) about a high school boy forbidden to go to university by his mother and her lover.

Ieki's films reveal the influence of his mentor Gosho in their subtle, unshowy technique, realist texture, and human detail. He was adept at suggesting the emotions of his characters through subtleties of gesture and expression and at addressing political themes through personal drama. His work merits international exposure.

**1944  Gekiryū** / Torrent
**1947  Wakaki hi no chi wa moete** /
Young Blood Is Burning

1949 **Kanashiki kuchibue** / Sad Whistle
1950 **Hana no omokage** / Appearance of a Flower
1953 **Kumo nagaruru hate ni** / Beyond the Clouds
1954 **Tomoshibi** / Tomoshibi (lit. Light)
1955 **Shimai** / Sisters
**Mune yori mune ni** / From Breast to Breast
1956 **Kobushi no hana no saku koro** / When the Magnolias Bloom
1957 **Ibo kyōdai** / Half Brothers
1958 **Hadaka no taiyō** / The Naked Sun
1959 **Subarashiki musumetachi** / Those Wonderful Girls
1960 **Himitsu** / The Secret
**Dangan taishō** / The Brass-Pickers / General Bullet (lit.)
1961 **Machi** / The City
1962 **Wakamonotachi no yoru to hiru** / Young People by Night and Day
1963 **Minna waga ko** / All Our Children
1964 **Robō no ishi** / A Pebble by the Wayside
1965 **Tōbō** / The Runaway
1967 **Kurohime monogatari** / The Kurohime Story
1968 **Chikara Tarō** / Strong Taro
1969 **Hitorikko** / The Only Child
1974 **Koi wa midori no kaze no naka** / Love Is in the Green Valley

**IKEHIRO Kazuo**
**(b. October 25, 1929)**
池広一夫

One of Daiei's most flamboyant directors of *chanbara*, Ikehiro served as assistant to such luminaries as Kōzaburō Yoshimura, Kenji Mizoguchi, Kon Ichikawa, and Kaneto Shindō before making his debut with *The Rose Daimyo* (*Bara daimyō*, 1960). His third film, the Shin Hasegawa adaptation *Tokijiro of Kutsukake* (*Kutsu-*

*kake Tokijirō*, 1961), initiated a fruitful collaboration with actor Raizō Ichikawa. Ichikawa also starred in *Seven Miles to Nakayama* (*Nakayama shichiri*, 1962), the story of a wandering gambler who rescues a woman resembling his murdered wife; this was thought to bring a freshness of touch to the *matatabi* (wandering yakuza) genre, as Ikehiro sought to stress the melancholy and solitude of the hero. The revenge drama *Lone Wolf* (*Hitori ōkami*, 1968), another *matatabi-eiga*, also has a high reputation among devotees of the genre.

Ikehiro's own reputation may have suffered because many of his films were contributions to long-running series, in which installments were shared between various studio artisans. *Zatoichi and the Chest of Gold* (*Zatōichi senryō kubi*, 1964), the first of his three entries in the sequence of films starring Shintarō Katsu as the blind swordsman, was less interesting than the episodes by Kenji Misumi and Issei Mori. However, *Kyoshiro Nemuri: Sword of Seduction* (*Nemuri Kyōshirō: Joyōken*, 1964), the fourth in an eccentric series, generally known in English as *Sleepy Eyes of Death*, with Raizō Ichikawa as the warrior son of a corrupted foreign missionary and a Japanese Christian, was a remarkable film which drew out the tortured psychology of the anti-hero through its bold use of color, expressionist camera angles, and overt symbolism. The stylized plot allowed Ikehiro's imagination free rein, and he later contributed two further installments, apparently even more outlandish.

In terms of sheer visual invention, Ikehiro may have been the most brilliant of Daiei's sixties contract directors, but this brilliance tended to be relatively shallow: thus, his version of the much-retold legend of folk hero

Yasubei, *Broken Swords* (*Hiken yaburi*, 1969) was more stylish, but less psychologically perceptive and less harrowing, than Issei Mori's 1959 version *Samurai Vendetta* (*Hakuōki*). In his last years at Daiei, Ikehiro helmed the three *Trail of Blood* (*Mushukunin Mikogami no Jōkichi*) films, another sequence of movies about a lone avenger. By now his style had become a little coarse, and the physical violence was unnecessarily emphatic. After Daiei's collapse, he went into television where, with the exception of one Shochiku-produced theatrical feature, *Make-Up* (*Keshō*, 1984), he was to spend the rest of his career.

1960 **Bara daimyō** / The Rose Daimyo
1961 **Tenka ayatsurigumi** / The Power Behind the Throne
   **Kutsukake Tokijirō** / Tokijiro of Kutsukake
   **Kodachi o tsukau onna** / Woman with a Shortsword
   **Kagerō samurai** / The Phantom Samurai / The Missing Leaf / Heat-Haze Samurai (lit.)
   **Hana no kyōdai** / Flower Brothers / Bringing Up His Elder Brother
1962 **Nakayama shichiri** / Seven Miles to Nakayama / The One and Only Girl I Ever Loved (lit. Seven Ri to Nakayama)
   **Jigoku no shikyaku** / Hell's Assassin
1963 **Kage o kiru** / Cut the Shadow
   **Zōhyō monogatari** / Rabble Tactics / Tale of the Rank and File (lit.)
   **Dokonjō ichidai** / The Disposition of a Generation / Life of Bad Temper / Nothing but Guts
1964 **Zatōichi senryōkubi** / Zatoichi and the Chest of Gold / Zatoichi's 1000-ryo Bounty (lit.)
   **Zatōichi abaredako** / Zatoichi's Flashing Sword / Zatoichi: A Tough Kite (lit.)
   **Nemuri Kyōshirō: Joyōken** / Kyoshiro Nemuri: Sword of

Seduction / Sleepy Eyes of Death: Sword of Seduction
   **Shinobi no mono: Zoku Kirigakure Saizō** / Band of Assassins: Return of Saizo of the Mist
1965 **Waka oyabun** / Young Boss
   **Waka oyabun shutsugoku** / Young Boss: Released from Prison
1966 **Waka oyabun: Kenkajō** / Young Boss: Invitation to Fight
   **Dorobō banzuke** / The Thieves' Who's Who / Rank of Thieves
   **Gan** / Wild Geese
   **Zatōichi umi o wataru** / Zatoichi's Pilgrimage / Zatoichi's Trip across the Sea (lit.)
   **Shinsho: Shinobi no mono** / A New Beginning: Band of Assassins / The Three Enemies
1967 **Nemuri Kyōshirō burai hikae** / Kyoshiro Nemuri: Trail of Traps / Sleepy Eyes of Death: Trail of Traps
   **Datsugokusha** / Jailbreaker
   **Waka oyabun senryō hada** / Young Boss: Leader's Flesh
1968 **Hitori ōkami** / Lone Wolf / The Lone Stalker
   **Zoku yakuza bōzu** / Return of the Hoodlum Priest / The Priest and the Gold Mint
   **Ama kuzure** / The Daring Nun
1969 **Nemuri Kyōshirō: Akujogari** / Kyoshiro Nemuri: Castle Menagerie / Kyoshiro Nemuri: Hunt for the Wicked Women (lit.) / Sleepy Eyes of Death: Castle Menagerie
   **Koroshiya o barase** / Kill the Killers
   **Hiken yaburi** / Broken Swords
   **Keimusho yaburi** / Prison Break
   **Nemuri Kyōshirō: Manjigiri** / Kyoshiro Nemuri: Fylfot Swordplay / Sleepy Eyes of Death: Fylfot Swordplay
1970 **Onna gokuakuchō** / Naked Ambition / Notebooks on Heinous Women (lit.)
   **Mama itsu made mo ikite ne** /

Mama, Won't You Live Forever? /
Live My Share, Mother
**Kenka ichidai: Dodekai yatsu**
/ Fighting Man's Life: Useless
Creature / Soft-Boiled Goro
1971 **Kataashi no ēsu** / The One-
Legged Ace
1972 **Mushukunin Mikogami no
Jōkichi: Kiba wa hikisaita** / Trail
of Blood / Jokichi Mikogami,
Wanderer: Pulling the Fangs that
Rip and Tear (lit.)
**Mushukunin Mikogami no
Jōkichi: Kawakaze ni kako wa
nagareta** / Trail of Blood 2 / Jokichi
Mikogami, Wanderer: Drifting in
the River Wind (lit.)
1973 **Mushukunin Mikogami no
Jōkichi: Tasogare ni senkō ga
tonda** / Trail of Blood 3 / Jokichi
Mikogami, Wanderer: Leaping
Glint in the Twilight (lit.)
1984 **Keshō** / Make-Up

## IMAI Tadashi
**(January 8, 1912–November 22, 1991)**
今井正

Critically acclaimed in Japan but the
victim of relative neglect abroad, Imai
assisted Tamizō Ishida and Nobuo Nakagawa at J.O. Studios before directing.
Despite his subsequent reputation as a
leftist, he worked initially on militarist
propaganda. His debut, *Numazu Military Academy* (*Numazu heigakkō*, 1939),
was a heroic account of the conflict between Shogun and Emperor at the end
of the Edo period, while *Love and Vows*
(*Ai to chikai*, 1945), co-directed with
Korean Sai To, was distressingly made
in order to encourage Koreans to enlist
as kamikaze pilots. Imai's most notable
propaganda piece was *Suicide Troops of
the Watchtower* (*Bōrō no kesshitai*, 1942),
about Japanese fighting the resistance

in Northern Korea; politics notwithstanding, it apparently displayed great
technical expertise. Imai, who later described these films as "the biggest mis-
take of my life," made amends after the
war with *An Enemy of the People* (*Minshū
no teki*, 1946), a trenchant attack on the
Imperial system, and an expression of
his allegiance to the Japanese Communist Party.

Thereafter Imai embarked on a
career as a polemical filmmaker addressing socially conscious themes.
The subject of *Blue Mountains* (*Aoi sanmyaku*, 1949) and *Echo School* (*Yamabiko
gakkō*, 1952) was education. In the former, an engagingly acted lyrical comedy
with an appealing freshness of touch,
the love between students in a newly
co-educational school overcomes the
feudal attitudes of the more conservative adults. In the latter, a teacher and
his pupils keep studying despite their
poverty. *And Yet We Live* (*Dokkoi ikiteiru*, 1951) chronicled the lives of the
urban poor: produced independently
and shot on location, it was inspired by
Italian neo-realism. Later, *Rice* (*Kome*,
1957) focused in comparable neo-realist
terms on rural life, though glossy color
and sentimental plotting rather romanticized the subject matter.

Elsewhere, Imai depicted those marginalized by reason of race or gender.
*Kiku and Isamu* (*Kiku to Isamu*, 1959)
was a sensitive study of the prejudice
endured by the mixed-race offspring
fathered by a black American soldier.
*Muddy Waters* (*Nigorie*, 1953), based on
three Ichiyō Higuchi stories of Meiji-
period women, showed the limited options for females in every social class. Its
detailed atmosphere and intelligent use
of staging in depth were reminiscent of
Heinosuke Gosho, who would adapt
the same author's work in *Growing Up*

©Dokuritsu Pro

Nigorie / Muddy Waters *(1953): Imai's study of female experience in the Meiji era treated socially conscious themes with uncharacteristic subtlety.*

(*Takekurabe*, 1955). Imai's most feminist work was the *jidai-geki Night Drum* (*Yoru no tsuzumi*, 1958), a scathing attack on the repressive social codes of feudal Japan, which lead a nobleman to kill his wife after she commits adultery. Here, especially in the stunning climax, Imai's social critique achieved a rare emotional intensity. *Cruel Story of Bushido* (*Bushidō zankoku monogatari*, 1963) was another interesting period film, chronicling the bitter relations between masters and servants down the generations; though the script was schematic, the last, present-day sequence intriguingly highlighted the continuing prevalence of feudal attitudes in the modern corporate structure.

Imai's most persistent subject, however, was war. *Tower of Lilies* (*Himeyuri* *no tō*, 1953) focused on combat nurses killed during the American invasion of Okinawa. *Until We Meet Again* (*Mata au hi made*, 1950) was a tragedy about lovers parted by the conflict: she dies in an air raid, he in combat. In *Story of Pure Love* (*Jun'ai monogatari*, 1957), two delinquents reform when they become lovers, only for the girl to die of radiation sickness contracted through a childhood visit to Hiroshima. Imai continued to focus on the war in his later career, remaking *Tower of Lilies* in 1982 and directing *Eternal Cause* (*Kaigun tokubetsu nenshōhei*, 1972), a story of class distinctions among the officers and men at Iwo Jima. His last film, *War and Youth* (*Sensō to seishun*, 1991), rather blandly chronicled the 1945 incendiary bombings of Tokyo.

Japanese critics traditionally referred to Imai's style as "*nakanai realism*" ("realism without tears"), in implicit contrast to the more melodramatic and sentimental approach of such directors as Keisuke Kinoshita. In fact, Imai's work manifested intriguing similarities to Kinoshita's. *Until We Meet Again* and *Story of Pure Love* (the latter a title Kinoshita might have chosen) celebrated simple, chaste, youthful romances, and personalized the horror of war by showing its destructive effect on the lovers. *Cruel Story of Bushido* resembled *The River Fuefuki* (*Fuefukigawa*, 1960) in exposing the futility of the warrior code through its impact on several generations of a single family. The limitation of Imai's work, as of Kinoshita's, was that the stress on the tragic consequences of a problem tended to overshadow analysis of its causes. Joan Mellen aptly commented that "he works close to the sentimental, suggesting too often that there is a special nobility among the oppressed."

Imai's films were generally well-made, but he did not achieve a particularly consistent or expressive style. He was adept at conveying meaning through simple, powerful images or juxtapositions: for instance, the military march drowning out classical music in *Until We Meet Again*. Sometimes, however, his devices seemed ill judged: in *Darkness at Noon* (*Mahiru no ankoku*, 1956), about three youths tendentiously accused of murder, the use of fast motion in an imagined depiction of the crime served to make the prosecutor's argument seem farcical, preventing the audience from judging the case on its merits. Only occasionally did he succeed in applying a consistent style to a whole film: if *Night Drum* remains his masterpiece, that fact is due largely to the vivid use of offscreen space to reflect a society where privacy is non-existent. Still, despite its stylistic unevenness, Imai's work was consistently moving. In Max Tessier's words, "If Imai's options lead him at times to prefer propaganda to art and the didacticism of simple statement, his sincere humanism always protects him from the dangerous temptations of dogmatism."

1939 **Numazu heigakkō** / Numazu Military Academy

**Warera ga kyōkan** / Our Instructor

1940 **Tajinko mura** / Tajinko Village

**Onna no machi** / Woman's Town

**Kakka** / The General

1941 **Kekkon no seitai** / Married Life

1942 **Bōrō no kesshitai** / Suicide Troops of the Watchtower

1944 **Ikari no umi** / The Angry Sea

1945 **Ai to chikai** / Love and Vows (*co-director*)

1946 **Minshū no teki** / An Enemy of the People

**Jinsei tombogaeri** / Life Is Like a Somersault

1947 **Chikagai nijūyojikan** / Twenty-Four Hours Underground / Twenty-Four Hours of a Secret Life (*co-director*)

1949 **Aoi sanmyaku (Zenpen; Kōhen)** / Blue Mountains (Parts 1 and 2)

**Onna no kao** / A Woman's Face

1950 **Mata au hi made** / Until We Meet Again

1951 **Dokkoi ikiteiru** / And Yet We Live

1952 **Yamabiko gakkō** / Echo School

1953 **Himeyuri no tō** / Tower of Lilies / The Girls of Okinawa

**Nigorie** / Muddy Waters

1955 **Ai sureba koso** / Because I Love / If You Love Me (*co-director*)

**Koko ni izumi ari** / Here Is a Spring

**Yukiko**

| 1956 | **Mahiru no ankoku** / Darkness at Noon / Shadows in Sunlight |
| 1957 | **Kome** / Rice |
| | **Jun'ai monogatari** / Story of Pure Love |
| 1958 | **Yoru no tsuzumi** / Night Drum / The Adulteress |
| 1959 | **Kiku to Isamu** / Kiku and Isamu |
| 1960 | **Shiroi gake** / The Cliff (lit. The White Cliff) |
| 1961 | **Are ga minato no hi da** / Pan Chopali (lit. There Are the Harbor Lights) |
| 1962 | **Kigeki: Nippon no obāchan** / Old Japanese Woman / The Old Woman's Paradise |
| 1963 | **Bushidō zankoku monogatari** / Cruel Story of Bushido / Samurai Saga / Oath of Obedience |
| 1964 | **Echigo tsutsuishi oya shirazu** / The Story of Echigo |
| | **Adauchi** / Revenge |
| 1967 | **Satōgashi ga kowareru toki** / When the Cookie Crumbles |
| 1968 | **Fushin no toki** / The Time of Reckoning (lit. Time of Disbelief) |
| 1969 | **Hashi no nai kawa** / The River without a Bridge |
| 1970 | **Hashi no nai kawa: Dainibu** / The River without a Bridge: Part 2 |
| 1971 | **En to iu onna** / A Woman Called En |
| 1972 | **Ā, koe naki tomo** / My Voiceless Friends |
| | **Kaigun tokubetsu nenshōhei** / Eternal Cause / Special Navy Junior Corps (lit.) |
| 1974 | **Kobayashi Takiji** / Life of a Communist Writer (lit. Takiji Kobayashi) |
| 1976 | **Yōba** / The Possessed / The Old Woman Ghost |
| | **Ani imōto** / Ino and Mon / Brother and Sister (lit. Older Brother, Younger Sister) |
| 1979 | **Kosodate gokko** / Rika / The Proper Way / Bringing Up the Children |
| 1981 | **Yuki** / The Snow Fairy |

| 1982 | **Himeyuri no tō** / Tower of Lilies / The Eternal Monument |
| 1991 | **Sensō to seishun** / War and Youth |

## IMAMURA Shōhei
### (September 15, 1926–May 30, 2006)
今村昌平

In a career bridging fiction and documentary, Imamura carried out an icy, iconoclastic investigation into "the relationship of the lower half of the human body and the lower half of the social structure." He directed after serving as assistant at Shochiku to Yasujirō Ozu, and at Nikkatsu to Yūzō Kawashima. Like Ozu, Imamura made films about the Japanese family, but he rejected Ozu's gentility: his families were characterized by violence, overt sexuality (including incest), and oppressive power structures. Kawashima's influence was more direct, particularly in *Pigs and Battleships* (*Buta to gunkan*, 1961), the energy and wild humor of which recalled the older director's freewheeling satires. More generally, Kawashima's spirit manifested itself in Imamura's talent for juggling numerous plot strands and in his materialist outlook: his characters, like Kawashima's, were physical beings, whose motivation was animal and instinctual.

Imamura's oeuvre may be read as an alternative social history, focusing on those excluded from the official postwar narrative of peace, reconstruction, and economic growth. His businesspeople were not the tycoons and obedient salaried workers of Japan's economic miracle, but entrepreneurs outside the margins of respectable society: the brothel keeper of *The Insect Woman* (*Nippon konchūki*, 1963), the in-

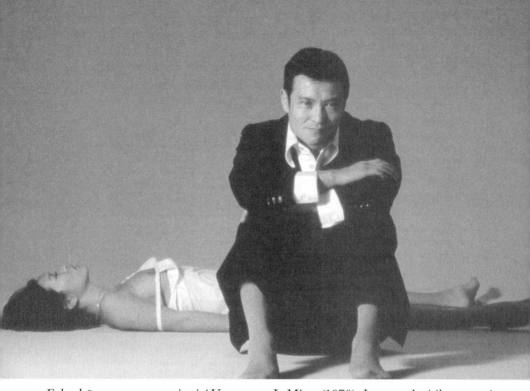

Fukushū suru wa ware ni ari / Vengeance Is Mine *(1979): Imamura's pitiless portrait of a serial killer viewed crime with an entomologist's detachment.*

decent filmmakers of *The Pornographers* (*"Erogotoshitachi" yori: Jinruigaku nyū-mon*, 1966), and the prewar pimp who, anticipating Japan's imperial expansion, opens a chain of brothels across Asia in *Zegen* (1987). *My Second Brother* (*Nian-chan*, 1959)—an early, uncharacteristi-cally tender film—focused on resident Koreans in a poor mining town, while the protagonists of two of Imamura's documentaries, *History of Postwar Japan as Told by a Bar Hostess* (*Nippon sengo shi: Madamu Onboro no seikatsu*, 1970) and *Karayuki-san, the Making of a Prostitute* (*Karayuki-san*, 1975), were members of the *burakumin* underclass. These films were socially critical, but Imamura had little faith in the power of politics to ef-fect change. The hostess in *History of Postwar Japan* watches newsreel foot-age of war and student protest, but sees no connection with her own life. Later,

in *Eijanaika* (*Ējanaika*, 1981), Imamura viewed the political ruptures of the Meiji Restoration largely through the eyes of the lower classes, who will gain nothing from the replacement of one authority by another. Here, for once, an anger at injustice spoke out in the climax, where the rioting poor are gunned down by the authorities.

Imamura's interest in the lower strata of society led him away from the classi-cal civilization of Kansai and the West-ernized modernity of Tokyo towards regional and folk cultures characterized by primitive vitality and superstition. *The Insect Woman, Intentions of Murder* (*Akai satsui*, 1964), and *The Ballad of Na-rayama* (*Narayama bushikō*, 1983) were set among the landowners and peasants of northern Japan, while *The Profound Desire of the Gods* (*Kamigami no fukaki yokubō*, 1968) was an epic account of the clash between the animist traditions of a far-flung southern island and the materialism of the Tokyo engineer who comes to develop it. Imamura's characters, though pragmatists, were not rationalists. Often, he showed that superstition endured despite the technological advances of modern Japan: thus, in the pseudo-documentary, *A Man Vanishes* (*Ningen jōhatsu*, 1967), the family of a missing person seek help from a shaman, while in *The Pornographers*, a woman believes her pet carp to be the reincarnation of her late husband.

As suggested by the titles of *The Insect Woman* (literally, *Entomological Chronicles of Japan*) and *The Pornographers* (*An Introduction to Anthropology*), Imamura observed these phenomena with a scientific detachment. In *The Pornographers*, the camera views the characters through bars or glass, like caged animals, while in numerous films, especially *The Profound Desire of the Gods*, the director drew parallels between human and animal life. *The Ballad of Narayama*, a realist fable about a community which abandons its elderly folk to starvation, saw human relations as subject to Darwinian principles. Though his wheeling tracking shots often followed human movement on screen closely, proximity did not create sympathy. Rather, Imamura's camera resembled the entomologist's microscope, scrutinizing people and their behavior in pitiless close up. The method achieved clarity, but lacked compassion, Imamura's Darwinist philosophy expressing itself logically in a contempt for human weakness.

Some have found feminist themes in Imamura's work; the truth is more that he saw women as supremely pragmatic, able to respond to changing circumstances with an adaptability generally denied to his weak or stupid men. *The*

*Insect Woman* and *Intentions of Murder* were both about the triumphs of amoral women over circumstances: their heroines were survivors, using any means necessary to endure. Imamura's men, by contrast, overreach themselves, with often fatal consequences: the hapless hero of *Pigs and Battleships* dies attempting to get rich through a criminal scam; the ambitious rapist of *Intentions of Murder* succumbs to heart disease on the way to a new life in Tokyo; the father in *The Profound Desire of the Gods* is slaughtered by his kinsmen as he tries to escape his island home; the serial killer of *Vengeance Is Mine* (*Fukushū suru wa ware ni ari*, 1979) meets death protesting at the unfairness of his fate.

In his later years, Imamura mellowed. *Black Rain* (*Kuroi ame*, 1989), based on Masuji Ibuse's novel, studied the after-effects of Hiroshima with an almost Ozu-like quietism, even approaching its subject through the Ozu-like plot formation of a middle-aged couple's attempts to marry off their niece despite her radiation-induced illness. *The Eel* (*Unagi*, 1997) was an unexpectedly humane account of the moral and psychological rehabilitation of a murderer after his release from prison, while Imamura's last feature, *Warm Water under a Red Bridge* (*Akai hashi no shita no nurui mizu*, 2001), was a sly Freudian comedy about a woman who gushes water on orgasm. The tenderness of these films, however, was bought at the cost of the subversive insights offered by Imamura's earlier misanthropy. Nevertheless, it was in the last decades of his life that the director earned a reputation abroad; *The Ballad of Narayama* and *The Eel* both won the Palme d'Or at Cannes, and Imamura was honored with international distribution and successful retrospectives in the West. Ironically, as his own work softened in tone, the generally grim outlook of his earlier films chimed increasingly with an age that had lost faith in politics and progress.

1958 **Nusumareta yokujō** / Stolen Desire
      **Nishi Ginza ekimae** / Nishi-Ginza Station
      **Hateshi naki yokujō** / Endless Desire
1959 **Nianchan** / My Second Brother
1961 **Buta to gunkan** / Pigs and Battleships / Hogs and Warships
1963 **Nippon konchūki** / The Insect Woman
1964 **Akai satsui** / Intentions of Murder
1966 **"Erogotoshitachi" yori: Jinruigaku nyūmon** / The Pornographers: Introduction to Anthropology
1967 **Ningen jōhatsu** / A Man Vanishes
1968 **Kamigami no fukaki yokubō** / The Profound Desire of the Gods / Kuragejima: Tales from a Southern Island
1970 **Nippon sengo shi: Madamu Onboro no seikatsu** / History of Postwar Japan as Told By a Bar Hostess
1975 **Karayuki-san** / Karayuki-san, the Making of a Prostitute
1979 **Fukushū suru wa ware ni ari** / Vengeance Is Mine
1981 **Ējanaika** / Eijanaika / Why Not?
1983 **Narayama bushikō** / The Ballad of Narayama
1987 **Zegen** / Zegen / The Pimp
1989 **Kuroi ame** / Black Rain
1997 **Unagi** / The Eel
1998 **Kanzō-sensei** / Dr. Akagi (lit. Doctor Liver)
2001 **Akai hashi no shita no nurui mizu** / Warm Water under a Red Bridge
2002 **11'09"01 September 11** (*co-director*)

## INAGAKI Hiroshi
## (December 30, 1905–May 21, 1980)
## 稲垣浩

A skilled and versatile filmmaker best known for his *jidai-geki*, Inagaki worked as an actor before directing. In the silent era, he narrated traditional stories with visual flair and melodramatic intensity: his extant second film, *Vagabond Gambler* (*Hōrō zanmai*, 1928), reveals his instinctive talent for choreographing action. *Long-Sought Mother* (*Mabuta no haha*, 1931), his best-known early work, told the story of a ronin's search for and rejection by his long-lost mother; also preserved today, it remains an outstanding example of the lyrical pessimism of the silent period film. After the coming of sound he continued to handle *jidai-geki* adeptly and achieved a major critical and commercial success with a multi-part version of the much-filmed *Daibosatsu Pass* (*Daibosatsu tōge*, 1935–36), about a sadistic samurai.

Inagaki's liberal attitudes also led him to produce some unusual films during the thirties and forties: *A Thousand and One Nights on the Road* (*Matatabi sen'ichiya*, 1936) transposed Frank Capra's *It Happened One Night* (1934) to Japan and apparently supported the common man against the authorities, while *The Sea-Crossing Festival* (*Umi o wataru sairei*, 1941), an allegory about the infiltration of a port town by a group of sinister horsemen, has been described by Motohiko Fujita as "the last representative of the liberal spirit in Japanese film until the end of the war." Even as late as 1943, *The Life of Matsu the Untamed* (*Muhō Matsu no isshō*), scripted by fellow liberal, Mansaku Itami, eschewed propagandistic elements in favor of subtle personal drama. In this story of a rickshaw driver's rela-

Muhō Matsu no isshō / The Life of Matsu the Untamed *(1943): Inagaki's delicate direction and Tsumasaburō Bandō's poignant acting yielded one of the best films of the war years.*

tions with a widow and her young son, Inagaki elicited a marvelously detailed performance from Tsumasaburō Bandō, and created a delicate balance between humor and poignancy. The result was one of the finest and most moving films produced during the war years.

After the war, Inagaki won international acclaim, including an Academy Award, for his *Musashi Miyamoto* trilogy (*Miyamoto Musashi*, 1954–56), distributed in the West as *Samurai*. This was a well-made but academic remake, starring Toshirō Mifune, of his 1940s film sequence of the same name. His 1958 version of *The Life of Matsu the Untamed*, again with Mifune, also earned foreign distribution as *The Rickshaw Man*; though virtually a shot-for-shot remake, it lacked the power and humanity of the

original. With *Life of a Swordsman* (*Aru kengō no shōgai*, 1959), Inagaki transposed the Cyrano de Bergerac story to the beginning of the Tokugawa era, but in fact some of his most interesting postwar films were set in more recent times. *Children Hand in Hand* (*Te o tsunagu kora*, 1948), based, like *The Life of Matsu the Untamed*, on a Mansaku Itami script, was a compassionate and engaging account of the experiences at school of a child with learning difficulties, a subject that might have appealed to Hiroshi Shimizu. *Storm* (*Arashi*, 1956), based on a novel by Tōson Shimazaki, was a delicate and beautifully acted Taisho-era story about a widower bringing up his young sons. *Geisha in the Old City* ("*Kottai-san*" *yori: Nyotai wa kanashiku*, 1957) was a complex account of the relationships within a Kyoto geisha house, shot in exquisite color. In its perceptive use of social changes in the old capital as a microcosm of Japan's postwar evolution, it resembled Kōzaburō Yoshimura's postwar work, which it almost rivaled for quality.

In the last years of his career, Inagaki continued to produce expertly crafted films in a traditional idiom. Among these, his version of the much-filmed *Chūshingura* story (1962) was rather pedestrian; but his last big-budget film, *Samurai Banners* (*Fūrin kazan*, 1969), a heroic epic chronicling the unification of Japan into a nation state, was given a certain poignancy by the performance of Toshiko Sakuma as the princess whose happiness is sacrificed on the altar of national unity. By the seventies, Inagaki was judged old-fashioned and found himself unemployed. It was an ironic fate, since the last film he directed, *Ambush* (*Machibuse*, 1970), had a distinctly modern tone of absurdism, reminiscent of a spaghetti Western: the hero protects the inhabitants of a besieged teahouse before learning that he was hired to fight for the other side. However, Inagaki's last contribution to the cinema was nostalgic: in 1978, in collaboration with silent film enthusiast Shunsei Matsuda, he served as producer of a modern silent *chanbara*, *The Worms of Hell* (*Jigoku no mushi*). In recalling the tone of his earliest work, this emphasized the classical consistency of his approach to filmmaking.

1928 **Tenka Taiheiki** / All's Right with the World / Peace on Earth

**Hōrō zanmai** / Vagabond Gambler

**Genji kozō** / Genji Boy

**Ginneko Samon** / Samon of the Silver Cat

1929 **Mekuragumo** / Blind Spider

**Zoku banka jigoku: Dainihen** / Hell of Ten Thousand Flowers 2: Part 2 (*co-director*)

**Zoku banka jigoku: Kanketsu hen** / Hell of Ten Thousand Flowers 2: Final Part

**Oshidori tabi nikki** / Lovebirds' Travel Diary

**Sōma Daisaku: Zenpen: Budō kassatsu no maki** / Daisaku Soma: Part 1: Bushido, Life and Death

**Ehon musha shugyō** / Picture Book on Knight Errantry / A Samurai's Career

**Koroshita hito** / The Murdered Man

**Samezaya** / Sharkskin Scabbard

1930 **Uzushio** / Whirlpool

**Kaigyaku sanrōshi** / Three Joking Warriors

**Isshin Tasuke** / Tasuke Isshin

1931 **On'ai gojūryō** / Kind Gift of 50 Ryo

**Mabuta no haha** / Long-Sought Mother / The Image of a Mother (lit. Mother in his Mind's Eye)

**Genroku jūsannen** / The Thirteenth Year of the Genroku Era

**Otokodate bayari** / Manly Men Are Popular

**Ippongatana dohyōiri** / A Sword and the Sumo Ring / Into the Sumo Ring with a Sword

1932 **Yatarōgasa: Kyorai no maki** / Yataro's Sedge Hat: Past and Future Reel / Yataro Walks Alone: Past and Future Reel

**Yatarōgasa: Doppo no maki** / Yataro's Sedge Hat: Independence Reel / Yataro Walks Alone: Independence Reel

**Tabi wa aozora** / Travel under a Blue Sky

**Jidai no kyōji** / Egotist of the Time

1933 **Kunisada Chūji: Tabi to kokyō no maki** / Chuji Kunisada: Travel and Home

**Kunisada Chūji: Rurō tenpin no**

maki / Chuji Kunisada: Wandering and Change

**Kunisada Chūji: Hareru Akagi no maki** / Chuji Kunisada: Weather Clearing over Akagi

**Sasano Gonzaburō: Mikazuki sasahokiri** / Gonzaburo Sasano: Spear Fight under New Moon

**Fūun: Zenpen** / Wind and Clouds: Part 1

1934 **Fūun: Kōhen** / Wind and Clouds: Part 2

**Naohachi kodomo tabi** / Childhood Travels of Naohachi

**Tenpō Chūshingura** / Tenpo-Era Chushingura

**Shinsengumi (Zenpen; Kōhen)** / Shinsengumi (Parts 1 and 2)

1935 **Tone no kawagiri** / Fog over the River at Tone

**Fuji no shirayuki** / White Snows of Fuji

**Seki no Yatappe** / Yatappe of Seki (*co-director*)

**Senryō tsubute** / The 1000-ryo Stone

**Daibosatsu Tōge: Daiippen: Kōgen ittōryū no maki** / Daibosatsu Pass: Part 1: Fencing School Reel (*co-director*)

1936 **Daibosatsu Tōge: Dainihen: Suzukayama no maki** / Daibosatsu Pass: Part 2: Mount Suzuka Reel

**Daibosatsu Tōge: Kanketsu hen: Mibu Shimabara no maki** / Daibosatsu Pass: Final Part: Mibu Shimabara Reel

**Matatabi sen'ichiya** / A Thousand and One Nights on the Road

1937 **Koichi Tanbei: Oitsu owaretsu no maki** / Tanbei Koichi: Chasing Reel

**Kōgen no tamashii** / Spirit of the Plain

**Hiryū no tsurugi** / Sword of the Flying Dragon

**Chikemuri Takadanobaba** / Duel at Takadanobaba / Blood Spattered at Takadanobaba (lit.) (*co-director*)

1938 **Muhōmono Ginpei** / Ginpei the Untamed

**Shusse Taikōki** / The Rise of Hideyoshi

**Yami no kagebōshi** / Shadow in Darkness

**Jigoku no mushi** / The Worms of Hell

**Mazō** / Image of the Devil

1939 **Zoku mazō: Ibara Ukon** / Image of the Devil 2: Ukon Ibara

**Kesa to Moritō** / Kesa and Morito (*co-director*)

**Sonnō sonjuku** / Respect the Emperor, Village School

1940 **Miyamoto Musashi: Daiichibu: Kusawake no hitobito** / Musashi Miyamoto: Part 1: The Pioneers

**Miyamoto Musashi: Dainibu: Eitatsu no mon** / Musashi Miyamoto: Part 2: Gate to Success

**Miyamoto Musashi: Kenshin ichiro** / Musashi Miyamoto: The Path of Fighting Spirit

1941 **Umi o wataru sairei** / The Sea-Crossing Festival

**Edo saigo no hi** / The Last Days of Edo

1942 **Miyamoto Musashi: Ichijō-ji kettō** / Musashi Miyamoto: Duel at Ichijoji Temple

**Dokuganryū Masamune** / Masamune the One-Eyed Dragon

1943 **Muhō Matsu no isshō** / The Life of Matsu the Untamed / The Rickshaw Man

1944 **Rōka wa Shanhai ni agaru: Shunkō ikon** / Flaming Shanghai / Signal Fires of Shanghai: Chunjie Revenge

1945 **Tōkai Suikoden** / Tokai-Region Water Margin

**Saigo no jōitō** / The Last Nationalist Party

1946 **Okagura kyōdai** / Brothers in the Band

1947 **Sōshi gekijō** / Political Theater
**Kokoro tsuki no gotoku** / My Heart Is Like the Moon

1948 **Te o tsunagu kora** / Children Hand in Hand
**Kurouma no Danshichi** / Danshichi of the Black Horse

1949 **Shirozukin arawaru** / The White-Hooded One Arrives
**Wasurerareta kora** / Forgotten Children

1950 **Ore wa yōjinbō** / I Am a Bodyguard
**Giyaman no yado: Guntō nanbansen** / Giyaman's Inn: Bandits and the Barbarian Ship
**Sasaki Kojirō** / Kojiro Sasaki

1951 **Zoku Sasaki Kojiro** / Kojiro Sasaki 2
**Kaizokusen** / Pirate Ship
**Kanketsu Sasaki Kojirō: Ganryūjima kettō** / Kojiro Sasaki: Conclusion: Duel at Ganryujima

1952 **Sengoku burai** / Sword for Hire (lit. Ruffian in the Time of Warring States)
**Shanhai no onna** / A Woman of Shanghai
**Fūun senryōsen** / Wind, Clouds, and the 1000-ryo Boat

1953 **Tabi wa soyokaze** / Travel in a Breeze
**Omatsuri Hanjirō** / Hanjiro of the Festival

1954 **Miyamoto Musashi** / Musashi Miyamoto / Samurai

1955 **Miyamoto Musashi: Ichijō-ji kettō** / Musashi Miyamoto: Duel at Ichijoji Temple / Samurai II: Duel at Ichijoji Temple
**Tabiji** / Journey / The Lone Journey

1956 **Miyamoto Musashi: Kettō Ganryūjima** / Musashi Miyamoto: Duel at Ganryujima / Samurai III: Duel at Ganryujima
**Shūjinsen** / Prison Ship
**Arashi** / Storm

1957 **Yagyū bugeichō** / Secret Scrolls / Notes on Martial Arts of Yagyu (lit.)
**"Kottai-san" yori: Nyotai wa kanashiku** / Geisha in the Old City (lit. From "Courtesan": Sadness of a Woman's Body)

1958 **Yagyū bugeichō: Sōryū hiken** / Secret Scrolls: Part 2 / Notes on Martial Arts of Yagyu: Twin Dragon Style
**Muhō Matsu no isshō** / The Rickshaw Man / The Life of Matsu the Untamed (lit.)
**Tabisugata Nezumi kozō** / The Ratkid on a Journey

1959 **Aru kengō no shōgai** / Life of a Swordsman / Samurai Saga
**Nihon tanjō** / The Three Treasures / Birth of Japan (lit.)

1960 **Fundoshi isha** / The Country Doctor

1961 **Ōsaka-jō monogatari** / Daredevil in the Castle / Tale of Osaka Castle (lit.)
**Gen to Fudōmyō'o** / Gen and Acala / A Youth and His Amulet
**Yatō kaze no naka o hashiru** / Bandits in the Wind

1962 **Doburoku no Tatsu** / "Home-brewed" Tatsu / Sake Dragon
**Chūshingura (Hana no maki; Yuki no maki)** / Chushingura / The Loyal 47 Ronin (Flower Reel; Snow Reel)

1963 **Hiken** / The Young Swordsman / Secret Sword (lit.)

1964 **Shikon madō: Dairyū maki** / Whirlwind (lit. Warrior Spirit, Devil's Path: Great Dragon Reel)
**Garakuta** / The Rabble

1966 **Abare Goemon** / Rise Against the Sword / Wild Goemon (lit.)

1967 **Sasaki Kojirō** / Kojiro Sasaki

1969 **Fūrin kazan** / Samurai Banners (lit. Wind in the Woods, Fire on the Mountains)

1970 **Machibuse** / Ambush / Ambush at Blood Pass / Incident at Blood Pass

## INOUE Umetsugu
## (b. May 31, 1923)
井上梅次

A prolific director of commercial films at Nikkatsu and elsewhere, Inoue is remembered particularly for his musicals. Among his early work, *Tokyo Cinderella* (*Jazu onparēdo 1954-nen: Tōkyō Shinderera musume*, 1954) was apparently the first jazz movie made in Japan. Inoue was also one of Yūjirō Ishihara's more sympathetic directors: their most famous collaboration, *The Man Who Raised a Storm* (*Arashi o yobu otoko*, 1957), was another musical, which chronicled the burgeoning career of an ambitious drummer. Ishihara's likeable bad-boy persona, the popular theme song, and the bold color images made it a huge popular success. Inoue also directed Ishihara in several action films: for instance, *The Winner* (*Shōrisha*, 1957), a boxing movie, and *The Eagle and the Hawk* (*Washi to taka*, 1957), a revenge melodrama set entirely on board ship. Among Inoue's other films were several thrillers with *noir*ish plots: *The Last Betrayal* (*Sannin no kaoyaku*, 1960) was a story about a gang boss who finds himself betrayed by his henchman and mistress, while *The Scarlet Rose* (*Makkana koi no monogatari*, 1963) focused on an undercover cop investigating a narcotics ring, only to fall for the *femme fatale* ringleader. Inoue also made a colorful version of *The Black Lizard* (*Kurotokage*, 1962), adapted from the Mishima play in turn derived from Gothic writer Edogawa Ranpo. Forays into period costume were rarer, but included *The Thief in Black* (*Kuro no tōzoku*, 1964), a somewhat whimsical but lively romp about a Tokugawa court official and his long-lost bandit brother.

From the mid-sixties into the early seventies, Inoue continued to direct for various Japanese studios, but spent three months of each year working at the Hong Kong-based Shaw Brothers studio. Some of his Hong Kong films were remakes of stories he had previously used in Japan: *The Man Who Raised a Storm* was recycled as *King Drummer* (*Cing ceon gu wong*, 1967), and the Shochiku musical *The Night I Want to Dance* (*Odoritai yoru*, 1963) became *Hong Kong Nocturne* (*Hoeng gong faa jyut je*, 1966). Among his Japanese films of the period was *The Performers* (*Hana to namida to honoo*, 1970), a melodramatic vehicle for popular singer Hibari Misora, which marked her final screen appearance.

Permanently back in Japan from the early seventies, Inoue continued to direct for both the small and the big screen. Among his last films were another remake of *The Man Who Raised a Storm* (*Arashi o yobu otoko*, 1983) and the feminist-themed *Bird! Lend Me Your Wings* (*Zesshō haha o yobu uta: Tori yo tsubasa o kashite*, 1985). Growing attention to popular genres within the Japanese cinema has recently stimulated something of a revival of interest in Inoue's work. He was certainly capable of creating eyecatching images, and at its best his direction displayed a genuine intelligence: for instance, in *The Man Who Raised a Storm*, the pan from the drunken hero and his girlfriend embracing to an idealized kissing couple on a record sleeve offers an ironic comment on the star image. For the most part, however, Inoue seems to have been an efficient but anonymous commercial director.

1952 **Koi no ōendanchō** / Love's Cheerleader
**Sararīman kenka sandaiki** / Record of Three Generations of Quarreling Salarymen

1953 **Santa gambare** / Santa, Do Your Best

**Achako seishun techō: Daiyonwa: Medetaku kekkon no maki** / Achako's Notebook of Youth: Happy Marriage

**Waga koi no rira no kokage ni** / Our Love in the Shade of the Lilac Tree

1954 **Musume jūroku jazu matsuri** / A 16-Year-Old Girl's Jazz Festival

**Haruka naru yama no yobigoe** / Call from the Mountains

**Jazu onparēdo 1954-nen: Tōkyō Shinderera musume** / Tokyo Cinderella (lit. Jazz on Parade 1954: Tokyo Cinderella Girl)

**Kanpai! Jogakusei** / Here's to the Student Girls

**Kekkonki** / Time of Marriage

1955 **Jazu musume kanpai!** / Here's to the Jazz Girls

**Sarutobi Sasuke**

**Midori haruka ni** / Green Far Away

**Mittsu no kao** / Three Faces

**Miseinen** / Underage

1956 **Uramachi no otenba musume** / The Tomboy from the Back Streets

**Shi no jūjiro** / Crossroads of Death

**Hinotori** / The Phoenix

**Nikoyon monogatari** / Story of a Day Laborer

**Gesshoku** / Lunar Eclipse

1957 **Otenba sannin shimai: Odoru taiyō** / Three Tomboy Sisters: The Dancing Sun

**Kikenna kankei** / Dangerous Liaisons

**Shōrisha** / The Winner / The Champion

**Jūnanasai no teikō** / The 17-Year-Old Rebel

**Washi to taka** / The Eagle and the Hawk

**Arashi o yobu otoko** / The Man Who Raised a Storm / A Man Called Storm / The Stormy Man

1958 **Yoru no kiba** / Fangs of the Night

**Fūfu hyakkei** / One Hundred Views of a Couple / The Husband Wore the Apron

**Ashita wa ashita no kaze ga fuku** / Tomorrow Is Another Day (lit. Tomorrow's Wind Will Blow Tomorrow)

**Subarashiki dansei** / That Wonderful Guy

**Zoku fūfu hyakkei** / One Hundred Views of a Couple 2

1959 **Arashi o yobu yūjō** / The Friendship That Raised a Storm / Friendship of Jazz

**Gunshū no naka no taiyō** / Sun in the Crowd

**Tōkyō no kodoku** / Alone in Tokyo

**Seishun banka** / Elegy to Youth

**Yogiri no kettō** / Duel in the Night Fog

1960 **Arashi o yobu gakudan** / The Band That Raised a Storm

**Shōri to haiboku** / Victory and Defeat

**Taiyō o idake** / Embrace the Sun / The Poem of the Blue Star

**Sannin no kaoyaku** / The Last Betrayal / Three Bosses (lit.)

**Dairoku no yōgisha** / Suspect No. 6 / Six Suspects

1961 **Ginzakko monogatari** / Story of Three Boys from Ginza

**Onna wa yoru keshō suru** / A Woman Makes Up at Night / Nocturne of a Woman

**Higashi kara kita otoko** / The Man from the East

**Gonin no totsugekitai** / Five Men of the Attack Squad / The Last-Ditch Glory

**Nyōbō gakkō** / Refresher Course for Wives

**Tsuma ari ko ari tomo arite** / With Wife, Child and Friend / Tokyo Detective Saga

1962 **Onna to san'akunin** / The Actress

and the Three Rascals (lit. A Woman and Three Bad Men)

**Kurotokage** / The Black Lizard

**Heiten jikan** / Closing Time

**Hōseki dorobō** / The Jewel Thief

**Ankokugai saigo no hi** / Hell's Kitchen / The Last Days of the Underworld (lit.)

**Yakuza no kunshō** / Medal for Gangsters

1963 **Daisan no kagemusha** / The Third Shadow Warrior

**Watashi o fukaku umete** / Bury Me Deep

**Ankokugai saidai no kettō** / Duel of the Underworld

**Makkana koi no monogatari** / The Scarlet Rose (lit. Story of Pure-Red Love)

**Hanzai sakusen No. 1** / Crime Operation No. 1

**Odoritai yoru** / The Night I Want to Dance

1964 **Hanzai no merodī** / Melody of Crime

**Ankokugai ōdōri** / The Main Street of the Underworld

**Kuro no kirifuda** / The Black Trump Card

**Modae** / Agony / The Night of the Honeymoon

**Kuro no tōzoku** / The Thief in Black

1965 **Ura kaidan** / The Back Stairs

**Ōshōbu** / The Big Game

**Fukushū no kiba** / Fang of Revenge

**Mushukumono jingi** / A Wanderer's Honor / The Hoodlum Brothers

**Kuroi yūwaku** / Black Seduction

**Gyangu chōjō sakusen** / Gang Summit Operation / The Dice of Gold

**Akai taka** / The Red Hawk

1966 **Honoo to okite** / Flames and the Law

**Hoeng gong faa jyut je** / Hong Kong Nocturne (*Hong Kong*)

**Dip mong giu waa** / Operation Lipstick (*Hong Kong*)

**Koi to namida no taiyō** / The Sun of Love and Tears

**Fōku de ikō: Ginrei wa koi shiteru** / Let's Go Folk Music: The Silver-Capped Mountain of Love

**Shutsugoku no sakazuki** / Cup of Release

1967 **Mesu ga osu o kuikorosu: Kamakiri** / The Female Devours the Male: Mantis

**Cing ceon gu wong** / King Drummer (*Hong Kong*)

**Faa jyut loeng siu** / Hong Kong Rhapsody (*Hong Kong*)

**Gekiryū** / Swift Current

**Mesu ga osu o kuikorosu: Sanbiki no kamakiri** / The Stronger Sex (lit. The Female Devours the Male: Three Mantises)

1968 **Dip hoi faa** / The Brain Stealers (*Hong Kong*)

**Diu gam gau** / The Millionaire Chase (*Hong Kong*)

**Kushiro no yoru** / Kushiro Nights

**Neoi gaau ceon sik** / Whose Baby's in the Classroom (*Hong Kong*)

**Cing ceon maan sui** / The Singing Escort (*Hong Kong*)

1969 **Koi no kisetsu** / Season of Love

**Yoru no nettaigyo** / Tropical Fish of Night / BGS of Ginza

**Wai chan ng jik jyun** / The Five Million Dollar Legacy (*Hong Kong*)

**Yūhi no koibito** / Lovers of the Setting Sun

**Taiyō no yarōdomo** / Guys in the Sun / A Marine Camera

**Neoi zi gung jyu** / Apartment for Ladies (*Hong Kong*)

1970 **Misora Hibari: Mori Shin'ichi no Hana to namida to honoo** / The Performers (lit. Hibari Misora in Shin'ichi Mori's Flowers, Tears, and Flames)

**Zai jan lok** / The Man with Two Wives (*Hong Kong*)

**Ng zi hung hang** / Long Road to Freedom (*Hong Kong*)

**Kigeki: Dokyō ichiban** / The Most Courageous

**Cing ceon lyun** / Young Lovers (*Hong Kong*)

**Hana no fushichō** / Flower Phoenix

**Ceon sek jim dou** / The Venus' Tear Diamond (*Hong Kong*)

**Ngo oi gam gau sai** / We Love Millionaires (*Hong Kong*)

1971 **Zik joeng lyun jan** / Sunset (*Hong Kong*)

**Juk neoi hei ceon** / The Yellow Muffler (*Hong Kong*)

**Ningen hyōteki** / Human Target

**Kawaii akujo** / My Darling Witch (lit. Cute Bad Woman)

**Hibari no subete** / All About Hibari

1972 **Kawaii akujo: Koroshi no mae ni kuchizuke o** / My Darling Witch: A Kiss before Death (lit. Cute Bad Woman: A Kiss before Killing)

1973 **Otoko ja nai ka: Tōshi manman** / Aren't You a Man: Full of Fighting Spirit

1974 **Mokugekisha o kese: Ikare dokuhebi** / Eliminate the Witness: Get Angry, Poisonous Snake

1975 **Yogiri no hōmonsha** / The Visitor in the Night Fog

1976 **Utareru mae ni ute** / Shoot before You Get Shot

1983 **Toshi in Takarazuka: Love Forever**

**Arashi o yobu otoko** / The Man Who Raised a Storm

1985 **Zesshō haha o yobu uta: Tori yo tsubasa o kashite** / Bird! Lend Me Your Wings (lit. Mother-Calling Song: Bird! Lend Me Your Wings)

1987 **Kōdonēmu: Burakku kyatto o oe!** / Codename: Chase the Black Cat

## ISAKA Satoshi
## (b. January 2, 1960)
## 井坂聡

Isaka's reputation rests mainly on his extraordinary debut, *Focus* (1996), an economical and disturbing thriller following the grim chain of events initiated when a television crew sets up an interview with an *otaku* (nerd) whose hobby is eavesdropping on two-way radio conversations. A subtle critique of the methods of Reality TV and a cautionary tale about the power of the media, it turned a low budget to its advantage, skillfully using handheld camera techniques to implicate the viewer in the action. The theme of media irresponsibility was again central to *The Frame* (*Hasen no marisu*, 2000), a gripping account of a television editor who uses dubious methods to slant the news and finds herself haunted by a murder suspect whose guilt was implied in one of her programs. Though more conventionally shot than *Focus*, this intelligent and chilling film posed important questions about the role of the media while refusing to provide easy answers. On a related topic, *Doubles* (*Daburusu*, 2001) investigated the criminal potential of technology, depicting a heist committed against a consultancy firm by a locksmith and a computer ace fired by the company.

Despite their interest in the media and technology, these films were essentially concerned with character. Tadanobu Asano's nervy performance brought plausibility to the narrative convolutions of *Focus*, while much of the complexity of *The Frame* derived from the skill of star Hitomi Kuroki in conveying the frustrations of a woman struggling to hold her own in a man's world. The heroine of *Detective Riko*

(*Onna keiji Riko: Seibo no fukakifuchi*, 1998) was another woman working in a traditionally male profession; here, Isaka deepened a generic plot about a murder investigation by concentrating on her personal life and her relationship with her child.

*G@me* (2003), proved to be Isaka's most conventional thriller to date: a glossy, labyrinthine Hollywood-style account of a kidnapping carried out with the connivance of the victim, a duplicitous *femme fatale*. Though gripping in its way, it was shallow compared to the director's best work, the distinction of which has derived from his ability to make generic plots a vehicle for meaningful criticism. However, Isaka's range may yet prove wider than his early films indicated, since his recent work has begun to move away from the thriller. Thus, *Embraced by Mana* (*Mana ni dakarete*, 2003) was a romance set in Hawaii, while *The Back of the Elephant* (*Zō no senaka*, 2007) was a poignant drama about the responses of a middle-aged professional to a diagnosis of terminal cancer.

1996  **Focus**
1998  **Onna keiji Riko: Seibo no fukakifuchi** / Detective Riko
2000  **Hasen no marisu** / The Frame
2001  **Daburusu** / Doubles
2002  **Mr. Rookie**
2003  **Mana ni dakarete** / Embraced by Mana
       **G@me**
2007  **Zō no senaka** / The Back of the Elephant

**ISHIDA Tamizō**
**(June 7, 1901–October 1, 1972)**
石田民三

Though his reputation rests largely on one film, *Fallen Blossoms* (*Hana chirinu*, 1938), Ishida was a prolific director through the late silent and early sound eras. His films during the twenties and early thirties were largely *chanbara*, of which few survive; the extant *Rokusuke of Keya Village* (*Keyamura Rokusuke*, 1927), a story of revenge, seems typical in style of its period and genre. From the mid-thirties, however, beginning with *Osen* (1934), Ishida achieved a reputation as a director of literary adaptations, often made in collaboration with the members of a Western-style theater group, the Bungaku-za. Ishida's films tended to focus on the lower strata of society: thus, *Fallen Blossoms* was a geisha story; *Dove of Night* (*Yoru no hato*, 1937), set in Tokyo's old *shitamachi* district, examined the life of a bar hostess disappointed in her love for a theater director; and *Keshoyuki* (*Keshōyuki*, 1940), from a story by Mikio Naruse, depicted a family managing a failing vaudeville theater, again in the *shitamachi* area of Tokyo.

Ishida's best films displayed a considerable formal imagination and an ability to analyze the material and psychological impact of social and political change on individuals. He had a particular interest in the upheavals of the late Edo and early Meiji periods: *War-Song for a Misty Dawn* (*Asagiri gunka*, 1943) dramatized the last stand of warriors defending the Tokugawa Shogunate. More commonly, Ishida focused on those indirectly affected by, rather than participating in, these changes. His acknowledged masterpiece, *Fallen Blossoms*, was a superb portrait of life among Kyoto geisha during the fighting which heralded the Shogunate's collapse. Filming wholly within the confines of the geisha house and with an entirely female cast, Ishida used a highly fragmented technique, in which no two shots are identically composed, to express the varying perspectives of the women and their contrasting emotional responses to their circumstances. The combination of stylistic imagination and a profound sympathy for its heroines made this one of the outstanding Japanese films of the thirties.

Somewhat less formally experimental, but still richly atmospheric in its portrayal of Meiji-period Osaka, was *Old Songs* (*Mukashi no uta*, 1939), which, through its story of the relations between two families, explored the rise of the merchant class and the decline of the former samurai. Again, Ishida's concern was with the psychological impact of social change, a theme seen most clearly in the decision by an ex-samurai, now fallen on hard times, to join the Satsuma Rebellion in quest of a heroic death. The decline of the samurai class was also central to *Street of Fireworks* (*Hanabi no machi*, 1937), the protagonists of which were a former warrior turned wholesaler and a girl of samurai stock living in Yokohama's foreigners' quarter in preparation for studying abroad.

Though Noel Burch championed *Fallen Blossoms*, Ishida's work is still barely known in the West; indeed, the loss of much of his output, coupled with his retirement early in the postwar period, have made him seem a marginal figure even in Japan. His extant films are overdue for wider exposure and re-evaluation.

1926 **Aishō** / Scars of Love
**Kentō** / Swordfight
**Yūken** / Chinese Sword
**Akki** / Wicked Devil
1927 **Keyamura Rokusuke** / Rokusuke of Keya Village
**Setsuen** / Proof of Innocence
**Isamihara** / Manliness

**Kengeki no sōryū** / Fighting Twin Dragons
**Kozaru Shichinosuke** / Shichinosuke Kozaru
**Kennan jonan** / Trouble over Swords and Women
**Aitō** / Love Fight
**Date Hiroku: Matsumae Tetsunosuke** / Hiroku Date: Tetsunosuke Matsumae
**Minamikaze** / South Wind
1928 **Akagaki Genzō** / Genzo Akagaki
**Danchō no sakebi** / Cry from the Heart
**Akagiya sōdō** / Trouble at the Akagiya
**Dasshutsu fukushūki** / Record of Escape and Revenge
**Kyōren tomoe zōshi** / Illuminated Chronicle of Love and Chivalry
**Gan kirai** / Migration of Wild Geese
**Sanjūrokkei** / The Thirty-Six Strategies
**Shinpan botan dōrō** / Peony Lantern: New Version
**Kyōren jumon (Zenpen; Kōhen)** / Spell of Crazed Love (Parts 1 and 2)
1929 **Bukotsumono** / The Rustic
**Ukiyoe sōmatō** / Ukiyo-e Phantasmagoria
**Yūgiri no Senta** / Senta of the Evening Mist
**Adauchi Jōrurizaka** / Revenge at Jorurizaka
**Sozoku ninjutsu banashi** / A Tale of Petty Theft and Ninja Art
1930 **Joraiya (Zenpen; Kōhen)** / Joraiya (Parts 1 and 2)
**Tengu sōdōki** / Record of Tengu's Troubles
**Meisō ketsukinpu** / Bloody Fight of the Famous Spear
**Kiyokawa Hachirō** / Hachiro Kiyokawa
**Kega kōmyō adauchi dan** / Tale of Injury, Ambition, and Revenge
**Uragiri Shōtengu** / Treacherous Little Tengu

Kirare Otomi / Scarred Otomi

Taishokkan jigoku ōrai / Street of Hellish Gluttons

1931 Kaien taichō Sakamoto Ryōma: Kyōraku hen / Ryoma Sakamoto, Head of the Kaientai: Kyoto Episode

Fūryū ichidai otoko / The Life of an Elegant Man

Adauchi nihonbare / Revenge and Clear Skies

Fūryū yakko mai / The Dance of an Elegant Person

Sasano meisōden: Orisuke Gonzō / Tale of the Famous Spear at Sasano: Gonzo Orisuke

Jiraikagumi / The Jiraika Group

1932 Hanafubuki samurai Senta / Samurai Senta of the Falling Cherry Blossoms

Ōedo yami no uta / Song of Darkness in Great Edo

Masumitsu Yasunosuke / Yasunosuke Masumitsu

1933 Yōma no egoyomi / Illustrated Almanac of Bewitching Devils

Renbo fubuki / Falling Blossoms of Love

Yashima kyōkakujin / Chivalrous War in Japan

Nanban karuta: Inochi no hibana / Cards, Foreign-Style: Spark of Life

Enma jigoku / King of Hell

Yatagorō zange / Yatagoro's Penitence

Osada no adauchi / Osada's Revenge

1934 Osen

Zenkamono no futari onna / Two Women with Criminal Records

Adauchi Tsumakoizaka / Revenge at Tsumakoizaka

1935 Ōedo haru keshō / Edo's Spring Finery

Meiji jūsannen / The Thirteenth Year of Meiji

Oden jigoku / Oden's Hell

Aogiri no uta / Song of the Parasol Tree

Yōen bosatsu / Bewitching Fire and Bodhisattva

1936 Shunshoku gonin onna / Five Women in Spring Scenery

Bunsei yōfuden / Legend of Bewitching Woman in the Bunsei Era

Satsukibare ippon yari / One Spear in Sunny Intervals during the Rainy Season

Kaidō hyakuri / A Hundred Ri on the Sea Road

1937 Hanabi no machi / Street of Fireworks

Yoru no hato / Dove of Night

Tōkai bijoden / Legend of a Beautiful Woman of the Tokai Region

1938 Hahaoya ningyō / Mother Doll

Hana chirinu / Fallen Blossoms / The Blossoms Have Fallen

1939 Mukashi no uta / Old Songs / Old Sweet Song

Kenka tobi (Zenpen; Kōhen) / Fighting Kites (Parts 1 and 2)

Hanatsumi nikki / Diary of Flowerpicking

1940 Keshōyuki / Keshoyuki / Light Dusting of Snow

Tsuriganesō / The Bellflower

Tatakau otoko / The Fighting Man

1941 Enoken, Torazō no Shunpū senri / Enoken and Torazo: A Thousand Ri in the Spring Wind

Orizuru shichi henge (Zenpen; kōhen) / Seven Changes of a Paper Crane (Parts 1 and 2)

Kumotsuki no imōto no uta / Song of Kumotsuki's Sister

Danshi yūjō / Friendship between Men

1942 Yamamatsuri bonten uta / Song of Brahma at the Mountain Festival

1943 Asagiri gunka / War-Song for a Misty Dawn

Rōkyoku Chūshingura / Recitation of the Chushingura

1944 **Sanjaku Sagohei** / Sagohei Sanjaku
1947 **En wa ina mono** / Relationships
Are Complicated Things

## ISHII Sōgo
(b. January 15, 1957)
石井聰亙

Ishii's career divides into two distinct halves: the brash early films, which earned him a reputation as a punk filmmaker, and the slower, pictorial, sometimes meditative work of his mature period. His early features were the fruit of the amateur short films he directed, while still a student, on 8 and 16mm; at Nikkatsu's invitation, he remade one of them, *Panic High School* (*Kōkō daipanikku*, 1977; remade 1978) in featurelength form. Dramatizing a rebellion by students after one of their number commits suicide because of academic pressure, this revealed anti-establishment leanings sustained in Ishii's next features. His graduation film, *Crazy Thunder Road* (*Kuruizaki sandā rōdo*, 1980), which also earned theatrical distribution, was a rowdy account of gang warfare in the streets of Tokyo; its raw intensity was some compensation for its lack of finish.

The success of these student films earned Ishii the opportunity to direct two further features in the same wild style. *Burst City* (*Bakuretsu toshi*, 1982) intertwined the story of a group of punk rockers protesting against the construction of a nuclear power plant with that of two bikers seeking revenge for a murder. *Crazy Family* (*Gyakufunsha kazoku*, 1984) was a scattershot satire on the Japanese nuclear family, whose characters respectively personified the underlying militarist tendencies of the elder gen-

eration, the materialism of the postwar generation, and the academic pressure on the young. Ishii's best-known film abroad, it was certainly subversive, but suggested the limitations of the director's early manner. The apparent madness of the family made them seem too extreme a case to be representative, and while superficially arresting, the film was less penetrating than Yoshimitsu Morita's similarly themed *Family Game* (*Kazoku gēmu*, 1983).

Its domestic failure left Ishii unable to finance further features for ten years, but his comeback, *Angel Dust* (*Enjeru dasuto*, 1994), was an eerie thriller which displayed a new stylistic discipline and psychological depth in its story of a psychiatrist who begins to feel implicated in a series of murders committed by a former lover. Its themes of urban and pre-millenial angst were also central to *August in the Water* (*Mizu no naka no hachigatsu*, 1995), in which Ishii returned to his native Fukuoka to narrate a curious story of adolescent emotions set against the backdrop of an apocalyptic plague. Ultimately inconsequential, the film still had a certain beauty, its shimmering images conveying the feel of stifling summer heat. Ishii next made *Labyrinth of Dreams* (*Yume no ginga*, 1997), like *Angel Dust* a story of a woman's equivocal fascination with a murderer. This, too, was a highly atmospheric film, shot imaginatively in a monochrome which reflected the visual textures of the cinema of the fifties, when its story was set. Although these films lacked the satiric edge of Ishii's early work, their elegant, small-scale approach seemed fruitful. By contrast, *Gojoe* (*Gojō reisenki*, 2000), Ishii's first *jidai-geki*, was a cavalier reworking of Japanese history, visually striking, but marred by trite elements of fantasy. It proved a costly flop, which bankrupted the company of producer Takenori Sentō.

Apart from his feature films, Ishii has also sustained a career as a director of shorts, experimental works, and music videos for such Japanese punk banks as Anarchy and The Stalin. Among his *avant-garde* films, *Shuffle* (*Shaffuru*, 1981), *Electric Dragon 80,000V* (2001) and *Dead End Run* (2003) all rejected narrative detail for a near-abstract distillation of generic plots, used mainly as a vehicle for formal experimentation. In *Mirrored Mind* (*Kyūshin: 3D Saundo kanzenpan*, 2005), he seems to have combined this formalism with a renewed interest in character, focusing on an alienated actress and her emotional regeneration during a trip to Bali. Since even Ishii's commercial films have revealed a consistent interest in innovation and experimentation, one may expect that his oeuvre will continue to develop in unpredictable directions.

1977 **Kōkō daipanikku** / Panic High School (*8mm short*)

1978 **1/880000 no kodoku** / The Solitude of One Divided by 880,000 (*8mm short*)

**Totsugeki! Hakata gurentai** / Charge! Hooligans of Hakata (*8mm short*)

**Kōkō daipanikku** / Panic High School (*feature-length remake*)

1979 **Hashiru** / Running (*8mm short*)

1980 **Kuruizaki sandā rōdo** / Crazy Thunder Road (*16mm*)

1981 **Shaffuru** / Shuffle (*16mm short*)

1982 **Bakuretsu toshi** / Burst City

1983 **Ajia no gyakushū** / Asia Strikes Back (*short*)

1984 **Gyakufunsha kazoku** / Crazy Family

1985 **Hanbun ningen: Ainshuturushende Noibauten** / ½ Mensch / Half Human

1989 **Shiatsu ōja** / The Master of Shiatsu (*short*)

1993 **J-Movie Wars** (*co-director*)

1994 **Enjeru dasuto** / Angel Dust

1995 **Mizu no naka no hachigatsu** / August in the Water

1997 **Yume no ginga** / Labyrinth of Dreams

2000 **Gojō reisenki** / Gojoe

2001 **Electric Dragon 80,000V**

2003 **Dead End Run**

2005 **Kyūshin: 3D Saundo kanzenpan** / Mirrored Mind

## ISHII Takashi
## (b. July 11, 1946)
## 石井隆

A sometime manga artist, Ishii entered the film industry as a writer, scripting Roman Porno at Nikkatsu for such directors as Chūsei Sone, Noboru Tanaka, Shun Nakahara, and Shinji Sōmai. Many of his scripts were based on his own manga *Angel Guts* (*Tenshi no harawata*), which Nikkatsu adapted into a series, Ishii making his own directorial debut with one of the later installments. These stories all featured a woman named Nami and a man named Muraki, an authorial quirk still present in much of Ishii's later work. He obtained good notices for his second film as director, *Original Sin* (*Shinde mo ii*, 1992), a grimly engrossing *film noir* with effectively crafted suspense sequences and some intelligent psychological insights, albeit marred by the distasteful genre staple of a heroine who falls in love with her rapist.

Ishii's subsequent films have generally unfolded as a variation on a theme, focusing on women in extreme situations. *Alone in the Night* (*Yoru ga mata*

Nūdo no yoru / A Night in Nude *(1993): Ishii skillfully adapted the screen persona of comedian Naoto Takenaka to the violent thriller genre.*

*kuru*, 1994) was another neo-*noir* thriller about a bereaved wife seeking revenge on the yakuza who raped her and killed her cop husband; its climax displayed the director's characteristic aestheticized violence. *A Night in Nude* (*Nūdo no yoru*, 1993) blended this brutality with very black comedy as the heroine, having murdered her violent gangster lover, tricks her agent into disposing of the body. In *Freeze Me* (*Furīzu mī*, 2000), about a rape victim who avenges herself on the three perpetrators, the director's treatment of his themes descended into self-parody. The tortured sexual politics of these films seem even more discomforting when one takes into account Ishii's admission that he had based the character of Nami on his wife.

The exception to these exercises in putting women and the audience through it was the male-centered, fatalistic heist movie *Gonin* (1995). Stylistically this was Ishii's most flamboyant work, with shifting patterns of light and shade visually suggesting the instability not only of the criminal lifestyle, but also of mainstream existence in an insecure post-bubble Japan. It was perhaps Ishii's most powerful and least distasteful film. However, its sequel, in which the five men of the title were replaced by five women, was poorly received.

Ishii is a technically skilled filmmaker: his staging of scenes of violence, often in long takes, rises at times to an excruciating intensity. His direction of actors is also generally good, and has sometimes been startling: witness the novel way in which the star persona of comedian Naoto Takenaka was adapted to the thriller genre in *Gonin* and *A Night in Nude*. However, there is a contradiction between the grim intensity of Ishii's narratives and the self-conscious elements of homage and parody: *Original Sin* was a deliberate reworking of *The Postman Always Rings Twice*, while pastiches of the shower murder scene from *Psycho* (1960, Alfred Hitchcock) occur in *Original Sin*, *Gonin*, *A Night in Nude*, and *Freeze Me*. This contradiction tends to unbalance his films, and makes their cruelties seem more exploitative than they might otherwise. Latterly, Ishii has returned to his roots in Roman Porno, realizing the two *Flower and Snake* (*Hana to hebi*, 2004 and 2005) films, adapted from Oniroku Dan's sexually explicit, sado-masochistic novel, and *The Brutal Hopelessness of Love* (*Hito ga hito o aisuru koto no dō shiyō mo nasa*, 2007), a softcore study of an actress who begins to prostitute herself in response to her husband's philandering.

1988   **Tenshi no harawata: Akai memai** / Angel Guts: Red Dizziness / Angel Guts: Red Vertigo

1992   **Shinde mo ii** / Original Sin (lit. Die If You Want)

1993   **Nūdo no yoru** / A Night in Nude

1994   **Tenshi no harawata: Akai senkō** / Angel Guts: Red Flash

        **Yoru ga mata kuru** / Alone in the Night (lit. Night Falls Again)

1995   **Gonin** / Gonin / The Five

1996   **Gonin 2**

1998   **Kuro no tenshi: Vol. 1** / The Black Angel: Vol. 1

1999   **Kuro no tenshi: Vol. 2** / The Black Angel: Vol. 2

2000   **Furīzu mī** / Freeze Me

2001   **Tokyo G.P.**

2004   **Hana to hebi** / Flower and Snake

2005   **Hana to hebi 2: Pari/Shizuko** / Flower and Snake 2

2007   **Hito ga hito o aisuru koto no dō shiyō mo nasa** / The Brutal Hopelessness of Love

## ISHII Teruo
### (January 1, 1924–August 12, 2005)
### 石井輝男

A prolific director of B-movies during the sixties and seventies, Ishii worked initially at ShinToho on the children's science fiction series *Super Giant* (*Sūpā Jaiantsu*). More typical of his approach were his several contributions to the *Line* (*Chitai*) series, set in the red-light districts of various Japanese cities among prostitutes, drug addicts, drug dealers, and their antagonists on the police force. *Black Line* (*Kurosen chitai*, 1960) memorably captured the atmosphere of both salubrious and sordid districts of Yokohama, while *Yellow Line* (*Iero rain*, 1960) contained some tense sequences as the heroine tries to alert the police to the fact that her companion is a murderer. Ishii's ShinToho B-movies outside this series generally gravitated towards similar racy and sensationalist subject matter: *Flesh Pier* (*Nyotai sanbashi*, 1958), for instance, was the story of a criminal ring conveying Japanese girls into prostitution in Asia. Despite hints of social commentary, these films did not succeed in transcending their exploitation format, but they were directed with a certain brusque power.

After transferring to Toei, Ishii made several well-regarded thrillers, among them *The Rogues* (*Narazumono*, 1964), shot on location in Macao, which apparently influenced Hong Kong action filmmaker John Woo. His most famous film of the period, however, was *Abashiri Prison* (*Abashiri bangaichi*, 1965), an account of prison life in a remote region of Hokkaido, centering on the experiences of a basically good-hearted inmate played by Ken Takakura. The snowscapes were an impressive backdrop to the hero's dilemmas, and this was arguably Ishii's most humane film, with a moving conclusion in which the hero throws away his chance of escape to assist his wounded antagonist. Its popularity spawned a long-running series, Ishii directing another nine installments before tiring of the material; he was, however, to essay similar subject matter in *The Big Escape* (*Daidatsugoku*, 1975), which reunited him with Takakura in a Hokkaido-set jailbreak story.

In the meantime, Ishii continued to direct exploitation films in various genres, including such notorious *zankoku* (cruelty) films as *Joys of Torture* (*Tokugawa onna keibatsu shi*, 1968), the sole *raison d'être* of which appeared to be the inventive depiction of extreme violence. This interest in shock effects was sustained with *Horror of Malformed Men* (*Edogawa Ranpo zenshū: Kyōfu kikei ningen*, 1969), a controversial adaptation of Edogawa Ranpo's macabre stories, which has been both praised for its visual imagination and damned for its exploitative portrayal of its disfigured "monsters." In truth, its occasional stylistic brilliance was overwhelmed by the incoherence of the plotting. In the seventies, Ishii made several films in a then popular subgenre featuring female yakuza, among them *Female Yakuza Tale: Inquisition and Torture* (*Yasagure anegoden: Sōkatsu rinchi*, 1973), about yakuza using addicted women to transport drugs. Had it been less prurient, the climax, which the abused women take revenge on their exploiters, might almost be read as a feminist statement. A curious hybrid of Ishii's preferred

genres was *Blind Woman's Curse* (*Kaidan noboriryū*, 1970), which seasoned the story of a female yakuza with such horror movie elements as a blood-drinking cat; esteemed in cult circles, it was fairly dismissed by Ishii himself as "nonsensical." Most of these films were distinguished by colorfully stylized art direction, but due to their absurd stories and the crudity of Ishii's camera style, they did not match the emotional depth of the best B-movies by Nobuo Nakagawa or Issei Mori.

After a long hiatus spent in television, Ishii finally made several independent films, including a trilogy based on the work of manga author Yoshiharu Tsuge and two low-budget horror movies. These confirmed his limitations: his loose reworking of Nakagawa's *Hell* (*Jigoku*, 1999) uncomfortably melded gruesome images of posthumous torture with unsubtle satire on the Aum Shinrikyo cult, while *Blind Beast vs. The Dwarf* (*Mōjū vs. Issunbōshi*, 2001), another Edogawa Ranpo adaptation, was if possible more sadistic, and certainly less visually striking, than Yasuzō Masumura's 1969 *Blind Beast* (*Mōjū*). Though Ishii's extensive oeuvre has its moments, it is likely to remain primarily of interest to connoisseurs of stylish savagery.

**1957** **Ringu no ōja: Eikō no sekai** / King of the Ring: World of Glory

**Kōtetsu no kyojin / Sūpā jaiantsu** / Super Giant

**Zoku kōtetsu no kyojin / Zoku sūpā jaiantsu** / Super Giant 2

**Sūpā jaiantsu: Kaseijin no majō** / Super Giant: Invaders from Space

**Sūpā jaiantsu: Chikyū metsubō sunzen** / Super Giant: The Earth in Danger

**Gonin no hanzaisha** / Five Criminals

**Sūpā jaiantsu: Jinkō eisei to**

jinrui no hametsu / Super Giant: Spaceship of Human Destruction

**1958** Sūpā jaiantsu: Uchūtei to jinkō eisei gekitotsu / Super Giant: Destruction of the Space Fleet

Amagi shinjū: Tengoku o musubu koi / Love Suicides at Amagi: Love Requited in Heaven

Nyotai sanbashi / Flesh Pier / A Woman's Body and the Wharf (lit.)

Hakusen himitsu chitai / Secret White Line / Call Girl Territory

Joōbachi no ikari / Queen Bee's Anger

**1959** Senjō no nadeshiko / Pink Battlefield / Broken Blossoms

Mōfubuki no shitō / Fight to the Death in a Blizzard

**1960** Kurosen chitai / Black Line

Nyotai uzumakijima / Women without Return Tickets

Iero rain / Ōsen chitai / Yellow Line

Joōbachi to daigaku no ryū / Queen Bee and the School for Dragons

**1961** Sekushī rain / Sexy Line

Ren'ai zubari kōza / Candid Course in Love (*co-director*)

Hana to arashi to gyangu / The Flower, the Storm and the Gang

Kiri to kage / Mist and Shadows

**1962** Koi to taiyō to gyangu / Love and the Sun and the Gang / All Rascals

Taiheiyō no G-men / G-Men of the Pacific

Gyangu tai gyangu / Gang vs. Gang

**1963** Ankokugai no kaoyaku: Jūichinin no gyangu / Underworld Boss: Gang of Eleven

Gyangu tai G-men: Shūdan kinko yaburi / Gang vs. G-men: Breaking the Company Safe

Bosu o taose / Kill the Boss

Shōwa kyōkakuden / Tale of Showa Era Chivalry

**1964** Tōkyō gyangu tai Honkon gyangu / Tokyo Gang vs. Hong Kong Gang

Narazumono / The Rogues / The Rascals

Gokinzō yaburi / The Safe Breakers / Robbing the Shogun's Gold (lit.)

Irezumi totsugekitai / Tattooed Sudden Attack / Shock Troop of Outlaws

**1965** Kaoyaku / The Boss

Abashiri bangaichi / Abashiri Prison / The Man from Abashiri Jail

Zoku Abashiri bangaichi / Return from Abashiri Prison

Abashiri bangaichi: Bōkyō hen / Abashiri Prison: Saga of Homesickness

Abashiri bangaichi: Hokkai hen / Abashiri Prison: Northern Seacoast Story

**1966** Nihon zero chitai: Yoru o nerae / Japan's Zero Zone: Nightwatch / The Flesh Market

Abashiri bangaichi: Kōya no taiketsu / Abashiri Prison: Duel in the Wilderness / Abashiri Prison: Duel in the Wind

Daiakutō sakusen / The Great Villain's Strategy

Abashiri bangaichi: Nankoku no taiketsu / Abashiri Prison: Duel in the South

Shinka 101: Koroshi no yōjinbō / Sacred Fire 101: Bodyguard's Murder

Abashiri bangaichi: Daisetsugen no taiketsu / Abashiri Prison: Duel in the Snow Country

**1967** Abashiri bangaichi: Kettō reika 30-do / Abashiri Prison: Duel at 30 Below

Otoshimae / The Settlement / Three Gamblers

Abashiri bangaichi: Aku e no chōsen / Abashiri Prison: Challenging the Wicked

Abashiri bangaichi: Fubuki no tōsō / Abashiri Prison: Duel in the Blizzard / Abashiri Prison: Duel in the Snowstorm

**1968** **Zoku otoshimae** / The Settlement 2 / The Final Decision

**Tokugawa onna keizu** / Shogun and Three Thousand Women / Tokugawa Women's Pedigree (lit.)

**Onsen anma geisha** / Spa Masseur Geisha

**Tokugawa onna keibatsu shi** / Joys of Torture / Tokugawa Women's Punishment (lit.)

**1969** **Zankoku ijō gyakutai monogatari: Genroku onna keizu** / Orgies of Edo / Story of Cruel and Strange Oppression: Genroku Era Women's Pedigree (lit.)

**Ijōsei ai kiroku: Harenchi** / Record of Abnormal Love: Shameless

**Noboriryū tekka hada** / Iron Flesh of the Rising Dragon / The Friendly Killer

**Tokugawa irezumi shi: Seme jigoku** / Hell's Tattooers / Inferno of Torture (lit. History of Tokugawa Tattoos: Torture Hell)

**Yakuza keibatsu shi: Rinchi** / Yakuza Punishment: Lynch Law

**Meiji Taishō Shōwa: Ryōki onna hanzai shi** / Love and Crime / Meiji, Taisho, and Showa Eras: Search for Bizarre Female Crimes (lit.)

**Edogawa Ranpo zenshū: Kyōfu kikei ningen** / Horror of Malformed Men

**1970** **Koroshiya ninbetsuchō** / Killer's Hit List / Killer's Census List

**Kaigoku ninbetsuchō** / Prisoners' Black List / Prison Census List

**Kaidan noboriryū** / Blind Woman's Curse / Black Cat's Revenge / Rising Dragon Ghost Story (lit.) / The Tattooed Swordswoman

**1972** **Hijirimen bakuto** / The Silk Gambler / Tiger Lily

**1973** **Poruno jidaigeki: Bōhachi bushidō** / Porno Period Film: Bohachi Bushido

**Yasagure anegoden: Sōkatsu rinchi** / Female Yakuza Tale:

Inquisition and Torture / Story of a Wild Elder Sister: Widespread Lynch Law (lit.)

**Gendai ninkyō shi** / Modern Chivalry

**1974** **Chokugeki! Jigokuken** / The Executioner / Direct Hit: Hell Fist (lit.)

**Chokugeki! Jigokuken daigyaku den** / The Executioner 2 / Direct Hit! Hell Fist: The Big Turnabout (lit.) / The Karate Inferno

**1975** **Daidatsugoku** / The Big Escape

**Bakuhatsu! Bōsōzoku** / Detonation! Violent Tribe

**Jitsuroku san'oku-en jiken: Jikō seiritsu** / True Account of the 300 million-yen Case: Statute of Limitations

**1976** **Bakuhatsu! Bōsō yūgi** / Detonation! Violent Games

**Kinkin no runpen taishō** / Kinkin the General of the Unemployed

**Bōsō no kisetsu** / Season of Violence

**1977** **Wakusei Robo: Dangādo A tai Konchū robotto gundan** / Planetary Robots: Danguard A vs. Bug Robot Army Corps

**1979** **Bōryoku senshi** / Violent Warrior

**1993** **Gensankan shujin** / The Master of Gensankan Inn

**1995** **Burai heiya** / Villain Field / Vagabond Plain / Ruffians

**1998** **Nejishiki** / Wind-Up Type / Screwed

**1999** **Jigoku** / Hell

**2001** **Mōjū vs Issunbōshi** / Blind Beast vs. The Dwarf

## ITAMI Jūzō
### (May 15, 1933–December 20, 1997)
伊丹十三

The son of Mansaku Itami, prewar director of satiric *jidai-geki*, Jūzō worked initially as an actor, appearing regularly in Japan and occasionally in English-language productions such as *Lord Jim* (1965, Richard Brooks). After a major success playing the father in Yoshimitsu Morita's *Family Game* (*Kazoku gēmu*, 1983), he privately financed his first and best film as director, *The Funeral* (*Osōshiki*, 1984), a pointed black comedy following a family preparing for their father's cremation. Though there were occasional sight gags, the main source of the comedy was incongruity: the awkwardness of people unfamiliar with established rituals, or the tactlessness of the crematorium assistant explaining the grisly details of the process to the bereaved relatives. Itami followed this film with an international hit, *Tampopo* (*Tanpopo*, 1985), in which the proprietor of a small restaurant learns to make the perfect bowl of *ramen* noodles, this saga unfolding alongside various sketches on the theme of food. Blending pastiche of the American Western with seasonings of pseudo-Oriental mysticism, this was actually more farce than satire, and one of Itami's less typical films; his most lightweight work, it was, nevertheless, his funniest.

Itami's most characteristic vein, however, was one of hectic social satire, typified by the two *Taxing Woman* films (*Marusa no onna*, 1987, and *Marusa no onna 2*, 1988), about a government agent pursuing tax evaders, by *A Woman against Extortion* (*Minbō no onna*, 1992), about a lawyer fighting yakuza intimidation in a luxury hotel, and by *Ageman* (1990), about a former geisha who brings luck to every man who beds her. All were distinguished by feisty performances from Itami's wife and regular star, Nobuko Miyamoto. The least successful, *Ageman*, was an uncomfortably broad critique of political corruption and plutocratic greed. The *Taxing Woman* films, however, were pointed attacks on the unscrupulous rich: not only tax evaders, but also, in the sequel, construction companies breaking up neighborhoods and resorting to intimidation in the pursuit of profit. *A Woman against Extortion* offered a deglamorized presentation of the yakuza as brutal thugs, a portrayal which had consequences for Itami himself when he was stabbed outside his home shortly after the film's release. This event was to inspire the director's final work, *Woman of the Witness Protection Program* (*Marutai no onna*, 1997), an unusually grim, if still comedic, drama about a woman threatened by the cultist perpetrators of a murder she has witnessed.

Itami's most typical films belonged to the era of the bubble economy, whose extravagances were fertile ground for satire. After its collapse, he attempted to expand his range with two relatively serious films. *The Last Dance* (*Daibyōnin*, 1993) was the story of a filmmaker diagnosed with cancer while directing a melodrama about a married couple both dying from the same disease. The contrast between the messy reality of death and the sentimentality of the film-within-a-film was effective, though the ending succumbed to the same kind of schmaltz that Itami had previously sent up. *A Quiet Life* (*Shizukana seikatsu*, 1995) was a flawed but fascinating story, based on events surrounding the family of Itami's brother-in-law, author Kenzaburō Ōe, and particularly his mentally handicapped son; the mixture of pathos and violence was effectively handled. Less well judged, in both these films, were the intrusive fantasy sequences and elements of farce. *Supermarket Woman* (*Sūpā no onna*, 1996) returned to more characteristic territory: a failing store restores its reputation. Though engaging, it was toothless as satire; indeed, Itami seemed by now to be celebrating the commercial values he had once mocked.

Although he often used eccentric camera angles to humorous effect, Itami's comedy derived less from style than from situation, and from the resourcefulness of his heroines in the face of adversity. His gags, especially in the *Taxing Woman* films, were suavely timed and slickly executed, but none of his later films equalled the gravity of *The Funeral* or the hilarity of *Tampopo*, and latterly his work became less barbed and somewhat formulaic. Mark Schilling has spoken ironically of his "ability to package his social comedies as adroitly and consistently as McDonald's packages Big Macs." Although Itami's suicide was a personal tragedy, it seems likely that his best work was behind him.

1984  **Osōshiki** / The Funeral
1985  **Tanpopo** / Tampopo
1987  **Marusa no onna** / A Taxing Woman
1988  **Marusa no onna 2** / A Taxing Woman Returns
1990  **Ageman** / Ageman / Tales of a Golden Geisha
1992  **Minbō no onna** / A Woman against Extortion / A Woman of "Minbo" / "Minbo," or the Gentle Art of Japanese Extortion
1993  **Daibyōnin** / The Last Dance (lit. A Seriously Ill Patient)
1995  **Shizukana seikatsu** / A Quiet Life
1996  **Sūpā no onna** / Supermarket Woman
1997  **Marutai no onna** / Woman of the Witness Protection Program

**ITAMI Mansaku**
**(January 2, 1900–September 21, 1946)**
伊丹万作

Considered among the best directors of prewar *jidai-geki*, Itami adopted a satiric approach to the genre, in contrast to the heroic melodrama of Daisuke Itō and the pessimistic realism of Sadao Yamanaka. Before directing, he had assisted Itō on *The Long Grudge* (*Chōkon*, 1926) and *The Diary of Chuji's Travels* (*Chūji tabi nikki*, 1927) and written scenarios for some of Hiroshi Inagaki's early films, including *Genji Boy* (*Genji Kozō*, 1928) where his taste for a comic treatment of period themes was already visible. Most of Itami's own early films as director are lost, but it appears that his debut, *Vicissitudes of Revenge* (*Adauchi ruten*, 1928), was already a subversive critique of the rigid codes of bushidō.

By the early thirties, he had begun to direct comedies in period settings, often starring the versatile Chiezō Kataoka. These films, like Yamanaka's roughly contemporary *jidai-geki*, tended to overlook the higher ranks of society—samurai and daimyo—to focus on ronin, merchants, and criminals. *Beyond the Spring Wind* (*Harukaze no kanata e*, 1930) was about a convict, released from jail, trying and failing to go straight, while *Fireworks* (*Hanabi*, 1931) was the story of a cowardly samurai obliged to seek revenge for his father's murder. The most famous of these satires was *Unrivaled Hero* (*Kokushi musō*, 1932), in which an impostor masquerades convincingly as a master swordsman. Surviving fragments reveal Itami's wit and comic timing, and suggest a refreshingly irreverent attitude to authority.

Itami's work, both silent and sound, displayed a marked Western influence. The story of *Rikitaro Kinteki* (*Kinteki*

Courtesy of the Kawakita Memorial Film Institute

Kokushi musō / Unrivaled Hero *(1932): Here Itami, Sr. essayed an irreverent satiric twist on the traditional period film.*

*Rikitarō*, 1931) is said to have been influenced by Molnar's *Liliom*, while *Tattooed Gambler* (*Shisei kigū*, 1933), a melodrama about a yakuza who marries a woman of ill repute after saving her from suicide, apparently recalled Sternberg's *The Docks of New York* (1928). *Capricious Young Man* (*Sengoku kitan: Kimagure kanja*, 1935) resembled the Marx Brothers' film *Duck Soup* (1933) in its farcical representation of belligerent generals, a theme which expressed Itami's hostility to the escalating militarism of the time. Similarly critical of the prevailing mood was *Bushido Handbook* (*Budō taikan*, 1934), about a daimyo who prefers to solve problems through negotiation rather than by violence.

Itami made two outstanding films early in the sound era. *Chuji Makes a Name for Himself* (*Chūji uridasu*, 1935), sadly now lost, was apparently a cri-tique of social injustice and totalitarianism, focusing on the folk hero Chūji Kunisada after excessive taxation and government tyranny force him to abandon farming for gambling. The hero of *Kakita Akanishi* (*Akanishi Kakita*, 1936) was a distinctly deglamorized, pragmatic, anti-heroic figure, willing to shame himself to achieve a goal. In this film, fortunately still extant, Itami incorporated touches of political allegory, sent up sacred cows such as the ritual of *seppuku*, and displayed an engagingly mellow humor.

After this, Itami reluctantly collaborated on a Japanese-German co-production, *The New Earth* (*Atarashiki tsuchi*, 1937), scripted by Nazi filmmaker Arnold Fanck. The story, of a Japanese returning from an extended stay in Germany and finding himself torn between his own country and Europe, was essentially fascist propaganda, to which the liberal Itami was distinctly ill-suited; indeed, mutual animosity eventually led the two directors to shoot separate versions of the film on the same set.

In his last films as director, Itami seems to have been attempting to widen his range of subject matter. *Hometown* (*Kokyō*, 1937) was a rare excursion into *gendai-geki*, relating the story of a woman who returns from Tokyo to her rural birthplace to work as a teacher. *The Giant* (*Kyojinden*, 1938) relocated *Les Misérables* to Kyushu and the era of the Satsuma Rebellion; the transposition felt somewhat contrived, but Denjirō Ōkōchi made an imposing Jean Valjean, and again the story's anti-authoritarian sentiments were subversive in the era of militarism. After this, failing health curtailed Itami's directorial career, but he continued until his death to write essays and screenplays, including fine, subtly characterized scripts for Hiroshi Inagaki's *The Life of Matsu the Untamed* (*Muhō Matsu no isshō*, 1943) and *Children Hand in Hand* (*Te o tsunagu kora*, 1948). Despite his short career, Itami's influence has been lasting: his taste for barbed irony and pastiche is detectable in the work of such postwar directors as Kon Ichikawa, and his son Takehiko, as Jūzō Itami, sustained his tradition of satire through the eighties and nineties.

1928 **Adauchi ruten** / Vicissitudes of Revenge
1929 **Zoku banka jigoku: Dainihen** / Hell of Ten Thousand Flowers 2: Part 2 (*co-director*)
1930 **Harukaze no kanata e** / Beyond the Spring Wind
**Genji kozō shutsugen** / Appearance of the Boy Genji
**Nigeyuku Kodenji** / Escape of Kodenji
1931 **Gozonji Genji kozō** / The Well-Known Boy Genji

**Kinteki Rikitarō** / Rikitaro Kinteki
**Hanabi** / Fireworks
1932 **Kokushi musō** / Unrivaled Hero / Peerless Patriot
**Yamiuchi tosei** / Professional Killer
**Kentatsu no utare** / Kentatsu's Vengeance
1933 **Shisei kigū** / Tattooed Gambler
1934 **Wataridori Kiso miyage** / A Migrating Bird's Souvenirs of the Kiso Valley
**Budō taikan** / Bushido Handbook
**Chūshingura** / The Loyal 47 Ronin (*co-director*)
1935 **Chūji uridasu** / Chuji Makes a Name for Himself / Chuji in His Heyday
**Sengoku kitan: Kimagure kanja** / Capricious Young Man (lit. Rare Story of the Era of Warring States: The Whimsical Youth)
1936 **Akanishi Kakita** / Kakita Akanishi / The Letter
1937 **Atarashiki tsuchi** / The New Earth (*co-director*)
**Kokyō** / Hometown
**Gonzō to Sukejū** / Gonzo and Sukeju
1938 **Kyojinden** / The Giant (lit. Story of a Giant)

# ITŌ Daisuke
## (October 12, 1898–July 19, 1981)
伊藤大輔

The acknowledged master of the silent *jidai-geki*, Itō worked initially as a scenarist for Henry Kotani and Norimasa Kaeriyama, both makers of films in a Westernized idiom. His earliest work as director partook of the fashionable Westernization of the twenties: *Smoke* (*Kemuri*, 1925) was an adaptation of Turgenev, while *The Living Soul* (*Seirei*, 1927) apparently evoked the German

*Chūji tabi nikki / The Diary of Chuji's Travels (1927): Sadly, only a fragmentary copy remains of this, the most famous work by the early master of the* jidai-geki.

"ballad films" scripted by Thea von Harbou. Itō found his true *métier*, however, in the samurai films he directed at Nikkatsu, which led Kesshū Tsukuda to call him "the great fighter who carries the Japanese cinema on his back." Most of these films are lost, but their brilliant technique, including flamboyant traveling shots and rapid montage, remains visible in the extant *Jirokichi the Rat* (*Oatsurae Jirokichi gōshi*, 1931), with its dazzling lantern-filled pursuit climax, and in surviving reels from the three-part epic *The Diary of Chuji's Travels* (*Chūji tabi nikki*, 1927), a two-reel condensation of *Man-Slashing, Horse-Piercing Sword* (*Zanjin zanbaken*, 1929), and various other fragments.

Multi-layered performances from regular star Denjirō Ōkōchi, who combined strength with sensitivity, gave these films depth, and Itō often subverted the established conventions of the genre. Thus, while the preserved fragment from the finale of *The Long Grudge* (*Chōkon*, 1926) shows a conventional bloodbath, the hero dying after defending himself against overwhelming odds, the outlaw Chūji in *The Diary of Chuji's Travels* succumbs to a paralyzing disease, and in the last scene is protected from his enemies by his gun-toting lover. This was typical of the way in which Itō extended the role of women in *chanbara*: *Jirokichi the Rat*, too, was remarkable for the rich characterizations of heroine and *femme fatale*. Itō also deepened the genre's social and political context, and expressed his own left-wing sympathies, by developing the concept of the "nihilist hero" in revolt against authority. Period settings enabled him to advance anti-authoritarian themes that would have been forbidden in *gendai-geki*. *The Servant* (*Gerō*, 1927), now lost, was a critique of feudal loyalty, the obedient servant of the title finally being betrayed and killed by his master. *Man-Slashing, Horse-Piercing Sword*, about a farmers' revolt against an oppressive lord, was a pioneering example of the left-leaning *keikō-eiga* genre, while *The Lordless Retainer* (*Sūrōnin Chūya*, 1930) was a sympathetic account of conspirators who plotted to overthrow the Tokugawa regime. In films such as *The Rise and Fall of the Shinsengumi* (*Kōgō Shinsengumi*, 1930) and *Tsuruchiyo Niino* (*Niinō Tsuruchiyo*, 1935), Itō courted censorship by dealing sceptically with events surrounding the fall of the Shogunate and the Meiji Restoration.

The quality of Itō's work declined in the late thirties, and during the war his interest in the Meiji period was co-opted for propagandistic purposes in films such as *International Smuggling Ring* (*Kokusai mitsuyudan*, 1944), about British smugglers operating in the treaty port of Yokohama. His best postwar films marked something of a return to form, though the stylistic flair of his earlier work had declined into an academic formalism. Even so, *The Humble Masterless Samurai Dares to Pass* (*Sūrōnin makaritōru*, 1947) was a vigorous and exciting film, while *Five Men from Edo* (*Ōedo gonin otoko*, 1951) and *The Inner Palace Conspiracy* (*Oborokago*, 1951) demonstrated his skill in creating a convincing period atmosphere. Itō also explored new subject matter during this period: *The Chess Master* (*Ōshō*, 1948), notable for its atmospherically detailed studio recreation of Meiji-era Osaka, was the story of a *shōgi* player's struggle to achieve recognition, while

*The Lion's Throne* (*Shishi no za*, 1953) was a touching drama that focused on a family of Noh actors preparing to appear before the Shogun. The theme of both films was how family bonds suffer through the pursuit of an ideal.

Nevertheless, many of Itō's late films harked back to his prewar triumphs, some of which he remade: *The Servant's Neck* (*Gerō no kubi*, 1955) and *Jirokichi* (*Jirokichi gōshi*, 1952) were both reworkings of stories he had filmed in the silent era. *Benten Boy* (*Benten Kozō*, 1958) and *Yosaburo* (*Kirare Yosaburō*, 1960), too, revived the nihilist hero of Itō's silents and recapitulated his signature climax of pursuit by lantern-light. Their tone, however, was softened by color cinematography and the somewhat feminine star persona of Raizō Ichikawa. *Yosaburo* in particular adopted a melodramatic approach, introducing quasi-incestuous themes into a traditional narrative.

In the last decade of his career, Itō made some subversive biopics of the major personalities of Japanese history. *The Conspirator* (*Hangyakuji*, 1961), about Shogun Ieyasu's son Nobuyasu, who committed *seppuku* on his father's orders, showed how family ties were sacrificed and the codes of bushidō exploited in the cause of political expediency. Itō's final work as director, *Bakumatsu* (1970), returned to the late Edo period and the themes of the *keikō-eiga*, exposing the iniquities of the Japanese class system through its portrait of assassinated pro-democracy statesman Ryōma Sakamoto. It was a creditable enough swansong, but despite the proficiency of many of these later films, it is clear from the admittedly scant surviving evidence that Itō's best work was made during the silent era. It is a tragedy that so little of it has been preserved.

1924 **Shuchū nikki** / Diary of a
Drunkard
**Rutsubo no naka ni** / Into the
Melting Pot
**Chi de chi o arau** / Washing Blood
with Blood
**Hoshi wa midaretobu** / Shooting
Stars
**Jōgashima** / Jogashima
**Ken wa sabaku** / Sword of
Judgment
**Nekketsu o hisomete** / Hide the
Warm Blood

1925 **Kemuri** / Smoke

1926 **Kyōko to Shizuko** / Kyoko and
Shizuko
**Nichirin: Zenpen** / The Sun:
Part 1
**Chōkon** / The Long Grudge
**Dohatsu** / Hair Standing on End

1927 **Idaten Kichiji** / Kichiji the Fast
Runner
**Chūji tabi nikki: Kōshū satsujin
hen** / The Diary of Chuji's Travels:
Death Squad in Koshu
**Seirei** / The Living Soul
**Ruten (Zenpen, Kōhen)** /
Vicissitudes (Parts 1 and 2)
**Chūji tabi nikki: Shinshū kesshō
hen** / The Diary of Chuji's Travels:
Bloody Smile in Shinshu
**Gerō** / The Servant
**Adauchi sōmatō** / Revolving
Lantern of Revenge
**Chūji tabi nikki: Goyō hen** /
The Diary of Chuji's Travels: On
Authority

1928 **Chikemuri Takadanobaba** / Blood
Spattered at Takadanobaba
**Shinban Ōoka seidan: Daiippen** /
Ooka's Trial: Part 1 (lit. Ooka's Trial,
New Version: Part 1)
**Shinban Ōoka seidan: Danihen** /
Ooka's Trial: Part 2 (lit. Ooka's Trial,
New Version: Part 2)
**Shinban Yotsuya kaidan** / Yotsuya
Ghost Story, New Version

**Shinban Ōoka seidan: Kaiketsu
hen** / Ooka's Trial: Final Part (lit.
Ooka's Trial, New Version: Final
Part)

1929 **Issatsu tashō ken** / The Sword
That Killed One and Saved Many
**Zanjin zanbaken** / Man-Slashing,
Horse-Piercing Sword

1930 **Zoku Ōoka seidan: Mazō hen
daiichi** / Ooka's Trial 2: Devil
Image, Part 1
**Surōnin Chūya** / The Lordless
Retainer / Humble Ronin Chuya
(lit.)
**Kōbō Shinsengumi (Zenpen;
Kōhen)** / The Rise and Fall of the
Shinsengumi (Parts 1 and 2)
**Tabisugata Jōshū namari** / Travel
Stories in Joshu Dialect

1931 **Samurai Nippon (Zenpen;
Kōhen)** / Samurai Japan (Parts 1
and 2)
**Nezumi kozō tabimakura** / The
Ratkid's Travel Pillow
**Zoku Ōoka seidan: Mazō
kaiketsu hen** / Ooka's Trial 2: Devil
Image, Final Part
**Oatsurae Jirokichi gōshi** /
Jirokichi the Rat / The Chivalrous
Robber Jirokichi (lit.)

1932 **Meiji gannen** / The First Year of
the Meiji Era
**Satsuma hikyaku** / Satsuma
Messenger

1933 **Hotta Hayato** / Hayato Hotta
**Tsukigata Hanpeita** / Hanpeita
Tsukigata
**Tange Sazen: Daippen** / Sazen
Tange: Part 1
**Nyonin mandara: Daiippen** /
Feminine Mandala: Part 1

1934 **Nyonin mandara: Dainihen** /
Feminine Mandala: Part 2
**Tange Sazen: Kengeki no maki** /
Sazen Tange: Weapons Reel
**Chūshingura: Katanakizu hen** /
The Loyal 47 Ronin: Sword Wound
Chapter

Chūshingura: Fukushū hen /
The Loyal 47 Ronin: Revenge
Chapter

Utamatsuri sandogasa / Sedge Hat
at Singing Festival

Kensetsu no hitobito /
Construction Workers

1935 Oroku gushi / The Comb of
Oroku

Niinō Tsuruchiyo / Tsuruchiyo
Niino

Edo miyage komoriuta / Souvenir
Lullaby from Edo

1936 Yonjūhachininme / The Forty-
Eighth Man

Asagiri tōge / Asagiri Pass

1937 Ihen Kurotegumi / Chance and the
Kurote Group

1938 Kengō Araki Mataemon /
Mataemon Araki of the Sword

Satsuma hikyaku / Satsuma
Messenger

1941 Washi no ō tōge / Pass of the Eagle
King

1942 Kurama Tengu: Yokohama ni
arawaru / Kurama Tengu Appears
in Yokohama

1943 Nitōryū kaigen / Swordfighting
School and Enlightenment

Kettō Hannyazaka / Duel at
Hannyazaka

1944 Kokusai mitsuyudan /
International Smuggling Ring

1945 Tōkai Suikoden / Tokai Region
Water Margin

1947 Surōnin makaritōru / The Humble
Masterless Samurai Dares to Pass /
The Paltry Ronin Forces His Way
Through

1948 Ōshō / The Chess Master

1949 Yama o tobu hanagasa / The
Flower that Crossed the Mountain

1950 Haruka nari haha no kuni / Far
from the Mother Country

Ware maboroshi no sakana mitari
/ I Saw a Dream Fish

Re Mizeraburu: Ā, mujō:
Daiichibu: Kami to akuma / Les

Misérables: Ah, Merciless: Part One:
God and the Devil

1951 Oborokago / The Inner Palace Conspiracy / Palanquin in the Haze (lit.)

Ōedo gonin otoko / Five Men
from Edo

1952 Jirokichi gōshi / Jirokichi

1953 Shishi no za / The Lion's Throne /
Throne of Noh

1954 Banchō sarayashiki: Okiku to
Harima / The Horror Mansions:
Okiku and Harima

Shunkin monogatari / Story of
Shunkin

1955 Meiji ichidai onna / The Life of a
Woman in the Meiji Period

Gerō no kubi / The Servant's Neck

Genroku bishōnen roku /
Chronicle of a Beautiful Boy in the
Genroku Era

1957 Itohan monogatari / Story of the
Young Mistress

Jigokubana / Flower of Hell

1958 Benten Kozō / Benten Boy / The
Gay Masquerade

1959 Onna to kaizoku / The Woman
and the Pirates

Jan Arima no shūgeki / Juan
Arima's Surprise Attack

1960 Kirare Yosaburō / Yosaburo (lit.
Scarred Yosaburo)

Tsukinode no kettō / Duel at
Moonrise

1961 Hangyakuji / The Conspirator

1962 Genji Kurō sōkaiki / A Fresh Tale
of Kuro Genji

Ōshō / The Chess Master

1963 Kono kubi ichimangoku / The
Man Worth 10,000 Bushels

1965 Tokugawa Ieyasu / Ieyasu
Tokugawa

1970 Bakumatsu / Bakumatsu / The
Shogunate's Downfall (lit.) / The
Ambitious

## IWAI Shunji
### (b. January 24, 1963)
岩井俊二

Stylish to a fault, Iwai's films glance obliquely at the realities but concentrate on the fantasies of modern Japanese youth. His first film to be screened in cinemas, *Undo* (1994), focused on the mental crisis of a woman in a troubled relationship. It received only a token release, but Iwai achieved a huge commercial success with *Love Letter* (1995), about a grieving woman who writes to her dead fiancé only to receive a reply from the woman who shares his name and was his high school classmate. The plot strained credulity, but Iwai directed fluently and with a beguiling freshness of touch. The film's popularity led to DVD and cinema releases for several of his television works, including *Ghost Soup* (1992), a silly and sentimental Christmas fable, and *Fireworks* (*Uchiage hanabi, shita kara miru ka? Yoko kara miru ka?*, 1993; cinema release 1995), which anticipated his later focus on the contrary emotions of children around puberty. Also shown at this time was the previously shelved *Picnic* (1996), which, like *Undo*, focused on mental illness: its characters were three patients in an institution who escape but dare not cross the perimeter wall.

The success of these films earned Iwai the freedom he needed to mount *Swallowtail Butterfly* (*Suwarōteiru*, 1996), a dark portrait of life among immigrants inhabiting a shanty town on the outskirts of a vaguely futuristic Tokyo and detailing their attempts, legitimate and criminal, to better their lot. The film's jittery camera style left little space for reflection, and it seemed finally to endorse widespread prejudices linking foreigners with crime.

Iwai has since worked relatively sparingly. *April Story* (*Shigatsu monogatari*, 1998) was a brief, simple, lyrical account of a college student, newly arrived in Tokyo, and her love for a young man she is too shy to speak to. Iwai's most recent fiction films have focused on children slightly estranged from reality. *All About Lily Chou Chou* (*Rirī Shushu no subete*, 2001) was a suggestive, if overlong, film about emotional alienation: its kids are unable to express their feelings except via a computer and in the context of their admiration for a pop star. Iwai touched on the consuming loneliness of modern Japanese life: for instance, the preponderance of families with only children. *Hana and Alice* (*Hana to Arisu*, 2004) was a lighter account of childhood, though not without its subtle cruelties in its depiction of the emotional confusion of the young at an age when new feelings transform old friendships. In contrast to these elaborate fictions, Iwai has also realized a documentary about veteran director Kon Ichikawa.

Iwai's recurrent theme is wish fulfilment: the heroine getting a reply to a letter she posts to a dead man in *Love Letter*; the poor immigrants chancing on a code which allows them to pass off 1,000-yen banknotes as 10,000 yen in *Swallowtail Butterfly*; the girl convincing the boy she fancies that they are a couple after an accident leaves him amnesiac in *Hana and Alice*. His style, with its restless, often handheld camera, stylized compositions, and rapid-fire cutting, is indebted to the techniques of advertising and pop video—those vehicles for the kind of shallow glamor of which Iwai's films are both critiques and expressions. The relative superficiality of his work is partly a by-product of that style, but also derives from the

Suwarōteiru / Swallowtail Butterfly *(1996): This dystopian vision is from a director who trades in fantasies.*

fact that his subject is the dreams that many prefer to reality.

1994 **Undo**

1995 **Love Letter**

   **Uchiage hanabi, shita kara miru ka? Yoko kara miru ka?** / Fireworks / Fireworks: Should We See It from the Side or from the Bottom (lit.) (*cinema release of 1993 TV movie*)

1996 **Fried Dragon Fish** (*cinema release of 1993 TV movie*)

   **Picnic**

   **Suwarōteiru** / Swallowtail Butterfly

   **¥en Town Band Swallowtail Butterfly** (*short*)

1998 **Shigatsu monogatari** / April Story

2001 **Rirī Shushu no subete** / All About Lily Chou Chou

2002 **Jam Films** (*co-director*)

2004 **Hana to Arisu** / Hana and Alice

2006 **Ichikawa Kon monogatari** / The Kon Ichikawa Story

## IZUTSU Kazuyuki
**(b. December 13, 1952)**
井筒和幸

Although little-known outside Japan, Izutsu has achieved a high profile in his native country thanks not only to the consistent commercial success of his films, but also to his status as a talk show host and media personality. He worked initially in the "pink" sector; his third film, *Rape Demon: Pearl Torture* (*Bōkōma shinju zeme*, 1979), initiated a successful collaboration with screenwriter Takuya Nishioka. ATG funding enabled him to make his first non-pornographic film,

*Empire of Kids* (*Gaki teikoku*, 1981), a brutal story about rival gangs of juvenile delinquents in the northern and southern districts of Osaka, which was popular enough to spawn a sequel. By the mid-eighties he was working on commercial films for Kadokawa and Nikkatsu. *The Second Is a Christian* (*Nidaime wa Kurisuchan*, 1985) was an amusing if shallow yakuza comedy with an extraordinary plot about a gangster who converts to Christianity to marry a nun; the stylized imagery was sometimes striking, and the heroine's final transformation from nun to warrior raised definite possibilities for cult appreciation among lovers of high camp. A more serious gangster film was *Shoot the Sun* (*Inujini seshi mono*, 1986), about two returned war veterans who operate as pirates on the Inland Sea.

Izutsu has since proved a versatile filmmaker, working on action films, comedy, and drama. *Universal Laws* (*Uchū no hōsoku*, 1990) detailed the obstacles faced and overcome by a Tokyo fashion designer who returns to his hometown to take over his late father's weaving mill. With *Boys, Be Ambitious* (*Kishiwada shōnen gurentai*, 1996), about a pair of delinquent teenage fighters, Izutsu returned to the Osaka setting and gang milieu of *Empire of Kids*, portraying delinquency as a response to Japanese expectations of conformity. *Nodo jiman* (1999) charted the experiences of a number of aspiring contestants on a popular television competition for amateur singers. *Get Up!* (*Geroppa!*, 2003) was an odd combination of sentimentality and black comedy, following a yakuza's attempts to locate his long-lost daughter before beginning a jail sentence; competent and professional, it was rather too pat and cozy. *Pacchigi!* (2005) was another film about teenage gangs and a story of star-crossed lovers, examining a romance between a Japanese boy and a Korean girl in 1960s Kyoto. An effectively made but curiously artificial film, it turned at the climax into an unabashed tearjerker. Nevertheless, it proved Izutsu's biggest critical success in Japan, winning the Kinema Junpō "Best One" award, and subsequently spawning a sequel. As yet, however, there seems little sign of the director's domestic celebrity translating into international distribution.

1975  **Iku iku maito gai: Seishun no monmon** / Come, Come, Mighty Guy: Youthful Sexual Frustration

1978  **Atsukute fukai majiwari: Nikuiro no umi** / Hot, Deep Intersection: Flesh-Colored Sea

1979  **Bōkōma shinju zeme** / Rape Demon: Pearl Torture

**Ashi no ura kara meiō made** / From the Sole to the Prince of Darkness

**Boku to Okishima-gō** / The Ferry to the Oki Islands and I (*short*)

1980  **Onna kyōshi: Nozokareta bōkō genba** / Woman Teacher: Spied-on Scene of Rape

1981  **Gaki teikoku** / Empire of Kids

**Shikijō mesugari** / Sexual Desire: Bitch Hunting

**Gaki teikoku: Akutare sensō** / Empire of Kids: Rowdy War

1982  **Akai fukushū: Bōkan** / Red Revenge: Violent Debauchery

1983  **Miyuki**

1984  **Hare tokidoki satsujin** / Fine with Occasional Murders

1985  **Marukin marubi no Kinkonkan** / Rich or Poor: The Yuppie Handbook

**Nidaime wa Kurisuchan** / The Second is a Christian

1986  **Inujini seshi mono** / Shoot the Sun

1989  **Abunai hanashi** / Dangerous Stories (*co-director*)

## JISSŌJI Akio
### (March 29, 1937–November 29, 2006)
### 実相寺昭雄

Jissōji's oeuvre contains a curious mixture of high art and pulp fiction. Directing for television during the sixties, he earned a reputation for visual invention with his contributions to the science fiction series *Ultraman* (*Urutoraman*). After the critical success of his big screen work during the seventies, a compilation of these episodes was released in cinemas. In the meantime, Jissōji had made a sequence of remarkable arthouse movies for ATG, starting with the featurette *When Twilight Draws Near* (*Yoiyami semareba*, 1969). Based on a Nagisa Ōshima script, this was originally intended for television, but was released in a double bill with Ōshima's *Diary of a Shinjuku Thief* (*Shinjuku dorobō nikki*, 1969).

Jissōji's first full-length feature, and acknowledged masterpiece, was *This Transient Life* (*Mujō*, 1970), a visually stunning account of an incestuous love affair. Not only the love scenes, but also the textures of wood, stone, and water, were filmed with an extraordinary sensuality, and Jissōji displayed a keen eye for the emotional resonances of traditional Japanese architecture and interior space. Though his elaborate tracking shots sometimes seemed more decorative than expressive, the film remained a powerful study of the destructive consequences of a single transgressive act. Jissōji also made *Mandala* (*Mandara*, 1971), *Poem* (*Uta*, 1972), and *Life in a Dream* (*Asaki yumemishi*, 1974) for ATG. These films displayed marked differences of approach: *Poem*, with its stark monochrome imagery and classical music score, seemed a companion piece to *This Transient Life*; *Life in a Dream* was a period film set during the Kamakura shogunate; while the context of *Mandala*, about a sexually predatory Buddhist sect, was the proliferation of militant groups in the late sixties and early seventies. Even so, all were variations on a theme, sharing common settings and motifs: the Kansai region; temples and graveyards; the sea, lakes, and waterfalls; clocks; traditional art forms. Their central concerns were sexual transgression and Buddhist theology: Roland Domenig has argued that "Jissōji's importance for Japanese cinema can be compared to that of Christian directors like Carl Dreyer or Robert Bresson for European cinema." Nevertheless, it may be argued that Jissōji was critical of Buddhism, hinting that its doctrines were inadequate as a response to human suffering.

After leaving ATG, Jissōji directed *Utamaro's World* (*Utamaro:*

*Yume to shiriseba*, 1977), a portrait of the eighteenth-century *ukiyo-e* artist. However, during the eighties he again worked mainly in television. Among his more important films in that medium was *Obon Waves* (*Nami no bon*, 1983), a story about the divided loyalties of Japanese emigrants to Hawaii during World War II. He returned to the cinema with *Tokyo: The Last Megalopolis* (*Teito monogatari*, 1988), a big-budget horror film about an evil spirit whose awakening threatens the capital. Though the plot was pure mumbo-jumbo, the recreation of Meiji, Taisho, and early-Showa era Tokyo was very picturesque. Jissōji's subsequent films were mainly in the horror genre: with *Watcher in the Attic* (*Yaneura no sanposha*, 1994), *The D-Slope Murder Case* (*D-zaka no satsujin jiken*, 1998), and a segment from *Rampo Noir* (*Ranpo jigoku*, 2005), he adapted the work of the early twentieth-century writer on macabre themes, Edogawa Ranpo, while *Ubume* (*Ubume no natsu*, 2005) was a version of a digressive avant-garde novel by Natsuhiko Kyōgoku. Here and in *Watcher in the Attic*, Jissōji again recreated the atmosphere of prewar Japan.

Jissōji's work was generally flawed; his artier conceits tended to lack discipline and there was perhaps something slightly opportunistic about his vacillation between the modernist and highbrow on the one hand and cultish genre pieces on the other. Nor, it seems, were any of his films perfectly achieved from start to finish. Nevertheless, his early films especially contain some of the most extraordinary individual images in Japanese cinema: the woman excavating a giant stone fish in *This Transient Life*; the boat with a mandala for its sail in *Mandala*; the desperate hero surrounded by discarded calligraphic manuscripts in *Poem*. His work is frustrating and rewarding in equal measure.

1969 **Yoiyami semareba** / When Twilight Draws Near
1970 **Mujō** / This Transient Life
1971 **Mandara** / Mandala
1972 **Uta** / Poem
1974 **Asaki yumemishi** / Life in a Dream / The Life of a Court Lady (lit. Transitory Dream)
1977 **Utamaro: Yume to shiriseba** / Utamaro's World (lit. Utamaro: If I Knew It Was a Dream)
1979 **Urutoraman** / Ultraman
1988 **Teito monogatari** / Tokyo: The Last Megalopolis
**Akutoku no sakae** / Glory of Corruption
1989 **Ijimete kudasai: Arietta** / Arietta
1990 **Ra varusu** / La Valse
**Urutora Q za Mūbī: Hoshi no densetsu** / Legend of the Stars
1992 **"Daraku": Aru hitozuma no tsuiseki hōkoku** / The Fallen: Report on a Followed Wife
1993 **Jissōji Akio kantoku sakuhin: Watashi nandemo shimasu** / The Films of Akio Jissōji: I'll Do Anything
1994 **Yaneura no sanposha** / Watcher in the Attic / Stroller in the Attic (lit.)
1998 **D-zaka no satsujin jiken** / The D-Slope Murder Case
2005 **Ubume no natsu** / Ubume / Summer of Ubume
**Ranpo jigoku** / Rampo Noir (*co-director*)
2006 **Yume jūya** / Ten Nights of Dreams (*co-director*)
**Shirubā kamen** / The Silver Mask (*co-director*)

## KAERIYAMA Norimasa
## (March 1, 1893–November 8, 1964)
## 帰山教正

Although all of his films are now lost, Kaeriyama was a figure of considerable importance in his day for his contribution to the Taisho-period "pure film" movement, which sought to modernize the technique and content of Japanese cinema. His early articles, published in the 'teens in *Kinema Record*, revealed a sophisticated awareness of the expressive potential of the medium, suggesting that cinematic art consisted neither purely of visual beauty, nor solely of dramatic effect, but derived from the fusion of pictorial and dramatic qualities. Kaeriyama put his theories into practice with his directorial debut, *The Glory of Life* (*Sei no kagayaki*, 1919), which apparently employed such innovative techniques as close ups and camera movements, and used an actress in the main female role instead of the customary *oyama*. The extant script suggests a combination of *shinpa*-style romantic melodrama with elements anticipating the "Kamata modernism" of Shochiku's late silents: for instance, the use of fashionable Western elements such as Christianity, and an ending where the protagonist resolves his problems by going abroad. Kaeriyama's second film, *The Girl in the Mountain* (*Miyama no otome*, 1919), released simultaneously with his first, is said also to have used innovative techniques such as flashbacks to juxtapose past and present in a story about a quarrel over an inheritance and a map showing the location of a gold mine.

The reception of these films was mixed, and they received only limited distribution. More successful commercially was *The Girl in His Dreams* (*Gen'ei no onna*, 1920), apparently a sophisticated comedy about "an amorous woman and an unresponsive man together on a desert island" (Joanne Bernardi's description). In *Tale of the White Chrysanthemums* (*Shiragiku monogatari*, 1920), Kaeriyama attempted to apply "pure film" techniques to the subject matter of *chanbara*; regrettably this film failed to find distribution. After this, Kaeriyama made educational films at Shochiku before retiring from direction to work as a lecturer and journalist.

1919 **Sei no kagayaki** / The Glory of Life / The Glow of Life
     **Miyama no otome** / The Girl in the Mountain
     **Nihon geigi no odori** / Japanese Geisha Dance (*short*)
1920 **Gen'ei no onna** / The Girl in His Dreams
     **Shiragiku monogatari** / Tale of the White Chrysanthemums (*unreleased*)
     **Kohan no kotori** / The Lakeside Bird
     **Saraba seishun** / Farewell to Youth
1921 **Higeki ni naru made** / Until Tragedy Strikes
     **Ai no mukuro** / Corpse of Love
     **Fumetsu no noroi** / The Eternal Curse
1922 **Kōkoku no kagayaki** / The Glory of the Empire
     **Kamiyo no bōken** / Adventure in the Time of the Gods
     **Dakuryū** / Turbid Current
     **Ā! sokoku** / Ah, Fatherland
1923 **Oshin-chan no koi** / The Love of Oshin-chan
     **Chichi yo izuko e** / Where Is Father?
1924 **Ai no kyoku** / Melody of Love
     **Sabishiki hitobito** / Lonely People
     **Shizen wa sabaku** / Nature Is the Judge
1926 **Shōnen kōshu** / The Boy Drummer

## KAMEI Fumio
## (April 1, 1908–February 27, 1987)
## 亀井文夫

A left-leaning documentarist who had trained at the Soviet Film Institute GIK, Kamei made his first films at Toho during the inhospitable era of militarism. After editing the successful *Through the Angry Waves* (*Dotō o koete*, 1937), the record of a naval vessel's official visit to Britain and Germany, he was assigned to direct two documentaries about major Chinese cities. In *Shanghai* (*Shanhai*, 1938), called "a masterpiece of subdued irony" by Peter High, he subverted pan-Asian propaganda by filming devastated landscapes and emphasizing the human cost of war, while in *Beijing* (*Pekin*, 1938), he concentrated on documenting the customs and culture of the Chinese capital. Kamei's next film, *Fighting Soldiers* (*Tatakau heitai*, 1939), shadowed the Japanese army on the Chinese front, but went unreleased when its unflinching portrayal of exhaustion and misery among the combatants courted official displeasure. *Song of Ina* (*Ina bushi*, 1940) and *Issa Kobayashi* (*"Shinano fūdoki" yori: Kobayashi Issa*, 1941), studies of life in rural Nagano, again courted controversy by exposing the region's poverty; and in 1941, the director was arrested and imprisoned for a year—the only Japanese filmmaker to meet this fate. After his release, during the last years of the war, he sadly capitulated to official requirements, working on propaganda films such as *Security of the Skies* (*Seikū*, 1945).

Kamei ironically suffered further censorship when his first postwar film, *The Japanese Tragedy* (*Nihon no higeki*, 1946), was banned for its pro-Communist stance. Using newsreel footage to chart the history of Japanese imperialism, it indicted both business leaders and the Emperor; one image famously superimposed a shot of the Emperor in military dress over another of him in civilian clothes. Kamei then collaborated with fellow leftist Satsuo Yamamoto on his first fiction feature, *War and Peace* (*Sensō to heiwa*, 1947), described by Tadao Satō as "the definitive anti-militarist film." Charting the experiences of a woman who remarries after being informed that her soldier husband has died, only for him to return alive, it combined this melodramatic premise with elements of realism, even incorporating some of the original documentary footage from *Fighting Soldiers*.

Kamei's later fiction features continued to examine socially committed themes. The well-regarded *A Woman's Life* (*Onna no isshō*, 1949) was an attack on the traditional family system, focusing on a woman who has no choice but to continue working to support her family even after she marries. This was Kamei's last film at Toho; he worked independently thereafter. Nevertheless, *As a Mother, as a Woman* (*Haha nareba, onna nareba*, 1952) had a more conventional *haha-mono* plot about a mother, played by Isuzu Yamada, sacrificing her chances of happiness for her son. *A Woman Walks the Earth Alone* (*Onna hitori daichi o iku*, 1953), funded by the Hokkaido Miners' Union, was a trenchant story about the exploitation of coal miners and their sufferings through accident, illness, and war.

The poor reception and commercial failure of this film led Kamei to return to documentary, realizing a sequence of radical films for his independent production company. The multi-part *Sunagawa* series prefigured Shinsuke Ogawa's *Sanrizuka* films in charting local opposition to the proposed expansion of an American air base. Kamei also worked on several films deploring nuclear proliferation: the most widely distributed was *The World Is Terrified: The Reality of the "Ash of Death"* (*Sekai wa kyōfu suru: Shi no hai no shōtai*, 1957), a polemical study of the effects of radiation on the human body. *Men Are All Brothers* (*Ningen mina kyōdai: Buraku sabetsu no kiroku*, 1960) detailed the discrimination faced by members of Japan's *burakumin* underclass. From the sixties onwards, Kamei was less involved in cinema. During his last years, however, he worked with a volunteer crew and a donated budget on *All Living Things Are Friends: Lullabies of Birds, Insects, and Fish* (*Seibutsu mina tomodachi: Tori, mushi, sakana no komoriuta*, 1987), a lengthy documentary on environmentalist themes, completed only weeks before his death. Considered among the most distinguished of documentary filmmakers in Japan, Kamei has had sadly little exposure abroad.

1937 **Gakkō hōsō** / School Broadcasting (*short*)
1938 **Shanhai** / Shanghai
**Pekin** / Beijing
1939 **Tatakau heitai** / Fighting Soldiers
1940 **Ina bushi** / Song of Ina
1941 **"Shinano fūdoki yori": Kobayashi Issa** / Issa Kobayashi
1944 **Niwatori** / Chicken
**Jagaimo no me** / Potato Sprout
**Bochō eiga** / Spy Protection Film
**Nihon no matsuri** / Festivals of Japan
1945 **Seikū** / Security of the Skies
1946 **Nihon no higeki** / The Japanese Tragedy
1947 **Sensō to heiwa** / War and Peace / Between War and Peace (*co-director*)
1949 **Onna no isshō** / A Woman's Life
**Buraikan Chōbei** / Chobei the Rogue

1952 **Haha nareba onna nareba** / As a Mother, as a Woman
**Kichi no kotachi** / Children of the Base (*short*)
1953 **Onna hitori daichi o iku** / A Woman Walks the Earth Alone
1955 **Sunagawa no hitobito: Kichi hantai tōsō no kiroku** / The People of Sunagawa
1956 **Ikiteite yokatta** / It's Good That We're Still Alive (*co-director*)
**Ryūketsu no kiroku: Sunagawa** / Record of Blood: Sunagawa
1957 **Sekai wa kyōfu suru: Shi no hai no shōtai** / The World Is Terrified: The Reality of the "Ash of Death"
1958 **Araumi ni ikiru: Maguro gyomin no seitai** / Living in a Rough Sea: The Life of Tuna Fishermen
1959 **Inochi no uta** / Poem of Life
**Nihon no kenchiku** / Invitation to Japanese Architecture
1960 **Ningen mina kyōdai: Buraku sabetsu no kiroku** / Men Are All Brothers (lit. Men Are All Brothers: Documentary on Discrimation against the Burakumin)
1961 **Shin Mitsubishi no zenbō** / The Entirety of the New Mitsubishi Corporation
1963 **Shizukana kenchiku kōhō** / Quiet Construction Methods
1984 **Minna ikinakereba naranai: Hito, mushi, tori, "nōji minzokukan"** / All Must Live: People, Insects, and Birds
1987 **Seibutsu mina tomodachi: Tori, mushi, sakana no komoriuta** / All Living Things Are Friends: Lullabies of Birds, Insects, and Fish

# KATŌ Tai
**(August 24, 1916–June 17, 1985)**
加藤泰

The nephew of *jidai-geki* master Sadao Yamanaka, Katō became an assistant at

Toho before serving in the war, after which he assisted Daisuke Itō on *The Chess Master* (*Ōshō*, 1948) and Kurosawa on *Rashomon* (*Rashōmon*, 1950). During the fifties, he initially directed *chanbara*, but, on joining Toei, began to specialize in the increasingly popular yakuza genre. Katō's yakuza were usually the vagabond gamblers of the Edo or Meiji periods, rather than the contemporary urban gangsters that populated Kinji Fukasaku's films. Films such as *Blood of Revenge* (*Meiji kyōkaku: Sandaime shūmei*, 1965) and *Fightin' Tatsu, the Rickshaw Man* (*Shafu yūkyōden: Kenka Tatsu*, 1964) were notable for their detailed historical atmosphere and for their unexpected shifts from bloodshed to comedy and pathos. With *Wind, Women, and Vagabonds* (*Kaze to onna to tabigarasu*, 1958), Katō initiated a regular collaboration with popular star Kinnosuke Nakamura, whose sensitive, youthful presence was well suited to two versions of Shin Hasegawa stories, *Long-Sought Mother* (*Mabuta no haha*, 1962) and *Tokijiro of Kutsukake, Lone Yakuza* (*Kutsukake Tokijirō: Yūkyō ippiki*, 1966), about yakuza seeking to establish or re-establish loving bonds. Of these, the former was markedly inferior to Inagaki's silent version, but the latter was extremely well realized, displaying an uncharacteristic tenderness and melodramatic intensity.

Katō frankly admitted that he worked in the yakuza genre for commercial reasons, but he also developed a distinctive personal style, characterized by the use of wide and low angles, which, in Shigehiko Hasumi and Sadao Yamane's words, serve to "accentuate the solitude of people sharing the same 'disorganized' space." This style, with its looming close ups and exaggerated deep focus compositions, was not subtle, but was well suited to the expression of simple, intense emotions. At their best, however, Katō's genre films also gave unexpectedly revealing insights into character. Among his more interesting later works were several contributions to the *Red Peony Gambler* (*Hibotan bakuto*) series, about a Meiji-period female Robin Hood, in which the characteristic machismo of the yakuza film was happily diluted by the delicate lead performances of Junko Fuji.

Occasionally Katō expressed *auteur*ist pretensions by making somewhat offbeat films, to varying degrees of success. *Cruel Story of the Shogunate's Downfall* (*Bakumatsu zankoku monogatari*, 1964), about the corruption of the elite *Shinsengumi* sect of pro-Tokugawa samurai, drew occasional parallels with the fascist mentality of World War II, but its depiction of violence was more often prurient than critical. Likewise, the gratuitous bloodshed in *History of a Man's Face* (*Otoko no kao wa rirekisho*, 1966) shifted a potentially interesting study of interracial relations in immediate postwar Japan towards irresponsible xenophobia. More successful among Katō's offbeat projects were *Sasuke and His Comedians* (*Sanada fūun roku*, 1963) and *I, the Executioner* (*Minagoroshi no reika*, 1968). The former was a comic riff on the samurai film, again starring Kinnosuke Nakamura, which drew out contemporary parallels with student protests against the U.S.-Japan Security Treaty through its playful use of anachronism. The latter was a grimly effective *film noir* about a serial killer, which painted a persuasive portrait of a seedy metropolitan underworld. Though his approach was often heavy-handed, such individual films elevated Katō's work somewhat above the level of the average genre filmmaker.

1941 **Sensuikan** / Submarine (*short*)

1943 **Awa** / Foam (*short*)

1944 **Shirami wa kowai** / Lice Are Scary (*short*)

**Gunkan gakkō** / Military School (*short*)

1951 **Kennan jonan: Joshin denshin no maki** / Trouble over Swords and Women: A Woman's Mind

**Kennan jonan: Kenkō ryūsei no maki** / Trouble over Swords and Women: Sword Light and Shooting Star

1952 **Shimizu minato wa oni yori kowai** / Shimizu Harbor Is More Frightening Than the Devil

**Hiyodori zōshi** / Chronicle of the Bulbul

1955 **Ninjutsu Jiraiya** / Ninja Arts of Jiraiya

**Gyakushū Daija maru** / Revenge of the Daija Maru

1957 **Koizome rōnin** / Lovestruck Ronin

**Genji Kurō sassōki: Nuregami nitōryū** / Chronicle of the Gallant Kuro Genji: Wet Hair Fighting School

1958 **Hizakura daimyō** / Red Cherry-Blossom Daimyo

**Genji Kurō sassōki: Byakko nitōryū** / Chronicle of the Gallant Kuro Genji: White Tiger Fighting School

**Kaze to onna to tabigarasu** / Wind, Women, and Vagabonds

1959 **Kōgan no misshi** / Mission to Hell (lit. Red-Faced Secret Messenger)

1960 **Ōedo no kyōji** / The Chivalrous Youth of Great Edo

**Ayamegasa: Kenka kaidō** / Iris Hat: Way of Strife

**Honoo no shiro** / Throne of Flame (lit. Castle of Flame)

1961 **Asagiri kaidō** / Way of Morning Mist

**Kaidan Oiwa no bōrei** / The Ghost of Oiwa

1962 **Mabuta no haha** / Long-Sought Mother (lit. Mother on His Mind)

**Tange Sazen: Kan'unkonryū no maki** / Sazen Tange: Masterpiece Sword (lit. Sazen Tange: Heavenly Clouds, Earthly Dragon)

1963 **Sanada fūun roku** / Sasuke and His Comedians / Records of the Brave Sanada Clan (lit.)

1964 **Kaze no bushi** / Warrior of the Wind

**Shafu yūkyōden: Kenka Tatsu** / Fightin' Tatsu, the Rickshaw Man

**Bakumatsu zankoku monogatari** / Cruel Story of the Shogunate's Downfall

1965 **Meiji kyōkaku: Sandaime shūmei** / Blood of Revenge / Tales of Meiji Era Chivalry: 3rd Boss (lit.)

1966 **Kutsukake Tokijirō: Yūkyō ippiki** / Tokijiro of Kutsukake, Lone Yakuza

**Hone made shaburu** / Gnawed to the Bone

**Otoko no kao wa rirekisho** / History of a Man's Face / By a Man's Face Shall You Know Him

**Ahen daichi: Jigoku butai totsugeki seyo** / Opium Plateau: Hell Squad, Charge!

1967 **Chōeki jūhachinen** / 18-Year Jail Term

1968 **Minagoroshi no reika** / I, the Executioner / Gospel Hymn of a Massacre (lit.)

1969 **Hibotan bakuto: Hanafuda shōbu** / Red Peony Gambler: Flower Cards Match

1970 **Hibotan bakuto: Oryū sanjō** / Red Peony Gambles Her Life (lit. Red Peony Gambler: Oryu's Visit)

1971 **Hibotan bakuto: Oinochi itadakimasu** / Red Peony Gambler: Death to the Wicked (lit. Red Peony Gambler: I Take Your Life)

1972 **Shōwa onna bakuto** / Showa-Era Woman Gambler

**Jinsei gekijō (Seishun hen; Aiyoku hen; Zankyō hen)** / Theater of Life: Story of Youth, Passion, and Spirit

1973 **Hana to ryū (Seiun hen; Aizō hen; Dotō hen)** / Flower and Dragon: Story of Ambition, Love, and Rage

**Miyamoto Musashi** / Musashi Miyamoto / Sword of Fury

**Nihon kyōkakuden** / Blossom and the Sword (lit. Japanese Tale of Chivalry)

1977 **Edogawa Ranpo no injū** / Scream from Nowhere (lit. Edogawa Ranpo's Shadow Beast)

1981 **Honoo no gotoku** / Like a Fire / Flames of Blood

1994 **Za Ondekoza** / The Ondeko-za (*filmed in 1981; released posthumously*)


# KAWASE Naomi
## (b. May 30, 1969)
河瀬直美

Kawase's films have explored the permeable boundaries between fiction and documentary and are rooted in their director's own background and experience. Her early short features, such as *Embracing* (*Ni tsutsumarete*, 1992) and *Katatsumori* (1994), reflected on the circumstances of her childhood; the former was a self-portrait taking her estrangement from her father as its starting point, while the latter was a portrait of the great aunt who raised her after her parents divorced. A later documentary, *The Weald* (*Somaudo monogatari*, 1997), recorded the lifestyles and local customs among the ageing inhabitants of Nishi Yoshino, a mountainous village in Kawase's native Nara Prefecture.

Kawase's fiction features have also been set in Nara Prefecture, Nishi Yoshino itself being the location for *Suzaku* (*Moe no Suzaku*, 1997), a melancholic drama about the disintegration of a local family. Wider concerns with the decay of rural communities were kept implicit; the film's central focus was on individual experience and emotions. Kawase's subsequent features, *Hotaru*

(2000), *Shara* (*Sharasōju*, 2003), and *The Mourning Forest* (*Mogari no mori*, 2007) were all quiet studies of people whose lives are affected by traumatic events. In *Hotaru*, the stripper heroine enters a relationship with a potter as a means of seeking solace from the unhappiness caused by an abusive lover, the illness of her sister, and the memory of her mother's suicide. In *Shara*, a Nara family lives under the shadow of a son's mysterious disappearance years before. *The Mourning Forest*, which won the Camera d'Or at Cannes, depicted the relationship between an elderly man with dementia and a young caretaker, both trying to come to terms with bereavement.

In these films, Kawase's style has remained close to documentary, using location shooting and natural light, and eschewing melodramatic incident or convoluted narrative. Also reminiscent of documentary was her use of handheld camera, though this jittery technique has sometimes felt at odds with the quiet observation in which she specializes. More telling are the raw, improvisational performances that she has elicited from mainly amateur actors and her ability to capture nuances of behavior, creating an art rooted in the everyday, the intimate, and the momentary. At the same time, Kawase's hyperrealist style has at times derived a symbolic intensity from chance events: for instance, the cleansing rain that falls during the festival in *Shara*.

Alongside her fiction films, Kawase has continued to direct true documentaries delving into private experience. *Sky, Wind, Fire, Water, Earth* (*Kya ka ra ba a*, 2001), made for television, glanced again at her painful childhood, while *Tarachime* (2006) juxtaposed the director's own pregnancy and the birth of her son with the approaching death of her now 90-year-old great aunt. *Letters from a Yellow Cherry Blossom* (*Tsuioku no dansu*, 2002), meanwhile, recorded the last hours of terminally ill critic and photographer Kazuo Nishi, a subject which took Kawase's realist observation to a ruthlessly invasive extreme.

1988 **Watashi ga tsuyoku kyōmi o motta mono o ōkiku fix de kiritoru** / I Focus on That Which Interests Me (*8mm short*)

**Watashi ga ikiiki to kakawatte ikō to suru jibutsu no gutaika** / The Concretization of These Things Flying around Me (*8mm short*)

**My J-W-F** (*8mm short*)

**Papa no sofutokurīmu** / Papa's Ice Cream (*16mm short*)

1989 **Tatta hitori no kazoku** / My Solo Family (*8mm short*)

**Ima** / Presently (*8mm short*)

**Chiisana ōkisa** / A Small Largeness (*16mm short*)

1990 **Megamitachi no pan** / The Girls' Daily Bread (*16mm short*)

1991 **Shiawase modoki** / Like Happiness (*8mm short*)

1992 **Ni tsutsumarete** / Embracing (*8mm*)

1993 **Shiroi tsuki** / White Moon (*16mm*)

1994 **Katatsumori** (*8mm*)

1995 **Ten mitake** / See the Heavens (*16mm short*)

1996 **Arawashiyo** / This World (*co-director*)

**Hi wa katabuki** / The Setting Sun (*8mm*)

1997 **Moe no suzaku** / Suzaku

**Somaudo monogatari** / The Weald (*8mm*)

**Mangekyō** / Kaleidoscope (*16mm*)

2000 **Hotaru** / Hotaru / Firefly

2001 **Kya ka ra ba a** / Sky, Wind, Fire, Water, Earth (*8 & 16mm*)

2002 **Tsuioku no dansu** / Letter from a Yellow Cherry Blossom (*video*)

2003 **Sharasōju** / Shara

2004 **Kage** / Shadow (*short*)

2006 **Tarachime** / Tarachime / Birth/Mother (*short*)

2007 **Mogari no mori** / The Mourning Forest

# KAWASHIMA Yūzō
## (February 4, 1918–June 11, 1963)
## 川島雄三

Little known outside Japan, the wry, wild work of Yūzō Kawashima is the missing link between the classical Japanese cinema of the fifties and the modernism of the sixties. He first directed during the wartime period, then and afterwards working on second features—largely melodramas and comedies—at Shochiku. Although *The Follower* (*Tsuisekisha*, 1948) was a critical success and *O, Citizens* (*Shimikin no Ō! shimin shokun*, 1948) apparently revealed elements of Kawashima's future style, these early films were mostly poorly received. Kawashima did not acquire a critical standing until the mid fifties, after transferring to Nikkatsu. His first film there, *Burden of Love* (*Ai no onimotsu*, 1955), was a social satire in the context of the postwar baby boom, about a government minister who advocates birth control even as all the women in his family become pregnant. This work demonstrated his skill in juggling a large number of characters, as did *Our Town* (*Waga machi*, 1956), an account of life in an Osaka suburb from the Meiji period to the 1930s. At around the same time, *Ginza* (*Ginza nijūyonjō*, 1955) and *Suzaki Paradise: Red Signal* (*Suzaki Paradaisu: Akashingō*, 1956), both set in the nocturnal milieu of Tokyo bars and brothels, made clear Kawashima's interest in the seamier side of Japanese soci-

©Nikkatsu Corporation

Bakumatsu taiyōden / The Shinagawa Path *(1957): Kawashima's witty, ribald work formed a missing link between the classical Japanese cinema and the New Wave.*

ety; the latter was Kawashima's personal favorite among his own films. However, his mature style was fully formed with a rare historical story, *The Shinagawa Path (Bakumatsu taiyōden*, 1957), a witty and ribald account of events in a brothel around the time of the Meiji Restoration. History, in fact, was kept in the wings, while Kawashima focused on the immediate concerns, sexual and financial, of his characters.

The success of this film initiated a sequence of freewheeling comedies, part satire and part farce, which were animated by an extraordinary vitality thanks to Kawashima's hectic direction and excellent ensemble acting. Particularly significant was the engaging presence of regular star Frankie Sakai, whose practical, resourceful characters incarnated what Shōhei Imamura, the

director's assistant on numerous films and screenwriter of *The Shinagawa Path*, described as "Kawashima's ideal image: not a well-groomed, clean-cut boy so much as a clever one." Perhaps the most characteristic of these films was *Room to Let (Kashima ari*, 1959), a barbed, hilarious portrait of Osaka low life distinguished by Kawashima's inventive choreography of actors and use of the 'Scope frame. But he also worked successfully with more traditional dramatic material: *Temple of Wild Geese (Gan no tera*, 1962), based on a novel by Tsutomu Mizukami, was an expertly crafted melodrama about the ambiguous relationship between a corrupt priest, his lover, and his acolyte, while *Shadow of a Flower (Kaei*, 1961) and *A Woman Is Born Twice (Onna wa nido umareru*, 1961) were delicate and touching studies of the unhappy lives of bar hostesses and geisha, notable for their subtle delineation of character and sympathy for the pain of fallen women.

Kawashima's primary concern, however, was less with emotional life than with material realities. Sex and money were a consistent focus and death was a constant backdrop: suicides concluded *Shadow of a Flower* and *Elegant Beast* (*Shitoyakana kemono*, 1962), while the cemetery was a recurrent location in his work. Kawashima's own untimely death was a misfortune for the Japanese cinema. *Elegant Beast*, his last notable film, narrated the story of a family of fraudsters in a faintly modernist style: the theatrical artificiality of its use of an elaborate single set mirrored some of Ōshima's techniques and hinted that Kawashima might have adapted well to the age of the art movie. His influence is visible especially in the work of his pupil Imamura, who shared Kawashima's interest in the instinctive, animal aspects of human behavior, though his own films as director tended to lack the lively humor that gave Kawashima's work its piquancy and leavened his cynicism.

1944 **Kaette kita otoko** / The Man Who Came Back
1946 **Nikoniko taikai** / Smiling Competition (*co-director*)
   **Owarai shūkan** / Comical Week (*co-director*)
1947 **Shin'ya no shichō** / Mayor at Midnight
1948 **Tsuisekisha** / The Follower
   **Shimikin no Ō! Shimin shokun** / O Citizens (lit. Shimikin's O Citizens)
1949 **Shimikin no Supōtsu-ō** / King of Sports (lit. Shimikin the King of Sports)
1950 **Yume o meshimase** / Just Dream
   **Joyū to meitantei** / The Actress and the Detective (*short*)

1951 **Tenshi mo yume o miru** / Even Angels Dream
   **Tekirei sannin musume** / Three Nice Nubile Girls
1952 **Tonkatsu taishō** / Fried Pork General
   **Aibore tokoton dōshi** / A Couple Very Much in Love
   **Musume wa kaku kōgi suru** / Girls Claim Their Rights
   **Konna watashi ja nakatta ni** / I Wasn't Like That
   **Asu wa gekkyūbi** / Tomorrow Is Payday
1953 **Gakusei shachō** / Student President
   **Hana fuku kaze** / Flowers in the Wind
   **Shin Tōkyō kōshinkyoku** / New Tokyo March
   **Junketsu kakumei** / Sexual Revolution
   **Tōkyō madamu to Ōsaka fujin** / Madame Tokyo and Lady Osaka
1954 **Ojōsan shachō** / Miss President
   **Shinjitsu ichiro** / The Road of Truth
   **Kinō to asu no aida** / Between Yesterday and Tomorrow
1955 **Ai no onimotsu** / Burden of Love
   **Ashita kuru hito** / The Man Who Comes Tomorrow
   **Ginza nijūyonjō** / Ginza / Twenty-four Views of Ginza (lit.)
1956 **Fūsen** / Balloon
   **Suzaki Paradaisu: Akashingō** / Suzaki Paradise: Red Light District
   **Waga machi** / Our Town
   **Ueru tamashii** / Hungry Souls
   **Zoku ueru tamashii** / Hungry Souls 2
1957 **Bakumatsu taiyōden** / The Shinagawa Path / Sun Legend of the Shogunate's Downfall (lit.) / Not Long after Leaving Shinagawa
1958 **Onna de aru koto** / Being a Woman
   **Noren** / The Shop Curtain

**1959 Gurama-tō no yūwaku /**
Temptation on Glamor Island
**Kashima ari /** Room to Let
**1960 Hito mo arukeba /** If a Man Could
Walk
**Seppun dorobō /** The Thief of
Kisses / The Dangerous Kiss
**Yoru no nagare /** Evening Stream
(*co-director*)
**Akasaka no shimai: Yoru no hada**
/ The Akasaka Sisters: Skin of Night
/ Soft Touch of Night
**1961 Shima no sebiro no oyabunshō /**
Pin-Stripe Bosses
**Tokkyū Nippon /** Japan Express
**Onna wa nido umareru /** A
Woman Is Born Twice / A Geisha's
Diary
**Kaei /** Shadow of a Flower
**1962 Gan no tera /** Temple of Wild
Geese
**Aobeka monogatari /** The Story of
Aobeka / This Madding Crowd
**Hakoneyama /** Hakone Mountain
**Shitoyakana kemono /** Elegant
Beast
**1963 Kigeki: Tonkatsu ichidai /** A Life
in the Fried Pork Business
**Ichi ka bachi ka /** Take a Chance

## KIMURA Sotoji
(September 4, 1903–August 10, 1988)
木村荘十二

A talented filmmaker of left-wing inclinations, Kimura assisted Shigeyoshi Suzuki on the famous *keikō-eiga What Made Her Do It?* (*Nani ga kanojo o sō saseta ka*, 1930) before directing his own contributions to this socially aware genre, mostly at Shinko Kinema. *Hail to the Farmers* (*Hyakushō banzai*, 1930) and *Youth across the River* (*Kawamukō no seishun*, 1933), both now lost, were admired in their time; the latter, according

to Kyoko Hirano, "is regarded as the last prewar 'proletarian film.'" Kimura was also active in studio politics, and eventually left Shinko over an industrial dispute. Migrating to the fledgling PCL company, he realized Japan's first musical, *Intoxicated Life* (*Ongaku kigeki: Horoyoi jinsei*, 1933) and, later, his most famous film, *Ino and Mon* (*Ani imōto*, 1936), a realist melodrama about the ambiguous relationship between a brother and sister. Kimura's background in the *keikō-eiga* was still apparent in the representation of the workers by the river in the opening sequence, which echoed Soviet silent films. In general the film displayed a considerable flair for editing and composition, though the drama lacked the psychological depth of Naruse's postwar remake, *Older Brother, Younger Sister* (*Ani imōto*, 1953).

Later in the thirties, Kimura capitulated to government expectations, directing war documentaries such as *The Yangtse River Fleet* (*Yōsukō kantai*, 1939) and *Naval Bomber Squadron* (*Kaigun bakugekitai*, 1940). During the war he went to work in Manchuria, but completed only one film there; nevertheless, he remained in China until 1953. On his return he resumed his career and worked into the seventies, largely on children's films in a socially conscious vein. Of these, *A Thousand Paper Cranes* (*Senbazuru*, 1958) retold the story of schoolgirl Sadako Sasaki, who contracted leukemia after exposure to the Hiroshima bomb, while the well-regarded *Sea Children, Mountain Children* (*Umikko yamakko*, 1959) focused on the mutual antipathy of two groups of children in an Izu village. Kimura's reputation, however, rests mainly on his prewar work.

**1925 Futsū senkyo wa kokumin
no yōkyū de aru /** The Nation
Demands a General Election

1930 **Shichiya to hanayome to shinshi /** The Pawnbroker, the Bride, and the Gentleman

**Hyakushō banzai /** Hail to the Farmers

1931 **Tokaibyō kanja /** Patient with Urban Disease

**Chinmoku no ai /** Silent Love

**Kokyō /** Hometown

1932 **Yōkina shokkaku /** The Cheerful Freeloader

**Warau chichi /** Laughing Father

1933 **Kawamukō no seishun /** Youth across the River

**Ongaku kigeki: Horoyoi jinsei /** Intoxicated Life

**Junjō no miyako /** Capital of Pure Love

1934 **Tadano bonji: Jinsei benkyō /** The Average Man Tadano: Life Lessons

**Sakura ondo: Namida no haha /** Cherry Blossom Dance: Mother in Tears

**Zoku Tadano bonji /** The Average Man Tadano 2

1935 **Hōrōki /** Diary of a Wanderer

**Sanshokki birudingu /** Tricolor on the Buildings

**Tokai no kaii shichiji sanpun /** Strange Incident in the City at 7:03

1936 **Jogun totsugekitai /** Women's Army Assault Group

**Majutsu no joō /** Queen of Magic

**Ani imōto /** Ino and Mon / Older Brother, Younger Sister (lit.)

**Haha nareba koso /** Since I Am a Mother

**Hikoroku ōi ni warau /** Hikoroku Laughs Hard

**Nihon no katei seikatsu /** Home Life in Japan

1937 **Karayuki-san**

**Nihon josei dokuhon /** Manual for Japanese Women

**Shinsengumi**

1938 **Bokujō monogatari /** Pasture Story

1939 **Yōsukō kantai /** The Yangtse River Fleet

1940 **Kaigun bakugekitai /** Naval Bomber Squadron

1945 **Su shaomei /** Little Miss Su (*Manchuria*)

1956 **Mori wa ikiteiru /** The Living Forest

1957 **Nagasaki no ko /** Children of Nagasaki

**Okāsan no kōfuku /** Mother's Happiness

**Unagitori /** Children by the River (lit. Eel Fisherman)

1958 **Senbazuru /** A Thousand Paper Cranes

**Dendenmushi no uta /** Song of a Snail

**Hitofusa no budō /** One Bunch of Grapes

1959 **Aisuru koto to ikiru koto /** To Love and Live

**Umikko yamakko /** Sea Children, Mountain Children

1960 **Umi no koibitotachi /** Lovers of the Sea

**Suekko taishō /** Bossy Youngest Child

**Nihon no dōyō /** Japanese Children's Songs

**Abarenbō taishō /** The Roughneck General

1962 **Mirai ni tsunagaru kora /** Children Are the Link to the Future

1963 **Kōan to sennin no wakamonotachi /** Dr. Koan and One Thousand Youths

**Chiisana hi o mamoru hitobito /** People Protecting a Small Light

1964 **Uchū ryokō /** Space Travel

1968 **Tonegawa suikei /** Tonegawa River System

1970 **Tōkyō-wan kanjō dōro /** Tokyo Bay Circular

1971 **Nihon no dentō ongaku /** Traditional Japanese Music

**Ōanamuchi no bōken /** Adventures of the God Oanamuchi

1976 **Tōkyō no shitamachi /** Old Town of Tokyo

## KINOSHITA Keisuke
## (December 5, 1912–December 30, 1998)
## 木下恵介

Having served as assistant at Shochiku to pioneering *shomin-geki* director Yasujirō Shimazu, Kinoshita became one of the leading postwar exponents of the studio's bittersweet, subtly sentimental "Ōfuna flavor." He began to direct in the repressive wartime period, but his earliest films nevertheless anticipated his future manner. *The Blossoming Port* (*Hana saku minato*, 1943) was a light-hearted comedy about the clash of rural innocence and urban cynicism. *Army* (*Rikugun*, 1944), a saga following three generations of a military family from the Meiji era to the Pacific War, was superficially conformist, but Kinoshita's anti-militarist sentiments were apparent in the famous last scene, which stressed a mother's grief as her son leaves for the front.

These films opened up the two main veins of Kinoshita's work: comedy and melodrama. His comedies focused on themes of culture clash and the generation gap. *Broken Drum* (*Yaburedaiko*, 1949) was a study of the difficult relationship between a traditional father and his modern children, a theme to which Kinoshita would return in his, and Japan's, first color film, *Carmen Comes Home* (*Karumen kokyō ni kaeru*, 1951), about a stripper, played by Hideko Takamine, who causes uproar when she visits her conservative country hometown. The new Fujicolor process attractively captured the hues of mountainous Nagano Prefecture in autumn, and Kinoshita extended an impartial sympathy to both the transgressive heroine and the distressed townsfolk. The tender humor of this film gave way to bitterness in its se-

quel, *Carmen's Pure Love* (*Karumen junjōsu*, 1952), an uneasy, somewhat misanthropic satire on modern Tokyo life and Japanese politics. The quirkily enjoyable *Spring Dreams* (*Haru no yume*, 1960) was also a satire, which somewhat resembled *Boudu sauvé des eaux* (1932) in its story of a wealthy family whose lives are overturned when a poor sweet-potato vendor collapses in their home.

Kinoshita's most typical melodramas might be described as "intimate epics": chronicles of families, or communities, over time. *Twenty-Four Eyes* (*Nijūshi no hitomi*, 1954) was a touching account of the relationship between a teacher and her pupils on an island in the Inland Sea from 1928 through to the aftermath of the war; in Tadao Satō's words, it "has probably wrung more tears out of Japanese audiences than any other postwar film." *The River Fuefuki* (*Fuefukigawa*, 1960) was a historical saga about the sufferings of several generations in the wars of the sixteenth and seventeenth centuries, while *Times of Joy and Sorrow* (*Yorokobi mo kanashimi mo ikutoshitsuki*, 1957) chronicled twenty-five years in the lives of a family of lighthouse keepers. *Snow Flurry* (*Kazabana*, 1959), a more experimental film, told another family saga in a fragmented, non-chronological fashion; *The Bitter Spirit* (*Eien no hito*, 1961) followed two decades in an unhappy marriage; and the powerful geisha story *The Scent of Incense* (*Kōge*, 1964) focused on the bitter relations between mother and daughter, spanning the years of the Russo-Japanese War to the present day.

These films, *The Scent of Incense* in particular, were attempts to narrate national history in personal terms. However, Kinoshita's approach to politics was less analytical than intuitive. He

Nogiku no gotoki kimi nariki / She Was Like a Wild Chrysanthemum *(1955):*
*Nostalgic imagery and visual artifice did not detract from the immediacy of one of Kino-*
*shita's most moving films.*

admired, in his own words, "beautiful, simple, pure relationships between
individuals," and opposed whatever
undermined them. His films often centered on the sufferings of children in
oppressive circumstances: for instance,
the schoolgirl driven to suicide by her
teacher's discriminatory treatment in
*Garden of Women (Onna no sono,* 1954),
or the lonely wartime evacuee in *Record of Youth (Shōnenki,* 1951). The evil
of war was, indeed, an abiding theme,
but Kinoshita barely investigated its
causes. The point of *The River Fuefuki*
was ultimately a simplistic pacifism.
*Morning for the Osone Family (Ōsone-ke
no asa,* 1946), a contribution to postwar democratization, dramatized the
wartime sufferings of a liberal family
by dividing its characters neatly into

villains and passive victims. The main
focus of *Twenty-Four Eyes,* too, was the
innocent victims of war, though here
Kinoshita did show the indoctrination
of the children with militarist propaganda. *A Japanese Tragedy (Nihon no
higeki,* 1953) used newsreel footage to
relate its melodramatic story to postwar
social realities, but the wider context
was less vivid than the personal conflict
between a self-sacrificing mother, superbly acted by Yūko Mochizuki, and
her selfish offspring.

In fact, Kinoshita's films were often
most memorable when most personal
in focus. *She Was Like a Wild Chrysanthemum (Nogiku no gotoki kimi nariki,*
1955), a Meiji-era melodrama about a
forbidden teenage romance, and *The
Ballad of Narayama (Narayama bushikō,*

1958), the fable of a community which abandons its elderly to starve on a nearby mountain, were, in part, critiques of oppressive customs that destroy the natural affections between young lovers in the former or mother and son in the latter. Their main concern, however, was with individual hopes, desires, and sorrows, and the former was exceptionally affecting. The subject of the lyrically shot *The Outcast* (*Hakai*, 1948) was the oppression of the *burakumin* underclass, but again the film's strength was in dramatizing the feelings of the protagonist, including an implied homosexuality; Kinoshita's own homosexuality perhaps inspired a general sympathy with the socially marginalized.

Though an intelligent visual stylist, Kinoshita had a weakness for somewhat schematic visual effects: the pastiche of expressionist camera angles in *Carmen's Pure Love*; the Van Gogh-like colors and elements of Kabuki in *The Ballad of Narayama*; the addition of color washes to the monochrome images of *The River Fuefuki*. These were often more distracting than meaningful: for instance, the artifice in *The Ballad of Narayama* somewhat drained the life from the drama. The silent-era-style masking of *She Was Like a Wild Chrysanthemum* did give the film an appropriately nostalgic tone, but the power of that film and of Kinoshita's best work in general lay in his use of simple techniques. A judicious choice of camera position and excellent performances, especially from his regular collaborator, Hideko Takamine, brought emotional subtlety to unashamedly melodramatic narratives, and placed *Twenty-Four Eyes* and *She Was Like a Wild Chrysanthemum*, despite their occasional naivety, among the most purely moving of Japanese films.

1943 **Hana saku minato** / The Blossoming Port
**Ikiteiru Magoroku** / The Living Magoroku
1944 **Kanko no machi** / Jubilation Street
**Rikugun** / Army
1946 **Ōsone-ke no asa** / Morning for the Osone Family
**Waga koi seshi otome** / The Girl I Loved
1947 **Kekkon** / Marriage
**Fushichō** / Phoenix
1948 **Onna** / Woman
**Shōzō** / The Portrait
**Hakai** / The Outcast / The Sin / Apostasy
1949 **Ojōsan kanpai** / A Toast to the Young Miss / Here's to the Girls
**Yotsuya kaidan: (Zenpen; Kōhen)** / The Yotsuya Ghost Story (Parts 1 and 2)
**Yaburedaiko** / Broken Drum
1950 **Engēji ringu** / Engagement Ring
1951 **Zenma** / The Good Fairy
**Karumen kokyō ni kaeru** / Carmen Comes Home
**Shōnenki** / Record of Youth
**Umi no hanabi** / Fireworks over the Sea
1952 **Karumen junjōsu** / Carmen's Pure Love
1953 **Nihon no higeki** / A Japanese Tragedy
1954 **Onna no sono** / The Garden of Women
**Nijūshi no hitomi** / Twenty-Four Eyes
1955 **Tōi kumo** / Distant Clouds
**Nogiku no gotoki kimi nariki** / She Was Like a Wild Chrysanthemum / You Were Like a Wild Chrysanthemum (lit.) / My First Love Affair
1956 **Yūyakegumo** / Clouds at Twilight
**Taiyō to bara** / The Rose on His Arm (lit. The Sun and the Rose)
1957 **Yorokobi mo kanashimi mo**

ikutoshitsuki / Times of Joy and
Sorrow / The Lighthouse

**Fūzen no tomoshibi** / A Candle
in the Wind / Danger Stalks Near /
Hanging by a Thread

1958 **Narayama bushikō** / The Ballad of
Narayama

**Kono ten no niji** / The Eternal
Rainbow / The Rainbow of This
Sky (lit.)

1959 **Kazabana** / Snow Flurry

**Sekishunchō** / The Bird of Springs
Past

**Kyō mo mata kakute ari nan** /
Thus Another Day

1960 **Haru no yume** / Spring Dreams

**Fuefukigawa** / The River Fuefuki

1961 **Eien no hito** / The Bitter Spirit /
Immortal Love

1962 **Kotoshi no koi** / This Year's Love /
New Year's Love

**Futari de aruita iku shunjū** / The
Seasons We Walked Together /
Ballad of a Worker

1963 **Utae wakōdotachi** / Sing, Young
People!

**Shitō no densetsu** / Legend of a
Duel to the Death

1964 **Kōge** / The Scent of Incense

1967 **Natsukashiki fue ya taiko** / Those
Dear Old Flutes and Drums /
Lovely Flute and Drum / Eyes, the
Sea and a Ball

1976 **Suri Ranka no ai to wakare** / Love
and Separation in Sri Lanka

1979 **Shōdō satsujin: musuko yo** /
Impulse Murder: Only Son / My
Son! My Son!

1980 **Chichi yo haha yo** / Parents,
Awake!

1983 **Kono ko o nokoshite** / Children of
Nagasaki / These Children Survive
Me (lit.)

1986 **Shin yorokobi mo kanashimi
mo ikutoshitsuki** / New Times of
Joy and Sorrow / Big Joys, Small
Sorrows

1988 **Chichi** / Father

## KINUGASA Teinosuke
**(January 1, 1896–February 26, 1982)**
衣笠貞之助

Kinugasa became a director after spending several years acting in films as an *oyama*. He is better known internationally than the average standard of his work would justify, having been discovered in the West not once, but three times. In the late twenties, *Crossroads* (*Jūjiro*, 1928), a flamboyant melodrama about a young man's physical and psychological sufferings after he is wounded, then blinded, in a quarrel over the geisha he loves, became one of the first Japanese films to be exported, winning praise for a highly pictorial style reflecting the expressionist mannerisms of much contemporary European cinema. More than forty years later, the rediscovered *avant-garde* silent *A Page of Madness* (*Kurutta ippēji*, 1926), about a janitor trying to free his wife from an asylum, proved a revelation to a generation of *cinéphiles* weaned on the experimentation of the modern art movie; its narrative complexity, visual brilliance, and ambiguous melding of reality and fantasy remain astonishing. In the fifties, meanwhile, Western cinemagoers had seen a more conservative side to Kinugasa, when the cosmetic values of the period melodrama, *Gate of Hell* (*Jigokumon*, 1953), earned it unjustified plaudits, including the Palme d'Or at Cannes and an Oscar for Best Foreign Film. Seen today, the film disappoints: rich Eastmancolor cinematography does not conceal the conventional mechanics of the plot and the stolidity of the staging.

These experimental films on the one hand, and this classical drama on the other, represent the opposite poles of Kinugasa's art. Even in the twenties, his *avant-garde* work was atypical,

Courtesy of the Kawakita Memorial Film Institute

Kurutta ippēji / A Page of Madness *(1926): One of the great avant-garde silent films, Kinugasa's early masterpiece remains astonishing.*

though the lost *The Sun* (*Nichirin*, 1925) is said to have broken new ground and courted censorship by representing the legendary shamaness and ruler Himiko onscreen. Another innovative early film, admired for its original montage techniques, was the lost *Before Dawn* (*Reimei izen*, 1931), one of the best-regarded of the left-wing *keikō-eiga* genre, about the sufferings, and subsequent revolt, of a group of prostitutes. Most of Kinugasa's prewar films, though, were more conventional *jidai-geki*. Even his version of *An Actor's Revenge* (*Yukinojō henge*, 1935–36), later to be filmed in modernist style by Kon Ichikawa, was basically a well-made commercial film. Nevertheless, Kinugasa's reputation remained high within the industry, and at Shochiku he was trusted with prestigious projects, such as the picturesque first sound ver-

sion of the perennially popular story of *The Loyal 47 Ronin* (*Chūshingura*, 1932) and the lost *The Summer Battle of Osaka* (*Ōsaka natsu no jin*, 1937), an epic account of the military campaign which led to the final unification of Japan under the rule of the Tokugawa Shogunate. Among his surviving period films, *The Battle of Kawanakajima* (*Kawanakajima kassen*, 1941), focusing on a young soldier's transient romance, before going to war, with a local woman, has been praised by Daryl William Davis for its visual beauty and humane attitudes.

During the Occupation era, Kinugasa made *Lord for a Night* (*Aru yo no tonosama*, 1946), a diverting Meiji-period satire on the feudal code, and *Actress* (*Joyū*, 1947) in which Isuzu Yamada played the pioneer star of Western-style theater, Sumako Matsui. Japanese critics generally consider this superior to Mizoguchi's competing account of her life story, *The Love of Sumako the Actress* (*Joyū Sumako no koi*), released the same year. In addition to *Gate of Hell*, Kinugasa's later work, made mainly at Daiei, included a sequel to Mizoguchi's *Tales of the Taira Clan* (*Shin Heike monogatari: Yoshinaka o meguru sannin no onna*, 1956) and *The Dedication of the Great Buddha* (*Daibutsu kaigan*, 1952), a pretty but superficial account of events surrounding the casting of the bronze Buddha at Nara. He also made various films based on melodramatic novels by authors such as Kyōka Izumi and Jun'ichirō Tanizaki: these included *The White Heron* (*Shirasagi*, 1958), *Okoto and Sasuke* (*Okoto to Sasuke*, 1961), and *The Song Lantern* (*Uta andon*, 1960). The stylization of these films has earned comparison with Douglas Sirk, but in fact they tended to be rather old-fashioned in approach and more interesting for their scripts than for their images. Nevertheless, though much of his output was second-rate, the individuality and imagination of Kinugasa's best work suggest a first-rate talent, and it is likely that some of his lesser-known films deserve wider exposure.

1920 **Imōto no shi** / The Death of My Younger Sister (*co-director*)

1922 **Ā, Konishi junsa** / Ah, Constable Konishi (*co-director*)

**Hibana** / Spark

**Aru shinbunkisha no shuki** / Memorandum of a Newspaper Journalist

1923 **Shiranui** / Sea-Fire

**Niwa no kotori** / Two Little Birds

**Kano yama koete** / Crossing That Mountain

**Jinsei o mitsumete** / Ways of Life (lit. Contemplating Life)

**Tsubame no uta** / Swallow's Song

**Konjiki yasha: Miya no maki** / The Golden Demon: Miya's Reel

**Ma no ike** / Spirit of the Pond

**Chōraku no kanata e** / Beyond Decline

**Konjiki yasha: Kan'ichi no maki** / The Golden Demon: Kan'ichi's Reel

1924 **Tsuma no himitsu** / Secret of a Wife

**Kanojo no unmei (Zenpen; Kōhen)** / She Has Lived Her Destiny (Parts 1 and 2) (lit. Her Destiny)

**Koi** / Love

**Kiri no ame** / Paulownia Rain

**Sabishiki mura** / Lonely Village

**Hanasakajiji** / Hanasakajiji / Happy Old Men

**Onigami Yuri keiji** / Fierce God: Yuri the Detective

**Kyōren no butō** / Dance of Passion

**Arashi no seirei** / Spirit of the Tempest

**Koi to wa narinu** / It Turned into Love

**Shōhinshū: Ashi** / Little Story: Foot

**Shōhinshū: Nusumi** / Little Story: Theft

**Seki no fūfumatsu** / Twin Pines at the Barrier

1925 **Jashūmon no onna** / A Woman's Heresy

**Koi to bushi** / Love and a Warrior

**Shinjū yoimachigusa** / Love Suicide: Evening Primrose

**Tsukigata Hanpeita** / Hanpeita Tsukigata

**Midagahara no satsujin** / Slaughter at Midagahara

**Nichirin** / The Sun (*re-edited version released in 1927 as* Josei no Kagayaki / Glory of Women)

**Ekisutora gāru** / Extra Girl

1926 **Ten'ichibō to Iganosuke** / Ten'ichibo and Iganosuke (*co-director*)

**Kurutta ippēji** / A Page of Madness

/ A Page Out of Order / A Crazy
Page
**Teru hi kumoru hi: Daiippen /**
Bright Day, Cloudy Day: Part 1
**Hanashi** / Story
**Kirinji** / The Prodigy
**Teru hi kumoru hi: Dainihen /**
Bright Day, Cloudy Day: Part 2
1927 **Inazuma zōshi** / Chronicle of
Lightning
**Ojō Kichizō** / Miss Thief Kichizo
**Oniazami** / The Horse Thistle
**Kin'ō jidai** / Epoch of Loyalty
**Myōtoboshi** / Vega
**Goyōsen** / The Government Vessel
**Hikuidori** / Cassowary
**Akatsuki no yūshi** / A Brave
Soldier at Dawn
**Dōchū Sugoroku: Kago /**
Backgammon on the Road: The
Palanquin
**Gekka no kyōjin** / Crazed Blades
under the Moon
1928 **Benten kozō** / Benten Boy / The
Gay Masquerade
**Kyōraku hijō** / Secret Story of
Kyoto / The Secret Documents
**Kaikokki** / Tales from a Country by
the Sea
**Dōchū Sugoroku: Fune /**
Backgammon on the Road: The
Boat
**Chōkon yasha** / Female Demon
(lit. Demon with a Grudge)
**Jūjiro** / Crossroads / Crossways /
Shadows of the Yoshiwara
1931 **Reimei izen** / Before Dawn
**Tōjin Okichi** / Okichi, Mistress of
a Foreigner
1932 **Nezumi kozō Jirokichi** / Jirokichi
the Ratkid
**Ikinokotta Shinsengumi** / The
Surviving Shinsengumi
**Chūshingura: Akō Kyō no maki**
/ The Loyal 47 Ronin: Ako and
Kyoto Reel
**Chūshingura: Edo no maki** / The
Loyal 47 Ronin: Edo Reel

1933 **Ten'ichibō to Iganosuke /**
Ten'ichibo and Iganosuke
**Futatsu dōrō** / Two Stone Lanterns
**Koina no Ginpei** / Ginpei from
Koina
1934 **Kutsukake Tokijirō** / Tokijiro of
Kutsukake
**Fuyuki shinjū** / Double Suicide in
Winter
**Ippongatana dohyōiri** / Into the
Sumo Ring with a Sword
**Nagurareta Kōchiyama** / The
Beaten Kochiyama
1935 **Kurayami no Ushimatsu /**
Ushimatsu in Darkness
**Yukinojō Henge (Daiippen;
Dainihen)** / An Actor's Revenge /
The Revenge of Yukinojo (lit. The
Avenging Ghost of Yukinojo) (Parts
1 and 2)
1936 **Yukinojō Henge, Kanketsu hen /**
An Actor's Revenge / The Revenge
of Yukinojo (lit. The Avenging
Ghost of Yukinojo) (Part 3)
1937 **Ōsaka natsu no jin** / The Summer
Battle of Osaka
**Hitohada Kannon** / The Helping
Hand of the Goddess of Mercy /
Sacred Protector
1938 **Kuroda seichū roku** / Loyalism at
Kuroda
1940 **Hebihimesama** / Snake Princess
**Zoku Hebihimesama** / Snake
Princess 2
1941 **Kawanakajima kassen** / The Battle
of Kawanakajima
1943 **Susume dokuritsu ki** / Forward,
Flag of Independence!
1945 **Kanchō: Umi no bara** / Spy: Rose
of the Sea
1946 **Aru yo no tonosama** / Lord for a
Night / A Certain Night's Lord
1947 **Yottsu no koi no monogatari /**
Four Love Stories (*co-director*)
**Joyū** / Actress
1948 **Kobanzame: Daiichibu: Dotō hen**
/ Remora: Part One: Angry Waves
Chapter

**1949** **Kobanzame: Dainibu: Aizō hen /** Remora: Part Two: Love and Hate Chapter

**Kōga yashiki /** House of the Koga Family

**1950** **Satsujinsha no kao /** Face of a Murderer

**Beni kōmori /** The Red Bat

**1951** **Tsuki no wataridori /** Migratory Bird under the Moon

**Meigetsu sōmatō /** Lantern under a Full Moon

**1952** **Shura-jō hibun: Sōryū no maki /** Castle of Carnage: Twin Dragon Reel

**Shura-jō hibun: Hiryū no maki /** Castle of Carnage: Flying Dragon Reel

**Daibutsu kaigan /** The Dedication of the Great Buddha

**1953** **Jigokumon /** Gate of Hell

**1954** **Yuki no yo no kettō /** Duel on a Snowy Night

**Hana no nagadosu /** Flowers and Long Sword / End of a Prolonged Journey

**Tekka bugyō /** The Great Administrator

**1955** **Kawa no aru shitamachi no hanashi /** It Happened in Tokyo / The Story of a River Downtown (lit.)

**Bara ikutabi ka /** A Girl Isn't Allowed to Love / How Often Do Roses Bloom? (lit.)

**Onna keizu: Yushima no shiraume /** Genealogy of Women: White Plums at Yushima

**1956** **Shin Heike monogatari: Yoshinaka o meguru sannin no onna /** New Tales of the Taira Clan: Three Women Around Yoshinaka

**Hibana /** Spark

**Tsukigata Hanpeita: Hana no maki /** Hanpeita Tsukigata: Flower Reel

**Tsukigata Hanpeita: Arashi no maki /** Hanpeita Tsukigata: Storm Reel

**1957** **Genji monogatari: Ukifune /** The Tale of Genji: The Floating Boat

**Naruto hichō /** Secret of Naruto

**1958** **Haru kōrō no hana no en /** A Spring Bouquet / Symphony of Love

**Ōsaka no onna /** A Woman of Osaka

**Shirasagi /** The White Heron

**1959** **Jōen /** The Affair / Tormented Flame

**Kagerō ezu /** Picture of Heat-Haze / Stop the Old Fox

**1960** **Uta andon /** The Song Lantern

**1961** **Midaregami /** Disheveled Hair / Blind Devotion

**Okoto to Sasuke /** Okoto and Sasuke

**1963** **Uso /** Lies / When Women Lie (*co-director*)

**Yōsō /** The Sorcerer / Bronze Magician / Priest and Emperor

**1966** **Chiisai tōbōsha /** The Little Runaway (*co-director*)

## KITAMURA Ryūhei
(b. May 30, 1969)
北村龍平

Kitamura's wild and ridiculous action pictures have avowedly been influenced by such English-language genre films as *Mad Max* (1979, George Miller), *The Evil Dead* (1982, Sam Raimi), and the early work of Peter Jackson and James Cameron. Having studied filmmaking at Sydney's School of Visual Arts, he began to direct films for his own independent company, aptly named Napalm Productions. His theatrical debut, *Heat after Dark* (*Hīto afutā dāku*, 1999), was a medium-length *noir*ish thriller about two men trying to conceal a murdered body. Kitamura acquired cult status with *Versus* (2000), a two-hour long combat involving two quasi-supernatural antagonists, a gang of yakuza, a pair of cops, and a large number of zombies. Shot cheaply on location, it displayed a surface gloss that belied its low budget; it deserved credit for enterprise, but was basically an excuse to pack as much gore and noise into two hours as humanly possible.

Kitamura has since run the gamut of action genres. *Alive* (2002) was a science fiction movie about a condemned murderer who survives electrocution, only to become a pawn in a scientific experiment. *Azumi* (2003) was a flamboyant *chanbara* about a group of assassins trained to eliminate the corrupt officials responsible for civil strife in medieval Japan. *Sky High* (*Sukai hai: Gekijōban*, 2003) was a confused supernatural horror film in which a serial killer collects human hearts to trigger the return of the dead to earth. With *Godzilla: Final Wars* (*Gojira: Final Wars*, 2004), Kitamura helmed Toho's fiftieth-anniversary celebration of Japan's most popular monster, but he returned to independent production with *LoveDeath* (2006) about a couple on the run from cops and criminals alike. Kitamura has jokingly described his work as "non-stop freefall ultraviolence action entertainment," a description which fairly sums up the vacuous flair of these slick, stupid blockbusters. Although they have all been well-made within the limitations of the genre, it is difficult to ignore the sheer unpleasantness of their ideas, particularly the Nietzschean connotations of *Azumi*.

In his less commercial work, Kitamura has seemed to be aiming for a *reductio ad absurdum* of action motifs: *Aragami* (2003), about a duel between a samurai and a demon, was made when fellow director Yukihiko Tsutsumi challenged him to make an action film with only two combatants and one setting, while *Longinus* (2004), a 40-minute work made for DVD release, seemed like the filmed synopsis of a feature length horror/science fiction movie. At the time of writing, Kitamura is in Hollywood, completing work on an adaptation of Clive Barker's short story *The Midnight Meat Train*. This transition is unsurprising, since his films have always looked abroad for inspiration. Though Kitamura himself has argued that he is returning to a Japanese tradition of pure action typified by such sixties *chanbara* as the *Zatoichi* and *Baby Cart* (*Kozure ōkami*) series, his shortcomings are fairly summed up by his stated belief that the Japanese film industry should be imitating *The Last Samurai* (2003, Ed Zwick). Kitamura's defenders have championed his work on the grounds that it is entertaining. This, of course, is a matter of opinion.

**1988** **Exit** (*short*)
**1997** **Down to Hell**
**1999** **Hīto afutā dāku** / Heat After Dark
**2000** **Versus**
**2002** **Jam Films** (*co-director*)
 **Alive**
**2003** **Azumi**
 **Aragami**
 **Sukai hai: Gekijōban** / Sky High
**2004** **Longinus** (*video*)
 **Gojira: Final Wars** / Godzilla: Final Wars
**2006** **LoveDeath**

## KITANO Takeshi
**(b. January 18, 1947)**
北野武

Arguably the most internationally recognized figure working in Japanese cinema today, Kitano began his career as a *manzai* stand-up comic, a background apparent in his feature work in the sexual and scatological farce *Getting Any* (*Minna yatteru ka*, 1995) and in *Glory to the Filmmaker* (*Kantoku: Banzai*, 2007), a slapstick parody of various film genres. He entered the cinema as an actor, most notably as the prisoner-of-war camp officer in Nagisa Oshima's *Merry Christmas, Mr. Lawrence* (*Senjō no Merī Kurisumasu*, 1983). He was memorable, too, as a yakuza in Yasuo Furuhata's *Demon* (*Yasha*, 1985), and has continued to act in the bulk of his own films. Indeed, he made his directorial debut only when Kinji Fukasaku, hired to make the Kitano star vehicle *Violent Cop* (*Sono otoko kyōbō ni tsuki*, 1989), stepped down due to illness.

In contrast with Fukasaku's hectic manner, Kitano opted for a stylistic restraint, which intriguingly offset the brutalities of the story. Generally using a static camera, employing pans and tracks only occasionally and functionally, to follow the movement of characters or vehicles, Kitano made this impassive style the trademark of such subsequent crime films as the blackly comic *Boiling Point* (*3-4 X jūgatsu*, 1990) and the immaculately constructed *Sonatine* (*Sonachine*, 1993), both set in Okinawa. The latter film benefited particularly from the laid-back score of Joe Hisaishi, composer on most of Kitano's films, and from the lush beauty of the island's subtropical landscape. The account of a gang gradually being eliminated against these pacific backdrops achieved an eerie cumulative power, although its fatalism was ultimately numbing. Fatalism also marred Kitano's most acclaimed crime film, *Hana-bi* (1997), though a new depth was perceptible in the touching depiction of the relationship between a guilt-ridden cop-turned-criminal and his dying wife. Here, too, the use of painting—the hobby taken up by the protagonist's wheelchair-bound former colleague—hinted at the therapeutic power of art.

Kitano's most humane films, however, were two non-genre pieces. With *A Scene at the Sea* (*Ano natsu ichiban shizukana umi*, 1991), his mellow style found perhaps its perfect complement in the subject of a deaf-mute surfer. The character was treated with slight sentimentality, but the film subtly highlighted the condescension he suffers, his fellow surfers failing to inform him when his name is called at a surfing competition. Kitano also beautifully captured the atmosphere of lazy summer days at the beach. Arguably his best film was *Kids Return* (*Kizzu ritān*, 1996), an ironic account of the different paths taken by two high school delinquents. Here, displacing fatalism, was an intelligent grasp of the role of chance events in shaping lives: for instance, when the kids take boxing lessons after being beating up, one proves a natural and embarks on a career in the ring.

The quality of Kitano's work has subsequently declined. *Kikujiro* (*Kikujirō no natsu*, 1999) was a flimsy road movie in which a drifter escorts a boy to visit his long-lost mother: its combination of slapstick and sentimentality was poorly judged, and its pace was slow. *Brother* (2000), which transposed yakuza violence to America, was a pure exercise in sadism, its tone fairly summed up by the image of corpses arranged in the shape of the Chinese character reading "Death." With *Zatoichi* (*Zatōichi*, 2003), Kitano essayed *jidai-geki* subject matter for the first time, albeit that he had spoofed the story of the legendary blind masseur in one of the movie skits in *Getting Any?* Though striking in the title role, Kitano did not erase memories of Shintarō Katsu, and while the film had its quirkier elements (the avenger in drag, the tap dance finale), it was basically a conventionally well-made *chanbara*.

In recent years, Kitano has also made two unashamed art movies. In *Dolls* (2002), extracts from a Bunraku puppet play bookended three interwoven stories of romantic obsession, while *Takeshis'* (2005) was a self-conscious examination of Kitano's star persona, recounting the actor's meeting with his convenience store clerk *alter ego*. Though *Dolls* was pictorially beautiful, both films were poorly received. *Glory to the Filmmaker* was self-consciously about Kitano's desire to avoid being pigeonholed as a director of gangster movies, but while his attempts to broaden his range are commendable, his recent work has achieved neither the humanity of *Kids Return* nor the nihilistic intensity of *Sonatine*. Nevertheless, he remains a technically expert filmmaker, and his importance in re-establishing an international audience for the Japanese cinema during the nineties is undeniable.

1989 **Sono otoko kyōbō ni tsuki** / Violent Cop (lit. That Man Is Brutal)
1990 **3-4 X jūgatsu** / Boiling Point
1991 **Ano natsu ichiban shizukana umi** / A Scene at the Sea (lit. That Summer, a Most Quiet Ocean)
1993 **Sonachine** / Sonatine
1995 **Minna yatteru ka** / Getting Any?
1996 **Kizzu ritān** / Kids Return
1997 **Hana-bi** / Hana-bi / Fireworks
1999 **Kikujirō no natsu** / Kikujiro (lit. Kikujiro's Summer)
2000 **Brother**
2002 **Dolls**

2003 **Zatōichi** / Zatoichi / The Blind Swordsman: Zatoichi
2005 **Takeshis'**
2007 **Chacun son Cinéma ou Ce petit coup au coeur quand la lumière s'éteint et que le film commence** / To Each His Cinema (*co-director*)
    **Kantoku: Banzai** / Glory to the Filmmaker

## KOBAYASHI Masaki
(February 14, 1916–October 4, 1996)
小林正樹

Of the generation of directors who entered the industry during or shortly after the Pacific War, Kobayashi was to become perhaps the most self-conscious social critic. His distinctive concerns took some years to develop: his early work displayed the influence of Keisuke Kinoshita, whom he had assisted on such films as *Broken Drum* (*Yaburedaiko*, 1949), the *Carmen* comedies, and *A Japanese Tragedy* (*Nihon no higeki*, 1953). Kinoshita himself scripted Kobayashi's second film, *Sincerity* (*Magokoro*, 1953), and his sister Yoshiko Kusuda wrote the script for *Somewhere under the Broad Sky* (*Kono hiroi sora no doko ka ni*, 1954). These, and other early films such as *My Sons' Youth* (*Musuko no seishun*, 1952), *Beautiful Days* (*Uruwashiki saigetsu*, 1955), and *The Spring* (*Izumi*, 1956) were sentimental romances or domestic dramas with the "Ōfuna flavor" typical of Kinoshita and of Shochiku productions in general.

Kobayashi's true manner was established with *The Thick-Walled Room* (*Kabe atsuki heya*, 1953; released 1956), an angry account of those imprisoned, perhaps unfairly, for war crimes, which was shelved for fear of offending the United

States. After its belated release, his films began to manifest a consistent social concern. *I'll Buy You* (*Anata kaimasu*, 1956) was a critique of commercial values in the world of sport, showing the machinations of scouts trying to snare a college baseball star for a professional team, which benefited from the hangdog persona of Yūnosuke Itō. The noirish *Black River* (*Kuroi kawa*, 1957) again focused on the Occupation, showing how crime and prostitution flourished around American military bases. It marked the first starring role for Kobayashi's regular actor, Tatsuya Nakadai, who later brought conviction and intensity to Kobayashi's most personal project, *The Human Condition* (*Ningen no jōken*, 1959-61). Though sometimes heavy-handed, this three-part epic, tracing the experiences of a liberal conscript in Manchuria, was an impressively comprehensive account of wartime experience, which dealt honestly both with atrocities committed by the Japanese and with the sufferings of ordinary Japanese soldiers on the battlefield.

Kobayashi's best-known films of the sixties are his *jidai-geki*: the visually flamboyant *Kwaidan* (*Kaidan*, 1964), drawn from Lafcadio Hearn's ghost stories, and two austerely ritualistic yet subversive samurai films, *Hara-Kiri* (*Seppuku*, 1962) and *Rebellion* (*Jōiuchi: Hairyō tsuma shimatsu*, 1967), both critiques of the arbitrary abuse of power. Kobayashi himself maintained that there was "absolutely no difference [...] in the feeling of making period or contemporary films," and though set in the distant past, these works recapitulated the anti-authoritarian sentiments of *The Human Condition*. Of Kobayashi's sixties *gendai-geki*, *The Inheritance* (*Karamiai*, 1962) was an uncharacteristically sardonic film, reminiscent of a Kon Ichi-

kawa or Yasuzō Masumura satire, which exposed the purely commercial values of the selfish rich through its story of the scheming initiated when a dying businessman attempts to leave his wealth to his three absent children. *Youth of Japan* (*Nihon no seishun*, 1968) was the story of a father and son and their divergent attitudes and feelings, shaped by contrasting experiences of youth during war and peacetime. From this time, Kobayashi's sympathies rested increasingly with the older generation. *Kaseki* (1975) chronicled the responses of an ageing executive to a diagnosis of cancer, while *The Empty Table* (*Shokutaku no nai ie*, 1985) was the story of a middle-aged father trying to come to terms with his son's participation in a terrorist act. In his later years, Kobayashi also revisited the subject of war criminals with *Tokyo Trial* (*Tōkyō saiban*, 1983), a documentary compilation of newsreel footage from the International Military Tribunal that tried the Japanese generals and politicians responsible for the war.

This documentary treatment was atypical, since Kobayashi generally preferred to address social and political themes in psychological terms, charting the mental and emotional responses of individuals to traumatic events. *The Human Condition* was the clearest example of this approach, chronicling the horrors of war through the sufferings and reactions of a single everyman figure. *Youth of Japan*, similarly, showed the effects of war through the character of the father, scarred physically and mentally by the after-effects of a beating received from a superior officer, while in *The Empty Table*, the enormity of terrorism was expressed through the disintegration of the culprit's family. Kobayashi's most sympathetic characters tended to be the powerless victims of larger events: the low-ranking war criminals of *The Thick-Walled Room*, imprisoned for minor crimes while many of their more culpable superiors escaped punishment; the naive youth sadistically compelled to attempt ritual suicide with a bamboo sword in *Hara-Kiri*; the courtly woman mistreated and manipulated by her lord in *Rebellion*.

Kobayashi's early films were efficiently but rather plainly made; they achieved dramatic power, but lacked nuance and stylistic individuality. *Black River*, however, displayed a new flair for striking compositions and inventive editing, and from *The Human Condition* onwards, the adoption of the 'Scope frame allowed him to perfect a more precise, pictorial style, grouping characters onscreen in elaborately composed tableaux, the stasis of which was punctuated by sudden eruptions of movement. This somewhat arid, academic technique proved particularly effective in his samurai films, where the balance of stillness and violent motion served to reflect both the suffocating formality of aristocratic society and the disruptive effect of the private rebellions that the films chronicled. Kobayashi's *jidai-geki* were also distinguished by their enthralling set pieces, such as the action climaxes of *Rebellion* and *Inn of Evil* (*Inochi bō ni furō*, 1971). *Kwaidan*, with its rich color cinematography and boldly stylized sets, was his most decorative film, but something of an exercise; indeed, the visual splendor rendered the supernatural more enticing than frightening. In general, Kobayashi's films tended to lack subtlety; his images were often contrived to convey clear points. But in its integrity and seriousness of purpose, his work commands respect.

1952 **Musuko no seishun** / My Sons' Youth
1953 **Magokoro** / Sincerity
1954 **Mittsu no ai** / Three Loves
**Kono hiroi sora no doko ka ni** / Somewhere under the Broad Sky
1955 **Uruwashiki saigetsu** / Beautiful Days
1956 **Izumi** / The Spring
**Anata kaimasu** / I'll Buy You
**Kabe atsuki heya** / The Thick-Walled Room (*made in 1953*)
1957 **Kuroi kawa** / Black River
1959 **Ningen no jōken (Daichibu: Jun'ai hen; Dainibu: Gekido hen)** / The Human Condition: Part 1: No Greater Love
**Ningen no jōken (Daisanbu: Bōkyō hen; Daishibu: Sen'un hen)** / The Human Condition: Part 2: Road to Eternity
1961 **Ningen no jōken: Kanketsu hen (Daigobu: Shi no dassatsu; Dairokubu: Arano no hōkō)** / The Human Condition: Part 3: A Soldier's Prayer
1962 **Karamiai** / The Inheritance
**Seppuku** / Hara-Kiri
1964 **Kaidan** / Kwaidan
1967 **Jōiuchi: Hairyō tsuma shimatsu** / Rebellion / Samurai Rebellion
1968 **Nihon no seishun** / Youth of Japan / Hymn to a Tired Man
1971 **Inochi bō ni furō** / Inn of Evil / At the Risk of My Life (lit.)
1975 **Kaseki** / Kaseki / Fossil
1979 **Moeru aki** / Glowing Autumn
1983 **Tōkyō saiban** / Tokyo Trial
1985 **Shokutaku no nai ie** / The Empty Table / Family without a Dinner Table (lit.)

# KOREEDA Hirokazu
(b. June 6, 1962)
是枝裕和

One of the most interesting younger di-

Wandāfuru raifu / After Life *(1998): Koreeda's work to date has made him one of the most respected artists in modern Japanese cinema.*

rectors in Japan today, Koreeda worked initially on television documentaries. These already displayed an individual talent with an interest in both social realities and existential truths: *However...* (*Shikashi... fukushi kirisute no jidai ni,* 1991) was an examination of political corruption focused through the context of the suicide of a frustrated bureaucrat, while *August without Him* (*Kare no inai hachigatsu ga,* 1994) chronicled the death of AIDS victim Yutaka Hirata. Koreeda's training in documentary was still apparent in the delicate observation of his fiction films. His cinema debut, *Maboroshi* (*Maboroshi no hikari,* 1995), was a subtle account of the experiences and feelings of a bereaved wife; the restraint of the direction earned comparisons with Ozu, but the sense of disquiet

and emotional dislocation was all Koreeda's own. His original vision flowered in the wonderfully affecting fantasy of *After Life* (*Wandāfuru Raifu,* 1998), a bittersweet film which used an allegorical story—souls in limbo trying to decide on the happiest memory of their lives—as the basis for an investigation into the thoughts, feelings, and memories that give meaning to life. Despite its supernatural premise, the film's real strength lay in its precise and compassionate delineation of character.

*Distance* (2001), an attempt to analyze the mindset of the members of a religious cult, was a response to the 1995 Aum Shinrikyo attacks on the Tokyo subway; though it displayed a topicality previously absent from Koreeda's fiction films, it lacked the human depth and stylistic discipline of its director's best work. *Nobody Knows* (*Dare mo shiranai*, 2004), however, was a return to form, charting the daily lives of a group of children left by their mother to fend for themselves in a Tokyo apartment. In this small masterpiece, Koreeda rejected conventional dramatic effect and returned to his roots in documentary, recording in minute detail and with exquisite poignancy the children's responses to their situation. He also elicited a magnificent performance from child star Yūya Yagira. The mellow and witty *Hana* (*Hana yori mo naho*, 2006) marked a new departure, turning to historical subject matter to narrate an unheroic variation on a story of revenge. In its critical attitude to bushidō values and its richly delineated portrait of interconnected lives in an Edo-era tenement, it evoked the work of prewar master Sadao Yamanaka.

Koreeda's themes are isolation, loss, death, memory, and the search for meaning; his excellence lies in his ability to anchor these philosophical concerns in the concrete realities of daily life and individual emotion. In consequence, his work displays a power and humanity that ensure that the release of his new films remains among the most eagerly awaited events in Japanese cinema today. If Koreeda's future films match the quality of his best work to date, he is likely to rank as one of the finest Japanese filmmakers of the twenty-first century.

**1995  Maboroshi no hikari** / Maboroshi / Maborosi (lit. The Phantom Light)
**1996  Arawashiyo** / This World (*co-director*)
**1997  Kioku ga ushinawareta toki** / Without Memory
**1998  Wandafuru raifu** / After Life
**2001  Distance**

**2003  Kaette kita deka matsuri** / Cop Festival Returns (*co-director*)
**2004  Dare mo shiranai** / Nobody Knows
**2006  Hana yori mo naho** / Hana

## KOTANI Henrii
### (April 25, 1887–April 8, 1972)
小谷ヘンリー

One of several American-trained filmmakers who attempted to bring modern techniques to Japanese cinema during the Taisho period, Kotani returned to Japan at the invitation of Shochiku after working as an actor and cameraman in Hollywood. His Shochiku films, which he often wrote and photographed as well as directed, are held to have introduced Hollywood-style lighting techniques into Japanese film. Among these were the studio's inaugural production, *Island Woman* (*Shima no onna*, 1920), about a girl living on an island who meets a lover while swimming, and *The Field Poppy* (*Gubijinsō*, 1921), a spectacular production which made a star of its lead actress, Sumiko Kurishima. The presence of actresses rather than *oyama* in these films was a novelty, but their visual style was apparently somewhat conservative and theatrical, eschewing close-ups and camera movements.

Kotani's only surviving film as director is his last feature, *Lights of Sympathy* (*Nasake no hikari*, 1926), a sentimental, socially conscious education film about a teenage flower-seller's struggle to support his ailing mother and his own schooling. Though somewhat complacent in its message of "class harmonization," it assimilated American techniques gracefully and its delicacy of touch makes the loss of Kotani's other films seem regrettable.

1920  **Shima no onna** / Island Woman
1921  **Gubijinsō** / The Field Poppy
      **Denkō to sono tsuma** / An Electrical Engineer and His Wife
      **Toranku** / Trunk
      **Mantetsu no zenbō** / Complete Picture of the South Manchurian Railway
      **Yūhi no mura** / Village of Evening Sun
      **Yami no michi** / Path in the Darkness
      **Tomu no kichō** / Tom's Return to Korea
1923  **Shitakiri suzume** / The Sparrow Whose Tongue Was Cut Out
1924  **Koi no misshi** / Secret Messenger of Love
      **Kurobōshi** / The Black Priest
      **Chidori naku yoru** / Night of the Crying Plovers
      **Migiwa no sakura** / Waterside Cherry
      **Meguru himitsu** / Surrounded by Secrecy (lit. Relevant Secret)
      **Miyako no fune** / Boat in the Capital
1926  **Nasake no hikari** / Lights of Sympathy
1932  **Daigaku no uta** / Song of College (*short*)

## KUDŌ Eiichi
(July 17, 1929–September 23, 2000)
工藤栄一

A director of films in masculine genres, based almost exclusively at Toei, Kudō cut his teeth on such conventional studio programmers as the *Bloody Account of Jirocho* (*Jirochō kesshōki*) tetralogy. The whimsical *Flowers on the Road* (*Hanakago dōchū*, 1961), about the humorous and dangerous misadventures of two young women traveling along the Tokaido highway, was typical of the Toei approach at that time, combining action, comedy, sentimentality, and a lively theme song. *A Fisher Wife's Tale* (*Uogashi no onna Ishimatsu*, 1961) was a rare excursion at this period of Kudō's career into *gendai-geki*: though its story, about a young woman's encounter with the businessman father who abandoned her as a child, was predictably handled, it was directed with some vitality.

Kudō's reputation rests, however, on the loose trilogy of *Thirteen Assassins* (*Jūsannin no shikaku*, 1963), *The Great Melee* (*Daisatsujin*, 1964), and *Eleven Samurai* (*Jūichinin no samurai*, 1967), all shot in black and white and 'Scope and all concerned with the arbitrary abuse of power and the violent measures necessary to oppose it. Though *The Great Melee* was apparently conceived as an allegory on the sixties student protest movement, these films were not simply anarchic in tone, but examinations of the fine line between legitimate and tyrannical authority. *The Great Melee* was about a reformist conspiracy to assassinate a prince and thus destroy the influence at court of his wicked patron; *Eleven Samurai* focused on a provincial clan's efforts to avenge their daimyo, murdered by a court official after protesting against the latter's slaying of a local farmer; *Thirteen Assassins*, by contrast, detailed an attempt by central government to assassinate a cruel provincial lord who threatens to destabilize the realm. That film in particular, with its austere, regimented compositions, had something of the ritualistic quality of Masaki Kobayashi's *Hara-Kiri* (*Seppuku*, 1962). The style of *The Great Melee* and *Eleven Samurai* was more informal: the former used handheld camera in the action sequences, while the latter made use of rapid, wheeling tracking shots. Both films still achieved a thunderous intensity.

In the samurai genre, Kudō also made *Castle of Owls* (*Ninja hichō: Fukurō no shiro*, 1963) on similar anti-authoritarian themes: a ninja plots the assassination of warlord Hideyoshi. However, this was less tautly plotted and more conventional in style than the trilogy. From the late sixties, the director began to work more frequently with contemporary subject matter. Among his thrillers, *Industrial Spy* (*Sangyō supai*, 1968) has been praised by Chris D. for its sharp examination of business hypocrisy, its tycoons despising the blackmailer whose skills ensure their success. Otherwise, Kudō contributed to several long-running series of yakuza films, including *Japan's Underworld History* (*Nihon ankokushi*), *Viper Brothers* (*Mamushi no kyōdai*), and *Battles without Honor and Humanity* (*Jingi naki tatakai*), of which he directed the last installment in 1979. During the eighties, he worked predominantly in television, but his big-screen work included the successful thriller *Yokohama BJ Blues* (*Yokohama BJ Burūsu*, 1981), a vehicle for hard-boiled star Yūsaku Matsuda. In the late features *Passion's Red and Black* (*Aka to kuro no netsujō*, 1992) and *Tale of a Scarface* (*Andō-gumi gaiden: Gunrō no keifu*, 1997), Kudō consciously attempted a more character-driven approach to gangster material: the theme of these films, in his own words, was "the instability of emotions, the uncertainty of human relationships."

Kudō was not a top-rank filmmaker: the quality of his work was dependent on studio politics and he was not able to transcend second-rate material. Even so, given good actors and good scripts, such as those of Kaneo Ikegami for the trilogy, he was capable of crafting films of remarkable visual flair and emotional intensity.

1959 **Fugaku hichō** / Secret Story of Mount Fuji

**Fugaku hichō: Kanketsu hen** / Secret Story of Mount Fuji: Conclusion

1960 **Jirochō kesshōki: Akiba no taiketsu** / Bloody Account of Jirocho: Duel at Akiba

**Jirochō kesshōki: Nagurikomi dōchū** / Bloody Account of Jirocho: Raid on the Road

**Hebigami maden** / Snake God and Demon Palace

**Hibari torimonochō: Orizuru kago** / Hibari's Casebooks: Paper Crane Palanquin

**Jirochō kesshōki: Fujimi tōge no taiketsu** / Bloody Account of Jirocho: Duel at Fujimi Pass

**Jirochō kesshōki: Nagurikomi kōjin'yama** / Bloody Account of Jirocho: Raid on the Holy Mountain

**Tenryū hahakoigasa** / The Tenryu River: Hat of Mother Love

1961 **Hanakago dōchū** / Flowers on the Road

**Hakkōryū kitai** / Hakko-Style Chivalry

**Uogashi no onna Ishimatsu** / A Fisher Wife's Tale (lit. A Female Ishimatsu of the Fish Market)

**Umon torimonochō: Maboroshi tōrō no onna** / The Casebooks of Detective Umon: The Woman with the Phantom Lantern

**Hana no Oedo no yakuza hime** / Lady Yakuza, Flower of Great Edo

**Gonkurō tabi nikki** / Gonkuro's Travel Diary

1962 **Ohimesama to hige daimyō** / The Princess and the Bearded Daimyo

**Kochō kagerō ken** / Butterfly-Mayfly Sword

**Chimoji yashiki** / Mansion of Characters Written in Blood

1963 **Hengen murasaki zukin** / Changes of the Purple Hood

Ninja hichō: Fukurō no shiro / Castle of Owls (lit. Secret Story of Ninja: Castle of Owls)

Wakasama yakuza: Edokko tengu / Young Master Yakuza: Edoite Goblin

Jūsannin no shikaku / Thirteen Assassins

1964 Daisatsujin / The Great Melee / The Great Killing (lit.)

1965 Ninkyō Kiso garasu / Chivalrous Crow of the Kiso Valley

Yakuza tai G-men: Meiji ankokugai / Yakuza vs. G-men: Meiji Underworld

1966 Nyoban hakai / The Broken Vow of Chastity

1967 Nihon ankoku shi: Chi no kōsō / Japan's Underworld History: Blood Feud

Jūichinin no samurai / Eleven Samurai

1968 Nihon ankoku shi: Nasake muyō / Japan's Underworld History: Compassion Is Futile

Sangyō supai / Industrial Spy

1969 Gonin no shōkinkasegi / Five Bounty Hunters / Fort of Death

1973 Yakuza tai G-men: Otori / Yakuza vs. G-men: Decoy

1974 Mamushi no kyōdai: Futari awasete sanjuppan / Viper Brothers: Up on Thirty Charges

1979 Sono go no jingi naki tatakai / Aftermath of Battles without Honor and Humanity

1980 Kage no gundan: Hattori Hanzō / Shadow Warrior: Hanzo Hattori

1981 Yokohama BJ burūsu / Yokohama BJ Blues

1982 Yajū deka / Beast Detective / The Dropout

1983 Nogare no machi / Escape Route

1986 Hissatsu! Ura ka omote ka / Sure Death! 3

1988 Takasebune / Flatboat

1989 Wōtāmūn / Watermoon

1991 Nakibokuro / The Mole under the Eye

1992 Aka to kuro no netsujō / Passion's Red and Black / Passion

1993 Ringu ringu ringu: Namida no chanpion beruto / Ring, Ring Ring: Championship Belt of Tears

1997 Andō-gumi gaiden: Gunrō no keifu / Tale of a Scarface / Supplementary Biography of the Ando Gang: The Gang of Wolves' Family Tree (lit.)

## KUMAGAI Hisatora
**(March 8, 1904–May 22, 1986)**
熊谷久虎

Like many of his generation, Kumagai moved from left-leaning, class-conscious filmmaking in the early thirties to patriotic propaganda in the forties; his politically diverse films were united, in Peter High's words, by "the ferocious passion he imprinted as his trademark on all his works." Such early films as *Mobilization Orders* (*Dōinrei*, 1931) and *A Scout in North China* (*Hokuman no teisatsu*, 1931) apparently subverted militarist plots by stressing the poverty of the rural proletariat. Kumagai achieved wider critical acclaim in the mid-thirties with the now lost *Takuboku, Poet of Passion* (*Jōnetsu no shijin Takuboku*, 1936) a biopic of a famous poet and non-conformist. Among his other notable films of the period was *Many People* (*Sōbō*, 1937), an interesting if somewhat politically compromised group portrait of working class emigrants departing Japan for Brazil in the Meiji era.

Kumagai's most famous film today is *The Abe Clan* (*Abe ichizoku*, 1938), a period film based an Ōgai Mori story about a retainer who commits *seppuku* in defiance of his daimyo's command, a deed which ultimately leads to the destruction of his entire household.

Except for the action climax, the film was austerely ritualistic in style, concentrating on the characters and the way in which bushidō ideals shape their actions. It is difficult at this remove to decide whether the film should be interpreted as an endorsement of the feudal code or a satire on it.

Thereafter, however, Kumagai, working with nationalist screenwriter Tsutomu Sawamura, directed such unambiguously pro-militarist films as *Naval Brigade at Shanghai* (*Shanhai rikusentai*, 1939), a semi-documentary account of the Japanese war effort in China, and *A Story of Leadership* (*Shidō monogatari*, 1941) about a railway engineer training a young soldier. After this, he left the film industry to become a leading figure of the Sumera-juku Association, a nationalist cult. He returned briefly to direction in the fifties, but his later films were not considered to match his prewar output in quality.

**1931** **Ren'ai kyōgijō** / Love's Competition Ground
**Tama o migaku** / Polishing the Jewel
**Honruida** / Home Run
**Dōinrei** / Mobilization Orders
**Hokuman no teisatsu** / A Scout in North China
**1932** **Saraba Tōkyō** / Farewell, Tokyo
**Yoshigaya-kun ni kike** / Ask Yoshigaya-kun
**1933** **Kanojo no michi** / Her Road
**Seishun no koro** / Time of Youth
**Kyoka: Den'en hen** / Torchlight: Pastoral Episode
**Gunmō yūzai** / The Blind Crowd Is Guilty
**1934** **Kyoka: Tokai hen** / Torchlight: Urban Episode
**Sankatei** / Three Households
**Gantō no shojo** / Virgin on the Great Rock

**1935** **Watashi ga oyome ni itta nara** / If I Become a Bride
**Seishun ondo** / Dance of Youth
**1936** **Jōnetsu no shijin Takuboku** / Takuboku, Poet of Passion
**Nankyoku mōgeiryō** / Antarctic Whale Hunt
**Kimagure fūfu** / Whimsical Couple
**1937** **Sōbō** / Many People / Common People / Wandering People
**1938** **Abe ichizoku** / The Abe Clan
**1939** **Shanhai rikusentai** / Naval Brigade at Shanghai
**1941** **Shidō monogatari** / A Story of Leadership
**1953** **Shirauo** / White Fish
**1954** **Kakute jiyū no kane wa naru** / Thus the Bell of Freedom Rings
**1955** **Utsukushiki haha** / Beautiful Mother
**1957** **Chieko shō** / The Chieko Story / Portrait of Chieko
**1958** **Mikkokusha wa dare ka** / Who Is the Informer?

## KUMAI Kei
**(June 1, 1930–May 23, 2007)**
熊井啓

Kumai's relatively slender output testifies to the integrity of a director determined to work with material of his own choosing along socially committed lines. His first films were thrillers of considerable intelligence, which used murder investigations as vehicles to examine the legacy of Japan's wartime aggression and defeat. *The Long Death* (*Teigin jiken: Shikeishū*, 1964), based on the true story of a notorious 1948 mass poisoning, touched on Japanese war guilt with the suggestion that the poison originated in a Manchurian chemical weapons factory, while in *Japanese Archipelago* (*Nihon rettō*, 1965), the murder of an American solder was used as the catalyst for a complex examination of postwar Japan's sense of its status as a U.S. colony and more obliquely, a critique of American foreign policy in Asia.

Unexpectedly, Kumai next directed *Kurobe Dam* (*Kurobe no taiyō*, 1968), essentially a celebration of one of Japan's largest public works projects. As if a riposte to this, *Rise, Fair Sun* (*Asayake no uta*, 1973) was a savage indictment of the Japanese construction state, its devastation of nature for financial gain, and its callous treatment of farmers initially encouraged by government intervention to cultivate remote land, but later perceived as an inconvenience in the face of expanding tourism. This was Kumai's richest period; in the early seventies, he also made *The Swarming Earth* (*Chi no mure*, 1970), an account of the discrimination suffered by such minority groups as *hibakusha*, *burakumin*, and resident Koreans; and *Sandakan 8* (*Sandakan hachibanshōkan: Bōkyō*, 1974), which examined the taboo subject of the *karayuki-san*: Japanese women sold into prostitution in Southeast Asia early in the twentieth century. Told in flashback, this film was given depth by the poignant performance of Kinuyo Tanaka as a former *karayuki-san* still ostracized because of her past. Less explicitly political, and perhaps Kumai's most humanly affecting film, was *The Long Darkness* (*Shinobugawa*, 1972), a delicate study of the relationship between two disillusioned young people whose mutual affection teaches them the strength to face the vicissitudes of life. As with *Sandakan 8*, this was a film about people coming to terms with a traumatic past: a theme given telling visual expression by Kumai's depiction of the decaying lumberyards of the Fukagawa district in Tokyo

and the inhospitable snowscapes and traditional homes of Tōhoku.

The best of Kumai's more recent films, and arguably his overall masterpiece, was *The Sea and Poison* (*Umi to dokuyaku*, 1986), a brilliant interrogation of the motives of Japanese medical personnel who participated in the vivisection of American prisoners-of-war. Kumai pursued his theme with breathtaking clarity, explaining everything but excusing nothing. The film was based on a novel by Shūsaku Endō, with whose earnest morality Kumai had a clear temperamental affinity; he later adapted *Deep River* (*Fukai kawa*, 1995), Endō's chronicle of Japanese tourists trying to lay the ghosts of the past during a trip to India. Among Kumai's other later films, *To Love* (*Aisuru*, 1997) dealt with the ostracism of sufferers from leprosy, but its melodramatic effects seemed too obviously calculated. *Darkness in the Light* (*Nihon no kuroi natsu: Enzai*, 2001), however, was a gripping account of the terrorist attacks committed in Matsumoto by the cult Aum Shinrikyo in preparation for their later attack on the Tokyo subway. Kumai indicted both the police and the mass media, which rushed to accuse an innocent man.

Skilled at tackling themes of contemporary relevance and at interrogating Japan's recent history, Kumai tended to seem uncomfortable in more remote period settings. *An Ocean to Cross* (*Tenpyō no iraka*, 1980) was notable only as the first postwar Japanese film shot in mainland China. *Love and Faith* (*Ogin-sama*, 1978) recounted the fatal quarrel between warlord Hideyoshi and tea master Sen no Rikyū; despite excellent credentials, including a script by Mizoguchi's screenwriter Yoshikata Yoda and lead performances from Kurosawa's regular stars Toshirō Mifune and Takashi Shimura, it was overlong and pedestrian. Kumai returned to the same subject matter in his later *Death of a Tea Master* (*Sen no Rikyū: Honkakubō ibun*, 1989); here Mifune, who had played Hideyoshi in the earlier film, essayed the role of Rikyū. This film, however, was overshadowed by Teshigahara's elaborately aestheticized *Rikyu* (*Rikyū*), made the same year. Kumai's final film, *The Sea Is Watching* (*Umi wa miteita*, 2002) was an account of life and love in a Meiji-period brothel, based on a script that Kurosawa left unrealized at his death: it was marred both by the sentimental humanism typical of Kurosawa's last works and by Kumai's rather bland direction.

In his best films, however, Kumai displayed an intelligent restraint, keeping his camera largely in the middle distance and eschewing emphatic visual rhetoric. The decision to use black and white in *The Long Darkness* and *The Sea and Poison* was characteristic; it saved the former from sentimentality and ensured that the viewer's response to the latter was one of moral rather than physical revulsion. Kumai's skill was in refusing to tell his audience what to think; rather, he was willing to let the facts speak for themselves.

1964    **Teigin jiken: Shikeishū** / The Long Death (lit. Imperial Bank Incident: Condemned Criminal)

1965    **Nihon rettō** / Japanese Archipelago / Chain of Islands

1968    **Kurobe no taiyō** / Kurobe Dam / Sun over the Kurobe Dam (lit.) / A Tunnel to the Sun

1970    **Chi no mure** / The Swarming Earth / Apart from Life

1972    **Shinobugawa** / The Long Darkness / Shinobugawa

1973    **Asayake no uta** / Rise, Fair Sun (lit. Song of Sunrise)

1974    **Sandakan hachibanshōkan:** **Bōkyō** / Sandakan 8 (lit. Sandakan 8 Brothel: Memories of Home)

1976    **Kita no misaki** / The North Cape

1978    **Ogin-sama** / Love and Faith / The Love and Faith of Ogin (lit. Lady Ogin)

1980    **Tenpyō no iraka** / An Ocean to Cross (lit. Tiled Roofs of Tenpyo )

1981    **Nihon no atsui hibi: Bōsatsu: Shimoyama jiken** / Willful Murder (lit. Hot Days in Japan: Willful Murder: Shimoyama Incident)

1986    **Umi to dokuyaku** / The Sea and Poison

1989    **Sen no Rikyū: Honkakubō ibun** / Death of a Tea Master (lit. Sen no Rikyu: Testament of Honkakubo)

1990    **Shikibu monogatari** / Mount Aso's Passion / Tale of Shikibu (lit.)

1992    **Hikarigoke** / Luminous Moss

1995    **Fukai kawa** / Deep River

1997    **Aisuru** / To Love

2001    **Nihon no kuroi natsu: Enzai** / Darkness in the Light (lit. Japan's Black Summer: False Accusation)

2002    **Umi wa miteita** / The Sea Is Watching

## KUMAKIRI Kazuyoshi
**(b. September 1, 1974)**
熊切和嘉

The first of several graduates of Osaka University of Arts who began to make films in the late nineties, Kumakiri achieved instant notoriety with his graphically gory debut feature, *Kichiku* (*Kichiku daienkai*, 1997), made as his graduation project. This account of the violent disintegration of a group of seventies student radicals was initially interesting in charting the way in which individual instability, malice, and suspicion undermine the unit, but became less so once its characters descended into psychopathic madness. Nevertheless, it displayed a rough-edged talent, particularly in the creative use of sound.

Kumakiri essayed gentler subject matter with his second film, *Hole in the Sky* (*Sora no ana*, 2001), an account of the relationship between the introverted chef of a Hokkaido roadside diner and the jilted, penniless woman he hires as a waitress after she leaves without paying for a meal. A similar unlikely relationship was at the heart of *The Volatile Woman* (*Kihatsusei no onna*, 2004), about a woman who begins an ambiguous affair with the burglar who tries to rob the gas station she runs. More widely distributed abroad was *Antenna* (*Antena*, 2003), a haunting but overextended account of the responses of a family to the trauma of the disappearance of one of the children. Though the story had its sensationalist elements, particularly in the depiction of the masochistic activities through which the hero strives to expiate his guilt, it was directed with considerable restraint, the tone of unease being conveyed visually only by the occasional startling camera angle.

*Green Minds, Metal Bats* (*Seishun kinzoku batto*, 2006) was an unexpected departure into comedy, albeit of a rather melancholy kind: it traced the lives of three disappointed men who have seen youthful ambitions of sporting success thwarted. Veteran "pink" director Kōji Wakamatsu gave an amusing performance as the spirit of Babe Ruth, but overall the film was slightly bland. Nevertheless, it seems likely that Kumakiri will continue to probe the darker corners of society and experience. *Freesia: Icy Tears* (*Furīja*, 2007) was a dystopian fantasy set in a near-future Japan where the Edo-period custom of paid avengers has been revived, and here again, the director focused on characters cruelly afflicted by the impact of a past trauma.

1997 **Kichiku daienkai** / Kichiku / Satanic Banquet
2001 **Sora no ana** / Hole in the Sky
2003 **Mottomo kikenna deka matsuri** / The Most Dangerous Cop Festival (*co-director*)
**Antena** / Antenna
2004 **Tadareta ie: "Zōroku no kibyō" yori** / The Ravaged House: Zoroku's Disease
**Kihatsusei no onna** / The Volatile Woman
2006 **Seishun kinzoku batto** / Green Minds, Metal Bats
2007 **Furīja** / Freesia: Icy Tears / Freesia: Bullets over Tears

## KUMASHIRO Tatsumi
## (April 24, 1927–February 24, 1995)
神代辰巳

Considered, along with Noboru Tanaka, to be the most important director of Nikkatsu Roman Porno, Kumashiro served a lengthy apprenticeship before making his first film, *A Thirsty Life* (*Kaburitsuki jinsei*, 1968), at the age of 41. After its failure, he worked in television for a few years, but returned to the cinema when Nikkatsu began to specialize in erotic films, achieving notice with *Sayuri Ichijo: Wet Desire* (*Ichijō Sayuri: Nureta yokujō*, 1972), a story of rival strippers starring a real-life striptease artist who had been prosecuted for obscenity. Its strong female characters were unusual for the genre; Chiseko Tanaka has noted that the director tended to focus on active women and passive men.

Kumashiro's most admired Roman Porno film, *The World of Geisha* (*Yojōhan fusuma no urabari*, 1973) focused on tensions among the inhabitants of a geisha house and was notable for its picturesque art direction. In general, however, Kumashiro essayed a style of gritty realism, often using long takes, which contrasted with Tanaka's usually more stylized manner. *Street of Joy* (*Akasen tamanoi: Nukeraremasu*, 1974) was a chronicle of a prostitute who sets out to break the record for clients serviced on the New Year's Eve before her profession is made illegal, while *Twisted Path of Love* (*Koibitotachi wa nureta*, 1973) and the later *The Woman with Red Hair* (*Akai kami no onna*, 1979), which ranked among Kinema Junpō's annual Top Ten, anchored stories of sexual conduct in well-drawn portraits of working-class milieux. The plain visual style of these films suited the exploration of sordid subjects, but sometimes made Kumashiro's work seem pedestrian and exploitative. He was capable, however, of moments of piercing clarity, such as the ironic use of the national anthem in the last minutes of *Street of Joy*.

Among Kumashiro's more original erotic films was *Ascent of the Black Rose* (*Kurobara shōten*, 1975), a self-referential work about a pornographic filmmaker encountering difficulties with his latest film. In the seventies he also made several films outside the Roman Porno genre, most notably *Bitterness of Youth* (*Seishun no satetsu*, 1974), about a law student who rejects the activism of his fellows. In his later years, Kumashiro's career was restricted by ill-health, but he was able to make the erotic thriller *Love Bites Back* (*Kamu onna*, 1988), about the consequences of an extra-marital affair, and a well-regarded Taisho-period melodrama, *Appassionata* (*Modorigawa*, 1983), about a *tanka* poet who seeks publicity by attempting to fake double

suicide pacts with two of his lovers. His last film, *Like a Rolling Stone* (*Bō no kanashimi*, 1994), was a violent character study of a yakuza who emerges from prison to find himself sidelined by his boss. Though more respectable in subject matter than Kumashiro's seventies work, these later films were still characterized by the nihilism that marked and marred his output.

**1968** **Kaburitsuki jinsei** / A Thirsty Life / The Life of a Striptease Lover

**1972** **Nureta kuchibiru** / Wet Lips

**Ichijō Sayuri: Nureta yokujō** / Sayuri Ichijo: Wet Desire / Stripper Sayuri: Wet Desires / Following Desire

**1973** **Koibitotachi wa nureta** / Twisted Path of Love / Wet Lovers (lit.)

**Onna jigoku: Mori wa nureta** / Female Hell: The Wet Forest / Woods Are Wet

**Yakuza kannon iro jingi** / Yakuza Justice: Erotic Code of Honor

**Yojōhan fusuma no urabari** / The World of Geisha / Behind the Sliding Door (lit.)

**1974** **Nureta yokujō: Tekudashi 21-nin** / Wet Desires: 21 Take-off Girls / The World of Stripteasers

**Yojōhan fusuma no urabari: Shinobihada** / World of Geisha 2: The Precocious Lad / The Secret Skin / Behind the Sliding Door: Chaste Skin (lit.)

**Kagi** / The Key

**Seishun no satetsu** / Bitterness of Youth

**Akasen tamanoi: Nukeraremasu** / Street of Joy

**Yoimachigusa** / Evening Primrose / Flower Waiting for the Night

**1975** **Kushi no hi** / The Golden Fleece / Love in a Small Room

**Afurika no hikari** / Light of Africa

**Kurobara shōten** / Ascent of the Black Rose / Professional Specialists

**Nureta yokujō: Hirake chūrippu**

/ Wet Desires: The Open Tulip /
Pachinko Professionals
**1976 Dannoura yomakura kassenki /**
Dan-no-Ura Night
**Monzetsu: Dondengaeshi** / Erotic
Ecstasy: Sexual Sensations / The
Peculiar Triangle
**1979 Akai kami no onna** / The Woman
with Red Hair
**Jigoku** / Hell / The Inferno
**Tōi ashita** / Far Tomorrow
**1980 Shōjo shōfu: Kemonomichi /**
Whore Girl: Trail of the Beast
**Kairaku gakuen: Kinjirareta asobi**
/ School of Pleasure: Forbidden
Games
**Misutā Misesu Misu Ronrī** / Mr.
Mrs. Miss Lonely
**1981 Hiwai no uta** / Obscene Games
**Ā! Onnatachi waika** / Ah! Women:
Obscene Songs
**1982 Akai bōshi no onna** / The Woman
in a Red Hat
**1983 Modorigawa** / Appassionata / River
of No Return
**1984 Mika Madoka: Yubi o nurasu
onna** / Mika Madoka: A Woman
Who Wets Her Fingers
**1985 Koibumi** / Love Letter
**1986 Rikon shinai onna** / A Woman
Who Doesn't Divorce
**1987 Beddotaimu aizu** / Bedtime Eyes
**1988 Kamu onna** / Love Bites Back (lit.
The Woman Who Bites)
**1994 Bō no kanashimi** / Like a Rolling
Stone / Hard-Headed Fool (lit.
Sadness of the Rod)

# KURAHARA Koreyoshi
**(May 31, 1927–December 28, 2002)**
蔵原惟繕

Best known abroad for his Nikkatsu action films, Kurahara directed after assisting Eisuke Takizawa at that studio.

His debut *I Am Waiting* (*Ore wa matteiru ze*, 1957) was a thriller about a
restaurant manager and former boxer
who saves a suicidal girl, but whose previous association with the yakuza comes
back to haunt him. This film apparently
set the tone for Nikkatsu's subsequent
action movies, particularly, as Mark
Schilling has commented, in its "air
of being in Japan but not quite of it."
Its star, tough guy and teen idol Yūjirō
Ishihara, also acted for Kurahara in *A
Man Who Rode the Typhoon* (*Fūsoku 40-
mētoru*, 1958), *Ginza Love Story* (*Ginza
no koi no monogatari*, 1962), and *I Hate
But Love* (*Nikui anchikushō*, 1962); the
latter two works co-starred Ruriko Asa-
oka and were major hits. Both featured
implausible but diverting narratives: in
*Ginza Love Story* a car accident and subsequent amnesia impede the course of
true love, while in *I Hate But Love* a star
escapes from his celebrity lifestyle to
deliver a jeep to a country doctor, only
to be pursued by his furious manager/
girlfriend.

Kurahara's films were noted for
their use of jazz soundtracks, and that
form of music was a narrative element
in *Black Sun* (*Kuroi taiyō*, 1964), about a
Japanese jazz fan helping a black soldier
who has gone AWOL after killing a
white man. Praised for the intelligence
with which it treated its theme of cross-
cultural assumptions and disappointments, this was one of several films on
more serious subjects that Kurahara
made at Nikkatsu. Among these were
*Flame of Devotion* (*Shūen*, 1964), a poetic account of a marriage destroyed by
war; *A Record of Love and Death* (*Ai to shi
no kiroku*, 1966), about a girl's love for a
youth afflicted with radiation sickness;
and *Thirst for Love* (*Ai no kawaki*, 1967),
an adaptation of a Mishima novel about
the sexual tensions between a widow,

her landowner father-in-law, and the manservant she loves.

The non-commercial qualities of the last film led Nikkatsu to shelve it, and Kurahara left the studio to work freelance, making a series of commercial hits filmed on location abroad. Among these was another collaboration with Yūjirō Ishihara, the African-set *Safari 5000* (*Eikō e no 5000-kiro*, 1969). Kurahara's talent for location shooting made him a suitable choice to realize *The Glacier Fox* (*Kita kitsune monogatari*, 1978), a documentary about wild foxes in Hokkaido, and another commercial success. He followed this with *Elephant Story* (*Zō monogatari*, 1980) and *Antarctica* (*Nankyoku monogatari*, 1983), a sentimentally anthropomorphic, if visually striking account of the epic journey of a group of dogs abandoned by an Antarctic expedition. Thereafter, with diminishing success, he continued to helm big-budget, location-shot films: *To the Sea* (*Umi e*, 1988) followed the Paris-Dakar rally, while *Strawberry Road* (*Sutoroberī Rōdo*, 1991) chronicled the experiences of a Japanese emigrant working on a California strawberry farm. Despite the popularity of many of his later films, it seems that Kurahara's most individual work belonged to his Nikkatsu period.

1957 **Ore wa matteiru ze** / I Am Waiting / I'll Be Waiting
1958 **Kiri no naka no otoko** / A Man in the Fog
**Fūsoku 40-mētoru** / A Man Who Rode the Typhoon (lit. Wind Speed 40 Meters)
**Arashi no naka o tsuppashire** / Showdown in the Storm (lit. Run Fast in the Storm)
1959 **Daisan no shikaku** / The Third Blind Spot
**Bakuyaku ni hi o tsukero** / Light the Explosive!
**Kaitei kara kita otoko** / The Man

Who Came from the Bottom of the Sea
**Jigoku no magarikado** / Hell's Corner / A Turning to Hell
**Warera no jidai** / The Age of Our Own
1960 **Aru kyōhaku** / A Certain Menace
**Kyōnetsu no kisetsu** / The Hot Season / The Warped Ones / The Wanted Ones
1961 **Yabure kabure** / Desperation
**Kono wakasa aru kagiri** / So Long as We Have Youth
**Umi no shōbushi** / Gambler in the Sea
**Arashi o tsukkiru jettoki** / The Jet That Cuts through the Storm
1962 **Mekishiko mushuku** / Mexico Wanderer
**Ginza no koi no monogatari** / Ginza Love Story
**Nikui anchikushō** / I Hate But Love / I Love You, Damnit!
**Garasu no Jonī: Yajū no yōni miete** / Glass Johnny: Look Like a Beast
1963 **Nani ka omoshiroi koto nai ka** / Isn't There Anything Interesting?
1964 **Kuroi taiyō** / Black Sun
**Shūen** / Flame of Devotion / Running Fever
1965 **Yoake no uta** / Song of Daybreak
1966 **Ai to shi no kiroku** / A Record of Love and Death / The Heart of Hiroshima
1967 **Ai no kawaki** / Thirst for Love
1969 **Eikō e no 5000-kiro** / Safari 5,000 (lit. 5000 Kilometers to Glory)
1971 **Furyō shōjo Mako** / Bad Girl Mako / Wet Highway
1973 **Hi wa shizumi hi wa noboru** / Sunset, Sunrise
1975 **Ame no Amusuterudamu** / It Happened in Amsterdam / Two in the Amsterdam Rain / Rainy Amsterdam (lit.)
1978 **Kita kitsune monogatari** / The Glacier Fox / Story of the Northern Fox (lit.)

1980  Zō monogatari / Elephant Story
1981  Seishun no mon / The Gate of
      Youth (*co-director*)
1982  Seishun no mon: Jiritsu hen /
      The Gate of Youth: Independence
      Chapter
1983  Nankyoku monogatari / Antarctica
      (lit. Antarctica Story)
1985  Haru no kane / Spring Bell
1986  Michi / The Road / Hopeless Love
1988  Umi e / To the Sea / See You
1991  Sutoroberī Rōdo / Strawberry
      Road

## KURIHARA Tōmasu
**(January 24, 1885–September 8, 1926)**
栗原トーマス

An emigrant who had worked as an actor for Thomas Ince in Hollywood, Kurihara (born Kisaburō Kurihara) returned to Japan in 1918 and soon became one of the leading figures in the "pure film" movement, which sought to modernize the style and content of Japanese cinema. The preserved fragment of *Sanji Goto* (*Gotō Sanji*, 1918, released in 1920), a slapstick comedy set partly in America and starring an actor, Iwajirō Nakajima, billed as "Japan's Chaplin," testifies to the influence of American modes on his early work. Kurihara's most famous film, the lost *Amateur Club* (*Amachua kurabu*, 1920), was another comedy, with a scenario by noted author Jun'ichirō Tanizaki, then in a Western-influenced phase of his career. The script and extant stills suggest a lively account of the mores of the fashionable rich at play; in Joanne Bernardi's words, "Kurihara's Hollywood background, Tanizaki's original story, a cast of amateurs, and the conscious exploitation of familiar locations made the film unquestionably the

furthest removed from the theater of all pure film attempts until then."

Tanizaki and Kurihara subsequently collaborated on *The Lust of the White Serpent* (*Jasei no in*, 1921), an attempt to apply modern film techniques to classical material; the plot was derived from a story in Akinari Ueda's *Ugetsu Monogatari*, later to be filmed by Mizoguchi. Regrettably these experiments met with little commercial success, and Kurihara abandoned "pure film" for educational films and documentaries until failing health curtailed his career. It is his early work that is considered of historical importance in marking an advance on the predominant theatricality of Taisho-period *shinpa*-based cinema.

1920  Meiji-jingū chinzasai / The
      Dedication Festival of Meiji-Jingu
      Amachua kurabu / Amateur Club
      Utsukushii Nihon / Beautiful Japan
      Katsushika Sunako / Sunako
      Katsushika
      Gotō Sanji / Sanji Goto / Sanji
      Goto, or a Japanese Enoch Arden
      (*filmed in 1918*)
1921  Gantan no satsuei / Filming on
      New Year's Day
      Doro no sainan / Disaster in the Mud
      Goman-en / 50,000 Yen
      Kami no setsuri / Divine
      Providence
      Hinamatsuri no yoru / Night of
      the Doll Festival
      Yume no tabiji / Dream Journey
      Beikoku kyokugei hikō / American
      Stunt Flight
      Shuppan mae: Kaishimon /
      Before Setting Sail: The Mysterious
      Fingerprint
      Kisen hōshi / The Merry Priest
      Kashū daigaku yakyudan rai
      Chōsen jikkyō / The University
      of California Baseball Team Visits
      Korea: Live Commentary
      Iwami Jūtarō buyūden: Jakusha

no yume / Heroic Legend of Jūtarō
Iwami: A Weak Man's Dream

**Hozugawa kudari** / Downstream
on the Hozu River

**Kurueru akuma** / Crazed Demon

**Narikin** / The Nouveau Riche
(*recut version of* "Gotō Sanji")

**Jasei no in** / The Lust of the White
Serpent / The Lasciviousness of the
Viper

**Tōgū denka dairan bōtorēsu** /
The Crown Prince Attends a Boat
Race

**Dainippon teikoku** / The Greater
Japanese Empire

**Tabakoya no musume** / The Girl
from the Tobacconist's

**Yukidoke no yoru** / The Night the
Snow Melts

**Beni zōshi** / The Crimson
Storybook

**Hakumei no onna** / The Woman
Who Died Young

1922  **Ōkuma-kō no kokuminsō** / The
State Funeral of Count Okuma

**Gunkan Mutsu** / Warship Mutsu

**Eikoku kōtaishi denka dairan no
gaishōtei no Musume Dōjōji** /
The British Crown Prince Attends
a Performance of "A Girl at Dojo
Temple" at the Foreign Minister's
House

1923  **Zoku amachua kurabu** / Amateur
Club 2

1924  **Haru wa kaeru** / Spring Returns

**Kuon no hibiki** / Eternal Sound

**Koke no musu made: Shugi no
tatakai** / Until the Moss Covers the
Stone: Struggle of Principles

# KUROKI Kazuo
(November 20, 1930–April 12, 2006)
黒木和雄

Though he began to direct features
some years after his official New Wave

contemporaries, Kuroki's imaginative, elliptical, and individual films mark him as a belated contributor to the movement's style and ethos. Like Susumu Hani, he started out working in documentary for Iwanami Productions and throughout his career continued to make documentaries, both for cinema and television, alongside his feature work. Among the most notable was *True Record of a Marathon Runner* (*Aru marason rannā no kiroku*, 1964), about 1964 Olympic athlete Kenji Kimihara. His first fiction film, *Silence Has No Wings* (*Tobenai chinmoku*, 1966), was an extraordinary fantasy which obliquely explored such themes as the legacy of war and the rise of international organized crime through a sequence of stylized human stories, linked by the device of a caterpillar being accidentally transported from Nagasaki to Hokkaido. The film's remarkable visual lyricism and rich ambiguities of implication made it an auspicious feature debut.

Kuroki's next feature was *Cuban Lovers* (*Kyūba no koibito*, 1969), filmed on location on the Caribbean island and tracing the relationship between a non-political Japanese fisherman and a girl in the Cuban People's Army. *Evil Spirits of Japan* (*Nihon no akuryō*, 1970) was an offbeat yakuza film in which both cop and criminal were played by the same actor, Kei Satō. Kuroki's most widely admired work, however, was *The Assassination of Ryoma* (*Ryōma ansatsu*, 1974), an iconoclastic account of events leading up to the death of a famous pro-democracy statesman in the last days of the Shogunate. Kuroki stressed the man's physical plainness, his fearfulness, and his human ordinariness, suggesting that his heroic stature was a fabrication of historians. A certain nihilism marred the film, but it achieved an aus-

©Nippon Eiga Shinsha Ltd.

Tobenai chinmoku / Silence Has No Wings *(1966): The history and society of postwar Japan are examined through a series of intimate and intricate connections.*

tere power. Mellower in tone, with a strain of black humor, was *Preparations for the Festival* (*Matsuri no junbi*, 1975), a story about a sexually frustrated young man facing up to an uncertain future. Though its attitude to some of the minor characters was unfairly patronizing, the film was nevertheless an intelligent account of the limited options open to rural youth.

Kuroki, who as a teenager had narrowly escaped death in an Allied bombing raid, touched in several films on the atomic bombings of Hiroshima and Nagasaki. One story in *Silence Has No Wings* concerned a young woman, born in the year of the bombing, dying from a radiation-induced illness. Among his later films, *Tomorrow* (*Ashita*, 1988) was an account of the last day in the lives of a Nagasaki family, destined to die in the bombing. It was notable for its original treatment of a well-worn theme, as was Kuroki's penultimate film, *The Face of Jizo* (*Chichi to kuraseba*, 2004), a haunting two-hander that examined the trauma of Hiroshima through the device of a series of imaginary conversations between a survivor and her late father, an A-bomb victim. Kuroki also directed two films about life on the home front during the last year of the war. The semi-autobiographical *A Boy's Summer in Kirishima* (*Utsukushii natsu Kirishima*, 2002) was a psychological study of the responses of a sensitive youth to an act of cowardice committed during an air raid. The director's last film, *The Youth of Etsuko Kamiya* (*Kamiya Etsuko no seishun*, 2006), was a odd, melancholy comedy about a young woman's meeting with the army officer her brother wants her to marry. Confined mostly to a single set, it was realized with deliberate theatricality and extreme, perhaps excessive, understatement.

The most widely circulated of Kuroki's later films was perhaps his least typical: *Roningai* (*Rōningai*, 1990), a loose remake of Masahiro Makino's famous 1929 *jidai-geki*, which deliberately mimicked the visual style of the silent *chanbara*. Though enjoyable and well crafted, this was an unusually conventional film in theme for a director whose distinction lay in his intransigent individualism.

**1958** **Electric Rolling Stock of Toshiba** (*short*)

**1959** **Kaiheki** / The Seawall (*short*)
**Arau: Okusama techō** / Washing: A Wife's Handbook (*short*)

**1960** **Ruporutāju: Honoo** / Reportage: Fire (*short*)

**1961** **Koi no hitsuji ga umi ippai** / The Seas Are Full of Sheep in Love (*short*)

1962 **Waga ai Hokkaido** / Hokkaido, My Love (*short*)
1963 **Taiyō no ito** / The Solar Thread (*short*)
1964 **Aru marason rannā no kiroku** / Record of a Marathon Runner (*short*)
1965 **Tanin no chi** / Another's Blood (*short*)
1966 **Tobenai chinmoku** / Silence Has No Wings
1968 **Isu o sagasu otoko** / Man Searching for a Chair (*short*)
1969 **Kyūba no koibito** / Cuban Lovers / Love in Cuba
1970 **Nihon no akuryō** / Evil Spirits of Japan
1974 **Ryōma ansatsu** / The Assassination of Ryoma
1975 **Matsuri no junbi** / Preparations for the Festival
1978 **Genshiryoku sensō: Lost Love** / Nuclear War (lit. Nuclear War: Lost Love)
1980 **Yūgure made** / Until Twilight
1983 **Namidabashi** / The Bridge of Tears
1988 **Ashita** / Tomorrow
1990 **Rōningai** / Roningai / Street of Masterless Samurai
2000 **Suri** / Pickpocket
2002 **Utsukushii natsu Kirishima** / A Boy's Summer in Kirishima / A Boy's Summer in 1945
2004 **Chichi to kuraseba** / The Face of Jizo (lit. Living with Father)
2006 **Kamiya Etsuko no seishun** / The Youth of Etsuko Kamiya / The Blossoming of Etsuko Kamiya

## KUROSAWA Akira
**(March 23, 1910–September 6, 1998)**
黒澤明

A filmmaker of worldwide reputation, Kurosawa served as assistant to Kajirō Yamamoto and Mikio Naruse and first directed at Toho in the fraught wartime period. The promise of his debut feature, an accomplished martial arts film with a superbly staged climax, took some years to be fulfilled. Among his forties films, *No Regrets for Our Youth* (*Waga seishun ni kui nashi*, 1946) was an interesting, if somewhat heavy-handed, account of the sufferings of the liberal middle class during the era of militarism, while *Drunken Angel* (*Yoidore tenshi*, 1948) and *Stray Dog* (*Nora inu*, 1949) were outstanding urban thrillers remarkable for their baroque visuals, psychological complexity, and compelling evocation of Occupation-era Tokyo. *Stray Dog*, about a cop's obsessive search for the criminal who stole his gun, ranks with Kurosawa's best work. International acclaim, however, came with *Rashomon* (*Rashōmon*, 1950), a striking historical parable which narrated the events leading to a murder from the conflicting perspectives of several characters. Though the film's treatment of its thematic concerns was slightly portentous, its visual splendor and structural ingenuity were justly admired.

From this film, and increasingly through the fifties, Kurosawa became a self-conscious artist with a desire to tackle grand themes: for instance, terminal illness in *Ikiru* (1952) and the threat of nuclear war in *Record of a Living Being* (*Ikimono no kiroku*, 1955). Similarly, his modern thrillers, *The Bad Sleep Well* (*Warui yatsu hodo yoku nemuru*, 1960) and *High and Low* (*Tengoku to jigoku*, 1963), focused respectively on corporate corruption and on class differences. The didacticism of Kurosawa's approach sometimes led him into stylistic overstatement, but he was skilled at anchoring his philosophical and political concerns in the concrete details of human experience. Honesty was a key

©Shochiku Company Ltd.

Hakuchi / The Idiot *(1951): An admirer of Western culture, Kurosawa based films on Shakespeare, Gorky, and, in this work, Dostoyevsky.*

theme: *Ikiru* and *Record of a Living Being* were essentially about people facing up squarely to a fact—the reality of death—which most prefer not to think about. *Rashomon*, as Robin Wood has argued, is less about the subjectivity of truth than about the need for personal integrity, in which light the much-criticized sentimental ending seems more appropriate. Equally, the social concerns of the thrillers were expressed through personal dilemmas centering on the question of how the individual can act with integrity in a corrupt world.

Kurosawa's method of approaching abstract concerns through individual experience contributed to the curious balance between involvement and distance in his films. The intensity of the acting (in particular, from Kurosawa's regular stars Toshirō Mifune and Ta-

kashi Shimura) and the baroque visuals made the impact of his work very direct: the dynamism of the action sequences in such period epics as *Seven Samurai (Shichinin no samurai*, 1954) and *The Hidden Fortress (Kakushi toride no san'akunin*, 1958) was often breathtaking, while the use of Tokyo's urban wastelands in *Stray Dog* and *The Bad Sleep Well* was hauntingly atmospheric. Yet Kurosawa's work often displayed a deliberate formalism at odds with the immediacy of the drama. The narrative experimentation of *Rashomon* was carried over to *Ikiru*, where the climax took place after the death of the hero, and to *High and Low*, where the psychological and moral emphasis of the confined first half gave way to the procedural detail of the extended climactic chase. *The Lower Depths (Donzoko*, 1957) was deliberately restricted to a single set, and seemed an investigation of how cinematic techniques could be used in a theatrical space. The formal and structural artifice of these films invited an analytical rather than an emotional response.

An admirer of Western culture, Kurosawa based several films on works by Western authors: thus *The Idiot* (*Hakuchi*, 1951) transposed Dostoyevsky to Japan's northern island of Hokkaido; *The Lower Depths* relocated Gorky's account of life among the urban poor to the shanty towns of Edo; and *High and Low* was adapted from an Ed McBain thriller. Shakespeare was also a key influence: the characterization of the doubting, prevaricating hero of *The Bad Sleep Well* owed something to *Hamlet*, and perhaps Kurosawa's masterpiece was *Throne of Blood* (*Kumonosujō*, 1957), a samurai version of *Macbeth* which essayed an ambitious fusion of Japanese and Jacobean theatrical techniques. Given this cultural affinity, it was perhaps unsurprising that Kurosawa should have become the most popular of Japanese directors in the West. *Seven Samurai*, a sweeping epic about a group of samurai training a village to defend itself against bandits, won wide praise for the brilliance of its combat scenes and for the vividly archetypal characterizations of its warrior heroes. It ultimately inspired a Hollywood remake in *The Magnificent Seven* (1960, John Sturges); Kurosawa returned the compliment by fusing samurai conventions with those of the American Western in *Yojimbo* (*Yōjinbō*, 1961) and *Sanjuro* (*Tsubaki Sanjurō*, 1962), uncharacteristically cynical films which were in turn remade as spaghetti Westerns by Sergio Leone.

The demise of the Japanese studio system made Kurosawa's position in the industry precarious, and his attempt to establish an independent production company foundered with the failure of its first film, *Dodes'kaden* (*Dodesukaden*, 1970), an eccentric, humorous variation on the themes of *The Lower Depths*. By the seventies, he found work unobtainable in Japan, and his later films were made with foreign backing. *Dersu Uzala* (1975), the story of an explorer's relationship with a local tribesman, was shot in Siberia with a Russian-speaking cast; its main distinction was the grandeur of the landscapes. In the eighties, Kurosawa directed two epic samurai films, *Kagemusha* (1980) and *Ran* (1985), the latter based on *King Lear*. These were hailed as marking a triumphant return to form, though Kurosawa's earlier urgency was lacking. Even so, *Ran* was an austerely powerful account of a nation's descent into chaos, true to Shakespeare, but rooted equally in the historical realities of medieval Japan. Kurosawa's subsequent films, however, were largely undistinguished.

Over the years, Kurosawa has had his detractors, who have found his humanism naive and judged his vigorous, montage-based technique inferior to Mizoguchi's elegant long takes. Nevertheless, if Kurosawa's images lacked the subtlety and depth of implication of Mizoguchi's, his visual flair and emotional sincerity remain undeniable. Nor can one deny Kurosawa's preeminent importance in winning an international audience for Japanese film. It is appropriate that, more than half a century after the breakthrough of *Rashomon*, his work continues to serve new generations as their introduction to its riches.

**1943  Sugata Sanshirō** / Sanshiro Sugata
**1944  Ichiban utsukushiku** / The Most Beautiful

1945 **Zoku Sugata Sanshirō** / Sanshiro Sugata II

1946 **Asu o tsukuru hitobito** / Those Who Make Tomorrow (*co-director*)

**Waga seishun ni kui nashi** / No Regrets for Our Youth

1947 **Subarashiki nichiyōbi** / One Wonderful Sunday

1948 **Yoidore tenshi** / Drunken Angel

1949 **Shizuka naru kettō** / The Quiet Duel / The Silent Duel

**Nora inu** / Stray Dog

1950 **Sukyandaru** / Scandal

**Rashōmon** / Rashomon

1951 **Hakuchi** / The Idiot

1952 **Tora no o o fumu otokotachi** / The Men Who Tread on the Tiger's Tail (*filmed in 1945*)

**Ikiru** / Ikiru / Living / To Live

1954 **Shichinin no samurai** / Seven Samurai

1955 **Ikimono no kiroku** / Record of a Living Being / I Live in Fear

1957 **Kumonosu-jō** / Throne of Blood / Cobweb Castle (lit.)

**Donzoko** / The Lower Depths

1958 **Kakushi toride no san'akunin** / The Hidden Fortress / Three Bad Men in a Hidden Fortress (lit.)

1960 **Warui yatsu hodo yoku nemuru** / The Bad Sleep Well

1961 **Yōjinbō** / Yojimbo / The Bodyguard

1962 **Tsubaki Sanjurō** / Sanjuro (lit. Sanjuro of the Camellias)

1963 **Tengoku to jigoku** / High and Low (lit. Heaven and Hell)

1965 **Akahige** / Red Beard

1970 **Dodesukaden** / Dodes'kaden

1975 **Derusu Uzāra** / Dersu Uzala

1980 **Kagemusha** / Kagemusha / The Shadow Warrior

1985 **Ran** / Ran (lit. Chaos)

1990 **Yume** / Akira Kurosawa's Dreams

1991 **Hachigatsu no rapusodī** / Rhapsody in August

1993 **Mādadayo** / Madadayo / Not Yet

## KUROSAWA Kiyoshi
### (b. July 19, 1955)
黒沢清

Of the directors who came to international prominence in the J-horror boom of the nineties, Kurosawa (no relation to Akira) is arguably the most talented and original. He has remarked that he uses genres "in order to better distance myself from them," and he displayed a certain intransigence even in his early erotic films. *Kandagawa Wars* (*Kandagawa inran sensō*, 1983) and *The Excitement of the DoReMiFa Girl* (*Doremifa musume no chi wa sawagu*, 1985) both offended their producers by concentrating less on sex than style; the latter apparently recalled the artificiality of Jean-Luc Godard. Kurosawa also quarreled with his producer, Jūzō Itami, when Itami reshot parts of his first horror film, *Sweet Home* (*Suīto Hōmu*, 1989). This cliché-ridden haunted house shocker showed few indications of future talent, but Kurosawa won decent reviews for the low-budget slasher, *The Guard from Underground* (*Jigoku no keibiin*, 1992).

In the mid-nineties, Kurosawa worked prolifically in television and on straight-to-video releases, most notably the six-film series *Suit Yourself or Shoot Yourself!* (*Katte ni shiyagere*, 1995–96), which salvaged his reputation as a reliable professional. His real breakthrough, however, came with *Cure* (*Kyua*, 1997), an original and darkly engrossing horror thriller about a cop forced to confront his own violent instincts when he investigates a series of identical but apparently unrelated murders. The violence, initiated by a hypnotist unlocking the suppressed desires of his victims, was juxtaposed with a bleakly compassionate portrait of the hero's frustrations as he cares for his mentally handicapped

©Nikkatsu Corporation

Karisuma / Charisma *(1999): Trancending genre, Kurosawa's best films have examined their themes through allegory and symbolism.*

wife, the stories being synthesized in a grimly logical conclusion.

In this film, too, Kurosawa perfected an understated style, using long takes and generally keeping the camera at a distance from his characters. The method, influenced by Kurosawa's Rikkyō University professor Shigehiko Hasumi, was also reminiscent of Shinji Sōmai, whom Kurosawa had assisted on *Terrible Couple (Tonda kappuru*, 1980). It allowed him to draw out the ambiguities of his material and to build tension without explicit shocks, relying instead on the creation of atmosphere and the exploration of disturbing themes. In Kurosawa's best horror film, *Pulse (Kairo*, 2001), students commit suicide after seeing a ghost inside their computer screens. The film's real concern, however, was the loneliness engendered by technology which discourages human contact; the use of staging in depth,

which kept characters at a distance from each other on screen, expressed this theme so subtly that the supernatural elements seemed almost superfluous. The plot, particularly in the apocalyptic climax, was almost allegorical; even more so was that of *Charisma (Karisuma*, 1999), where a stylized story about a dying forest suggested themes of individuality versus conformity and the potential for renewal. This film admirably demonstrated Kurosawa's ability to distill emotional and philosophical implications from the shapes and textures of landscape.

It is limiting to pigeonhole Kurosawa as a director of horror films. *Charisma* and the eerie, almost plotless *Barren Illusion (Ōinaru gen'ei*, 1999) were actually dystopian fantasies that kept supernatural elements to a minimum. *The Serpent's Path (Hebi no michi*, 1998) was a disturbing thriller about two vigilantes pursuing those responsible for the murders of children in snuff movies. Claustrophobically confined mainly to one warehouse, it plumbed depths of moral ambiguity as responsibility for the crime becomes unclear. *License to Live* (*Ningen gōkaku*, 1999) was a subdued drama about a young man who wakes from a ten-year coma to find his family circumstances transformed. Kurosawa's most touching film, it subtly conveyed the role of chance in shaping lives and the futility of holding onto the past. *Bright Future* (*Akarui mirai*, 2003) was a quirky, if not perfectly achieved, work, with intriguing psychosexual undercurrents, again centering on alienated youth; here, the hero's attempt to acclimatize a jellyfish to fresh water seemed a metaphor for the human ability to adapt to circumstances.

Kurosawa's focus is on human personality; his characters often suffer because they learn too much about themselves. Examples include the tormented detective of *Cure*; the students in *Pulse*, dying when they realize their own loneliness; and the hero of the unsuccessful but intriguing *Doppelgänger* (*Dopperugengā*, 2003), whose suppressed urges are enacted by his double. Against this destructive inwardness, Kurosawa sets human contact and interaction: the central love affair in *Pulse*; the relationship between the recovered patient and his friend in *License to Live*. In that film as elsewhere Kurosawa focused on an unusual relationship between men; similarly, the hero of *Bright Future* is torn between rival father figures, while in *The Serpent's Path* the vigilantes are both fathers of murdered children.

Recently, with *Loft* (*Rofuto*, 2005) and *Retribution* (*Sakebi*, 2006), Kurosawa has returned to the horror film. *Retribution* was one of his most visually enthralling films, but its plot was something of a retread of *Cure*, a fact which, coupled with the mediocrity of *Loft*, suggested that Kurosawa may have exhausted the possibilities of the genre. In fact, despite the melodramatic and fantastic aspects of his stories, his real strength is in the delineation of character. His films contain consistently rich performances, notably from Shō Aikawa and Kōji Yakusho, and were he so inclined he could doubtless work ably with domestic and intimate subject matter.

**1973** **Rokkō** / Rokko (*8mm short*)

**1975** **Bōryoku kyōshi: Hakuchū daisatsuriku** / Teacher of Violence: Massacre in Broad Daylight (*8mm short*)

**1976** **Fukakutei ryokōki** / Record of Indefinite Travel (*8mm short*)

**Shingō chikachika** / The Flashing Signal (*8mm short*)

**1977** **Shiroi hada ni kuruu kiba** / Fangs Crazy for White Skin (*8mm short*)

**1978** **School Days** (*8mm*)

**1980** **Shigarami gakuen** / Vertigo College (*8mm*)

**1982** **Tōsō zen'ya** / The Night Before the Escape (*8mm short; co-director*)

**1983** **Kandagawa inran sensō** / Kandagawa Wars

**Ningensei no kejime** / Human Nature: The Line between Right and Wrong (*8mm short; co-director*)

**1985** **Doremifa musume no chi wa sawagu** / The Excitement of the Do-Re-Mi-Fa Girl / Bumpkin Soup

**1988** **Fuyuko no omokage** / Girl! Girl! Girl! (*8mm short*)

**1989** **Suīto hōmu** / Sweet Home

**Abunai hanashi** / Dangerous Stories (*co-director*)

**1992** **Jigoku no keibiin** / The Guard from Underground

**1995** **Katte ni shiyagare!!: Gōdatsu keikaku** / Suit Yourself or Shoot Yourself!: The Heist

Katte ni shiyagare!!: Datsugoku keikaku / Suit Yourself or Shoot Yourself! 2: The Escape

1996 **Katte ni shiyagare!!: Ōgon keikaku** / Suit Yourself or Shoot Yourself! 3: The Loot

**Katte ni shiyagare!!: Gyakuten keikaku** / Suit Yourself or Shoot Yourself! 4: The Gamble

**Door III**

**Katte ni shiyagare!!: Narikin keikaku** / Suit Yourself or Shoot Yourself! 5: The Nouveau Riche

**Katte ni shiyagare!!: Eiyū keikaku** / Suit Yourself or Shoot Yourself! 6: The Hero

1997 **Fukushū: Unmei no hōmonsha** / The Revenge: A Visit from Fate

**Fukushū: Kienai kizu** / The Revenge: The Scar That Never Fades

**Kyua** / Cure

1998 **Hebi no michi** / The Serpent's Path

**Kumo no hitomi** / Eyes of the Spider

1999 **Ningen gōkaku** / License to Live

**Ōinaru gen'ei** / Barren Illusion

**Karisuma** / Charisma

2001 **Kairo** / Pulse

**Kōrei** / Séance

2003 **Deka matsuri** / Cop Festival (*co-director*)

**Akarui mirai** / Bright Future

**Dopperugengā** / Doppelgänger

2005 **Umezu Kazuo: Kyōfu gekijō: Mushitachi no ie** / Kazuo Umezu's Horror Theater: Bug's House

**Rofuto** / Loft

2006 **Sakebi** / Retribution (lit. Cry)

## MAKINO Masahiro
(February 29, 1908–October 29, 1993)
マキノ雅弘

The son of Shōzō Makino, Masahiro first directed at the age of 18 for his father's company, initiating a productive career in which he was to make 261 films. Specializing in *jidai-geki*, he first achieved critical esteem during the silent era with two downbeat samurai films. *Beheading Place* (*Kubi no za*, 1929) told the story of a ronin falsely accused of a crime and unable to convince others of his innocence. The three-part *Street of Masterless Samurai* (*Rōningai*, 1928-29) was an epic account of a group of unemployed samurai in Edo; a surviving hour-long fragment illustrates its deglamorized portrait of Tokugawa-period low life, with a strong stress on the tedium of everyday experience.

Makino continued to work on period films throughout the thirties; it appears that these were generally in a rather more conventional mode, dramatizing famous historical incidents and the lives of folk heroes, and working with such genre stars as Tsumasaburō Bandō. Some of them, such as the engagingly lightweight *Duel at Takadanobaba* (*Chikemuri Takadanobaba*, 1937) and the samurai musical *Singing Lovebirds* (*Oshidori uta gassen*, 1939), brought a comic inflection to their handling of generic motifs. Makino made more eccentric use of a period setting in another humorous *jidai-geki*, *The Man Who Disappeared Yesterday* (*Kinō kieta otoko*, 1941), a well-cast murder mystery which transposed the plot of the American comic thriller *The Thin Man* (1934, W.S. Van Dyke) to the tenements of Edo. In the era of militarism, even before Pearl Harbor, such borrowings from Hollywood surprise; still more extraordinary was *The Opium War* (*Ahen sensō*, 1943), which relocated the story of D.W. Griffith's *Orphans of the Storm* (1922) from Revolutionary France to nineteenth-century Canton. Setsuko Hara and Hideko Takamine played the suffering sisters acted in the original by Lillian and Dorothy Gish, but despite their talents and the spectacular effects, the film proved a broadly caricatured account of British imperialism in China, aiming to promote notions of pan-Asian brotherhood. A more straightforward propaganda piece was *Sinking the Unsinkable Battleship* (*Fuchinkan gekichin*, 1944), about an engineer inspiring factory workers to meet a tough new quota.

Immediately after the war, with *jidai-geki* officially discouraged by the Occupation authorities, Makino made a number of socially conscious films, including *Gate of Flesh* (*Nikutai no mon*, 1948), apparently a dour, realist version of a Taijirō Tamura novel about prostitution later to be reworked in a stylized exploitation format by Seijun Suzuki. From the fifties, however, Makino returned to period subjects, directing program pictures, mainly at Toei, with efficiency and flair. Although these tended to be relatively conventional in plotting, they often focused interestingly on character and psychology. For instance, in *Vendetta at Sozenji Temple* (*Adauchi Sōzen-ji baba*, 1957), the hero, having killed an enemy, is pursued by the dead man's brothers; saved by the intervention of a mob but feeling that he has betrayed the codes of bushidō, he descends into madness. *Princess Sen and Hideyori* (*Senhime to Hideyori*, 1962) dramatized the embitterment of the princess whose happiness is dashed when her Tokugawa father and grandfather engineer her husband's death. Admittedly, the psychological complexities of these films were more a consequence of the talents of Makino's actors than of his proficient but shallow direction. Nonetheless, his expert choreography sometimes brought a haunting intensity

to the climaxes: witness the power of the *Tale of Two Cities*-like twist in *Echo of Love* (*Koi yamabiko*, 1959), where the hero's life is saved by the double who dies in his stead.

In the sixties, Makino became associated with the burgeoning *ninkyō-eiga* genre, realizing numerous films set among the mythically chivalrous yakuza of the Meiji to early Showa periods. Among these were many contributions to the *Japanese Yakuza* (*Nihon kyōkakuden*) series, starring a young Ken Takakura. Makino's last film, *Red Cherry Blossom Family of Kanto* (*Kantō hizakura ikka*, 1972), was made to commemorate the retirement of *Red Peony Gambler* (*Hibotan bakuto*) star Junko Fuji; featuring an all-star cast, it was filmed in an appropriately old-fashioned style. Although Makino's work was neither particularly original nor particularly profound, its unobtrusive expertise serves to illustrate the genius of the system.

1926 **Aoi me no ningyō** / The Doll with Blue Eyes
1927 **Nazo no ichiya** / One Mysterious Night
 **Shūkan kugyō** / Week of Penance
 **Gakusei gonin otoko: Ranman hen** / Five Male Students: Innocence Chapter
 **Gakusei gonin otoko: Ankoku hen** / Five Male Students: Darkness Chapter
 **Kagiana** / Keyhole
 **Gakusei gonin otoko: Hiyaku hen** / Five Male Students: Great Step Forward Chapter
 **Seishun o suritorareta hanashi** / Story of Stolen Youth
 **Yōfu** / The Temptress
 **Hachishōnin** / Eight Smiling People
1928 **Itoshiki kare** / A Beloved Man
 **Moyuru kahen** / The Burning Petal

**Adauchi junjō roku** / A Story of Heartfelt Revenge
**Kanja** / The Spy
**Keaidori** / Fighting Cocks
**Dokubana** / Poison Flower
**Rōningai: Daiichiwa: Utsukushiki emono** / Street of Masterless Samurai: Story 1: Beautiful Prey
**Sōzen-ji baba** / The Stable at Sozen-ji Temple

1929 **Rōningai: Dainiwa: Gakuyaburo daiippen** / Street of Masterless Samurai: Story 2: The Dressing Room Bath, Part 1
**Rōningai: Dainiwa: Gakuyaburo kanketsu hen** / Street of Masterless Samurai: Story 2: The Dressing Room Bath, Conclusion
**Yajikita: Daisanpen** / Yaji and Kita: Part 3
**Modoribashi** / The Modori Bridge
**Kubi no za** / Beheading Place
**Araki Mataemon** / Mataemon Araki
**Rōningai: Daisanwa: Tsukareta hitobito** / Street of Masterless Samurai: Story 3: The Possessed

1930 **Unmei senjō ni odoru hitobito** / People Who Dance on the Fate Line
**Nisekon shinkon** / False Marriage, True Marriage
**Gakusei sandaiki: Meiji jidai** / Record of Three Generations of Students: Meiji Era
**Gakusei sandaiki: Shōwa jidai** / Record of Three Generations of Students: Showa Era
**Eijigoroshi** / Killing the Newborn
**Hara no tatsu Chūshingura** / The Furious 47 Ronin
**Kōtō ichidai onna** / The Life of a Woman with a Red Light
**Kyōen sannin onna** / Three Temptresses

1931 **Bakumatsu fūunki** / Record of Affairs at the End of the Shogunate
**Pinkoro Chōji** / "Charmed Life" Choji

**Dorodarake no tenshi** / Mud-Spattered Angel
**Rōnin Taiheiki** / The Ronin's Taiheiki

1932 **Shichinin no hanayome** / Seven Brides
**Heijūrō koban** / Heijuro's Money
**Byakuya no kyōen** / Banquet of the Midnight Sun
**Nibante Akō rōshi** / The Second Account of the Ako Wariors
**Reimei** / Dawn

1933 **Moyuru kahen** / The Burning Petal

1934 **Iwami Jūtarō** / Jutaro Iwami
**Sakura ondo** / Sakura Dance
**Shura hototogisu: Zenpen** / Cuckoo of Hell: Part 1 (*co-director*)
**Awadatsu bīru** / Foaming Beer

1935 **Narihira kozō: Harugasumi happyakuyachō** / Narihira the Kid: Spring Haze in Edo
**Katsujinken: Araki Mataemon** / The Swordman Mataemon Araki
**Edo banashi Nezumi kozō** / Story of the Ratkid in Edo

1936 **Hana no haru Tōyamazakura** / Young Toyama Kinsan (lit. Toyama Kinsan of the Spring Flowers) (*co-director*)
**Saigo no doyōbi** / The Last Saturday
**Shiranami gonin otoko** / Five Men of the White Waves
**Kunisada Chūji: Shinshū komoriuta** / Chuji Kunisada: Shinshu Lullaby
**Tange Sazen: Kan'un hissatsu no maki** / Sazen Tange: Killing under the Clouds of Heaven
**Tange Sazen: Konryū jubaku no maki** / Sazen Tange: Curse of the Female Dragon
**Renbo no kinuta** / Love Play
**Jirochō hadaka tabi** / The Naked Journey of Jirocho
**Sange kenpō** / Sange's Swordsmanship

**Kaga Miyama** / Miyama in Kaga
**Yatarōgasa** / Yataro's Sedge Hat
**Hiragana ren'aichō** / Notes in
Hiragana on Love
**Edo no hana oshō** / Flower-Monk
of Edo
**Shura hakkō (Daiippen;
Dainihen; Daisanpen)** / The Pains
of Hell (Parts 1, 2, and 3)
**Shibahama no kawazaifu** / Leather
Wallet on Shiba Beach
**Hasshu kyōkakujin** / The
Chivalrous Men of Japan
**Kaitō kagebōshi** / A Thief in the
Shadows
**Goronbogai** / Street of Ruffians
**Kenka daimyōjin** / The Fighting
God
**Nagaregumo sandogasa** / Drifting
Clouds and a Low-Brimmed Hat
**Chūji kesshōki** / Record of Chuji's
Bloody Smile
**Ninjutsu mōjūkoku tanken** / A
Ninja Explores the Land of Beasts
**Maiōgi** / Fan Dance
**Kessen kōjin'yama** / The Battle of
the Sacred Mountain
**Chūretsu nikudan sanyūshi** / The
Loyal Human Bullet: Three Heroes
**Chūji kassatsuken** / Chuji's Fatal
Sword
**Akagaki Genzō tokkuri no wakare**
/ Genzo Akagaki's Farewell Toast
**Hatsutobi yagura ondo** / The
Steeplejack's New Year Dance
1937 **Yōjutsu shiranui henge** /
Supernatural Change of Sea Fire
**Seishun gonin otoko (Zenpen;
Kōhen)** / Five Young Men (Parts 1
and 2)
**Onna Sazen: Daiippen: Yōka no
maki** / A Female Sazen: Part 1:
Bewitching Fire
**Kenka bosatsu** / The Fighting
Bodhisattva
**Maken** / Demon Sword
**Hanamuko hyakumangoku** / A
Million-koku Bridegroom

**Koi yamabiko** / Echo of Love /
Shamisen Royale
**Yūkyō Taiheiki** / The Gentleman's
Taiheiki
**Dotō** / The Angry Waves
**Yōkiden** / Legend of Enchanted
Shogi
**Kunisada Chūji** / Chuji Kunisada
**Edo no arawashi** / Wild Eagle of
Edo
**Chikemuri Takadanobaba** / Duel
at Takadanobaba / Blood Spilled at
Takadanobaba (lit.) (*co-director*)
**Jiraiya**
1938 **Edo no hanaoshō** / Edo Flower
Monk
**Oshidori dōchū** / Traveling
Lovebirds
**Kurama Tengu: Kakubei jishi no
maki** / Kurama Tengu: Kakubei the
Lion (*co-director*)
**Chūshingura: Ten no maki** / The
Loyal 47 Ronin: Heavenly Reel
**Chūji komoriuta** / Chuji's Lullaby
**Shinsengumi**
**Moyuru reimei** / Flaming Dawn
**Yajikita dōchūki** / Yaji and Kita on
the Road
1939 **Ukina kōji** / Bad Reception on a
Narrow Road
**Kesa to Moritō** / Kesa and Morito
(*co-director*)
**Edo no akutarō** / Bad Guy of Edo
**Rōningai** / Street of Masterless
Samurai
**Shimizu minato** / Shimizu Harbor
**Oshidori uta gassen** / Singing
Lovebirds / A Friendly Singing
Contest / Samurai Musical
1940 **Yajikita: Meikun hatsunobori** /
Yaji and Kita: A Clever Guy's First
Visit to the City
**Zoku Shimizu minato** / Shimizu
Harbor 2
**Oda Nobunaga** / Nobunaga Oda
1941 **Kinō kieta otoko** / The Man Who
Disappeared Yesterday
**Hasegawa Roppa no Iemitsu to**

Hikoza / Hasegawa and Roppa as Shogun Iemitsu and His Mentor Hikozaemon

Awa no odoriko / A Dancing Girl of Awa

Seiki wa warau / The Century Laughs

Otoko no hanamichi / A Man's Triumph

1942 Matteita otoko / The Man Who Was Waiting

Onna keizu / Genealogy of Women

Zoku onna keizu / Genealogy of Women 2

1943 Ahen sensō / The Opium War

Hanako-san / Miss Hanako

Konjinchō / Notes on Fundraising for a Buddhist Statue

1944 Fuchinkan gekichin / Sinking the Unsinkable Battleship

Yasen gungakutai / Military Combat Band

1945 Hisshōka / Victory Song (co-director)

Sennichimae fukin / The Neighborhood of Sennichimae

1946 Gurandoshō 1946-nen / Grand Show of 1946

Ikina fūraibō / The Sophisticated Wanderer

Machibōke no onna / A Woman Kept Waiting

Nonkina tōsan / Carefree Father

Mangetsu-jō no uta gassen / Singing Contest at Full Moon Castle

1947 Hijōsen / Cordon of Police

Shukujo to sākasu / The Lady and the Circus

Yukaina nakama / Funny Friend

1948 Konjiki yasha (Zenpen; Kōhen) / The Golden Demon (Parts 1 and 2)

Nikutai no mon / Gate of Flesh

Yūrei akatsuki ni shisu / The Ghost Died at Dawn

1949 Bosu / Boss

Bangoku Edo e iku / Bangoku Goes to Edo

Saheiji torimonochō: Murasaki zukin (Zenpen; Kaiketsu hen) / Saheiji's Casebooks: The Purple Hood (Parts 1 and 2)

1950 Kizudarake no otoko / The Scarred Man

Kumagai jin'ya / Kumagai Camp

Terakoya / Temple Elementary School

Tateshi Danpei / Fencing Master

Re Mizeraburu: Ā mujō: Dainibu: Ai to jiyū no hata / Les Misérables: Ah, Merciless: Part 2: Flag of Love and Liberty

Sengoku matoi / A Thousand Standards of Stone

1951 Nyozoku to hankan / The Lady Thief and the Judge

Otsuya goroshi / The Killing of Otsuya

Gōkai sannin otoko / Three Heroic Men

Ginjirō tabi nikki / Ginjiro's Travel Diary

Yoidore hachimanki / A Horde of Drunken Knights

1952 Okaru Kanpei / Okaru and Kanpei

Ukigumo nikki / Diary of Floating Clouds

Yaguradaiko / Drumbeat

Rikon / Divorce

Suttobi kago / The Hurrying Palanquin

Musashi to Kojirō / Musashi and Kojiro

Yatarōgasa (Zenpen; Kōhen) / Yataro's Sedge Hat (Parts 1 and 2)

Jirochō sangokushi / Jirocho's Tale of Three Provinces

1953 Hawai no yoru / A Night in Hawaii

Jirochō sangokushi: Dainibu: Hatsutabi / Jirocho's Tale of Three Provinces: Part 2: First Journey

Hōyō / Last Embrace

Jirochō sangokushi: Daisanbu: Jirochō to Ishimatsu / Jirocho's Tale of Three Provinces: Part 3: Jirocho and Ishimatsu

Jirochō sangokushi: Daiyonbu:
Seizoroi Shimizu minato /
Jirocho's Tale of Three Provinces:
Part 4: All Gathered at Shimizu
Harbor
Tange Sazen / Sazen Tange
Zoku Tange Sazen / Sazen Tange 2
Jirochō sangokushi: Daigobu:
Nagurikomi Kōshūji / Jirocho's
Tale of Three Provinces: Part 5:
Violence on the Koshu Road
Jirochō sangokushi: Dairokubu:
Tabigarasu Jirochō ikka / Jirocho's
Tale of Three Provinces: Part 6:
Jirocho's Family of Wanderers
1954 Jirochō sangokushi: Daishichibu:
Hatsuiwai Shimizu minato /
Jirocho's Tale of Three Provinces:
Part 7: First Celebration at Shimizu
Harbor
Utsukushiki taka / The Beautiful
Hawk
Gohiiki rokkasen: Suttobi otoko
/ Six Favorite Songs: The Man in a
Hurry
Jirochō sangokushi: Daihachibu:
Kaidō ichi no abarenbō / Jirocho's
Tale of Three Provinces: Part 8:
The Most Violent Man on the Road
Yakuza bayashi / Yakuza Festival
Music
Jirochō sangokushi: Daikyūbu:
Kōjin'yama / Jirocho's Tale of
Three Provinces: Part 9: The Holy
Mountain
Konomura Daikichi / Daikichi
Konomura
1955 Jirochō yūkyōden: Akiba no
himatsuri / Chronicle of Jirocho
the Gambler: Akiba Fire Festival
Ningyō Sashichi torimonochō:
Mekura ōkami / Casebooks of
Dandy Sashichi: The Blind Wolf
Jirochō yūkyōden: Amagi karasu
/ Chronicle of Jirocho the Gambler:
Crow of Amagi
Ryanko no Yatarō / Tough Guy
Yataro
Akagi no chimatsuri / Blood
Festival of Akagi

Jinsei tonbogaeri / Life Is a
Somersault
1956 Tange Sazen: Kan'un no maki /
Sazen Tange: Heavenly Clouds Reel
Asayake kessenjō / Decisive Battle
at Sunrise
Tange Sazen: Konryū no maki /
Sazen Tange: Earthly Dragon Reel
Tange Sazen: Daisanbu: Shōryū
no maki / Sazen Tange: Part 3:
Rising Dragon Reel
Kyōfu no tōbō / Fearful Escape
Tōyama no Kinsan
torimonohikae: Kage ni ita otoko
/ Casebooks of Toyoma Kinsan:
Man in the Shadows
1957 Junjō butai / Pure-Hearted Unit
Rōningai / Street of Masterless
Samurai
Adauchi Sōzen-ji baba / Vendetta
at Sozenji Temple (lit. Vendetta at
Sozenji Track)
Awa odori: Naruto no kaizoku /
Awa Dance: Pirates of Naruto
Ippongatana dohyōiri / Into the
Sumo Ring with a Sword
1958 Oshidori kago / Lovebirds'
Palanquin / A Bullseye for Love
Hijōsen / Cordon of Police
Futeki naru hankō / Fearless
Opposition
Shimizu minato no meibutsu
otoko: Enshū Mori no Ishimatsu /
A Famous Man of Shimizu Harbor:
Ishimatsu of the Forest of Enshu
Province
Suteuri Kanbei / A Rough and
Love (lit. Kanbei's Bargain Sale)
Kenkagasa / Fighting Hat /
Traveling Rough
1959 Kurama Tengu / Kurama Tengu /
Black-Masked Reformer
Tatsumaki bugyō / The Tornado
Magistrate / Vanished Gold Case
Koi yamabiko / Echo of Love
Edo no akutarō / Bad Guy of Edo
Yukinojō henge / An Actor's
Revenge / The Avenging Ghost of
Yukinojo (lit.)

1960 **Yatarōgasa** / Yataro's Sedge Hat
**Tenpō rokkasen: Jigoku no hanamichi** / Six Great Men of the Tenpo Era: Pathway to Hell
**Shimizu minato ni kita otoko** / The Man Who Came to Shimizu Harbor
**Kanda matsuri: Kenkagasa** / Kanda Festival: Fighting Hat
**Wakaki hi no Jirochō: Tōkai no kaoyaku** / Jirocho's Days of Youth: Boss of the Tokai Region

1961 **Edokko hada** / The Nature of the Edoite
**Tsukigata Hanpeita** / Hanpeita Tsukigata
**Wakaki hi no Jirochō: Tōkai ichi no wakaoyabun** / Jirocho's Days of Youth: The Youngest Boss in the Tokai Region
**Edokko hanshōki** / Record of a Prosperous Edoite
**Minato matsuri ni kita otoko** / The Man Who Came to the Harbor Festival

1962 **Wakaki hi no Jirochō: Tōkaidō no tsumujikaze** / Jirocho's Days of Youth: Whirlwind on the Tokaido
**Senhime to Hideyori** / Princess Sen and Hideyori
**Hashizō no yakuza hankan** / Hashizo the Unlawful Judge
**Jirochō to kotengu: Nagurikomi Kōshūji** / Jirocho and the Small Goblin: Violence on the Koshu Road

1963 **Ōabare gojūsantsugi** / Great Violence on the Tokaido
**Irezumi Hantarō** / Tattooed Hantaro
**Hasshū yūkyōden: Otoko no sakazuki** / Chronicle of a Japanese Gambler: A Man's Sake Cup
**Kyū-chan katana o nuite** / Kyu-chan Draws His Sword
**Jirochō sangokushi** / Jirocho's Tale of Three Provinces
**Zoku Jirochō sangokushi** / Jirocho's Tale of Three Provinces: Part 2

1964 **Jirochō sangokushi: Daisanbu** / Jirocho's Tale of Three Provinces: Part 3
**Nihon kyōkakuden** / Japanese Yakuza / A Story of Japanese Yakuza / An Account of the Chivalrous Commoners of Japan / Chivalrous Chronicles of Japan (lit.)

1965 **Nihon kyōkakuden: Naniwa hen** / Japanese Yakuza: Osaka Chapter
**Irogotoshi Harudanji** / Amorous Harudanji
**Chōchō Yūji no meoto zenzai** / Chocho and Yuji's Marital Relations
**Nihon kyōkakuden: Kantō hen** / Japanese Yakuza: Kanto Chapter
**Jirochō sangokushi: Kōshūji nagurikomi** / Jirocho's Tale of Three Provinces: Violence on the Koshu Road
**Ninkyō otoko ippiki** / One Chivalrous Man

1966 **Kettō Kanda matsuri** / Bloody Festival at Kanda
**Nihon daikyōkaku** / Great Chivalry of Japan
**Nihon kyōkakuden: Raimon no kettō** / Japanese Yakuza: Fight at Thunder Gate
**Otoko no kao wa kirifuda** / A Man's Face Is His Trump Card

1967 **Nihon kyōkakuden: Shiraha no sakazuki** / Japanese Yakuza: Sake Cup and Drawn Sword
**Shōwa zankyōden: Chizome no karajishi** / Tales of Showa Era Chivalry: Bloodstained Lion Tattoo
**Nihon kyōkakuden: Kirikomi** / Japanese Yakuza: Deep Cut
**Kyōkotsu ichidai** / The Chivalrous Life

1968 **Nihon kyōkakuden: Zetsuenjō** / Japanese Yakuza: Note of Farewell
**Kyōkaku retsuden** / Biographies of Chivalrous Men
**Gorotsuki** / The Rogue

**Shin Abashiri bangaichi** / New
Abashiri Prison

1969 **Shōwa zankyōden: Karajishi jingi**
/ Tales of Showa Era Chivalry: The
Lion's Honor / The Man With the
Dragon Tattoo

**Nihon kyōkakuden: Hana to Ryū**
/ Japanese Yakuza: The Flower and
the Dragon

**Nihon zankyōden** / Tales of
Remnants of Japanese Chivalry

**Akumyō ichiban shōbu** / Battle to
be the No. 1 Bad Guy

1970 **Onna kumichō** / Woman Boss

**Botan to ryū** / Peony and Dragon

**Genkai yūkyōden: Yabure kabure**
/ Chivalrous Chronicle of Fukuoka:
Desperation

**Shōwa zankyōden: Shinde
moraimasu** / Tales of Showa Era
Chivalry: I Accept Your Life / Hell
Is Man's Destiny

1971 **Nihon yakuza den: Sōchō e no
michi** / The Path of the King (lit.
Chronicle of Japanese Yakuza: The
Way to the Top)

1972 **Kantō hizakura ikka** / Red Cherry
Blossom Family of Kanto

# MAKINO Shōzō
## (September 22, 1878–July 25, 1929)
牧野省三

Often called the "father of Japanese cinema," Makino directed films from 1908. The bulk of his early work consisted of one-reelers, turned out at a rate of one every three days. From 1909, at Nikkatsu, he collaborated with Matsunosuke Onoe, considered Japan's first film star, on films derived from Kabuki or popular *kōdan* narratives. Rather than working from a script, Makino apparently recited lines to his actors while the camera was rolling, in a declamatory style known as *kuchidate*.

In common with almost all Japanese cinema of that date, the bulk of his work from the teens has been lost, although an important compilation of his early *Chūshingura* films is extant. It appears that Makino's work was stylistically conservative, its technique barely changing through most of his career. The evidence of a rare surviving film such as *Heroic Thunder Boy* (*Gōketsu Jiraiya*, 1921) demonstrates that in the early twenties he was still staging entire scenes in single, static shots and placing the camera at a sufficient distance to record the entire setting in one composition. This contrasts with the extremely sophisticated use of editing in Minoru Murata's exactly contemporary film, *Souls on the Road* (*Rojō no reikon*, 1921). Nevertheless, it may be argued that Makino's persistent use of long takes and long shot marked an early stage in the evolution of a specifically Japanese style which would reach its zenith in the creative use of sequence shots and camera distance by directors such as Kenji Mizoguchi and Hiroshi Shimizu during the thirties.

In any case, the stylistic archaism of Makino's early films may have been due to Onoe's sceptical attitude to new techniques. Makino's subsequent work with the younger period film star Tsumasaburō Bandō seems to have grown gradually more advanced; the extant *Mystery of a Million Ryo* (*Hyakumanryō hibun*, 1927) shows that by that date he was making use of rapid cutting, close-ups, and camera movements. Furthermore, Makino's own production company, founded in 1921, was responsible for some of the more innovative *jidai-geki* of the twenties. By the early Showa period, nevertheless, his work as director had been surpassed by that of younger filmmakers such as

Courtesy of the Kawakita Memorial Film Institute

Chūshingura / The Loyal 47 Ronin *(1914): The father of Japanese cinema narrates one of the earliest versions of Japan's most potent legends.*

Daisuke Itō and his own son, Masahiro Makino, who made *Street of Masterless Samurai (Rōningai*, 1928–29) for his father's company. Makino, Sr. celebrated his fiftieth birthday with his last version of the *Chūshingura* story, *The True Story of Loyal Retainers (Chūkon giretsu: Jitsuroku Chūshingura*, 1928), released not long before his death.

1908 **Honnō-ji gassen (Taikōki no Honnō-ji)** / Battle at Honnō-ji Temple (Honnō-ji from the Chronicle of Hideyoshi)

1909 **Sugawara denju tenarai kagami (Sugawara tenjinki)** / Model for the Initiation of Sugawara (Record of the Divine Sugawara)

**Akegarasu yume no awayuki /** The Pale Crow: Dream of a Light Snowfall

**Kojima Takanori homare no sakura** / Takanori Kojima's Glorious Cherry Tree

**Adachigahara sandanme sodehagi saibun no jō (Ōshū Adachigahara)**

/ Adachigahara: Third Scene: Sleeves and Bush Clover: Scene of the Song to the Gods (Adachigahara in the North Country)

**Goban chūshin Genji: Ishizue** / Faithful Genji of the Go Board: Foundation Stone

1910 **Ishiyama gunki** / War Chronicle of Ishiyama

**Sanjūsangen-dō tōyurai** / The Origins of Sanjusangen-do

**Chūshingura** / The Loyal 47 Ronin

1911 **Yamanaka Shikanosuke /** Shikanosuke Yamanaka

**Akita giminden** / Chronicle of a Public-Spirited Man of Akita

**Iwami Jūtarō** / Jutaro Iwami

**Sekiguchi Yatarō** / Yataro of Sekiguchi

**Shimizu no Jirochō** / Jirocho of Shimizu

**Ieyasu-kō (Tokugawa eitatsu monogatari)** / Lord Ieyasu (Story of the Rise of the Tokugawa)

**Katakiuchi Sōzen-ji baba /** Vendetta at Sozen-ji Temple Track

**1912** Chūshingura / The Loyal 47 Ronin

Shiobara Tasuke no ichidaiki / Record of the Life of Tasuke Shiobara

Sano Jirōzaemon / Jirozaemon Sano

Kyūbi no kitsune / The Fox of Kyubi

Yotsuya kaidan / The Yotsuya Ghost Story

Nogi shōgun to shōgai / Life and General Nogi

Chūshingura / The Loyal 47 Ronin

Hanagasa Bunshichi / Flower-Hat Bunshichi

Yodoya Tatsugorō / Tatsugoro of Yodoya

Akushichibei Kagekiyo / Kagekiyo Akushichibei

Shin Nihon (Kondō Jūzō) / The New Japan (Juzo Kondo)

Ryūjin Otama / The Dragon God Otama

Oni no Umekichi / The Demon Umekichi

Shunkan ichidaiki / Record of the Life of Shunkan

Shōki no Hanbei / Hanbei the Plague Fighter

Benkei no ichidaiki / Record of the Life of Benkei

**1913** Hakkenden / Legend of Eight Samurai

Tanuma sōdō / Strife at Tanuma

Shaka hassōki / Record of Eight Phases in the Life of Buddha

Mikazuki Jirokichi (Zenpen; Kōhen) / Jirokichi under the Crescent Moon (Parts 1 and 2)

Kanzaki Yogorō / Yogoro of Kanzaki

Yanagisawa sōdō / Strife at Yanagisawa

Matsumaeya Gorobei / Gorobei of the Matsumaeya

Iwami Jūtarō ichidaiki / Record of the Life of Jutaro Iwami

Karainu Gonbei / Gonbei the Foreign Dog

Araki Mataemon / Mataemon Araki

Kawanakajima

Sarashina Otama / Otama of Sarashina

Daianji tsutsumi / Daianji Riverbank

Katayama Manzō / Manzo Katayama

Chōshi no Gorōzō / Gorozo the Drunkard

Sanada man'yūki / Sanada Pleasure Trip

Sakuragi Ochō / Ocho Sakuragi

Sakura Sōgorō / Sogoro of Sakura

Kaminari Yoshigorō / "Thunder" Yoshigoro

Ōishi Kuranosuke ichidaiki / Record of the Life of Kuranosuke Oishi

Araoni Shinpachi / Shinpachi the Wild Devil

Fuwa Kazuemon / Kazuemon Fuwa

Musume taihai daimyō Ohatsu / The Girl Gives the Cup to Ohatsu and the Daimyo

Shashin no adauchi / Revenge on Film

Izutsu Menosuke / Menosuke Izutsu

Mongaku Shōnin ichidaiki / The Life of Mongaku the Saint

Murakumo Ohide / Ohide of Murakumo

Ōkubo tenka man'yūki / Okubo and the Shogun's Pleasure Trip

Asahi Gongorō / Gongoro of the Dawn

Yui to Marubashi / Yui and Marubashi

Owari Kunimaru / Kunimaru Owari

Tokugawa Ten'ichibō / Ten'ichibo Tokugawa

Yakko no Ohatsu / Ohatsu the Servant

Date daihyōjō / Date's Great Consultation

Sakura Sōgorō (Sakura Sōgo) / Sogoro (Sogo) Sakura

Genkotsu no Yūzō (Jōhen; Gehen) / Yuzo the Fistfighter (Parts 1 and 2)

Zeniya Gohei / Gohei the Moneychanger

Akao no Rinzō / Rinzo of Akao

Yūdachi Kangorō / Kangoro Yudachi

Tsurugi no Denji / Denji of the Sword

Zōho Chūshingura / The Loyal 47 Ronin, Expanded Version

Yoshiwara kaidan Kozakura Chōji / Yoshiwara Ghost Story: Choji of the Kozakura

Buyūden Amako jūyūshi / Tale of Martial Arts: Ten Heroes of Amako

Tokugawa Yoshinobu-kō ichidaiki / Record of the Life of Lord Yoshinobu Tokugawa

Sannin Kichizō (Sannin Okichi) / Three People Named Kichizo (Three People Named Okichi)

Sagamasa (Sagamiya Masagorō ichidaiki) / Sagamasa (Record of the Life of Masagoro Sagamiya)

Ii Tairō to Mito Rekkō / Minister Ii and Lord Mito

Kachū no Oyuki / Oyuki in the Flames

Ōmi no Okane / Okane of Omi

Nochi no hakkenden / A Later Legend of Eight Samurai

Bishamon Otatsu / Otatsu of Bishamon

Saga sanyūshi (Yamanaka Shikanosuke) / Three Heroes of Saga (Shikanosuke Yamanaka)

Mikazuki Tokuji / Tokuji under a Crescent Moon

Jōrurizaka no adauchi / Revenge at Jorurizaka

Tengu Tarō / Taro the Goblin

Hanaregoma Gonpachi / Gonpachi of Hanaregoma

Horibe Yasubei (Horibe Yasubei monogatari) / Yasubei Horibe (Story of Yasubei Horibe)

Akechi Mitsuhide / Mitsuhide Akechi

Kimura Nagatonokami / Nagatonokami Kimura

Kizu Kansuke / Kansuke Kizu

Yoritomo kozō / Yoritomo the Boy

Motojime Kangorō / Kangoro the Manager

Taishō sanyūshi / Three Heroes of the Taisho Era

1914 Katakiuchi Takadanobaba / Revenge at Takadanobaba

Kyōkaku Yoritomo kozō / The Chivalrous Boy Yoritomo

Tsuchigumo / Earth Spider

Ogasawara kitsune (Ogasawara sōdō) / The Ogasawara Fox (The Ogasawara Affair)

Arima Gennosuke / Gennosuke Arima

Kuriyama Daizen / Daizen Kuriyama

Ban no Tarō: Isshin Tasuke yōkai taiji (Yōkai taiji) / Taro of Ban: Tasuke Isshin Exterminates Ghosts (Extermination of Ghosts)

Hanagasa Bunshichi / Flower-Hat Bunshichi

Jiraiya

Kogitsune Reizō / Reizo the Fox Cub

Sakamoto Ryōma / Ryoma Sakamoto

Kume no Heinai / Heinai of Kume

Utsunomiya tsuritenjō / The Ceiling at Utsunomiya

Onna junrei (Musume junrei) / A Woman's Pilgrimage (A Girl's Pilgrimage)

Tenjiku Tokubei / "Indian" Tokubei

**Batō Matagorō** / Matagoro the Horse-Headed

**Miyamoto Musashi** / Musashi Miyamoto

**Sasano Gonzaburō** / Gonzaburo Sasano

**Kōchiyama Sōshun** / Kochiyama Soshun

**Furisode bikuni** / The Priestess in the Long-Sleeved Kimono

**Okazaki no neko** / The Cat of Okazaki

**Oguri hankan** / Magistrate Oguri

**Heikegani** / The Heike Crab

**Ōshio Heihachirō** / Heihachiro Oshio

**Akechi Samanosuke** / Samanosuke Akechi

**Yoshiwara kaidan teburi bōzu** / Yoshiwara Ghost Story: Gestures of the Bonze

**Yumiharizuki (Minamoto no Tametomo)** / Crescent Moon (The Adventures of Tametomo)

**Iwami Jūtarō** / Jutaro Iwami

**Shiranui monogatari (Shiranui hime)** / Story of Sea Fire (The Sea Fire Princess)

**Hanakawado Sukeroku** / Sukeroku of Hanakawado

**Nichiren shōnin ichidaiki** / Record of the Life of Saint Nichiren

**Happyakuya kitsune** / The City Fox

**Nogitsune Sanji** / Sanji the Wild Fox

**Banchō sarayashiki** / Broken Dishes at the Haunted Mansion

**Honjo nanafushigi** / The Seven Wonders of Honjo

**Sugawara Michizane-kō** / Prince Michizane Sugawara

**Kezori Kyūemon** / Kyuemon Kezori

**Matsuyama tanuki sōdō** / Trouble with Raccoon Dogs at Matsuyama

**Funayūrei** / Spirits of the Deep

**Ran no meitō** / The Inscribed Sword of Chaos

**Miyajima ōadauchi** / Great Revenge at Miyajima

**Botan dōrō** / Peony Stone Lantern

**Ishikawa Torajirō** / Torajiro of Ishikawa

**Kunisada Chūji (Nikkō Enzō to Kunisada Chūji)** / Chūji Kunisada (Enzo of Nikko and Chuji Kunisada)

**Natsumatsuri Danshichi Kurobei** / Danshichi and Kurobei at the Summer Festival

**Sannō no bakeneko** / Ghost Cat of Sanno

**Furisode kaji** / The Fire of the Long Sleeves

**Tengu kozō Kiritarō** / Goblin Boy Kiritaro

**Hashiba no Chōkichi** / Chokichi of Hashiba

**Reppu Katsuyama** / A Chaste Woman of Katsuyama

**Kataomoi Otowa Tanshichi** / The Unrequited Love of Otowa and Tanshichi

**Daimyō Saburōmaru** / The Daimyo Saburomaru

**Komachi musume to bishōnen** / The Town Belle and the Beautiful Youth

**Anego no Ohyaku** / Ohyaku the Elder Sister

**Matsudaira Chōshichirō** / Choshichiro Matsudaira

**Isshin Tasuke** / Tasuke Isshin

**Torisashi Kimosuke** / Kimosuke Torisashi

**Kitsune sōdō** / Fox Trouble

**Tenpō Suikoden** / Tenpo Era Water Margin

**Nezumi kozō Jirokichi** / Jirokichi the Ratkid

**Muromachi goten hyakkaiden** / A Hundred Ghost Tales of the Muromachi Palace

**Akogi no Heiji (Akogi no hatakaze)** / Heiji of Akogi (Wind in the Flags at Akogi)

**Ichikawa Danjūrō** / Danjuro Ichikawa

**Gyōten Hoshigorō** / Hoshigoro at Dawn

**Shōjiki Seibei** / Honest Seibei

**Sarasaya Kinbei (Chigatana Kinbei)** / Calico Night Kinbei (Kinbei of the Bloody Sword)

**Nihon Ginji** / Ginji of Japan

**Hiyama sōdō (Sōdō Hiyama nidaime)** / Strife at Hiyama Mountain (Strife at Hiyama: The Second Generation)

**Oniyakko** / The Demon Servant

**Kamakura denchū neko sōdō** / Trouble with a Cat in the Kamakura Palace

**Heike no yōma (Heikegani)** / The Heike Ghost (Heike Crab)

**Chūshingura** / The Loyal 47 Ronin

**Arao Hidemaru** / Hidemaru Arao

**Kumakiri Nizaemon** / Nizaemon Kumakiri

**Konjin Tatsugorō** / Tatsugorō the Golden God

**Shiraume Genji** / Genji of the White Plums

**Asamagatake (Kaidan Asamagatake)** / Asama Peak (Ghost Story of Asama Peak)

**Okuruma Ohatsu** / Ohatsu of the Carriage

**Kaibutsu taiji** / Extermination of Monsters

**Minamoto Yorimitsu** / Yorimitsu Minamoto

**Hitogiri jōgo** / Drunk with Killing

1915  **Me-gumi kenka** / The Me-Gang Feud

**Keyamura Rokusuke** / Rokusuke of Keya Village

**Kongōden (Kamo Kotarō)** / Adamantine Legend (Kotaro at the Kamo Shrine)

**Raimei Rokurō** / "Thunder" Rokuro

**Hida naishō** / Secret Craftsmen of Hida

**Echigo Tenkichi** / Tenkichi of Echigo

**Kaisoden** / Legend of the Ghost Mouse

**Hakone reigen Iinuma Katsugorō (Izari Katsugorō)** / The Ghost of Katsugoro Iinuma at Hakone (Crippled Katsugoro)

**Akegarasu jūyūshi** / Ten Heroes and a Pale Crow

**Mito Kōmon ki** / Record of Mito Komon

**Nozarashi Gosuke** / Gosuke Nozarashi

**Hakamadare Yasusuke** / Hakamadare and Yasusuke

**Ōkubo Hikozaemon Kiso man'yūki** / Record of Hikozaemon Okubo's Pleasure Trip to Kiso

**Hōzō-in Kakuzen** / Kakuzen of the Hozo-in

**Sōzen-ji baba adauchi** / Revenge at Sozen-ji Temple Track

**Shuntokumaru**

**Sendai sōdō** / Ancestral Strife

**Momoyama chitenjō** / The Bloody Ceiling of Momoyama

**Nanba senki: Gojitsudan** / Military History of Nanba: Sequel

**Higo no komageta** / Low Wooden Clogs of Higo

1916  **Matsumae Tetsunosuke** / Tetsunosuke of Matsumae

**Yoshida goten** / The Yoshida Palace

**Inuyama keibu** / Place of Punishment at Inuyama

**Shimizu Jirochō** / Jirocho of Shimizu

**Sayuri-hime Jinzūgawa no tatari: Tenshō no kaika bakeichō** / Princess Sayuri and the Curse of Jinzū River: Mysterious Fire on a Gingko Tree in the Tensho Era

1917  **Genroku kaikyo: Jūniji Chūshingura** / The Brilliant Achievement of the Genroku Era: The 47 Ronin at Midnight

**Awa Jūrobei** / Jurobei of Awa

Ten'ichibō azumakudari / Ten'ichibo Travels East from Kyoto

Meisō Takada Matabei / The Famous Spear of Matabei Takada

Byakkotai / The White Tiger Corps

Ōmura Masujirō / Masujiro Omura

Kanadehon Chūshingura / The 47 Ronin: Kana Copybook Version

Nagoya Sanzō / Sanzo of Nagoya

1918 Sumidagawa no adauchi / Revenge on the Sumida River

Sendai hagi / Ancestral Bush Clover

Yaguchi no watashi / The Crossing at Yaguchi

Kusarigama kōjo no adauchi / Sickle and Chain: A Filial Daughter's Revenge

Jūmonji Hidegorō / Hidegoro of the Cross

Marubashi Chūya / Chuya Marubashi

Mikazuki Jirokichi / Jirokichi under the Crescent Moon

Araki Mataemon / Mataemon Araki

Miyamoto Musashi / Musashi Miyamoto

Mito man'yū Takada sōdō / Mito's Pleasure Trip: Strife at Takada

1919 Shusse taikō Hiyoshimaru / The Success of the Young Hideyoshi

Mito Kōmon ki: Daiyonhen / Record of Mito Komon: Part 4

Nitta man'yūki: Daiippen / Record of Nitta's Pleasure Trip: Part 1

Keyamura Rokusuke / Rokusuke of Keya Village

1920 Ichijō Ōkura kyō (Heike monogatari) / The Finance Minister Ichijo (Tale of the Heike)

Iwami Jūtaro: Zenpen / Jutaro Iwami: Part 1

Kishū no tonosama / The Lord of Kishu

Ogasawara Hayato / Hayato Ogasawara

Tengu yawa / The Goblin Talks at Night

1921 Gōketsu Jiraiya / Heroic Thunder Boy / Jiraiya the Hero (lit.)

Jitsuroku Chūshingura / True Record of the 47 Ronin

Kinkanban Jinkurō / Jinkuro of the Golden Sign

Kanadehon Chūshingura / The 47 Ronin: Kana Copybook Version

Kōshi yōrō / A Filial Child Makes Provision for the Elderly

Kojima Takanori / Takanori Kojima

Dainankō fujin / The Wife of Masashige Kusunoki

1922 Jitsuroku Chūshingura / True Record of the 47 Ronin

Kunisada Chūji / Chuji Kunisada

Ōgon no tora / The Golden Tiger

Yamanouchi Kazutoyo no tsuma / The Wife of Kazutoyo Yamanouchi

Masuhime

1923 Sado no wakatake: Kumawakamaru / Youth of Sado: Kumawakamaru

Nogitsune Sanji / Sanji the Wild Fox

Ōishi Kuranosuke / Kuranosuke Oishi

Yōkai Jiraiya / The Ghost of Jiraiya

Nezumi kozō Jirokichi / Jirokichi the Ratkid

Matsudaira Chōshichirō / Choshichiro Matsudaira

Ōkubo Hikozaemon / Hikozaemon Okubo

Shimizu Jirochō / Jirocho of Shimizu

Yaji to Kitahachi (Daiippen; Dainihen) / Yaji and Kitahachi: (Parts 1 and 2)

Omatsuri Sashichi / Sashichi of the Festivals

Banzuiin to Gonpachi / Banzuiin and Gonpachi

Kanadehon Chūshingura / The 47 Ronin: Kana Copybook Version

Kanjinchō Ataka no seki / The Subscription List: The Ataka Barrier

Ogasawara kitsune / The Ogasawara Fox

Murasaki zukin ukiyoeshi / The Purple-Hooded Printmaker

Sorori to Goemon / Sorori and Goemon

Dainankō fujin / The Wife of Masashige Kusunoki

Fujiwara no Kamatari

Futari Seiriki Tomigorō / Two Men Named Tomigoro Seiriki

Ahōshige (Iwami Jūtarō) / Ahoshige (Jutaro Itami)

Ushi nusutto / The Cow Thief

Kaga no wakatono / The Young Lord of Kaga

Mikazuki Jirokichi / Jirokichi under the Crescent Moon

Kanzaki Yogorō / Yogoro of Kanzaki

1924 Kyōfu no yasha / The Dreadful Demon

1925 Kunisada Chūji / Chuji Kunisada

Onshū no kanata ni / Beyond Love and Hate

Ikedaya sōdō / Trouble at the Ikedaya

Kamahara / Death by Disembowelment

Gishi to kyōkaku / The Warrior and the Chivalrous Man

1926 Chūya meshitoru / Chuya Captures

Sanzoku / The Brigand

Kaiketsu yashaō / The Mysterious Demon King

Ten'ichibō to Iganosuke / Ten'ichibo and Iganosuke (co-director)

Oshare kyōjo / The Smartly Dressed Madwoman

Shado / Red Ochre

Ōedo no ushimitsudoki / The Small Hours in Great Edo

1927 Tenaraigoya / Elementary School

Kanadehon Chūshingura

shichidanme / The 47 Ronin: Kana Copybook Version: Seventh Scene

Moritsuna

Hyakumanryō hibun (Daiippen; Dainihen; Saishūhen) / Mystery of a Million Ryo (Part 1, Part 2, and Final Part)

Gatten Kanji / Kanji Consents

1928 Chūkon giretsu: Jitsuroku Chūshingura / The True Story of Loyal Retainers

Raiden / Thunder

Saheiji torimonochō / The Casebooks of Saheiji

## MASUDA Toshio
(b. October 5, 1927)
舛田利雄

Although his colleague Seijun Suzuki has gained wider recognition abroad, Masuda was the most commercially successful of Nikkatsu's action directors during the fifties and sixties. Having served as assistant to Umetsugu Inoue and Kon Ichikawa, he achieved critical notice with the third film he directed, *Rusty Knife* (*Sabita naifu*, 1958), a taut *noir*ish thriller about two gangsters whose attempts to go straight are derailed when they witness a murder. This gave Yūjirō Ishihara one of his most three-dimensional characterizations, and Masuda became Ishihara's most frequent director, collaborating with him on twenty-four films. Many of these were thrillers, such as *Red Handkerchief* (*Akai hankachi*, 1964), about a detective expelled from the force when he kills a witness. They also included two films in which Ishihara played a pilot: the war movie *The Zero Fighter* (*Zerosen kuro-kumo ikka*, 1962) and the action melodrama *The Man Who Risked Heaven and Earth* (*Ten to chi o kakeru otoko*, 1959)

Kurenai no nagareboshi / Velvet Hustler *(1967): Masuda's gangster thrillers exemplified the trademark style of Nikkatsu action.*

about a daredevil whose methods earn the disapproval of his instructors. Masuda also worked with another popular young star, Akira Kobayashi, who appeared alongside Ishihara in *Rusty Knife* and starred as the naive hero of *The Perfect Game* (*Kanzenna yūgi*, 1958), conscious-stricken after his fellow students commit a crime.

Some of Masuda's films were loosely based on foreign originals: *Red Quay* (*Akai hatoba*, 1958), about a gangster who escapes to Kobe after murdering his rivals in Tokyo, was a reworking of the classic French poetic realist thriller *Pepé le Moko* (1936, Julien Duvivier), while *We Live Today* (*Kyō ni ikiru*, 1959) echoed *Shane* (1953, George Stevens) in its story of a wanderer (Ishihara again) who brings order to a violent mining town. This internationalized flavor

was typical of Nikkatsu product at that time, but Masuda's action films tended to have a certain surface realism which contrasted with Suzuki's deliberate stylization. His preference for location shooting allowed him to anchor generic narratives in the distinctive attributes of a specific place: thus *Rusty Knife*, despite expressionist touches, painted a plausible portrait of a small harbor town, while *Velvet Hustler* (*Kurenai no nagareboshi*, 1967), actually a reworking of *Red Quay* with the embellishment of color, was distinguished by its atmospheric Kobe settings.

Masuda left Nikkatsu to work freelance in 1968 and was hired, along with Kinji Fukasaku, to realize the Japanese scenes of *Tora! Tora! Tora!* (1970). *Shadow Hunters* (*Kagegari*, 1972) reunited him with Yūjirō Ishihara in a period story about a trio of warriors hunting government spies; regrettably, its stylistic overstatement made it seem crass compared to the classical economy of his Nikkatsu period. Thereafter, Masuda's reputation as a reliable commercial filmmaker enabled him to helm various big-budget films, starting with the dystopian science fiction movie *Catastrophe 1999: The Prophecies of Nostradamus* (*Nosutoradamusu no daiyogen*, 1974). He later made three war movies for Toei and *Doten* (*Dōten*, 1991), a Yokohama-set epic depicting events surrounding the nineteenth-century opening of Japan to foreigners. Better received by the critics was *Company Funeral* (*Shasō*, 1989), an account of a battle for succession in a large corporation, which ranked in the annual Kinema Junpō Top Ten. Nevertheless, Masuda is likely to be remembered primarily for his contribution to the Nikkatsu action genre.

1958 **Kokoro to nikutai no tabi** / Body and Soul / A Journey of Body and Soul (lit.)
**Yogiri no daini kokudō** / Highway in the Fog
**Sabita naifu** / Rusty Knife
**Haneda hatsu 7-ji 50-ppun** / Flight Time 7:50
**Akai hatoba** / Red Quay / The Left Hand of Jiro
**Kanzenna yūgi** / The Perfect Game / The Tragedy of Today

1959 **Onna o wasero** / Forget About Women
**Kyō ni ikiru** / We Live Today
**Otoko ga bakuhatsu suru** / The Man Explodes / The Explosion Came
**Ten to chi o kakeru otoko** / The Man Who Risked Heaven and Earth / The Sky Is Mine
**Seishun o fukinarase** / Trumpeting Youth

1960 **Yakuza no uta** / Yakuza Song

**Seinen no ki** / Tree of Youth
**Kenka Tarō** / The Brawler / The Tough Guy
**Tōgyū ni kakeru otoko** / The Man at the Bullfight

1961 **Ikiteita nora inu** / The Living Stray Dog / Hotbed of Crime
**Yōjinbō kagyō** / Bodyguard Work / Joy of Aces: Bodyguard Work
**Taiyō umi o someru toki** / When the Sun Colors the Sea / Where the Horizon Meets the Sun
**Taiyō wa kurutteiru** / The Sun Is Mad / Lost in the Sun
**Ankokugai no shizukana otoko** / Quiet Man of the Underworld

1962 **Otoko to otoko no ikiru machi** / The Town Where Men Live in Harmony
**Ue o muite arukō** / Keep Your Chin Up
**Zerosen kurokumo ikka** / The Zero Fighter
**Hitoribotchi no futari da ga** / Two Lonely People
**Hana to Ryū** / Flower and Dragon / A Man with a Dragon Tattoo

1963 **Taiyō e no dasshutsu** / Escape to the Sun / Escape into Terror
**Ōkami no ōji** / Prince of Wolves

1964 **Akai hankachi** / Red Handkerchief
**Jinsei gekijō** / Theater of Life
**Kawachi zoro dokechimushi** / Lowlife of Kawachi
**Satsujinsha o kese** / Kill the Killer
**Kawachi zoro kenka shamo** / Fighting Birds of Kawachi

1965 **Shirotori** / Taking the Castle
**Seishun to wa nan da** / What Is Youth?
**Akai tanima no kettō** / Battle in the Red Valley

1966 **Nihon ninkyōden: Chimatsuri kenkajō** / The Bloodstained Challenge (lit. Tales of Japanese Chivalry: Invitation to a Bloodbath)
**Yoru no bara o kese** / Kill the Night Rose

**Eikō e no chōsen** / Challenge for Glory

**Arashi o yobu otoko** / The Man Who Raised a Storm

1967 **Hoshi yo nageku na: Shōri no otoko** / Stars, Don't Cry: The Winning Guy / The Man of Victory

**Arashi kitari saru** / The Storm Comes and Goes

**Taiketsu** / Friendly Enemies (lit. Showdown)

**Kurenai no nagareboshi** / Velvet Hustler / Like a Shooting Star (lit. Crimson Shooting Star)

**Kettō** / The Endless Duel

1968 **Burai yori: Daikanbu** / Gangster VIP

**Waga inochi no uta: Enka** / Song of my Life: Enka

**Shōwa no inochi** / Stormy Era (lit. Life in the Showa Era)

**Ā, himeyuri no tō** / Ah, Tower of Lilies

1969 **Jigoku no hamonjō** / Exiled to Hell

**Daikanbu: Nagurikomi** / The Big Boss: Attack!

**Arashi no yūshatachi** / The Cleanup (lit. Heroes in a Storm)

1970 **Tora! Tora! Tora!** (*co-director*)

**Suparuta kyōiku: Kutabare oyaji** / Spartan Education: Go to Hell, Dad

1971 **Akatsuki no chōsen** / Challenge at Dawn / Battle at Dawn

**Saraba okite** / Goodbye Gangster Code / Law of the Outlaw

1972 **Oitsumeru** / Cornered / Chase That Man

**Ken to hana** / The Sword and the Flower

**Kagegari** / Shadow Hunters

**Kagegari: Hoero taihō** / Shadow Hunters: Echo of Destiny

1973 **Ningen kakumei** / The Human Revolution

1974 **Nosutoradamusu no daiyogen** / Catastrophe 1999: The Prophecies of Nostradamus

**Ore no chi wa tanin no chi** / My Blood Is Another's Blood

1976 **Zoku ningen kakumei** / The Human Revolution 2

1977 **Uchū senkan Yamato** / Space Battleship Yamato

1978 **Saraba uchū senkan Yamato: Ai no senshitachi** / Farewell to Space Battleship Yamato: In the Name of Love

**Teiku ofu** / Take Off

1980 **Nihyakusan kōchi** / The Battle of Port Arthur / Port Arthur (lit. Hill 203)

**Yamato yo towa ni** / Be Forever, Yamato

1981 **Uchū senkan Yamato: Arata naru tabidachi** / Space Battleship Yamato: The New Voyage

1982 **Dainippon teikoku** / The Great Japanese Empire / Empire of Japan

**Hai tīn bugi** / High Teen Boogie

**Future War 198X-nen** / Future War, 198X

1983 **Uchū senkan Yamato: Kanketsu hen** / Space Battlehip Yamato: Final Part

**Nihonkai daikaisen: Umi yukaba** / The Battle of the Sea of Japan: To Go to Sea

**Eru ō vi ai NG** / L o v i N G

1984 **Zerosen moyu** / Zero Fighter in Flames

1985 **Ai: Tabidachi** / Love: Take Off

**Ōdīn: Kōshi hobune Sutāraito** / Odin (lit. Odin Photon Sailing Ship Starlight)

1986 **Katayoku dake no tenshi** / The Angel with One Wing / Angel's Love

1987 **Shuto shōshitsu** / Tokyo Blackout

**Kono ai no monogatari** / This Story of Love

1989 **Shasō** / Company Funeral / Company Executives

1991 **Dōten** / Doten (lit. Earthshaking Event)

**Edo-jō tairan** / The Great

Shogunate Battle (lit. Great
Uprising at Edo Castle)
**Hissatsu! V: Ōgon no chi** / Sure
Death V: Blood of Gold
1992 **Tengoku no daizai** / Heavenly Sin

## MASUMURA Yasuzō
**(August 25, 1924–November 23, 1986)**
增村保造

An inventive satirist and melodrama-
tist, Masumura began to direct at Daiei
after training in Rome and serving as
assistant to Kon Ichikawa. His debut,
*Kisses* (*Kuchizuke*, 1957), was admired
by Nagisa Ōshima for its mobile camerawork and amoral plot. Masumura
pursued a similar iconoclastic approach
in *Warm Current* (*Danryū*, 1957*)*, a remake of Kōzaburō Yoshimura's classic
weepie which, in Tadao Satō's words,
"increase[ed] the tempo to the violent
pitch of an action film," and substituted
an "audacious frankness" for the subdued romanticism of the original.

Nevertheless, Masumura was not
really part of the Japanese New Wave
and his style was more classical than
modernist. Though he was later critical of Ichikawa in print, his most interesting early films, especially *Kisses* and
*Giants and Toys* (*Kyojin to gangu*, 1958),
display a considerable debt to the older
director's example: in particular, to the
diptych of *Punishment Room* (*Shokei no
heya*, 1956) and *A Full-Up Train* (*Man'in
densha*, 1957). Masumura used the same
young male lead, Hiroshi Kawaguchi,
and, as Ichikawa had done, produced
opposite but complementary accounts
of delinquency and conformity among
postwar youth. Masumura's striking
widescreen compositions also owed
something to Ichikawa, but his satirical

accounts of Japanese society tended to
be bleaker and more outrageous. *Giants
and Toys* and *The Black Test Car* (*Kuro
no tesutokā*, 1962) were both scathing
indictments of the excesses of corporate
culture, but despite his sceptical attitude to big business, Masumura did not
approach society from an orthodox left-
wing viewpoint. *A False Student* (*Nise
daigakusei*, 1960), indeed, was a genuinely frightening film about a young
man who enters university under false
pretences and is kidnapped by Marxist
fellow students on suspicion of being a
police plant. Both the student militants
and the complicit authority figures were
subjected to bitter criticism, and Masumura pursued the film's political implications through to a grimly logical
conclusion.

Among Masumura's other early
films, *A Man Blown by the Wind* (*Karakkaze yarō*, 1960) was a routine yakuza
movie, chiefly notable for the presence in the lead role of novelist Yukio
Mishima. More characteristic in theme
and style were *Precipice* (*Hyōheki*, 1958)
and *A Wife Confesses* (*Tsuma wa kokuhaku suru*, 1961), interesting melodramas which used climbing accidents as
catalysts for investigations into sexual
guilt. These films initiated a concern
with triangular relationships also visible
in two literary adaptations: *A Thousand
Cranes* (*Senbazuru*, 1969), a bleak drama
based on a novel by Yasunari Kawabata, and *Manji* (1964), a black comedy
about a bisexual *ménage à trois*, and the
first of three Masumura films based on
Jun'ichirō Tanizaki. Its theme of a love
affair culminating in a suicide pact was
to be recapitulated in *Blind Beast* (*Mōjū*,
1969), a horror movie based on an
Edogawa Ranpo story about the sado-
masochistic relationship between an
artist's model and her blind kidnapper.

©Kadokawa Pictures

*Akai tenshi / The Red Angel (1966):*
*This is one of the Japanese cinema's most*
*intense depictions of the horrors of war.*

This repulsive film was notable mainly for its surreal art direction.

Of Masumura's other literary adaptations, *Tattoo (Irezumi,* 1966), also based on Tanizaki, and *A Lustful Man (Kōshoku ichidai otoko,* 1961), loosely adapted from Saikaku's account of an obsessive womanizer, were excursions into period settings. Neither was especially distinguished, though both were handsomely mounted. Masumura's most critically acclaimed works were two war movies, *The Hoodlum Soldier (Heitai yakuza,* 1965) and *The Red Angel (Akai tenshi,* 1966), which depicted the horrors of war in contrasting tones of dark humor and violent intensity. Both were subversive films: the former frankly described a young soldier's hatred of army life, while the latter saw sexual activity as one of the few redeeming forces amidst the brutality of the battlefield.

Masumura continued to work under contract at Daiei until the studio's demise in the early seventies, after which he became a freelancer. In the more commercially motivated environment of the period, he tended to be assigned to unsuitable material, though the ATG-financed Kabuki adaptation *Love Suicides at Sonezaki (Sonezaki shinjū,* 1978), another story of a tragic love affair ending in suicide, has a high reputation, and Jonathan Rosenbaum has praised *Lullaby for the Good Earth (Daichi no komoriuta,* 1976), about a village girl who becomes a prostitute.

In general, Masumura's art was shocking without being truly profound: Donald Richie has commented that "a certain shallowness of characterization is perhaps the price exacted by a restless camera and fast editing." In fact, Masumura's visuals tended to shift his stories towards parody: the cartoon-like imagery of *Giants and Toys* and the exaggeration of *noir*ish tropes in *The Black Test Car* seemed at odds with the harshness of the scripts. Perhaps the director's most poignant film was one of his least typical: *The Wife of Seishu Hanaoka (Hanaoka Seishū no tsuma,* 1967), which recounted the life of a doctor who invented a primitive anaesthetic. As the hero's scientific discoveries benefit the world while leaving him powerless to cure the ills or save the lives of his own family, the film rose to a level of genuine tragedy, achieving a depth rare in Masumura's work.

1957  **Kuchizuke** / Kisses
      **Aozora musume** / The Blue Sky Girl / A Cheerful Girl
      **Danryū** / Warm Current
1958  **Hyōheki** / Precipice (lit. Icy Precipice)
      **Kyojin to gangu** / Giants and Toys
      **Futeki no otoko** / The Fearless Man / The Lowest Man
      **Oya fukō dōri** / Disobedience / Street of Parental Sorrow (lit.)
1959  **Saikō shukun fujin** / The Most Distinguished Wife / Most Valuable Madam

Hanran / Inundation / The Castoff

**Bibō ni tsumi ari** / So Beautiful It's a Sin / Beauty the Enemy

**Yami o yokogiri** / Across the Darkness

1960 **Jokyō** / A Woman's Testament (*co-director*)

**Karakkaze yarō** / A Man Blown by the Wind / Afraid to Die

**Ashi ni sawatta onna** / The Woman Who Touched the Legs

**Nise daigakusei** / A False Student

1961 **Koi ni inochi o** / Love and Life

**Kōshoku ichidai otoko** / A Lustful Man / The Life of an Amorous Man (lit.) / The Man Who Loved Love / All for Love

**Tsuma wa kokuhaku suru** / A Wife Confesses / Her Confession

**Urusai imōtotachi** / The Burdened Sisters (lit. Noisy Younger Sisters)

1962 **Tadare** / Stolen Pleasures / Indulgence (lit. Inflammation)

**Kuro no tesutokā** / The Black Test Car

**Onna no isshō** / The Life of a Woman

1963 **Kuro no hōkokusho** / The Black Report / Black Statement Book / Secret Report

**Uso** / Lies / When Women Lie (*co-director*)

**Gurentai junjōha** / Band of Pure-Hearted Hoodlums

1964 **Gendai inchiki monogatari: Damashiya** / Modern Fraud Story: Cheat

**Manji** / Manji / Passion

**Kuro no chōtokkyū** / The Black Superexpress / Black Mark Express

1965 **Heitai yakuza** / The Hoodlum Soldier

**Seisaku no tsuma** / Seisaku's Wife

1966 **Irezumi** / Tattoo / The Spider Tattoo / Spider Girl

**Rikugun Nakano gakkō** / Nakano Army School / School for Spies

**Akai tenshi** / The Red Angel

1967 **Tsuma futari** / Two Wives

**Chijin no ai** / A Fool's Love / An Idiot in Love / Naomi

**Hanaoka Seishū no tsuma** / The Wife of Seishu Hanaoka

1968 **Daiakutō** / The Great Villain / The Most Corrupt / Evil Trio

**Sekkusu chekku: Daini no sei** / Sex Check: The Second Sex

**Tsumiki no hako** / The House of Wooden Blocks

**Nureta futari** / One Day at Summer's End (lit. Wet Couple)

1969 **Mōjū** / Blind Beast

**Senbazuru** / A Thousand Cranes

**Nyotai** / A Woman's Body / Vixen

1970 **Denki kurage** / The Electric Jellyfish / Play It Cool

**Yakuza zesshō** / Ode to a Gangster / The Yakuza Song / The Final Payoff / A Yakuza Masterpiece

**Shibire kurage** / The Electric Medusa / The Hot Little Girl

1971 **Asobi** / Games

1972 **Shin heitai yakuza: Kasen** / New Hoodlum Soldier: Firing Line

**Ongaku** / Music

1973 **Goyōkiba: Kamisori Hanzō jigokuzeme** / The Razor 2: The Snare / Tortures of Hell (lit. Fangs of Public Office: Razor Hanzo's Torture Hell)

1974 **Akumyō: Shima arashi** / Notorious Dragon (lit. Bad Reputation: Turf War)

1975 **Dōmyaku rettō** / Hardened Arteries / Pulsating Island / Archipelago of Arteries (lit.)

1976 **Daichi no komoriuta** / Lullaby for the Good Earth

1978 **Sonezaki shinjū** / Love Suicides at Sonezaki

1980 **Eden no sono** / Garden of Eden

1982 **Kono ko no nanatsu no oiwai ni** / Happy Seventh Birthday (lit. For the Seventh Birthday of His Child)

## MATSUDA Sadatsugu
### (November 17, 1906–January 20, 2003)
### 松田定次

Matsuda is included here as a representative example of the proficient but anonymous artisans working in *jidai-geki* between the twenties and the sixties. The illegitimate son of the "father of Japanese cinema," Shōzō Makino, he made his debut, *Poor Daikuro* (*Kawaisōna Daikurō*, 1928), at Makino Productions shortly before the pioneer's death. Matsuda subsequently worked at Makino Talkie (the company founded by his half-brother Masahiro Makino), Nikkatsu, and Daiei; among the best appreciated of his prewar films were *Young Toyama Kinsan* (*Hana no haru Tōyamazakura*, 1936) and *Drawing the Sword* (*Katana o nuite*, 1937). In the postwar era he worked mainly at Toei, where his films displayed the blend of violence, humor and pathos typical of the studio. Throughout his career he specialized in period films, often based on famous stories and legends, and starring such genre fixtures as Utaemon Ichikawa and Chiezō Kataoka; the latter also appeared in Matsuda's sequence of popular detective films based on novels by Seishi Yokomizo. Of his Toei *jidai-geki*, *Chronicle of Ako* (*Akō rōshi*, 1961) was one of the more humane retellings of the story of the 47 ronin, with a stronger than expected emphasis on the personal lives and feelings of the participants.

Matsuda has a footnote in film history as the director of *Samurai Bride Hunter* (*Hō-jō no hanayome*, 1957), the first Japanese film in color and 'Scope. This very lightweight period comedy was, like Hollywood's first Cinemascope film, *The Robe* (1953, Henry Koster), more notable for its pioneering status than for any inherent merit, but Matsuda earned some appreciation thereafter for his adept use of the 'Scope frame. However, apart from the change of format, his Toei *jidai-geki* of the fifties and sixties showed scant evolution from the techniques of the silent era. Indeed, the occasional zip pans in *Road of Chivalry* (*Ninkyō nakasendō*, 1960) recalled the pre-sound style of Daisuke Itō, of whose frenetic manner Matsuda may be considered a second-rank imitator. Nevertheless, his films displayed the virtues of a classical training: economy, pace, and graceful choreography of action. These assets speak for the strength of the Japanese studio system and the vitality of its classical approach, a vitality demonstrated as much by the proficiency of its minor talents as by the genius of its masters.

1928 **Kawaisōna Daikurō** / Poor Daikuro

1929 **Muriyari sanzengoku** / An Ill-Gotten 3,000-koku
**Nusumareta Daikurō** / Stolen Daikuro

1930 **Oikora kōshinkyoku** / Hey! March
**Gakusei sandaiki: Tenpō jidai** / Chronicle of Three Generations of Students: Tenpo Era
**Gorōnin yokochō** / Alley of Masterless Samurai

1931 **Aiaigasa sanryō samurai** / Samurai with 3 Ryo and a Shared Umbrella
**Tabimakura Matsudaira Chōshichirō** / The Travels of Choshichiro Matsudaira
**Bushū no sōryū** / Twin Dragons of Musashi Province

1932 **Ninkyō daimyō Gorōzō** / The Chivalrous Daimyo Gorozo
**Idahachi jima** / Stripes of Idahachi
**Meian sansesō** / Light and Dark: Three Aspects of Society

1933 **Somewake furiko** / The Parti-Colored Pendulum

**Sakebu raichō** / The Crying Snow Grouse

**Hanji tsukiyo no uta** / Hanji's Song of a Moonlit Night

**Hare hare Samon** / Clear, Clear Samon

1934 **Fujizō gyōjōki (Zenpen; Kōhen)** / Conduct Report on Fujizo (Parts 1 and 2)

**Tenpō Suikoden** / Tenpo-Era Water Margin

**Onnagokoro sōjōki** / A Woman's Heart: Record of Two Passions

**Kikyorai tōge** / The Pass Home

1935 **Aizō ichidai** / A Life of Love and Hate

**Jigoku bayashi** / Festival Music of Hell

**Fūryū yakkohige** / The Elegant Moustache

1936 **Hana no haru Tōyamazakura** / Young Toyama Kinsan (lit. Toyama Kinsan of the Spring Flowers) (*co-director*)

**Tabi no Baka Yasu** / The Travels of Yasu the Stupid

**Matsudaira gaiki** / Story of Matsudaira

**Yatarōgasa (Zenpen; Kōhen)** / Yataro's Sedge Hat (Parts 1 and 2)

**Edo sodachi omatsuri Sashichi** / Sashichi of the Festivals, Born and Bred in Edo

**Hadaka no haritsuke** / The Naked Crucifixion

**Kabuki kenpō** / Kabuki Fencing

1937 **Katana o nuite** / Drawing the Sword

**Sengoku jidai** / Era of Warring States

1938 **Kurama Tengu: Kakubei shishi no maki** / Kurama Tengu: Kakubei the Lion (*co-director*)

**Jirochō ikka** / The Family of Jirocho

**Dokyō senryō** / Courage and a Thousand Ryo

**Kurama Tengu: Ryūjōkohaku no maki** / Kurama Tengu: Fierce Fighting

**Arajishi** / Violent Lion

1939 **Chōhachirō emaki: Tsuki no maki** / The Scroll of Chohachiro: Moon Reel

**Chōhachirō emaki: Hana no maki** / The Scroll of Chohachiro: Flower Reel

**Matatabi no uta** / Wanderers' Song

**Kurama Tengu: Edo nikki** / Kurama Tengu: Edo Diary

**Kurama Tengu: Kyōfu hen** / Kurama Tengu: Terror Chapter

**Mumei yūmei (Zenpen; Kōhen)** / Obscure and Famous (Parts 1 and 2)

**Junjō ichidai otoko** / The Life of an Innocent Man

1940 **Namida no torinawa** / Snare of Tears

**Akō no hitozuma** / A Wife of Ako

**Rōgoku no ōkami** / Prison Wolf

**Gokoku no oni** / The Devil Who Defends the Country

**Hokkai ni sakebu bushi** / The Warrior Who Calls toward the North Sea

1941 **Sangaku bushi** / The Warrior in the Mountains

**Sugata naki fukushū** / Secret Revenge

1943 **Chingisu Kan** / Genghis Khan (*co-director*)

1944 **Takadanobaba (Zenpen; Kōhen)** / Takadanobaba (Parts 1 and 2)

**Kappa taishō** / General Kappa

1946 **Meiji no kyōdai** / Brothers of the Meiji Era

**Kunisada Chūji** / Chuji Kunisada

1947 **Yami o hashiru basha** / Chariot in the Dark

**Jūsan no me** / Thirteen Eyes

**Yoimatsuri happyakuyachō** / Edo on the Eve of a Festival

**Sanbon yubi no otoko** / The Man with Three Fingers

1948 **Kiso no tengu** / A Goblin in Kiso

Nijūichi no shimon / Twenty-One
Fingerprints
Gonin no mokugekisha / Five
Witnesses
Nippon G-men / G-Men of Japan
Kurokumo kaidō / Road of Black
Clouds
Sanjūsan no ashiato / 33
Footprints
1949 Byakko / White Tiger
Gokumontō / Island of Horrors
Gokumontō: Kaimei hen / Island
of Horrors: The Solution
1950 Nippon G-men: Dainiwa:
Nansenzaki no kettō / G-Men
of Japan: Part 2: Bloody Duel at
Shipwreck Cape
Shishi no wana / The Lion Trap
Yami ni hikaru me / Eyes Alight in
Darkness
Hatamoto taikutsu otoko
torimonobikae: Shichinin no
hanayome / Notes on a Boring
Retainer: Seven Brides
Hatamoto taikutsu otoko
torimonobikae: Dokusatsu maden
/ Notes on a Boring Retainer:
Mysterious Mansion of Poisoning
1951 Tengu no Yasu / Yasu the Goblin
Yatsuhakamura / Village of Eight
Gravestones
Edo koi sugoroku / Love and
Games in Edo
1952 Yūmingai no yashū / Night Attack
on the Street of Idlers
Kojiki taishō / The Beggar General
Shura hakkō / The Pains of Hell
Tange Sazen / Sazen Tange
Ryūzoku kuromatai: Akatsuki
no kyūshū / Wandering Thieves:
Black Horse Gang: Sudden Attack at
Dawn
Ryūzoku kuromatai: Gekka no
taiketsu / Wandering Thieves:
Black Horse Gang: Duel under the
Moon
1953 Asayake Fuji (Zenpen; Kōhen) /
Mount Fuji in Dawn Light (Parts 1
and 2)

Shinsho Taikōki: Kyūshū
Okehazama / Chronicle of
Hideyoshi, New Book: Sudden
Attack on Okehazama
Yama o mamoru kyōdai / Brothers
Protecting the Mountains
Onibuse kaidō / Street of the
Devils' Ambush
Chūji tabi nikki: Kenka daiko /
Chuji's Travel Diary: Battle Drum
1954 Hatamoto taikutsu otoko:
Dokuro yashiki / The Boring
Retainer: Skull Mansion
Denshichi torimonochō:
Hitohada senryō / Notebooks of
Denshichi: Skin and 1,000 Ryo
Akuma ga kitarite fue o fuku /
The Devil Comes Whistling
Kagebōshi ichiban tegara: Yōi
Chūshingura / The Shadow's
Greatest Exploit: Uncanny
Chushingura
Yaoya Oshichi: Furisode tsukiyo
/ Oshichi of the Grocer's: Long
Sleeves on a Moonlit Night
Zangetsu ikkiuchi / One-to-One
Fight under the Morning Moon
1955 Tarao Bannai shirīzu: Hayabusa
no maō / Bannai Tarao Series: The
Demon King of Falcons
Fūun shōgidani / Wind and Clouds
in the Valley of Shogi
Seiryūgai no ōkami / The Wolf of
Blue Dragon Street
Yatarōgasa / Yataro's Sedge Hat
Tarao Bannai shirīzu:
Daihachiwa: Fukushū no
shichikamen / Bannai Tarao Series:
Part 8: Seven Masks of Revenge
1956 Tarao Bannai shirīzu: Senritsu no
shichikamen / Bannai Tarao Series:
Seven Horrible Masks
Akō rōshi / Warriors of Ako
Kengō nitōryū / The Master Two-
Handed Swordsman
Fushitaka / Father and Chick Hawk
Hatamoto taikutsu otoko: Nazo
no yūreisen / The Boring Retainer:
The Mysterious Ghost Ship

Dokuro zeni / Skull Money

Yōja no maden / The Mysterious Snake Mansion

1957 Ninkyō Shimizu minato / Port of Honor (lit. Chivalry at Shimizu Harbor)

Hatamoto taikutsu otoko: Nazo no gurentō / The Boring Retainer: The Mysterious Red Lotus Flower

Hō-jō no hanayome / Samurai Bride Hunter / The Lord Takes a Bride / The Bride of Phoenix Castle (lit.)

Hayatozoku no hanran / Rebellion (lit. Rebellion of the Hayato Clan)

Yūreisen: Dotō hen / Ghost Ship: Angry Waves Chapter

Yūreisen: Kōhen / Ghost Ship: Part 2

Koikaze dōchū / Breeze of Love

1958 Ninkyō Tōkaidō / A Chivalrous Spirit / Fighters on Passage (lit. Chivalry on the Tokaido)

Tarao Bannai: Jūsan no maō / Bannai Tarao: The Thirteenth King of Hell / Man of Thirteen Eyes

Tange Sazen / Sazen Tange / Secret of the Bronze Dragon

Ōedo shichinin shū / Seven from Edo (co-director)

Yatsu no kenjū wa jigoku da ze / The Guy's Gun Is Hell

Hatamoto taikutsu otoko / The Boring Retainer

Onmitsu shichishōki / The Abandoned Swords / Destiny of Credential Agent (lit. Record of the Seven Lives of a Secret Messenger)

1959 Tange Sazen: Dotō hen / Sazen Tange: Angry Waves Chapter / Secret of the Golden Spell

Chūshingura / The Great Avengers / The Loyal 47 Ronin

Shingo jūban shōbu / Shingo's Original Challenge / Ten Duels of Young Shingo (lit.)

Fūryū shisha: Tenka musō no ken / The Elegant Messenger: The Shogun's Unrivaled Sword

Mito Kōmon: Tenka no fukushōgun / Komon Mito: The Shogun's Adjutant

Tenka no Igagoe: Akatsuki no kessen / The Shogun Crosses Iga: Duel at Dawn

1960 Ninkyō Nakasendō / Road of Chivalry / Gamblers' Code on the Nakasendo (lit.)

Tange Sazen: Yōtō nuretsubame / Sazen Tange: The Mysterious Sword (lit. Sazen Tange: The Mysterious Sword and the Damp Swallow)

Shingo jūban shōbu: Daisanbu / Shingo's Original Challenge: Part 3

Shingo jūban shōbu: Kanketsu hen / Shingo's Original Challenge: Conclusion

Hatamoto taikutsu otoko: Nazo no ansatsutai / The Boring Retainer: The Mysterious Group of Assassins

Mito Kōmon / Mito Komon

Shōsuke buyūden: Aizu Bandai-san / Chronicle of Shosuke's Bravery: Mount Bandai in Aizu

1961 Shingo nijūban shōbu / Shingo's Challenge / Twenty Duels of Shingo (lit.)

Akō rōshi / Chronicle of Ako / Warriors of Ako / The 47 Ronin

Tange Sazen: Nuretsubame ittōryū / Sazen Tange: The Sword Flies Like a Swallow

Shingo nijūban shōbu: Dainibu / Shingo's Challenge: Part 2

Ishin no kagaribi / Bonfires of the Restoration

1962 Tenka no goikenban / His Excellency's Advisor

Minamoto Kurō Yoshitsune / Kuro Yoshitsune Minamoto

Umon torimonochō: Beni tokage / The Casebooks of Detective Umon: The Crimson Lizard

Chikemurigasa / Hat of Bloodshed

Wakasama samurai torimonochō / Notebooks of a Young Master Samurai

1963  **Seizoroi Tōkaidō** / Mustered on
the Tokaido
**Nakasendō no tsumujikaze /**
Whirlwind on the Nakasendo
**Shingo nijūban shōbu: Kanketsu
hen** / Shingo's Challenge:
Conclusion
**Chi to suna no kettō** / Duel of
Blood and Sand
1964  **Hitokirigasa** / Killer's Hat
**Shingo bangai shōbu** / Shingo's
Extra Challenge
1965  **Baraketsu shōbu** / Three Young
Rebels
1969  **Mekura no Oichi monogatari:
Makkana nagaredori** / Story
of Blind Oichi: Red Bird in
Flight / Crimson Bat: The Blind
Swordswoman
**Mekura no Oichi: Jigokuhada**
/ Trapped: The Crimson Bat (lit.
Blind Oichi: Skin of Hell)

## MATSUMOTO Toshio
**(b. March 26, 1932)**
松本俊夫

Matsumoto is one of Japan's most distinguished *avant-garde* filmmakers; his work has fused a range of eclectic influences, including mythology, neo-realism, classical theater, and the theories of Brecht. His leftist inclinations were given expression in such early documentaries as *The Bends* (*Senkan*, 1956) and *Children Calling Spring* (*Haru o yobu kora*, 1959), both socially conscious studies of the exploitation of workers from the poor north of Japan. However, Matsumoto quickly became dissatisfied with this social realist approach, and his sixties shorts, such as *Nishijin* (1961) and *The Song of Stones* (*Ishi no uta*, 1963), were more concerned with formal experimentation. His belief that cinema

"dissolves the binary divisions between fact and fiction, between objective and subjective" was expressed in the synthesis of a fictional narrative with documentary and *avant-garde* techniques in his first feature, *Funeral Parade of Roses* (*Bara no sōretsu*, 1969), which relocated the Oedipus myth to the gay subculture of Tokyo's Shinjuku district. Though interesting and provocative, the film was somewhat undisciplined in its experimentation. Nevertheless, its subversive approach to traditional film grammar was remarkable, as witness the climactic forward tracking point-of-view shot, filmed in disorienting fashion as if through the eyes of the blinded hero.

A new stylistic integrity was visible in *Pandemonium* (*Shura*, 1971), Matsumoto's masterpiece and a film of astonishing emotional intensity. Like *Funeral Parade of Roses*, it was an iconoclastic reworking of a famous story, in this case the historical vendetta of the 47 ronin; Matsumoto subverted the grand tragedy of the traditional narrative by instead recounting a sordid revenger's tragedy in which multiple murder, motivated solely by misunderstanding, is committed by a would-be participant in the vendetta. The film's deliberate artificiality, employing stylized sets and the device of staging scenes repeatedly with different outcomes, unsettlingly blurred the distinction between reality and the protagonist's obsessive fantasies.

Matsumoto's next film was *War of Sixteen* (*Jūrokusai no sensō*, 1973; released 1976), a story about a youthful romance overshadowed by unresolved wartime traumas among the older generation. Despite creative camerawork, this was Matsumoto's most conventional film, but also his most tender. From the mid-seventies onwards, however, he devoted himself increasingly to experimental shorts, making use of new media such as video. His most recent feature, *Dogra Magra* (*Dogura magura*, 1988), sustained his preoccupation with the ambiguous borderline between reality and fantasy: recounting an amnesiac's struggle to remember the truth of events which led him to be sent to an asylum, it unfolded as a mystery without a solution, in which flashbacks served as hypotheses rather than explanations. Subversively, the film hinted that science is not simply an objective way of exploring reality, but also a mechanism for exerting power over others. Though lacking the savage brilliance of *Pandemonium*, it confirmed Matsumoto's ability to undermine audience assumptions and challenge complacency.

1955  **Ginrin** / Bicycle in Dream (*short, co-director*)

1956  **Senkan** / The Bends / Caisson (*short*)

1959  **Haru o yobu kora** / Children Calling Spring (*short*)

   **300-ton torērā** / 300-Ton Trailer (*short*)

   **Anpo jōyaku** / The U.S.-Japan Treaty (*short*)

1960  **Shiroi nagai sen no kiroku** / Document of a Long White Line (*short*)

1961  **Nishijin** / Nishijin / Weavers of Nishijin (*short*)

1963  **Ishi no uta** / The Song of Stones (*short*)

1967  **Hahatachi** / Mothers (*short*)

1968  **Tsuburekakatta migime no tameni** / For My Crushed Right Eye (*short*)

   **Magunechikku: Sukuranburu** / Magnetic: Scramble (*short*)

   **Ekusutashisu = Kōkotsu** / Ecstasis (*short*)

1969  **Bara no sōretsu** / Funeral Parade of Roses

   **Ikon no tame no purojekushon /**
Projection for the Benefit of an Icon (*short*)

   **Shadō** / Shadow (*short*)

1970  **Supēsu purojekushon AKO** / Space Projection AKO (*short*)

1971  **Shura** / Pandemonium / Hell / The Demon

   **Metasutashisu = Shinchintaisha** / Metastasis (*short*)

1972  **Ōtonomī = Jiritsusei** / Autonomy (*short*)

   **Ekusupanshon = Kakuchō** / Expansion (*short*)

1973  **Mona Risa** / Mona Lisa (*short*)

1974  **Furai = Tobu** / Fly (*short*)

   **Andi Wōhoro = Fukufukusei** / A.W.: Re-reproduction (*short*)

   **Mōningu dyū (Asatsuyu)** / Morning Dew (*short*)

1975  **Seijo** / Blue Woman (*short*)

   **Tōtaru shiatā: Aoi no ue** / Total Theater: Aoi no ue (*short*)

   **Fantomu: Genmō** / Phantom (*short*)

   **Shikisoku zekū** / Everything Visible is Empty (*short*)

   **Ātoman** / Atman (*short*)

1976  **Jūrokusai no sensō** / War of Sixteen (lit. War of 16-Year-Olds) (*made in 1973*)

   **Tako** / Kite (*short*)

   **Yūterasu = Shikyū** / Uterus (*short*)

1977  **Burakku hōru** / Black Hole (*short*)

   **Iryuminēshon** / Illumination (*short*)

   **Nijūzō** / Double Image (*short*)

1978  **Eniguma = Nazo** / Enigma (*short*)

1979  **Howaito hōru** / White Hole (*short*)

   **Suizokukan** / Aquarium (*short*)

1980  **Kosumikku rirēshon** / Cosmic Relation (*short*)

   **Ki = Breathing** / Breathing (*short*)

1981  **Konekushon** / Connection (*short*)

1982  **Ema** / Votive Tablet (*short*)

   **Rirēshon = Kankei** / Relation (*short*)

   **Shifuto** / Shift (*short*)

1983  **Fōmeishon = Keisei** / Formation (*short*)

1984 **Wave** (*short*)

   **Dirē ekusupōjā** / Delayed
   Exposure (*8mm short*)

1985 **EE kontorōru** / EE Control (*8mm short*)

   **Baiburēshon** / Vibration (*8mm short*)

   **Suwei = Yuragi** / Sway (*short*)

1986 **Maruchi konekushon** / Multi
   Connection (*short*)

   **Āchikurēshon = Bunsetsu** /
   Articulation (*short*)

1987 **Enguramu = Kioku kizuato** /
   Engram (*short*)

   **Ruminasu gurōbu** / Luminous
   Globe (*short*)

1988 **Dogura magura** / Dogra Magra /
   Abracadabra

1989 **Torauma** / Trauma (*short*)

1990 **Kihai** / Indication (*short*)

1992 **Naratorojī no wana** / The Trap of
   Narratology (*short*)

   **Dishimyurēshon** / Dissimulation
   (*short*)


## MATSUOKA Jōji
**(b. November 7, 1961)**
松岡錠司

Matsuoka's intelligent, perceptive films are notable for their unconventional treatment of genre themes. His early amateur work, on 8 and 16mm formats, included a trilogy on the theme of homecoming. He made his professional debut with *Swimming Upstream* (*Bata-ashi kingyo*, 1990), a film about a teenage boy who joins the school swimming team to impress the girl he loves. The unusually aggressive performances and jagged editing patterns conveyed the intensity of young love, imbuing familiar material with an engrossing quality of emotional violence.

Matsuoka's next film, *Twinkle* (*Kira kira hikaru*, 1992), broke new ground as the first mainstream Japanese film with a gay man as its leading character. Recounting the triangular story of a doctor's relationship with his student boyfriend and his marriage of convenience with an alcoholic woman, it was, in Mark Schilling's words, "an honest, sympathetic portrayal of three people who don't fit Japanese society's rigid definitions of normality." Similarly focused on unconventional relationships was *When We Were in Love* (*Watashi-tachi ga suki datta koto*, 1997), in which two women, one a victim of disabling panic attacks, invite themselves to move into the luxury apartment of two male housemates. Darker in theme was *Acacia Walk* (*Akashia no michi*, 2001), a film of compassionate severity about a woman caring for her mother, a victim of Alzheimer's disease. Here Matsuoka ruthlessly exposed the emotional frustrations of a woman torn between her duty as a daughter and her desire for personal fulfilment. Stylistic echoes of Ozu in the prevalence of static interior shots suggested the disintegration of traditional family ties in the modern world, and again the film was notable for subtle characterization and fine acting.

Regrettably, in *Sayonara, Kuro* (2003), Matsuoka proved unable to bring depth to a schematic, sentimental, and clumsily structured story about a stray dog that becomes a school mascot. The director subsequently realized his biggest commercial hit with *Tokyo Tower: Mom and Me and Sometimes Dad* (*Tōkyō Tawā: Okan to boku to tokidoki oton*, 2007), another sentimental film, made at Shochiku in the tradition of the old-fashioned *haha-mono*, about a feckless young man remembering his childhood while he cares for his cancer-stricken mother. Despite occasional disappointments, Matsuoka has already created an impressive body of work, and it seems likely that he will continue to produce humane and individual films.

1978  **Dainashi (Dainashi)** / Ruin (Untitled) (*8mm short*)
       **Natsu no ashioto** / Summer Footfalls (*8mm short*)
1981  **Sangatsu** / March (*8mm*)
1982  **Watashi o saratta yakuza** / The Yakuza Who Snatched Me (*8mm short*)
1983  **Aojiri musume** / The Immature Girl (*8mm*)
1984  **Inaka no hōsoku** / Laws of the Countryside (*8mm short*)
1985  **Itoshi no haigūsha** / Loving Spouse (*16mm short*)
1986  **Aza** / The Quarter (*8mm short*)
1990  **Bataashi kingyo** / Swimming Upstream / Goldfish (lit. The Thrashing Goldfish)
1992  **Kira kira hikaru** / Twinkle (lit. Twinkle Twinkle Little Star)
1995  **Toire no Hanako-san** / Hanako / School Mystery / Phantom of the Toilet (lit. Hanako in the Toilet)
1997  **Watashitachi ga suki datta koto** / When We Were in Love / The Things We Liked
1998  **Beru epokku** / Belle Epoque
2001  **Akashia no michi** / Acacia Walk
2003  **Sayonara, Kuro** / Goodbye, Kuro
2007  **Tōkyō tawā: Okan to boku to tokidoki oton** / Tokyo Tower: Mom and Me and Sometimes Dad

## MIIKE Takashi
(b. August 24, 1960)
三池 崇史

A prolific director of offbeat, often controversial genre movies, Miike came to international notice with his most harrowing film, *Audition* (*Ōdishon*, 1999). A grim cautionary tale about a complacent filmmaker and the apparently demure woman he chooses as his second wife, this was an exceptionally well-crafted shocker, building slowly towards an intense climax, and featuring a chilling performance from Eihi Shiina. In fact, it proved atypical of Miike in its seriousness and concentration; the director played tricks on his audience, but did not send up his story, with the result that the violence was genuinely shocking.

Miike's work as a whole is notable for extreme violence, but this has more often been presented in a deliberately theatrical, stylized fashion which owes something to the techniques of manga. *Fudoh* (*Gokudō sengokushi: Fudō*, 1996), a campy saga of the conflict between a teenage gangster and his father, was actually based on a manga, as was the notorious *Ichi the Killer* (*Koroshiya 1*, 2001), starring Tadanobu Asano as a sadomasochistic yakuza hitman. Miike has also essayed *outré* variations on traditional action genres: *Izo* (2004), a fantasy about an executed samurai transformed after death into a supernatural killing machine, was a parodic variation on the *chanbara*, while *Sukiyaki Western Django* (*Sukiyaki: Uesutan Jango*, 2007) transposed the conventions of the spaghetti Western to medieval Japan.

The portrayal of violence in Miike's work is characterized by a sadistic inventiveness: one victim is sliced in half in *Ichi the Killer*, while the gangster boss in *Gozu* (*Gokudō kyōfu daigekijō: Gozu*, 2003) dies in a manner which defies polite description. During the final confrontation in the overblown gangster film *Dead or Alive* (*DOA: Dead or Alive: Hanzaisha*, 1999), the cop tears off his own wounded arm, and the film actually seems to end with the destruction of the entire world. Certain critics have suggested that this very excess generates a sophisticated commentary on the representation of violence in film, but since Miike's manner typically distances the viewer from such real-life consequences as pain or grief, these claims seem far-fetched.

Nevertheless, these deliberately outrageous films have been balanced in Miike's oeuvre by a number of more straightforward thrillers, including the long, convoluted yakuza film *Agitator* (*Araburu tamashiitachi*, 2002) and a remake of Kinji Fukasaku's *Graveyard of Honor* (*Shin jingi no hakaba*, 2002). Perhaps most notable among these was an early trilogy of films focusing on Sino-Japanese relations. *Shinjuku Triad Society* (*Shinjuku kuroshakai: Chaina mafia sensō*, 1995) was relatively conventional in execution; nevertheless, as Tom Mes argues, the mixed-race cop hero's obsessive pursuit of a Taiwanese gangster was an intriguing metaphor for Japanese attitudes towards race. Its follow-up, *Rainy Dog* (*Gokudō kuroshakai: Rainy Dog*, 1997), was perhaps Miike's most completely acceptable picture, subtly and without sensationalism chronicling the last days of a doomed Japanese gangster adrift in Taiwan. Here, for once, the final bloodshed was genuinely cathartic. With *Ley Lines* (*Nihon kuroshakai: Ley Lines*, 1999), Miike explored the dark experiences of a group of young resident Chinese sucked into crime after they move from the countryside to Tokyo. Not a crime film, but also concerned with Sino-Japanese relations, was *The Bird People in China* (*Chūgoku no chōjin*, 1998), a sentimental depiction of two Japanese discovering a paradisial village in remote Yunnan province; regrettably, life in the village was too thinly sketched to be convincing.

This gentle film seemed atypical of Miike, but his range is in fact relatively wide. *One Missed Call* (*Chakushin ari*, 2003) was a more typical J-horror film which, like Hideo Nakata's *Ring* (*Ringu*, 1998) perceived technology (here, mobile phones) as a threat. *Sabu* (2002), made for television, was a relatively low-key, character-driven period film. Less generic was *Visitor Q* (*Bijitā Q*, 2001), an outrageous portrayal of the nuclear family which touched on every taboo subject from necrophilia to drug addiction; its intention seemed more to shock than to satirize, and it would have taken Fassbinder to reconcile the two aims. The nuclear family was also central to the mellower *The Happiness of the Katakuris* (*Katakuri-ke no kōfuku*, 2001), in which the Katakuri family open a country motel only for their success to be threatened by the sudden deaths of several guests. Punctuated by musical numbers and animated sequences, it was too shallow to succeed as a critique of Japanese aspirations, but took Miike's love of stylization to an interesting extreme.

The shaggy dog story *Gozu* was also an exceptionally stylized film, and proof of Miike's limitations: he allowed the potentially interesting play with sexual identity to be sidelined by grotesque happenings, shock effects, and an obsessive fascination with every conceivable bodily fluid. Ultimately, the image of a can being kicked into and breaking the camera lens in the last shot of *The City of Lost Souls* (*Hyōryūgai*, 2000) is typical of Miike's in-your-face approach. His films are inevitably inventive, but he would seem overall to be more interested in provoking his viewers than in enlightening them.

**1995 Daisan no gokudō** / The Third Gangster
**Shinjuku kuroshakai: Chaina mafia sensō** / Shinjuku Triad Society

1996 **Gokudō sengoku shi: Fudō /** Fudoh: The New Generation

1997 **Kishiwada shōnen gurentai: Chikemuri junjō hen /** Young Thugs: Innocent Blood

**Gokudō kuroshakai: Rainy Dog /** Rainy Dog / Criminal Underworld: Rainy Dog (lit.)

1998 **Chūgoku no tōjin /** The Bird People in China

**Andoromedia /** Andromedia

**Blues Harp**

**Kishiwada shōnen gurentai: Bōkyō /** Young Thugs: Nostalgia

**Zuiketsu gensō: Tonkararin yume densetsu /** Illusions of the Tunnel: Tonkararin's Dream Legend (short)

1999 **Nihon kuroshakai: Ley Lines /** Ley Lines (lit. Japanese Underworld: Ley Lines)

**Ōdishon /** Audition

**DOA: Dead or Alive: Hanzaisha /** Dead or Alive

**Sararīman Kintarō /** Salaryman Kintaro / White-Collar Worker Kintaro

2000 **Kikuchi-jō monogatari: Sakimoritachi no uta /** Story of Kikuchi Castle: Song of the Kyushu Garrison (short)

**Tengoku kara kita otokotachi /** The Guys from Paradise

**Hyōryūgai /** The City of Lost Souls / The City of Strangers / The Hazard City

**Dead or Alive 2: Tōbōsha /** Dead or Alive 2: Birds / Dead or Alive: Runaway (lit.)

2001 **Family**

**Bijitā Q /** Visitor Q

**Koroshiya 1 /** Ichi the Killer

**Katakuri-ke no kōfuku /** The Happiness of the Katakuris

2002 **Dead or Alive: Final**

**Onna: Kunishū ikki /** Woman: Riot of the Masses

**Araburu tamashiitachi /** Agitator / The Outlaw Souls (lit.)

**Shin jingi no hakaba /** Graveyard of Honor / New Graveyard of Honor (lit.)

**Kin'yū hametsu Nippon: Tōgenkyō no hitobito /** Shangri-La (lit. Japan's Credit Crisis: People of Shangri-La)

**Jitsuroku: Andō Noboru kyōdōden: Rekka /** Deadly Outlaw: Rekka / Violent Fire (lit. True Record of the Chivalrous Way of Noboru Ando: Violent Fire)

**Sabu**

2003 **Yurusarezaru mono /** The Man in White

**Gokudō kyōfu daigekijō: Gozu /** Gozu (lit. Yakuza Horror Theater: Gozu)

**Chakushin ari /** One Missed Call

2004 **Zeburāman /** Zebraman

**Izo**

**Saam gaang yi /** Three . . . Extremes (co-director)

2005 **Yōkai daisensō /** The Great Yokai War / The Great Hobgoblin War

2006 **46-okunen no koi /** Big Bang Love: Juvenile A / 4.6 Billion Years of Love (lit.)

**Waru**

**Taiyō no kizu /** Scars of the Sun / Sun-Scarred

2007 **Ryū ga gotoku: Gekijōban /** Like a Dragon

**Sukiyaki: Uesutan Jango /** Sukiyaki Western Django

**Tantei monogatari /** Detective Story

**Kurōzu Zero /** Crows: Episode 0

## MISUMI Kenji
**(March 2, 1921–September 24, 1975)**
三隅研次

One of the more interesting specialists in *chanbara*, Misumi entered Daiei after being repatriated from a prisoner-of-war camp in Siberia, and directed after serv-

Kiru / Destiny's Son *(1962): Misumi's flamboyant style brought flair and psychological complexity to the* chanbara.

ing as assistant to Teinosuke Kinugasa and Daisuke Itō. He is best known internationally for his contributions to two long-running series: *Zatoichi* and *Lone Wolf and Cub* (*Kozure ōkami,* known in the West as "Baby Cart"). He had originally come to notice in Japan through his confident handling of the first two episodes of an earlier sequence of films, *Daibosatsu Pass* (*Daibosatsu tōge,* 1960), about a psychopathic samurai played by Raizō Ichikawa. The success of this earned him the opportunity to direct a big-budget, 70mm epic about the life of Buddha; however, he continued to specialize in samurai films throughout his career. Even his one *gendai-geki,* the visually stunning *Ken* (1964), based on a Yukio Mishima novel, evoked the bushidō spirit through its story of a college *kendō* champion and his fanatical devotion to the martial art.

Misumi's best films were lifted above the average standard of *chanbara* by their depth of characterization, attention to historical detail, and the visual flamboyance which earned him the nickname of "Little Mizoguchi." Genuine stylistic similarities were few, Misumi lacking Mizoguchi's subtlety and delicacy of touch. Nevertheless, Misumi did bring a certain feminine sensibility to a stereotypically male genre. Women were occasionally the central focus of his films: examples included *River of Tears* (*Namidagawa,* 1967), about the loves of two sisters in Edo, and *What Price Love* (*Shirokoya Komako,* 1960), a melodrama about an innocent girl forced by her employer to marry for financial gain. Even in Misumi's samurai films the most intense moments often involved women. For instance, *Shinsengumi* (*Shinsengumi shimatsuki,* 1963) was for the most part a conventional if expertly made account of the elite corps of warriors defending the Shogunate in the years before the Meiji Restoration, but its powerful climax echoed the final scene of Kinoshita's *Army* (*Rikugun*, 1944) in shifting the focus from the departing warriors to the distress of the hero's watching lover.

Misumi's unusual concentration on human emotion rather than swordplay was also assisted by the sensitive persona of his regular male lead, Raizō Ichikawa, in films such as *Destiny's Son* (*Kiru*, 1962). Widely considered Misumi's finest achievement, this visually extraordinary work moved the *chanbara* into melodramatic territory, exploring "quasi-Freudian areas of the samurai psyche" (Robin Gatto's words). Ichikawa's hero is traumatized by the revelation of his true parentage and the murder of his foster family; subsequently, the traumas are repeated as he tries and fails to prevent the deaths of their surrogates. Slightly less complex in psychological terms, but even more visually flamboyant, was *Sword Devil* (*Kenki*, 1965), about a gardener exploited by his clan officials. Here, the bold colors and stylized compositions almost approached the artificiality of animation.

This taste for stylized imagery made Misumi a suitable choice, after Daiei's collapse, to direct four out of six episodes of the *Lone Wolf and Cub* series, based on a popular manga, for Toho. These earned him a reputation in cult circles as a purveyor of visually striking ultra-violence. However, the director's final film, *The Last Samurai* (*Ōkami yo rakujitsu o kire*, 1974), which he scripted himself, was a return to history, portraying a samurai hesitating between commitment to bushidō ideals and acceptance of modernity at the end of the Tokugawa era. Intelligently detailed in

its portrayal of a time of change and notable for a conclusion which eschewed the genre's characteristic fatalism, it confirmed that Misumi's true interest was in the moral and emotional dilemmas of those caught between duty and desire. It was this attention to character, coupled with his stylistic imagination, which gave Misumi's best films their unforced gravity. He died sadly young.

**1954** **Tange Sazen: Kokezaru no tsubo** / Sazen Tange: The Monkey Pot

**1955** **Nanatsu no kao no Ginji** / Ginji of the Seven Faces

**Tsuki o kiru kagebōshi** / The Shadow that Kills the Moon

**Kankanmushi wa utau** / The Rust-Cleaner Sings

**1956** **Asatarō karasu** / Asataro the Crow

**Hana no kyōdai** / Flower Brothers

**Shiranui bugyō** / The Fiery Magistrate

**Amigasa Gonpachi** / "Woven Hat" Gonpachi

**1957** **Mikazuki hibun** / Secret Letter of the Crescent Moon

**Momotarō samurai** / Freelance Samurai (lit. Peach Boy Samurai)

**1958** **Furisode matoe** / Wearing a Long-Sleeved Kimono

**Kaibyō noroi no kabe** / The Cursed Wall / The Ghost Cat's Cursed Wall (lit.)

**Shūnen no hebi** / Obsessive Snake

**Mito Kōmon man'yūki** / Record of Mito Komon's Pleasure Trip

**1959** **Kagerōgasa** / Halo of Heat Haze

**Senbazuru hichō** / A Thousand Flying Cranes (lit. Secret Notes on a Thousand Cranes)

**Yotsuya kaidan** / The Yotsuya Ghost Story

**Machi bugyō nikki: Tekka botan** / Diary of a Town Magistrate: Gambling Peony

**1960** **Senhime goten** / Palace of Princess Sen

**Zenigata Heiji no torimonokō: Bijingumo** / The Casebooks of Heiji Zenigata: The Beautiful Spider

**Joyō** / Patterns of Love (lit. The Phantom Woman)

**Shirakoya Komako** / What Price Love / Komako of Shirakoya (lit.)

**Daibosatsu tōge** / Satan's Sword / Daibosatsu Pass (lit.)

**Daibosatsu tōge: Ryūjin no maki** / Satan's Sword 2 / Daibosatsu Pass: The Dragon God (lit.)

1961 **Shaka** / Buddha

**Zenigata Heiji torimonokō: Bijinzame** / The Casebooks of Heiji Zenigata: The Beautiful Shark

1962 **Onna keizu** / Genealogy of Women / Her Hidden Past

**Zatōichi monogatari** / The Story of Zatoichi / The Life and Opinions of Masseur Ichi

**Kiru** / Destiny's Son (lit. Kill)

**Aoba-jō no oni** / The Devil of Aoba Castle

1963 **Shinsengumi shimatsuki** / Shinsengumi / I Want to Die a Samurai (lit. Record of the Beginning and End of the Shinsengumi)

**Jokei kazoku** / Family of Women / The Third Wall

**Maiko to ansatsusha** / The Maiko and the Assassin

**Kyojin: Ōkuma Shigenobu** / The Giant Shigenobu Okuma

1964 **Nemuri Kyōshirō shōbu** / Kyoshiro Nemuri's Showdown / Sleepy Eyes of Death: Sword of Adventure

**Ken** / Ken / Sword

**Mushukumono** / The Vagabond

**Zatōichi kesshō tabi** / Fight, Zatoichi, Fight / Zatoichi's Journey of Laughter and Blood (lit.)

1965 **Nemuri Kyōshirō enjōken** / Kyoshiro Nemuri: Sword of Fire / Sleepy Eyes of Death: Sword of Fire

**Nezumi kozō Jirokichi** / Jirokichi the Ratkid

**Muhōmatsu no isshō** / The Life of Matsu the Untamed / The Wild One

**Kenki** / Sword Devil

**Zatōichi jigoku tabi** / Zatoichi's Trip to Hell / Zatoichi and the Chess Expert

1966 **Shojo ga mita** / The Virgin Witness

**Yoidore hakase** / The Drunken Doctor / Dynamite Doctor

**Daimajin ikaru** / The Wrath of Daimajin / The Return of Giant Majin

**Nemuri Kyōshirō buraiken** / Sleepy Eyes of Death: Villain Sword / Kyoshiro Nemuri: Villain Sword

1967 **Yuki no moshō** / Shroud of Snow

**Koto yūshū** / Sorrow in the Old Capital

**Namidagawa** / River of Tears / The Namida River (lit.)

**Zatōichi chikemuri kaidō** / Zatoichi Challenged / Zatoichi's Bloodstained Path (lit.)

1968 **Tomuraishitachi** / The Undertakers / The Funeral Racket

**Nihiki no yōjinbō** / Two Bodyguards

**Zatōichi kenka daiko** / Zatoichi and the Battle Drum / The Blind Swordsman Samaritan

1969 **Oni no sumu yakata** / The Devil's Temple

**Shirikurae Magoichi** / The Magoichi Saga

1970 **Kyōjō nagaredosu** / The Angry Sword

**Zatōichi abare himatsuri** / Zatoichi's Festival of Fire

1971 **Shin onna tobakushi: Tsubo gure hada** / New Woman Gambler: Iron Rule

**Kitsune no kureta akanbō** / Gift of the Fox (lit. The Baby Given by the Fox)

1972 **Kozure ōkami : Ko o kashi udekashi tsukamatsuru** / Lone Wolf and Cub: Sword of Vengeance

/ Lone Wolf and Cub: Sword and Child for Rent (lit.)

**Kozure ōkami: Sanzunokawa no ubaguruma** / Lone Wolf and Cub: Baby Cart at the River Styx

**Kozure ōkami: Shi ni kaze ni mukau ubaguruma** / Lone Wolf and Cub: Baby Cart on the Winds of Death / Lone Wolf and Cub: Lightning Swords of Death

**Goyōkiba** / Fangs of Public Office

1973 **Sakura no daimon** / Cherry Blossom Crest

**Kozure ōkami: Meifu madō** / Lone Wolf and Cub: Baby Cart in the Land of Demons / Lone Wolf and Cub: The Path Between Heaven and Hell

1974 **Ōkami yo rakujitsu o kire** / The Last Samurai / Wolf, Cut Down the Setting Sun (lit.)

# MIZOGUCHI Kenji
## (May 16, 1898–August 23, 1956)
溝口健二

One of Japan's greatest filmmakers, Mizoguchi achieved international acclaim only in the last years of his life when European festivals began to screen his bleak, beautiful, and serenely moving period films. These late works remain his best known, but form only part of an oeuvre of unsurpassed variety, grace, and complexity, which stretches back to the silent era. Mizoguchi's work in the twenties is almost all lost, but surviving reviews and synopses suggest a considerable eclecticism and openness to Western influence: thus *Foggy Harbor* (*Kiri no minato*, 1923) was a version of *Anna Christie*, while *Blood and Soul* (*Chi to rei*, 1923) imitated the techniques of German expressionism. Within a few years, however, Mizoguchi had turned

towards native Japanese subject matter: *Nihonbashi* (1929), *Cascading White Threads* (*Taki no shiraito*, 1933), and *The Downfall of Osen* (*Orizuru Osen*, 1935) adapted *shinpa* stories by the melodramatic novelist, Kyōka Izumi. The last two of these, of which prints fortunately have been preserved, possessed a remarkable emotional intensity; moreover, despite their adherence to the conventionalized dramaturgy of *shinpa*, they displayed in embryo their director's capacity for rich atmospheric detail and his abiding concern with the oppression of women.

During the silent period, Mizoguchi also contributed to the leftist *keikō-eiga* genre with *And Yet They Go On* (*Shikamo karera wa yuku*, 1931); this story about a mother and daughter forced into prostitution was admired for its increasingly direct social criticism. Mizoguchi himself, however, felt that he did not reach artistic maturity until the extraordinary diptych of *Osaka Elegy* (*Naniwa erejii*, 1936) and *Sisters of Gion* (*Gion no kyōdai*, 1936), stories of the difficult lives of a modern Osaka girl and of Kyoto geisha respectively. Here the greater realism of the sound film allowed him to anchor his concern with female experience in a more exact and detailed recreation of milieu and culture; *Sisters of Gion*, in particular, dissected its theme with a scalpel-like precision. In these films and in their lesser-known but equally distinguished companion piece, *The Straits of Love and Hate* (*Aien kyō*, 1937), he developed an austere, contemplative style, characterized by the use of long take and long shot, which exposed the repressive mechanisms of Japanese society with extraordinary clarity.

By the late thirties, the growing power of militarism had forced Mizoguchi to mute his social criticism, but

Utamaro o meguru gonin no onna / Five Women around Utamaro *(1946): Here is the emblem of Mizoguchi's art: beautiful and refined, collaborative yet supremely personal.*

he continued his formal experimentation in a sequence of melodramas about the performing arts, including the lost *A Woman of Osaka (Naniwa onna*, 1940), which marked his first collaboration with actress Kinuyo Tanaka, and the emotionally overwhelming *The Story of the Late Chrysanthemums (Zangiku monogatari*, 1939), which imaginatively melded *avant-garde* techniques with traditional dramatics in its story of a woman who steers her actor lover to greatness at the cost of her own life. Even his version of the old patriotic warhorse, *The Loyal 47 Ronin of the Genroku Era (Genroku Chūshingura*, 1941–42), executed at official request, was an exquisite exercise in *mise-en-scène*, the delicacy and restraint of which went some way to subverting its propagandistic intentions.

Under the Occupation, Mizoguchi adapted to Allied dictates regarding democratization, examining themes of social justice and personal liberty in films about art (*Five Women around Utamaro* [*Utamaro o meguru gonin no onna*, 1946]), the law (*Victory of Women* [*Josei no shōri*, 1946]), theater (*The Love of Sumako the Actress* [*Joyū Sumako no koi*, 1947]), prostitution (*Women of the Night* [*Yoru no onnatachi*, 1948]), and politics (*My Love Has Been Burning* [*Waga koi wa moenu*, 1949]). These were among Mizoguchi's most outspoken films. *My Love Has Been Burning*, in particular, was a startlingly trenchant study of female emancipation and an exposure of the complacencies of liberal thought; its conclusion, the heroine leaving her philandering politician husband to found a feminist school, remains unparalleled in Western popular film. *Five Women around Utamaro*, on the other hand, was Mizoguchi's mellowest work: a portrait of the artist and a richly atmospheric panorama of Edo-period life, which examined the intricate, indirect relationship between the artist and society.

In his last years Mizoguchi continued his investigation of female experience in a wide variety of social milieux: *Portrait of Madame Yuki* (*Yuki fujin ezu*, 1950), *Miss Oyu* (*Oyū-sama*, 1951), and *The Lady from Musashino* (*Musashino fujin*, 1951) were studies of the troubled emotional lives of bourgeois women, while *Gion Festival Music* (*Gion bayashi*, 1953), *A Woman of Rumor* (*Uwasa no onna*, 1954), and *Street of Shame* (*Akasen chitai*, 1956) focused on the suffering of geisha and prostitutes. These films were penetrating social and psychological studies, dramatizing the interlinked motives and pressures which shape human behavior. Especially fine were *Portrait of Madame Yuki*, a poignant study of the destructive power of sexual impulse, with a keen eye for the symbolic connotations of water, and *A Woman of Rumor*, a complex examination of family relationships within a geisha house, which with economy and power explored the postwar decline of the geisha system and the corruption of human feelings by financial priorities.

At the same time, Mizoguchi essayed literary adaptations, set in the past, which examined the role of the individual in history and the effect of society on the individual through the experiences of everyman figures and the sufferings of women. The finest of these were *The Life of Oharu* (*Saikaku ichidai onna*, 1952), an impassive chronicle of the decline and fall of a courtly woman; *Ugetsu* (*Ugetsu Monogatari*, 1953), a haunting ghost story which used the su-

pernatural as a metaphor for the human desire to evade reality and responsibility; and *Sansho the Bailiff* (*Sanshō Dayū*, 1954), a historical panorama centering on a man's struggle to retain his innate decency in the face of human cruelty. Slightly more academic in approach, but still distinguished, were the Bunraku adaptation *Crucified Lovers* (*Chikamatsu monogatari*, 1954) and the Heian-period epic *Tales of the Taira Clan* (*Shin Heike monogatari*, 1955). Diverse in subject matter, these late films were unified by Mizoguchi's mature style, influenced by traditional painting but using minimal cutting, exquisite choreography of actors, and complex camera movements to wholly cinematic effect. Remarkable for its beauty, this style also achieved an unparalleled depth of implication, imbuing scenes such as the murder of the heroine in *Ugetsu*, or the final reunion in *Sansho the Bailiff*, with a cathartic intensity that has occasioned deserved comparisons with Shakespeare.

In the West, a difference of opinion exists as to the relative value of Mizoguchi's work at different periods: the traditional, liberal humanist line, exemplified most recently by the criticism of Mark Le Fanu, exalts the later work for its moral complexity, dramatic power and visual beauty; the formalist line, represented by Noel Burch, prefers the prewar films for their supposedly more radical formal qualities; while feminist critics such as Freda Freiburg have praised the more overtly political films of the immediate postwar period. My own feeling is that masterpieces were produced throughout Mizoguchi's career, and that the explicitly feminist narratives of *Sisters of Gion* and *My Love Has Been Burning* remain as satisfying dramatically as politically; conversely, a sense of outrage against oppression was still apparent in *The Life of Oharu*, *Ugetsu*, or *Sansho the Bailiff*.

Mizoguchi's collaborators should not be overlooked; his achievement was founded in no small part on the subtle performances of Kinuyo Tanaka and Isuzu Yamada, the complex scripts of Yoshikata Yoda, and the rich photography of Kazuo Miyagawa. Indeed, artistic collaboration was a key theme of *Five Women around Utamaro*, where the image of the artist painting on the naked back of a courtesan seemed the emblem of Mizoguchi's approach. Nevertheless, Mizoguchi's achievement was personal and unique, and his oeuvre includes, among many distinguished films, at least half a dozen that rank, for their beauty, delicacy, and humanity, among the supreme achievements of world cinema.

1923    **Ai ni yomigaeru hi** / The Resurrection of Love (lit. The Day of Love's Resurrection)
**Kokyō** / Hometown
**Seishun no yumeji** / The Dream Path of Youth
**Jōen no chimata** / City of Desire
**Haizan no uta wa kanashi** / Sad Song of Failure
**813** / 813: The Adventures of Arsène Lupin
**Kiri no minato** / Foggy Harbor
**Yoru** / The Night
**Haikyo no naka** / In the Ruins
**Chi to rei** / Blood and Soul
**Tōge no uta** / Song of the Mountain Pass

1924    **Kanashiki hakuchi** / The Sad Idiot
**Akatsuki no shi** / Death at Dawn
**Gendai no joō** / The Queen of Modern Times
**Josei wa tsuyoshi** / Women Are Strong
**Jinkyō** / This Dusty World
**Shichimenchō no yukue** / Turkeys in a Row / The Trace of a Turkey (lit.)

**Itō junsa no shi** / The Death of a Police Officer (lit. The Death of Constable Ito) (*co-director*)
**Samidare zōshi** / Chronicle of the May Rain (lit. Chronicle of the Rainy Season)
**Koi o tatsu ono** / Love-Breaking Axe (*co-director*)
**Kanraku no onna** / A Woman of Pleasure
**Kyokubadan no joō** / Queen of the Circus

1925    **Ā tokumukan Kantō** / Ah, Special Battleship Kanto (*co-director*)
**Uchien Puchan** (sometimes listed as "Musen Fusen" and mistranslated "No Money, No Fight"; actually a Chinese name)
**Gakusō o idete** / Out of College
**Daichi wa hohoemu: Daiichibu** / The Earth Smiles: Part 1
**Shirayuri wa nageku** / The White Lily Laments
**Akai yūhi ni terasarete** / Shining in the Red Sunset
**Furusato no uta** / The Song of Home
**Shōhin eigashū: Machi no suketchi** / Street Sketches (*co-director*)
**Ningen** / The Human Being
**Nogi Taishō to Kuma-san** / General Nogi and Kuma-san

1926    **Dōkaō** / The Copper Coin King
**Ka’miningyō haru no sasayaki** / A Paper Doll's Whisper of Spring
**Shinsetsu ono ga tsumi** / My Fault, New Version
**Kyōren no onna shishō** / Passion of a Woman Teacher
**Kaikoku danji** / The Boy of the Sea
**Kane** / Money

1927    **Kōon** / The Imperial Grace
**Jihishinchō** / The Cuckoo / A Loving Heart

1928    **Hito no isshō: Jinsei banji kane no maki** / A Man's Life: Money Is Everything in Life

Hito no isshō: Ukiyo wa tsurai ne no maki / A Man's Life: This Floating World Is Hard

Hito no isshō: Kuma to Tora saikai no maki / A Man's Life: Bear and Tiger Meet Again

Musume kawaiya / My Lovely Daughter

1929 Nihonbashi / Nihonbashi / Bridge of Japan

Asahi wa kagayaku / The Morning Sun Shines (co-director)

Tōkyō kōshinkyoku / Tokyo March

Tokai kokyōkyoku / Metropolitan Symphony

1930 Fujiwara Yoshie no Furusato / Hometown (lit. Yoshie Fujiwara's Hometown)

Tōjin Okichi / Okichi, Mistress of a Foreigner

1931 Shikamo karera wa yuku (Zenpen; Kōhen) / And Yet They Go On (Parts 1 and 2)

1932 Toki no ujigami / The Man of the Moment / Timely Mediator

Manmō kenkoku no reimei / The Dawn of Manchuria and Mongolia

1933 Taki no shiraito / Cascading White Threads / White Threads of the Waterfall / The Water Magician

Gion matsuri / Gion Festival

1934 Jinpūren / The Jinpu Group

Aizō tōge / The Mountain Pass of Love and Hate

1935 Orizuru Osen / The Downfall of Osen / Osen of the Paper Cranes (lit.)

Maria no Oyuki / Oyuki the Virgin / Oyuki the Madonna

Ojō Okichi / Miss Okichi (supervisor; sometimes credited as co-director)

Gubijinsō / The Field Poppy / Poppies

1936 Naniwa erejī / Osaka Elegy

Gion no kyōdai / Sisters of Gion

1937 Aien kyō / The Straits of Love and Hate

1938 Roei no uta / Song of the Camp

Ā, furusato / Ah, My Hometown

1939 Zangiku monogatari / The Story of the Late Chrysanthemums

1940 Naniwa onna / A Woman of Osaka

1941 Geidō ichidai otoko / The Life of an Actor

Genroku Chūshingura: Zenpen / The Loyal 47 Ronin of the Genroku Era: Part 1

1942 Genroku Chūshingura: Kōhen / The Loyal 47 Ronin of the Genroku Era: Part 2

1944 Danjurō sandai / Three Generations of Danjuro

Miyamoto Musashi / Musashi Miyamoto / The Swordsman

1945 Meitō Bijomaru / The Famous Sword

Hisshōka / Victory Song (co-director)

1946 Josei no shōri / Victory of Women

Utamaro o meguru gonin no onna / Five Women around Utamaro / Utamaro and His Five Women

1947 Joyū Sumako no koi / The Love of Sumako the Actress

1948 Yoru no onnatachi / Women of the Night

1949 Waga koi wa moenu / My Love Has Been Burning

1950 Yuki fujin ezu / Portrait of Madame Yuki

1951 Oyū-sama / Miss Oyu

Musashino fujin / The Lady from Musashino

1952 Saikaku ichidai onna / The Life of Oharu / The Life of a Woman by Saikaku (lit.)

1953 Ugetsu monogatari / Ugetsu / Ugetsu Monogatari / Tales of the Pale and Silvery Moon after the Rain / Tales of Moonlight and Rain (lit.)

Gion bayashi / Gion Festival Music / A Geisha

1954 Sanshō dayū / Sansho the Bailiff

**Uwasa no onna** / A Woman of Rumor / The Crucified Woman

**Chikamatsu monogatari** / Crucified Lovers / A Story from Chikamatsu (lit.)

1955 **Yōkihi** / The Princess Yang Kwei Fei / The Empress Yang Kwei Fei

**Shin Heike monogatari** / Tales of the Taira Clan / New Tales of the Taira Clan (lit.)

1956 **Akasen chitai** / Street of Shame / Red Light District (lit.)


# MOCHIZUKI Rokurō
## (b. May 9, 1957)
## 望月六郎

A director of intermittent excellence, Mochizuki worked initially and prolifically on pornography, generally for straight-to-video release. His first mainstream feature *Skinless Night* (*Sukinresu naito*, 1991) was the semi-autobiographical story of a filmmaker who has abandoned his youthful artistic intentions to work on erotic films. If this plot suggested disillusionment with the milieu, Mochizuki has never entirely abandoned erotica. *Currency and Blonde* (*Tsūka to Kinpatsu*, 2000), for instance, was a bizarre account of the sado-masochistic affair between a university lecturer in economics and his American lover, allegedly intended as an allegory for American-Japanese relations. Subsequently, Mochizuki has continued to direct pornographic videos in addition to his feature work.

After *Skinless Night*, Mochizuki achieved a major commercial hit with *The Wicked Reporter* (*Gokudō kisha*, 1993), about a feckless journalist played by Eiji Okuda. Tom Mes has commented on this film's "affinity for those that have fallen by the wayside

of the national quest for ever more financial gain." It spawned two sequels and its success paved the way for Mochizuki's most distinguished work: the sequence of low-key crime movies he directed during the nineties. Lacking the pared-down mechanics of Takeshi Kitano or the bizarre stylization and extreme content of Takashi Miike, these films focused, with intelligence and restraint, on three-dimensional characters whose illegal activities were placed in the context of plausible situations and relationships. Though it was, in fact, one of his wilder films, the title of *A Yakuza in Love* (*Koi gokudō*, 1997) aptly expressed Mochizuki's interest in emotions more delicate than the genre typically allows.

The finest example, and one of the outstanding crime movies of the nineties, was *Onibi: The Fire Within* (*Onibi*, 1997), an engrossing study of a middle-aged yakuza whose efforts to go straight are undermined when he falls for a woman seeking revenge on the man who has exploited her. A generally static camera enabled the viewer to concentrate on nuances of behavior and expression, and the tone was less fatalistic than tragic, with a real sense of the gravity of death. Less consistently remarkable in style, but still powerful, was *Another Lonely Hitman* (*Shin kanashiki hittoman*, 1995), another story of an old-fashioned yakuza out of touch with the modern world, with a genuinely cathartic climax. *Mobster's Confession* (*Gokudō zange roku*, 1998), an ironic account of the activities of a small-time hood during the era of the bubble economy, was more comic in tone. Sometimes cynical, it was ultimately affecting in balancing the purely material values of the protagonist against the loyalty and love of his henchman and girlfriend, whose selflessness guarantees his success and ultimate survival.

Outside the gangster genre, Mochizuki made *Apron Stage* (*Debeso*, 1996), about a group of itinerant actors. This interest in artists was taken up again in *Kamachi* (2004), the biopic of a precocious poet and painter who died accidentally in 1977 aged 17, but the film was criticized for presenting its hero as an uncomplicated golden boy. *Wet Red Thread* (*Nureta akai ito*, 2005) was the story of two former prostitutes trying to make a new life for themselves, a plot which might be taken as a female variation on Mochizuki's earlier concern with gangsters trying to leave the mob. However, his work in recent years seems not to have matched his best nineties films; a pity, since his ability to distill emotional complexities from generic plots is admirable.

1985 **Honban bideo: Hagu** / Unrehearsed Video: Stripping
**Onanie jō: Midarana shiseikatsu** / The Masturbating Woman: Loose Private Life

1986 **Aido ningyō: I ka se te** / Love Slave Doll: Let Me Come

1991 **Sukinresu naito** / Skinless Night

1993 **Gokudō kisha** / The Wicked Reporter

1994 **Gokudō kisha 2: Baken tenshō hen** / The Wicked Reporter 2: (lit. The Wicked Reporter 2: Reincarnation of a Betting Ticket)

1995 **Shin kanashiki hittoman** / Another Lonely Hitman
**Kitanai yatsu** / Dirty Guy

1996 **Debeso** / Apron Stage (lit. Protruding Belly Button)
**Shin gokudō kisha: Nigema densetsu** / The Wicked Reporter 3: The One That Got Away

1997 **Onibi** / Onibi: The Fire Within
**Mukokuseki no otoko: Chi no shūkaku** / Pinocchio: Man without

Nationality (lit. Man without Nationality: Blood Harvest)
**Koi gokudō** / A Yakuza in Love

1998 **Gokudō zangeroku** / Mobster's Confession
**Gedō** / The Outer Way (lit. The Heresy)

1999 **Minazuki**

2000 **Tsūka to kinpatsu** / Currency and Blonde
**Chinpira** / Coward

2001 **Shishi no ketsumyaku** / The Lion's Vein

2002 **Konjaku denki: Kashin** / Legend of Past and Present: Flower God
**Jam Films** (*co-director*)

2004 **Kamachi**
**Koharu Komachi** / Beautiful Koharu

2005 **Nureta akai ito** / Wet Red Thread

## MORI Issei
(January 15, 1911–June 29, 1989)
森一生

One of the best-regarded directors of second features in pre- and postwar Japan, Mori (sometimes known as Kazuo Mori) rather resembled such maverick American directors as Samuel Fuller and Don Siegel, whose formal intelligence and imagination allowed them to impose a personal stamp on generic plots. Directing *jidai-geki* as assignments for Shinko Kinema from 1936, he quickly earned a reputation for his imaginative technique: in *Kichimatsu Yuten* (*Yūten Kichimatsu*, 1937), for instance, a famous cut between successive shots of a stone lantern in the road actually marked the lapse of time between the hero's setting out in search of his wife and child and his disconsolate return. Mori's last Shinko film, *Masujiro*

*Omura* (*Ōmura Masujirō*, 1942), was particularly well received, but soon after this his career was interrupted by war service. After the war, he continued to direct assignments at Daiei, Shinko's successor, for which he was to work almost exclusively.

During the Occupation, official discouragement of period films led him to widen his range by directing several notable *gendai-geki*, which revealed a sympathetic interest in female protagonists. *My Name Is Mistress* (*Watashi no na wa jōfu*, 1949), scripted by Mizoguchi's regular screenwriter Yoshikata Yoda, was a socially critical film about a journalist pursuing a woman thought to be a criminal's mistress, while *Mountain Cat Woman* (*Yamaneko reijō*, 1948), about the affection between a poor mother and daughter, initiated Daiei's sequence of postwar *haha-mono*. In the fifties and sixties, however, Mori was again usually assigned to period material, collaborating regularly with such genre stars as Kazuo Hasegawa, Raizō Ichikawa, and Shintarō Katsu, all three of whom appeared in *Jirocho at Mount Fuji* (*Jirochō Fuji*, 1959), an atypically comical retelling of the exploits of a nineteenth-century folk hero. *Duel at Kagiyanotsuji* (*Araki Mataemon: Kettō Kagiyanotsuji*, 1952) was notable for its basis in a Kurosawa script, but *Samurai Vendetta* (*Hakuōki*, 1959) is widely considered Mori's masterpiece, most completely expressing the style and outlook that Sadao Yamane has described as "lyricism full of pathos [...] a gentle kind of nihilism." Mori directed this unusual samurai film with an extraordinary intensity, and Ichikawa's tortured performance gave full rein to the script's psychological complexity and subversive take on bushidō ideals. Among Ichikawa's other collaborations with Mori, *A*

*Certain Killer* (*Aru koroshiya*, 1967) was an efficient thriller about a professional hitman, played out against a backdrop of wastelands and graveyards, and setting its crimes obliquely in the context of the wider violence in Vietnam.

Also remarkable among Mori's later films was *Shiranui Kengyo* (*Shiranui kengyō*, 1960), a bleak cautionary tale tracing the criminal career of a blind *masseur*. Mori drew out the ironies of the story, avoided sentimentalizing the villain's disability, and elicited a performance of cruel vitality from Shintarō Katsu. Katsu subsequently achieved fame playing another blind *masseur*, the folk hero Zatōichi, in a popular series of films. The second of these was capably directed by Mori, who also handled installments in other popular series such as *Heiji Zenigata*, *Kyoshiro Nemuri* (*Nemuri Kyōshiro*) and *Band of Assassins* (*Shinobi no mono*). His ability to imbue these genre pieces with both visual flair and emotional depth is proof of his flexibility, imagination, and stylistic integrity.

1936 **Adauchi Hizakurige** / Journey to Revenge / Yaji and Kita's Revenge

1937 **Yūten Kichimatsu** / Kichimatsu Yuten

**Okano Kin'emon** / Kin'emon Okano

**Genroku jūrokunen** / The Sixteenth Year of the Genroku Era

1938 **Miyamoto Musashi** / Musashi Miyamoto

**Ninjutsu Sekigahara: Sarutobi Sasuke** / Ninja Arts: Sarutobi Sasuke

**Kaibyō akakabe daimyōjin** / Monster Cat: God of the Red Wall

1939 **Nishikie Edo sugata: Hatamoto to machiyakko** / Figures of Edo in Nishiki-e Painting: Samurai and Townspeople

**Yoshino kinnōtō** / The Emperor's Followers in Yoshino

Oisemairi / Journey to Ise

Konpirabune / Ship of Neptune (lit. Ship of Konpira)

Oniazami / Plumed Thistle

1940 Kondō Isami / Isami Kondo

Zoku Awa tanuki gassen / Battle of the Raccoon Dogs in Awa 2

Oyakodori / Family of Birds

1941 Tsumi naki machi / A Town without Crime

Meoto daiko / The Drum Couple

1942 Ōmura Masujirō / Masujiro Omura

Ōsaka chōnin / Osaka Townspeople

Sandai no sakazuki / Three Generations, One Sake Cup

1946 Tebukuro o nugasu otoko / The Man Who Took off the Gloves

Yari odori gojūsantsugi / Spear Dance on the Tokaido

1947 Fujin keisatsukan / Policewomen

Ryūkoden / Legend of the Dragon and the Tiger

Seikatsu no ki / Tree of Life

1948 Oshidorigasa / The Bamboo Hat

Yamaneko reijō / Mountain Cat Woman

Nerawareta onna / Target Woman

Kurogumo kaidō / Black Cloud Road

1949 Kōren bosatsu / Red Lotus Bodhisattva

Chikagai no dankon / A Bullet Hole Underground

Watashi no na wa jōfu / My Name Is Mistress

Enoken Kasagi no Gokuraku fūfu / A Couple in the Seventh Heaven (lit. Enoken and Kasagi: A Couple in the Seventh Heaven)

1950 Tsukinode fune / Ship of the Rising Moon

Watashi wa nerawareteiru / I'm the Target

Aru fujinkai no kokuhaku / Confessions of a Gynaecologist

Minami no bara / Southern Rose

Gorotsukibune / Pirate Ship

1951 Ashura hangan / Judge of the Ashuras

Zenigata Heiji / Heiji Zenigata

Hana aru dotō / The Angry Waves with Flowers

Ōmagatsuji no kettō / Duel at Omagatsuji

1952 Araki Mataemon: Kettō Kagiyanotsuji / Duel at Kagiyanotsuji (lit. Araki Mataemon: Duel at Kagiyanotsuji)

Zenigata Heiji torimonohikae: Jigoku no mon / Notebooks of Heiji Zenigata: Gate to Hell

Shin Yajikita dōchū / New Journey of Yaji and Kita

Koshinuke Ganryūjima / Cowards on Ganryujima

1953 Zenigata Heiji torimonohikae: Karakuri yashiki / Notebooks of Heiji Zenigata: House of Tricks

Ehon Sarutobi Sasuke / Picture Book of Sarutobi Sasuke

Hana no Kōdōkan / Judo Hall of Flowers

Irezumi satsujin jiken / The Case of the Tattoo Murder

Zenigata Heiji torimonohikae: Kin'iro no ōkami / Notebooks of Heiji Zenigata: The Golden Wolf

1954 Koina no Ginpei / Ginpei of the Carp

Yoidore nitōryū / The Drunken Master with Two Swords

Shirazu no Yatarō / Ignorant Yataro

Midori no nakama / Green Comrades

1955 Hotaru no hikari / Firefly Light

Hanazakari otoko ichidai / A Florid Life

Fūsetsu Kōdōkan / Wind and Snow in the Judo Hall

Tōjūrō no koi / The Loves of Tojuro

Nagasaki no yoru / Nagasaki Nights

Ore wa Tōkichirō / I Am Tokichiro

1956 **Marason samurai** / Marathon
Samurai
**Keijibeya** / The Detectives' Room
**Zenigata Heiji torimonohikae:
Hitohada gumo** / Notebooks of
Heiji Zenigata: Spider on the Skin
**Abaretobi** / Violent Hawk

1957 **Suzakumon** / Suzaku Gate
**Yatarōgasa** / Yataro's Sedge Hat
**Mangorō tengu** / Mangoro the
Goblin
**Inazuma kaidō** / Thunder Road
**Nichiro sensō shōri no hishi:
Tekichū ōdan sanbyakuri** / Secrets
of the Russo-Japanese War: 300 Ri
into Enemy Territory

1958 **Akadō Suzunosuke: Mitsume no
chōjin** / Suzunosuke of the Red
Sash: Bird Man With Three Eyes
**Nanabanme no misshi** / The
Seventh Secret Messenger
**Hitohada kujaku** / Peacock on the
Skin / The Swishing Sword

1959 **Hitohada botan** / Peony on the
Skin
**Wakaki hi no Nobunaga** / The
Youth of Nobunaga
**Jirochō Fuji** / Jirocho at Mount
Fuji
**Hakuōki** / Samurai Vendetta / Saga
of Pale Cherry Blossoms (lit.)

1960 **Nuregami kenka tabi** / The Battle
of the Wet-Haired Men
**Zoku Jirochō Fuji** / Jirocho at
Mount Fuji 2
**Shiranui kengyō** / Shiranui Kengyo
/ Blinded by Sea Fire
**Tadanao gyōjōki** / Conduct Report
on Sergeant Tadanao

1961 **Kaze to kumo to toride** / Wind,
Clouds, and a Fortress
**Okesa utaeba** / Singing Okesa
**Daibosatsu tōge: Kanketsu hen** /
Satan's Sword 3 / Daibosatsu Pass:
Final Chapter (lit.)
**Kaidan: Kakuidori** / Ghost Stories
of the Mosquito-Eating Bird

**Shin Genji monogatari** / New Tale
of Genji

1962 **Keshin** / Incarnation
**Sandai no sakazuki** / Three
Generations, One Sake Cup
**Shin akumyō** / The Unknown,
New Version
**Edo e hyakunanajūri** / 170 Ri to
Edo
**Zoku Zatōichi monogatari** / The
Return of Zatoichi
**Yōkina tonosama** / The Cheerful
Lord

1963 **Yaburegasa Chōan** / Choan with a
Broken Umbrella
**Akumyō ichiba** / Market of the
Unknown
**Ten'ya wan'ya Jirochō dōchū** /
The Confusing Journey of Jirocho
**Akumyō hatoba** / Harbor of the
Unknown
**Shin shinobi no mono** / New Band
of Assassins

1964 **Dokonjō monogatari: Zubutoi
yatsu** / A Heroic Tale: The
Impertinent Fellow
**Kinō kieta otoko** / The Man Who
Disappeared Yesterday
**Suruga yūkyōden: Toba arashi** /
The Life of a Chivalrous Man in
Suruga: The Casino Robbery
**Akumyō daiko** / Drum of the
Unknown
**Bakuto zamurai** / The Gambling
Samurai

1965 **Suruga yūkyōden: Dokyō garasu**
/ The Life of a Chivalrous Man in
Suruga: The Courageous Crow
**Abareinu** / Wild Dog
**Shinobi no mono: Iga yashiki** /
Band of Assassins: Iga Mansion
**Zatōichi sakategiri** / Zatoichi and
the Doomed Man (lit. Zatochi and
the Sword With the Reverse Grip)
**Hondara kenpō** / The Stupid
Swordsman

1966 **Shinobi no mono: Shin**

Kirigakure Saizō / Band of
Assassins: New Saizo Kirigakure

Hondara torimonochō / Crazy
Casebooks

Heitai yakuza: Datsugoku / The
Hoodlum Soldier: Jailbreak

Rikugun Nakano gakkō: Kumo
ichigō shirei / Nakano Army
School: Assignment Cloud

Daimajin gyakushū / Majin Strikes
Again

1967 Ano shisōsha o nerae / Aim at
That Testcar! / Spy on That Masked
Car

Aru koroshiya / A Certain Killer

Waka oyabun gyōjō tabi /
Criminal Journey of a Young Boss

Aru koroshiya no kagi / A Certain
Killer's Key

1968 Akumyō jūhachiban / The
Unknown, Number 18

Teppō den raiki / The First Rifles
in Japan / The Saga of Tanegashima

Hiroku onnagura / The
Storehouse Woman

1969 Shutsugoku yonjūhachijikan / 48-
Hour Jailbreak

Kantō onna gokudō / Woman
Yakuza of Kanto

Kantō onna akumyō / Unknown
Woman of Kanto

Yotsuya kaidan: Oiwa no bōrei
/ The Yotsuya Ghost Story: The
Ghost of Oiwa / Curse of the Ghost

Nemuri Kyōshirō: Engetsu sappō
/ Kyoshiro Nemuri: Murder at Full
Moon

1970 Shinobi no shū / The Last Iga Spy
/ Mission: Iron Castle

Abuku zeni / Bubble Money

Minagoroshi no Sukyatto /
Massacre Scat

1971 Wakaki hi no Kōdōkan / Early
Days at the Judo Hall

1972 Zatōichi goyōtabi / Zatoichi at
Large (lit. Zatoichi on Official
Business)

## MORITA Yoshimitsu
(b. January 25, 1950)
森田芳光

A fascinating but inconsistent director, Morita tends to defy traditional *auteur*ist analysis; Aaron Gerow has argued that he "jumps from genre to genre, trend to trend, trying to be at the forefront of what is popular." His work is unified, however, by the creative reworking of genres which marks him as a quintessential postmodern filmmaker. He spent some years directing amateur 8mm films before realizing his earliest features, which were comedies on sexual themes, including two Nikkatsu Roman Porno projects. His comedic talent was confirmed by the ATG production *Family Game* (*Kazoku gēmu*, 1983), a scabrous, funny, and visually inventive satire on the Japanese family and the bourgeois obsession with academic achievement. Morita's technique in this film, using a generally static camera and frequent frontal compositions, has been identified as a pastiche of Ozu's style, which served to emphasize the obsolescence of traditional family values. A talent for pastiche was also visible in *And Then* (*Sore kara*, 1985), a melodrama adapted from a Sōseki Natsume novel about a man's enduring passion for the woman he gave up when a classmate declared his love for her. Here, the use of decentered compositions, long takes, and long shot subtly parodied the style of prewar cinema, while subdued, near-Bressonian performances admirably expressed the emotional repression of Meiji-era society.

Also well-received among Morita's early films were *Deaths in Tokimeki* (*Tokimeki ni shisu*, 1984), about a hitman hired to assassinate a cult leader, and *For Business* (*Sorobanzuku*, 1986), a satire on the practices of rival advertising agencies. *24 Hour Playboy* (*Ai to Heisei no irootoko*, 1989), about the neurotic efforts of an insomniac dentist and saxophonist to avoid romantic commitment, was another satire, aimed at the affluent yet feckless bubble-era generation, but marred by its indulgent treatment of its protagonist. *Kitchen* (*Kitchin*, 1989) was the first adaptation of Banana Yoshimoto's eccentric novel, later to be filmed, with greater success, in Hong Kong by Yim Ho. *Happy Wedding* (*Oishii kekkon*, 1991), was conceived as a comic gloss on the work of Ozu, about a young woman who asks a coworker to pose as her boyfriend in order to avoid an arranged marriage.

During the nineties, Morita abandoned satiric irony for love stories and fantasies, directing, in Mark Schilling's words, "feelgood entertainment that is at once strenuously with-it and timelessly romantic." Some of these were sophisticated in premise: *Last Christmas* (*Mirai no omoide: Rasuto Kurisumasu*, 1992) was about two deceased women given the chance to relive the last ten years of their lives with the advantage of foreknowledge, while *haru* (1996) was an account of an online romance. Morita's biggest popular success, however, was his most straightforward film, *Lost Paradise* (*Shitsurakuen*, 1997), a melodrama about an adulterous love affair which, despite its modern trappings, was basically an unabashedly traditional account of *amour fou* culminating in a double suicide. *Inseparable* (*Umineko*, 2004), another drama of adultery, was less well received. Subsequently, Morita returned to comedy with *The Mamiya Brothers* (*Mamiya kyōdai*, 2006), a wry story about two nerdish brothers looking for romance, and remade Kurosawa's classic period action film *Sanjuro* (*Tsubaki Sanjūrō*, 2007).

Also in recent years, Morita has made some accomplished thrillers: *Keiho* (*39 keihō daisanjūkyūjō*, 1999), a courtroom drama about a psychologist assigned to assess the sanity of a murderer; *The Black House* (*Kuroi ie*, 1999), a darkly humorous film about an insurance adjuster probing the circumstances of a suspicious death; and the intricately structured *Copycat Killer* (*Mohōhan*, 2002), where the events surrounding a series of killings were used to satirize a media-driven, celebrity-obsessed culture which allows even murderers their fifteen minutes of fame. Here, Morita's rapid editing, use of onscreen text, and visual pyrotechnics at once reflected and parodied this culture, making this perhaps his most suggestive film since *Family Game*.

Morita's work has returned repeatedly to the theme of human separation and the impossibility of wholly knowing another person or of achieving a complete perspective on events. The members of the family in *Family Game* share the confines of a small apartment but live in different mental worlds. The lovers in *haru*, though soulmates, choose to remain physically separated, communicating via the internet and withholding basic information such as their real names. *Keiho* pivoted on the ambiguity of the killer's state of mind, while *Copycat Killer* told its story twice from different perspectives, motivation in both films remaining uncertain. The stylized acting in Morita's films speaks for his sense that communication is inevitably interpretative. If his work has sometimes seemed a little superficial, this is perhaps because its implication is that the surface is as deep as one can see.

**1970 POS I-?** (*8mm short*)
  **Hex (Junko e no jumon)** / Hex

(Junko's Incantation) (*8mm short*)
**Sky** (*8mm short*)
1971 **Eiga** / Film (*8mm short*)
**Seaside** (*8mm short*)
**Eating** (*8mm short*)
**Midnight** (*8mm short*)
**Light** (*8mm short*)
**Mother** (*8mm short*)
**Tenki yohō** / Weather Forecast (*8mm short*)
**Nude** (*8mm short*)
**Film** (*8mm short*)
**Denwa** / Telephone (*8mm short*)
1972 **Enkinjutsu** / Techniques of Perspective (*8mm*)
**Kenkō shindan** / Physical Check-Up (*8mm short*)
**Kōjō chitai** / Industrial Zone (*8mm short*)
1973 **Tōkyō kinkō chitai** / Tokyo Suburbs (*8mm short*)
1974 **Shōjo shumi** / Girlish Taste (*8mm short*)
**Kaiga kyōshitsu** / Drawing Class (*8mm short*)
1976 **Suijōki kyūkō** / The Steam Express (*8mm*)
1978 **Raibu in Chigasaki** / Live in Chigasaki (*8mm*)
1981 **No yōna mono** / Something Like It / Something Like Yoshiwara
1982 **Shibugakitai: Bōizu & Gāruzu** / Shibugakitai: Boys and Girls
**Zūmu appu: Maruhon uwasa no sutorippā** / The Stripteaser (lit. Zoom Up: Confidential Book About a Stripper in the Rumor)
1983 **Pinku katto: Futoku aishite fukaku aishite** / Love Hard, Love Deep
**Kazoku gēmu** / Family Game
1984 **Tokimeki ni shizu** / Deaths in Tokimeki
**Mein Tēma** / Main Theme
1985 **Sore kara** / And Then
1986 **Sorobanzuku** / For Business

1988 **Kanashii iroyanen** / Getting Blue in Color / Love and Action in Osaka
1989 **Ai to Heisei no irootoko** / 24-Hour Playboy (lit. Love and a Heisei-era Playboy)
**Kitchin** / Kitchen
1991 **Oishii kekkon** / Happy Wedding
1992 **Mirai no omoide: Rasuto Kurisumasu** / Last Christmas (lit. Future Memories: Last Christmas)
1996 **(haru)**
1997 **Shitsurakuen** / Lost Paradise
1999 **39 keihō daisanjūkyūjō** / Keiho / Criminal Code Article 39 (lit.)
**Kuroi ie** / The Black House
2002 **Mohōhan** / Copycat Killer
2003 **Ashura no gotoku** / Like Ashura
2004 **Umineko** / Inseparable (lit. Black-Tailed Gull)
2006 **Mamiya kyōdai** / The Mamiya Brothers
2007 **Sausubaundo** / Southbound
**Tsubaki Sanjurō** / Sanjuro

**MURATA Minoru**
**(March 2, 1894–June 26, 1937)**
村田実

Though few of his films survive today, Murata was once rated alongside Mizoguchi as one of the outstanding filmmakers of the twenties. His fame rested on his talent for blending realism and symbolism: he used non-professional actors and filmed on location, while, in Anderson and Richie's words, creating characters "whose actions and personalities had symbolic, almost allegorical meanings." This talent remains visible in his most famous extant film, *Souls on the Road* (*Rojō no reikon*, 1921), a melodrama remarkable for its rapid intercutting between plot strands. Here, the characterizations and events were

©Nikkatsu Corporation

*Kaijin / Ashes (1929): This is one of many lost films that earned Murata a towering reputation in the silent era.*

contrived to point out a didactic moral about the human need for compassion. A certain didacticism appears to have been typical of Murata's work, which often examined political themes: *Ashes* (*Kaijin*, 1929) was an account of the sufferings of a liberal idealist who joins Takamori Saigō's abortive rebellion in the Meiji period, while *The Skyscraper* (*Matenrō*, 1929–30) was a critique of the sharper practices of big business.

Murata was among the first Japanese directors to earn foreign distribution, *The Street Juggler* (*Machi no tejinashi*, 1925) and *Ashes*, both now lost, having been shown in Europe shortly after their Japanese release. The content and style of his films were much influenced by Western models: thus, *Souls on*

*the Road* took its storyline from Gorky while faintly echoing the structure of D.W. Griffith's *Intolerance* (1916); *Seisaku's Wife* (*Seisaku no tsuma*, 1924), about a wife who blinds her husband to ensure that he will not leave her, apparently borrowed techniques from German expressionism; and *The Lady of the Camellias* (*Tsubaki hime*, 1927) was an adaptation of Dumas. *Foghorns* (*Muteki*, 1934), a tragic melodrama set in Meiji-period Yokohama, ironically brought the moody atmosphere and fluent tracking shots of F.W. Murnau to a strikingly xenophobic triangular narrative about a foreign merchant's ill-treatment of his Japanese lover and servant. Although derivative in some ways, Murata's surviving films also display an individual talent, and are stylish enough to make one regret both the loss of much of his output and his early death.

| 1920 | **Hikari ni tatsu onna (Joyūden)** / The Woman Standing in the Light (Chronicle of an Actress) |
|---|---|
| 1921 | **Rojō no reikon** / Souls on the Road |
| | **Kimi yo shirazu ya** / You Who Don't Know |
| | **Hōshi no bara** / Rose of Service |
| 1923 | **Chichi no tsumi** / A Father's Sin |
| | **Jigoku no butō** / Dance of Hell |
| | **Omitsu to Seizaburō** / Omitsu and Seizaburo |
| 1924 | **Seisaku no tsuma** / Seisaku's Wife |
| | **Mōken no himitsu** / Secret of the Fierce Dogs |
| | **Natsukashi no sato** / Dear Old Hometown |
| | **Shingō** / The Signal |
| | **Osumi to haha** / Osumi and Her Mother |
| | **Konjiki yasha** / The Golden Demon |
| | **Shin kago no tori** / Caged Bird, New Version |
| | **Untenshu Eikichi** / Driver Eikichi |

**Seishun no uta** / Song of Youth
**Omitsu to Seizaburō** / Omitsu and Seizaburo
**Honmoku yawa** / The Night Tales of Honmoku

1925 **Machi no tejinashi** / The Street Juggler
**Hō o shitau onna** / The Woman Who Longs for Justice

1926 **Kujaku no hikari (Daiippen; Dainihen)** / Peacock Light (Parts 1 and 2)
**Nichirin (Zenpen; Kōhen)** / The Sun (Parts 1 and 2)
**Sutekina bijin** / The Wonderful Beauty
**Shinshū danji no iki** / The Spirit of a Man from Japan (lit. The Spirit of a Man from the Land of the Gods)

1927 **Tsubaki hime** / The Lady of the Camellias

1928 **Kekkon nijūsō (Zenpen; Kōhen)** / Wedding Duet (Parts 1 and 2)
**Gekiryū (Zenpen; Kōhen)** / Torrent (Parts 1 and 2)

1929 **Kaijin** / Ashes
**Matenrō: Sōtō hen** / The Skyscraper: Fighting Chapter

1930 **Matenrō: Aiyoku hen** / The Skyscraper: Chapter of Love and Lust
**Kono taiyō (Daiippen; Dainihen; Daisanpen)** / This Sun (Parts 1, 2 and 3)

1931 **Misutā Nippon** / Mr. Japan
**Umi no nai minato** / The Harbor without a Sea
**Shiroi ane (Zenpen; Kōhen)** / White Elder Sister (Parts 1 and 2)

1932 **Shanhai** / Shanghai
**Senkyūhyakusanjūninen no haha** / A Mother of 1932
**Shōwa Shinsengumi** / Showa Era Shinsengumi (co-director)

1933 **Seishungai** / Street of Youth
1934 **Haru no mezame** / Spring Awakening
**Muteki** / Foghorns

**Yama no yobigoe** / Call of the Mountains
**Hana saku ki: Zenpen: Namiko no maki** / The Blossoming Tree: Part 1: Namiko's Reel
**Hana saku ki: Kōhen: Emako no maki** / The Blossoming Tree: Part 2: Emako's Reel

1935 **Onna no yūjō** / A Woman's Friendship
**Jōnetsu no shiranui** / Sea Fire of Passion
**Toppa muden** / Breakthrough Wireless

1936 **Sakura no sono** / The Cherry Orchard
**Shingetsu shō** / Story of the New Moon (co-director)

## NAGASAKI Shun'ichi
(b. June 18, 1956)
長崎俊一

Since Nagasaki's most individual films have tended to circulate abroad only on the festival circuit, his name is less widely known than those of many of his contemporaries. Like his friend Sōgo Ishii, he came to notice initially through the 8mm films he directed while a student. His best-known 8mm work, the feature-length *Heart, Beating in the Dark* (*Yamiutsu shinzō*, 1982), was a claustrophobic two-hander about young lovers on the run, the details of whose circumstances emerge gradually through their stylized dialogues. Despite its stylistic inadequacies, the film's originality earned it international festival screenings; Nagasaki's trip to London for its festival showing there became the subject of a later short, *London Calling* (*Rondon kōringu*, 1985). By this time the director had gained funding from ATG to make his first 35mm film, *The*

*Lonely Hearts Club Band in September* (*Kugatsu no jōdan kurabubando*, 1982), about biker gangs. Another youth film was *Rock Requiem* (*Rokku yo, shizuka ni nagare yo*, 1988), about four high school boys dreaming of forming a band.

Nagasaki's next film was his first thriller, *The Vamp* (*Yōjo no jidai*, 1988), and his later career in commercial cinema has included several suspense pieces notable for inventively reworking genre plots. *The Enchantment* (*Yūwakusha*, 1989) was a wry psychological thriller about a psychiatrist's involvement with a woman who claims that she is being abused by a lesbian lover. Elaborate plot twists served not only to startle the viewer, but also to undermine conventional assumptions about the authority of the medical profession and the rationality of men. Of his subsequent thrillers, *Stranger* (*Yoru no sutorenjā: Kyōfu*, 1991), made for video release but shown at festivals abroad, was the story of a female taxi driver stalked by a psychopathic passenger, while *Dogs* (*Doggusu*, 1998) focused on the psychological impact of a policewoman's decision to lie about a murder she has witnessed.

Nagasaki's films in other genres, such as the hospital drama *Nurse Call* (*Nāsu kōru*, 1993) and the triangular romance *Some Kinda Love* (*Romansu*, 1996), have not been so well received. Ironically, his best-known work internationally is probably his most ordinary film, *Shikoku* (1999), a mechanical and derivative horror movie marred by the clumsy use of handheld camera and most interesting for its rural locations. However, he achieved a major critical success with *A Tender Place* (*Yawarakana hoo*, 2001), a domestic epic recounting the attempts of a woman to come to terms with the disappearance of her 5-year-old daughter during a holiday in Hokkaido, which

won praise for its subtlety of observation and psychological insight. The director went back to his roots with the sequel to/remake of *Heart, Beating in the Dark* (*Yamiutsu shinzō*, 2005), which combined a restaging of the original film with scenes focusing on the now middle-aged characters of that original, alongside ostensible documentary footage of the making of the new version. The result, despite its pretensions, commented intelligently on the gulf between the flexible process of remaking a fictional film and the impossibility of changing the actual past. If the subject matter of *Black Belt* (*Kuroobi*, 2007), about karate trainees vying to succeed their late master as head of his *dōjō*, suggested a return to a more commercial vein, the decision to cast genuine karate masters in the lead roles demonstrated Nagasaki's concern for authenticity.

Though Nagasaki has never evolved an especially distinctive visual style, his use of the camera is generally intelligent and precise, and he is remarkable for his sympathetic interest in female psychology, a concern which has united his genre films and his art movies. Indeed, in the context of the industry he is noteworthy as an artist who has bridged the gap between arthouse and commercial filmmaking.

1975  **25-ji no butōha** / Dance at One in the Morning (*8mm short*)
**Baku o bukkorose** / Kill the Tapir That Feeds on Dreams (*8mm short*)
**Zōka no kareru kisetsu** / The Season When Artifical Flowers Die (*8mm short*)

1977  **Yumeko zanshi** / The Cruel Death of Yumeko (*16mm short*)

1978  **Kurējī rabu** / Crazy Love (*16mm short*)
**Yuki ga rokku o suteta natsu** / The Summer Yuki Gave Up Rock Music (*16mm short*)

1979  **Happī sutorīto ura** / The Back of Happy Street (*16mm short*)
      **Eiko, yoru ni nare** / Eiko Becomes Evening (*8mm short*)

1982  **Kugatsu no jōdan kurabubando** / The Lonely Hearts Club Band in September
      **Yamiutsu shinzō** / Heart, Beating in the Dark (*8mm*)
      **Sono ato** / After That (*short*)

1985  **Rondon kōringu** / London Calling (*16mm short*)
      **Shinario: Yamaguchi Momoe no haishin** / Scenario: Betrayed by Momoe Yamaguchi (*16mm short*)

1988  **Rokku yo, shizuka ni nagare yo** / Rock Requiem / Rock in a Minor Key
      **Yōjo no jidai** / The Vamp (lit. Age of the Temptress)

1989  **Yūwakusha** / The Enchantment

1991  **Yoru no sutorenjā, kyōfu!** / Stranger (lit. Stranger in the Night, Fear!)

1992  **Saigo no doraibu** / The Last Drive / The Drive

1993  **Nāsu kōru** / Nurse Call / Nurses
      **J-Movie Wars** (*co-director*)

1996  **Romansu** / Some Kinda Love

1998  **Doggusu** / Dogs

1999  **Shikoku**

2001  **Yawarakana hoo** / A Tender Place

2005  **Yamiutsu shinzō** / Heart, Beating in the Dark (*remake*)
      **Hachigatsu no kurisumasu** / Christmas in August

2007  **Kuroobi** / Black Belt

# NAKAGAWA Nobuo
## (April 18, 1905–June 17, 1984)
中川信夫

Nakagawa's reputation rests on the sequence of horror films he directed at Shin Toho in the late fifties and sixties. Like Roger Corman, who had made a roughly contemporary cycle of Poe adaptations in Hollywood, he often drew on literary sources, the Kabuki theater furnishing plots for two of his best supernatural films, *The Yotsuya Ghost Story* (*Tokaidō Yotsuya kaidan*, 1959) and *The Ghost of Kasane* (*Kaidan Kasanegafuchi*, 1957). These, along with *Mansion of the Ghost Cat* (*Bōrei kaibyō yashiki*, 1958) and the later *Snake Woman's Curse* (*Kaidan hebi onna*, 1968), were Nakagawa's most characteristic studies of sin and retribution. *Grand guignol* sequences notwithstanding, they were generally psychological in emphasis; their ghosts were usually conceived as externalizations of guilt and so do not directly harm their victims. The ghostly strangler in *Mansion of the Ghost Cat* was an exception; more often, the mere presence of the supernatural drives Nakagawa's protagonists to self-destruction. In the films mentioned above, and others such as *The Ceiling at Utsunomiya* (*Kaii Utsunomiya tsuritenjō*, 1956), the haunted villain or anti-hero kills family, lovers, friends, or associates, and often finally himself, thinking that he is attacking the ghost. Nakagawa explored similar themes in his most personal film, *Hell* (*Jigoku*, 1960), a brooding account of the fatal repercussions of a single tragedy, which imaginatively recreated the Buddhist underworld.

The flair and polish of these films belied their low budgets. Some credit is due to Haruyasu Kurosawa, Nakagawa's art director in this period, responsible for convincing evocations of old Edo in *The Yotsuya Ghost Story* and of Meiji-era Tokyo in *Wicked Woman* (*Dokufu Takahashi Oden*, 1958). Nevertheless, the distinction of these films derived ultimately from Nakagawa's elegant long takes, elaborate camera movements, striking

Bōrei kaibyō yashiki / The Mansion of the Ghost Cat *(1958): This is one of the stylish and chilling ghost stories by the Roger Corman of Japan.*

compositions, and interest in formal experimentation. The underworld in *Hell* was consciously based on traditional scroll paintings. *Mansion of the Ghost Cat*, divided into color and monochrome sequences, deliberately applied a distinct camera technique to each. Nakagawa's last film, *The Living Koheiji* (*Kaiidan: Ikiteiru Koheiji*, 1982), made for ATG after many years' inactivity, expressively fused Kabuki techniques with those of experimental cinema to craft a haunting study of alienation.

Elsewhere, Nakagawa's films were characterized by an elegant simplicity. The baroque climax of *The Ghost of Kasane* was less memorable than the affecting low-key domestic scenes, often shot with a static camera, which gave the actors space to develop their characters. Nakagawa was also adept at charging props and decor with symbolic mean-

ing: in *The Yotsuya Ghost Story*, a dolly from white to blood-red strips of cloth was used to give visual expression to the anti-hero's decision to murder his wife, while in *Hell*, the cheerfully colored umbrellas begin to function ironically as guilt images. Kōyō Udagawa has discussed the symbolic function of such motifs as wheels, water, and bridges in Nakagawa's work and related these to the director's interest in the Buddhist concept of *gō* (karma). The last shots of *Hell* famously showed the hero trapped on a spinning wheel in the underworld; *The Ghost of Kasane*, *The Yotsuya Ghost Story*, and *Snake Woman's Curse* also depicted an afterlife, the tormented characters achieving posthumous salvation. Given this Buddhist outlook, it is significant that *Vampire Woman* (*Onna kyūket-suki*, 1959), admittedly a minor film, presented Christianity as the sinister "other," the vampire being a descendant of Christian martyr Shirō Amakusa.

The fame of Nakagawa's horror films has led some critics to neglect his work in other genres. Many of his prewar films were comedies, often starring popular clown Enoken. *The Grass-Cutter Girl* (*Shishun no izumi*, 1953) was also a comedy, about a young couple's courtship in a northern farming village. *Lynch* (*Rinchi*, 1949) was an efficiently made *film noir* about the long-term consequences of crime; again, the theme of karma was suggested as Nakagawa charted the impact of the father's sin—the theft of a Buddhist statue—on the next generation. *Wandering Journey* (*Sasurai no tabiji*, 1951), about a selfish singer who, after becoming famous, rejects the woman who supported him in obscurity, was an intelligent variation on melodramatic themes, given psychological depth by its director's grasp of the emotional resonances of interior space. *Kaachan* ("*Nendo no omen*" *yori: Kāchan*, 1961) was a neo-realist chronicle of a family of traditional craftsmen in Tokyo's old *shitamachi* neighborhood. Perhaps Nakagawa's best non-horror film was *Wicked Woman*, a subtle story about a Meiji-era lady thief. Lucid and economical, it detailed the circumstances which lead a basically decent woman into crime and depicted her impossible love for a sympathetic policeman with a balance of humanity and sharp irony. Though in some ways atypical, it was characteristic of the tenderness Nakagawa extended to those damned by circumstances beyond their control.

1934 **Yumiya hachiman ken** / Sword of the God of War
1935 **Tōkai no kaoyaku** / Boss of the Tokai Region
**Haji o shiru mono** / The Man Who Felt Ashamed

**Goyōuta Nezumi kozō** / The Ratkid's Official Song
**Hakone hachiri** / Eight Ri to Hakone
1936 **Akutarō jishi** / Bad Boy Lion
**Shura hakkō: Daisanbu** / The Pains of Hell: Part 3
**Yarimochi kaidō** / The Spear-Carrier's Road
1937 **Hatamoto hachimanki** / 80,000 Mounted Vassals
**Onna Sazen: Daiippen: Yōka no maki** / A Female Sazen: Part 1: The Mysterious Fire
**Onna Sazen: Dainihen: Maken no maki** / A Female Sazen: Part 2: The Demon Sword
1938 **Nippon'ichi no okappiki** / Japan's Best Secret Policeman
**Itahachi jima** / Stripes of Itahachi
**Gekka no wakamusha** / Young Warrior in the Moonlight
1939 **Enoken no Mori no Ishimatsu** / Enoken's Ishimatsu of the Forest
**Enoken no Ganbari senjutsu** / Rivals / Enoken's Rivals (lit.)
**Shinpen Tange Sazen: Sekigan no maki** / Sazen Tange: New Version: One-Eye Reel
**Enoken no Yajikita** / Enoken's Yaji and Kita
1940 **Kingorō no Musume monogatari** / The Story of Kingoro's Daughter
**Enoken no Homare no dohyōiri** / Enoken Honorably Enters the Ring
**Enoken no Wanwan taishō** / Enoken's Bow-Wow General
**Dengeki musuko** / Electric Son
1941 **Akatsuki no shinpatsu** / Start at Dawn
**Gubijinsō** / Poppy
1948 **Basha monogatari** / Story of a Coach
1949 **Shin'ya no kokuhaku** / Midnight Confession
**Enoken no Tobisuke bōken ryokō** / The Adventures of Tobisuke / Enoken's Adventures of Tobisuke (lit.)
**Rinchi** / Lynch

1950  **Tsukinode no seppun** / Kiss at Moonrise

**Atariya Kinpachi torimonochō: Senri no tora** / Casebooks of Kinpachi the Accurate Archer: Tiger of a Thousand Ri

**Amakara chindōchū** / Strange Bittersweet Journey

**Wakasama samurai torimonochō: Nazo no nōmen yashiki** / Casebooks of the Young Master Samurai: The Mysterious Mansion of Noh Masks

1951  **Umon torimonochō: Katame ōkami** / Casebooks of Detective Umon: The One-Eyed Wolf

**Matashirō gyōjōki: Onihime shigure** / Conduct Report on Matashiro: The Devil Princess and Winter Rain

**Wakasama samurai torimonochō: Noroi no ningyōshi** / Casebooks of the Young Master Samurai: The Cursed Dollmaker

**Hatamoto taikutsu otoko: Tōjingai no oni** / The Boring Retainer: Demon of the Foreigners' Quarter

**Kōgen no eki yo sayonara** / Farewell to the Highland Station

**Sasurai no tabiji** / Wandering Journey

1952  **Umon torimonochō: Hikanoko ihen** / Casebooks of Detective Umon: The Incident of the Fawn-Pattern Cloth

**Inuhimesama** / The Dog Princess

**Koikaze gojūsantsugi** / Love's Zephyr along the Tokaido

**Itoshiko to taete yukamu** / Enduring with a Lovechild

**Kyō wa kaisha no gekkyūbi** / Today Is Payday

**Yūyake Fuji** / Sunset over Mount Fuji

1953  **Edokko hangan** / The Edoite Judge

**Haresugata: Izu no Satarō** / The Hour of Triumph: Sataro of Izu

**Kinsan torimonochō: Nazo no ningyōshi** / Casebooks of Kinsan: The Mysterious Dollmaker

**Edo no hanamichi** / The Theater of Edo

**Shishun no izumi** / The Grass-Cutter Girl (lit. Spring of Adolescence)

1954  **Wakaki hi no Takuboku: Kumo wa tensai de aru** / The Youth of Takuboku: Genius in a Cloud

**Ishinaka-sensei gyōjōki: Seishun musen ryokō** / Conduct Report on Professor Ishinaka: Youthful Hitchhikers

**Horafuki Tanji** / Tanji the Braggart

**Nīsan no aijō** / My Elder Brother's Love

1955  **Banba no Chūtarō** / Chutaro of Banba

**Natsume Sōseki no Sanshirō** / Soseki Natsume's Sanshiro

**Aogashima no kodomotachi: Onna kyōshi no kiroku** / Children of Aogashima: Record of a Woman Teacher

1956  **Kyūketsu ga** / Vampire Moth

**Koisugata kitsune goten** / The Palace of a Fox in Love

**Ashura sankenshi** / Three Swordsmen of Ashura

**Kaii Utsunomiya tsuritenjō** / The Ceiling at Utsunomiya

**Ningyō Sashichi torimonochō: Yōen rokushibijin** / Dandy Sashichi Detective Story: Six Famous Dead Beauties

1957  **Fūun kyū nari Ōsaka-jō: Sanada jūyūshi sōshingun** / The Sudden Importance of Osaka Castle: Ten Heroes of Sanada, the Whole Advancing Army

**Ningyō Sashichi torimonochō: Ōedo no ushimitsudoki** / Dandy Sashichi Detective Story: The Small Hours in Great Edo

**Kaidan Kasanegafuchi** / The Ghost of Kasane / The Ghost of Kasane Swamp (lit.) / The Depths

**Hibarigaoka no taiketsu /** Showdown at Hibarigaoka

**Shōgun Iemitsu to tenka no Hikoza /** Shogun Iemitsu and Hikozaemon

1958 **Dokufu Takahashi Oden /** Wicked Woman (lit. Wicked Woman Oden Takahashi)

**Tenka no fukushōgun: Mito man'yūki /** The Shogun's Adjutant: Mito's Pleasure Trip

**Bōrei kaibyō yashiki /** The Mansion of the Ghost Cat / Black Cat Mansion

**Kenpei to yūrei /** Ghost in the Regiment (lit. The Military Police and the Ghost)

**Kyōen kobanzame (Zenpen; Kōhen) /** The Chivalrous and Beautiful Remora (Parts 1 and 2)

1959 **Onna kyūketsuki /** Vampire Woman / The Lady Vampire

**Kagebōshi torimonochō /** Casebooks of the Shadow

**Nippon romansu ryokō /** Romantic Trip in Japan (*co-director*)

**Tōkaidō Yotsuya kaidan /** The Yotsuya Ghost Story (lit. Ghost Story of Yotsuya on the Tokaido)

**Raiden /** Thunder and Lightning

**Zoku raiden /** Thunder and Lightning 2

1960 **Onna shikeishū no datsugoku /** Death Row Woman (lit. Escape of a Woman Condemned to Death)

**Jigoku /** Hell / Jigoku / The Sinners of Hell

1961 **Hatamoto kenkataka /** The "Quarreling Falcon" Retainer

**"Nendo no omen" yori: Kāchan /** Kaachan (lit. From "The Clay Mask": Mother)

**Happyakumangoku ni idomu otoko /** The Man Who Contended for Eight Million Koku

1962 **Hatamoto taikutsu otoko: Nazo no sango yashiki /** The Boring Retainer: The Mysterious Coral Mansion

**Kanashimi wa itsu mo haha ni /** Sorrow Is Always for Mother

**Maboroshi tengu /** The Mysterious Goblin

**Kishū no abarenbō /** The Roughneck of Kishu

**Inazuma tōge no kettō /** Duel at Lightning Pass

1963 **Nihon zankoku monogatari /** Cruel Story of Japan (*co-director*)

**Otoko no arashi /** A Man's Storm

1968 **Kaidan hebi onna /** Snake Woman's Curse / Ghost Story of the Snake Woman (lit.)

1969 **Sakurahai: Gikyōdai /** Sakura Cup: Sworn Brothers

**Yōen dokufuden: Hitokiri Okatsu /** Okatsu the Avenger / Quick Draw Okatsu / Legend of a Wicked Temptress: Okatsu the Assassin (lit.)

**Yōen dokufuden: Okatsu kyōjō tabi /** Legend of a Wicked Temptress: Okatsu's Criminal Journey / Vendetta of a Samurai Girl

1982 **Kaiidan: Ikiteiru Koheiji /** The Living Koheiji

## NAKAHARA Shun
**(b. May 25, 1951)**
中原俊

An interesting if uneven filmmaker, Nakahara started out directing Roman Porno at Nikkatsu; this, he later argued, was "the best way to learn how to make films about human beings." Certainly, his first mainstream work, *The Cherry Orchard* (*Sakura no sono*, 1990), was a precisely judged, piercing human drama, unfolding in the hours before a student performance of Chekhov's play at a private girls' school. Conversations between the girls gradually shaded in their individual complexities, fears, and desires, while imaginatively composed group shots and

Sakura no sono / The Cherry Orchard *(1990): Nakahara entered the mainstream with this piercing story of emotional tensions among schoolgirls preparing for a play.*

well-chosen camera movements gave eloquent expression to the personal and sexual tensions between them.

Nakahara's talent for distinctively characterizing the various members of a specific group within a confined environment was also apparent in his next work, *The Gentle Twelve (Jūninin no yasashii Nihonjin*, 1991), set in an imaginary Japan that has adopted the system of trial by jury. Nakahara created an ironic reworking of *Twelve Angry Men* (1957, Sidney Lumet); here, a lone juror strives to convince his fellows of the guilt, not the innocence, of the accused. The director's next work, *Season Off (Shīzun ofu*, 1992), was even more confined in setting and in number of characters: it delved into the hidden cracks in two ostensibly happy marriages during the couples' stay at an island resort.

However, after a hiatus of some years, Nakahara began to make more obviously commercial films. *Lie Lie Lie* (1997) was an entertaining but flimsy and thinly characterized caper movie, well made, but with little directorial personality. *Coquille (Kokīyu*, 1999) was one of several accounts of doomed extra-marital affairs which emerged after the commercial success of Yoshimitsu Morita's *Lost Paradise (Shitsurakuen*, 1997); regrettably, Nakahara's sensitive, tasteful approach rendered this account of passion somewhat bland. Nakahara's later *Colorful (Karafuru*, 2000) was actually scripted by Morita, and its high-concept story of a deceased gangster sent back to earth to be reincarnated in the body of a teenage boy recalled Morita's *Last Christmas (Mirai no omoide: Rasuto Kurisumasu*, 1992).

In recent years, Nakahara has also made two interesting accounts of women responding to bereavement. *Concent* (*Konsento*, 2002) was an exceptionally bleak film about a freelance writer trying to come to terms with the death of a brother; the heroine's ability to smell illness was an intriguing plot device, but the sexual complications began to seem farcical by the fadeout. However, in *Ichigo Chips* (*Ichigo no kakera*, 2005), about a manga writer psychologically paralyzed by her indirect responsibility for her boyfriend's death, the contrast between tragic subject matter and the cartoon-like opulence of the visuals had something of the incongruous power of Fassbinder. The film was more visibly artificial than most of Nakahara's oeuvre, and it is difficult to judge how much was the contribution of co-director Tsutomu Takahashi. Nevertheless, it seemed a return to form, and one may hope that it bodes well for future developments.

1982   **Okasareta shigan** / Violated Desire
**Dorei keiyakusho: Muchi to haihīru** / Slave's Contract: Whip and High Heels
**Seiko no futomata: Onnayu Komachi** / Seiko's Thighs: Komachi of the Women's Bath
1983   **Uno Kōichirō no shimai riyōshitsu** / Koichiro Uno's Sisters' Barber Shop
**3-nenme no uwaki** / The Third Year Affair
**Boku no oyaji to boku** / My Stiff-Necked Daddy and Me
1984   **Nawa shimai: Kimyō na kajitsu** / Rope Sisters: Strange Fruit
**Ivu-chan no hanabira** / Eve's Petals
**Shoya no umi** / Sea of the Bridal Night
1986   **Boku no onna ni te o dasuna** / Don't Touch My Woman
1987   **Meiku appu** / Make-Up

**Shakotan bugi** / Lowrider Boogie
1988   **Neko no yōni** / Like a Cat
1990   **Sakura no sono** / The Cherry Orchard
1991   **Jūnin no yasashii Nihonjin** / The Gentle Twelve
1992   **Shīzun ofu** / Season Off
1997   **Lie Lie Lie**
1999   **Kokīyu** / Coquille
2000   **Shikai** / The Dentist
**Karafuru** / Colorful
2002   **Konsento** / Concent (lit. Electrical Outlet)
**Tomie: Saishūshō: Kindan no kajitsu** / Tomie: Last Chapter: Forbidden Fruit
2004   **Derashine** / Déraciné
2005   **DV: Domesutikku baiorensu** / DV: Domestic Violence
**Ichigo no kakera** / Ichigo Chips (*co-director*)
2007   **Sutekina yoru, boku ni kudasai** / Give Me This Lovely Night

## NAKAHIRA Kō
**(January 3, 1926–September 11, 1978)**
中平康

A talented yet frustratingly unfulfilled director, Nakahira served an orthodox apprenticeship at Shochiku and Nikkatsu to such directors as Keisuke Kinoshita, Akira Kurosawa, Minoru Shibuya, Tomotaka Tasaka, and Kaneto Shindō. This classical training was belied by the freshness of his feature debut, *Crazed Fruit* (*Kurutta kajitsu*, 1956), a seminal *taiyōzoku* ("sun-tribe") melodrama based on a Shintarō Ishihara novel about sibling rivalry, set among the wealthy, feckless *après-guerre* youth of the Shōnan coast. Location shooting, sensual imagery and an eye for significant detail gave the film a physical

Kurutta kajitsu / Crazed Fruit *(1956): The* taiyōzoku *("sun tribe") genre brought a new frankness to Japanese cinema.*

realism that compensated for the more overblown aspects of the plotting, such as the famous motorboat climax.

Several of Nakahira's other early films at Nikkatsu achieved some favorable critical notice. Among them were *The Flesh Is Weak (Bitoku no yoromeki,* 1957), based on a Yukio Mishima novel, and again praised for its freshness of touch; *Four Seasons of Love (Shiki no aiyoku,* 1958), a satiric riff on the *haha-mono* genre in which a free-spirited mother's behavior outrages her strait-laced children; and *The Assignation (Mikkai,* 1959), a brief, brutal account of the fatal affair between a married woman and a student. Increasingly, however, Nakahira was assigned to more conventional dramatic material, particularly the action thrillers in which Nikkatsu specialized during the sixties.

In films such as *Crimson Wings (Kurenai no tsubasa,* 1958), *He and I (Aitsu to watashi,* 1961), and *The Arab Storm (Arabu no arashi,* 1961), he collaborated with popular tough-guy star Yūjirō Ishihara (Shintarō's brother), who had made his debut in *Crazed Fruit.* His most individual film of the period was perhaps *Monday Girl (Getsuyōbi no Yuka,* 1964), described by Steven Higgins as "a shrewdly observed portrait of a modern, sexually assertive woman," which, with its stylistic echoes of Godard and Truffaut, recalled Nakahira's original status as a precursor to the New Wave.

By this stage, however, Nikkatsu was not encouraging Nakahira's interest in experimentation, and during the late sixties he spent two years in Hong Kong working for Shaw Brothers, where he again directed action pictures.

On his return to Japan, he established an independent production company, for which he made *Soul to the Devil* (*Yami no naka no chimimōryō*, 1971) and *Melody of Love* (*Hensōkyoku*, 1976), both films on sexual themes, the latter shot on location in Europe. The former was screened in competition at Cannes, and it is possible that Nakahira might have achieved a new reputation as a director of art films had it not been for his premature death. Apart from *Crazed Fruit*, his work remains virtually unknown in the West, and his more personal films would benefit from wider exposure.

1956 **Kurutta kajitsu** / Crazed Fruit
**Nerawareta otoko** / The Pursued Man / A Man Spied Upon
**Natsu no arashi** / Summer Storm
**Gyūnyūya Furankī** / Frankie the Milkman

1957 **Koi to uwaki no seishun techō: Gaitō** / Youthful Notebooks of Love and Infidelity: Street Light
**Koroshita no wa dare ka** / Who Is the Murderer?
**Yūwaku** / Temptation
**Bitoku no yoromeki** / The Flesh Is Weak

1958 **Shiki no aiyoku** / Four Seasons of Love
**Kurenai no tsubasa** / Crimson Wings
**Saijo katagi** / The Talented Woman

1959 **Sono kabe o kudake** / Break That Wall!
**Mikkai** / The Assignation / A Secret Rendezvous

1960 **Kyanpasu 110-ban: Gakusei yarō to musumetachi** / The Girls and the Students (lit. Campus Dial 110: The Student Rascals and the Girls)
**Chizu no nai machi** / The Town without a Map / Jungle Block
**Ashita hareru ka** / Wait for Tomorrow (lit. Will It Be Fine Tomorrow?)

1961 **Aitsu to watashi** / He and I / That Guy and I
**Arabu no arashi** / The Arab Storm / Storm over Arabia

1962 **Atariya taishō** / The Lucky General
**Wakakute warukute sugoi koitsura** / The Young, Bad, Great Guys
**Yabai koto nara zeni ni naru** / Danger Pays

1963 **Dorodarake no junjō** / The Mud-Spattered Pure Heart
**Ore no senaka ni hi ga ataru** / With My Back to the Sun
**Gendaikko** / A Child of Modern Times
**Hikaru umi** / Bright Sea

1964 **Getsuyōbi no Yuka** / Monday Girl
**Ryōjin nikki** / The Hunter's Diary
**Suna no ue no shokubutsugun** / Plants from the Dunes
**Onna no uzu to fuchi to nagare** / Whirlpool of Flesh

1965 **Gendai akutō jingi** / A Modern Villain's Honor
**Kuroi tobakushi** / The Black Gambler
**Yarō ni kokkyō wa nai** / The Black Challenger (lit. To Rogues There Are No Borders)
**Kekkon sōdan** / Marriage Consultation

1966 **Kuroi tobakushi: Akuma no hidarite** / The Black Gambler: Left Hand of the Devil
**Akai gurasu** / Red Glass
**Dak ging ling ling gau** / Interpol (*Hong Kong*)

1967 **Kigeki: Ōburoshiki** / Bluster
**Seishun Tarō** / The Youth of Taro
**Kuroi tobakushi** / The Black Gambler
**Fei tin neoi long** / Trapeze Girl (*Hong Kong*)

1968 **Za Supaidāsu no daishingeki** / The Spiders a-Go-Go
**Kwong lyun si** / Summer Heat (*Hong Kong*)

**Lip jan** / Diary of a Ladykiller
(*Hong Kong*)

1970 **Eikō e no hangyaku** / The
Glorious Rebellion

1971 **Yami no naka no chimimōryō** /
Soul to the Devil (lit. Evil Spirits in
the Darkness)

1972 **Konketsuji Rika** / Rika the Mixed-
Blood Girl

1973 **Konketsuji Rika: Hitori yuku
sasurai tabi** / Rika the Mixed-Blood
Girl: Lonely Wanderer

1976 **Hensōkyoku** / Melody of Love (lit.
Variation)

# NAKAMURA Noboru
## (August 4, 1913–May 20, 1981)
## 中村登

A specialist in *gendai-geki* at Shochiku, Nakamura was a director of carefully made, well-acted, well-mounted, somewhat academic films, typified, in Arne Svensson's words, by an "elegiac harmony, which may seem a little cloying." He first directed during the wartime years, working then and in the early postwar era on romances. With *Natsuko's Adventure* (*Natsuko no bōken*, 1953), an adaptation in color of a Yukio Mishima story, he began to concentrate on literary adaptations. Among the most successful of his fifties films was *Payoff with Love* (*Shūkin ryokō*, 1957), based on a novel by Masuji Ibuse, in which a lodger in a boarding house goes on a quest to recover money from fellow boarders after the death of the proprietor leaves his orphan son in need. This became the first in a popular series.

Nakamura's most critically acclaimed films, however, were a sequence of female-centered melodramas made during the sixties, which commented intelligently on the place of women in Japanese society and on wider political issues. *Portrait of Chieko* (*Chieko shō*, 1967) was an intriguing account of a woman artist's descent into schizophrenia, albeit with ambiguous sexual politics, it being unclear whether her madness is triggered by the frustration of her artistic career or by her inability to bear children. *The Old Capital* (*Koto*, 1963), after Kawabata, was a moving account of a Kyoto girl who learns that she has a twin sister in a rural village. Shima Iwashita handled the dual role ably, and Nakamura effectively caught the atmosphere of the city, while implicitly condemning the corrosive effect of the Japanese class system on personal relationships. *The Kii River* (*Kinokawa*, 1966), also a richly atmospheric and beautifully acted film, followed three generations in the life of a provincial family in Wakayama Prefecture as a microcosm of Japan's economic, social, and political transformation from the Meiji period to the end of World War II. Another family saga unfolding over the decades was *The Song from My Heart* (*Waga koi waga uta*, 1969), about the troubled relations between a famous nationalist poet, Hideo Yoshino, and his children.

Nakamura's more notable films in his later years included *Love Stopped the Runaway Train* (*Shiokari tōge*, 1973), about a man who hates Christianity because his mother was expelled from her family after converting to the religion, and *Three Old Women* (*Sanbaba*, 1974), about the wife, sister and mistress of a deceased financier, each of whom claims the right to take up residence in his estate. Intended as a discreet comment on the situation of the elderly in Japan, this latter film also served as a vehicle for three distinguished veteran actresses: Aiko Mimasu, Kinuyo

Tanaka, and Michiyo Kogure. In his skill as a director of actresses, ability to create atmosphere, and general good taste, Nakamura somewhat resembled Shirō Toyoda or Kōzaburō Yoshimura, the latter of whom he had assisted on *The Story of Tank Commander Nishizumi* (*Nishizumi senshachōden*, 1940). Though lacking the formal precision that elevated the best work of those directors, he nevertheless upheld the classical tradition of Japanese filmmaking with sensitivity and grace.

1941 **Seikatsu to rizumu** / Life and Rhythm (*short*)
**Kekkon no risō** / Ideal of Marriage
1942 **Arata naru kōfuku** / Another Joy
**Ningen dōshi** / Human Comrades
**Otoko no iki** / A Man's Disposition
1943 **Kohan no wakare** / Lakeside Parting
1946 **Nikoniko taikai** / Smiling Competition (*co-director*)
**Ai no senkusha** / Pioneer of Love
**Omitsu no endan** / Omitsu's Proposal
1947 **Shojo wa shinju no gotoku** / A Virgin Is Like a Pearl
**Musume no gyakushū** / A Girl Strikes Back
1948 **Ryosō** / Traveling Suit
**Hi no bara** / Fiery Rose / Scarlet Rose
1949 **Kimi matedomo** / Although I Wait for You
**Shūkaidō** / The Begonia
**Ren'ai sanbagarasu** / Three Crows in Love
1950 **Eikō e no michi** / Road to Glory
**Haru no ushio (Zenpen; Kōhen)** / Spring Tide (Parts 1 and 2)
**Eden no umi** / Eden by the Sea
1951 **Wagaya wa tanoshi** / Our House Is Happy
**Koibumi saiban** / The Love-Letter Trial

1952 **Yume to shiriseba** / If I Knew It Was a Dream
**Nami** / Waves
1953 **Haru no koteki** / Spring Flute and Drum
**Natsuko no bōken** / Natsuko's Adventure
**Yume miru hitobito** / Dreaming People
**Ganpeki** / The Cliff
**Tabiji** / The Journey
1954 **Kazoku kaigi: Tōkyō hen** / Family Meeting: Tokyo Chapter
**Kazoku kaigi: Ōsaka hen** / Family Meeting: Osaka Chapter
**Hi wa shizumazu** / The Sun Never Sets
**Edo no yūbae** / Edo Sunset
1955 **Onna no isshō** / A Woman's Life
**Shuzenji monogatari** / A Tale of Shuzenji / The Mask of Destiny
**Akogare** / Yearning
**Kimi utsukushiku** / You Are Beautiful
1956 **Shiroi magyo** / The White Devil-Fish
**Shu to midori: Zenpen: Shu no maki** / Red and Green: Part 1: Red Reel
**Shu to midori: Kōhen: Midori no maki** / Red and Green: Part 2: Green Reel
**Tsuyu no atosaki** / Before and After the Rains
1957 **Doshaburi** / Cloudburst
**Shūkin ryokō** / Payoff with Love / Bill-Collecting Trip (lit.)
1958 **Hibi no haishin** / A Triple Betrayal
**Wataru sekai wa oni bakari: Boroya no shunjū** / This Passing World Is Full of Demons: Seasons of a Poor Family
**Kamitsukareta kaoyaku** / The Country Boss (lit. The Bitten Boss)
1959 **Haru o matsu hitobito** / People Awaiting Spring
**Itazura** / Mischief / Love Letters

**Kiken ryokō** / Vagabond Lovers / Dangerous Trip (lit.)

**Asu e no seisō** / Marry a Millionaire / Dressed for Tomorrow (lit.)

1960 **Koibito** / My Love

**Irohanihoheto** / ABC / Of Men and Women

**Nami no tō** / Tower of Waves

1961 **Madara onna** / Women of Tokyo (lit. Capricious Women)

**Onna no hashi** / A Lonely Geisha (lit. A Woman's Bridge)

**Kakō** / The Estuary

1962 **Senkyaku banrai** / A Roaring Trade

**Aizen katsura** / Tree of Promises / Yearning Laurel / The Love-Troth Tree / The Compassionate Buddha Tree

**Kyūjin ryokō** / Recruiting Trip

**Zoku aizen katsura** / Yearning Laurel 2

1963 **Koto** / The Old Capital / Twin Sisters of Kyoto

**Tsumujikaze** / Whirlwind

**Kekkonshiki kekkonshiki** / Marriage Ceremony

**Kagami no naka no razō** / Naked Image in the Mirror

1964 **Nijūissai no chichi** / A 21-Year-Old Father / Our Happiness Alone

**Yoru no henrin** / Beautiful People (lit. A Glimpse of Night)

1965 **Zettai tasū** / Absolute Majority

1966 **Danshun** / Springtime (lit. Warm Spring)

**Kinokawa: Haru no maki** / The Kii River: Haru's Reel

**Kinokawa: Fumio no maki** / The Kii River: Fumio's Reel

1967 **Sekishun** / Three Faces of Love (lit. Regret for Springs Past)

**Chieko shō** / Portrait of Chieko

1968 **Sōshun** / Refreshing Spring

**Waga tōsō** / Our Struggle

1969 **Hi mo tsuki mo** / Through Days and Months

**Kekkon shimasu** / I'll Get Married / Marriage, Japanese Style

**Waga koi waga uta** / The Song from My Heart / My Song of Love

1970 **Kaze no bojō** / Journey of Love / The Yearning of the Wind (lit.)

1971 **Yomigaeru daichi** / The Revived Earth

**Ai to shi** / Love and Death

1972 **Tsujigahana** / Tsujigahana Kimono

1973 **Shiokari tōge** / Love Stopped the Runaway Train (lit. Shiokari Pass)

1974 **Sanbaba** / Three Old Women

1976 **Isho: Shiroi shōjo** / Suicide Note: White Girl

1979 **Nichiren** / The Priest Nichiren

## NAKATA Hideo
## (b. July 19, 1961)
## 中田秀夫

Nakata is a typical film buff turned director, whose reference points are other movies rather than real life. His cinephilia has found overt expression in two documentaries devoted to film directors. *Joseph Losey: The Man with Four Names* (*Jōsefu Rōjī: Yottsu no na o motsu otoko*, 1998) chronicled the career of the blacklisted Anglo-American filmmaker, while *Sadistic and Masochistic* (*Sadisutikku & Mazokisutikku*, 2001) was a study of Roman Porno director Masaru Konuma, whom Nakata had assisted in the eighties. Some of Nakata's fiction films also had a markedly self-referential quality: *Ghost Actress* (*Joyūrei*, 1996) was a horror movie set in a film studio, while *Last Scene* (2002), a less generic film than most of Nakata's work, examined the relationship between a washed-up star, now reduced to working as an extra, and a young prop girl.

Nakata's international reputation, however, rests substantially on one overpraised horror film, *Ring* (*Ringu*, 1998). The plot device of a videotape which places a curse on the viewer fed effectively into modern anxieties about the power of technology; however, unlike Kiyoshi Kurosawa's *Pulse* (*Kairo*, 2001), Nakata's film barely related these anxieties to the cultural malaise of pre-millenial Japan. Although the rejection of overt bloodshed in favor of low-key unease was commendable, Nakata was still reliant for his effects on such standard horror movie techniques as shadowy lighting and spooky music. The film's popularity led to a needless sequel, which clumsily attempted to elaborate the mythology of the original. Within the horror genre, Nakata also made *Dark Water* (*Honogurai mizu no soko kara*, 2002) about the vengeful ghost of a murdered child. Sharpened by interesting psychological undercurrents relating to the heroine's real-life fears of losing her child in a custody battle, this was perhaps his most effective chiller.

Of his films outside the horror genre, *Sleeping Bride* (*Garasu no nō*, 2000) was a curious melodrama about the brief awakening of a girl in a coma since birth. Its one-dimensional characterizations and the sentimental handling of its fairytale premise testified to its origins in a manga strip, and again, it suffered by comparison with Kiyoshi Kurosawa's complex treatment of similar subject matter in *License to Live* (*Ningen gōkaku*, 1999). *Chaos* (*Kaosu*, 2000), a tautly paced thriller about a kidnapping, eschewed the linear narrative typical of Nakata for a non-chronological approach which repeatedly compelled the viewer to revise his assumptions. It was perhaps his most gripping film, but the structural intricacy tended to emphasize plot mechanics at the expense of character and motivation.

In general, Nakata's plain, televisual style has proved better suited to efficient storytelling than to emotional nuance. His solid craftsmanship and the worldwide success of *Ring* ultimately earned him an invitation to Hollywood, where he worked on one of the more dispiriting phenomena of modern popular cinema: a sequel to the remake of his own original. He returned to Japan to make his most traditional film to date: *Kaidan* (2007), an old-fashioned ghost story in the mould of Nobuo Nakagawa, with an Edo-period setting and a theme of karmic retribution. Despite this move towards the exploitation of native material, it seems likely that he will continue, whether in Japan or America, to be an exponent of the bland international style which has come to typify much commercial filmmaking in the twenty-first century.

1986   **Natsutsuki monogatari** / Story of the Summer Moon (*16mm short*)

1995   **Jokyōshi nikki: Kinjirareta sei** / Woman Teacher's Diary: Forbidden Sex

1996   **Joyūrei** / Ghost Actress

   **(Ura) Tōsatsu nanpadō** / Behind the Scenes: Hidden Camera Pickup Technique

1997   **Ansatsu no machi** / Town without Pity / Town of Assassins (lit.)

1998   **Ringu** / Ring

   **Josefu Rōjī: Yottsu no na o motsu otoko** / Joseph Losey: The Man with Four Names

1999   **Ringu 2** / Ring 2

2000   **Garasu no nō** / Sleeping Bride (lit. The Glass Brain)

   **Kaosu** / Chaos

2001   **Sadisutikku & mazohisutikku** / Sadistic and Masochistic

2002  Honogurai mizu no soko kara /
      Dark Water
      **Last Scene**
2005  **The Ring Two** (*American remake*)
2007  **Kaidan** / Kaidan / Ghost Story

## NARUSE Mikio
(August 20, 1905–July 2, 1969)
成瀬巳喜男

Japan's master of naturalistic pessimism ironically began his career in comedy, a background still apparent in the delicate affection and tentative optimism of his finest early film, *Wife, Be Like a Rose* (*Tsuma yo bara no yōni*, 1935). His distinctive vision was, however, more clearly foreshadowed in *Nightly Dreams* (*Yogoto no yume*, 1933), *Apart from You* (*Kimi to wakarete*, 1933), and *Street without End* (*Kagiri naki hodō*, 1934), silent melodramas of remarkable intensity, where potential happiness is thwarted by hostile environments and practical responsibilities. As well as demonstrating a considerable stylistic virtuosity, these films revealed their director's ability to delineate social milieux—the rough harbor town in *Nightly Dreams*, fashionable Ginza with its upwardly mobile inhabitants in *Street without End*—and initiated, in Acquarello's phrase, his "compassionate portrayal of courageous women faced with great adversity."

Naruse moved from Shochiku to P.C.L., a forward-thinking studio, to make his first sound films: *Three Sisters with Maiden Hearts* (*Otomegokoro sannin musume*, 1935), an intricate melodrama about a family of shamisen players, based on a Kawabata novel, and *Wife, Be Like a Rose*, a bittersweet comic melodrama distinguished by its innovative visual style, progressive social attitudes, and witty depiction of the foibles and pretensions of the Westernized middle class. Naruse's work later in the thirties is often unfairly denigrated. In fact, such realist melodramas as *Avalanche* (*Nadare*, 1937) and *A Woman's Sorrows* (*Nyonin aishū*, 1937) continued to display a lively formal experimentation and an intriguingly sceptical attitude to the institution of marriage and traditional family structures: the latter was a particularly fine film with an outstanding performance from Takako Irie. As late as 1939, *The Whole Family Works* (*Hataraku ikka*), about a printer's family struggling to make ends meet, daringly associated the oppressive demands of filial duty with the ideals of militarism. In other films made during this inhospitable period, Naruse, like Mizoguchi, attempted to evade political pressures by dramatizing the lives and loves of performing artists, in stories often distanced from contemporary realities by a Meiji-period setting. These displayed a certain variety, spanning the slapstick humor of *Traveling Actors* (*Tabi yakusha*, 1940) and the academic beauty of *The Song Lantern* (*Uta andon*, 1943), but overall did not rank among Naruse's major works.

Naruse's immediate postwar work was apparently undistinguished, but in 1951 he returned to form with *Ginza Cosmetics* (*Ginza geshō*, 1951), a characteristically melancholy story about a woman whose chances of happiness are dashed when the man she loves prefers her sister. At the same time, he found his ideal collaborator in the late Fumiko Hayashi, a novelist whose pessimistic outlook matched his own. He adapted almost all of her books for the screen and chronicled her sad life story in *Her Lonely Lane* (*Hōrōki*, 1962). His versions of her novels exemplify the three main strands of his later work: the film about unrequited passion (*Floating Clouds* [*Ukigumo*, 1955]), the film about unhappy families and marriages that have gone stale (*Repast* [*Meshi*, 1951], *Wife* [*Tsuma*, 1953], *Lightning* [*Inazuma*, 1952]), and the film about the struggle against material hardship and social oppression (*Late Chrysanthemums* [*Bangiku*, 1954]). His protagonists were always women, but Naruse's studies of female experience spanned a wide range of social milieux, professions, and situations. *Ginza Cosmetics*, *Flowing* (*Nagareru*, 1956), and *When a Woman Ascends the Stairs* (*Onna ga kaidan o agaru toki*, 1960) were accounts of bar hostesses and geisha, while the heroine of *Yearning* (*Midareru*, 1964) is a businesswoman. *Wife, Mother* (*Okāsan*, 1952) and *Older Brother, Younger Sister* (*Ani imōto*, 1953), as their titles suggest, focused on the position of women within the family; the last of these was an uncharacteristically brutal film in which the emotional tensions between a brother and sister explode into physical violence.

The tone of these films (apart from the uncharacteristically mellow *Mother*) was austerely downbeat, illustrating Naruse's belief that "the world we live in betrays us." Only rarely, as in the delicate adaptation of Kawabata's *Sound of the Mountain* (*Yama no oto*, 1954), where the heroine finds relief from marital unhappiness in the friendship of her father-in-law, did his characters achieve a positive resolution of their problems. *Floating Clouds* and *Yearning* were both bitter love stories culminating in death, but even this tragic catharsis was exceptional. More often, Naruse's conclusions affirmed the impossibility of escape: the discontented wives returning to un-

©Kokusai Hoei Company Ltd.

Ginza geshō / Ginza Cosmetics *(1951): Here is one of Naruse's subtle chronicles of the life of a bar hostess, in this case affectingly played by Kinuyo Tanaka.*

happy marriages in *Repast* and *Anzukko* (1958), the ageing bar hostess climbing to work again in *When a Woman Ascends the Stairs*. Similarly, several of his fifties films ended with an expenditure of physical energy which seems a substitute for emotional catharsis. Examples include the nearly estranged couple throwing a balloon back and forth at the end of *Sudden Rain* (*Shūu*, 1956), the retired geisha in *Late Chrysanthemums* essaying a comic walk patterned on Marilyn Monroe, and the heroine of *Summer Clouds* (*Iwashigumo*, 1958) laboriously ploughing the fields after the rest of her family leave for the city. This physical activity seems to provide an outlet for the frustrations of Naruse's characters, expressing their problems without resolving them. Nevertheless, these films were not despairing: rather, they found hope in the strength and resilience of their heroines, who endure despite the pressure of circumstances.

During the last decade of his life, Naruse was sometimes assigned to atypical projects, with mixed results. *Hit and Run* (*Hikinige*, 1966) was an exceptionally hollow thriller. *Approach of Autumn* (*Aki tachinu*, 1960), however, was a precise, clear-eyed story of a child's emotional life, with something of the bittersweet quality of Shimizu. *Yearning* and Naruse's last film *Scattered Clouds* (*Midaregumo*, 1967) were both enriched by the elements of melodrama which offset the director's characteristic understatement.

In the postwar era, Naruse was not an especially innovative visual stylist, but his films boasted an unobtrusive intelligence in camera placement and staging which contributed to their tone of compassionate severity. Akira Kurosawa, who had assisted him on *Avalanche*, rightly admired his skill in editing together a sequence of brief, ostensibly unremarkable shots to create the effect of "the flow of a deep river, with a calm surface hiding a rushing, turbulent current below." His work was also distinguished by its structural elegance: *Summer Clouds*, for instance, expertly juggled half a dozen separate stories as it recounted the history of a farming family. This meticulous artifice was a counterweight to Naruse's stress on realistic detail, his reiterative method allowing places and objects gradually to accrue symbolic meaning. Naruse also elicited outstanding performances from such actresses as Setsuko Hara, Kinuyo Tanaka, Chikage Awashima, and particularly Hideko Takamine, whose sensitive yet resourceful persona proved ideal to incarnate Naruse's suffering, persevering heroines. Ken Uehara and

Masayuki Mori were likewise compelling as his selfish, vacillating, and untrustworthy anti-heroes. If Naruse never achieved a mastery of a specific cinematic style comparable to that of Ozu and Mizoguchi, his dedication and seriousness of purpose remain unquestionable. He was, above all, a supremely intelligent dramatist, and he crafted some of the Japanese cinema's most profound chronicles of human experience and motivation.

1930 **Chanbara fūfu** / Mr. and Mrs. Swordplay
**Junjō** / Pure Love
**Fukeiki jidai** / Hard Times
**Ai wa chikara da** / Love Is Strength
**Oshikiri shinkonki** / A Record of Shameless Newlyweds
1931 **Nē kōfun shitara iya yo** / Now Don't Get Excited
**Nikai no himei** / Screams from the Second Floor
**Koshiben ganbare** / Flunky, Work Hard!
**Uwaki wa kisha ni notte** / Fickleness Gets on the Train
**Hige no chikara** / The Strength of a Moustache
**Tonari no yane no shita** / Under the Neighbors' Roof
1932 **Onna wa tamoto o goyōjin** / Ladies, Be Careful of Your Sleeves
**Aozora ni naku** / Crying to the Blue Sky
**Eraku nare** / Be Great
**Mushibameru haru** / Motheaten Spring
**Chokorēto gāru** / Chocolate Girl
**Nasanu naka** / Not Blood Relations
**Kashi no aru Tōkyō fūkei** / Scenes of Tokyo with Sweets
1933 **Kimi to wakarete** / Apart from You / After Our Separation
**Yogoto no yume** / Nightly Dreams / Every Night Dreams

**Boku no marumage** / A Man with a Married Woman's Hairdo

**Sōbō** / Two Eyes

**Kinga shinnen** / New Year Greetings

1934 **Kagiri naki hodō** / Street without End

1935 **Otomegokoro sannin musume** / Three Sisters with Maiden Hearts / The Asakusa Sisters

**Joyū to shijin** / The Actress and the Poet

**Tsuma yo bara no yōni** / Wife, Be Like a Rose / Kimiko

**Sākasu goningumi** / Five Men in the Circus

**Uwasa no musume** / The Girl in the Rumor

1936 **Tōchūken Kumoemon** / Kumoemon Tochuken

**Kimi to iku michi** / The Road I Travel with You

**Asa no namikimichi** / Morning's Tree-Lined Street

1937 **Nyonin aishū** / A Woman's Sorrows / Feminine Melancholy

**Nadare** / Avalanche

**Kafuku (Zenpen; Kōhen)** / Learn from Experience / Ups and Downs (lit.) (Parts 1 and 2)

1938 **Tsuruhachi Tsurujirō** / Tsuruhachi and Tsurujiro

1939 **Hataraku ikka** / The Whole Family Works

**Magokoro** / Sincerity

1940 **Tabi yakusha** / Traveling Actors

1941 **Natsukashi no kao** / A Face from the Past

**Shanhai no tsuki** / Shanghai Moon

**Hideko no shashō-san** / Hideko the Bus Conductress

1942 **Haha wa shinazu** / Mother Never Dies

1943 **Uta andon** / The Song Lantern

1944 **Tanoshiki kana jinsei** / This Happy Life

**Shibaidō** / The Way of Drama

1945 **Shōri no hi made** / Until Victory Day

**Sanjūsangen-dō tōshiya monogatari** / A Tale of Archery at the Sanjusangen-do

1946 **Urashima Tarō no kōei** / The Descendants of Taro Urashima

**Ore mo omae mo** / Both You and I

1947 **Yottsu no koi no monogatari** / Four Love Stories (co-director)

**Haru no mezame** / Spring Awakens

1949 **Furyō shōjo** / Delinquent Girl

1950 **Ishinaka-sensei gyōjōki** / A Conduct Report on Professor Ishinaka

**Ikari no machi** / Angry Street

**Shiroi yajū** / White Beast

**Bara gassen** / Battle of Roses

1951 **Ginza geshō** / Ginza Cosmetics / Light and Darkness of Ginza

**Maihime** / Dancing Girl

**Meshi** / Repast

1952 **Okuni to Gohei** / Okuni and Gohei

**Okāsan** / Mother

**Inazuma** / Lightning

1953 **Fūfu** / Husband and Wife

**Tsuma** / Wife

**Ani imōto** / Older Brother, Younger Sister

1954 **Yama no oto** / Sound of the Mountain / Sounds from the Mountain

**Bangiku** / Late Chrysanthemums

1955 **Ukigumo** / Floating Clouds

**Kuchizuke** / Kisses (co-director)

1956 **Shūu** / Sudden Rain

**Tsuma no kokoro** / A Wife's Heart

**Nagareru** / Flowing

1957 **Arakure** / Untamed / Untamed Woman

1958 **Anzukko**

**Iwashigumo** / Summer Clouds / Herringbone Clouds (lit.)

1959 **Kotan no kuchibue** / Whistling in Kotan / Whistle in My Heart

1960  **Onna ga kaidan o agaru toki** /
When a Woman Ascends the Stairs
**Musume tsuma haha** / Daughters,
Wives, and a Mother
**Yoru no nagare** / Evening Stream
(*co-director*)
**Aki tachinu** / Approach of Autumn

1961  **Tsuma toshite onna toshite** / As
a Wife, as a Woman / The Other
Woman

1962  **Onna no za** / A Woman's Place
**Hōrōki** / Her Lonely Lane / A
Wanderer's Notebook

1963  **Onna no rekishi** / A Woman's
Story

1964  **Midareru** / Yearning (lit.
Turbulence)

1966  **Onna no naka ni iru tanin** / The
Stranger within a Woman / The
Thin Line
**Hikinige** / Hit and Run / Moment
of Terror

1967  **Midaregumo** / Scattered Clouds /
Two in the Shadow

## NARUSHIMA Tōichirō
### (November 19, 1925–October 8, 1993)
### 成島東一郎

The bulk of Narushima's career was
spent as a cinematographer, in which
capacity he did outstanding work for
many of the major directors of the Japanese New Wave, including Yoshishige
Yoshida (*Akitsu Spa* [*Akitsu Onsen*,
1962], *18 Who Cause a Storm* [*Arashi o
yobu jūhachinin*, 1963]), Masahiro Shinoda (*Double Suicide* [*Shinjū: Ten no
Amijima*, 1969], *Buraikan* [1970]), and
Nagisa Ōshima (*The Man Who Left
His Will on Film* [*Tōkyō sensō sengo hiwa*,
1970], *Ceremonies* [*Gishiki*, 1971]). He
was nearly fifty by the time he made his
directorial debut, *Time within Memory*
(*Seigenki*, 1973), an affecting story

about a middle-aged man remembering
his childhood and the events leading
up to his mother's death. Narushima's
approach was generally more classical
than those of the New Wave filmmakers he had worked with as cinematographer, though he occasionally used the
avant-garde technique of filming the
adult protagonist and his childhood self
in the same shot, thus conveying the
psychological weight of his past traumas. Though this aspect of the story
gave clear expression to Narushima's
avowed interest in Freudian psychology, the film, shot on location on the
southern island of Okinoerabujima, was
also, in part, a documentary portrait of
the vanishing folk customs of Japan's re-
motest regions.

Though *Time within Memory* was
critically esteemed, Narushima was unable to find funding for other directorial
projects. Instead, he returned to cinematography, notably for Ōshima, again, on
*Merry Christmas, Mr. Lawrence* (*Senjō no
merī kurisumasu*, 1983). He was finally
able to direct a second film, *Blade of Oedipus* (*Oidipusu no yaiba*), in 1986; this was
a suspense piece, also with Freudian undercurrents, in which an antique sword
exposes the tensions between three siblings. Regrettably, this was the last work
as director that Narushima managed to
realize before his death.

1973  **Seigenki** / Time within Memory
1986  **Oidipusu no yaiba** / Blade of
Oedipus

## NEGISHI Kichitarō
### (b. August 24, 1950)
### 根岸吉太郎

Though little-known abroad, Negishi
has achieved consistent critical success

within Japan, where his films are admired for their subtlety and intelligence. He worked initially on Roman Porno at Nikkatsu; among his films of that period was a sexually explicit remake of the classic youth film *Crazed Fruit* (*Kurutta kajitsu*, 1981). He made his artistic breakthrough, however, with the ATG-financed *Far Thunder* (*Enrai*, 1981), a low-key account of a farmer persisting in his profession despite urbanization and modernization. Eliciting outstanding performances from his actors, especially from Toshiyuki Nagashima in the lead role, Negishi achieved a scrupulous, detailed realism which brought complexity and depth to the drama. After directing one more Roman Porno, the satirical *Cabaret Diary* (*Kyabarē nikki*, 1982) at Nikkatsu, he left the studio to make the heartwarming comedy *My Wedding* (*Oretchi no uedingu*, 1983) and the thriller *Story of a Detective* (*Tantei monogatari*, 1983), about the budding relationship between a young woman and the detective hired to trail her. The latter, a rather lightweight film in outline, was again deepened somewhat by excellent acting. During the eighties Negishi also achieved favorable notice with the youth film *Half of Eternity* (*Eien no ½* 1987) and with *The Hours of Wedlock* (*Uhohho tankentai*, 1986), a domestic drama about the consequence of a divorce, scripted by fellow director Yoshimitsu Morita. This was described by Masahiro Hirose as "one of the forerunners of Japanese new age movies in the 80s."

Negishi has worked more sparingly in recent years. *Nipple* (*Chibusa*, 1993) was a short feature about a middle-aged man caring for a wife stricken with leukemia. *Ties* (*Kizuna*, 1998) was a well-characterized thriller about a former yakuza who returns to the criminal

life to protect his sister's reputation; it displayed a sure grasp of human motivation, and Negishi again elicited a multi-layered performance from his star, Kōji Yakusho. More recently, Negishi received good notices for *Embers* (*Tōkō no ki*, 2004) and for *What the Snow Brings* (*Yuki ni negau koto*, 2005). The former was a bleak romantic melodrama about the relationship between a cancer-stricken documentary filmmaker and the daughter of the swordsmith whom he once made the subject of a film. The latter was a Hokkaido-set story about a prodigal who turns over a new leaf when he returns home and agrees to become a stable hand in a stable owned by his brother.

Though Negishi has not developed an especially distinctive visual style, he has consistently directed with unobtrusive intelligence, often bringing subtlety and humanity to conventional material. It is a matter of regret that his critical success in Japan has not yet translated into international esteem.

1978   **"Orion no satsui" yori: Jōji no hōteishiki** / Orion's Will to Kill / From Orion's Testimony: Formula for Murder (lit. From "Orion's Intentions of Murder": Equation for a Love Affair)

1979   **Joseito** / High School Girls
       **Nureta shūmatsu** / Wet Weekend

1980   **Bōkō gishiki** / Assault Ceremony
       **Asa wa dame yo!** / Never in the Morning

1981   **Jokyōshi: Yogoreta hōkago** / Woman Teacher: Dirty After School
       **Kurutta kajitsu** / Crazed Fruit
       **Enrai** / Far Thunder

1982   **Kyabarē nikki** / Cabaret Diary

1983   **Oretchi no uedingu** / My Wedding
       **Tantei monogatari** / Story of a Detective

1985   **Hitohira no yuki** / One Flake of Snow / Flakes of Snow

1986 **Uhohho tankentai** / The Hours
   of Wedlock (lit. Ooh! Exploration
   Party)
1987 **Eien no 1/2** / Half of Eternity
1992 **Kachō Shima Kōsaku** / Assistant
   Manager Kosaku Shima
1993 **Chibusa** / Nipple
1998 **Kizuna** / Ties / Bonds / Eternal
   Bond
2004 **Tōkō no ki** / Embers / Transluscent
   Tree (lit.)
2005 **Yuki ni negau koto** / What the
   Snow Brings
2007 **Saidokā ni inu** / The Dog in the
   Sidecar

## NISHIKAWA Katsumi
## (b. July 1, 1918)
西河克己

An assistant at Shochiku from 1939, Nishikawa transferred to Nikkatsu shortly after being promoted to director. His early films displayed the influence of both studios: thus, *Everything That Lives* (*Ikitoshi ikerumono*, 1955), based on a Yūzō Yamamoto novel, echoed the social realist melodrama of Nikkatsu's prewar output; *The Young Cyclone* (*Wakai toppū*, 1960), about a teenager's efforts to break up a narcotics ring, was an action film in Nikkatsu's characteristic postwar vein; while *Red Buds and White Flowers* (*Akai tsubomi to shiroi hana*, 1962), about the efforts of two young friends to unite their surviving parents, recalled the bittersweet sentimentality of Shochiku's "Ōfuna flavor." By the sixties, such films had earned Nishikawa a reputation as a sensitive director of young actors, and he became something of a specialist in remaking classics, often based on admired literary sources, as vehicles for budding stars. Among these were versions of Kawabata's much-adapted mel-

ancholy romance, *The Izu Dancer* (*Izu no odoriko*, 1963), and *Blue Mountains* (*Aoi sanmyaku*, 1963), a story of conflicts among high school students that Tadashi Imai had filmed in 1949.

This trend continued into the seventies, when Nishikawa made a series of star vehicles for teenage pop star Momoe Yamaguchi at Toho. *Flag in the Mist* (*Kiri no hata*, 1977) was a pedestrian adaptation of a Seichō Matsumoto thriller, inferior to Yoshitarō Nomura's versions of books by the same writer. Yamaguchi also starred in Nishikawa's second take on *The Izu Dancer* (*Izu no odoriko*, 1974); in *Acorn Kid* (*Dongurikko*, 1976), a remake of Tasaka's *The Maid's Kid* (*Jochūkko*, 1955); and in new versions of novels by Mishima (*The Sound of Waves* [*Shiosai*, 1975]) and Tanizaki (*A Portrait of Shunkin* [*Shunkin shō*, 1976]). This last, though virtually a shot-for-shot remake of Yasujirō Shimazu's 1935 *Okoto and Sasuke* (*Shunkin shō: Okoto to Sasuke*), was perhaps the best; in general, however, these films were prettily photographed stories of passion without sexuality, proficient but anonymous, and alienated from modern realities. Nishikawa continued to work in this vein until the nineties; his last film, *One Bowl of Noodles* (*Ippai no kakesoba*, 1992), was a popular tearjerker about a struggling family finding comfort in a New Year bowl of noodles. As Mark Schilling commented, Nishikawa allows us "to be moved without being made to think."

1952 **Izu no enkashi** / The Ballad Singer
   of Izu
   **Let's See Japan**
1953 **Yome no tachiba** / A Daughter-in-
   Law's Point of View
   **Nanairo no hanafubuki** / Falling
   Blossoms of Seven Colors
1955 **Ikitoshi ikerumono** / Everything
   That Lives

**Haru no yo no dekigoto** / Events on a Spring Night

1956 **Yukaina nakama** / Funny Friend

**Tōkyō no hito (Zenpen; Kōhen)** / A Person of Tokyo (Parts 1 and 2)

**Shiawase wa doko ni** / Where Is Happiness?

1957 **Kodoku no hito** / A Lonely Person

**Eien ni kotaezu** / Never to Reply

1958 **Eien ni kotaezu: Kanketsu hen** / Never to Reply: Conclusion

**Utsukushii Anju-san** / The Beautiful Foundling / The Nun

**Asu o kakeru otoko** / The Man Who Wagers Tomorrow

1959 **Fudōtoku kyōiku kōza** / An Unethical Lecture on Education

**Kōshudai no shita** / Under the Gallows

**Wakai keisha** / A Young Person's Descent

**Kaze no aru michi** / Windy Street

**Mugon no ranto** / The Silent Drunkard

1960 **Rokusansei gurentai** / High School Delinquents

**Suttobi kozō** / Kid in a Hurry

**Wakai toppū** / The Young Cyclone / Cyclone Kid

**Shippū kozō** / The Young Gale / Galeforce Kid (lit.)

**Tatsumaki kozō** / The Young Tornado / Tornado Kid (lit.)

**Ore no kokyō wa uesutan** / I Come from the West

1961 **Arigataya bushi: Ā, arigataya, arigataya** / Doing What I Please (lit. Song of Thanks: Ah, Thankyou, Thankyou)

**Tatakai tsuzukeru otoko** / Never Admit Defeat (lit. The Man Who Keeps Fighting)

**Tsuiseki** / Pursuit

**Kusa o karu musume** / The Grass-Cutter Girl / The Grass Mowers

1962 **Kimagure tosei** / Changing Jobs on a Whim

**Seinen no isu** / The Seat of Youth

**Akai tsubomi to shiroi hana** / Red Buds and White Flowers

**Hoshi no hitomi o motsu otoko** / The Man with Stars in His Eyes

**Wakai hito** / Young People / Fresh Lovers

1963 **Aoi sanmyaku** / Blue Mountains / Beyond the Green Hill

**Ame no naka ni kiete** / Lost in the Rain

**Izu no odoriko** / The Izu Dancer / Love Comes with Youth

**Eden no umi** / Eden by the Sea

1964 **Izuko e** / Where To?

**Kikyō** / Homecoming

1965 **Kanashiki wakare no uta** / Sad Song of Separation

**Yottsu no koi no monogatari** / Four Love Stories / The Four Loves

1966 **Aishū no yoru** / Night of Sorrow

**Tomo o okuru uta** / Song of Seeing off a Friend

**Zesshō** / The Last Song

**Hakuchō** / The Swan

1967 **Kitaguni no ryojō** / A Traveler's Mood in the North Country

**Hi no ataru sakamichi** / Slope in the Sun

**Yūbue** / Evening Flute

1968 **Zansetsu** / Eternal Love / Lingering Snow (lit.)

**Za Supaidās no Bari-tō chindōchū** / The Spiders' Unusual Trip to Bali

1969 **Yoru no mesu: Hana to chō** / Night Female: Flowers and Butterflies

**Yoru no mesu: Toshiue no onna** / Night Female: Older Woman

1974 **Izu no odoriko** / The Izu Dancer / The Dancing Girl of Izu

1975 **Shiosai** / The Sound of Waves

**Zesshō** / The Last Song

1976 **Eden no umi** / Eden by the Sea

**Dongurikko** / Acorn Kid

**Shunkin shō** / A Portrait of Shunkin

1977 **Koibito misaki** / Cape of Lovers
**Kiri no hata** / Flag in the Mist /
Sweet Revenge
1978 **Oyome ni yukimasu** / I'm Getting
Married
1979 **Hanamachi no haha** / Mother of
the Pleasure Quarters
1983 **Suparuta no umi** / Sea of Sparta
(*unreleased*)
1984 **Chī-chan gomen ne** / Sorry,
Chi-chan
1985 **Bājin Rōdo** / Virgin Road
(*unreleased*)
1989 **Mai Fenikkusu** / My Phoenix
1992 **Ippai no kakesoba** / One Bowl of
Noodles

## NOMURA Hiromasa
(August 16, 1905–July 8, 1979)
野村浩将

Best-known today for a single film, *Yearning Laurel* (*Aizen katsura*, 1938), Nomura was one of the most commercially successful of house directors at Shochiku in the thirties. Having been trained by distinguished silent-era filmmaker Kiyohiko Ushihara, he made his debut with *The Beating* (*Tekken seisai*, 1930), a vehicle for popular romantic duo Kinuyo Tanaka and Denmei Suzuki, who had starred in several of Ushihara's own films. Many of his early works were comedies; among them, the extant *The Layabout and the Town Belle* (*Yotamono to Komachi musume*, 1935), one of a popular series, suggests a talent for humorous slapstick and retains a certain freshness thanks to outdoor shooting in the mountains.

Nomura's breakthrough, however, came with the melodrama *Tsubaki, a Married Woman* (*Hitozuma tsubaki*, 1936), which was a major hit. After another commercial success, *A Man's*

*Recompense* (*Otoko no tsugunai*, 1937), he was assigned to *Yearning Laurel*, a convoluted melodrama following the romantic travails of a nurse and doctor, played touchingly by Kinuyo Tanaka and Ken Uehara. Though critically despised, this three-part film was extraordinarily popular thanks to the stars' charisma and Nomura's efficiency as a director of tearjerking material. It established a genre known as *surechigai* (literally "brushing past") melodrama, in which lovers repeatedly come close to meeting, but miss each other by meters or moments.

During the war, Nomura made *Suchow Night* (*Soshū no yoru*, 1942), another film with a hospital setting, and a vehicle for singer and actress Ri Koran (Yoshiko Yamaguchi), born in China to Japanese parents. Despite its reprehensible pro-colonial message, the film intriguingly caught the atmosphere of occupied China. Nomura left Shochiku after the war, and in his later years worked at various studios. Among his more notable postwar films were several musicals, and he also remade Mizoguchi's *Sisters of Gion* (*Gion no kyōdai*, 1956). After retiring from theatrical filmmaking, he worked in television, particularly on educational programs.

1930 **Tekken seisai** / The Beating
**Kaishain kubiyoke senjutsu** /
A Company Man's Strategy for
Avoiding the Sack
**Rusuchū hatten** / Developments
During Absence
1931 **Watashi no papa-san mama ga
suki** / My Dad Loves My Mom
**Otto yo naze naku ka?** / Husband,
Why Do You Cry?
**Haru no himitsu** / Secret of Spring
**Namida no aikyōmono** / A
Charmer in Tears

**Kiken shingō** / Danger Signal
**Momoiro no yūwaku** / Pink Seduction
**Reijō to yotamono** / The Well-Born Girl and the Layabout
1932 **Hatsukoi to yotamono** / First Love and the Layabout
**Sensō to yotamono** / War and the Layabout
**Kagayake Nihon josei** / Shine, Women of Japan
**Yotamono to endan** / The Layabout and a Proposal
**Nokosareta Okiku-chan** / Okiku-chan Left Behind
1933 **Yotamono to geisha** / The Layabout and the Geisha
**Ōendanchō no koi** / Love of a Cheerleader
**Chikara to onna no yo no naka** / Strength and a Woman's World (*dialogue director*)
**Wasurarenu hana** / Unforgettable Flower
**Yotamono to kyakusenbi** / The Layabout and the Beautiful Legs
**Yomeiri mae** / Before Becoming a Bride
**Yotamono to kaisuiyoku** / The Layabout and Seabathing
**Ureshii koro** / Happy Times
**Jogakusei to yotamono** / The Girl Student and the Layabout
1934 **Genkanban to ojōsan** / The Doorman and the Young Miss
**Yume miru koro** / Time of Dreams
**Musume sannin kangeki jidai** / Three Girls' Age of Deep Emotion
**Shinkon ryokō** / Honeymoon
**Yotamono to hanayome** / The Layabout and the Bride
**Harue no kekkon** / Harue's Marriage
1935 **Yotamono to Komachi musume** / The Layabout and the Town Belle
**Hitotsu no teisō** / One Virtue
**Haha no koibumi** / A Mother's Love Letter

**Yume utsutsu** / Half Asleep
**Reijin shakōjō** / The Belle in Society
**Yotamono to wakafūfu** / The Layabout and a Young Couple
1936 **Subarashiki kūsō** / Wonderful Fantasy
**Irimuko gassen** / Contest for Marrying into the Wife's Family
**Hitozuma tsubaki (Zenpen; Kōhen)** / Tsubaki, a Married Woman (Parts 1 and 2)
**Marumage konseki** / Oval Chignon and Crossed Line
1937 **Joi Kinuyo sensei** / Kinuyo the Lady Doctor
**Otoko no tsugunai (Zenpen; Kōhen)** / A Man's Recompense (Parts 1 and 2)
**Musume yo naze sakarau ka** / Daughter, Why Do You Defy Me?
**Utae kanko no haru** / Sing, Spring of Cheer
1938 **Kokumin no chikai** / The People's Vow
**Kanojo wa nani o oboeta ka** / What Did She Remember?
**Aizen katsura (Zenpen; Kōhen)** / Yearning Laurel / The Compassionate Buddha Tree / The Love-Troth Tree (Parts 1 and 2)
**Akutarō** / The Bastard
**Ganbari musume** / The Girl Who Does Her Best
1939 **Zoku aizen katsura** / Yearning Laurel 2
**Subarashiki kana kanojo** / Ah, How Wonderful She Is
**Aizen katsura: Kanketsu hen** / Yearning Laurel: Conclusion
**Niizuma mondō** / New Wives: Questions and Answers
1940 **Kinuyo no hatsukoi** / Kinuyo's First Love
**Ai no bōfū** / Gale of Love
**Butai sugata** / View of the Stage
**Okinu to bantō** / Okinu and the Head Clerk

1941 **Genki de ikō yo** / Let's Go in Good
Spirits
**Soshū no yoru** / Suchow Night

1942 **Kyōraku no mai** / Dance of Kyoto

1943 **Tekki kūshū** / Enemy Air Raid (*co-director*)

1944 **Santarō ganbaru** / Santaro Does
His Best

1945 **Tengoku no hanayome** / Bride of
Heaven

1946 **Kanojo no hatsugen** / Her Words

1947 **Hazukashii koro** / Time of
Embarrassment

1948 **Shimikin no Kekkon senshu** /
Shimikin's Marriage Athlete
**Komadori fujin** / Madame
Redbreast

1949 **Yume yo mō ichido** / To Dream
Once More
**Kekkon sanjūshi** / The Marriage of
Three Musketeers
**Yu no machi erejī** / Spa Town
Elegy
**Kage o shitaite** / Yearning for
Shadows

1950 **Yotamono to tenshi** / The
Layabout and the Angel
**Yume wa hakanaku** / Dreams Are
Fleeting
**Ren'ai taifūken** / Typhoon Zone of
Love

1951 **Jōen ichidai onna** / The Life of a
Passionate Woman
**Waga ko to utawan** / I Will Sing
with My Child
**Kenjū jigoku** / Hell of Guns

1952 **Wakaki hi no ayamachi** / Mistakes
of Young Days
**Achako seishun techō: Tōkyō
hen** / Achako's Notebook of Youth:
Tokyo Chapter
**Achako seishun techō: Ōsaka
hen** / Achako's Notebook of Youth:
Osaka Chapter

1953 **Kenpei** / Military Policeman
**Yasen kangofu** / Field Nurse
**Ninjutsu makaritōru** / Ninja Arts
Win Through

1954 **Kimi yueni** / Because of You
**Sensuikan rogō imada fujō sezu** /
Submarine "Ro" Hasn't Surfaced Yet

1955 **Hibotanki** / Record of a Red Peony
**Santōshain to onna hisho** / Grade
3 Employee and Female Secretary
**Haha futari** / Two Mothers

1956 **Gion no kyōdai** / Sisters of Gion
**Akogare no renshūsen** / Training
Ship of Yearning

1957 **Akebonosō no satsujin** / Murder at
the Akebono Apartment
**Kosui monogatari** / Tale of a Lake
**Sen'un Ajia no joō** / Queen of Asia
(lit. War Clouds over the Queen of
Asia)

1958 **Sekai no haha** / Mother of the
World
**Zekkai no rajo** / Naked Woman in
the Distant Sea

1959 **Kyōfu no wana** / Trap of Fear

# NOMURA Hōtei
## (November 13, 1880–August 23, 1934)
野村芳亭

Nomura was involved in cinema from its
beginnings, having served as projection
assistant to Katsutarō Inahata when, in
1897, he first brought the Lumière *ci-
nématographe* to Japan. Thereafter he
worked in lighting, set design, and distribution before joining Shochiku as a
manager and director. Due to the loss
of much of his output, he is little known
today, but in his time he achieved both
commercial and critical success. His
early films, such as *The Woman and the
Pirates* (*Onna to kaizoku*, 1923) and *Jirocho of Shimizu* (*Shimizu no Jirochō*,
1922), both scripted by Daisuke Itō,
apparently marked a novel approach
to period drama, achieving a new realism by using actors previously associ-

ated with *gendai-geki* rather than with Kabuki. Nomura also made comedies, including the critically admired *Collar Button* (*Kara botan*, 1926), an early *shomin-geki*, about a clerk who receives a payrise when he replaces his boss's lost button, but quarrels with his wife when he starts spending the money on treating his colleagues to drinks.

However, Nomura worked most frequently in melodrama, usually focusing on women. Indeed, his films are considered of importance in developing the Shochiku tradition of female-centered melodrama. *Mother* (*Haha*, 1929), which recounted the tragedy of a woman who rejects a suitor for the sake of her children, marked the debut of a 5-year-old Hideko Takamine. Nomura also adapted popular *shinpa*-style novels such as Yūhō Kikuchi's *Foster Sisters* (*Chikyōdai*, 1932), about a woman who masquerades as the daughter of an aristocrat, and Kōyō Ozaki's *The Golden Demon* (*Konjiki yasha*, 1932), the chronicle of a student who becomes a usurer after poverty separates him from his fiancée. *Foster Sisters* was unattractively moralistic in tone, but possessed some of the narrative drive of a Hiroshi Shimizu silent; still fortunately preserved, it suggests a distinct talent. *The Golden Demon* extended the range of male star Chōjūrō Hayashi, who appeared for the first time in a contemporary setting, and became the first in a sequence of Nomura-directed melodramas featuring his co-star Kinuyo Tanaka. She, coincidentally, had made her debut in one of the director's earlier films, *Woman of the Genroku Era* (*Genroku onna*, 1924), and in the early thirties was approaching the height of her popularity. Nomura, too, was at his most successful at the time of his relatively early death, and it is likely that he would have continued to pro-

duce interesting work had he lived. His son, Yoshitarō Nomura, later worked as a director.

1921  **Yūkan'uri (Futari yūkan'uri)** / Evening Newspaper Sellers (Two Evening Newspaper Sellers)
**Hō no namida** / Tears of the Law
**Tokkuri** / Sake Bottle

1922  **Jigokubune** / Hell Ship
**Shimizu no Jirochō** / Jirocho of Shimizu
**Umi no yobigoe (Umi no sakebi)** / Call of the Sea (The Sea Is Crying Out)
**Eien no nazo** / Eternal Mystery
**Otto toshite tsuma toshite** / As a Husband, As a Wife
**Kessaku shūsui** / Anthology of Masterpieces (*co-director*)

1923  **Shi ni yuku tsuma** / The Dying Wife
**Kon'ya no musume** / The Dyer's Daughter
**Warae wakamono** / Smile, Young People
**Nasuna koi** / Do Not Love
**Haha** / Mother
**Dai Tōkyō no ushimitsudoki** / The Small Hours in Greater Tokyo (*co-director*)
**Onna to kaizoku** / The Woman and the Pirates
**Jissetsu Kunisada Chūji: Kari no mure** / The True Story of Chūji Kunisada: Flock of Wild Geese
**Hagi-dera shinjū** / Double Suicide at Hagi-dera
**Murai Chōan** / Choan Murai
**Jigoku (Shōnetsu jigoku)** / Hell (Burning Hell)
**Ohimegusa** / Princess Grass
**Yūhōshū** / Stories from Yuho (*co-director*)

1924  **Kanojo no unmei** / Her Destiny
**Wakamono yo** / Young People
**Eijigoroshi** / Infanticide
**Kanji no yoi eigashū** / Films That Make You Feel Good (*co-director*)

Uso / Lie

Onnagoroshi abura jigoku / Oil Hell Murder

Yamato damashii / Spirit of Japan

Shirakabe no ie / The White-Walled House

Taii no musume / The Captain's Daughter

Genroku onna / A Woman of the Genroku Era

Nanba no fuku / Pleasures of Nanba

Kaminari Oshin / Oshin of the Thunder

Koi no Kenshin / Kenshin the Lover

Shirokiya Okoma / Okoma of Shirokiya

Mikazuki Oroku: Zenpen / Oroku of the Crescent Moon: Part 1

1925 Mikazuki Oroku: Kōhen / Oroku of the Crescent Moon: Part 2

Oden jigoku (Zenpen; Chūhen; Kōhen) / The Hell of Oden (Parts 1, 2, and 3)

Kyōya no Oito / Oita of the Kyōya

Kaizoku dokurobune / The Pirates' Skull Ship

Fukkatsu / Resurrection

1926 Dainankō / The Great Kusunoki

Shin Ohatsu jizō / The Jizo of Ohatsu, New Version

Kara botan / Collar Button

Niwaka gyosha / An Inexperienced Driver

Kosumosu saku koro / When the Cosmos Blooms

Yōfu gonin onna / Five Bewitching Women (co-director)

1927 Kyūkanchō / The Mynah

Kawaii yatsu / Sweet One

Chichi kaeru / Father Returns

Byakkotai / The White Tiger Company

Akikusa dōrō: Otsuyu no maki / Autumn Flower Lantern: Dew Reel

Akikusa dōrō: Kohagi no maki / Autumn Flower Lantern: Bush Clover Reel

Dokushin / Poisoned Lips

Ai no gaika / Victory Song of Love

1928 Tengoku no hito / People of Heaven

Dōroku-hakase / Dr. Doroku

Asakusa kōshinkyoku / Asakusa March

Bijin kashima / The Beauty Rents a Room

Tomioka-sensei / Dr. Tomioka

Dōtonbori kōshinkyoku / Dotonbori March

Toge no rakuen / Paradise of Thorns

Koi no kyanpu / Love's Camp

Natsu no hi no koi / Love on a Summer's Day

Butai sugata / View of the Stage

Minzoku no sakebi / Cry of the Nation

Ren'ai kōshinkyoku / March of Love

Seishun kōkyōkyoku / Symphony of Youth

1929 Hibari naku sato / The Village Where the Skylark Sings

Midori no asa / Green Morning

3-zennin / Three Good People

Haha / Mother

1930 Haha: Shimai hen / Mother: Sisters Chapter

1931 Moyuru hanabira / The Burning Petal

Kudake yuku tama / Crushing Gemstones

Bōfū no bara / Rose in the Storm

Ichitarō ya ai / Hey! Ichitaro

Kaitō X-dan / Mysterious Thieves: The X-Gang

Shinri no haru / Spring of Truth

Reijin no hohoemi / Smile of the Belle

Junan no onna / A Woman of Ordeals

1932 **Konjiki yasha** / The Golden
Demon
**Hitowana** / Mantrap
**Chikyōdai** / Foster Sisters
**Shin Yotsuya kaidan** / The New
Yotsuya Ghost Story
**Namida no hitomi** / Tearful Eyes
**Josei no kirifuda** / Women's Trump
Card
1933 **Biwa uta** / Song of the Lute
**Namida no wataridori** / Migratory
Bird of Tears
**Ōendanchō no koi** / Loves of a
Cheerleader
**Shima no musume** / Island Girl
**Seidon** / Fine and Cloudy Weather
**Tenryū kudareba** / When the
Heavenly Dragon Descends
**Sasurai no otome** / A Wandering
Maid
**Tōkyō ondo** / Tokyo Dance
**Chinchōge** / The Daphne
**Hatsukoi no haru** / Spring of First
Love
1934 **Onna keizu** / The Genealogy of
Women
**Chijō no seiza: Chijō hen** /
Constellation on Earth: Earth
Chapter
**Chijō no seiza: Seiza hen**
/ Constellation on Earth:
Constellation Chapter
**Tone no asagiri** / Morning Mist on
the Tone River
**Machi no bōfū** / Storm in Town

# NOMURA Yoshitarō
**(April 23, 1919–April 8, 2005)**
野村芳太郎

The son of silent era director Hōtei Nomura, Yoshitarō, like his father, spent his
career at Shochiku, becoming a prolific,
proficient director of commercial entertainment films. He worked initially
in a range of genres, including musicals,
melodramas, comedies, and period films.
*The Izu Dancer* (*Izu no odoriko*, 1954), an
adaptation of Yasunari Kawabata's story
of the brief romance between a student
and an itinerant dancer in the rural Izu
Peninsula, initiated a persistent interest in provincial settings. Among Nomura's more individual sixties films was
*Dear Emperor* (*Haikei tennō heika-sama*,
1963), an ironic account of the experiences of a conscript who finds the army
preferable to civilian life and writes to
the Emperor begging to be allowed to
stay in the service. *Tokyo Bay* (*Hidarikiki no sogekisha: Tōkyō-wan*, 1962),
about a detective whose investigation
into the murder of a government agent
leads him to suspect a wartime friend,
also commands a reputation as a distinguished thriller.

The thriller was to prove Nomura's
most fruitful vein, particularly with a sequence of films adapted from novels by
Seichō Matsumoto, in which he proved
adept at drawing out the emotional resonances and social connotations of generic plots. The first of these, *Stakeout*
(*Harikomi*, 1958), an expertly crafted
thriller about two detectives tracking a
suspect to the house of his former lover
in a Kyushu town, used the region's
picturesque towns and countryside as
an incongruous backdrop to its bleak
story. It has been praised for its critique
of the oppression of women in Japan,
while the later *Castle of Sand* (*Suna no
utsuwa*, 1974) touched on the ostracism
of sufferers from leprosy. This latter
was acclaimed as Nomura's masterpiece
in Japan, though in most respects it unfolded as a rather conventional *policier*,
structurally flawed by the long flashback denouement which laboriously
provided the solution to the mystery.
More effective were *Zero Focus* (*Zero no*

Kage no kuruma / The Shadow Within *(1970): Nomura's thrillers drew out the emotional resonances and social connotations of generic plots.*

*shōten*, 1961) and *The Demon* (*Kichiku*, 1978), two grimly compelling films which again used location skillfully, expertly distilling a mood of subtle unease from the beautiful yet bleak scenery of the Noto Peninsula. *Zero Focus* chronicled the aftermath of the disappearance of a newly married man and effectively portrayed the psychological torment of a wife forced to the realization that she knows almost nothing about her husband. *The Demon* was a genuinely shocking film about violence against children, made more unsettling by Nomura's stylistic detachment and by the relatively sympathetic characterization of the unwillingly abusive protagonist. Among Nomura's other Matsumoto adaptations, *The Shadow Within* (*Kage no kuruma*, 1970) was about a man who comes to believe that his lover's disaffected son is plotting to kill him, while *Suspicion* (*Giwaku*, 1982), focused on a female lawyer assigned to defend a woman suspected of murdering her husband.

Even when Nomura was not adapting Matsumoto's originals, he tended in his later years to gravitate towards similar subject matter. *Perennial Weed* (*Shōwa karesusuki*, 1975) was the story of a policeman's sister accused of killing her gangster lover. *Village of Eight Gravestones* (*Yatsuhakamura*, 1977), though a less psychologically acute, more generic mystery with supernatural lineaments, still benefited from its director's ability to make idyllic country locations seem threatening. The same sense of menace distinguished *The Writhing Tongue* (*Furueru shita*, 1980), a visually pedestrian but psychologically acute hospital drama, focusing on the anguish of parents when their daughter contracts tetanus. Though his work was relatively conventional in style, Nomura was never less than a competent filmmaker, and he displayed, at his best, a subtlety and finesse rare among studio artisans.

1952 **Hato** / Pigeons
**Haru wa kyamera ni notte** / The Camera Catches Spring
1953 **Jinanbō** / The Second Son
**Gutei kenkei** / Stupid Younger Brother, Clever Elder Brother
**Kinpira-sensei to ojōsan** / Mr. Kinpira the Teacher and the Young Miss
**Kurama Tengu: Seimen yasha** / Kurama Tengu: Blue-Masked Demon
**Seishun sanbagarasu** / The Youth of Three Crows
1954 **Keian Suikoden** / Keian-Era Water Margin
**Izu no odoriko** / The Izu Dancer
**Seishun romansu shīto** / Youth's Romance Seat
**Bikkuri gojūsantsugi** / Surprise on the Tokaido
1955 **Daigaku wa deta keredo** / I Graduated, But…
**Zoku otoko daigaku: Shinkon kyōshitsu** / A Man's College 2: Class of Newlyweds
**Bōmeiki** / Record of Exile / Refugee
**Tōkyō-Honkon: Mitsugetsu ryokō** / Tokyo-Hong Kong Honeymoon
**Hanayome wa doko ni iru** / Where Is the Bride?
**Taiyō wa hibi ni arata nari** / The Sun Is Renewed Each Day
1956 **Kakubō sanbagarasu** / Three Crows in Student Caps
**Tabigarasu Itarō** / Itaro the Vagrant

**Jinanbō kokyō e iku** / The Second Son Goes Home
**Hanayome boshūchū** / Bride Wanted
**Koko wa shizuka nari** / It's Quiet Here
**Odoru matenrō** / The Dancing Skyscraper
1957 **Banjun Morishige no Funnyōdan** / A Tale of Dung and Urine (lit. Banjun and Morishige's Tale of Dung and Urine)
1958 **Hanayome no onoroke** / The Bride's Fond Talk of Love
**Harikomi** / Stakeout / The Chase
**Gekkyū 13,000-en** / Monthly Salary 13,000 yen
**Modan dōchū: Sono koi mattanashi** / Modern Journey: Don't Give Up on Love
1959 **Donto ikōze** / Let's Go!
1960 **Ginza no onīchan chōsensu** / A Brother of Ginza Sets a Challenge
**Kiiroi sakuranbo** / The Yellow Cherry
**Kanshōyō dansei** / The Man They Idolized
**Saigo no kirifuda** / The Last Trump Card / The Grave Tells All
1961 **Zero no shōten** / Zero Focus
**Koi no gashū** / Love's Book of Paintings
**Haitoku no mesu** / Scalpel of Immorality
1962 **Haru no sanmyaku** / Mountains in Spring
**Hidarikiki no sogekisha: Tokyo-wan** / Tokyo Bay (lit. Left-Handed Sniper: Tokyo Bay)
**Ano hashi no hotori de** / By That Bridge
**Ano hashi no hotori de: Dainibu** / By That Bridge: Part 2
1963 **Ano hashi no hotori de: Daisanbu** / By That Bridge: Part 3
**Haikei Tennō heika-sama** / Dear Emperor / To Your Majesty the Emperor

Ano hashi no hotori de: Kanketsu hen / By That Bridge: Conclusion

1964 **Zoku haikei Tennō heika-sama** / Dear Emperor 2

**Haikei Sōri daijin-sama** / Dear Prime Minister

**Goben no tsubaki** / The Scarlet Camellia

1965 **Sutekina konban wa** / A Nice Good Evening

1966 **Bōkyō to okite** / Homesickness and the Rules / The Betrayers Out

**Danryū** / Warm Current

**Ohana-han (Daiichibu; Dainibu)** / Miss Ohana (Parts 1 and 2)

**Inochi hateru hi made** / Until the Last Day of Our Lives

1967 **Ā, kimi ga ai** / Oh, Your Love

**Onnatachi no niwa** / Garden of Women

**Onna no isshō** / A Woman's Life / Une Vie

**Otoko nara furimukuna** / If You're a Man, Don't Look Back

1968 **Yoake no futari** / A Couple at Dawn

**Hakuchū dōdō** / In Broad Daylight, without Inhibitions

**Konto 55-gō to Suizenji Kiyoko no kamisama no koibito** / Conte 55 and Kiyoko Suizenji's Divine Lover

1969 **Dekkai dekkai yarō** / Big, Big Fellow

**Hibari Hashi no Hana to kenka** / Hibari and Hashi's Flowers and Quarrels

**Konto 55-gō to Suizenji Kiyoko no wan tsū panchi: Sanbyakurokujūgoho no māchi** / Conte 55 and Kiyoko Suizenji's One Two Punch: 365 Steps' March

**Chinchin 55-gō buttobase: Shuppatsu shinkō** / The Street Car Game / Tram No. 55 Go! Departing! (lit.)

1970 **Kage no kuruma** / The Shadow Within / Car in the Shadows (lit.) / Shadow Doom

**Sandogasa da yo jinsei wa** / Life Is Just a Traveler's Hat

**Kochira 55-gō ōtō seyo: Kiki hyappatsu** / No. 55 Calling, Over: A Hundred Dangers

**Nani ga nandemo Tamegorō** / Tamegoro, No Matter What

**Konto 55-gō to Suizenji Kiyoko no Daishōbu** / Conte 55 and Kiyoko Suizenji's Big Gamble

1971 **Yaruzo mite ore Tamegorō** / Watch Your Heart, Tamegoro

**Hana mo mi mo aru Tamegorō** / Tamegoro with Flowers and Fruit

**Konto 55-gō to Mīko no zettai zetsumei** / Conte 55 and Miko's Desperate Situation

1972 **Hatsuwarai: Bikkuri bushidō** / First Smile: Surprising Bushido

1973 **Shinanogawa** / The River Shinano

**Dame oyaji** / No-Good Father

1974 **Tōkyō domannaka** / Heart of Tokyo

**Suna no utsuwa** / Castle of Sand (lit.Vessel of Sand)

1975 **Shōwa karesusuki** / Perennial Weed (lit. Shōwa-Era Withered Pampas Grass)

1977 **Yatsuhakamura** / Village of Eight Gravestones

1978 **Jiken** / The Incident

**Kichiku** / The Demon

1979 **Haitatsu sarenai santsū no tegami** / The Three Undelivered Letters

1980 **Warui yatsura** / Bad Sorts

**Furueru shita** / The Writhing Tongue

1981 **Mayonaka no shōtaijō** / Invitation at Midnight

1982 **Giwaku** / Suspicion

1983 **Meisō chizu** / Wanderer's Map

1984 **Nezumi kozō kaitōden** / Legend of the Ratkid's Mysterious Thefts

1985 **Kikenna onnatachi** / Dangerous Women

# ŌBA Hideo
## (February 28, 1910–March 10, 1997)
大庭秀雄

Ōba's reputation in Japan rests largely on one film, the three-part *What Is Your Name?* (*Kimi no na wa*, 1953–54), a romantic epic following the trials of a couple who fall in love when they meet on a bridge during an air raid, but must endure a long separation before they are united. Considered the quintessential example of Shochiku's "Ōfuna flavor" understated melodrama, the film actually lacked the domestic focus and human detail essayed by Yasujirō Ozu, Keisuke Kinoshita, and others. Nevertheless, its sentimentality and narrative contrivances were redeemed by its visual flair and the conviction of the acting.

Ōba had been directing melodramas and home dramas at Shochiku since the late thirties. In films such as *Woman in the Typhoon Zone* (*Taifūken no onna*, 1948), a taut thriller about a group of pirates who take shelter from an approaching typhoon at an island weather station, his style displayed a clear Hollywood influence. Likewise, the climax of *Homecoming* (*Kikyō*, 1950) was a rather Hawksian sequence where the hero and heroine agree to decide whether they will marry or part on the basis of a game of cards. That film, however, used melodramatic conventions intelligently to examine the effect of World War II on Japanese family relations. The war was also the subject of *Bells of Nagasaki* (*Nagasaki no kane*, 1950), the first Japanese film to deal directly with the atomic bomb. This told the life story of the Catholic Dr. Takashi Nagai, who contracted leukemia while working as a radiologist and was exposed again in the bombing of Nagasaki. Its Christian themes, and the fact that Nagai's illness

was not solely due to the bomb, enabled Ōba to make the film despite Occupation censorship.

Also in the early fifties, Ōba directed *The Pure White Night* (*Junpaku no yoru*, 1951), adapted from an early Mishima novel, and *Life Is Beautiful* (*Inochi uruwashi*, 1951), about a family who, living near a place notorious for suicides, repeatedly have to save despairing young people. After the success of *What Is Your Name?*, he continued to make literary adaptations and melodramas through the fifties and sixties. *Enraptured* (*Onna mai*, 1961), chronicling a dancer's affair with a famous Noh teacher, was prettily photographed in color and contained a superb performance from Mariko Okada. Ōba also remade *The Story of the Late Chrysanthemums* (*Zangiku monogatari*, 1963), originally filmed by Mizoguchi, and *Snow Country* (*Yukiguni*, 1965), based on a Kawabata novel adapted previously by Shirō Toyoda. With its story about a student's love for the widow of a naval officer, Ōba's last film, *Farewell, My Beloved* (*Wakare*, 1969), returned to the war and its destructive effect on interpersonal relations. Though he was basically a minor artist, Ōba's professionalism reaffirms the abiding strengths of the old Japanese studio system in general and of Shochiku in particular.

1939 **Ryōnin no kachi** / Worth of a Husband
**Ane no himitsu** / Older Sister's Secret
**Kangeki no koro** / Time of Deep Emotion
**Wagako no kekkon** / Our Child's Marriage
1940 **Katei no hata** / Flag of Home
**Utsukushii rinjin** / Beautiful Neighbor
**Katei kyōshi** / Private Tutor

Tanoshiki wagaya / Our Happy Home

Himetaru kokoro / Burdened Heart

Fuyuki-hakase no kazoku / The Family of Dr. Fuyuki

1941 Hana wa itsuwarazu / The Flower Does Not Deceive

Kokoro wa itsuwarazu / The Heart Does Not Deceive

1942 Kaze kaoru niwa / The Wind-Scented Garden

Chikai no minato / Harbor of Vows

Futari sugata / Appearance of a Couple

1943 Musume / Girl

Atatakaki kaze / Warm Wind

1944 Kachidoki ondo / Dance of Triumph

1946 Kigeki wa owarinu / The Comedy Has Finished

Nikoniko taikai / Smiling Competition (co-director)

Jinsei gajō / Picture Album of Life

1947 Saigo no tetsuwan / The Last Strong Arm

1948 Idai naru X / The Great X

Taifūken no onna / Woman in the Typhoon Zone / Typhoon Woman

Shachō to onna ten'in / The Boss and the Lady Shop Assistant

1949 Utsukushiki batsu / Beautiful Punishment

Dassen jōnetsu musume / A Passionate Girl Derailed

1950 Otome no seiten / A Virgin's Sex Manual

Niizuma no seiten / New Wives' Sex Manual

Nagasaki no kane / Bells of Nagasaki

Kikyō / Homecoming

1951 Zakuzaku musume / The Crunch Crunch Girl

Junpaku no yoru / The Pure White Night

Inochi uruwashi / Life Is Beautiful

1952 Futatsu no hana / Two Flowers

Jōka / Passion Fire

1953 Aiyoku no sabaki / Judgment of Lust

Kimi no na wa / What Is Your Name? / Always in My Heart

Kimi no na wa: Dainibu / What Is Your Name?: Part 2 / Always in My Heart: Part 2

1954 Kimi no na wa: Daisanbu / What Is Your Name?: Part 3 / Always in My Heart: Part 3

Shinjitsu no aijō o motomete: Izuko e / Seeking True Love: Where?

1955 Anata to tomo ni / With You

Ejima Ikushima / Ejima and Ikushima

1956 Shiroi hashi / The White Bridge

Hareta hi ni / On a Fine Day

1957 Tenshi no jikan / Time of Angels

1958 Kuroi kafun / Black Pollen / True Love

Hana no uzushio / The Invisible Wall (lit. Whirlpool of Flowers)

Me no kabe / The Wall of Eyes

1959 Aru rakujitsu / A Certain Setting Sun

Wakai sugao / Young Naked Face

1960 Shu no kafun / Red Pollen

Rishū / Sadness of Parting

1961 Onna mai / Enraptured (lit. A Woman's Dance)

Kyō geshō / Kyoto Cosmetics

1962 Ai to kanashimi to / With Love and Sorrow

1963 Ano hito wa ima / That Person Is Now

Zangiku monogatari / The Story of the Late Chrysanthemums

1965 Yukiguni / Snow Country

1966 Yokoborigawa / The River Yokobori

1967 Harubiyori / Springlike Weather

Inazuma / Lightning

1969 Wakare / Farewell, My Beloved / Farewell

## ŌBAYASHI Nobuhiko
(b. January 9, 1938)
大林宣彦

An amateur filmmaker from the age of six, Ōbayashi directed experimental shorts on 8mm and 16mm formats until the seventies. *The Man Who Was Eaten* (*Tabeta hito*, 1964) was well received at the time, earning festival screenings abroad; more famous today is *Complexe* (*Complexe = Binetsu no ruri*, 1966), a dada-influenced, broadly anarchistic film in which Ōbayashi interlinked various small stories. A similar outrageous imagination was visible in his feature debut, *House* (*Hausu*, 1977), an incoherent and shoddily made horror spoof notable mainly for such quasi-surreal imagery as a girl being devoured by a piano. Among his other early commercial features were a sentimental San Francisco-set melodrama, *Take Me Away* (*Furimukeba ai*, 1978), starring the popular duo of Momoe Yamaguchi and Tomokazu Miura, and *The Adventures of Kosuke Kindaichi* (*Kindaichi Kōsuke no bōken*, 1979), an entry in a long-running detective series.

Fantasy continued to be his preferred genre, however, and during the eighties he made several popular high-concept films. In *Exchange Students* (*Ten-kōsei*, 1982), the souls of two classmates, boy and girl, swap bodies with humorous consequences, while in *Girl of Time* (*Toki o kakeru shōjo*, 1983)—an especially engaging film, acted with deadpan wit by its teenage stars—a schoolgirl begins to anticipate or experience events before they happen. These two films, together with *Lonelyheart* (*Sabishinbō*, 1985), formed a trilogy of youth films set in Ōbayashi's native Onomichi, a picturesque small town whose cozily old-fashioned charm was an incongruous backdrop to bizarre happenings. Also fantastic in its premise was the Tokyo-set *The Disincarnates* (*Ijintachi tono natsu*, 1988), a ghost story about a divorced screenwriter who encounters the spirits of his deceased parents. Despite occasional stylistic crudities, it was often touching, and it unfolded as an intelligently sustained metaphor for the unhealthiness of living in the past.

During the nineties, Ōbayashi directed a second Onomichi trilogy consisting of *Chizuko's Younger Sister* (*Futari*, 1991), *Goodbye for Tomorrow* (*Ashita*, 1995), and *One Summer's Day* (*Ano natsu no hi: Tondero jīchan*, 1999). The first of these was another ghost story, in which the return of the dead allows the bereaved to come to terms with their grief. Here, Ōbayashi's handling of fantastic material seemed less sure-footed than in his eighties films, but he nevertheless persisted with similar supernatural themes in *Goodbye for Tomorrow*. *One Summer's Day*, however, was a drama about the relationship between a boy and his senile grandfather.

Some of Ōbayashi's more recent films have focused more directly on social realities. *I Want to Hear the Wind's Song* (*Kaze no uta ga kikitai*, 1998) was a story about deaf people triumphing over their disability; *Turning Point* (*Onna zakari*, 1994) depicted a woman journalist who encounters difficulties when she tries to write about a former Prime Minister's anti-abortion stance; while *The Motive* (*Riyū*, 2004) used a murder investigation involving more than a hundred characters to create a panorama of twenty-first-century Japanese society. Also notable was *Sada* (1998), a historical drama about a geisha who strangled her lover and amputated his sexual organ. Reworking the story told by Ōshima in *In the Realm of the Senses*

Toki o kakeru shōjo / Girl of Time *(1983): Ōbayashi's engaging fantasies were among the most commercially successful films of the 1980s.*

(*Ai no korīda*, 1976), Ōbayashi eschewed explicit sex for psychological emphasis, recounting the roots of the heroine's actions in her personal history.

Echoes of Ōbayashi's training in experimental cinema, and of his subsequent career making commercials, remain in his feature films, which have adapted New Wave distancing devices to the context of popular narrative cinema. He has frequently used artificial backdrops, silent-style intertitles, hard-edged wipes, and switches from black and white to color. These stylistic quirks have generally worked well in his more fantastic films, where they seem to complement the whimsy of the plots. Occasionally, too, Ōbayashi has used this artificiality to make pointed comments: in *Beijing Watermelon* (*Pekinteki suika*, 1989), about the relationship between a Japanese grocer and Chinese students, the final studio recreation of a trip to China drew attention to the incident which had prevented location shooting there: the Tiananmen Square massacre. On the other hand, the parodic elements in *Sada* detracted from the integrity of the story, making the unhappy heroine a subject for mockery. While Ōbayashi's films are generally lively and interesting, such ceaseless camera tricks tend to make them seem arch; overall, they are ultimately less than meets the eye.

1944 **Popai no takarajima** / Popeye's Treasure Island (*animated short*)

1945 **Manuke-sensei** / Mr. Blockhead (*animated short*)

1957 **Seishun: Kumo** / Youth: Cloud (*8mm short*)

1958 **E no naka no shōjo** / The Girl in the Picture (*8mm short*)

1959 **Dandango** (*8mm short*)
**Nemuri no kioku** / Memory of Sleep (*8mm short*)

1960 **Mokuyōbi** / Thursday (*8mm short*)
**Onomichi** (*8mm short*)

1961 **Nakasendō** / Nakasendo (*8mm short*)

1962 **T-shi no gogo** / Mr. T's Afternoon (*8mm short*)

1963 **Katami** / Memento (*8mm short*)

1964 **Tabeta hito** / The Man Who Was Eaten (*16mm short*)

1966 **Complexe = Binetsu no ruri** / Complexe (lit. Complexe = Lapiz Lazuli in Fever) (*16mm short*)
**Arui wa kanashii jōzetsu: Warutsu ni notte sōretsu no sanpomichi** / Or Sad Loquacity: Waltz-Accompanied Funeral Parade Path (*16mm short*)

1967 **Emotion = Densetsu no gogo = Itsu ka mita Dorakyura** / Emotion = Legendary Afternoon = One Day I Saw Dracula (*16mm short*)

1968 **Confession = Haruka naru akogare girochin koi no tabi** / Confession = Distant Yearning, Guillotine, Loving Journey (*16mm*)

1970 **Umi no kioku = Sabishinbō: Jo** / Memories of the Sea = The Lonely One: Opening (*16mm short*)

1971 **Orere: Orara** (*16mm short*)
**Jerumi: In: Rio** / Jeremy in Rio (*16mm short*)

1972 **Sutanpīdo kantorī** / Stampede Country (*16mm short*)
**Happī dainanosaurusu: Arubamu** / Happy Dinanosaurus: Album (*16mm short*)

1977 **Hausu** / House
**Hitomi no naka no hōmonsha** / Visitor in the Eye

1978 **Utau reitōshokuhin** / Singing Frozen Food (*16mm short*)
**Furimukeba ai** / Take Me Away / If She Looks Back, It's Love (lit.)
**Pinku redī: Konsāto** / Pink Lady: Concert (*16mm short*)

1979 **Kindaichi Kōsuke no bōken** / The Adventures of Kosuke Kindaichi

1981 **Nerawareta gakuen** / School in the Crosshairs

1982 **Tenkōsei** / Exchange Students / Transfer Students / I Am You, You Are Me

1983 **Toki o kakeru shōjo** / Girl of Time / The Little Girl Who Conquered Time / The Girl Who Transcends Time

1984 **Haishi** / The Deserted City (*16mm*)
**Shōnen Keniya** / Kenya Boy
**Tengoku ni ichiban chikai shima** / The Island Closest to Heaven

1985 **Sabishinbō** / Lonelyheart / Miss Lonely
**Shimaizaka** / Four Sisters / Sister Hills (lit.)

1986 **Kare no ōtobai, kanojo no shima** / His Motorbike, Her Island
**Shigatsu no sakana** / April Fish
**Noyuki yamayuki umibeyuki** / The Young and Wild (lit. To the Fields, To the Mountains, To the Beach)

1987 **Hyōryū kyōshitsu** / The Drifting Classroom

1988 **Nihon junjōden: Okashina futari: Monokuru hoshiki hitobito no mure** / The Strange Couple (lit. Chronicle of Japanese Impulsiveness: Strange Couple: Herd of Nearly Crazy People)
**Ijintachi tono natsu** / The Disincarnates / Summer with Ghosts (lit.)

1989 **Pekinteki suika** / Beijing Watermelon

1991 **Futari** / Chizuko's Younger Sister / Us Two (lit.)

1992 **Watashi no kokoro wa papa no mono** / My Heart Is Dad's
**Kanojo ga kekkon shinai wake** / The Reason She Doesn't Get Married
**Seishun dendekedekedeke** / The Rocking Horseman

1993 **Haruka, nosutarujī** / Nostalgie

©Kadokawa Pictures

Mizu no tabibito: Samurai Kids /
Samurai Kids / The Water Traveler

1994 Onna zakari / Turning Point / A
Mature Woman

1995 Ashita / Goodbye for Tomorrow
(lit. Tomorrow)

1998 Mikeneko Hōmuzu no suiri:
Direkutāzu katto / Tortoiseshell
Cat Holmes' Deduction: Director's
Cut (re-edited version of 1996 TV
movie)

Sada

Kaze no uta ga kikitai / I Want to
Hear the Wind's Song

Reibyō densetsu: Gekijōban
/ Legend of the Beautiful Cat:
Theatrical Version (re-edited version
of 1983 TV movie)

1999 Ano natsu no hi: Tondero jīchan /
One Summer's Day

2000 Yodogawa Nagaharu monogatari:
Kobe hen: Sainara / The Story of
Nagaharu Yodogawa: Kobe Episode:
Bye-bye

2001 Kokubetsu / Valediction

2002 Nagoriyuki / Remaining Snow

2004 Riyū / The Motive

2006 22-sai no wakare: Lycoris:
Hamizu hanamizu monogatari /
Song of Goodbye (lit. Parting at 22:
Lycoris: Story of Unseen Leaves and
Flowers)

2007 Tenkōsei: Sayonara anata /
Exchange Students: Goodbye You /
Switching: Goodbye Me

# OGAWA Shinsuke
(June 25, 1936–February 7, 1992)
小川紳介

Ogawa's fiercely committed documentaries charted the experiences of those overlooked or adversely affected by the postwar phenomena of economic growth and modernization. His earliest films focused on student protest: *Sea of Youth* (*Seinen no umi: Yonin no tsūshin kyōikuseitachi*, 1966) was an account of the campaign run by part-time students whose chances of graduation are threatened by a new law requiring them to complete their courses in a limited number of years. Ogawa emphasized their marginalization within the student body and consequent lack of support. His next film, *Forest of Pressure* (*Assatsu no mori: Takasaki keizai daigaku tōsō no kiroku*, 1967), charted the protests at Takasaki College of Economics against preferential treatment given to applicants related to leading politicians or industrialists. *Report from Haneda* (*Gennin hōkokusho: Haneda tōsō no kiroku*, 1967) chronicled clashes between riot police and students demonstrating at Haneda Airport against Prime Minister Eisaku Satō's visit to the United States; Ogawa sought to prove police responsibility for a protestor's death.

The theme of revolt against authority was at the heart of Ogawa's most important project: the seven-film *Sanrizuka* sequence, beginning with *Summer in Narita* (*Nihon kaihō sensen: Sanrizuka no natsu*, 1968), which followed a campaign by peasant farmers to prevent the appropriation of land chosen as the site for Tokyo's new international airport at Narita. These films combined extensive footage of the violent confrontations between police and farmers with scenes in which the peasants discuss their motives and strategies. The focus was less on ideological debate than on the practical details of the campaign: for instance, much of the last half hour of *People of the Second Fortress* (*Dainitoride no hitobito*, 1971) consisted of scenes in which a protestor describes the construction and use of an underground fortress.

Ogawa next made *A Song of the Bottom* (*Dokkoi! Ningenbushi: Kotobuki jiyū*

©Athenée Français Cultural Center

Nippon-koku: Furuyashiki-mura / Furuyashiki Village *(1982): To make his docu-mentaries, Ogawa chose to live and work alongside his subjects, such as this Tōhoku farmer.*

*rōdōsha no machi*, 1975), an account of the lives of poor casual laborers in Yoho-hama. Ogawa stressed the consequences of poverty, recording the illnesses and deaths of some of his participants, but also revealed their dignity and vitality, with the result that this was perhaps his most moving film. While making it, Ogawa lived for a year in the same Yo-kohama suburb as his subjects. A larger project was initiated when farmers complained that the *Sanrizuka* films be-trayed ignorance of rural life; accepting their offer of a field in Yamagata Prefec-ture, Ogawa set up a farm in collabo-ration with his production company. The cinematic fruits of this experience were *Furuyashiki Village* (*Nippon-koku: Furuyashiki-mura*, 1982) and *Magino Village* (*1000-nen kizami no hidokei: Magino-mura monogatari*, 1987). The former, perhaps Ogawa's finest film, was a richly layered chronicle of village life

and culture, loosely structured around the events of one year, but intertwining footage about the practicalities of deal-ing with a bad harvest with sequences recording the thoughts and memories of the mostly elderly villagers, their individual and collective histories. The latter placed rural customs in a political context through dramatic reconstruc-tions of an Edo-period peasants' revolt against unjust taxation; it was, however, less humanly engaging than its prede-cessor. In his last years, Ogawa helped to found the Yamagata International Documentary Film Festival, and be-gan another film about country life, *Red Persimmons* (*Manzan benigaki*, 2001), which was completed by his Chinese pupil, Peng Xiaolian, after his untimely death.

Although Ogawa has often been called a leftist director, it is more ac-curate to describe him as anti-authoritarian. The *Sanrizuka* documentaries might be read as eminently conservative in upholding individual property rights against excessive state power; the plight of the students in *Sea of Youth* stemmed more from misguided government policy than wider economic issues; and the later films were celebrations of tradition. The partisan qualities of Ogawa's work derived more from what he filmed than from how it was filmed: his hand-held camera did not editorialize, but merely moved to cover the action, and obviously rhetorical camerawork, such as the aerial shots of the threatened farmland which conclude *Summer in Narita*, was rare. More typically, Ogawa's sympathies were expressed through his selection of material. In David Desser's words, he "is unabashedly on the side of his subjects so that he literally allows them to speak for themselves," offering farmers and laborers the chance to address the camera and explain their situations and attitudes. By contrast, the police, government, and construction industry were portrayed in the *Sanrizuka* films as a faceless enemy and denied the opportunity to put their case. Depending on the viewer's perspective, this partisanship may be considered a virtue or a vice; Ogawa himself would doubtless have claimed that his work was a corrective to mainstream media outlets which favored the establishment position. He was certainly admirable in his determination to speak for the dispossessed, and to let them speak for themselves.

1966   **Seinen no umi: Yonin no tsūshin kyōikusei** / Sea of Youth / Sea of Youth: Four Correspondence Course Students (lit.)

1967   **Assatsu no mori: Takasaki keizai daigaku tōsō no kiroku** / Forest of Pressure / The Oppressed Students / Forest of Oppression: A Record of the Struggle at Takasaki City University of Economics (lit.)

**Gennin hōkokusho: Haneda tōsō no kiroku** / Report from Haneda / Eyewitness Report: Chronicle of the Haneda Struggle (lit.)

1968   **Nihon kaihō sensen: Sanrizuka no natsu** / Summer in Narita / Japan Liberation Front: Summer in Sanrizuka (lit.)

1970   **Nihon kaihō sensen: Sanrizuka** / Winter in Narita / Japan Liberation Front: Sanrizuka: Winter

**Sanrizuka: Daisanji kyōsei sokuryō soshi tōsen** / Sanrizuka: The Three-Day War in Narita / Sanrizuka: The Third Struggle Against Forced Surveying (lit.)

1971   **Sanrizuka: Dainitoride no hitobito** / People of the Second Fortress / Sanrizuka: Peasants of the Second Fortress

**Sanrizuka: Iwayama ni tettō ga dekita** / Sanrizuka: The Construction of Iwayama Tower / The Building of the Iwayama Tower

1973   **Sanrizuka: Heta buraku** / Sanrizuka: Heta Village

1975   **Dokkoi! Ningenbushi: Kotobuki jiyū rōdōsha no machi** / A Song of the Bottom / A Song of Common Humanity / Song of the Humans

1976   **Kurīn sentā hōmonki** / Interview at Clean Center

1977   **Sanrizuka: Gogatsu no sora: Sato no kayoiji** / Sanrizuka: The Skies of May: The Road to the Village / Narita: The Skies of May

**Magino monogatari: Yōsan hen** / The Magino Village Story: Raising Silkworms

1978   **Magino monogatari sono 2: Tōge: Zaō to Makabe Jin** / The Magino Village Story: Pass

1982   **Nippon-koku: Furuyashiki-mura** / Furuyashiki Village / A Japanese Village: Furuyashikimura

1987   **1000-nen kizami no hidokei: Magino-mura monogatari** / Magino Village / The Sundial

Carved with a Thousand Years of Notches: The Magino Village Story (lit.)

**Kyōto oni ichiba: Sennen shiatā /** Kyoto Demon Market: The Theater of a Thousand Years (*short*)

2001  **Manzan benigaki** / Red Persimmons (*co-director; released posthumously*)

## OGURI Kōhei
## (b. October 29, 1945)
## 小栗康平

Oguri's short filmography bears witness to his determination to explore chosen themes and evolve a personal style while refusing to submit to commercial pressures. After working as an assistant director on a freelance basis, he obtained private funding for his debut, *Muddy River* (*Doro no kawa*, 1981), a sombre and poignant study of childhood in postwar Osaka, and a small masterpiece. Many critics drew comparisons with Ozu, to whose work the predominantly static camera, spare black and white images, and mid-fifties setting seemed a deliberate homage. However, in its focus on working-class rather than bourgeois characters, its way of setting the injustice and cruelty of the adult world against the emotional purity of the young, and its ultimate hard-won faith in human decency, the film more closely evoked the tone of social realist filmmaker Kirio Urayama, whom Oguri had assisted on *Gate of Youth* (*Seishun no mon*, 1975). Like Urayama's best work, Oguri's film was an affecting personal drama broadened in implication by social concern.

A similar blend of human observation with social commentary was also apparent in the director's second film, *For Kayako* (*Kayako no tameni*, 1984), a downbeat study of the prejudice faced by resident Koreans in Japan. Here, however, the social concern was somewhat compromised by the obsessively pictorial compositions, which aestheticized the protagonist's situation and heralded the more stylized approach of Oguri's later work. His third film, *Sting of Death* (*Shi no toge*, 1990) nominally revisited the fifties setting of *Muddy River* and *For Kayako*, but dramatized the mutual animosity between an adulterous husband and his wife in a deliberately timeless, theatrical fashion. Again Oguri's images were precisely composed and visibly contrived, but in this case the technique suggestively conveyed the sense that the couple's recriminations were less an expression of spontaneous anger than a form of elaborate and dangerous gameplaying. Though the film's bitterness was ultimately monotonous, it achieved moments of piercing intensity, particularly in the haunting use of the couple's children as silent onlookers to their parents' strife.

Oguri took this stylization further with *The Sleeping Man* (*Nemuru otoko*, 1996) and *The Buried Forest* (*Umoregi*, 2005), both magic realist accounts of rural life. In the former, the passive presence of a young man, comatose after an accident in the mountains, was used to illuminate the experiences, emotions, and desires of the other villagers. The latter, which again interwove various small stories in a country town, centered around the discovery, after a storm, of the petrified stumps of ancient trees beneath a nearby forest; Oguri intended this as a metaphor for the traditional Japanese spirit of harmony with nature, now buried beneath the accoutrements of modern life. Both these films were set in Oguri's native

©Kimura Production

Doro no kawa / Muddy River *(1981): This sombre study of childhood was an auspicious debut for a unique filmmaker.*

Gunma Prefecture, which financed *The Sleeping Man*, but this setting seemed almost incidental. Their real concern was with more universal themes: the passing of time, the life cycle, the role of tradition in local communities. It may be argued that Oguri's decision to address such timeless concerns and his deliberately poetic approach have deprived his more recent work of the specificity which made his debut so humanly moving. Nevertheless, *The Sleeping Man* remains one of the most purely beautiful films produced in Japan in recent decades, and among modern Japanese directors, Oguri seems almost alone in aspiring to film the transcendent.

1981  **Doro no kawa** / Muddy River
1984  **Kayako no tameni** / For Kayako
1990  **Shi no toge** / Sting of Death

1996  **Nemuru otoko** / The Sleeping Man
2005  **Umoregi** / The Buried Forest

## OKAMOTO Kihachi
### (February 17, 1924–February 19, 2005)
岡本喜八

A specialist in action cinema, Okamoto served as assistant at Toho to Senkichi Taniguchi and Masahiro Makino, whose influence may have contributed to his flair for choreographing violence. His early gangster movies, such as *Underworld Boss* (*Ankokugai no kaoyaku*, 1959) and its sequels, apparently owed much to Hollywood models: Chris D. has praised the "hard-boiled, *noir*ish edginess" of *Procurers of Hell* (*Jigoku no kyōen*, 1961), which traced the destructive consequences of an attempt to extort money from a wealthy industrialist. Okamoto's most notable early film was *Desperado Outpost* (*Dokuritsu gurentai*, 1959), in which the director, himself a combat veteran, exposed the absurdities of war through a black comic treatment of corruption in a Manchurian base. The later *The Human Bullet* (*Nikudan*, 1968), made for ATG, was another absurdist story, considered Okamoto's masterpiece in some quarters, about a young soldier preparing for a kamikaze mission. Elsewhere, Okamoto treated the war in more serious fashion: *Fort Graveyard* (*Chi to suna*, 1965) was a bleak account of the training and futile deaths of a youthful marching band. *Japan's Longest Day* (*Nihon no ichiban nagai hi*, 1967) depicted the conflicts between politicians and the military in the last hours before the country's surrender at the end of World War II; Joan Mellen has condemned this as "a shameless film" for whitewashing the leading militarists.

Okamoto's international reputation rests on the sequence of *chanbara* he directed in the sixties. Apart from *Sword of Doom* (*Daibosatsu Tōge*, 1966), a version of the classic *kōdan* story *Daibosatsu Pass*, all focused on politically turbulent eras of Japan's past: in *Warring Clans* (*Sengoku yarō*, 1963), the civil wars of the sixteenth century; in *Samurai Assassin* (*Samurai*, 1965), *Kill!* (*Kiru*, 1968), and *The Red Lion* (*Akage*, 1969), the conflicts leading up to and following the Meiji Restoration. Like his accounts of the Pacific War, they varied in approach between the severity of *Samurai Assassin* and the dark humor of *Warring Clans* and *Kill!* This latter work has elicited comparisons with the spaghetti Western, and even Okamoto's more humorous films, like Sergio Leone's, tended

towards nihilism. In *Warring Clans*, a group of warriors risk their lives to smuggle weapons through enemy territory, only to discover, after many have died, that their cargo was merely a decoy. *The Red Lion* suggested that authority of whatever kind will always exploit the poor; it ended with Toshirō Mifune's hero killed by his treacherous employers, while the local peasants chant "*Eijanaika*" ("What the hell!").

Though rarely subtle, these films displayed a considerable expertise, as the comparison of *Sword of Doom* with the 1960 *Daibosatsu Pass* by Kenji Misumi (himself a talented filmmaker) suggests. The precision and violent intensity of Okamoto's direction conveyed with particular clarity the theme of bushidō values used as a cover for individual psychopathy. Memorable among Okamoto's set pieces was the climax of *Samurai Assassin*: a battle in a snowstorm which dramatically concluded a largely static, dialogue-centered film. His work was notable, too, for good performances, not only from such established genre stars as Tatsuya Nakadai and Toshirō Mifune, but also from character actor Yūnosuke Itō, who had acted for Okamoto in the comedy *Oh, My Bomb* (*Ā bakudan*, 1964), and whose lugubrious persona brought an unusual, seedy edge to the villains in *Samurai Assassin* and *The Red Lion*.

Okamoto's later work was less successful. *Battle Cry* (*Tokkan*, 1975), another *chanbara* set at the time of the Meiji Restoration, lacked his characteristic flair, the use of handheld camera seeming clumsy. This was another low-budget ATG film, as was *At Long Last, the Charleston* (*Chikagoro naze ka Chārusuton*, 1981), a bizarre, improvisational, ultimately unsuccessful art movie, filmed in dreamy monochrome, about a group of elderly peace campaigners. Latterly, Okamoto directed some curious hybrids of Japanese and American modes: *Dixieland Daimyo* (*Jazu daimyō*, 1986) was about a group of black slaves adrift in Meiji-era Japan, while *East Meets West* (1995) told the story of a samurai sent to San Francisco to prevent the signing of a treaty between the United States and Japan. However, his last film, *Vengeance for Sale* (*Sukedachiya Sukeroku*, 2001), was a reunion with actor Nakadai and a return to his most fruitful vein of samurai action laced with humor.

**1958  Kekkon no subete** / All About Marriage

**Wakai musumetachi** / Young Daughters

**1959  Ankokugai no kaoyaku** / Underworld Boss / The Big Boss

**Aru hi watashi wa** / Some Day I'll Know

**Dokuritsu gurentai** / Desperado Outpost

**1960  Ankokugai no taiketsu** / Underworld Duel / The Last Gunfight

**Daigaku no sanzokutachi** / Bad Boys in University / The Spook Cottage / The University Scamps

**Dokuritsu gurentai nishi e** / Westward Desperado

**1961  Ankokugai no dankon** / Underworld Bullets / Blueprint of Murder

**Kaoyaku akatsuki ni shisu** / Big Shots Die at Dawn / Death of the Boss

**Jigoku no kyōen** / Procurers of Hell / Banquet in Hell (lit.)

**1962  Dobunezumi sakusen** / Operation Sewer Rats / Operation X

**Gekkyū dorobō** / Salary Robber

**1963  Sengoku yarō** / Warring Clans

**Eburiman-shi no yūgana seikatsu** / The Elegant Life of Mr. Everyman

**1964  Ā bakudan** / Oh, My Bomb

**1965  Samurai** / Samurai Assassin / Samurai (lit.)

**Chi to suna** / Fort Graveyard / Blood and Sand (lit.)

**1966  Daibosatsu Tōge** / Sword of Doom / Daibosatsu Pass (lit.)

**1967  Satsujinkyō jidai** / The Age of Assassins / Epoch of Murder Madness (lit.)

**Nihon no ichiban nagai hi** / Japan's Longest Day / The Emperor and the General

**1968  Kiru** / Kill!

**Nikudan** / The Human Bullet

**1969  Akage** / The Red Lion (lit. Red Hair)

**1970  Zatōichi to Yōjinbō** / Zatoichi Meets Yojimbo

**1971  Gekidō no Shōwa shi: Okinawa kessen** / The Battle of Okinawa

**1972  Nippon sanjūshi: Osaraba Tōkyō no maki** / Musketeers of Japan: Farewell, Tokyo

**1973  Nippon sanjūshi: Hakata obishime ippon dokko no maki** / Musketeers of Japan: The Pattern of a Hakata Obi

**1974  Aoba shigereru** / Green Leaves Grow Thick

**1975  Tokkan** / Battle Cry

**1977  Sugata Sanshirō** / Sanshiro Sugata

**1978  Dainamaito dondon** / Dynamite Bang Bang

**Burū kurisumasu** / Blue Christmas

**1979  Eireitachi no ōenka: Saigo no Sōkeisen** / The Last Game (lit. Cheerleaders' Song for the Spirits of War Dead: The Last Waseda-Keio Match)

**1981  Chikagoro naze ka Chārusuton** / At Long Last, the Charleston

**1986  Jazu daimyō** / Dixieland Daimyo / Jazz Daimyo (lit.)

**1991  Daiyūkai** / Rainbow Kids

**1995  East Meets West**

**2001  Sukedachiya Sukeroku** / Vengeance for Sale

## ŌMORI Kazuki
### (b. March 3, 1952)
大森一樹

Little known outside Japan, Ōmori has achieved both critical and commercial success at home during the course of a prolific career. During the seventies, while a medical student in Kyoto, he made a number of admired amateur films on 8 and 16mm formats; these apparently displayed the influence of Jean-Luc Godard. His success in this field earned him an invitation to make a feature, *Orange Road Express* (*Orenji rōdo ekusupuresu*, 1978) at Shochiku; as with most of his early work, he scripted this himself. ATG financed Ōmori's next film, *Disciples of Hippocrates* (*Hipokuratesu-tachi*, 1980), a semi-autobiographical account of the lives of a group of Kyoto medical students; visually rather indifferent, it nevertheless conveyed a real sense of the varied facets of student life.

After making *Hear the Song of the Wind* (*Kaze no uta o kike*, 1981), based on a Haruki Murakami novel, Ōmori helped to establish the Director's Company with Kazuhiko Hasegawa and other younger directors. Such films as the youth film *Paupers' Walk* (*Sukanpin wōku*, 1984) bolstered his reputation, and by the mid-eighties he was working at Toho. There he made *Young Girls in Love* (*Koisuru onnatachi*, 1986), which juxtaposed a high school girl's experience of first love with a number of other love stories, and *Sayonara, Fraulein* ("*Sayonara*" *no onnatachi*, 1987), a road movie about a woman who leaves her native Hokkaido to search for work in the Kansai region. At the same time he also directed several successful television dramas, including some set again among medical students. For Kado-

kawa, he made *Afternoon When Flowers Fell* (*Hana no furu gogo*, 1989), a celebration of the 100th anniversary of the foundation of the port city of Kobe.

By the nineties, Ōmori's work had grown more commercial in tone, but he has continued to essay a wide range of genres and subjects. He scripted several and directed two installments in an updated sequence of *Godzilla* (*Gojira*) movies. *Hit the Goal* (*Shūto*, 1994) was a story about teenage soccer players, somewhat sentimental in tone, but with a sharp eye for the homoerotic dimension of adolescent hero worship. *Succession Ceremony* (*Keishō sakazuki*, 1992) was a comic riff on the yakuza genre, about the complications which ensue when a young gangster has to persuade the boss of an allied clan to preside at a succession ceremony; Ōmori satirized the elaborate codes of the gangster world. *Night Train to the Stars* (*Waga kokoro no Ginga tetsudō: Miyazawa Kenji monogatari*, 1996) was another centenary tribute: to Tohoku-born poet and children's author Kenji Miyazawa. More recently, *Those Were the Days* (*Kanashiki tenshi*, 2006) was a thriller about male and female detectives investigating a murder.

Ōmori has realized several international co-productions and films made or set abroad. *Emergency Call* (*Kinkyū yobidashi: Emājenshī kōru*, 1995), in which he again focused on the medical profession, was shot on location in the Philippines, while *T.R.Y.* (2003) was a Sino-Korean-Japanese co-production with Ken Watanabe as a Japanese swindler selling arms to anti-government factions in early twentieth-century Shanghai. *Natu: Dance! Ninja Legend* (*Natu: Odoru! Ninja densetsu*, 2000) was a film in the style of Bollywood, with Hindi-language song-and-dance numbers. This high-profile career in Asia contrasts with Ōmori's

general lack of recognition in the West—
perhaps because, *Godzilla* aside, he has
rarely worked in the masculine genres
that tend to win distribution in Europe
and North America.

1969 **Kakumeikyō jidai** / Revolution
Crazy Age (*8mm short*)
**Shiroi koibitotachi** / White Lovers
(*8mm short*)

1972 **Death Cover Japan** (*8mm short*)
**Hiroshima kara tōku hanarete** /
Far from Hiroshima (*8mm short*)
**Sora tobu enban o mita otoko** /
The Man Who Saw the Disk Flying
in the Sky (*8mm short*)
**Ashita ni mukatte hashirenai!** /
I Can't Run Towards Tomorrow
(*8mm*)

1973 **Shinu ni wa ma ni awanai!** / Death
Won't Do! (*8mm*)

1975 **Kuraku naru made matenai!** / I
Can't Wait Till It's Dark / Never
Wait Until Dark (*16mm*)
**Sora tobu enban o mita otoko:
Ginmaku shitōhen** / The Man
Who Saw the Disk Flying in the
Sky: Battle to the Death on Screen
(*8mm short*)

1978 **Orenji rōdo ekusupuresu** /
Orange Road Express
**Natsuko to, rongu guddobai** / A
Long Goodbye to Natsuko (*16mm
short*)

1980 **Hipokuratesu-tachi** / Disciples of
Hippocrates

1981 **Zenritsusen no byōki to yobō** /
The Prevention of Prostatic Disease
(*16mm short*)
**Sora tobu enban o mita otoko
3: Enerugīman** / The Man Who
Saw the Disk Flying in the Sky:
Energyman (*8mm short*)
**Kaze no uta o kike** / Hear the
Song of the Wind

1984 **Sukanpin wōku** / Paupers' Walk
**Nyōro kesseki bishōhappa** /
Blasting Kidney Stones in the
Urinary Tract (*16mm short*)

1985 **Yū gatta chansu** / You've Got a
Chance

1986 **Teiku itto ījī** / Take It Easy
**Koisuru onnatachi** / Young Girls in
Love

1987 **Totto channeru** / Totto Channel
**"Sayonara" no onnatachi** /
Sayonara, Fraulein / Goodbye to the
Girls

1989 **Hana no furu gogo** / Afternoon
When Flowers Fell
**Gojira vs. Biorante** / Godzilla vs.
Biorante

1990 **Boku ga byōki ni natta wake** / The
Reason I Got Sick (*co-director*)

1991 **Mangetsu** / Mr. Moonlight
**Gojira vs. Kingu Gidora** / Godzilla
vs. King Ghidora

1992 **Keishō sakazuki** / Succession
Ceremony

1994 **Shūto** / Hit the Goal / Shoot

1995 **Daishitsuren** / The Great
Heartbreak
**Kinkyū yobidashi: Emājenshī
kōru** / Emergency Call

1996 **Waga kokoro no Ginga tetsudō:
Miyazawa Kenji monogatari** /
Night Train to the Stars (lit. My
Heart's Railway to the Milky Way:
The Story of Kenji Miyazawa)

1997 **Dorīmu sutajiamu** / Dream
Stadium

1998 **Jūn buraido: 6-gatsu 19-nichi no
hanayome** / June Bride

2000 **Kaze o mita shōnen** / The Boy
Who Saw the Wind
**Hakata mūbī: Chinchiromai** /
Hakata Movie: Chinchiromai
**Natu: Odoru! Ninja densetsu** /
Natu: Dance! Ninja Legend

2001 **Hashire! Ichirō** / Run, Ichiro!

2003 **T.R.Y.**

2005 **Gekijōban: Chōsei kantai seizā X
tatakae! Hoshi no senshitachi** /
Theatrical Version: Super Star Fleet
Sazer X Fight! Star Warriors

2006 **Kanashiki tenshi** / Those Were the
Days (lit. The Sad Angel)

# ŌSHIMA Nagisa
## (b. March 31, 1932)
大島渚

Arguably the most formally innovative and politically provocative director of the Japanese New Wave, Ōshima was certainly its most acclaimed artist internationally, although his reputation has latterly been eclipsed somewhat by that of his older contemporary Shōhei Imamura. As a critic in the fifties, he rejected the conservatism he saw embodied in Shochiku's sentimental "Ōfuna flavor"; nevertheless, he directed initially at Shochiku, then seeking to emulate the success of the *Nouvelle Vague*. His debut feature, *A Town of Love and Hope* (*Ai to kibō no machi*, 1959), was a merciless anecdote about a poor boy criminalized for an insignificant fraud, while *The Sun's Burial* (*Taiyō no hakaba*, 1960) and *Cruel Story of Youth* (*Seishun zankoku monogatari*, 1960) were nihilistic accounts of young delinquents, which recalled the *taiyōzoku* ("sun tribe") movement of the fifties. These films established Ōshima's recurrent tactic of using crime to suggest the underlying rottenness of society. *Night and Fog in Japan* (*Nihon no yoru to kiri*, 1960), a more directly political film, confronted the disunity of the radical left in the context of its failure to stop the ratification of the U.S.-Japan (Anpo) Security Treaty. After Shochiku withdrew this work from circulation, Ōshima's next two films tackled controversial subject matter under cover of historical distance. *The Catch* (*Shiiku*, 1961) detailed the ill-treatment and ultimate murder of a black American airman captured by the inhabitants of a remote village during World War II, while *The Rebel* (*Amakusa Shirō Tokisada*, 1962) dramatized the seventeenth-century Christian

rebellion in Shimabara, apparently as an allegory of the fate of the postwar student movement.

Ōshima reached artistic maturity, however, later in the sixties, with an independently produced sequence of complex and subversive analyses of Japanese society. Again, his heroes were criminals: he saw crime as a symptom of social injustice and potentially a revolutionary act. *Violence at Noon* (*Hakuchū no tōrima*, 1966) juxtaposed the murders committed by the protagonist with the collapse of a collective farm, the contrast implicitly expressing despair at the failure of progressive politics. In this film and *Death by Hanging* (*Kōshikei*, 1968), Ōshima treated murder in a non-judgmental fashion, believing that "as long as the state makes the absolute evil of murder legal through the waging of wars and the exercise of capital punishment, we are all innocent." Though persuasively argued, this proposition was morally questionable. With *Boy* (*Shōnen*, 1969), however, Ōshima produced a more nuanced account of guilt and responsibility, focusing on a child used by his family to fake car accidents so that compensation can be extorted from the drivers. Here, in his most moving film, he showed the helplessness of those for whom no option exists but criminality.

Several of Ōshima's sixties films examined issues related to Korea. *Yunbogi's Diary* (*Yunbogi no nikki*, 1965) was a photomontage focusing on child poverty in that country; while with *A Treatise on Japanese Bawdy Song* (*Nihon shunkakō*, 1967) Ōshima began to detail the prejudice experienced by Koreans in Japan. *Death by Hanging* and *Three Resurrected Drunkards* (*Kaette kita yopparai*, 1968) were in part fables about the artificial construction of ethnic identity. In

©Shochiku Company Ltd.

Hakuchū no tōrima / Violence at Noon *(1966): New Wave master Ōshima portrayed crime as a symptom of injustice and an act of revolution.*

*Death by Hanging*, a botched execution leaves its Korean victim an amnesiac, and the film charted the re-creation of his identity as a "typical" Korean: both his Japanese captors, who re-enact his childhood as they imagine it according to ethnic stereotypes, and the compatriot who urges him to become a militant encourage him to define his identity along racial lines. In *Three Resurrected Drunkards*, identity became a matter of surface appearances: when a Korean army deserter steals the clothes of three Japanese students and substitutes Korean costumes, they begin to experience the ill-treatment suffered by racial minorities in Japan.

Another recurrent concern, particularly in Ōshima's later work, was sexuality, and its ambivalent relation to power politics. *Diary of a Shinjuku Thief (Shin-juku dorobō nikki*, 1969) suggested a link between crime, sexual liberation, and political change; and a similar implication was offered by Ōshima's last film, *Gohatto* (1999), which showed how homosexual desire undermined discipline among the elite *Shinsengumi* corps of samurai at the time of the Shogunate's downfall. By contrast, in Ōshima's most notorious work, the hardcore *In the Realm of the Senses (Ai no korīda*, 1976), a couple's obsessive sado-masochism was seen as a retreat from politics: their erotic gameplaying was set discreetly against the backdrop of Japan's pre-war descent into fascism. Another film about transgressive love was *Max, Mon Amour* (1986), a Bunuelian satire about a bourgeois woman's relationship with a chimpanzee. By the time of these later works, Ōshima was reliant on foreign funding, a fact that sometimes influenced their subject matter and setting: *Max, Mon Amour* was filmed in Paris and mainly in French, while *Merry Christmas, Mr Lawrence* (*Senjō no merī Kurisumasu*, 1983), an Anglo-Japanese co-production with much English-language dialogue, was an account of the relationship between Japanese officers and their British captives in a prisoner-of-war camp.

Ōshima's style has varied dramatically from film to film, drawing on an eclectic range of influences. *Violence at Noon* was an exercise in Soviet-style montage, where constant reframing reflected societal fragmentation. *Diary of a Shinjuku Thief* mimicked the freewheeling artifice of Godard. By contrast, *Night and Fog in Japan*, *Boy*, and *Death by Hanging* explored the expressive potential of the long take as a means of achieving both dramatic efficacy and theatrical artificiality. The unifying factor in Ōshima's technique was a tension between overtly stylized devices and realist or documentary elements. Thus, *Death by Hanging* opened with a matter-of-fact description of the practical details of implementing an execution before developing into a theatrical fantasy; *Boy*, generally naturalistic in approach, drained the color from the image at climactic moments; *Diary of a Shinjuku Thief* combined disruptive text inserts with scenes of apparent improvisation.

The most assured example of this method was *Ceremonies* (*Gishiki*, 1971), a masterly account of the history of postwar Japan reflected through the microcosm of one family. Here every character was fully rounded, but also personified a facet of Japanese society; melodrama encouraged emotional involvement, while structural formality and overt symbolism invited a detached, analytical response. Ōshima also explored the complex relationship between the filmed image and reality in *The Man Who Left His Will on Film* (*Tōkyō sensō sengo hiwa*, 1970), a more self-conscious work about a Marxist student trying to discover the motive behind the suicide of a comrade through clues left in a documentary, only to find that the film shapes his own actions. Both here and in *Ceremonies*, which exposed the persistence of feudal values in postwar Japan, Ōshima suggested that only violence can overcome the oppressive weight of the past.

The doctrinaire aspects of Ōshima's films sometimes made them excessively arid in tone, and some of his political concerns now seem specific to their time and place, a fact which may account for his relative neglect in the twenty-first century. Nevertheless, his best work retains its power and remains both suggestive and formally imaginative.

1959  **Asu no taiyō** / Tomorrow's Sun (*short*)
**Ai to kibō no machi** / A Town of Love and Hope
1960  **Seishun zankoku monogatari** / Cruel Story of Youth / Naked Youth
**Taiyō no hakaba** / The Sun's Burial
**Nihon no yoru to kiri** / Night and Fog in Japan
1961  **Shiiku** / The Catch
1962  **Amakusa Shirō Tokisada** / The Rebel / Shiro Tokisada from Amakusa
1963  **Chiisana bōken ryokō** / Little Adventure Trip (*short*)
1964  **Watashi no beretto** / My Beretto (*short*)
1965  **Etsuraku** / Pleasures of the Flesh
**Yunbogi no nikki** / Yunbogi's Diary (*short*)
1966  **Hakuchū no tōrima** / Violence at

Noon / Violence at High Noon /
The Daylight Demon

1967 **Ninja bugeichō** / Band of Ninja
**Nihon shunkakō** / A Treatise on
Japanese Bawdy Song / Sing a Song
of Sex
**Muri shinjū Nihon no natsu** /
Japanese Summer: Double Suicide /
Night of the Killer

1968 **Kōshikei** / Death by Hanging
**Kaette kita yopparai** / Three
Resurrected Drunkards / Sinner in
Paradise

1969 **Shinjuku dorobō nikki** / Diary of a
Shinjuku Thief
**Shōnen** / Boy

1970 **Tōkyō sensō sengo hiwa** / The
Man Who Left His Will on Film /
He Died After the War

1971 **Gishiki** / Ceremonies / The
Ceremony

1972 **Natsu no imōto** / Dear Summer
Sister

1976 **Ai no korīda** / In the Realm of the
Senses / Empire of the Senses (lit.
Bullfight of Love)

1978 **Ai no bōrei** / Empire of Passion

1983 **Senjō no merī kurisumasu** / Merry
Christmas, Mr. Lawrence (lit. Merry
Christmas on the Battlefield)

1986 **Makkusu mon amūru** / Max, Mon
Amour

1991 **Kyoto, My Mother's Place** (*short*)

1999 **Gohatto** / Gohatto / Taboo

# OZU Yasujirō
## (December 12, 1903–December 12, 1963)
小津安二郎

One of Japan's greatest directors and a towering figure in world cinema, Ozu has nevertheless been represented in partial and misleading terms in many Western accounts. The standard view

is exemplified by Paul Schrader's assertion that "Ozu is the filmmaker who doesn't do certain things": thus, he was the maker of subdued, contemplative dramas of family life; he elicited restrained, understated performances from his actors; and he used an invariably static camera. It has become something of a cliche to refer to him as "the most Japanese of Japanese directors": the serenity of his films has been related to his adherence to Zen Buddhism, and his distinctive low camera positions explained as marking the viewpoint of a person kneeling on a tatami mat. As a corrective to this, it should be noted that Ozu himself dismissed the connection with Zen, and that, as David Bordwell has shown, his camera was often closer to ground level than to the height of a seated observer. Moreover, though the subject matter of his later films was distinctively Japanese, Ozu admired Chaplin, Lubitsch, and Harold Lloyd, and his silent films included slapstick comedies such as *Days of Youth* (*Gakusei romansu: Wakaki hi*, 1929), melodramas like *A Woman of Tokyo* (*Tōkyō no onna*, 1933), and thrillers and gangster movies such as *That Night's Wife* (*Sono yo no tsuma*, 1930) and *Dragnet Girl* (*Hijōsen no onna*, 1933), all influenced to a greater or lesser degree by Hollywood. Indeed, as late as 1956, the opening shots of *Early Spring* (*Sōshun*), with their René Clair-like, rhythmic depiction of the morning awakening and activity of the city, testified to the continuing influence of Western popular cinema.

Nevertheless, the homogeneity of Ozu's work remains remarkable, and his films may be interpreted as a chronicle of the experiences of his generation, from student days (*I Flunked, But...* [*Rakudai wa shita keredo*, 1930]) to early

Tōkyō no kōrasu / Tokyo Chorus *(1931): In a film that helped form his style, we see one of Ozu's first nuclear families: the girl is a young Hideko Takamine.*

parenthood (*I Was Born, But…*[*Otona no ehon: Umarete wa mita keredo*, 1932]) to a middle age characterized in the post-war films by nostalgia, disillusionment, and the indifference of grown-up children (Ozu, ironically, never attended university and was childless). Even in the early thirties, he was already the acknowledged master of the *shomin-geki* genre, focusing on the realities of daily life for lower middle class Japanese. Films such as *Tokyo Chorus* (*Tōkyō no kōrasu*, 1931) and the masterly *I Was Born, But…* essayed the delicate fusion of comedy and pathos for which Ozu and his studio, Shochiku, would be renowned, and focused discreetly on the alienation of the salaryman at a time of poverty and unemployment. *A Story of Floating Weeds* (*Ukigusa monogatari*, 1934), a poignant low-key melodrama about generational conflict, was set in a

more traditional milieu among a troupe of traveling actors.

In these films, too, Ozu began to refine his style, gradually eliminating fades, dissolves, and pans, and developing his trademark "pillow shots"—cuts away from the action to surrounding objects or scenery, which gave the viewer space to contemplate the drama. His mature style was fully established with his first sound film, *The Only Son* (*Hitori musuko*, 1936), which was also one of his richest and most moving accounts of the sorrows and disappointments of family life. This film, about a mother who has sacrificed her own happiness for her son's well-being, also marked a shift in Ozu's sympathies towards the older generation: subsequently, *The Brothers and Sisters of the Toda Family* (*Toda-ke no kyōdai*, 1941), focused on the indifference of grown-up children to their mother's well-being after their father's death, while *There Was a Father* (*Chichi ariki*, 1942) studied the loneliness of a father forced for professional reasons to live at a distance from his son. Despite occasional injunctions to do one's duty, these wartime films seemed largely unaffected by the troubles of the time. In the immediate postwar period, however, Ozu made some films which focused with uncharacteristic directness on contemporary social problems: thus, *Record of a Tenement Gentleman* (*Nagaya shinshi roku*, 1947) depicted the experiences of an abandoned child and *A Hen in the Wind* (*Kaze no naka no mendori*, 1948) was a melodrama about a repatriated soldier who finds that his wife has had to support herself through prostitution.

The bulk of Ozu's postwar work, however, conforms more closely to the standard account and constitutes a searching examination of the Japanese family system in an era of change. In films such as *Tokyo Story* (*Tōkyō monogatari*, 1953), *Early Summer* (*Bakushū*, 1951), *The End of Summer* (*Kohayagawa-ke no aki*, 1961), and *Late Spring* (*Banshun*, 1949)—plus its reworkings or remakes, *Late Autumn* (*Akibiyori*, 1960) and *An Autumn Afternoon* (*Sanma no aji*, 1962)—he examined the emotional gulfs between individuals and especially between the generations. The tone of these films was one of gentle melancholy, with the bleakness of the subject matter redeemed by the tenderness of Ozu's approach. For Ozu, as for Renoir, "Everyone has his reasons," but he showed that the needs and desires even of people who love each other are often mutually incompatible. His films about the family ended almost invariably with its disintegration, through death or geographical separation, and his closing

scenes often focused on the loneliness of those left isolated, such as the widower of *Tokyo Story*, or the parents of married children in *The Only Son*, *Late Spring*, and *Early Summer*.

Noel Burch has compared Ozu's technique to that of classical Japanese painters, who sought to explore every possible variation on a chosen theme. Thus, *Late Autumn* substituted a widowed mother for the widowed father of *Late Spring*, while *Good Morning* (*Ohayō*, 1959), about brothers who go "on strike" when their parents refuse to buy a television set, updated the silent *I Was Born, But...* to the context of the postwar economic boom. Especially in Ozu's later films, this approach was enriched by the presence of a repertory company of actors, pre-eminently Chishū Ryū and Setsuko Hara, who essayed subtle variations on set roles, and contributed to the creation of a uniquely nuanced portrait of human interaction, where simplicities of style elucidated complexities of feeling. Though the consistency of his later work threatens to make some of the minor films redundant, all of Ozu is rewarding, and his finest films rank, in their formal perfection and humanity, among the summits of cinematic art.

1927 **Zange no yaiba** / Sword of Penitence
1928 **Wakōdo no yume** / The Dreams of Youth
**Nyōbō funshitsu** / Wife Lost
**Kabocha** / Pumpkin
**Hikkoshi fūfu** / A Couple on the Move
**Nikutaibi** / Body Beautiful
1929 **Takara no yama** / Treasure Mountain
**Gakusei romansu: Wakaki hi** / Days of Youth
**Wasei kenka tomodachi** / Fighting Friends, Japanese Style

Daigaku wa deta keredo / I Graduated, But…

Kaishain seikatsu / The Life of an Office Worker

Tokkan kozō / A Straightforward Boy

1930 Kekkongaku nyūmon / An Introduction to Marriage

Hogaraka ni ayume / Walk Cheerfully

Rakudai wa shita keredo / I Flunked, But…

Sono yo no tsuma / That Night's Wife

Erogami no onryō / The Revengeful Spirit of Eros

Ashi ni sawatta kōun / Lost Luck / The Luck Which Touched the Leg (lit.)

Ojōsan / Young Miss

1931 Shukujo to hige / The Lady and the Beard / The Lady and her Favorite

Bijin aishū / Beauty's Sorrows

Tōkyō no kōrasu / Tokyo Chorus

1932 Haru wa gofujin kara / Spring Comes from the Ladies

Otona no miru ehon: Umarete wa mita keredo / I Was Born, But… (lit. Picture Book for Adults: I Was Born, But...)

Seishun no yume ima izuko / Where Now Are the Dreams of Youth?

Mata au hi made / Until the Day We Meet Again

1933 Tōkyō no onna / A Woman of Tokyo

Hijōsen no onna / Dragnet Girl / Woman on the Firing Line

Dekigokoro / Passing Fancy

1934 Haha o kowazuya / A Mother Should Be Loved

Ukigusa monogatari / A Story of Floating Weeds

1935 Hakoiri musume / An Innocent Maid

Tōkyō no yado / An Inn in Tokyo

1936 Kikugorō no Kagamijishi / Kagamijishi (*short*)

Daigaku yoi toko / College Is a Nice Place

Hitori musuko / The Only Son

1937 Shukujo wa nani o wasureta ka / What Did the Lady Forget?

1941 Toda-ke no kyōdai / The Brothers and Sisters of the Toda Family / Toda Brother and Sister

1942 Chichi ariki / There Was a Father

1947 Nagaya shinshi roku / Record of a Tenement Gentleman

1948 Kaze no naka no mendori / A Hen in the Wind

1949 Banshun / Late Spring

1950 Munekata kyōdai / The Munekata Sisters

1951 Bakushū / Early Summer

1952 Ochazuke no aji / The Flavor of Green Tea over Rice

1953 Tōkyō monogatari / Tokyo Story / Their First Trip to Tokyo

1956 Sōshun / Early Spring

1957 Tōkyō boshoku / Tokyo Twilight

1958 Higanbana / Equinox Flower (lit. Cluster Amaryllis)

1959 Ohayō / Ohayo / Good Morning

Ukigusa / Floating Weeds

1960 Akibiyori / Late Autumn (lit. A Clear Autumn Day)

1961 Kohayagawa-ke no aki / The End of Summer / Early Autumn / The Autumn of the Kohayagawa Family (lit.)

1962 Sanma no aji / An Autumn Afternoon (lit. The Taste of Mackerel)

## SABU
(b. November 18, 1964)
サブ

An actor under his real name of Hiroyuki Tanaka before he turned to direction, Sabu quickly became known for a quirky, instantly recognizable but somewhat vacuous brand of moviemaking. He has directed a series of variations on a trivial theme, consisting primarily of extended chase sequences, whether by foot (*Dangan Runner* [*Dangan rannā*, 1996]), bicycle (*Postman Blues* [*Posutoman burūsu*, 1997]), or car (*Hard Luck Hero* [*Hādo rakku hīrō*, 2003]). Usually these are set in motion by absurd coincidences: in *Unlucky Monkey* (*Anrakkī monkī*, 1998), a bank robber's plans are thrown into disarray when another robber beats him to it by moments, while in *Postman Blues*, the postman hero is hunted by both the mob and the police after a chance encounter with a former classmate, now a gangster, leaves him with a severed finger in his bag. The postman was typical of Sabu's hapless, usually doomed heroes, often played by everyman figure Shin'ichi Tsutsumi, who typically remain oblivious to events shaping their lives. Thus, the salaryman in *Monday* (2000) wakes in a hotel room and tries frantically to piece together the events of the night before from clues scattered around the room. In recent years, Sabu seems to have approached the reductio ad absurdum of his method: *Hard Luck Hero* followed six men who flee from an illegal kickboxing match, only to be reunited in a three-way car crash, while *Hold Up Down* (*Hōrudo appu daun*, 2005) contained some of his most breathtakingly silly plot twists to date.

Sabu is at his best with sudden, outrageous shock moments: the salaryman in *Monday* glancing from the window and realizing that he is surrounded by armed police; the apparently dead and buried gangster boss being pulled out of the ground alive in *Unlucky Monkey*. The most elaborate of such shocks are his catastrophic chain reactions: for instance, in *Drive* (2002) one character spills a glass of wine and an elaborate sequence of tiny consequences leads to another being stabbed in the throat. This scene was typical of Sabu both in its ingenuity and in its callousness: death in his films is usually presented as a gag and denied its real gravity (he has sometimes made light of mortality by including ghosts as characters). Some commentators have compared this approach with the often violent slapstick of Hollywood's silent comedians, but that rarely proved fatal. Nor has Sabu's visual style matched the grace of Buster Keaton's. His characters have generally seemed most plausible when most shallow. Shin'ichi Tsutsumi has proved entertaining when reacting abruptly to wildly changing circumstances, but the actor's attempts to dramatize his characters' agonies of conscience in *Unlucky Monkey* were embarrassing, while his speech against gun ownership in *Monday* was rhetorical and sentimental.

More recently, *The Blessing Bell* (*Kōfuku no kane*, 2002) was hailed as a subtler, more socially conscious work. Nevertheless, despite the focus on a manual worker laid off and the vivid evocation of urban decay, it was basically another journey through a stylized Tokyo peopled by eccentrics, and its narrative was again powered by a chain of coincidences and ironies. *Dead Run* (*Shissō*, 2005) was a definite departure, but into a curious David Lynch–like brand of sinister weirdness. Its portrayal of teenage angst was occasionally harrowing, but its abstraction of setting was, if anything, a step back from the distorted but recognizable Tokyo of Sabu's earlier films, and overall it suggested that he is more likely to alter than to improve. At the time of writing, he was attempting to set up projects abroad, and this might well be the most fruitful path he could now take.

1996 **Dangan rannā** / Dangan Runner / Non-Stop
1997 **Posutoman burūsu** / Postman Blues
1998 **Anrakkī monkī** / Unlucky Monkey
2000 **Monday**
2002 **A1012K** (*short*)
 **Drive**
 **Kōfuku no kane** / The Blessing Bell
2003 **Hādo rakku hīrō** / Hard Luck Hero
2005 **Hōrudo appu daun** / Hold Up Down
 **Shissō** / Dead Run

**SAI Yōichi**
**(b. July 6, 1949)**
崔洋一

Sai began to direct after serving as assistant to Nagisa Ōshima on *In the Realm of the Senses* (*Ai no korīda*, 1976), earning a reputation as a director of hard-boiled material with films such as *Mosquito on the Tenth Floor* (*Jukkai no mosukīto*, 1983) and *Sleep Quietly, Friend* (*Tomo yo, shizuka ni nemure*, 1985). This aspect of his talent was still visible in *MARKS* (*Mākusu no yama*, 1995), an elaborate and violent procedural thriller about a police investigation into a series of murders. His most interesting work, however, has focused on the situation of ethnic minorities in Japan, a theme which has personal resonance for Sai, himself a second-generation resident Korean. His most critically successful film, *All under the Moon* (*Tsuki wa dotchi ni deteiru*, 1993), was a sharp-edged comedy, directed with infectious en-

ergy, about an ethnic Korean taxi driver, his bumpy romance with a Filipino bar hostess, and his experience of prejudice in Japanese society. Though some scenes were close to slapstick, others, such as the protagonist's awkward encounter with an ostensibly sympathetic passenger, effectively conveyed the condescension faced by immigrants in Japan.

A concern with immigrant experience has been sustained by several of Sai's other films. *Dog Race* (*Inu, hashiru*, 1998) was a comic thriller about the unlikely triangular relationship between a Japanese cop, a Korean gangster, and a Chinese prostitute, the latter two involved in smuggling illegal immigrants into Japan. The domestic epic *Blood and Bones* (*Chi to hone*, 2004) recounted the experiences of a Korean family in Osaka from the twenties to the eighties, centering on the character of the brutal, bestial father played by Takeshi Kitano. An uncompromising study of a man with no redeeming features, it was sweetened only by its heartrending musical score. Sai has also made two films about Okinawan issues. *Via Okinawa* (*A-saindeizu*, 1989), set at the time of the Vietnam war, focused on a half-American woman and her struggle for success; Donald Richie has compared Sai's film to Imamura's portraits of scheming, indomitable women. *The Curse of the Pig* (*Buta no mukui*, 1999) used pigs as symbols of Okinawan ethnicity, pork being an Okinawan specialty; the film emphasized the separate culture and identity of the southern islands.

Sai has remarked that he is not interested in "stories about honorable lives and upstanding families," and even his more mainstream films have tended to deal with socially marginalized characters. *Doing Time* (*Keimusho no naka*, 2002) was an account of prison life, which balanced a semi-documentary realism with visualizations of the prisoners' thoughts and fantasies. *Quill* (*Kuīru*, 2004) was a drama about the relationship between a guide dog and his blind master. Both these films were somewhat sentimental, the former in presenting the experience of imprisonment as relatively pleasant, the latter in its anthropomorphic treatment of its canine hero. Though he has consistently tackled offbeat subject matter, Sai's films are often flawed by uncertainties of tone; in particular, they seem torn between social commentary and straightforward dramatic effect. Arguably, he has not developed a visual style precise enough to reconcile the two aims. Nevertheless, Sai's consciousness of his Korean heritage makes him an important figure in modern Japanese cinema. He returned to his roots by making *Double Casting* (*Soo*, 2007), a violent revenge thriller, in South Korea, and it will be interesting to see whether he begins to work more regularly on that side of the Sea of Japan.

1983 **Jukkai no mosukīto** / Mosquito on the Tenth Floor

 **Seiteki hanzai** / Sexual Crime

1984 **Itsu ka dare ka korosareru** / Someday Someone Will Be Killed

1985 **Tomo yo, shizuka ni nemure** / Sleep Quietly, Friend / Rest in Peace, My Friend

1987 **Kuroi doresu no onna** / The Woman in the Black Dress

1988 **Hana no Asuka-gumi** / The Wonderful Asuka Gang

1989 **A-Saindeizu** / Via Okinawa

1993 **J-Movie Wars** (*co-director*)

 **Tsuki wa dotchi ni deteiru** / All under the Moon

1995 **Heisei musekinin ikka: Tōkyō derakkusu** / Tokyo Deluxe (lit. Irresponsible Family of the Heisei Era: Tokyo Deluxe)

 **Mākusu no yama** / MARKS

1998 **Inu, hashiru** / Dog Race

1999 **Buta no mukui** / The Curse of the Pig

2002 **Keimusho no naka** / Doing Time

2004 **Kuīru** / Quill

 **Chi to hone** / Blood and Bones

2007 **Soo** / Double Casting (*South Korea*)

## SAITŌ Kōichi
## (b. February 3, 1929)
斎藤耕一

Saitō became a director after working as a still photographer, mainly at Nikkatsu, through the fifties and sixties, taking production stills for films by Tadashi Imai, Kon Ichikawa, and Shōhei Imamura. His low-budget, independently made directorial debut, *Whispering Joe* (*Sasayaki no Jō*, 1967), used the story of a young murderer to comment on modern Japanese youth and earned comparisons with Claude Lelouch for its visual polish. It also gained him an invitation to make musicals at Shochiku; these, despite using popular songs and stars, apparently hinted at darker issues in their portrayal of unstable young people.

By the seventies Saitō was able to make more personal films, which betrayed the influence of Imamura, particularly in their use of undeveloped remote locations where traditional lifestyles and beliefs had not yet given way to modernity. His most widely admired film, *Tsugaru Folk Song* (*Tsugaru jongarabushi*, 1973), was an account of a woman's return to her native region in northern Japan. Joan Mellen has claimed that this film advocated a return to primitivism, but its portrait of traditional life was so suffocatingly

©Shochiku Company Ltd.

Tabi no omosa / Journey into Solitude *(1972): A Buddhist pilgrimage becomes a voyage of self-discovery in this record of vanishing customs and culture.*

bleak as to make modernity seem rather desirable. More positive in its vision was *Journey into Solitude (Tabi no omosa,* 1972), in which a 20-year-old woman grows into maturity while hiking the 88-temple pilgrimage around Shikoku. With its picturesque settings and feel for the atmosphere of rural Japan, this film was a loving and often beautiful record of vanishing customs and culture.

In other films, such as *Le Rendezvous (Yakusoku,* 1972) and *Shadow of Deception (Naikai no wa,* 1971), Saitō used provincial settings as a backdrop for doomed romances. The former, about a wanted criminal's love for a woman prisoner on temporary release, was perhaps his most humanly engaging work, building with subtle assurance to an emotionally devastating climax. The latter was a darker, more arid film about an adulterous love

affair that disintegrates through mutual mistrust.

The commercial and critical success of these films enabled Saitō to continue working regularly through the seventies, at a time when many of his contemporaries were hard pressed to find work in Japan. He has continued to work, albeit more sparingly, since; however, his later films were less highly regarded than his work in the early seventies. Among them were *And the Ship of Happiness Sails On (Kōfukugō shuppan,* 1980), adapted from a Mishima novel about a family in dispute over an inheritance; *Blue Mountains '88 (Aoi sanmyaku '88,* 1988), an updated version of a popular high school story, first filmed by Tadashi Imai in 1949; *Human Wilderness (Ningen no sabaku,* 1990), a prison drama based on a script left unrealized by the late social realist filmmaker Kirio Urayama; and *Mission Barabba* (*Oyabun wa Iesu-sama*, 2001), an international co-production, shot partly in Korea, about a gangster who reforms after converting to Christianity. Saitō interspersed these fiction features with documentaries on various subjects, including the Noh theater and, for television, Beijing's Forbidden City.

Saitō has consistently worked with intriguing subject matter and elicited fine performances from his actors. His work has suffered, however, from a relative lack of stylistic individuality and a tendency to heavy-handedness. Consequently, his films have often proved more interesting for what they say than for how they say it.

1967  **Sasayaki no Jō** / Whispering Joe
1968  **Omoide no yubiwa** / Ring of Memory
      **Niji no naka no remon** / Lemon in the Rainbow
      **Chiisana sunakku** / The Little Snack Bar
1969  **Ochiba to kuchizuke** / Fallen Leaves and Kisses
      **Aisuru ashita** / To Love Tomorrow
      **Umi wa furimukanai** / The Tide Does Not Return
1970  **Tōkyō-Pari: Seishun no jōken** / Rainbow Over Paris (lit. Tokyo-Paris: The Condition of Youth)
      **Hatoba onna no burūsu** / Waterfront Blues
1971  **Naikai no wa** / Shadow of Deception (lit. The Ring of the Inland Sea)
      **Memai** / Dizziness
      **Tabiji: "Ofukurosan" yori** / Journey (from "Mother")
      **Kigeki: Hanayome sensō** / War of the Brides
1972  **Yakusoku** / Le Rendezvous
      **Tabi no omosa** / Journey into Solitude (lit. The Weight of Travel)
1973  **Kigeki: Koko kara hajimaru**

**monogatari** / The Story That Starts Here
      **Hana shinjū** / Double Suicide of Flowers
      **Tsugaru jongarabushi** / Tsugaru Folk Song / Jongara
1974  **Yadonashi** / Homeless
1975  **Saikai** / Someday, Somewhere / Reunion (lit.)
      **Takehisa Yumeji monogatari: Koisuru** / The Story of Yumeji Takehisa: To Love
1976  **Tōga** / The Frozen River
1977  **Akogare** / Yearning
      **Kisetsufū** / Seasonal Wind
1978  **Nagisa no shiroi ie** / The White House on the Shore
1979  **Shiawase o sekai no tomo e** / May Our Friends across the World Be Happy
1980  **Kōfukugō shuppan** / And the Ship of Happiness Sails On
1983  **Nankyoku** / Antarctica
1985  **Shōchū: Inochi no mizu** / Shochu: The Water of Life
      **Iseki to ningen** / Ruins and Humans
1986  **Nō no subete** / All About Noh
1988  **Aoi sanmyaku '88** / Blue Mountains '88
1990  **Ningen no sabaku** / Human Wilderness
1993  **Bōkyō** / Homesickness
1996  **Bara hoteru** / The Rose Hotel
1999  **Wakkanai hatsu: Manabiza** / From Wakkanai: The Manabiza
2001  **Oyabun wa Iesu-sama** / Mission Barabba / Jesus Is My Boss (lit.)
2004  **Onigiri**

## SAITŌ Torajirō
**(January 30, 1905–May 1, 1982)**
斎藤寅次郎

A specialist in comedy, Saitō is best remembered for the fast-paced slapstick of his silent shorts. Directing at Shochiku's Kamata studios from 1926, he worked initially in *jidai-geki*, all now lost; his earliest surviving film, *The Dawning Sky* (*Akeyuku sora*, 1929), is a sentimental melodrama interesting for its offbeat setting in a Christian community. From the early thirties, however, he specialized in the farcical *nansensu-eiga* ("nonsense film") genre, imbuing frivolous stories with charm through the flair and timing of his direction. Although few of his prewar films survive, his talent for physical comedy is preserved in the absurdist ghost story, *A Buddhist Mass for Goemon Ishikawa* (*Ishikawa Goemon no hōji*, 1930), and in the gracefully choreographed chase climax of *Dynamite Bride* (*Bakudan hanayome*, 1932; released 1935). However, Saitō's humor was not always purely farcical; sometimes it contained elements of pastiche or social criticism. *Chaplin, Why Do You Cry?* (*Chappurin yo naze naku ka*, 1932) transposed *City Lights* (1931) to a Japanese setting; *King Kong, Japanese Style* (*Wasei Kingu Kongu*, 1933) did the same for the Cooper/Schoedsack fantasy; while *What Made Her Naked?* (*Nani ga kanojo o hadaka ni shita ka*, 1931) was a parody of the then fashionable left-leaning *keikō-eiga* genre. The *keikō-eiga* theme of class distinctions was also visible in *The Treasure That Is Children* (*Kodakara sōdō*, 1935), which used slapstick to underline the gulf between rich and poor in Depression-era Japan, as an unemployed father tries to earn a 500-yen reward by catching a nobleman's lost pig.

After joining Toho in 1937, Saitō made feature-length films, some of which starred popular comedians Enoken and Roppa. At times, his comic talent was harnessed to serve the war effort: thus, *The Brash Stationmaster* (*Tokkan ekichō*, 1945) apparently focused on the training of women to work on the home front while their menfolk are at war. Among Saitō's more notable postwar films were *Tokyo Kid* (*Tōkyō kiddo*, 1950), a sentimental vehicle for child star Hibari Misora, which created a cross-section of Occupation-era working class society; *The Emperor's Hat* (*Tennō no bōshi*, 1950), an irreverent comedy about the consequences of the theft of the emperor's hat from a museum; and *Unusual Trip to Hawaii* (*Hawai chindōchū*, 1954), which enlivened a story about the reunion of a mother and her child with location photography of Hawaii in Eastmancolor. None of Saitō's later features, however, were considered to match his best silent shorts in quality.

1926 **Katsura Kogorō to Ikumatsu** / Kogoro Katsura and Ikumatsu
**Hiren Shinjūgaoka** / Hill of Sad Love Suicides
**Dotō** / The Angry Waves
**Kyokubadan no shimai** / Sisters of the Circus
**Ā Kawano junsa** / Ah, Constable Kawano
1927 **Antō** / Secret Feud
**Takadanobaba**
**Madō** / Way of the Demon
**Tate jidai** / Era of Swordfighting
**Adauchi chigai** / Mistaken Revenge
**Shimabara bishōnen roku** / Chronicle of a Beautiful Boy in Shimabara
**Fukeiki seibatsu** / Conquering the Recession
1928 **Uwaki seibatsu** / Conquering the Affair
**Katsudōkyō** / Movie Crazy
**Kahō wa nete mate** / Everything Comes to Those Who Wait
**Chindon'ya** / The Musical Sandwich Man

**Isoge ya isoge** / Hurry! Hurry!
**Konsen shichiningumi** / Seven on Crossed Lines
**Musume ganbare** / Girl, Work Hard!
**Appare bidanshi** / Bravo, Handsome!
**Kanojo to umi** / She and the Sea
**Kame-kō** / Sir Turtle
**Kōkō yarinaoshi** / Redoing Filial Piety
1929 **Banzai**
**U no me taka no me** / Keeping Eyes Peeled
**Iroke tappuri** / So Sexy!
**Akeyuku sora** / The Dawning Sky
**Okatatsu oshikirichō** / Okatatsu's Notebook of Monies Received
**Ichioku-en** / One Hundred Million Yen
**Aishite chōdai** / Love Me Please!
**Jonan kangei udekurabe** / Welcome Woman Trouble Competition
**Mikansei no koi** / Unfinished Love
**Zenbu seishin ijō ari** / They All Have Mental Problems
1930 **Bijin bōryokudan** / The Beautiful Thugs
**Tatakare teishu** / The Beaten Husband
**Suki de issho ni natta no yo** / Because We Loved Each Other, We Got Together
**Ara! Sono shunkan yo** / Oh! That Moment
**Ishikawa Goemon no hōji** / A Buddhist Mass for Goemon Ishikawa
**Ubawareta kuchibiru** / Plundered Lips
**Umibōzu nayamashi** / The Seductive Sea Monster
**Ara! Tairyō da ne** / Oh! Isn't It a Big Catch
**Koi no shakkin gurui no senjutsu** / Debt of Love: Crazy Strategy

**Iroke dango sōdōki** / Trouble About Sex Appeal and Dumplings
**Entotsu otoko** / Chimney Man
1931 **Seiryoku nyōbō** / An Energetic Wife
**Modan kago no tori** / Modern Caged Bird
**Kono ana o miyo** / Look at This Hole
**Onna wa tsuyokute hitorimono** / A Strong Woman Is Single
**Nani ga kanojo o hadaka ni shita ka** / What Made Her Naked?
**Musume no iki takashi** / The Girl in High Spirits
**Kanojo no kōfun** / Her Excitement
**Shin'ya no tameiki** / Midnight Sigh
1932 **Santarō Manshū shussei** / Santaro Goes to the Manchurian Front
**Kuma no yatsugiri jiken** / The Incident of the Bear Cut Into Eight Pieces / The Story of the Man-Eating Bear
**Chappurin yo naze naku ka** / Chaplin, Why Do You Cry?
**Tokochō-san** / Mr. Tokocho
**Kawaii goke-san** / Sweet Widow
**Onna wa nete mate** / A Woman Comes to Those Who Wait
**Suttonkyō** / Eccentric
1933 **Okugata no mōryoku** / The Power of Wives
**Taihenna shojo** / The Terrible Virgin
**Kanojo to kinkai** / She and Gold Bars
**Otokoyamome no Gen-san** / Gen the Widower
**Awatemono no Kuma-san** / Hasty Kuma
**Wasei Kingu Kongu** / King Kong, Japanese Style
**Shikkari seyo to dakiokoshi** / Cheer Up and Let Me Help
1934 **Namerareta aitsu** / He Was Treated Lightly
**Koshi no nuketa onna** / The Spineless Woman

Debeso no chikara / The Strength of a Protruding Belly Button

1935 Ā hakujō / Ah, Cold-Hearted!

Kodakara sōdō / The Treasure That Is Children / Kid Commotion

Uma kaeru / The Horse Returns

Kono ko sutezareba / If I Abandon This Child / If We Don't Abandon This Child

Bakudan hanayome / Dynamite Bride (*made in 1932; co-director*)

Yajikita kōshinkyoku / Yaji and Kita's March

Shinkon sanruida / Newlyweds' Third Base Hit

1936 Watashi no raba-san / My Mule

Kuruma ni tsunda takaramono / The Treasure in the Car

Onna wa naze kowai / Why Are Women Frightening?

Jinsei wa rokujū kara: Oite masumasu sakan nari / Life Begins at Sixty: Things Get Better as You Get Older

Yūrei ga shindara / If the Ghost Dies

Kurohyō dassō kyoku / Melody of the Black Leopard's Escape

Nakasete ne / Let Me Cry

Shichiten battō / Writhing in Pain

1937 Nanatsugo tanjō / The Birth of Septuplets

On'ai futasujimichi / Benevolent Love at the Crossroads

Kono oya ni tsumi ariya / This Parent Has Sinned

Aogeba tōtoshi / Song of Gratitude

Hoero Gin-chan / Howl, Gin-chan!

Haha no shōri / A Mother's Victory

1938 Enoken no Hōkaibō / Enoken's Monk

Mito Kōmon man'yūki: Tōkaidō no maki / Mito Komon's Pleasure Trip: Tokaido Reel

Mito Kōmon man'yūki: Nihonbare no maki / Mito Komon's Pleasure Trip: Fine Weather Reel

Roppa no Otōchan / Roppa's Father

1939 Roppa no Ōkubo Hikozaemon / Roppa's Hikozaemon Okubo

Musume no negai wa tada hitotsu / Her Only Wish (lit. A Girl Has Only One Wish)

Omoitsuki fujin / The Impulsive Wife

Roppa no Komoriuta / Roppa's Lullaby

Entatsu, Achako no Shinkon obakeyashiki / Entatsu and Achako: Newlyweds' Haunted Mansion

Tōkyō burūsu / Tokyo Blues

Entatsu, Achako, Torazō no Hatsuwarai Kunisada Chūji / Entatsu, Achako and Torazo: Chuji Kunisada's First Smile of the New Year

1940 Roppa no Dadakko tōchan / Roppa's Fretful Dad

Meirō gonin otoko / Five Cheerful Men

Oyako kujira / Parent-and-Child Whale

1941 Kodakara fūfu / The Treasure That Is Children and a Couple

Jinsei wa rokujūichi kara / Life Begins at Sixty-One

Subarashiki kinkō / The Splendid Gold Mine

1942 Minami kara kaetta hito / The Person Who Returned from the South

Isokawa Heisuke kōmyōbanashi / Story of the Exploits of Heisuke Isokawa

1944 Teki wa ikuman ari totemo / Although There Are Thousands of Enemies

1945 Tokkan ekichō / The Brash Stationmaster

Tōkyō gonin otoko / Five Tokyo Men

1947 Mukoiri gōkasen / The Groom Brings a Luxury Liner

Mitari kiitari tameshitari / Look, Listen, and Try

Ukiyo mo tengoku / This Floating World Is Heaven Too

1948 Dare ga tameni kane wa aru / For Whom the Gold Swells

Sore wa aru yo no koto datta / That Was What Happened on a Certain Night

Utamatsuri hyakumanryō / The Song Festival and a Million Ryo

Yakyūkyō jidai / The Age of Baseball Fever

1949 Yomeiri mukotori hana gassen / Happy Battle of Marriage

Nodo jimankyō jidai / The Age of Singing Competition Fever

Shin Tōkyō ondo: Bikkuri gonin otoko / New Tokyo Dance: Five Surprised Men

Otoko no namida / A Man's Tears

Akireta musumetachi / The Shocked Girls

Odoroki ikka / A Surprised Family

1950 Akogare no Hawai kōro / Longed-For Trip to Hawaii

Zoku mukō sangen ryōdonari: Daisanwa: Donguri uta gassen / Near Neighbors Again: Third Story: Acorn Song Contest

Sengoha oyaji / A Father of the Postwar School

Zoku mukō sangen ryōdonari: Daiyonwa: Koi no mikeneko / Near Neighbors Again: Fourth Story: Love's Tortoiseshell Cat

Aozora tenshi / The Blue Sky Angel

Tōkyō kiddo / Tokyo Kid

Tennō no bōshi / The Emperor's Hat

Tonbogaeri dōchū / Somersault on the Way

1951 Umi o wataru senman chōja / The Millionaire Crossing the Sea

Hatsukoi tonko musume / First Love of a Tonko Girl

Haha o shitaite / Yearning for Mother

Tōkyō kappa matsuri / Tokyo Water Goblin Festival

Domori Shichi torimonochō: Ichiban tegara / Casebooks of Stammering Shichi: The Greatest Achievement

1952 Utakurabe seishun sanjūshi / Singing Competition of Three Young Musketeers

Ōatari pachinko musume / The Girls Who Win at Pachinko

Musume jūhachi bikkuri tengoku / A Girl at Eighteen: Surprised Heaven

Koshinuke Date sōdō / Trouble about Spineless Date

Tonchinkan mittsu no uta / Three Absurd Songs

Utakurabe kōjin'yama / Singing Competition at the Holy Mountain

Tonchinkan torimonochō: Maboroshi no onna / Absurd Notebooks: The Phantom Woman

Bikkuri sanjūshi / The Three Musketeers Surprised

Sokonuke seishun ondo / The Hilarious Dance of Youth

1953 Chinsetsu Chūshingura / Rare Story of the 47 Ronin

Sōri daijin no koibumi / The Prime Minister's Love Letters

Tonchinkan: Kaitō hi no tama kozō / Absurdity: The Mysterious Thief: Will o' the Wisp Boy

Ajapā tengoku / Crazy Heaven

Appare gonin otoko / Bravo! Five Men

Hibari torimonochō: Utamatsuri happyakuyachō / Hibari's Notebooks: Song Festival across Edo

Udekurabe senryō yakusha / Competition of Prima Donnas

Kappa rokujūshi / The Water Goblin and Six Musketeers

Ōoka seidan: Bikkuri Taiheiki / Ooka's Trial: A Surprising Version of the Taiheiki

Seizoroi Ōedo rokuninshū / Six Men Mustered in Great Edo

Hatsuwarai Kan'ei gozenjiai

/ New Year's Laughing Contest before the Shogun in the Kan'ei Era

**1954** **Hanamatsuri sokonuke sen'ichiya** / Hilarious Flower Festival: 1001 Nights

**Hanafubuki gozonji shichinin otoko** / Seven Well-Known Men under Falling Cherry Blossoms

**Takarasagashi hyakumanryō** / Treasure Hunt for a Million Ryo

**Koshinuke kyōsōkyoku** / Wild Music of a Spineless Man

**Hawai chindōchū** / Unusual Trip to Hawaii

**Adauchi chinkenpō** / Revenge: Rare Art of Fencing

**Kaibyō koshinuke daisōdō** / Weak-Kneed from Fear of the Ghost Cat

**Ukaregitsune senbonzakura** / The Highspirited Fox and a Thousand Cherry Trees

**1955** **Bakushō seishun ressha** / Violent Laughter on the Train of Youth

**Utamatsuri mangetsu tanuki gassen** / Song Festival, Full Moon, and the Battle of the Raccoon Dogs

**Hana no nijūhachininshū** / Twenty-Eight Happy Men

**Otōsan wa ohitoyoshi** / Dad Is Gullible

**Oyabaka komoriuta** / A Doting Parent's Lullaby

**Toei kateigeki shirīzu: Hanagoyomi hachishōnin** / Toei Domestic Series: Flower-Illustrated Calendar and Eight Laughing People

**Toei kateigeki shirīzu: Kechinbo chōja** / Toei Domestic Series: The Stingy Millionaire

**Kaette kita yūrei** / The Ghost Who Returned

**1956** **Otōsan wa ohitoyoshi: Kakushigo sōdō** / Dad Is Gullible: Trouble about an Illegitimate Child

**Otōsan wa ohitoyoshi: Sanji museigen** / Dad Is Gullible: Birth Out of Control

**Otōsan wa ohitoyoshi: Yūtō rakudaisei** / Dad Is Gullible: Excellent Failing Student

**Otōsan wa ohitoyoshi: Mayoigo hiroigo** / Dad Is Gullible: Lost Child, Found Child

**Gonzō to Sukejū: Kagoya Taiheiki** / Gonzo and Sukeju: The Palanquin Bearers' Taiheiki

**Nakiwarai dohyōiri** / Into the Ring, Crying and Laughing

**Koi suredo monogatari** / Even Though I Love: A Story

**Yajikita dōchūki** / Record of Yaji and Kita on the Road

**Kingorō no Appare untenshu monogatari** / Kingoro's Story of a Praiseworthy Driver

**1957** **Ichiya no hyakuman chōja** / A Millionaire for One Night

**Dekoboko genkutsuō: Kaizokusen no maki** / The Rugged Count of Monte Cristo: Pirate Ship

**Dekoboko genkutsuō: Onizukijima no maki** / The Rugged Count of Monte Cristo: Devil Moon Island

**Taiatari satsujinkyō jidai** / Body Blow: Age of Homicidal Maniacs

**Ōedo ninki otoko** / A Popular Man in Great Edo

**Nanbanji no semushi otoko** / Return to Manhood

**Botchan daigaku** / College Boys

**Aozora tokkyū** / Blue Sky Express / Merry Detective Story

**1958** **Okesagarasu** / The Crow of Folk Music

**Itchome ichibanchi** / Happy-Go-Lucky Alley (lit. Block 1, Building 1)

**Itchome ichibanchi: Dainibu** / Happy-Go-Lucky Alley: Part 2

**Sokonuke ninja gassen** / Hilarious Battle of Ninja

**Sokonuke ninja gassen: Ore wa kieruze** / Hilarious Battle of Ninja: I'm Going to Vanish

**Seizoroi Edokko nagaya** / All Gathered in the Edoite Tenement

1959 **Ōwarai Edokko matsuri** / Big Laughs at the Edoites' Festival

**Bakushō Mito Kōmon man'yūki** / Violent Laughter: Mito Komon's Pleasure Trip

1960 **Shachō yarōdomo** / Boss, You Bastard!

**Nagurikomi onna shachō** / The Female Boss Storms In

1961 **Dare yori mo kane o aisu** / I Love Money More Than Anyone

**Watashi wa uso o mōshimasen** / I Don't Tell Lies

1962 **Ōwarai Jirochō ikka: Sanshita nichōkenjū** / The Laughing Family of Jirocho: Two-bit Gangster with Two Guns

## SAKAMOTO Junji
(b. October 1, 1958)
坂本順治

A maker of elegant, gripping but slightly superficial commercial films, Sakamoto served initially as assistant to Kazuyuki Izutsu and Sōgo Ishii before earning a reputation as a director of masculine genres with a sequence of boxing movies—*Knockout* (*Dotsuitarunen*, 1989), *Tekken* (1990) and *Boxer Joe* (1995)— and a thriller about a kidnapping, *Tokarev* (*Tokarefu*, 1994). More recently, he directed *Another Battle* (*Shin jingi naki tatakai*, 2000), a loose update of Kinji Fukasaku's 1970s *Battles without Honor and Humanity* series.

By this time Sakamoto had demonstrated some versatility with the whimsical *Billiken* (*Biriken*, 1996), a fantasy set in his native city of Osaka about a benevolent but fallible demigod striving to grant the wishes of his various clients. His most widely admired film,

*Face* (*Kao*, 2000), was his least conventional: though its premise—a woman on the run after murdering her abusive sister—was that of a thriller, it developed into a subtle character study and a morally ambiguous account of personal growth in extreme circumstances. Sakamoto used the hinterland of Kyushu's provincial cities and small towns as an effective backdrop to a story of disaffected people with no obvious destination. Also offbeat in theme was *Bokunchi* (2002), a manga-based film about two brothers learning to fend for themselves in their mother's absence.

Sakamoto's more recent male-centered films have tended towards sentimentality. *Battered Angels* (*Kizudarake no tenshi*, 1997) was a buddy movie about a private detective who promises a dying yakuza to escort his young son to the gangster's ex-wife; again, Sakamoto used provincial settings effectively, but the depiction of the relationship between the hero, his partner, and the boy was calculated to induce easy tears. *Out of This World* (*Kono yo no soto e: Kurabu Shinchūgun*, 2004) was a loving recreation of the Occupation era, about the relationship between a band of Japanese jazz musicians and the American troops they are hired to play for. Though it was mellow, charming, and sometimes touching, the tone of melancholy nostalgia allowed the real social problems and antagonisms of the era to dissolve into a fuzzy humanism. More politically astute was *KT* (2002), a gripping if convoluted Oliver Stone-style thriller recounting the events surrounding the kidnapping of South Korean opposition leader Kim Dae Jung from Tokyo by the Korean secret service. Sakamoto indicated the involvement of the Japanese Self-Defense Forces in the plot, and touched on the political influence of the United States in Asia.

Sakamoto's most recent films have suggested that the direction of his career is still unresolved. *Aegis* (*Bōkoku no Ījisu*, 2005), its professionalism notwithstanding, was a rather reprehensible return to machismo: a nationalistic action film described by Mark Schilling as "a feature-length recruiting poster for the Maritime Self-Defense Force." Its story of unspecified enemy agents hijacking a ship and threatening Tokyo with a biological weapon played on contemporary Japanese fears of North Korean belligerence, but its generic lineaments seemed to confirm that Sakamoto's inspiration stemmed less from his own national film culture than from Hollywood. On the other hand, *Awakening* (*Tamamoe!*, 2007), about a widow's response to the discovery that her late husband had been unfaithful, explored similar territory to *Face* as a sympathetic portrait of a woman in difficult circumstances.

1986  **Kiss** (*16mm short*)
1989  **Dotsuitarunen** / Knockout
1990  **Tekken** / Tekken (lit. Fist)
1991  **Ōte** / Checkmate
1994  **Tokarefu** / Tokarev
1995  **Boxer Joe**
1996  **Biriken** / Billiken
1997  **Kizudarake no tenshi** / Battered Angels / Injured Angels / Scarred Angels
1998  **Orokamono: Kizudarake no tenshi** / Battered Angels: The Goofball
2000  **Kao** / Face
       **Shin jingi naki tatakai** / Another Battle / New Battles without Honor and Humanity (lit.)
2002  **KT**
       **Bokunchi** / Bokunchi / My House
2004  **Kono yo no sotoe: Kurabu Shinchūgun** / Out of This World
2005  **Bōkoku no Ījisu** / Aegis
2007  **Tamamoe!** / Awakening

# SATŌ Jun'ya
## (b. November 6, 1932)
佐藤純彌

Among the most commercially successful studio directors of the seventies and eighties, Satō also has a cult reputation in some quarters for his earlier, apparently more personal films. He directed at Toei after assisting, among others, Daisuke Itō and Tadashi Imai; his debut, *Story of Military Cruelty* (*Rikugun zangyaku monogatari*, 1963), was an account of the dehumanizing training inflicted on Japanese army recruits during World War II. In comparison with most genre pictures of the time, his sixties yakuza movies seemed grittier and more realistic in approach, anticipating the manner of the seventies *jitsuroku-eiga*. The three *Organized Crime* (*Soshiki bōryoku*) films, based on the same events as Kinji Fukasaku's *Battles without Honor and Humanity* (*Jingi naki tatakai*) series, have earned praise for their uncompromising depiction of the struggle to survive in Occupation-era Japan. Similar themes were developed in *True Account of Ginza's Secret Enforcers* (*Jitsuroku: Shisetsu Ginza keisatsu*, 1973), about demobilized soldiers turning to crime. Satō remarked that these films tended to focus on "a character struggling against the system and authority"; and an element of social criticism was apparently present also in two romantic melodramas: *Red Light Breed* (*Kuruwa sodachi*, 1964), about a former prostitute whose past destroys her hopes for happiness, and *Passion* (*Aiyoku*, 1966), about a man whose choice between two lovers is motivated by financial concerns rather than affection.

Satō's biggest hits were his big-budget action films starring Ken Takakura. *Golgo 13* (*Gorugo 13*, 1973), adapted from a *manga* strip about a professional hitman and set in the Middle East, marked the director's first experience of location shooting abroad. *Bullet Train* (*Shinkansen daibakuha*, 1975), about a bomb planted on a *shinkansen* super-express and primed to detonate when it falls below a certain speed, served as partial inspiration for the Holly-wood action film *Speed* (1994, Jan de Bont). The thin characterizations of the threatened passengers reduced its im-pact, but the sympathetic depiction of a plausibly motivated villain was inter-esting. *Never Give Up* (*Yasei no shōmei*, 1978) was another anti-establishment action movie in which an investigation into the massacre of the inhabitants of a village threatens to expose political cor-ruption; marred by unnecessary super-natural elements, it boasted a powerful downbeat ending.

More recently, Satō departed from action material with *Hug Me, Then Kiss Me* (*Watashi o daite soshite kisu shite*, 1992), which used the conventions of women's melodrama to tackle the sub-ject of AIDS. Although rather manipu-lative, it successfully dramatized the irrational fears surrounding the disease, and was ultimately touching. However, Satō has continued to specialize in big-budget films, often set in period and abroad. *Dream of Russia* (*Oroshiya-koku suimutan*, 1992), based on fact, was the saga of an eighteenth-century sea cap-tain who spent ten years in Russia after being shipwrecked on the Kamchatka Peninsula. More frequently, Satō fo-cused on China, twice handling Sino-Japanese co-productions. *The Silk Road* (*Dun huang*, 1988), starring Japanese ac-tors but set in eleventh-century China, blended an account of romance between a scholar and an enemy princess with the story of the former's efforts to preserve a collection of Buddhist artifacts. *The Go Masters* (*Mikan no taikyoku*, 1982), co-directed with the Chinese Ji Shunduan, used the relationships between Chinese and Japanese *go* champions and their respective children as a microcosm of the troubled interactions between their countries in the twentieth century.

This film was basically humanist and anti-nationalist, but Satō's attitudes have sometimes seemed more equivocal. The inept fantasy *Peking Man* (*Pekin gen-jin*, 1997) took a cue from *Jurassic Park* (1993, Steven Spielberg) in its story of Chinese and Japanese scientists quarrel-ing over a group of early humans recre-ated from preserved DNA; it reached a conclusion of international solidarity only after milking stereotypes through its presentation of the Chinese villainess. *Battleship Yamato* (*Otokotachi no Yamato*, 2005), an account of the fatal last mis-sion of a famous World War II warship, was also controversial; some criticized it as a celebration of the military, while others praised it as antiwar. In general, the limitations of Satō's work are those of the commercial blockbuster: even where his material contains interesting social and political elements, his visual style is too glossily impersonal fully to develop them. His best films, neverthe-less, remain gripping.

**1963  Rikugun zangyaku monogatari** / Story of Military Cruelty / Cruel Story of the Army (lit.)
**Zoku ōshō** / The Chess Master Returns
**1964  Kuruwa sodachi** / Red Light Breed
**1966  Aiyoku** / Passion / The Grapes of Passion
**1967  Soshiki bōryoku** / Organized Crime
**Zoku soshiki bōryoku** / Organized Crime 2
**1968  Kōya no toseinin** / The Drifting

Avenger / Chivalrous Man in the Wilderness (lit.)

1969 **Tabi ni deta gokudō** / The Fast Liver's Return Trip from Prison

**Soshiki bōryoku: Kyōdai sakazuki** / Organized Crime: Loyalty Offering Brothers

**Nihon bōryokudan: Kumichō to shikaku** / Japan's Violent Gangs: The Boss and the Killers

1970 **Nihon dābī: Shōbu** / Japanese Derby: The Match

**Saigo no tokkōtai** / The Last Kamikaze

1971 **Bōryokudan saibusō** / Violent Gang Re-arms

**Bakuto kirikomitai** / Gamblers' Counterattack

1972 **Gyangu tai gyangu: Aka to kuro no burūsu** / Gang vs. Gang: Red and Black Blues

**Yakuza to kōsō** / Yakuza and Feuds

1973 **Yakuza to kōsō: Jitsuroku Andō-gumi** / Yakuza and Feuds: The True Account of the Ando Gang / The Ando File

**Jitsuroku: Shisetsu Ginza keisatsu** / True Account of Ginza's Secret Enforcers / True Account of Ginza Tortures

**Jitsuroku Andō-gumi: Shūgeki hen** / True Account of the Ando Gang: Story of Attack

**Gorugo 13** / Golgo 13

1974 **Rubangu-tō no kiseki: Rikugun Nakano gakkō** / The Miracle of Lubang Island: Nakano Army School

1975 **Shinkansen daibakuha** / Bullet Train

1976 **Kimi yo funnu no kawa o watare** / When You Cross a River of Rage

1977 **Ningen no shōmei** / Proof of a Man

1978 **Yasei no shōmei** / Never Give Up (lit. Proof of Wildness)

1980 **Yomigaere majo** / The Resurrected Witch

1982 **Mikan no taikyoku** / The Go Masters (lit. The Unfinished Match) (*co-director*)

1983 **Jinsei gekijō** / Theater of Life (*co-director*)

1984 **Kūkai** / Kobo Daishi

1986 **Uemura Naomi monogatari** / Lost in the Wilderness (lit. The Story of Naomi Uemura)

1988 **Dun-Huang / Tonkō** / The Silk Road

1992 **Oroshiya-koku suimutan** / Dream of Russia

**Watashi o daite soshite kisu shite** / Hug Me, Then Kiss Me

1994 **Chōnōryokusha: Michi e no tabibito** / The Man With Supernatural Powers: Voyager to the Unknown

1997 **Pekin genjin** / Peking Man

2005 **Otokotachi no Yamato** / Battleship Yamato / Yamato

## SHIBUYA Minoru
### (January 2, 1907–December 20, 1980)
### 渋谷実

One of Shochiku's stalwart directors, Shibuya served as assistant to Yasujirō Ozu and Heinosuke Gosho before directing. His early films were sentimental family melodramas: *Mother's Proposal* (*Mama no endan*, 1937) charted the relationship between a widow and her prospective second husband and the growing affection of their respective children. *Mother and Child* (*Haha to ko*, 1938), not unlike the work of Yasujirō Shimazu in tone and style, examined the moral dilemmas which arise when the daughter of a company president is engaged to her father's clerk, who has rejected his lover to make an advantageous marriage. Its conclusion was progressive, the daughter rejecting the clerk to pursue an independent lifestyle. Under wartime strictures, Shibuya's films grew more conservative: in *Cherry-Tree Country* (*Sakura no kuni*, 1941), shot on location in China, a youthful love affair ends when the girl's mother arranges her marriage to another man, affection here being sacrificed to duty.

Early in the postwar period, Shibuya made several topical problem pictures: *Passion Fire* (*Jōen*, 1947), about a couple contemplating divorce; *Topsy Turvy* (*Yassa mossa*, 1953), about mixed-race children; and most notably, *The Moderns* (*Gendaijin*, 1952), which ironically used the boyish persona of Ryō Ikebe in a drama about a young idealist who becomes involved in a bribery scandal. Shibuya's most characteristic vein, however, was an offbeat form of comedy, combining sentimentality, satire, and social commentary. The most representative and best-loved example was *Doctor's Day Off* (*Honjitsu kyūshin*, 1952), a droll yet gently affecting adaptation of stories by Masuji Ibuse, in which a doctor's holiday is interrupted by various people in need. The cast of victims, veterans, and criminals, all scarred in one way or another by war, constituted a cross-section of Tokyo's early postwar society, viewed reassuringly through the eyes of a dependable authority figure. *School of Freedom* (*Jiyū gakkō*, 1951) was an ironic account of a salaryman's quest for liberty, again set against the backdrop of a changing postwar society in which opportunity and criminality coexist. Shibuya's socially observant humor also examined country life: *Crazy Uproar* (*Ten'ya wan'ya*, 1950) was a hectic comedy of culture clash about the arrival of a metropolitan magazine editor in a traditional town on Shikoku, whose inhabitants are hoping to make the island an independent state. Later, *The Unbal-*

*anced Wheel* (*Kichigai buraku*, 1957) was a study of uneasy relationships among the inhabitants of a tiny rural community.

The late fifties marked a certain decline in Shibuya's art. *Christ in Bronze* (*Seidō no Kirisuto*, 1955) was a period film about the persecution of Japanese Christians in the Tokugawa era; this was not material which suited his talents. The visually striking *Season of Bad Women* (*Akujo ni kisetsu*, 1958), a black comedy about a mother and daughter conspiring to murder the former's husband for his fortune, was still faintly satirical, but the social awareness of Shibuya's earlier work had largely dissipated in favor of a cynical depiction of individual selfishness. Among his sixties films, *The Shrikes* (*Mozu*, 1961) was a bitter melodrama about the troubled relationship of a mother and daughter, reunited after twenty years' separation; lovely color photography ironically counterpointed the grim personal conflict. *Radishes and Carrots* (*Daikon to ninjin*, 1965) adapted a scenario inherited from Ozu on his death, though it also echoed Shibuya's own earlier work in its depiction of a cross-section of society, from salarymen to prostitutes.

Shibuya is not well known outside Japan. Anderson and Richie were critical of his "irregularities in direction" and "confused social criticism." But his stock is higher in his native country: Akira Iwasaki praised his "first-class movie techniques," and he is generally considered a significant figure in the development of Shochiku's bittersweet "Ōfuna flavor."

**1937 Okusama ni shirasu bekarazu /** Don't Tell the Wife

**Mama no endan /** Mother's Proposal

**1938 Hanauta ojōsan /** Humming Young Miss

Haha to ko / Mother and Child

**Wagaya ni haha are** / If Only Our House Had a Mother

1939 **Minamikaze** / South Wind

**Atarashiki kazoku** / New Family

**Kitsune** / Fox

1940 **Josei no kakugo: Daiichibu: Junjō no hana** / Woman's Resolution: Part One: Flower of Pure Love

**Josei no kakugo: Dainibu: Gisei no uta** / Woman's Resolution: Part Two: Song of Sacrifice

1941 **Tōkyō no fūzoku** / Customs of Tokyo

**Tōkakan no jinsei** / Ten Days of Life

**Sakura no kuni** / Cherry-Tree Country

1942 **Kazoku** / Family

**Aru onna** / A Certain Woman

**Yūrei ōi ni okoru** / The Ghost Gets Very Angry

1943 **Tekki kūshū** / Enemy Air Raid (*co-director*)

**Ojisan** / Middle-Aged Man

1947 **Jōen** / Passion Fire

**Tobidashita ojōsan** / The Young Miss Who Got Away

1948 **Jutai** / Conception

**Yoninme no shukujo** / The Fourth Lady

1949 **Beni imada kiezu** / Traces of Rouge

**Hana no sugao** / Naked Face of a Flower

1950 **Hatsukoi mondō** / First Love: Questions and Answers

**Ten'ya wan'ya** / Crazy Uproar

1951 **Jiyū gakkō** / School of Freedom

1952 **Honjitsu kyūshin** / Doctor's Day Off / No Consultations Today

**Gendaijin** / The Moderns

1953 **Yassa mossa** / Topsy Turvy

1954 **Kunshō** / Medals

1955 **Seidō no Kirisuto** / Christ in Bronze

1956 **Onna no ashiato** / A Woman's Footsteps

1957 **Seigiha** / The Righteous Ones

**Kichigai buraku** / The Unbalanced Wheel / Crazy Society

1958 **Akujo no kisetsu** / Season of Bad Women / Days of Evil Women

1959 **Kiri aru jōji** / Romance in the Fog

1960 **Banana**

1961 **Mozu** / The Shrikes

**Kōjin kōjitsu** / Loving Person, Day of Love

1962 **Yopparai tengoku** / Drunken Heaven

1963 **Futari dake no toride** / Fortress for Only Two / The Rats among the Cats

1964 **Monrō no yōna onna** / A Woman Like Monroe / Naked Girl

1965 **Daikon to ninjin** / Radishes and Carrots / Mr. Radish and Mr. Carrot / Twilight Path

1966 **Kigeki: Aogeba tōtoshi** / Graduation Song

## SHIMA Kōji
## (February 16, 1901–September 10, 1986)
島耕二

Initially an actor at Shinko Kinema, appearing in films by such directors as Tomotaka Tasaka and Tomu Uchida, Shima became a director in his own right in 1939, and soon began to specialize in literary adaptations. Some of the best appreciated of these focused on children; particularly fine was *The Tale of Jiro* (*Jirō monogatari*, 1941), a well-acted version of a famous story about a neglected child, later to be filmed by Hiroshi Shimizu. Shima's approach was more deliberately heart-tugging than Shimizu's, but the film was genuinely poignant. Also popular at the time was

*Big Wind at School* (*Kaze no Matasaburō*, 1940), a somewhat twee fantasy about a new boy believed by his classmates to be a legendary wind spirit.

In the postwar period, another children's story, the sentimental boy-and-horse saga *The Phantom Horse* (*Maboroshi no uma*, 1955), was curiously selected for competition at Cannes. Also shown abroad at the time was *The Golden Demon* (*Konjiki yasha*, 1954), the stylish first version in color of the old warhorse about a student who turns to usury after being disappointed in love. Shima's postwar work, mostly made under contract at Daiei, was an odd mixture of the lowbrow and the highbrow. On the one hand, he made popular musicals such as *Ginza Cancan Girls* (*Ginza kankan musume*, 1949) and science fiction such as *Warning from Space* (*Uchūjin Tōkyō ni arawaru*, 1956), an allegory of the threat of nuclear war. On the other, he continued to make literary adaptations, such as the second film version of *The Makioka Sisters* (*Sasameyuki*, 1959), Jun'ichirō Tanizaki's novel of prewar life among the Osaka bourgeoisie, and remakes of Mizoguchi's thirties melodramas, *Cascading White Threads* (*Taki no shiraito*, 1956) and *The Story of the Late Chrysanthemums* (*Zangiku monogatari*, 1956). Though by no means an *auteur*, Shima was clearly a competent journeyman director and his films also achieved considerable commercial success in their day.

1939 **Hibari** / Skylark
**Wagaya no taishō** / The General of Our House
**Utsukushiki kadode** / Beautiful Departure
**Watashi no taiyō** / My Sun
1940 **Machi no shōkatai** / Town Chorus
**Nonki megane** / Easy-Going Spectacles

**Tenraku no shishū** / Downfall: A Collection of Poems
**Kaze no Matasaburō** / Big Wind at School (lit. Matasaburo of the Wind)
1941 **Yamataka bōshi** / The Bowler Hat
**Umi no mieru ie** / The House with a Sea View
**Dengeki nijūsō** / Shocking Duet
**Jirō monogatari** / The Tale of Jiro
1942 **Yamasandō** / The Mountain Pilgrimage Route
1943 **Shingapōru sōkōgeki** / All-Out Attack on Singapore
**Shussei mae jūnijikan** / Twelve Hours Before Shipping Out
1946 **Kimi ka to omoite** / I Thought It Was You
1947 **Todoroki-sensei** / Mr. Todoroki
**Midori no kobako** / The Small Green Basket
1948 **Unmei no koyomi** / Calendar of Fate
**Enoken no Bikkuri shakkuri jidai** / Enoken's Age of Surprises and Hiccups
**Gekkō-jō no tōzoku** / The Thief of Moonlight Castle
1949 **Kyō ware ren'ai suru** / Today I Love
**Guddobai** / Goodbye
**Ginza Kankan musume** / Ginza Cancan Girls
1950 **Shojo takara** / Virgin's Treasure
**Mado kara tobidase** / Fly Out of the Window
**Kimi to iku Amerika kōro** / The Voyage to America with You
**Tōkyō no hiroin** / Tokyo Heroine
1951 **Kujaku no sono** / The Peacock Garden
**Hinageshi** / The Red Poppy
**Yoru no mibōjin** / Night Widows
**Hibari no Komoriuta** / Hibari's Lullaby
1952 **Aru yo no dekigoto** / Incidents on a Certain Night

**Shanhai-gaeri no Riru** / Lil's Return from Shanghai

**Kaze no uwasa no Riru** / Lil on the Grapevine

**Zoku bakurō ichidai** / One Generation of Horse Dealers 2

**Ringoen no shōjo** / Young Women of the Orchard

1953 **Jūdai no seiten** / Teenagers' Sex Manual

**Chatarē fujin wa Nihon ni mo ita** / There Was Also a Lady Chatterley in Japan

**Koshō musuko** / Pepper Son

**Asakusa monogatari** / Story of Asakusa

**Nippon sei** / Made in Japan

1954 **Konjiki yasha** / The Golden Demon

**Kaze tachinu** / The Wind Has Blown

**Asakusa no yoru** / Asakusa Nights

**Hi no onna** / A Woman of Fire

**Bazoku geisha** / A Geisha on Horseback

1955 **Maboroshi no uma** / The Phantom Horse / The Mysterious Horse

**Shin josei mondō** / New Women's Dialogue

1956 **Uchūjin Tōkyō ni arawaru** / Warning from Space / The Mysterious Satellite (lit. Aliens Appear in Tokyo)

**Niji ikutabi** / Rainbow: How Many Times?

**Zangiku monogatari** / The Story of the Late Chrysanthemums

**Taki no shiraito** / Cascading White Threads

**Shin Heike monogatari: Shizuka to Yoshitsune** / New Tales of the Taira Clan: Shizuka and Yoshitsune / The Dancer and the Warrior

1957 **Bojō no kawa** / River of Yearning

**Onna no hada** / A Woman's Skin

**Yūwaku kara no dasshutsu** / Escape from Seduction

**Kujikan no kyōfu** / Nine Hours of Fear

1958 **Yūrakuchō de aimashō** / Chance Meeting (lit. Let's Meet in Yurakucho)

**Edokko matsuri** / Shogun's Holiday (lit. Festival of Edoites)

**Neko wa shitteita** / The Cat Knew

**Kawaki** / Disillusion

**Musuko no kekkon** / My Son's Marriage / My Son's Revolt

**Tokai to iu minato** / The Port Called a City

**Musume no bōken** / My Daughter's Adventure / The Perfect Mate

1959 **Sasameyuki** / The Makioka Sisters (lit. A Light Snowfall)

**Itsu ka kita michi** / The Path I Remember

**Hana no daishōgai** / Great Obstacle Horse Race

**Sōkaiya nishikijō: Shōbushi to sono musume** / The Extortionist's Brocade Castle: The Gambler and His Daughter

1960 **Sekushī sain: Suki suki suki** / Sexy Sign: Love, Love, Love

**Otoko wa damasareru** / The Man Is Deceived

**Anchin to Kiyohime** / The Poet and the Beauty (lit. Anchin and Princess Kiyo)

**Kao** / The Beloved Image (lit. Face)

1961 **Wakai nakama** / Young Company

**Yūyake koyake no akatonbo** / The Red Dragonfly at Sunset

**Asu o yobu minato** / The Harbor That Calls for Tomorrow

1962 **Jōnetsu no shijin Takuboku** / Takuboku, Poet of Passion

**Otoko to onna no yo no naka** / The World of Man and Woman

**Goshin** / The Body

1963 **Teinen taishoku** / Retirement

**Sue wa hakase ka daijin ka** / He Has Prospects (lit. He'll End Up a Doctor or a Cabinet Minister)

1964 **Asufaruto gāru** / Asphalt Girl

Muchana yatsu / The Unreasonable Guy

1965 **Onna mekura monogatari** / Story of a Blind Woman

**Rokunin no onna o koroshita otoko** / The Man Who Killed Six Women

1966 **Waga ai o hoshi ni inorite** / Wishing for Love on a Star

**Fukuzatsuna kare** / A Complicated Man

**Shojo jutai** / Immaculate Conception

1967 **Rāmen taishi** / The Ramen Ambassador

1968 **Kaidan otoshiana** / The Ghostly Trap

1969 **Lo si han** / Dear Murderer (*Hong Kong*)

**Ye lam ceon lyun** / Tropical Interlude (*Hong Kong*)

1970 **Hoi ngoi cing go** / Love Song over the Sea (*Hong Kong*)

**Wu ji faa** / The Orchid (*Hong Kong*)

# SHIMAZU Yasujirō
## (June 3, 1897–September 18, 1945)
島津保次郎

Though his work is rarely shown today, Shimazu is a figure of somewhat legendary status, acclaimed as the pioneer of the *shomin-geki* genre, which became the specialty of his studio, Shochiku. His interest in the everyday life of the lower middle classes was established in silent comedies such as *Father* (*Otōsan*, 1923), about the relationship between a college baseball star and his father, and *Sunday* (*Nichiyōbi*, 1924), about a salaryman's love for a married typist. Shimazu's twenties films are almost all lost, but his best sound films, especially the domestic dramas *Our Neighbor Miss Yae* (*Tonari no Yae-chan*, 1934) and *An*

*Older Brother and His Younger Sister* (*Ani to sono imōto*, 1939), displayed a talent for realist observation, and (in David Shipman's words) "a faintly ironic detachment which almost rivals Jane Austen." These films were remarkable for their sense of lived-in detail: for instance, the play with the boy's worn-out, dirty socks in *Our Neighbor Miss Yae* or with a broken thermometer in *An Older Brother and His Younger Sister*. Touches such as these made each Shimazu family unique, for all that they seemed to exemplify "the Japanese family" as a whole.

This kind of realism, however, was not Shimazu's only mode: much of his work was more melodramatic in tone. *First Steps Ashore* (*Jōriku daiippo*, 1932), inspired by Sternberg's *The Docks of New York* (1928), was a Shanghai-set story of the relationship between a young girl and a gangster. *Okoto and Sasuke* (*Shunkin shō: Okoto to Sasuke*, 1935), about a youth who blinds himself for the love of a selfish woman, was a well-realized, sometimes chilling adaptation of one of Jun'ichirō Tanizaki's stories of perverse sexuality. *Family Meeting* (*Kazoku kaigi*, 1936) was an inventively shot and intricately plotted melodrama about a businessman's relationships with the three women in his life. *Three Crows' Engagement* (*Kon'yaku sanbagarasu*, 1937) was a popular romance that helped to propel its three male leads (Ken Uehara, Shin Saburi, and Shūji Sano) to stardom.

Shimazu's best films employed a subtle social criticism. Among his silent films, *Lifeline ABC* (*Seikatsusen ABC*, 1931) and *The Belle* (*Reijin*, 1930) were contributions to the left-leaning *keikō-eiga* genre; the latter was a trenchant critique of capitalist arrogance and its destructive effect on women and the working class. As late as 1939, *An*

Tonari no Yae-chan / Our Neighbor Miss Yae *(1934): A talent for realist observa-tion was visible in this famous drama from the pioneer of* shomin-geki.

*Older Brother and His Younger Sister* displayed clear feminist sympathies in its treatment of the heroine's rejection of a marriage proposal and satirized the un-friendly world of Tokyo business. The conclusions of Shimazu's films often made clear his antipathy to urban life. In *Lights of Asakusa (Asakusa no hi*, 1937), a melodrama with a theatrical setting, characters resolve their problems by leaving the capital; in *Family Meeting*, and the lost *Girl in a Storm (Arashi no naka no shojo*, 1932), by leaving the city for the countryside; and, in *Our Neigh-bor Miss Yae* and *An Older Brother and His Younger Sister*, by leaving Japan. In the last two films the destinations are, respectively, Korea and Manchuria, and these endings regrettably made implicit endorsement of Japanese imperialism. This became explicit in such wartime

films as *Green Earth (Midori no daichi*, 1942) and *The Daily Battle (Nichijō no tatakai*, 1944), which positively dra-matized the experiences of Japanese colonists in Asia; although, in fairness, the Manchurian-set *My Bush Warbler (Watashi no uguisu*, 1943) went unre-leased due to its failure to promote the war effort.

Shimazu's cinematic talents were variable: his best scenes were framed and staged with exquisite delicacy, but his lesser work was marred by moments of stylistic awkwardness. *An Older Brother and His Younger Sister*, probably his masterpiece, displayed a pleasing integrity of tone and style, and its best scenes rivaled Ozu in their tender se-renity. Often, however, the elegant and the clumsy co-existed, somewhat per-plexingly, within the same film. *Family*

*Meeting*, for example, made extremely slick use of rapid-fire Hollywood-style cutting in the opening scenes, but spoiled the emotional climaxes with heavy-handed track-ins. Nevertheless, Shimazu's legacy proved lasting: Heinosuke Gosho, Shirō Toyoda, Kōzaburō Yoshimura, Keisuke Kinoshita, and Yūzō Kawashima all served as his assistants, and his penchant for understated melodrama and the blending of humor and pathos influenced not only those immediate disciples but also the development of a tradition central to Japanese film art.

1921 **Sabishiki hitobito** / Lonely People
1922 **San'yabori** / The Moat of Sanya
**Wataridori** / Migratory Bird
**Yūkan naru teisōfu** / The Brave Messenger
**Kuzushichi no ie** / The House of Kuzushichi
**No ni saku shirayuri** / White Lilies of the Field
**Ihin no guntō (Kinen no guntō)** / Inherited Saber (Memorial Saber)
**Chirinishi hana** / A Fallen Flower
**Unmei no ko** / Child of Destiny
**Kagayaki no michi e** / To the Path of Glory
**Matsuri no yoru** / Festival Night
**Ai no kusabi** / Linchpin of Love
**Ā shinkō** / Ah, New School
**Kataki akushu** / Firm Handshake
**Ōgon** / Gold
1923 **Nogi Shōgun no uijin (Nogi Shōgun yōnen jidai)** / General Nogi's First War (The Early Childhood of General Nogi)
**Megumarenu hito** / An Unlucky Person
**Yama no senroban** / The Crossing Watchman of the Mountains
**Ninjutsu gokko** / Ninja Make-Believe
**Daigujin** / Imbecile

**Jikatsu suru onna** / An Independent Woman
**Kyōdai** / Brothers
**Shōnen shoki** / Boy Secretary
**Jinniku no ichi** / Market of Human Flesh
**Dai Tōkyō no ushimitsudoki** / The Small Hours in Greater Tokyo (*co-director*)
**Chi no sakebi** / Cry of Blood
**Kamisori** / Razor
**Kuroshōzoku** / Dressed in Black
**Kan'ichi to Mitsue** / Kan'ichi and Mitsue
**Tsumi no tobira** / Gate of Sin
**Jūichiji gojūhappun** / 11:58
**Otōsan (Chichi)** / Father
1924 **Sobaya no musume** / The Girl from the Noodle Bar
**Fukōmono** / The Unfilial One
**Nichiyōbi** / Sunday
**Gusha nareba koso** / Since He's Stupid
**Hone nusumi** / Stealing Bones
**Nageki no minato** / Harbor of Grief
**Cha o tsukuru ie** / The House That Makes Tea
**Umi wa warau** / The Sea Laughs
**Akutarō** / Stinker
**Sennin** / The Hermit
**Koutashū: Daisanpen: Kago no tori** / Collection of Short Songs: Part 3: The Caged Bird
**Jukensha** / The Candidate
**Jōgashima no ame** / Rain at Jogashima
**Norowaretaru misao** / Cursed Virginity
**Tengoku** / Heaven
1925 **Shin ono ga tsumi** / My Sin, New Version
**Shin chikyōdai** / Foster Sisters, New Version
**Yū no kane** / Evening Bell
**Nantō no haru** / Spring on Southern Islands

**Daichi wa hohoemu (Zenpen; Chūhen; Kōhen)** / The Earth Smiles (Parts 1, 2, and 3) (*co-director*)

**Mura no sensei** / The Village Teacher

**Sokoku** / Fatherland

**Bunkabyō** / Cultural Sickness

**Yūkan naru koi** / Brave Love

**Shizen wa sabaku** / Nature Is the Judge

**Yōseichi ni otsureba** / Falling in Fairyland

**Odoriko no yubiwa** / Ring of a Dancing Girl

**Aisai no himitsu** / Secret of a Beloved Wife

1926 **Fukumen no kage** / Shadow of the Mask

**Kōtō no kage** / Shadow of a Red Lantern

**Obotchan** / The Young Master

**Mankō** / Manko

**Nyōbō reisan** / Praise for the Wife

**Ai (Rabu)** / Love

**Nijibare** / Rainbow and Clear Skies

**Yōfu gonin onna** / Five Bewitching Women (*co-director*)

1927 **Ren'ai konsen** / Crossed Line of Love

**Namida no egao** / Tearstained Smiling Face

**Kyūzō rōjin** / Old Man Kyuzo

**Onna** / Woman

**Aratama** / The New Jewel

**Tōsei katagi** / The Way of the Modern World

**Onna no kage** / A Woman's Shadow

**Koi o hirotta otoko** / The Man Who Picked Up Love

**Umi no yūsha** / Hero of the Sea

**Bijo no himitsu** / The Beauty's Secret

**Tabi yakusha** / Traveling Players

1928 **Shūtome hanayome funsenki** / Battle Between the Bride and the Mother-in-Law

**Moshimo kanojo ga** / If She…

**Yowaki hitobito** / Weak People

**Shin'ya no okyaku** / Visitor in the Middle of the Night

**Kaminari oyaji** / Thunder Dad

**Ura kara oide** / Come in from the Back

**Marusēyu shuppan** / Departure for Marseilles

**Oi! Sandayū** / Hey! Sandayu

**Bōnasu** / Bonus

**Haru hiraku** / The Coming of Spring

**Kagayaku Shōwa** / The Glory of the Showa Era

1929 **Echigo jishi** / The Lion of Echigo

**Ren'ai fūkei** / Scenes of Love

**Kimi koishi** / Missing You

**Tājō busshin** / Fickle but Not Unfeeling

**Bijin wa kuroi** / The Beauty Is Dark

**Ashita tenki ni nāre** / May Tomorrow Be Fine

1930 **Revū no shimai** / Revue Sisters

**Reijin** / The Belle

**Kyosen** / The Great Ship

**Zattsu ō kē: Ii no ne chikatte ne** / That's OK. Is It All Right? Won't You Make a Vow?

**Kamata biggu parēdo** / Kamata Big Parade

1931 **Ai yo jinrui to tomo ni are** / May Love Be with Humanity

**Ai no tatakai** / Love's Struggle

**No ni sakebu mono: Seishun hen** / The One Crying in the Field: Youth Chapter

**No ni sakebu mono: Sōtō hen** / The One Crying in the Field: Conflict Chapter

**Seikatsusen ABC (Zenpen; Kōhen)** / Lifeline ABC (Parts 1 and 2)

1932 **Shōhai** / Win or Lose

**Jōriku daiippo** / First Steps Ashore

**Arashi no naka no shojo** / Girl in a Storm / Maiden in the Storm

Kanki no ichiya / One Night of
Pleasure
1933 Hoo o yosureba / Cheek to Cheek
1934 Jōen no toshi / City of Passion
Tonari no Yae-chan / Our
Neighbor Miss Yae
Kekkon kōfunki / Story of the
Excitement of Marriage
Osayo koi sugata / Osayo in Love
Sono yoru no onna / The Woman
That Night
Watashi no nīsan / My Older
Brother
1935 Shunkin shō: Okoto to Sasuke /
Okoto and Sasuke (lit. A Portrait of
Shunkin: Okoto and Sasuke)
Semete koyoi o / At Least Tonight
Kanojo wa iya to iimashita / She
Said "No"
Hanayome kurabe / Comparison
of Brides
1936 Kazoku kaigi / Family Meeting
Dansei tai josei / Male versus
Female
1937 Hanayome karuta / A Bride's
Game of Cards
Shu to midori: Shu no maki / Red
and Green: Red Reel
Shu to midori: Midori no maki /
Red and Green: Green Reel
Kon'yaku sanbagarasu / Three
Crows' Engagement
Jinsei no hatsutabi / The First Trip
in Life
Asakusa no hi / Lights of Asakusa
1938 Kamitsuita hanayome / The Bride
Who Bit
Ai yori ai e / From Love to Love
Nihonjin: Meiji hen / Japanese
People: Meiji Chapter
Nihonjin: Shōwa hen / Japanese
People: Showa Chapter
1939 Okayo no kakugo / Okayo's
Resolution
Ani to sono imōto / An Older
Brother and His Younger Sister
1940 Hikari to kage (Zenpen; Kōhen) /
Light and Shade (Parts 1 and 2)

Totsugu hi made / Until the
Wedding Day
Futari no sekai / A Couple's World
Toki no hanagata / The Star of the
Moment
1941 Ani no hanayome / My Older
Brother's Bride
Shirasagi / The White Heron
Tōgyo / Fighting Fish
1942 Midori no daichi / Green Earth
Haha no chizu / A Mother's Map
1943 Chikai no gasshō / Chorus of Vows
Watashi no uguisu / My Bush
Warbler (unreleased)
Shutsujin / Going to War
1944 Nichijō no tatakai / The Daily
Battle

## SHIMIZU Hiroshi
(March 28, 1903–June 23, 1966)
清水宏

A friend and contemporary at Shochiku of Yasujirō Ozu, Shimizu was one of the Japanese cinema's most individual talents, and seems at last to be receiving due recognition for his subtle, spontaneous technique and for the variety, intelligence, and humanity of his oeuvre. He specialized in films about children, and his reputation has traditionally rested on the charm and good humor of such works as *Children in the Wind* (*Kaze no naka no kodomo*, 1937) or *Four Seasons of Childhood* (*Kodomo no shiki*, 1939), both in fact among his more superficial films. Thus, Alan Stanbrook can claim that "the world of Hiroshi Shimizu is a sunny one, where the sadness of things rarely intrudes." It is worth emphasizing that the charm of Shimizu's work was usually tinged with melancholy and that his children were often lonely and rejected by their fellows. Moreover, they

©Planet Bibliotheque de Cinema

Hachi no su no kodomotachi / Children of the Beehive *(1948): In Shimizu's master-piece of neo-realism, a group of war orphans journeys across a scarred postwar Japan.*

included the war orphans of *Children of the Beehive* (*Hachi no su no kodomotachi*, 1948), the delinquents of *The Inspection Tower* (*Mikaeri no tō*, 1941), children afflicted with polio in *The Shiinomi School* (*Shiinomi gakuen*, 1955), children who (as in *The Tale of Jiro* [*Jirō monogatari*, 1955]) do not love their parents, or (as in *A Mother's Love* [*Bojō*, 1950]) are not loved by them. Often the experiences of Shimizu's children reflected in microcosm the attitudes of society as a whole; thus, the marginalization of Chinese boys in *Forget Love for Now* (*Koi mo wasurete*, 1937) and disabled children in *The Shiinomi School* was an implicit comment on the widespread prejudice against minority groups in Japanese society.

Nor was Shimizu only a director of kids. In the silent era, with such visually flamboyant and emotionally intense films as *Eternal Heart* (*Fue no shiratama*, 1929), *Seven Seas* (*Nanatsu no umi*, 1931–32), and *Japanese Girls at the Harbor* (*Minato no Nihon musume*, 1933), he used the conventions of romantic melodrama as a vehicle to examine the dilemmas of a nation poised between native and Western ideas, liberalism and traditionalism. Among his prewar sound films, *A Star Athlete* (*Hanagata senshu*, 1937) was an engaging and stylistically imaginative comedy about the rivalries between students on a military training exercise, while *Mr. Thankyou* (*Arigatō-san*, 1936), *The Masseurs and a Woman* (*Anma to onna*, 1938), and *Ornamental Hairpin* (*Kanzashi*, 1941) were bittersweet studies of grown-up feelings. These three films were group portraits set among temporary communities of travelers or holidaymakers, which concentrated more on the delineation of character than on plot. *Ornamental Hairpin*, in particular, boasted outstanding performances from Kinuyo Tanaka and Chishū Ryū, and had a wonderfully delicate way of highlighting the nuances of behavior which give expression to unspoken emotions.

Often Shimizu's adult dramas focused on vagrants or fallen women. The lost silent film *Windmill of Life* (*Jinsei no fūsha*, 1931), which is held to have established Shimizu's mature style, depicted the transient encounter between a man and a woman forced to leave the city. *Notes of an Itinerant Performer* (*Utajo oboegaki*, 1941) was a touching account of the experiences of a former strolling player who runs a tea wholesaler's business on behalf of the man she loves, but is spurned by the community due to her humble background. If the Meiji period setting distanced that film somewhat from contemporary realities, *Forget Love for Now*, a bleak portrait of the life of a bar hostess struggling to raise her only child set in present-day Yokohama, was as trenchant a critique of the status of women in Japanese society as almost any film by Mizoguchi, and, accordingly, suffered at the hands of the censors. Moreover, *A Star Athlete*, *Mr. Thankyou*, *Forget Love for Now*, and *A Hero of Tokyo* (*Tōkyō no eiyū*, 1935) were all implicitly opposed to the militaristic and colonial policies of the time. Shimizu's love for the countryside was eloquently expressed in the exquisite landscape photography of films shot on location in the remote Izu Peninsula, but neither this nor his affection for rural traditions (for instance, the strolling players in *A Mother's Love*) precluded an awareness of the problems of rural life. *Mr. Thankyou* stressed the extreme poverty of country dwellers during the Depression, while even *Children in the Wind* touched on the prejudices and petty rivaries of apparently close-knit communities.

This social concern was carried over into Shimizu's postwar work with the independently produced *Children in the Beehive*, a masterpiece of neo-realism, and its companion piece, *Children in the Great Buddha* (*Daibutsu-sama to kodomotachi*, 1952). Both were touching studies of the plight of children orphaned by war, a problem that affected Shimizu sufficiently for him to donate money to fund the foundation of an orphanage. This gesture was a characteristic expression of Shimizu's faith that small charitable actions can improve society, a faith expressed also in the conclusions of many of his films, where humane actions alleviate individual suffering. Thus, "Mr. Thankyou" will marry a girl to save her from prostitution; two of the Children of the Great Buddha are spontaneously adopted by concerned adults; and benevolent children's homes in *Children of the Beehive* and *The Inspection Tower* provide hope for at least a few of the hopeless.

Social conscience notwithstanding, Shimizu was not by nature a polemicist, and his style did not editorialize. Filming usually in long takes and long shot, with an improvisational technique that permitted his actors considerable freedom, he preferred to show rather than tell, and his political concerns were grounded in his sure sense of individual feelings and social reality. The essence of Shimizu's art was its deceptive simplicity. Few directors have succeeded in combining such lightness of touch with such human depth.

**1924  Tōge no kanata** / Beyond the Pass
**Yamaotoko no koi** / The Love of a Mountain Man

**Koi yori butai e** / Theater Before Love

**Shiragiku no uta** / Song of the White Chrysanthemum

**Koi ni kuruu yaiba** / Love-Crazed Blade

**Mura no bokujō** / The Village Pasture

1925 **Chiisaki tabi geinin** / The Little Traveling Player

**Kagaribi no yoru** / Bonfire Night

**Momoiro no toge** / The Pink Thorn

**Gekiryū no sakebi** / Roar of the Torrent

**Gijin no yaiba** / Blade of a Righteous Man

**Sutaremono** / The Outdated Man

**Isshin-ji no hyakuningiri** / The Killing of a Hundred Men at Isshin-ji Temple

**Kotetsu no kireaji** / Sharpness of the Blade

**Ochimusha** / The Fleeing Warrior

**Koi no honawa** / Snare of Love

1926 **Nayamashiki koro** / LovelornTimes

**Bijin to rōnin** / The Beauty and the Ronin

**Shinjū Satsuma uta** / Song of a Double Suicide in Satsuma

**Shinku no jōnetsu** / Crimson Passion

**Kyōko to Shizuko** / Kyoko and Shizuko

**Uragiraremono** / The Betrayed Man

**Yōtō** / The Amorous Blade

**Kyōdoranshin** / Feelings in Turmoil

**Nageki no bara** / Roses of Grief

1927 **Sannin no musume** / Three Daughters

**Oteru to Oyuki** / Oteru and Oyuki

**Kare to mibōjin** / He and the Widow

**Kyōren no Maria** / Love-Crazed Madonna

**Haru no ame** / Spring Rain

**Renbo yasha** / Idol of Love

**Koi wa kusemono** / Love Is Tricky

**Honoo no sora** / Flaming Sky

**Jinsei no namida** / Tears of Life

**Fukeiki seibatsu** / Victory over the Depression

**Shusse no chikamichi** / Shortcut to Success

**Inaka no dateotoko** / A Country Dandy

1928 **Aiyoku hensōzu** / A Portrait of Changing Love

**Umi ni sakebu onna** / The Woman Who Calls to the Sea

**Ren'ai futari angya** / A Couple's Pilgrimage of Love

**Odore wakamono** / Dance, Young People

**Shōwa no onna** / A Woman of the Showa Period

**Osana najimi** / Childhood Friends

**Hirotta hanayome** / A Picked-Up Bride

**Yamabiko** / Mountain Echo

**Utsukushiki hōhaitachi** / Beautiful Best Friends

1929 **Mori no kajiya** / The Village Blacksmith

**Ahiru onna** / Duck Woman

**Tōkyō no majutsu** / Magic of Tokyo

**Sutteki gāru** / Escort Girl

**Ukikusa musume tabifūzoku** / Travel Manners of a Vagrant Girl

**Mura no ōja** / The Village Champion

**Yōkina uta** / Cheerful Song

**Oya** / Parent

**Jiman no segare** / Proud of My Son

**Fue no shiratama** / Eternal Heart / Undying Pearl (lit.)

**Chichi no negai** / Father's Desire

**Renbo kouta** / Short Song of Love

**Ren'ai: Daiikka** / Love: Part One

1930 **Kōshin tsumi ari** / Sin on Red Lips

**Shinjitsu no ai** / True Love

Kiro ni tachite / Standing at a
Crossroads

Hōyō / Embrace

Umi no kōshinkyoku / March of
the Sea

Uwaki bakari wa betsumono da /
Flirtation Is Another Thing

Seishun no chi wa odoru /
Youthful Blood Dances

Kiri no naka no akebono /
Daybreak in the Mist

Shin jidai ni ikiru / Living in a
New Era

1931 Gaki daishō / Bully

Ginga / The Milky Way

Konsen nita fūfu / Crossed Line
Between Husband and Wife

Ureibana / Flower of Grief

Sorya jikkan yo / Chalk It Up to
Experience

Kagayaku ai / Shining Love

Kono haha ni tsumi ari ya / This
Mother Has Sinned

Jinsei no fūsha / Windmill of Life

Seishunzue / An Illustrated Guide
to Youth

Nanatsu no umi: Zenpen: Shojo
hen / Seven Seas: Part One:
Virginity Chapter

1932 Jōnetsu / Passion

Nanatsu no umi: Kōhen: Teisō
hen / Seven Seas: Part Two:
Chastity Chapter

Manshū kōshinkyoku /
Manchurian Marching Song

Rikugun daikōshin / The Army's
Big March (co-director)

Umi no ōja / King of the Sea

Ai no bōfūrin / Love's Windbreak

Byakuya wa akaruku / Dawn after
the Midnight Sun

Gakuseigai no hanagata / The Star
of the Student Quarter

Bōfūtai / Stormy Region

1933 Nemure haha no mune ni / Sleep,
at Mother's Breast

Nakinureta haru no onna yo /
The Lady Who Wept in Spring

Minato no Nihon musume /
Japanese Girls at the Harbor

Ren'ai ittōryū / Dexterity in Love

Tabine no yume / A Traveler's
Dream

Daigaku no wakadanna / The
Boss's Son at College / The Young
Master at College (lit.)

1934 Tōyō no haha / Mother from the
Far East

Koi o shirisome mōshisōrō / I
Want to Know about Love

Daigaku no wakadanna: Buyūden
/ The Boss's Son at College: Record
of Valor

Gion bayashi / Gion Festival Music

Daigaku no wakadanna:
Taiheiraku / The Boss's Son at
College: Shooting the Breeze

Kinkanshoku / Eclipse

Ren'ai shūgaku ryokō / Love on a
School Excursion

Daigaku no wakadanna:
Nihonbare / The Boss's Son:
Cloudless Skies

1935 Tokyo no eiyū / A Hero of Tokyo

Wakadanna haruranman / The
Boss's Son's Youthful Innocence

Kare to kanojo to shōnentachi /
The Man and the Woman and the
Boys

Sōshinzō / Double Heart

Ren'ai gōka ban / Love in Luxury

1936 Wakadanna hyakumangoku / The
Boss's Son Is a Millionaire

Kanjō sanmyaku / Mountain
Range of Emotion

Arigatō-san / Mr. Thankyou

Ai no hōsoku / Law of Love

Jiyū no tenchi / Heaven and Earth
Are Free

Kimi yo takaraka ni uta e / Sing in
a Loud Voice!

Seishun mankanshoku / Youth in
Full Dress

1937 **Ren'ai muteki kantai** / Loves of the Invincible Fleet

**Konjiki yasha** / The Golden Demon

**Koi mo wasurete** / Forget Love for Now

**Saraba sensen e** / Farewell, I Go to the Front (*co-director*)

**Hanagata senshu** / A Star Athlete

**Kaze no naka no kodomo** / Children in the Wind

1938 **Shin katei reki** / New Domestic History

**Shuppatsu** / Departure

**Ōenka** / Cheerleaders' Song

**Anma to onna** / The Masseurs and a Woman

**Katei nikki** / Family Diary

1939 **Isōrō wa takaibiki** / A Freeloader's Big Snore

**Kodomo no shiki** / Four Seasons of Childhood

**Onna no fūzoku: Daiichiwa: Ojōsan no nikki** / A Woman's Manners: Part One: Young Girl's Diary

**Hana aru zassō** / Flowering Weed

**Kuwa no mi wa akai** / Mulberries Are Red

1940 **Watashi ni wa otto ga aru** / I Have a Husband

**Nobuko** / Nobuko

**Tomodachi** / Friends

**Nyonin tenshin** / Woman's Fickle Heart

1941 **Mikaeri no tō** / The Inspection Tower / The Introspection Tower

**Utajo oboegaki** / Notes of an Itinerant Performer / Notes of a Female Singer (lit.)

**Donguri to shiinomi** / Acorns (*short*)

**Akatsuki no gasshō** / Dawn Chorus

**Kanzashi** / Ornamental Hairpin

1942 **Joi no kiroku** / Record of a Woman Doctor

**Kyōdai kaigi** / Meeting of a Brother and Sister

1943 **Sayon no kane** / Sayon's Bell

1945 **Hisshōka** / Victory Song (*co-director*)

1948 **Hachi no su no kodomotachi** / Children of the Beehive

**Asu wa nihonbare** / Tomorrow There Will Be Fine Weather

1949 **Musume jūhachi usotsuki jidai** / At Eighteen a Girl Tells Lies

**Ōhara Shōsuke-san** / Mr. Shosuke Ohara

1950 **Bojō** / A Mother's Love

1951 **Sono go no hachi no su no kodomotachi** / Children of the Beehive: What Happened Next

**Momo no hana no sakushita de** / Under the Blossoming Peach

1952 **Daibutsu-sama to kodomotachi** / Children of the Great Buddha

1953 **Mogura yokochō** / Mole Alley

**Nara ni wa furuki hotoketachi** / Ancient Buddhas of Nara (*short*)

**Tokai no yokogao** / Profile of a City

1954 **Daini no seppun** / The Second Kiss

**Tōshōdai-ji nite obāsan to kodomotachi** / Old Woman and Childen at Toshodai-ji (*short*)

1955 **Shiinomi gakuen** / The Shiinomi School

**Jirō monogatari** / The Tale of Jiro

1956 **Naze kanojora wa sō natta ka** / Why Did These Women Become Like This?

**Ninjō baka** / Stupid with Kindness

**Haha o motomeru kora** / Children Seeking a Mother

**Kiri no oto** / Sound in the Mist

1957 **Odoriko** / Dancing Girl

1958 **Haha no tabiji** / A Mother's Journey

1959 **Haha no omokage** / Image of a Mother

## SHIMIZU Takashi
(b. July 27, 1972)
清水崇

Shimizu has spun a career from a single profitable franchise: the *Juon* or *Grudge* series of horror movies, initiated in 2000 by two straight-to-video releases. These spawned a pair of Japanese big-screen remakes, followed by a Hollywood-financed, Tokyo-set reworking of the first film, which in turn generated a further sequel; at the time of writing, further installments both in Japan and America are in production. This seemingly unstoppable proliferation is ironically reminiscent of the theme of the films themselves, which concern a fatal curse passed to anyone who enters a house in which murder has been committed. The series' main claim to distinction is a non-chronological method of narration; other than this, Shimizu has proved content to exploit every cliche in the J-horror manual, from the ghostly child whose appearances herald the transmission of the curse to the way in which modern technology becomes a source of horror.

Although he became a director after studying under Kiyoshi Kurosawa, Shimizu's glossily impersonal style bears little trace of his mentor's brooding manner and is suited mainly to the efficient crafting of cheap shocks. Outside the *Grudge* series, *Reincarnation* (*Rinne*, 2005) proved no advance: its potentially interesting self-referential plot, about a horror movie shoot where the cast begin to re-enact the murders which inspired the film, was incoherently developed. However, *Marebito* (2004) was a surprising intense film about a freelance cameraman, hauntingly played by Shin'ya Tsukamoto, who is obsessed with the extremes of fear. Akin to Tsukamoto's

own directorial work in its discomforting focus on disturbed psychology and sexual perversion, the film opted for a deliberately rough-edged style, using digital video and handheld camera to create a pseudo-documentary mood which aptly dramatized the experiences of a character precisely observant of, yet estranged from, reality. Despite its pretensions, it was a genuine achievement. To date, however, it remains an exception in Shimizu's oeuvre, and one suspects that he will continue mainly to opt for Hollywood production values over this kind of low-budget innovation.

2000  **Juon** (*video version*) / Juon: The Curse
      **Juon 2** (*video version*) / Juon: The Curse 2
2001  **Tomie: Rebirth**
2003  **Juon** (*cinema version*) / Juon: The Grudge / The Grudge
      **Juon 2** (*cinema version*) / Juon: The Grudge 2 / The Grudge 2
2004  **Marebito**
      **The Grudge** (*American version*)
2005  **Rinne** / Reincarnation
2006  **The Grudge 2** (*American version*)
      **Yume jūya** / Ten Nights of Dreams (*co-director*)

## SHINDŌ Kaneto
(b. April 22, 1912)
新藤兼人

Shindō's more than five decades as a director constitute only part of a prolific career in cinema. Initially an assistant to Kenji Mizoguchi, he later wrote screenplays for Mizoguchi, Kon Ichikawa, Keisuke Kinoshita, Tadashi Imai, Seijun Suzuki, and especially Kōzaburō Yoshimura, the distinction of whose early postwar work owed something to

Hadaka no shima / The Island *(1960): This allegory set among an island family was praised for its humanism and visual poetry; the actress is Shindō's wife, Nobuko Otowa.*

Shindō's talent for dramatic construction. Yoshimura in turn produced several of Shindō's early films, which were made for the director's independent company, Kindai Eiga Productions.

Shindō's fifties films were mostly in a social realist vein. *Epitome (Shukuzu,* 1953) was a Tokyo riposte to Yoshimura's Shindō-scripted, Kyoto-set geisha story, *Clothes of Deception (Itsuwareru seisō,* 1951); its view of the geisha system was less resigned, and more bluntly critical, than Yoshimura's. *The Ditch (Dobu,* 1954) was a variation on the theme of *The Lower Depths,* examining the wretchedness of life in Tokyo's postwar shanty towns. *Sorrow Is Only for Women (Kanashimi wa onna dake ni,* 1958) was apparently a feminist critique of traditional family structures. Shindō also examined the topic of nuclear weapons: the touching *Children of the Atom Bomb*

*(Genbaku no ko,* 1952) followed a teacher's return to Hiroshima to track down those of her former pupils who had survived the blast, while *Lucky Dragon No. 5 (Daigo Fukuryū maru,* 1959) told the story of a Japanese fishing vessel contaminated by fallout from an American nuclear test. Shindō would return to the subject later in his career with *Sakuratai 8.6. (Sakuratai chiru,* 1988), a semi-documentary about a left-leaning theatrical troupe who became victims of the atomic bomb at Hiroshima.

Also political in theme among Shindō's later films were two well-regarded thrillers, *Heat Wave Island (Kagerō,* 1969) and *Live Today, Die Tomorrow (Hadaka no jūkyūsai,* 1970), which probed the roots of crime in social deprivation. In general, however, Shindō's post-1960 work was more aestheticized in approach. *The Island*

(*Hadaka no shima*, 1960) was a transitional work, chronicling the lives of a family struggling to cultivate a waterless island. Though widely praised for its humanism and visual poetry, it suffered from its rejection of local context and individual characterization, as typified by the implausible decision to eschew spoken dialogue. Its fable-like quality was carried further in *Onibaba* (1964) and *Kuroneko* (*Yabu no naka no kuroneko*, 1968), two visually opulent stories of the supernatural. Vestiges of class consciousness were apparent in the theme of strife between peasant and samurai, but these films were primarily concerned with psychological tensions within the family, the horror in both stemming from the conflicts between parent and child. Also in the sixties, Shindō directed several sexually explicit films; *Lost Sex* (*Honnō*, 1966), where the protagonist becomes impotent due to radiation sickness, again touched on the legacy of the bomb, but these were generally considered minor works.

The elaborate aestheticism of *Onibaba* and *Kuroneko* heralded an increasing focus in Shindō's later career on art and artist figures. As early as his debut, *Story of a Beloved Wife* (*Aisai monogatari*, 1951), he had essayed a semi-autobiographical account of a woman's devotion to her screenwriter husband, but from the seventies, portraits of the artist became a specialty. *Sanka* (1972), adapted from Jun'ichirō Tanizaki's *A Portrait of Shunkin*, cast Shindō himself as the author and, unlike more straightforward versions by Yasujirō Shimazu and Katsumi Nishikawa, tried to reflect the layered narration of the literary original. *Kenji Mizoguchi: The Life of a Film Director* (*Aru eiga kantoku no shōgai: Mizoguchi Kenji no kiroku*, 1975) was a documentary about the life and

work of Shindō's own mentor. Elsewhere, Shindō fictionalized the life stories of famous artists: *The Life of Chikuzan* (*Chikuzan hitori tabi*, 1977) traced the childhood and youth of a blind shamisen player in prewar Tohoku; *Edo Porn* (*Hokusai manga*, 1981) was a ribald portrait of *ukiyo-e* printmaker Hokusai, showing an artist motivated by both philosophical speculations and physical desires; and *The Strange Tale of Oyuki* (*Bokutō kidan*, 1992) was a biopic of author and *flaneur* Kafū Nagai, who chronicled the low life of Tokyo's old *shitamachi* district. It is significant that *Sakuratai 8.6.* used the experiences of actors to dramatize the bombing of Hiroshima.

Also in these later films, Shindō, who has remained active into his nineties, began to focus on the tribulations of age: the most vivid scenes of *Edo Porn* and *The Strange Tale of Oyuki* dramatized the responses of their protagonists to ebbing vitality. *Will to Live* (*Ikitai*, 1999) juxtaposed a retired chemist's fears of being sent to a nursing home with an ancient legend about a village which abandons its elderly to die on a nearby mountain. *A Last Note* (*Gogo no yuigonjō*, 1995) was a melancholy comedy about an octogenarian actress's reunion with a now senile colleague; maybe Shindō's most touching film, it explored ways of coming to terms with mortality, tinged by awareness that circumstances may not allow us to face death with dignity.

Shindō has proved an eclectic stylist. His early social realist films, especially *The Ditch*, were tilted towards sentimentality by somewhat heavy-handed camera rhetoric. His best-known films abroad, *The Island*, *Onibaba*, and *Kuroneko*, displayed a flamboyance and visual elegance which, while striking, arguably softened their depiction of suffering and horror. Similar criticisms may be leveled at *Children of the Atom Bomb*, where the bombing itself, depicted in a Soviet-style montage sequence, seemed pictorial rather than painful. Shindō's later manner was more restrained, but despite the beautiful snowscapes of *The Life of Chikuzan* and the atmospheric period trappings of *Edo Porn* and *The Strange Tale of Oyuki*, he never truly evolved a coherent visual style or a way of commenting on the world through images. His work is distinguished mainly by the literary virtues of construction and characterization and by excellent acting, especially from his wife, the versatile Nobuko Otowa, who appeared in almost all Shindō's films until her death. His scripts for other directors were also consistently outstanding, and he ultimately may merit admiration more as a writer than as a stylist.

1951　**Aisai monogatari** / Story of a Beloved Wife

1952　**Nadare** / Avalanche

　　　**Genbaku no ko** / Children of the Atom Bomb / Children of Hiroshima

1953　**Shukuzu** / Epitome

　　　**Onna no isshō** / A Woman's Life

1954　**Dobu** / The Ditch / The Gutter

1955　**Ōkami** / Wolves

1956　**Shirogane shinjū** / Double Suicide at Shirogane

　　　**Ryūri no kishi** / The Shore of Departure

　　　**Joyū** / An Actress

1957　**Umi no yarōdomo** / Harbor Rats / Guys of the Sea (lit.)

1958　**Kanashimi wa onna dake ni** / Sorrow Is Only for Women

1959　**Daigo Fukuryū maru** / Lucky Dragon No. 5

　　　**Hanayome-san wa sekaiichi** / The World's Best Bride / The Bride from Japan

1960　**Hadaka no shima** / The Island / Naked Island (lit.)

1962　**Ningen** / Human Being / The Man

1963　**Haha** / Mother

1964　**Onibaba** / Onibaba / The Hole / Devil Woman

1965　**Akutō** / A Scoundrel / The Conquest

1966　**Honnō** / Lost Sex (lit. Instinct)

　　　**Totsuseki iseki** / Monument of Totsuseki

　　　**Tateshina no shiki** / Four Seasons of Tateshina

1967　**Sei no kigen** / Libido

1968　**Yabu no naka no kuroneko** / Kuroneko / The Black Cat / Black Cat from the Grove

　　　**Tsuyomushi onna to yowamushi otoko** / Strong Women and Weak Men / Operation Negligee

1969　**Kagerō** / Heat Wave Island

1970　**Shokkaku** / Tentacles

　　　**Hadaka no jūkyūsai** / Live Today, Die Tomorrow / Naked Nineteen-Year-Olds (lit.)

1972　**Kanawa** / The Iron Crown

　　　**Sanka** / Sanka / A Paean

1973　**Kokoro** / The Heart / Love Betrayed

1974　**Waga michi** / My Way

1975　**Aru eiga kantoku no shōgai: Mizoguchi Kenji no kiroku** / Kenji Mizoguchi: The Life of a Film Director

1977　**Chikuzan hitori tabi** / The Life of Chikuzan / The Solitary Travels of Chikuzan (lit.)

1979　**Kōsatsu** / The Strangling

1981　**Hokusai manga** / Edo Porn (lit. Hokusai Manga)

1984　**Chiheisen** / The Horizon

1986　**Burakkubōdo** / Blackboard

　　　**Rakuyōju** / Tree without Leaves / Deciduous Tree

1988　**Sakuratai chiru** / Sakuratai 8.6.

1992　**Bokutō kigan** / The Strange Tale of Oyuki

1995 **Gogo no yuigonjō** / A Last Note
1999 **Ikitai** / Will to Live
2000 **Sanmon yakusha** / By-Player
2003 **Fukurō** / The Owl

## SHINODA Masahiro
(b. March 9, 1931)
篠田正浩

An imaginative, eclectic filmmaker, Shinoda moved from New Wave experimentalism to middle-aged conventionality; though his work has often proved more style than substance, his best films have combined visual flair with thematic complexity. He worked initially at Shochiku on assignments, some of which foreshadowed his future concerns. The film often considered his first truly personal project, *Pale Flower* (*Kawaita hana*, 1964), was a yakuza movie which resembled those of Seijun Suzuki in enlivening generic material with passages of abstract formal beauty. The elaborately edited gambling sequences and the climactic murder to the accompaniment of Purcell were memorable. Also notable among Shinoda's Shochiku films were *Assassination* (*Ansatsu*, 1964), a morally complex and visually astonishing account of power politics in the years leading up to the Meiji Restoration, and *With Beauty and Sorrow* (*Utsukushisa to kanashimi to*, 1965), a stylish if superficial adaptation of a Yasunari Kawabata novel about a woman seeking revenge on the middle-aged author who once exploited her lover.

Shinoda's professed admiration for Mizoguchi was intermittently detectable in his films of the sixties and seventies, in the use of extreme long shot to record the historical panorama of *Assassination*, in the occasional elaborate long takes of *Punishment Island* (*Shokei no shima*, 1966) and *Double Suicide* (*Shinjū: Ten no Amijima*, 1969), and in the delicate group compositions of *Banished Orin* (*Hanare goze Orin*, 1977). In fact, though, such direct stylistic influence was rare, and Shinoda's work lacked the compassion and emotional complexity of Mizoguchi's. It recalled Mizoguchi, however, in its detailed depiction of social milieux, particularly in period settings. His two finest films, *Double Suicide* and *Buraikan* (1970), were representations of Edo-period society which drew on Shinoda's background in theater studies at Waseda University, borrowing their imagery from Bunraku and Kabuki respectively. *Double Suicide*, based on a Chikamatsu play, was a powerful tragedy with a superb performance in a dual role from Shinoda's wife and regular star, Shima Iwashita. Filming in stark monochrome on confined sets, where domestic and public spaces are linked by empty portals and slatted windows, Shinoda created the impression of a society where privacy is non-existent and personal feelings are repressed by convention. *Buraikan*, a brilliant panorama of metropolitan life scripted by Shūji Terayama, was colorful, ribald, and funny; at its heart, however, was a scathing condemnation of a puritanical regime which bans popular theater and even fireworks, while failing to prevent crimes like kidnapping and murder.

Such anti-authoritarian sentiments were a consistent feature of Shinoda's work, an abiding theme of which was the oppressive legacy of the past. Sometimes this past was personal: *The Petrified Forest* (*Kaseki no mori*, 1973) ascribed the murderous actions of its student anti-hero to the childhood trauma of witnessing his mother's adultery. More often, Shinoda's concern was with

©Shochiku Company Ltd.

*Ansatsu / Assassination (1964): The aestheticization of history: Shinoda brings his visual flamboyance to a saga of the Meiji Restoration.*

history. *Himiko* (1974), depicting the legendary shamaness who once ruled Japan, showed the origins of power structures in Japanese society, subversively implying that the Imperial system draws its legitimacy from a historical fabrication. *Punishment Island*, about a man's vengeful search for the criminal who exploited him for slave labor during the war, dealt with the legacy of militarist tyranny in both political and psychological terms.

However, Shinoda, unlike Ōshima, was not led by his anti-authoritarian attitudes to a specific ideological commitment. Instead, his belief that "politics lead to nothing" resulted in a bitter nihilism. *Buraikan* ended with the failure of revolution and the realization that one power will always be replaced by another, while the early *Dry Lake*

*(Kawaita mizuumi,* 1960) focused on a disillusioned leftist who attempts to bomb protests against the U.S.-Japan security treaty. Shinoda's characters were often victims of divided loyalties or caught between two conflicting sides: examples include the dock worker torn between unions and management in *Tears on the Lion's Mane (Namida o shishi no tategami ni,* 1962), the ronin who shifts his support from Shogun to Emperor in *Assassination,* and the spy hunted by the forces of rival warlords Hideyoshi and Ieyasu in *Samurai Spy (Ibun Sarutobi Sasuke,* 1965). In *Silence (Chinmoku,* 1971), based on Shūsaku Endō's novel about the persecution of Christians in seventeenth-century Japan, a priest apostatizes to save his life. These characters' refusal of commitment spoke for Shinoda's own disillu-

sionment with politics, which led him to take solace in what Audie Bock terms an "icy aestheticism."

During the seventies Shinoda made several rather substandard films, in which formal imagination gave way to arid expertise. *Silence*, despite its interesting subject matter, was unusually heavy-handed in approach; *Under the Cherry Blossoms (Sakura no mori no mankai no shita*, 1975) was a stupidly stylish story about a demonic woman; and *Banished Orin* was a melancholy, picturesque but shallow drama about the doomed love affair between a musician and a deserter. All these films were proficiently made, but anonymous. *Demon Pond (Yashagaike*, 1979) and *Gonza the Spearman (Chikamatsu Monzaemon: Yari no Gonza*, 1986) were new attempts to draw on the plotting and imagery of traditional theater, but despite their striking surfaces they lacked the genuine formal imagination of *Double Suicide* and *Buraikan*.

Shinoda made a partial return to form with *MacArthur's Children (Setouchi shōnen yakyūdan*, 1984), *Takeshi: Childhood Days (Shōnen jidai*, 1990), and *Moonlight Serenade (Setouchi mūnraito serenāde*, 1997), a loose trilogy about children growing up during and just after the war, which led Mark Schilling to describe the director as "Japan's James Ivory." Though cozily sentimental and stylistically conventional, they were lovingly atmospheric recreations of time and place and displayed a welcome humanity after the grim tone of Shinoda's seventies work. In the last films he made before retiring, Shinoda experimented with computer-generated settings to recreate the Momoyama period in *Owl's Castle (Fukurō no shiro*, 1999), a dull account of the feud between two ninja, and the cityscapes of prewar Japan in

*Spy Sorge (Supai Zorge*, 2003*)*, an uneven but intermittently gripping biopic of the German spy who passed Japanese war strategies to the Russians. These films lacked, however, the genuine formal imagination which gave his best work its beauty and power. Overall, Shinoda would seem not quite to have fulfilled his potential, but *Double Suicide* and *Buraikan*, at least, are masterpieces, and almost all his films contain individual sequences that display a master's flair.

**1960** **Koi no katamichi kippu** / One-Way Ticket to Love
**Kawaita mizuumi** / Dry Lake / Youth in Fury
**1961** **Yūhi ni akai ore no kao** / My Face Red in the Sunset / Killers on Parade
**Waga koi no tabiji** / Epitaph to My Love (lit. Journey of My Love)
**Shamisen to ōtobai** / Shamisen and Motorcycle / Love Old and New
**1962** **Watakushitachi no kekkon** / Our Marriage
**Yama no sanka: Moyuru wakamonotachi** / Glory on the Summit: Burning Youth
**Namida o shishi no tategami ni** / Tears on the Lion's Mane
**1964** **Kawaita hana** / Pale Flower (lit. Dry Flower)
**Ansatsu** / Assassination
**1965** **Utsukushisa to kanashimi to** / With Beauty and Sorrow
**Ibun Sarutobi Sasuke** / Samurai Spy (lit. The Strange Tale of Sarutobi Sasuke)
**1966** **Shokei no shima** / Punishment Island / Captive's Island
**1967** **Akanegumo** / Clouds at Sunset
**1969** **Shinjū: Ten no Amijima** / Double Suicide
**1970** **Buraikan** / Buraikan / The Scandalous Adventures of Buraikan
**1971** **Chinmoku** / Silence
**1972** **Sapporo Orinpikku** / Sapporo Olympics

1973 Kaseki no mori / The Petrified Forest
1974 Himiko
1975 Sakura no mori no mankai no shita / Under the Cherry Blossoms
1976 Nippon maru / The Ship Nippon (*short*)
1977 Hanare goze Orin / Banished Orin / Ballad of Orin / Melody in Gray
1979 Yashagaike / Demon Pond
1981 Akuryōtō / Island of the Evil Spirits
1984 Setouchi shōnen yakyūdan / MacArthur's Children (lit. Inland Sea Youth Baseball Team)
1985 Allusion (*short*)
1986 Chikamatsu Monzaemon: Yari no Gonza / Gonza the Spearman
1989 Maihime / The Dancing Princess
1990 Shōnen jidai / Takeshi: Childhood Days / Takeshi: Days of Youth
1995 Sharaku
1997 Setouchi mūnraito serenāde / Moonlight Serenade
1999 Fukurō no shiro / Owl's Castle
2003 Supai Zorge / Spy Sorge

## SHINOZAKI Makoto
**(b. 1963, precise date unknown)**
篠崎誠

Like his contemporaries Shinji Aoyama and Akihiko Shiota and the slightly older Kiyoshi Kurosawa, Shinozaki studied at Rikkyō University, where he was influenced by film theorist and Ozu specialist Shigehiko Hasumi. He later assisted Kurosawa on *The Guard from Underground* (*Jigoku no keibiin*, 1992) and worked as a projectionist before making his feature debut, *Okaeri* (1995). This was more directly influenced by Ozu than most films by Rikkyō alumni; the title ("Welcome home"), the domestic setting, and the static, unobtrusive camera all evoked the old master, as

did the depiction of a husband and wife kept apart by work. The wife's developing schizophrenia served to expose the fragility of loving bonds, but the bleakness of the film, visually expressed by its chilly colors, was balanced by its humane observation and touching, partly improvised performances.

Shinozaki's next fiction film, *Not Forgotten* (*Wasurerarenu hitobito*, 2000), charted the experiences of three World War II veterans who take on a corrupt corporation seeking to fleece the elderly and regiment its young employees. The film touched on the generation gap in modern Japan and on the danger of repeating the mistakes of the past as living witnesses die. Among the stars was the elderly Tomio Aoki (formerly, as Tokkan-Kozō, a child actor in prewar Ozu movies), who also played bit parts in *Okaeri* and *Walking with the Dog* (*Inu to arukeba: Chirori to Tamara*, 2004). The latter was a low-key comic drama about a stray dog trained to work as a "therapy dog" comforting the elderly and dying. In a more humorous vein, and glancing back to a different chapter in film history, was *0093: Masao Kusakari On Her Majesty's Secret Service* (*0093 Joō heika no Kusakari Masao*, 2007), a parody of James Bond.

Shinozaki has also been associated with Takeshi Kitano, whom he interviewed regularly for *Switch* magazine during the nineties. He realized a feature-length documentary about the making of Kitano's *Kikujiro* (*Kikujirō no natsu*, 1999), and adapted Kitano's autobiography in *Asakusa Kid* (*Asakusa kiddo no Asakusa kiddo*, 2002), which focused on the actor/director's early days as a *manzai* stand-up comic. His close links with established artists speak for Shinozaki's sense of membership in a filmmaking tradition and community,

*Okaeri (1995): The film is a promising start to Shinozaki's career, though his future development still seems uncertain.*

and it was appropriate that he also served as producer of *Cop Festival* (*Deka matsuri*, 2003), to which he and various esteemed directors each contributed a ten-minute comic segment about a policeman featuring one gag a minute. The balance between individual and collaborative expression is perhaps Shinozaki's main strength as a filmmaker. The precise development of his career, however, seems at yet uncertain.

1990 **Rusuban bideo** / Nobody Home (*short*)

1995 **Okaeri** / Okaeri (lit. Welcome Home)

1998 **Yoru 9-ji 20-ppun no wanpīsu: Mazushisa to yutakasa to** / One-Piece Dress at 9:20 p.m.: Poverty and Wealth (*short*)

1999 **Jamu sesshon: Kikujirō no natsu kōshiki kaizokuban** / Jam Session: The Unofficial Bootleg of Kikujiro

2000 **Wasurerarenu hitobito** / Not Forgotten

2002 **Asakusa kiddo no Asakusa kiddo** / Asakusa Kid

2003 **Deka matsuri** / Cop Festival (*co-director*)

2004 **Inu to arukeba: Chirori to Tamara** / Walking with the Dog
    **Rusuban bideo** / Nobody Home (*short; remake*)

2007 **0093 Joō heika no Kusakari Masao** / 0093: Masao Kusakari On Her Majesty's Secret Service

## SHIOTA Akihiko
**(b. September 11, 1961)**
塩田明彦

A specialist in films about the young, Shiota is notable for his ability to eschew sentimentality and capture the awkwardness and violence of adolescent emotions. A student member of Rikkyō University's Ciné-Club, he was influenced by theorist Shigehiko Hasumi and future director Kiyoshi Kurosawa. One of his early 8mm projects, *Falala* (*Farara*, 1983) won the PIA Film Festival competition, but until the late nineties he worked primarily as a screenwriter, mainly on erotic films released straight to video. After directing *The Nude Woman* (*Roshutsukyō no onna*, 1996) for video release, he made his first theatrical feature, *Moonlight Whispers* (*Gekkō no sasayaki*, 1999). Directed with restraint and without sensationalism, this unsettling film began as a conventional high school romance, later moving into darker territory as it explored the masochistic tendencies of the boy, superbly acted by Kenji Mizuhashi. Released simultaneously, *Don't Look Back* (*Dokomademo ikō*, 1999) focused on slightly younger protagonists; its theme was the way in which simple childhood friendships are undermined by the complexities of adolescence.

Shiota next made *Gips* (*Gipusu*, 2000), shot cheaply on digital video. This story about a young woman who wears a plaster cast in order to be noticed was something of a retread of *Moonlight Whispers*, particularly in its wry coda, and felt superfluous as a result. However, a definite stylistic advance was apparent in the bleak *Harmful Insect* (*Gaichū*, 2001), which followed a young girl's fruitless attempts to find an emotional connection with those around her. Framing his heroine in silence and isolation against the scenery, Shiota emphasized her loneliness, and though the film was at times suffocatingly cruel, it was perhaps its director's most assured in style. *Canary* (*Kanaria*, 2005), some-

what more tender in tone, was a moving account of the experiences of a 12-year-old former member of a cult (based on the Aum Shinrikyo organization), as he attempts to re-integrate into society. Flawed by occasional contrivances and an overuse of handheld camera, the film was nevertheless intriguing in its sceptical attitude towards the nuclear family and celebration of the alternative bonds established with other ex-cultists and socially marginalized characters.

In these films, the experiences of children often served as a microcosm of society, Shiota himself commenting that "if you want to describe the problems of Japanese society today, teenagers are a fitting symbol." Less direct in relevance were two adaptations of novels by Shinji Kajio, in which Shiota essayed fantastic subject matter. In *Resurrection* (*Yomigaeri*, 2002), reminiscent of Kiyoshi Kurosawa in its non-sensational treatment of supernatural themes, the dead return to earth, not as ghosts but as living people. Focusing on the mixed responses of their bereaved relatives and friends, Shiota posed some probing questions about guilt and acceptance before the film subsided into strained melodrama. The theme of accepting or failing to accept the past was also central to *A Heartful of Love* (*Kono mune ippai no ai o*, 2005), a story about a 30-year-old advertising executive and a young gangster given the opportunity to travel back twenty years to correct things they regret. Here, unfortunately, a potentially touching idea was dealt with in the most sentimental fashion imaginable.

With *Dororo* (2007), an action film with supernatural elements adapted from a *manga* by Osamu Tezuka about a female thief raised as a boy, Shiota used period settings for the first time. This was further confirmation of his versatility and a commercial success in Japan; indeed, at the time of writing, Shiota is preparing two sequels. Reviews, however, were mixed, and it may be that the director's most memorable work will continue to be found in his disquieting investigations into the troubled feelings of the young.

1981 **Aria** (*8mm short*)
1982 **Yasashii musume** / Kind Girl (*8mm short*)
1983 **Farara** / Falala (*8mm*)
1985 **Hoshikage no warutsu** / Starlight Waltz (*8mm short*)
1999 **Gekkō no sasayaki** / Moonlight Whispers / Sasayaki
    **Doko made mo ikō** / Don't Look Back
2000 **Gipusu** / Gips (lit. Cast)
2001 **Gaichū** / Harmful Insect
2002 **Yomigaeri** / Resurrection
2003 **Kaette kita deka matsuri** / Cop Festival Returns (*co-director*)
2005 **Kanaria** / Canary
    **Kono mune ippai no ai o** / A Heartful of Love
2007 **Dororo**

## SŌMAI Shinji
**(January 13, 1948–September 9, 2001)**
相米慎二

Among the finest independent directors of the eighties and nineties, Sōmai began his career after assisting two other individual filmmakers: Kazuhiko Hasegawa and Shūji Terayama. With his earliest films, *Terrible Couple* (*Tonda kappuru*, 1980) and *Sailor Suit and Machine Gun* (*Sērāfuku to kikanjū*, 1981), he was already establishing a remarkable personal style, often using one shot per scene to observe the actions and interactions

of his characters in real time. Though *Sailor Suit and Machine Gun* was a rather absurd yakuza pastiche about a teenage girl who becomes the heir to a failing gang, and though Sōmai also directed a Roman Porno film, *Love Hotel* (*Rabu hoteru*, 1985), his method was best suited to understated human drama, where it enabled him to reveal nuances of behavior which shed light on the psychology and feelings of his characters.

Sōmai was particularly adept at examining the awkward feelings of children and adolescents. His debut focused on a teenage love affair. His most famous film, *Typhoon Club* (*Taifū kurabu*, 1985), filmed pitilessly in extreme long shot, was a dark account of psychological tensions among a group of junior high school kids waiting out a typhoon at school; Sōmai used the storm to externalize their violent emotions. *Moving* (*Ohikkoshi*, 1993), generally ranked among the director's best films, was another low-key examination of child psychology, following a young girl's reactions to her parents' divorce; the cathartic last scene of the girl's lonely wanderings through a town at festival time is considered one of the finest sequences in modern Japanese cinema. In *The Friends* (*Natsu no niwa*, 1994), three boys at elementary school begin to sneak into the garden of an elderly man whom they eventually befriend; here, however, Sōmai's adept exploration of childhood emotions contrasted with the schematic and sentimental handling of the old man's wartime guilt.

Despite their focus on the young, these films were darkened by their consciousness of the proximity of death. In *Typhoon Club*, one boy nearly drowns and another commits suicide, while the children in *The Friends* are obsessed with death, originally hoping to witness the old man's demise. Mortality was a prominent theme, too, in *Tokyo Heaven* (*Tōkyō jōkū irasshaimase*, 1990), a fantasy about a young woman given the chance to return to earth after her death in a traffic accident. The first and last scenes of Sōmai's penultimate film, *Wait and See* (*Ā, haru*, 1998) depicted funerals; this was, nevertheless, one of Sōmai's most affirmative dramas. Its story, vaguely reminiscent of Renoir's *Boudu sauvé des eaux* (1932), focused on the disruption of a bourgeois family by the arrival of an unwanted guest (the neglectful father of the salaryman hero, long presumed dead); its theme was the triumph of human affections over complacency, snobbery, and selfishness. Though even *Typhoon Club* had found tentative hope in the calm after the storm, a therapeutic quality was more apparent in Sōmai's later works: *The Friends* and *Wait and See* followed death with images of rebirth in nature, very movingly in the latter case. Sōmai's final film, *Kazahana* (2000), was an account of the moral and emotional rebirth of two lost souls during a journey through Hokkaido. Initially merciless in its portrayal of directionless lives, the film achieved a touching catharsis in its last sequences as the characters realize their need for each other.

Sōmai was capable of extraordinary stylistic virtuosity: the opening sequence shot of *Fragments in the Snow: Passion* (*Yuki no danshō: Jōnetsu*, 1985) was one of the most breathtakingly elaborate pieces of choreography in Japanese film, meriting comparison with Mizoguchi. By contrast, the slow, meticulous preparations for the suicide in *Typhoon Club* were made doubly chilling by the unflinching observation of an absolutely static camera. More often, however, Sōmai's use of the long take was essentially functional: subtle reframings followed the movements of the actors, while the rejection of editing allowed them to develop performances of depth and nuance. His cuts, when they did occur, were often jarring, seeming to leap over certain events and deprive the viewer of anticipated information. As Aaron Gerow has observed, this tension between continuity and discontinuity, expressed, too, in the concern with such human discontinuities as adolescence and death, was among the most fascinating features of Sōmai's art. His untimely death deprived the modern Japanese cinema of one of its most distinctive and distinguished artists, but his influence remains visible in the style of such younger directors as Kiyoshi Kurosawa. His relative neglect in the West is a matter of regret.

1980 **Tonda kappuru** / Terrible Couple / Dreamy Fifteen
1981 **Sērāfuku to kikanjū** / Sailor Suit and Machine Gun
1983 **Shonben raidā** / Shonben Rider
     **Gyoei no mure** / The Catch / The Big Catch
1985 **Rabu hoteru** / Love Hotel
     **Taifū kurabu** / Typhoon Club
     **Yuki no danshō: Jōnetsu** / Fragments in the Snow: Passion
1987 **Hikaru onna** / Luminous Woman
1990 **Tōkyō jōkū irasshaimase** / Tokyo Heaven
1993 **Ohikkoshi** / Moving
1994 **Natsu no niwa** / The Friends / The Summer Garden (lit.)
1998 **Ā, haru** / Wait and See (lit. Ah, Spring)
2000 **Kazahana** / Kaza-hana (lit. Snow Flurry)

## SUO Masayuki
### (b. October 29, 1956)
### 周防正行

Famous as the director of some of Japan's most engagingly quirky mainstream comedies, Suo worked initially in the "pink" sector, serving as assistant to Kōji Wakamatsu before realizing his infamous debut, *Abnormal Family* (*Hentai kazoku: Aniki no yome-san*, 1984). This wicked variation on the themes of the traditional home drama, depicting alcoholism, prostitution, and incest, was somewhat insubstantial as a satire on the nuclear family, but succeeded as an uncannily precise pastiche of the style of Yasujirō Ozu, mimicking his static camera and contemplative "pillow shots" of surrounding objects or scenery. During the eighties, Suo also shot two videos on the making of Juzō Itami's *Taxing Woman* (*Marusa no onna*) films.

Suo entered the mainstream with *Fancy Dance* (*Fanshī dansu*, 1989), the first of three comedies focusing, in the words of Tom Mes and Jasper Sharp, on "a group of men forced together by circumstance in a colorful milieu far removed from their usual element." *Fancy Dance* cast pop idol Masahiro Motoki as a singer obliged to spend a year in a Buddhist monastery in order to inherit it from his grandfather. The influence of Ozu was still apparent in the use of a static camera, and while the comedy was slightly callous in tone, the star's air of charming irresponsibility was well used. Motoki also starred in *Sumo Do, Sumo Don't* (*Shiko funjatta*, 1992), an endearingly predictable story about a bunch of no-hopers who lick themselves into shape to win a student sumo competition. The humor was sometimes too broad, particularly in the caricatured treatment of some of the minor characters, but the film had an undeniable feel-good charm and featured winning supporting perfomances from such talented farceurs as Naoto Takenaka and Hiromasa Taguchi.

Suo's international reputation rests on *Shall We Dance?* (*Shall we dansu*, 1996), which focused on the equally marginal pastime of ballroom dancing. The plotting was again slightly predictable as the middle-aged, conventional salaryman hero joins a dance class to indulge a mild obsession with its beautiful teacher, before growing into a committed dancer. However, in addition to characteristically expert comic timing, it displayed a new subtlety and depth thanks to Kōji Yakusho's warm, plausible performance and Suo's sympathetic engagement with the office worker's frustration in the face of stultifying routine. Curiously, despite its huge commercial success, it was ten years before Suo directed again. His comeback was his first non-comic film, *I Just Didn't Do It* (*Sore demo boku wa yatteinai*, 2006), which followed the experiences of a salaryman unjustly accused of groping a woman on a train. Although aptly scathing about a justice system that virtually assumes the guilt of the accused, this felt a little labored. Suo seemed not quite comfortable away from comedy, and his critique might well have been sharper had he opted for a satiric approach.

**1984  Hentai kazoku: Aniki no yome-san** / Abnormal Family

**1989  Fanshī dansu** / Fancy Dance

**1992  Shiko funjatta** / Sumo Do, Sumo Don't

**1996  Shall we dansu** / Shall We Dance?

**2006  Sore demo boku wa yatteinai** / I Just Didn't Do It

Sore demo boku ni wa yatteinai / I Just Didn't Do It *(2006): Suo moved away from comedy with this scathing study of the Japanese justice system.*

## SUWA Nobuhiro
### (b. May 28, 1960)
諏訪敦彦

Suwa began to direct features after a successful career in television documentary, a training which has left its mark on his fictional work. His debut feature, *2/Duo* (*2/Dyuo*, 1997), earned plaudits for the realism with which it detailed the disintegration of a superficially happy love affair. This realism developed from Suwa's method, which elicited comparisons with John Cassavetes; he used an outline rather than a detailed script and developed the film through improvisation in rehearsal. The same method was used in *M/other* (1999), a quiet masterpiece of human observation detailing the effect on the relationship of a divorced man and his girlfriend when his son comes to live with them after

his ex-wife is injured in a road accident. Tender yet ruthless in its interrogation of individual needs and desires, the film was superbly acted by Tomokazu Miura and Makiko Watanabe, and its spontaneity was belied by the precision of Suwa's framing, which used the cluttered interior geography of the couple's flat to claustrophobic effect.

Suwa's next work, *H Story* (2001), was an examination of the troubled shoot of a remake of *Hiroshima Mon Amour* (1959, Alain Resnais). The film touched on the way historical tragedies become less relevant with passing time and contrasted the freedom of Suwa's improvisational technique with the absolute premeditation of the film-within-a-film, a line-by-line remake of a classic. Though philosophically intriguing, it lacked the human depth of *M/other*. Having worked on *H Story* with both

*2/Dyuo / 2/Duo (1997):Suwa creates improvisational, realist accounts of human relations.*

French and Japanese actors, Suwa made his next film, *Un couple parfait* (2005), about a couple contemplating divorce, entirely in Europe with a French-speaking cast and a Parisian setting. It was less well-received, perhaps because Suwa lacked a detailed understanding of French life. Nevertheless, his concern with the difficulty of romantic relationships is a fairly universal one, and he has proved both an enquiring dramatist and a technically skilled filmmaker. His future career, whether in Japan or the West, should be worth following.

1982 **Santa ga machi ni yatte kuru /** Santa's Coming to Town (*16mm short*)
1985 **Hanasareru Gang /** The Gang Separates (*8mm short*)
1997 **2/Dyuo** / 2/Duo
1999 **M/other**
2001 **H Story**
2002 **Jeonjaeng geu ihu /** After War (*co-director, South Korea*)

2005 **Un couple parfait /** A Perfect Couple (*France*)
2006 **Paris, je t'aime /** Paris, I Love You (*co-director; France*)

## SUZUKI Seijun
**(b. May 24, 1923)**
鈴木清順

Suzuki achieved international fame belatedly, a quarter century after the visual flamboyance of his gangster pictures and his dismissal by a studio outraged by the liberties he took with generic material won him a cult reputation among students in Japan. By the nineties, the self-conscious, self-mocking exploitation of generic motifs in such films as *Tokyo Drifter* (*Tōkyō nagaremono*, 1966) and *Branded to Kill* (*Koroshi no rakuin*, 1967) seemed to have anticipated the ethos of postmodernism; as Mark Schilling observed, Suzuki's "aestheticized, absurdist worldview, in which the code of the tough guy devolves into choreographed grotesquerie, foretold the course of much of the popular culture over the next three decades, both in Japan and the West."

Under contract at Nikkatsu, Suzuki initially directed assignments in a variety of genres, including musicals, youth films, and literary adaptations. These were often professionally done: *Fighting Delinquents* (*Kutabare gurentai*, 1960), for instance, enlivened a rather predictable story with some startling color effects and striking compositions. *Underworld Beauty* (*Ankokugai no bijo*, 1958), for which the director first adopted the professional name Seijun, more closely anticipated the tone of his later work in its story of conflict among thieves, especially in the nihilistic climax where the diamonds which have motivated the drama are incinerated with a heap of coal. Suzuki's characteristic style, however, was only established from about 1963 onwards, particularly in his collaborations with talented art director Takeo Kimura. Films such as *Youth of the Beast* (*Yajū no seishun*, 1963) and *Tokyo Drifter* used parody and visual artifice to satirize the established conventions of the action thriller. Their brilliant stylization made these films foolishly enthralling, but in their resort to pastiche they were sometimes emotionally hollow. With *Tokyo Drifter*, in particular, the cartoon-like imagery and deliberately exaggerated acting actually overwhelmed a potentially moving story of the betrayal of a young gangster by his boss.

Nevertheless, Suzuki's best films in this vein displayed both emotional depth and complexity of implication. *Kanto Wanderer* (*Kantō mushuku*, 1963)

was a subtly subversive commentary on the obsolescence of the yakuza code; here, the protagonist's efforts to act honorably fail to avert bloodshed and, indeed, trigger the death of his own patron. *Branded to Kill* raised incoherence to an art form: the competition among professional hit men to be "Number One" became a metaphor for the rat race, while the disconnected narrative and choppy editing seemed to express the confusion and alienation of urban life.

Suzuki also at times set films in the past, obliquely charting the social history of his country through the twentieth century. His focus was on proletarian and socially marginalized characters: *One Generation of Tattoos* (*Irezumi ichidai*, 1965) and *The Flower and the Angry Waves* (*Hana to dotō*, 1964) were yakuza films set in the Taisho period, in which generic stories of honor and violence were given depth by a detailed recreation of specific milieux. The latter, in particular, contained some intelligent commentary on the links between organized labor and organized crime. Elsewhere, Suzuki dealt with prostitution in two remakes of Occupation-era films, both originally based on novels by Taijirō Tamura. *Story of a Prostitute* (*Shunpuden*, 1965), reworking Senkichi Taniguchi's *Escape to Tomorrow* (*Akatsuki no dassō*, 1950), charted the experiences of "comfort women" in wartime China. *Gate of Flesh* (*Nikutai no mon*, 1964), earlier filmed by Masahiro Makino, was a brutal account of the struggle for survival during the Occupation, centering on the experiences of a group of Tokyo prostitutes. In general, the exploitation format of these films somewhat compromised their social concern: thus, the humanism of Taniguchi's film gave way to a bleak nihilism in its remake, while

©Nikkatsu Corporation

*Kenka erejii / Fighting Elegy (1966): Suzuki's most politically sophisticated film traced the roots of fascism to the violent impulses and sexual frustrations of youth.*

*Gate of Flesh* treated its subject matter with unattractive prurience. *Fighting Elegy* (*Kenka erejii*, 1966), however, was a perfectly judged marriage of action and implication, and Suzuki's most politically sophisticated film: set against the backdrop of the February 26, 1936 militarist uprising, it traced the roots of fascism to the violent impulses and sexual frustrations of youth.

After his dismissal from Nikkatsu, Suzuki worked for ten years in television before re-establishing himself as an independent director. His comeback film, *Story of Sorrow and Sadness* (*Hishū monogatari*, 1977) was a curious critique of the cult of celebrity, the implications of which were not fully developed. Better received were *Zigeunerweisen* (*Tsigoineruwaizen*, 1980), *Heat-Haze Theater* (*Kageroza*, 1981), and *Yumeji*

(1991), a trilogy of atmospheric experimental films which returned to the Taisho period to explore themes of sexuality and the supernatural. Though digressive to the point of incoherence, these were visually sumptuous films, and Suzuki narrowly avoided slipping into pretension by including moments of quirky humor, particularly in *Yumeji*. In the twenty-first century, Suzuki has again essayed parodic variations on generic plots: *Pistol Opera* (*Pisutoru opera*, 2001) was a reworking of *Branded to Kill*, while *Princess Raccoon* (*Operetta: Tanuki goten*, 2005) was an inventive but inane postmodern musical, which retold a traditional legend on stylized sets, bizarrely fusing traditional and modern music. Like many of Suzuki's films, it was more interesting to look at than to think about, and it confirmed, perhaps, that his imagination was most effectively channeled by the restrictions of studio discipline.

1956 **Minato no kanpai: Shōri o wagate ni** / Harbor Toast: Victory Is in Our Grasp

**Hozuna wa utau: Umi no junjō** / Pure Emotions of the Sea

**Akuma no machi** / Satan's Town

1957 **Ukigusa no yado** / Inn of the Floating Weeds

**Hachijikan no kyōfu** / Eight Hours of Terror

**Rajo to kenjū** / The Naked Woman and the Gun

1958 **Ankokugai no bijo** / Underworld Beauty

**Fumihazushita haru** / The Spring That Didn't Come / The Boy Who Came Back

**Aoi chibusa** / Young Breasts

**Kage naki koe** / The Voice without a Shadow

1959 **Rabu retā** / Love Letter

**Ankoku no ryoken** / Passport to Darkness

**Suppadaka no nenrei** / Age of Nudity

1960 **"Jūsangō taihisen" yori: Sono gosōsha o nerae** / Aim at the Police Van (lit. From "No. 13 Breakdown Lane": Aim at the Police Van)

**Kemono no nemuri** / Sleep of the Beast

**Mikkō zero rain** / Clandestine Zero Line

**Subete ga kurutteru** / Everything Goes Wrong

**Kutabare gurentai** / Fighting Delinquents (lit. Go to Hell, Delinquents)

1961 **Tōkyō kishitai** / Tokyo Knights

**Muteppō taishō** / Reckless Boss / The Big Boss Who Needs No Gun

**Sandanjū no otoko** / The Man with the Hollow-Tip Bullets / The Man with a Shotgun

**Tōge o wataru wakai kaze** / The Wind-of-Youth Group Crosses the Mountain Pass / New Wind over the Mountain

**Kaikyō chi ni somete** / Blood Red Water in the Channel / Bloody Channel

**Hyakuman-doru o tatakidase** / Million Dollar Match / Million Dollar Smash and Grab

1962 **Haitīn yakuza** / High-Teen Yakuza

**Ore ni kaketa yatsura** / Those Who Bet on Me

1963 **Tantei jimusho 23: Kutabare akutōdomo** / Detective Bureau 23: Go to Hell, Bastards

**Yajū no seishun** / Youth of the Beast / The Brute

**Akutarō** / The Bastard

**Kantō mushuku** / Kanto Wanderer

1964 **Hana to dotō** / The Flower and the Angry Waves

**Nikutai no mon** / Gate of Flesh

**Oretachi no chi ga yurusanai** / Our Blood Won't Allow It / Our Blood Will Not Forgive

1965 **Shunpuden** / Story of a Prostitute / Joy Girls

**Akutarōden: Warui hoshi no shita demo** / Stories of Bastards: Despite Being Born under a Bad Star

**Irezumi ichidai** / One Generation of Tattoos / Tattooed Life / Life of a Tattooed Man

1966 **Kawachi Karumen** / Carmen from Kawachi

**Tōkyō nagaremono** / Tokyo Drifter

**Kenka erejii** / Fighting Elegy / Elegy to Violence / The Born Fighter

1967 **Koroshi no rakuin** / Branded to Kill

1977 **Hishū monogatari** / Story of Sorrow and Sadness

1980 **Tsigoineruwaizen** / Zigeunerweisen

**1981 Kagerōza** / Heat-Haze Theater / Kagero-za / Mirage Theater
**1985 Kapone ōi ni naku** / Capone Cries Hard
**Rupajidain sansei: Babiron no ōgon densetsu** / Lupin III: Legend of the Gold of Babylon (*animation; co-director*)
**1991 Yumeji**
**1993 Kekkon** / Marriage (*co-director*)
**2001 Pisutoru opera** / Pistol Opera
**2005 Operetta: Tanuki goten** / Princess Raccoon (lit. Princess Raccoon Dog)


## SUZUKI Shigeyoshi
### (June 25, 1900–October 17, 1976)
### 鈴木重吉

One of the outstanding directors of the silent era, Suzuki (sometimes called Jūkichi Suzuki) is best known in Japan and internationally for his contribution to the left-leaning *keikō-eiga* genre. His most famous film, the rediscovered *What Made Her Do It?* (*Nani ga kanojo o sō saseta ka*, 1930), recounted the sufferings of a naive orphan girl at the hands of relatives and employers; the desperation of the Depression era was well conveyed, while Suzuki's imaginative use of montage and vivid caricature revealed the influence of Soviet cinema. The example of foreign cinema had also been important to Suzuki's earlier work; indeed, his first hits were made for a Kyoto-based subsidiary of Universal Studios in collaboration with an American cinematographer, Harold Smith. *The Blue Moth* (*Ao ga*, 1927) and *Skylark* (*Hibari*, 1927), now lost, were praised at the time for their imaginative fusion of Japanese and Western techniques, while *The Coward* (*Yowamushi*, 1927) was a reworking of a Harold Lloyd comedy, *The Kid Brother* (1927, Ted Wilde). This blend of influences spoke for the director's cosmopolitan sensibility, as did the fact that in the late twenties he became a contributing writer for the *avant-garde* British film journal *Close Up*.

Cosmopolitanism notwithstanding, Suzuki's best films addressed specifically Japanese concerns. *Tears Behind Victory* (*Eikan namida ari*, 1931), an example of the student comedy genre also essayed by Ozu, was a sharp study of social relationships which moved skillfully from a register of light humor to melodrama; the focus, as in many prewar Japanese films, was on a heroine who accepts a demeaning profession to fund her brother's education. *The Reclaimed Land of Bears* (*Kuma no deru kaikonchi*, 1932), set in Hokkaido, was a visually splendid and politically incisive account of the struggles of pioneer farmers against capitalist encroachment. Though rarely shown, these two films rank among the finest Japanese silents preserved today.

Regrettably, Suzuki's political commitment mutated in the era of militarism. As early as 1933, he had directed propaganda documentaries for the Army (*The Tenth of March* [*Sangatsu tōka*]) and Navy (*This One Battle* [*Kono issen*]), while in 1938 he made the shamelessly propagandistic *The Road to Peace in the Orient* (*Tōyō heiwa no michi*), about Chinese refugees who learn to appreciate the kindness of the Japanese enemy. During the war he served as head of the Man'ei studio in China, and was not repatriated till 1950. His undistinguished postwar work reached a nadir with *Buruuba* (*Burūba*, 1955), a *Tarzan* clone made in California at MGM. Nevertheless, his surviving silent films retain their power and deserve wider exposure.

1926 **Tsuchi ni kagayaku** / Shining on the Earth

**Undōka** / The Sportsman

**Unmei no ko** / Child of Destiny

**Ningen ai** / Human Love

**Kiri no naka no tomoshibi** / Light in the Fog

**Hadaka sōdōki** / Record of Naked Trouble

**Rajo** / Naked Woman

**Kyokubadan no shimai** / Sisters of the Circus

**Otoshiana** / Pitfall

1927 **Fuyuyasumi** / Winter Holiday

**Ao ga** / The Blue Moth

**Hibari** / Skylark

**Yowamushi** / The Coward

**Yami no tejina** / Sleight of Hand in the Dark

1928 **Tanaka Saishō no shōnen jidai** / The Youth of Prime Minister Tanaka

1929 **Koi no jazu** / Jazz of Love

1930 **Nani ga kanojo o sō saseta ka** / What Made Her Do It?

**Odoru gen'ei** / The Dancing Phantom

**Komoriuta** / Lullaby

**Ude** / Arm

1931 **Ai subeku** / About Love

**Nani ga kanojo o koroshita ka** / What Killed Her?

**Eikan namida ari** / Tears Behind Victory

1932 **Kuma no deru kaikonchi** / The Reclaimed Land of Bears

**Konjiki yasha** / The Golden Demon

1933 **Ginrei Fuji ni yomigaeru** / Resurrection on Snow-Capped Mount Fuji

**Seishun mujō** / The Heartless Youth

**Sōbō kokubō** / Blue Eyes, Black Eyes

**Sangatsu tōka** / The Tenth of March

**Kono issen** / This One Battle

1934 **Misomerareta seinen** / The Youth Who Was Loved at First Sight

**Ushio** / The Tide

**Karisome no kuchibeni** / Trifling Lipstick

1935 **Teisō mondō: Kōgen no maki** / Dialogue about Chastity: Highlands Reel

**Teisō mondō: Tokai no maki** / Dialogue About Chastity: City Reel

**Uramachi no kanpai** / Here's to the Back Streets

**Hanayome gakkō** / Bridal School

1936 **Yōjō no kangeki** / Thrilled by the Ocean

**Raimei** / Thunder

**Shingetsu shō** / Story of the New Moon (*co-director*)

1937 **Gendai Nihon** / Modern Japan

**Jōkonki: Masago no maki** / Record of a Pure Marriage: Sand Reel

**Jōkonki: Hifumi no maki** / Record of a Pure Marriage: Hifumi's Reel

1938 **Shōkokumin** / Young Citizens

**Tōyō heiwa no michi** / The Road to Peace in the Orient

1939 **Fūki haru yume** / Fleeting Dream of Wealth (*Manchuria*)

**Hyōjō senreisai** / Baptism on the Ice (*Manchuria*)

**Shokujusetsu** / Time for Planting Trees (*Manchuria*)

**Rama chōki** / The Leaping Lama (*Manchuria*)

**Tenshin suika** / The Tianjin Flood (*Manchuria*)

1940 **Gyohitei** / The Imperial Stele Pavilion (*Manchuria*)

1941 **Kōsenden** / Legend of the Red Line (*Manchuria*)

1942 **Menka** / Cotton Flower (*Manchuria*)

1950 **Tōkyō rumuba** / Tokyo Rumba

**Aishū no minato** / Harbor of Grief

1954 **Atarashiki ten** / The New Heaven

**Haha chigusa** / A Mother and Many Plants

**1955** Ojōsan sensei / The Young Miss Is a Teacher

Tōkyō bōryokudan / Tokyo Gangsters

Burūba / Buruuba

**1956** Hyō no manako / The Leopard's Eye

Seiryū no dōkutsu / Cave of the Green Dragon

**1963** Tōkyō Orinpikku e no michi / Road to the Tokyo Olympics

# TAKAMINE Gō
## (b. November 12, 1948)
高嶺剛

Okinawa's most distinctive filmmaker, Takamine has devoted his career to exploring the separate regional identity of the southwestern archipelago. He worked initially on 8mm films while a student in Kyoto; his sense of alienation in Japan's cultural capital spurred him to document the landscapes and cultural heritage of his birthplace, then in the process of reverting to Japanese rule after nearly thirty years under U.S. control. The reversion itself was the backdrop of *Okinawan Dream Show* (*Uchinā imi manegatai*, 1974), which consisted of silent documentary footage of the region's life and changing landscapes around the time of the handover. *Okinawan Chirudai* (1978) was another impressionistic documentary, focusing on the cultural traditions and ways of life eroded by foreign influence. The term "chirudai" refers to "loafing around" or "chilling out," but Takamine used it to convey the relaxed Okinawan sense of time, supplanted by clock time with the coming of modernity. A melancholy background to these films was the

decimation of Okinawa's population in World War II. Among Takamine's more recent documentaries, *Kadekaru Rinsho: Songs and Stories* (*Kadekaru Rinshō: Uta to katari*, 1995) consisted of interviews with and songs by the eccentric local folk singer of the title, while *Private Images of Ryukyu: JM* (*Shiteki satsu mugen Ryūkyū: JM*, 2003) was another collection of images depicting Okinawan life and culture, woven around a visit to the island by *avant-garde* filmmaker Jonas Mekas.

Takamine's narrative films have addressed the same themes in a magical realist style blending Okinawan folklore with the director's own personal mythology. *Paradise View* (*Paradaisu Byū*, 1985) and *Untama Giru* (*Untama Girū*, 1989)—the latter named after a local Robin Hood figure—were languid yet pointed fables about the archipelago's status as a colony of two large and powerful nations. The commentary was not subtle: typical of Takamine's broad, vivid brand of satire was the scene in *Untama Giru* in which the American governor receives a blood transfusion from a pig. Nevertheless, the surreal wit of these films made them seem less angry than amused: Tony Rayns described *Untama Giru* as "doubtless the most spaced-out agit-prop ever filmed."

The later *Tsuru-Henry* (*Mugen Ryūkyū: Tsuru-Henrī*, 1998), about a folk singer and her half-American son trying to adapt a film script left unfinished by a local filmmaker, linked these concerns with cultural heritage and its dilution to a more self-conscious examination of the role of the artist in a colonial milieu. Alas, the use of video rather than celluloid deprived its images of the sensuality with which *Paradise View* and *Untama Giru* had recorded the Okinawan landscape. In general, Takamine's work may simply be too mellow, too lacking in urgency, for some tastes. But he remains a unique and often beguiling voice.

1970 **Redman** (*8mm short*)
1971 **Dorīmu shō No. 1** / Dream Show No. 1 (*8mm short*)
1972 **Sashinguwā** / Dear Photograph (*8mm short*)
1974 **Uchinā imi manegatai** / Okinawan Dream Show (*8mm*)
1975 **Sashingwā** / Dear Photograph (*16mm short*)
1978 **Okinawan chirudai** / Okinawan Chirudai (lit. Loafing Around, Okinawa Style) (*16mm*)
1981 **V.O.H.R.: Ningen kankei no nagame** / View of Human Relations (*16mm*)
1985 **Paradaisu Byū** / Paradise View
1989 **Untama Girū** / Untama Giru
1992 **Photo on the Stone** (*16mm short*)
1994 **A.S.O.P. Shu Lea Cheang no bāi** / A.S.O.P. In the Case of Shu Lea Cheang
1995 **Kadekaru Rinshō: Uta to katari** / Kadekaru Rinsho: Songs and Stories
1998 **Mugen Ryūkyū: Tsuru-Henrī** / Tsuru-Henry
2003 **Mugen Ryūkyū: Okinawa shimauta Pari no sora ni hibiku** / Okinawa Island Songs Echo in the Parisian Sky
     **Shiteki satsu mugen Ryūkyū: JM** / Private Images of Ryuku: JM

## TAKECHI Tetsuji
**(December 10, 1912–July 26, 1988)**
武智鉄二

Takechi is mentioned here less for his distinctly modest talent as a filmmaker than for his historical importance in pioneering the representation of ex-

plicit sexuality in Japanese film. Predominantly a director of experimental theater, he staged Noh and Kabuki with naked actors during the fifties. His first film, *A Night in Japan: Woman Woman Woman Story* (*Nihon no yoru: Onna onna onna monogatari*, 1963), was a semidocumentary about women working as bar hostesses, strippers, masseurs, and geisha, but he achieved notice and notoriety the following year with two Jun'ichirō Tanizaki adaptations: *Daydream* (*Hakujitsumu*, 1964) and *The Dream of the Red Chamber* (*Kōkeimu*, 1964). Both were sexually explicit experimental films; the latter was heavily cut by the censors. The former recounted the masochistic fantasies experienced by a woman under sedation for dental treatment. Though its minimal plotting and dream logic were innovative, it was clumsy in style, and Tanizaki himself publicly condemned it. Nevertheless, it was commercially successful and obtained international distribution.

Takechi's next film, *Black Snow* (*Kuroi yuki*, 1965) was an account of a young Japanese who murders the black GI who had slept with his prostitute mother. Intended as a satire on the American military presence in Japan, it again displayed scant stylistic finesse, with clumsily choreographed long takes and an undisciplined use of the zoom lens. Takechi claimed that the nude scenes were "psychological nude scenes symbolizing the defenselessness of the Japanese people in the face of the American invasion," but the film led to a celebrated trial for obscenity (the director was eventually cleared). After making an erotic adaptation of the classical novel, *The Tale of Genji* (*Genji monogatari*, 1966), and the two *Cruel Stories*, set respectively among prostitutes and artists, Takechi worked mainly in the theater until the eighties. During his last years, he moved from soft pornography to hard; among these late, sexually explicit films were a remake of *Daydream* (*Hakujitsumu*, 1981) and an adaptation of Kyōka Izumi's melodrama *The Saint of Mt. Koya* (*Kōya hijiri*, 1983), about a demonic temptress and a Buddhist monk. *Oiran* (1983) was a Nagasaki-set costume picture-cum-horror film, again loosely inspired by Tanizaki, about a courtesan loved by a street vendor and coveted by a tattoo artist who wants to work on her beautiful skin.

The aesthetic merit of Takechi's film work is dubious: he was an indifferent *metteur-en-scène* and has often been dismissed as a dilettante. However, his films retain both historical significance and symptomatic interest.

1963 **Nihon no yoru: Onna onna onna monogatari** / A Night in Japan: Woman Woman Woman Story / Women . . . Oh Women
1964 **Hakujitsumu** / Daydream
      **Kōkeimu** / The Dream of the Red Chamber
1965 **Kuroi yuki** / Black Snow
1966 **Genji monogatari** / The Tale of Genji
      **Genjitsu** / Parhelia
1968 **Sengo zankoku monogatari** / Cruel Story of the Postwar Era
      **Ukiyoe zankoku monogatari** / Cruel Story of the Floating World / Ukiyoe
1973 **Sukyandaru fujin** / The Lady of Scandal
1981 **Hakujitsumu** / Daydream
1983 **Oiran** / Oiran (lit. Prostitute)
      **Kōya hijiri** / The Saint of Mt. Koya
1987 **Hakujitsumu 2** / Daydream 2 / Captured for Sex

## TAKITA Yōjirō
(b. December 4, 1955)
滝田洋二郎

One of the more interesting directors to have graduated from "pink" film to the mainstream, Takita initially came to notice while working on eleven installments of a long-running series of sex comedies, *Molester Train* (*Chikan densha*). Such more serious "pink" films as *Serial Rape* (*Renzoku bōkan*, 1983) and *Daylight Ripper* (*Mahiru no kirisakima*, 1984) had already earned him a cult reputation before he made his mainstream breakthrough with *Comic Magazine* (*Komikku zasshi nanka iranai*, 1986), a scabrous episodic satire on the dubious practices of television journalism, inspired by actual news stories and precisely described by Vincent Canby as "a scurrilously funny picture of a technologically advanced society with an insatiable appetite for what's largely irrelevant." Certainly, its portrait of the way in which a fascination with the trivial leads people to lose sight of real moral issues is only more relevant in the twenty-first century.

Satiric comedy proved Takita's most fertile vein. *The Yen Family* (*Kimura-ke no hitobito*, 1988) was a critique of the materialism of the bubble era, focusing on a family whose sole priorities are financial: each member runs or helps to run one of numerous small businesses, the kids pay for their room and board, and the parents pay each other for sex. *Let's Go to the Hospital* (*Byōin e ikō*, 1990) was a humorous account of patients and staff in a hospital, while its sequel *Love Never Dies* (*Yamai wa ki kara: Byōin e ikō 2*, 1992), blended the theme of patients dealing with illness with a touch of satire on the cult of celebrity, which recalled the concerns of *Comic Magazine*. We

*Are Not Alone* (*Bokura wa minna ikiteru*, 1993) and *The Tropical People* (*Nettai rakuen kurabu*, 1994) both dealt with the relations between Japan and its poorer Asian neighbors: the former focused on a group of salarymen trying to cut deals with the corrupt government of a fictitious South-East Asian nation, while the latter was the story of a Japanese tour guide in Bangkok who revolts against her dislikeable customers and masterminds a scam selling stolen passports.

More domestic in focus was *The Exam* (*Ojuken*, 1999), an engaging satire depicting the pressures on the middle class in an era when expectations are high and prosperity precarious. Though slightly sentimentalized towards the end, this story of parents trying to get their only daughter into an exclusive school spoke volumes about the gap between aspiration and reality in modern Japan. Takita also played with conventional family roles in *Secret* (*Himitsu*, 1999), a fantasy about a mother fatally injured in a car crash who transfers her soul into her daughter's body, causing some complications in her relationship with her husband/father. Regrettably, Takita has since begun to concentrate on *jidai-geki*, producing such stylish but silly period spectaculars as *The Yin-Yang Master* (*Onmyōji*, 2001), *When the Last Sword Is Drawn* (*Mibu gishiden*, 2003), and *Ashura* (*Ashura-jō no hitomi*, 2005). Especially in *The Yin-Yang Master*, the willingness to bring deceased characters back to life robbed even death of its gravity. Nor were impressive set design, a heavy reliance on special effects, and comic-book action any substitute for the wry observation and unobtrusive intelligence which had characterized Takita's best work. One may trust he will eventually rediscover these qualities; *The Battery* (*Batterī*, 2007) was, at least,

a return to the present day, albeit with a relatively conventional story about the experiences of a talented young baseball player.

1981 **Chikan onna kyōshi** / Molester Woman Teacher
1982 **Chikan densha: Motto tsuzukete** / Molester Train: Keep Doing It
**Kannō danchi: Uwatsuki shitatsuki shigekitsuki** / Apartment of the Senses: Superscript, Subscript, Stimulus
1982 **Chikan densha: Man'in mame sagashi** / Molester Train: All Searching for Beans
1983 **Chikan densha: Rumiko no oshiri** / Molester Train: Rumiko's Buttocks
**Chikan densha: Keiko no hippu** / Molester Train: Keiko's Hips
**Chikan densha: Momoe no oshiri** / Molester Train: Momoe's Buttocks
**Renzoku bōkan** / Serial Rape
1984 **Chikan densha: Shitagi kensatsu** / Molester Train: Underwear Ticket Check
**Chikan densha: Chinchin hassha** / Molester Train: Ding Dick Departure
**Gubbai bōi** / Goodbye Boy
**OL 24-ji: Bishōjo** / 24-Hour Office Lady: The Attractive Harlot
**Mahiru no kirisakima** / Daylight Ripper
**Chikan densha: Gokuhi honban** / Molester Train: Secret Performance
**Chikan hokenshitsu** / Molestation in the Nurse's Office
**Za kinbaku** / Tightly Bound
1985 **Chikan densha: Seiko no oshiri** / Molester Train: Seiko's Buttocks
**Momoiro shintai kensa** / Pink Physical Check-Up
**Chikan densha: Shanai de ippatsu** / Molester Train: One Shot in the Train
**Chikan tsūkin basu** / Molester Commuter Bus
**Chikan densha: Ato oku made 1**

**cm** / Molester Train: 1cm Further Inside

**Zetsukin gyaru: Yaruki munmun** / The Matchless Girl: Fully Willing

1986 **Komikku zasshi nanka iranai** / Comic Magazine / No More Damn Comics! (lit.)

**Za Mania: Kaikan seitai jikken** / The Mania: Body Pleasure Experiment

**Chikan takuhaibin** / Molester Home Delivery

**Hamidashi sukūru mizugi** / Overflow School Swimsuit

**Taimu Abanchūru: Zetchō 5-byō mae** / Time Adventure: 5 Seconds Before Climax

1987 **Itoshi no hāfu mūn** / Lovely Half Moon

1988 **Kimura-ke no hitobito** / The Yen Family / The People of the Kimura Family (lit.)

1990 **Byōin e ikō** / Let's Go to the Hospital

1992 **Yamai wa ki kara: Byōin e ikō 2** / Love Never Dies (lit. Sickness Is in the Mind: Let's Go to the Hospital 2)

1993 **Bokura wa minna ikiteiru** / We Are Not Alone / Made in Japan (lit. We Are All Living)

**Nemuranai machi: Shinjuku same** / The City That Never Sleeps: Shinjuku Shark

1994 **Nettai rakuen kurabu** / The Tropical People / Tropical Paradise Club (lit.)

1997 **Sharan Q no enka no hanamichi** / Sharan Q's Success in Enka

1999 **Ojuken** / The Exam

**Himitsu** / Secret

2001 **Onmyōji** / The Yin-Yang Master

2003 **Mibu gishiden** / When the Last Sword is Drawn

**Onmyōji 2** / The Yin-Yang Master 2

2005 **Ashura-jō no hitomi** / Ashura / Blood Gets in Your Eyes

2007 **Batterī** / The Battery

## TAKIZAWA Eisuke
## (September 6, 1902–November 29, 1965)
## 滝沢英輔

The younger brother of *Orochi* director Buntarō Futagawa, Takizawa served as scenarist for his brother on *Swordfight* (*Rantō*, 1925) and as assistant to Masahiro Makino before directing. He achieved critical acclaim with his fourth film, *Sankichi of the Pipe* (*Paipu no Sankichi*, 1929), about a pickpocket who unknowingly causes a diplomatic incident by stealing a pipe in which is hidden' a vital scientific formula. During the thirties, he specialized in *jidai-geki*, including versions of such Japanese standbys as the *Chūshingura* story and the life of folk hero Musashi Miyamoto. More offbeat in theme was *A Tale of Thieves in Wartime* (*Sengoku guntōden*, 1937), based on a script by Sadao Yamanaka about a warrior seeking revenge on the lord who accused him of treachery; the plot was derived from Schiller and transposed to Sengoku-era Japan.

During the war, Takizawa directed some Meiji-period melodramas and contributed to the war effort with *The Sun of the Eighty-Eighth Year* (*Hachijūhachinenme no taiyō*, 1941), an account of shipyard workers managing to build a destroyer against the odds. Among his more admired postwar films were *The Saint of Mt. Koya* (*Byakuya no yōjo*, 1957), a full-blooded supernatural melodrama based on a Kyōka Izumi novel about a monk beguiled by a demonic temptress, and *Six Assassins* (*Rokunin no ansatsusha*, 1955), a samurai film set during the last years of the Tokugawa Shogunate, which used the story of a young man's quest to avenge the death of his pro-Western mentor to mount a critique of bushidō ideals. Though he continued to work mainly with historical material, Takizawa made occasional excursions into other genres: *Forever, My Love* (*Kajin*, 1958) and *The Last Song* (*Zesshō*, 1958) were both romantic tragedies about lovers divided by illness and war, and *Facing the Clouds* (*Kumo ni mukatte tatsu*, 1962) was a political thriller about an investigation into the assassination of a socialist politician. Takizawa remains almost unknown in the West.

1929 **Aru onna to gaka** / The Painter and a Certain Woman
**Shigekazu yāi** / Hey, Shigekazu
**Kuroi hitomi** / Dark Eyes
**Paipu no Sankichi** / Sankichi of the Pipe
**Kiri haruru** / The Fog Disperses
1930 **Ore wa tensai** / I Am a Genius
**Gakusei sandaiki** / Record of Three Generations of Students
**Waraenu gaika** / Unsmiling Song of Triumph
**Nankyoku ni tatsu onna** / A Woman at the South Pole
**Aisukurīmu** / Ice Cream
**Senkō sensen** / The Hidden Front
1931 **Sanada jūyūshi** / Ten Brave Men from Sanada
**Akasaya Yasubei** / Yasubei of Akasaya
**Furisode shōbu** / Competition in Long Sleeves
1932 **Karakusa Taiheiki** / Bur Clover Taiheiki
**Ōoka seidan: Jūsan'ya kenbutsu samurai** / Ooka's Trial: A Samurai Views the Moon on the Thirteenth Night
**Sukedachi tsuji kōshaku** / The Backup's Street Lectures
1933 **Jōshū shichinin arashi** / Seven Men in a Storm in Joshu
**Bushi jingi** / Warrior's Honor
1935 **Hareru Kisoji** / Fine Weather on the Kisoji
**Taikōki: Tōkichirō sōsotsu no maki** / Chronicle of Hideyoshi as a Young Foot Soldier
1936 **Kaidai musō** / The Unparalleled **Miyamoto Musashi** / Musashi Miyamoto
**Kaidō hyakuri** / 100 Ri on the Coast Road
1937 **Sengoku guntōden: Zenpen: Tora ōkami** / A Tale of Thieves in Wartime: Part 1: Tiger and Wolf / Saga of the Vagabonds: Part 1: Tiger and Wolf
**Sengoku guntōden: Kōhen: Akatsuki no zenshin** / A Tale of Thieves in Wartime: Part 2: Advance at Daybreak / Saga of the Vagabonds: Part 2: Advance at Daybreak
1938 **Chinetsu** / Subterranean Heat
**Ōma no tsuji: Edo no maki** / Street at Dusk : Edo Reel
**Budō sen'ichiya** / 1001 Nights of Bushido
1939 **Chūshingura (Zenpen; Kōhen)** / The Loyal 47 Ronin (Parts 1 and 2)
**Gozonji azuma otoko** / The Famous Man from Edo
1940 **Taiyō no miyako** / Capital of the Sun
1941 **Kaiketsu** / Solution
**Hachijūhachinenme no taiyō** / The Sun of the 88th Year
1942 **Umesato-sensei kōjōki: Ryūjinken** / The Life Story of Dr. Umesato: Sword of the Dragon God
1943 **Ina no Kantarō** / Kantaro of Ina
**Himetaru kakugo** / Secret Readiness
1945 **Nihon kengōden** / Great Swordsman of Japan
1947 **Osumi no jisankin** / Osumi's Dowry
1949 **Kirare no Senta** / Scarred Senta
1950 **Tsuma no heya** / The Wife's Room
**Shinsō gonin onna** / Five Well-Dressed Women
1951 **Heian guntōden: Hakamadare Yasusuke** / Tale of Heian-Era Thieves: Swords and Brocade

1952 **Yaguradaiko** / The Drumbeat
**Kenka Yasubei** / Fighting Yasubei

1953 **Yasugorō shusse** / Yasugoro's Success
**Yūdachi Kangorō** / The Vengeance Trail (lit. Kangoro in Evening Downpour)
**Tetsuwan namida ari** / Even the Mighty Shed Tears
**Uwaki tengoku** / Fickle Heaven

1954 **Kunisada Chūji** / Chuji Kunisada
**Jigoku no kengō: Hirate Zōshu** / Hell's Swordsman: Zoshu Hirate
**Hatsusugata Ushimatsu gōshi** / Ushimatsu Appears Through the Lattice

1955 **Rokunin no ansatsusha** / Six Assassins
**Oshun torimonochō: Nazo no amagoten** / Casebooks of Oshun: The Mysterious Nun's Palace
**Edo issun no mushi** / A Worm Will Turn in Edo

1956 **Kuroobi yōjō: Hana to arashi** / The Merciful Blackbelt: The Flower and the Storm

1957 **Kawakami Tetsuji monogatari: Sebangō 16** / The Story of Tetsuji Kawakami: Uniform No. 16
**"Kuruwa" yori: Muhō no ichidai** / From "Red-Light District": The Untamed Generation
**Byakuya no yōjo** / The Saint of Mt. Koya / The Temptress and the Monk / The Temptress (lit. Enchantress of a White Night)

1958 **Kajin** / Forever, My Love / The Beauty (lit.)
**Shi no kabe no dasshutsu** / The Face of Death (lit. Escape from the Wall of Death)
**Zesshō** / The Last Song / No Greater Love

1959 **Inoru hito** / The Praying Man
**Sekai o kakeru koi** / Love and Death (lit. A Love That Wagers the World)

1960 **Zassō no yōna inochi** / Trodden Blossoms (lit. Life Like a Weed)

**Ajisai no uta** / Blossoms of Love (lit. Song of Hydrangeas)
**Jūrokusai** / Sixteen

1961 **Shokei zen'ya** / The Night Before Execution
**Ore wa shinanaize** / I Refuse to Die

1962 **Dojokko no uta** / The Song of the Season
**Kumo ni mukatte tatsu** / Facing the Clouds
**Shirobanba** / White Fairy Dust

1963 **Kiriko no tango** / Kiriko's Tango

1964 **Shutsugeki** / Sortie
**Shin otoko no monshō: Dokyō ichiban** / A Man's Crest, New Version: The Most Courageous
**Otoko no monshō: Hana to nagadosu** / A Man's Crest: Flower and Long Sword

1965 **Otoko no monshō: Kenka kaidō** / A Man's Crest: Road of Fighting
**Otoko no monshō: Ruten no okite** / A Man's Crest: Vicissitudes of the Law

## TANAKA Eizō
**(November 3, 1886–June 13, 1968)**
田中栄三

Though very few of his films survive, Tanaka is a figure of considerable historical importance for his role in modernizing the technique of Taisho-era *shinpa*-based cinema. Working at Nikkatsu from 1917, he often directed films based on Western subject matter: thus, *The Living Corpse* (*Ikeru shikabane*, 1918) was a version of Tolstoy's *Resurrection* and *The Cherry Orchard* (*Sakura no sono*, 1918) was taken from Chekhov. He also adapted such Western-influenced Japanese novels as Yūhō Kikuchi's *Foster Sisters* (*Chikyōdai*), which he filmed in 1918 and again in 1922.

However, Tanaka's technique was apparently somewhat conservative, using one take per scene and continuing to employ *oyama* in female roles. Indeed, his most famous film, *The Kyoya Collar Shop* (*Kyōya erimise*, 1922), was the last major film to use *oyama* instead of actresses. Generally considered his masterpiece, this melodrama, about a violent merchant's obsessive love for a geisha and its destructive consequences for those around him, was praised for its meticulous set design and atmospheric lighting. Novelist Jun'ichirō Tanizaki commented that it "conjures the atmosphere of a disappearing Tokyo *shitamachi* in an aesthetic way and brings out the decadent beauty of the *onnagata* to the utmost degree." According to Anderson and Richie, it also presaged the "realistic stories of the lower classes" in which Nikkatsu would come to specialize later in the twenties.

Tanaka achieved a further success with *Dance of the Skull* (*Dokuro no mai*, 1923); here, he used actresses for the first time in a story about a monk reflecting on his youthful loves. However, his directorial career in silent film came to an end shortly afterwards, and he worked subsequently as an actor and scenarist. Although he directed two minor sound films in the thirties, his main contribution to cinema in his later years was as a teacher of film technique at university level. He also made acting appearances in Tadashi Imai's *Blue Mountains* (*Aoi sanmyaku*, 1949) and Shirō Toyoda's *Wild Geese* (*Gan*, 1953).

1918 **Akatsuki** / Dawn
**Ikeru shikabane** / The Living Corpse
**Konjiki yasha** / The Golden Demon
**Sakura no sono** / The Cherry Orchard

**Kurosuishō** / The Black Crystal
**Chikyōdai** / Foster Sisters
**Chichi no namida** / A Father's Tears
**Usuki en** / Weak Bond
**Kyōen roku** / Chronicle of Chivalry and Love
**Kobonnō** / The One Who Dotes on Children
**Tsukinu urami** / The Unending Grudge
**Chichiya no musume** / The Girl from the Chichiya
**Matsukaze Murasame** / Matsukaze and Murasame
**Ushio** / The Tide
**Shiranui** / Sea-Fire
**Hibiki** / The Echo
**Onna kuzuya** / The Female Rubbish Collector
**Kataomoi: Zenpen** / Unrequited Love: Part 1
**Haha no tsumi** / A Mother's Sin
1919 **Onna no inochi** / A Woman's Life
**Kachūsha** / Katusha
**Kataomoi: Kōhen** / Unrequited Love: Part 2
**Shinobinaki** / Silent Weeping
**Hikari no chimata** / Neighborhood of Light
**Osero** / Othello
**Hototogisu** / The Cuckoo
**Mayoi no hate** / After Wondering
**Haru no nagare** / Spring Stream
**Shin Nozaki mura** / New Nozaki Village
**Ukishizumi** / Rise and Fall
**Biwa uta** / Song of Biwa
**Shinbashi jōwa** / Love Story of Shinbashi
**Geisha no misao** / A Geisha's Chastity
**Kyōgeisha** / The Chivalrous Geisha
**Zangetsu** / The Moon at Dawn
**Jitensha Otama** / Otama on a Bicycle
**Ono ga tsumi** / My Sin

**Onna majutsushi** / The Female Magician

**Fushimiya**

1920 **Wakaki chishio** / Young Spirited Blood

**Nisei no chikai** / The Second Generation's Vow

**Kurokami (Koi no kurokami)** / Black Hair (Black Hair of Love)

**Ai no uzu** / Ripples of Love

**Hakuchō no uta** / Song of the Swan

**Renbo nagashi** / Love Floats

**Saisōki** / Romance of the West Chamber

**Chiriyuku hana** / The Flowers Will Fall

**Kataonami (Awabiuri)** / High Waves (The Abalone Seller)

**Yahataya no musume** / A Girl of Yahataya

**Unmei no kage** / Shadow of Fate

**Asahi sasu mae** / Before Daybreak

1921 **Shirayuri no kaori** / Scent of the White Lily

**Nagareyuku onna** / The Woman Will Change

**Chidorigafuchi** / The Palace Moat

**Menashidori** / Blind Man's Buff

**Ki no shita yami** / Darkness under the Tree

**Ukishizumi** / Rise and Fall

**Yae no shiokaze** / Yae's Sea Breeze

**Yasaka no homare** / The Honor of Yasaka

**Shisen no kanata** / Beyond the Verge of Death

1922 **Chikyōdai** / Foster Sisters

**Iro tazuna** / The Colorful Bridle

**Koi no wakaremichi** / Love's Path of Separation

**Tsuma to tsuma** / Wife Versus Wife

**Koi yori shi e** / From Love to Death

**Kyōya erimise** / The Kyoya Collar Shop / The Lapel Shop

1923 **Dokuro no mai** / Dance of the Skull

**Wasurenagusa** / Forget-Me-Not

**Mittsu no tamashii** / Three Souls

**Sannin zuma** / Three Wives

1932 **Namiko** / Namiko, "the Cuckoo"

1933 **Shōnen Chūshingura** / Boys' Chushingura

## TANAKA Kinuyo
### (November 29, 1909–March 21, 1977)
### 田中絹代

One of her country's finest and most versatile actresses, Tanaka also became the first woman to sustain a directorial career in Japan, realizing six creditable features which, in David Thomson's words, "displayed the same intelligence, taste, and intensity as her acting." Yasujirō Ozu, who had directed her in numerous films from the silent period on, paid her the compliment of scripting her second film, *The Moon Has Risen* (*Tsuki wa noborinu*, 1955). This story of a widowed mother and her two daughters accordingly had an Ozu-like flavor; more commonly, however, Tanaka worked in a melodramatic vein, imbuing stories of female emotions with contemporary relevance and subtle political undercurrents. Her debut, *Love Letter* (*Koibumi*, 1953), used the conventions of romantic melodrama to explore the problems of postwar women, particularly of those driven by material circumstances into unwanted marriages, relationships with foreign soldiers, or prostitution. *The Eternal Breasts* (*Chibusa yo eien nare*, 1955) was a touching account of a woman poet who divorces an unpleasant husband to pursue her writing career, only to succumb to breast cancer. *Girls of Dark* (*Onna bakari no yoru*, 1961) followed the experiences of prostitutes being rehabilitated after their trade was legally prohibited in Japan.

Tanaka also directed two intriguing historical films about women linked by love or marriage to male participants in major political events. *The Wandering Princess* (*Ruten no ōhi*, 1960) followed the wartime experiences of a Japanese woman married to the brother of the puppet Emperor of Manchuria. *Love under the Crucifix* (*Ogin-sama*, 1962) was about the daughter of tea master Sen no Rikyū and her love for a Christian. Both films focused on the way in which historical events shape individual lives.

Tanaka's films were all broadly feminist and progressive, but she tended to shy away from their more controversial implications. Thus, the most interesting theme of *The Eternal Breasts*—that a woman might willingly choose career over marriage—was obscured by the film's subsequent concentration on her terminal illness. Similarly, in *Girls of Dark*, the heroine's choice to work is motivated by the fact that, being an ex-prostitute, she cannot find acceptance as a wife. *The Wandering Princess*, meanwhile, presented war as an abstract evil, largely ignoring the issue of Japanese responsibility for Chinese suffering.

Stylistically, Tanaka's films were always tasteful and restrained, without ever achieving a truly individual style. As befits a former actress, her greatest strength was in eliciting subtle, suggestive performances from her stars; particularly affecting contributions came from Yoshiko Kuga in *Love Letter*, Yumeji Tsukioka in *The Eternal Breasts*, and Machiko Kyō in *The Wandering Princess*.

**1953  Koibumi** / Love Letter
**1955  Tsuki wa noborinu** / The Moon Has Risen

**Chibusa yo eien nare** / The Eternal Breasts
**1960  Ruten no ōhi** / The Wandering Princess
**1961  Onna bakari no yoru** / Girls of Dark
**1962  Ogin-sama** / Love under the Crucifix (lit. Lady Ogin)

**TANAKA Noboru**
**(August 15, 1937–October 4, 2006)**
田中登

Usually ranked among the most talented filmmakers working on Roman Porno during the seventies, Tanaka served a lengthy apprenticeship to directors such as Shōhei Imamura, Seijun Suzuki, and Kei Kumai, beginning to direct as Nikkatsu switched production to erotic material. He soon earned favorable notice for the visual beauty he brought to this originally disreputable genre in films such as *Night-Train Woman* (*Yogisha no onna*, 1972), a story about a woman dangerously possessive of her half-sister. *Confidential Report: Sex Market* (*Maruhi: Shikijō mesu ichiba*, 1974), about the grim lives of Osaka prostitutes, was particularly well-received; though exploitative to a degree, it achieved a certain rough integrity thanks to its harsh, mainly black and white cinematography, claustrophobic compositions and atmospheric location work among the city's seedier districts.

Tanaka himself asserted that he preferred to make films in a less realistic, more stylized vein. Shot largely on studio sets, *The True Story of Abe Sada* (*Jitsuroku Abe Sada*, 1975) was an opulent account of a famous love affair that culminated with the woman murder-

Maruhi: Shikijō mesu ichiba / Confidential Report: Sex Market *(1974)*: *Tanaka's atmospheric location work won plaudits for the disreputable new genre of Roman Porno.*

ing her lover and amputating his sexual organ. Though more prurient and less psychologically perceptive in its depiction of sexual obsession than Ōshima's contemporary hardcore version of the story *In the Realm of the Senses* (*Ai no korīda*, 1976), Tanaka's film was still powerful thanks to Junko Miyashita's haunting lead performance. Also interesting, though somewhat less intense, was *Watcher in the Attic* (*Edogawa Ranpo ryōkikan: Yaneura no sanposha*, 1976), a visually inventive adaptation of an Edogawa Ranpo story about a bored *voyeur* spying on the sexual conduct of the tenants of an apartment block.

Leaving Nikkatsu to work freelance in the eighties, Tanaka went to Shochiku to direct the bleak *Village of Doom* (*Ushimitsu no mura*, 1983), a non-pornographic film about a country boy who massacres the inhabitants of his village after tuberculosis renders him unfit for military service. The film effectively exposed the roots of violence in a culture which presents the warrior as admirable;

regrettably, the handling of the massacre itself undermined this by making the slaughter gripping. After making his last film, another erotic melodrama, Tanaka worked mainly in television. The distinction of his best work probably owes as much to Nikkatsu art direction as to his directorial contribution, and his use of handheld camera and the zoom lens was often heavy-handed. Nevertheless, he was capable of creating very striking compositions, and the limitations of his films are perhaps more those of the exploitation format in which he worked than of his own talent.

1972   **Kaben no shizuku** / Dewdrops on the Petal
**Mesunekotachi no yoru** / Night of the Female Cats
**Yogisha no onna** / Night-Train Woman
**Kōshoku kazoku: Kitsune to tanuki** / Amorous Family: Fox and Racoon Dog
**Kannō kyōshitsu: Ai no tekunikku** / Classroom of the Senses: Techniques of Love

1973   **Hirusagari no jōji: Henshin** / Love in the Afternoon: Metamorphosis
**Maruhi: Jorozeme jigoku** / The Ill-Fated Courtesan / Confidential Report: Hell of Tortured Prostitutes (lit.)
**Mayonaka no yōsei** / The Midnight Fairy / Strange Feelings During the Night
**Onna kyōshi: Shiseikatsu** / Private Life of a School Mistress

1974   **Maruhi: Shikijō mesu ichiba** / Confidential Report: Sex Market / The Oldest Profession

1975   **Jitsuroku Abe Sada** / The True Story of Abe Sada / A Woman Called Abe Sada
**Kōbe kokusai gyangu** / International Gang in Kobe

1976   **Edogawa Ranpo ryōkikan: Yaneura no sanposha** / Watcher

in the Attic / Stroller in the Attic
(lit. Edogawa Ranpo's House of the
Bizarre: Stroller in the Attic)

**Andō Noboru no waga tōbō to
sex no kiroku** / The Sex Life and
Escape of Gangster Noboru Ando

1977 **Hakkinbon "Bijin ranbu" yori:
Semeru** / Banned Play / To Torture
(lit. From the Banned Book "Wild
Dance of a Beautiful Woman": To
Torture)

**Onna kyōshi** / School Mistress

1978 **Hitozuma shūdan bōkō chishi
jiken** / Group of Married Women:
Fatal Case of Assault

**Pinku Saron: Kōshoku gonin no
onna** / Pink Salon: Five Amorous
Women

1979 **Tenshi no harawata: Nami** / Angel
Guts: Nami

**Aiyoku no tāgetto** / Target of
Sexual Passion

1980 **Hādo sukyandaru: Sei no
hyōryūsha** / Hard Scandal: Sex
Drifter

1981 **Motto hageshiku motto tsuyoku** /
Harder and Stronger

1983 **Ushimitsu no mura** / Village of
Doom / A Village at Dawn (lit. A
Village after Midnight)

1986 **Tsubomi no nagame** / View of the
Bud / The Sight

1988 **Yōjo densetsu '88** / Monster
Woman '88 / A Woman in the Net
(lit. Legend of a Temptress '88)

# TANIGUCHI Senkichi
**(February 19, 1912–October 29, 2007)**
谷口千吉

Taniguchi's career has been overshadowed by that of his colleague and mentor, Akira Kurosawa; they had met in the thirties while serving as assistants to Kajirō Yamamoto at PCL (later Toho). After the war, the three men worked closely together, founding an independent production company, Motion Picture Arts Association; Yamamoto and Kurosawa also co-scripted Taniguchi's first narrative feature, *Snow Trail* (*Ginrei no hate*, 1947), a thriller about three robbers hiding out in the Japan Alps, which marked the debut of Toshirō Mifune, who was to act regularly for both Taniguchi and Kurosawa. Its concern with a criminal's innate humanity and potential for reformation was of a piece with Kurosawa's humanist philosophy. However, Taniguchi's *mise-en-scène* lacked the baroque qualities of Kurosawa's, displaying a classical economy more reminiscent of Hollywood filmmakers such as Raoul Walsh. This technique made him an ideal director of action material.

Kurosawa also scripted several of Taniguchi's subsequent films: *Jakoman and Tetsu* (*Jakoman to Tetsu*, 1949), with Mifune as the son of a fishing baron defending a Hokkaido village against a powerful criminal; *Beyond Love and Hate* (*Ai to nikushimi no kanata e*, 1951), another story about a criminal seeking refuge in the mountains; and *Spring Breeze* (*Fukeyo harukaze*, 1953) which sketched a cross-section of postwar society through the characters of the passengers encountered by an idealistic taxi driver. Their finest collaboration was *Escape to Tomorrow* (*Akatsuki no dassō*, 1950), a powerful war film about the love of a soldier for a "comfort woman," which not only condemned the doctrines of militarism, but also surprisingly presented the Chinese enemy as exemplars of humane values. This liberalism was probably Kurosawa's contribution, since Taniguchi's subsequent films included such xenophobic stories as the Meiji-period melodrama *Foghorns* (*Muteki*, 1952) and the Occupation-set *Red-Light*

*Bases* (*Akasen kichi*, 1953), both of which portrayed Americans as sexual exploiters of Japanese women. Among his other fifties work, *The Sound of Waves* (*Shiosai*, 1954), based on Mishima's story of a teenage love affair on a remote island, was notable for its visual beauty; it suffered, however, from the schematic everyman characterizations carried over from its source. Its romantic concerns were somewhat atypical, but it shared with many of Taniguchi's other films an interest in distant locales, which would be apparent as late as his last film, *Asante Sana* (*Asante sāna*, 1975), a Tanzanian-set story about Japanese Peace Corps volunteers.

In the sixties, Taniguchi made occasional forays into comedy, but continued to specialize mainly in action films, directing gangster movies such as *Man against Man* (*Otoko tai otoko*, 1960), war films like *Outpost of Hell* (*Dokuritsu kikanjūtai imada shagekichu*, 1963), conventional *jidai-geki* like *Chuji Kunisada* (*Kunisada Chūji*, 1960), and period fantasies such as *The Great Thief* (*Daitōzoku*, 1963). His work grew steadily less distinguished: *The Great Thief* was a cavalier *mélange* of Japanese, Arabic and European decor and plot motifs, aptly dismissed by Tony Rayns for its "bland rejection of the entire Oriental fantasy tradition," which enabled it to be distributed abroad, dubbed, as a Sinbad movie. This practice may have inspired Woody Allen to make *What's Up, Tiger Lily?*, a version of Taniguchi's *Key of Keys* (*Kokusai himitsu keisatsu: Kagi no kagi*, 1965) redubbed with farcical English-language dialogue. His later decline and the perception that Kurosawa was responsible for the quality of his early work have adversely affected Taniguchi's reputation. Nevertheless, his best films still rank among the most purely gripping made in Japan, and their terse power was Taniguchi's own achievement.

**1946 Tōhō shōbōto** / Toho Showboat

**1947 Ginrei no hate** / Snow Trail / To the End of the Silver-Capped Mountains (lit.)

**1949 Jakoman to Tetsu** / Jakoman and Tetsu

**1950 Akatsuki no dassō** / Escape to Tomorrow / Escape at Dawn (lit.) / Deserter at Dawn

**Ma no ōgon** / The Devil's Gold

**1951 Ai to nikushimi no kanata e** / Beyond Love and Hate

**Dare ga watashi o sabaku no ka** / Who Judges Me?

**Shi no dangai** / Cliff of Death

**1952 Muteki** / Foghorns

**Gekiryū** / Swift Current

**1953 Fukeyo harukaze** / Spring Breeze / My Wonderful Yellow Car / Blow! Spring Wind (lit.)

**Yoru no owari** / The End of the Night

**Akasen kichi** / Red-Light Bases

**1954 Shiosai** / The Sound of Waves / The Surf (lit.)

**1955 Sanjūsangōsha ōtō nashi** / No Response from Car 33

**1956 Kuroobi Sangokushi** / Black Belt Sangokushi / Rainy Night Duel

**Furyō shōnen** / Juvenile Delinquents

**Hadashi no seishun** / Barefoot Youth

**1957 Arashi no naka no otoko** / The Man in the Storm

**Saigo no dassō** / The Last Escape / The Last Pursuit

**Haruka naru otoko** / The Distant Man

**1960 Kunisada Chūji** / Chuji Kunisada / The Gambling Samurai

**Otoko tai otoko** / Man against Man

**1961 Kurenai no umi** / The Crimson Sea / Blood on the Sea

## TASAKA Tomotaka
### (April 14, 1902–October 17, 1974)
田坂具隆

An interesting but erratic director, Tasaka worked under contract at Nikkatsu from the twenties. His earliest surviving film, *Town of Love* (*Ai no machi*, 1928), is a superb example of the Westernized cinema of the late twenties, with a visual flair rivaling F. W. Murnau or Frank Borzage: the story was conceived as a political allegory, plotting the reconciliation of capital and labor through the reunion of a working girl with her industrialist grandfather. A similar fusion of social conscience with melodramatic plotting was apparently visible in the lost *Behold This Mother* (*Kono haha o miyo*, 1930), Tasaka's contribution to the leftist *keikō-eiga* genre, which detailed the vicissitudes of a widowed mother trying to make ends meet as she raises her son.

Most of Tasaka's prewar sound films are lost, but he seems to have specialized mainly in romantic melodrama: his most popular film in that genre was *The Life of a Woman in the Meiji Era* (*Meiji ichidai onna*, 1935), starring Takako Irie. Later, with two films based on novels by Yūzō Yamamoto, he adopted a more realistic approach: *A Pebble by the Wayside* (*Robō no ishi*, 1938), a chronicle of the unhappy experiences of a young boy, was typical of the melancholy naturalism prevalent in the Japanese cinema of the time. This remains extant, but today Tasaka's most famous works of the thirties are two contributions to the war effort, *Five Scouts* (*Gonin no sekkōhei*, 1938) and *Earth and Soldiers* (*Tsuchi to heitai*, 1939), the latter impressively shot on location in China. These films have been praised for their "humanism," but they, like the later *Navy* (*Kaigun*, 1943), were essentially well-crafted propaganda pieces celebrating duty, sacrifice, and the strength of the group.

Tasaka, who enlisted in the last months of the war, had the misfortune to be training in Hiroshima on August 6, 1945; his injuries and subsequent radiation sickness halted his career for some years. The legacy of the atomic bomb was the theme of one of his earliest postwar films, *I'll Not Forget the Song of Nagasaki* (*Nagasaki no uta wa wasureji*, 1952), in which he struggled to bring conviction to a contrived narrative about an American serviceman visiting the bombed city. Tasaka's later work tended towards low-key melodrama, a recurrent motif being

Tsuchi to heitai / Earth and Soldiers *(1939): Tasaka made some of the most famous works of wartime propaganda, including this film, shot on location in China.*

the experiences of the naive country girl in the big city. The finest example of this motif, and Tasaka's masterpiece, was *The Maid's Kid* (*Jochūkko*, 1955), a touching account of culture clash told through the story of the relationship between a northern girl and the wealthy Tokyo family for whom she works as a maid. Tasaka captured the visual and behavioral contrasts between the prosperous capital and the traditional, rural north, and elicited an outstanding lead performance from Sachiko Hidari. Variations on the same theme recurred in films of disparate subject matter: for instance, in *Street in the Sun* (*Hi no ataru sakamichi*, 1958), a contrived story of a country girl's encounter with a dysfunctional family, conceived as a vehicle for that icon of rebellious youth, Yūjirō Ishihara; and in *Lake of Tears* (*Umi no koto*,

1966), a moving romantic tragedy set in the world of silk manufacture. The same plot formation was also the basis of perhaps Tasaka's best film of the sixties, *The House in the Quarter* (*Gobanchō yūgirirō*, 1963), an intelligent story set in the milieu of a Kyoto brothel, and focusing on the bitter relations between a newcomer, the temple novice she loves, and the businesslike yet compassionate madam memorably played by Michiyo Kogure. This film also echoed Kon Ichikawa's *Conflagration* (*Enjō*, 1958), in dramatising the true story of the disturbed monk who burned down Kyoto's Golden Pavilion.

Tasaka's visual style was not particularly distinctive, and even in some of his creditable minor films, such as the late *Carpenter and Children* (*Chiisakobe*, 1962), about a carpenter who takes in homeless children after a fire, his tasteful manner could seem bland. Moreover, he was sometimes capable of turning out very substandard films. His best work, however—*The Maid's Kid* above all—commands respect for its intelligent realism and complexity of characterization.

1926 **Kabocha sōdōki** / Trouble about a Pumpkin

**Haha o tazunete sanbyakuri** / 300 Ri in Search of Mother

**Jōnetsu no ukishizumi** / Rise and Fall of Love

**Ikiten o tsuku** / The Spirit Strikes the Sky

**Shi no hōko (Zenpen; Chūhen; Kōhen)** / The Treasure House of Death (Parts 1, 2 and 3)

1927 **Tetsuwan kisha** / The Strong-Armed Journalist

**Seigi no yūsha** / Hero's Justice

**Kurotaka maru** / Black Hawk

**Arisan no kyōji** / A Child of Alishan

**Fūfu zenshū** / A Couple's Complete Works

**Shabon musume** / Soap Girl

**Kōsei** / Rehabilitation

1928 **Kekkon nijūsō (Zenpen; Kōhen)** / Marriage Duet (Parts 1 and 2)

**Muteppō jidai** / The Reckless Age

**Chikyū wa mawaru: Daiichibu: Kako hen** / The World Turns: Part 1: Past Chapter

**Ai no machi** / Town of Love

**Omoide no suifu** / Sailor in the Memory

1929 **Kyōen: Daiippen** / Banquet: Part 1

**Watashi to kanojo** / She and I

**Nikkatsu kōshinkyoku** / Nikkatsu March (*co-director*)

**Ai no fūkei** / Scenery of Love

**Kumo no ōza** / Throne of Clouds

1930 **Kono haha o miyo /** Behold This Mother

1931 **Fukeyo harukaze** / Blow, Spring Wind

**Kankanmushi wa utau** / The Rust-Cleaner Sings

**Gonin no yukai naru aibō** / Five Delightful Companions

**Kokoro no nichigetsu: Retsujitsu hen** / Heart of Day and Night: Part 1: Heat of Day

**Kokoro no nichigetsu: Gekkō hen** / Heart of Day and Night: Part 2: Light of Moon

1932 **Hatobue o fuku onna** / A Woman Who Plays the Dove Whistle

**Haru to musume** / Spring and a Girl

**Shōwa Shinsengumi** / Showa-Era Shinsengumi (*co-director*)

1934 **Tsuki yori no shisha** / Messenger from the Moon

1935 **Meiji ichidai onna** / The Life of a Woman in the Meiji Era

1936 **Tsuioku no bara** / Memory of a Rose

1937 **Shinjitsu ichiro: Chichi no maki** / The Road of Truth: Father Reel

**Shinjitsu ichiro: Haha no maki** / The Road of Truth: Mother Reel

1938 **Gonin no sekkōhei** / Five Scouts

**Robō no ishi** / A Pebble by the Wayside

1939 **Bakuon** / Airplane Drone

**Kūshū** / Air Raid (*co-director*)

**Tsuchi to heitai** / Earth and Soldiers / Mud and Soldiers

1941 **Kimi to boku** / You and Me (*supervision*)

1942 **Hahakogusa** / Mother-and-Child Grass

1943 **Kaigun** / Navy

1945 **Hisshōka** / Victory Song (*co-director*)

1949 **Doburoku no Tatsu** / Hard-Drinking Tatsu

1951 **Yukiwarisō** / Hepatica

1952 **Nagasaki no uta wa wasureji** / I'll Not Forget the Song of Nagasaki

1955 **Jochūkko** / The Maid's Kid

1956 **Ubaguruma** / The Pram / The Baby Carriage

1957  **Kyō no inochi** / The Life of Today / Pleasure of Life

1958  **Hi no ataru sakamichi** / Street in the Sun / Slope in the Sun / The Sunny-Hill Path

1959  **Wakai kawa no nagare** / The Stream of Youth

1960  **Shinran** / Shinran
**Zoku Shinran** / Shinran 2

1961  **Hadakakko** / Naked Child / Run, Genta, Run

1962  **Chiisakobe** / Carpenter and Children

1963  **Gobanchō yūgirirō** / The House in the Quarter / A House of Shame

1964  **Same** / The Sharks

1965  **Hiyameshi to Osan to Chan** / Cold Rice, Osan and Chan

1966  **Umi no koto** / Lake of Tears / A Blighted Love at the Lake

1968  **Sukurappu shūdan** / Scrap Collectors

## TERAYAMA Shūji
**(December 10, 1935–May 4, 1983)**
寺山修司

Like many modernist artists, Terayama worked in various media, and his film career forms only part of an oeuvre which also encompasses poetry, novels, and plays. In the theater he wrote, directed, and was the founder of the Tenjōsajiki Troupe, a group which pledged to "reform the world through poetry and imagination." His plays favored audience participation and had actors directly address the audience in order to challenge conventional expectations that assumed an active artist and passive spectator. *Throw Away Your Books, Let's Go Into the Streets* (*Sho o suteyo, machi e deyō*), in which teenagers read their own poems on stage, was the basis for one of

Terayama's later films, while *The Heathen* (*Jashūmon*) established the recurrent Terayama figure of the monstrous mother.

In the late sixties, Terayama began to script films for other directors, including Susumu Hani's *Inferno of First Love* (*Hatsukoi: Jigoku hen*, 1968) and Masahiro Shinoda's masterpiece *Buraikan* (1970). These were followed by his first features as director, *The Emperor Tomato Ketchup* (*Tomato kechappu kōtei*, 1970) and *Throw Away Your Books, Let's Go Into the Streets* (*Sho o suteyo, machi e deyō*, 1971). The former was a playful study of a revolution in which children take power, persecute adults, and assert their right to freedom of action and sexual expression. The latter, loosely adapted from Terayama's play, was a stylized account of coming-of-age, focusing on a young man's sexual awakening and troubled family relationships. Both these films were original and provocative, but their low budgets restricted Terayama's ability to create images as striking as his concepts.

These limitations were overcome in Terayama's next feature, *Pastoral Hide-and-Seek* (*Den'en ni shisu*, 1974), a witty, fictionalized account of his own childhood, which expertly synthesized the influences of traditional Japanese art forms, Freud, surrealism, the circus, and the modernism of the New Wave. This was another account of a boy's difficult family relationships, centering around his fantasies of murdering his mother; its modernist aesthetic showed in the presence of the adult Terayama admitting that his reminiscences are largely imaginary and trying to influence the actions of his younger self. Colorful, poetic, and darkly humorous, it was arguably Terayama's masterpiece.

With *The Boxer* (*Bokusā*, 1977), Terayama fastened his customary conceits to a more conventional narrative about a boy seeking to make it as a professional fighter. Another venture into commercial film was the international co-production *Fruits of Passion* (*Shanhai ijin shōkan: Chaina dōru*, 1980), a sexually explicit work set in a Shanghai brothel. With *Grass Labyrinth* (*Kusa meikyū*, 1979), however, Terayama returned to the territory of *Pastoral Hide-and-Seek* in a poetic, loose yet economical recapitulation of his characteristic motifs; less witty than its precursor, it was perhaps even more visually striking. Another recapitulation, containing such classic Terayama elements as the family hoping to stop time by collecting clocks, was the posthumously released *Farewell to the Ark* (*Saraba hakobune*, 1984), which charted a century in the life of a single village.

A multimedia artist *par excellence*, Terayama arguably expressed himself on film rather than through film; his work in cinema displayed a remarkable conceptual sophistication, but while individual images were astonishing, he never really developed a consistently expressive camera style. His most distinguished contribution to the cinema was probably his script for *Buraikan*, which benefited in realization from Masahiro Shinoda's more sophisticated *mise-en-scène*. One might have reservations, too, about the recurrent notion of crime as a liberating force. Nonetheless, Terayama's films were consistently imaginative and suggestive, and he contrived some of the most extraordinary single moments in Japanese cinema, which was robbed by his premature death of one of its most individual and intransigent talents.

1960 **Nekogaku** / Catology (*16mm short*)

1964 **Ori** / Cage (*16mm short*)

1970 **Tomato kechappu kōtei** / The Emperor Tomato Ketchup (*16mm; short and feature versions*)

1971 **Janken sensō** / The War of Jan Ken Pon (*16mm short*)

**Sho o suteyo machi e deyō** / Throw Away Your Books, Let's Go into the Streets

1974 **Seishōnen no tame no eiga nyūmon** / Young Person's Guide to the Cinema / An Introduction to the Cinema for Boys and Young Men (*16mm short*)

**Chōfukuki** / Butterfly Dress Pledge (*16mm short*)

**Rōra** / Roller (*16mm short*)

**Den'en ni shisu** / Pastoral Hide-and-Seek / Death in the Country (lit.)

1975 **Meikyūtan** / Labyrinth Tale (*16mm short*)

**Hōsōtan** / Tales of Smallpox (*16mm short*)

**Shinpan** / Der Prozess (*16mm short*)

1977 **Keshigomu** / Eraser (*16mm short*)

**Marudorōru no uta** / Les Chants de Maldoror (*16mm short*)

**Issunbōshi o kijutsu suru kokoromi** / Attempt to Describe a Dwarf / Attempt to Describe the Measure of a Man (*16mm short*)

**Bokusā** / The Boxer

**Nitō onna: Kage no eiga** / Shadow Film: The Two-Headed Woman (*16mm short*)

**Shokenki** / The Reading Machine

1979 **Kusa meikyū** / Grass Labyrinth

1980 **Shanhai ijin shōkan: Chaina dōru** / Fruits of Passion / The Story of O Continued (lit. Shanghai Foreigners' Brothel: China Doll)

1984 **Saraba hakobune** / Farewell to the Ark

## TESHIGAHARA Hiroshi
### (January 28, 1927–April 14, 2001)
勅使河原宏

A modernist who worked in many media, Teshigahara initially directed documentaries, including some on aspects of traditional Japanese culture such as *ikebana* and the great woodblock artist Hokusai. He made his early feature films in collaboration with another *avant-garde* artist, novelist Kōbō Abe, whose fiction distilled existential themes from generic premises. His first and best feature, *Pitfall* (*Otoshiana*, 1962), detailed a series of murders in a mining town from the point of view of the victims' ghosts. Dan Harper has discussed the film's thematic connection with Antonioni's *L'Avventura* (1960) as a mystery without a solution, but the tone was less of melancholy than of bewilderment, alienation residing in the contrast between the straightforward desire of the dead for an explanation and the ambiguous tangle of motives and intentions among the living. *Woman of the Dunes* (*Suna no onna*, 1964) was a parable about an entomologist held hostage by the inhabitants of a village who compel him to sweep away the sand which constantly threatens to cover the community. Though the central irony—the entomologist himself becoming trapped like a fly in a web—was somewhat facile, the film's investigation of the way in which people use arbitrary tasks to give meaning to their lives was fascinating. Despite their thematic abstraction, these films were anchored in physical reality by their striking black and white imagery and location shooting; the industrial wastelands of *Pitfall* and the sands of *Woman of the Dunes* seemed tangible. Also impressive was the unsettling music by *avant-garde* composer Tōru

Takemitsu, who would compose scores for all of Teshigahara's films.

Teshigahara's subsequent collaborations with Abe were less remarkable. *The Face of Another* (*Tanin no kao*, 1966) was a flawed fantasy about the experiences of a badly burnt man who receives an artificial face. Though Teshigahara's imagery was again visually startling, the bland characterization of the anti-hero sapped conviction from the interesting thesis that appearance shapes personality. *The Man without a Map* (*Moetsukita chizu*, 1968) focused similarly on themes of identity with its story of a detective whose life merges with that of the man whose disappearance he is investigating. These existential concerns may have been more Abe's than Teshigahara's. *Summer Soldiers* (*Samā sorujā*, 1972), scripted by American writer John Nathan, essayed topical subject matter—the plight of American deserters from Vietnam hiding in Japan—and replaced the stylistic flamboyance of Teshigahara's sixties films with an informal, improvisational approach influenced by such independent filmmakers as John Cassavetes and Bob Rafelson.

After this, Teshigahara made no features for more than a decade, devoting himself increasingly to the Sōgetsu Foundation, the *ikebana* school of which he became *iemoto*, succeeding his father, in 1980. His later films encapsulated the duality of classical and *avant-garde* influences on his work. *Antonio Gaudi* (*Antonī Gaudī*, 1984), a documentary on the Catalan architect, was a tribute from one modernist to another, while *Rikyu* (*Rikyū*, 1989), the chronicle of the quarrel between tea master Sen no Rikyū and warlord Hideyoshi, was the clearest evidence in his narrative films of Teshigahara's background in the traditional arts. At the same time, it was a study of cultural pluralism, depicting such Japanese arts as *ikebana*, Noh, and tea ceremony, but using Renaissance-style music on the soundtrack, and examining the role of Portuguese traders and missionaries in Momoyama-era Japan. Teshigahara's interest was in the political function of the arts, and he implied that the aesthetic, even in so abstract a medium as *ikebana* or ceramics, is inescapably political. His last feature, *Basara: The Princess Goh* (*Gōhime*, 1992), was envisaged as a follow-up, narrating events at Hideyoshi's court after Rikyū's suicide; though visually beautiful, it was a relatively conventional period melodrama.

Teshigahara's themes were noncommunication and isolation; his characters often share the frame, but inhabit different worlds. This was literally the case with the ghosts of *Pitfall*, who can neither be seen nor heard by the living. Metaphorically, it applied to the entomologist of *Woman of the Dunes*, an educated urban professional bewildered by the primitivism of the society under the dunes; to the socially isolated disfigured protagonists of *The Face of Another*; to the American deserters of *Summer Soldiers*, helpless in a country where they understand neither the culture nor the language; and to the mutually hostile aesthete and politician of *Rikyu*. The investigation of these themes from both political and existential perspectives made Teshigahara's small body of work extremely rich and complex in implication; he was also one of the most imaginative visual stylists of the Japanese New Wave.

1953 Hokusai (*short*)
1955 12-nin no shashinka / 12 Photographers (*short*)
1956 Ikebana (*short*)
1958 Tōkyō 1958 / Tokyo 1958 (*short*)
1959 Hozē Toresu / Jose Torres (*short*)

1962 Otoshiana / Pitfall
1964 Suna no onna / Woman of the Dunes
1965 Shiroi asa / Ako (lit. White Morning) (*short*)
Hozē Toresu: Dainibu / Jose Torres Part 2 (*short*)
1966 Tanin no kao / The Face of Another
Indirēsu chōhen kiroku eiga: Bakuso / Bakuso (lit. Independent Race: Long Version Documentary: At Full Speed) (*short*)
1968 Moetsukita chizu / The Man without a Map / The Ruined Map (lit.)
1970 1-nichi 240-jikan / 240 Hours in One Day (*short*)
1972 Samā sorujā / Summer Soldiers
1981 Ugoku chōkoku : Jan Tingerī / Sculpture Mouvante: Jean Tinguely (*short*)
1984 Antonī Gaudī / Antonio Gaudi
1989 Rikyū / Rikyu
1992 Gōhime / Basara: The Princess Goh

## TOYODA Shirō
## (December 25, 1905–November 13, 1977)
## 豊田四郎

An expert craftsman who flourished under the classical studio system, Toyoda never really developed a personal style, but directed films of considerable intelligence and visual imagination. In the thirties, with films such as *Young People* (*Wakai hito*, 1937), about a schoolgirl's love for her teacher, and *The Bush Warbler* (*Uguisu*, 1938)—sketches of events in a rural police station—he contributed to the establishment of the *jun-bungaku* ("pure literature") movement, which looked to prestigious Japanese novels for source material. The bulk of his work after the war, too, was literary adaptation, made mainly at Toho; indeed, the list of authors whose books he filmed reads like an encyclopedia of twentieth-century Japanese novelists.

Though his adaptations were not slavishly faithful to their originals, Toyoda usually strove for a precise rendition of the tone and meaning of his source. Thus, he reproduced the melancholy realism of Fumiko Hayashi in *Crybaby Apprentice* (*Nakimushi kozō*, 1938), the story of a neglected child, and the melancholy romanticism of Ōgai Mori in *Wild Geese* (*Gan*, 1953), about an unhappy wife's love for a student. *Marital Relations* (*Meoto zenzai*, 1955), chronicling the affair between the son of a wealthy family and a geisha, transposed the tender comedy of Sakunosuke Oda to the screen; *A Cat, Shozo and Two Women* (*Neko to Shōzō to futari no onna*, 1956), in which an innocent animal becomes a symbol of the tensions between a hapless man and his first and second wives, successfully dramatized the perverse humor of Jun'ichirō Tanizaki; and *Snow Country* (*Yukiguni*, 1957), about a geisha's love for a selfish, introverted man, captured Yasunari Kawabata's subtle depiction of sexual tensions. *Twilight Story* (*Bokutō kidan*, 1960) was a representation of Kafū Nagai's Tokyo *demimonde* of prostitutes and low life, while *Portrait of Hell* (*Jigoku hen*, 1969), about an artist depicting hell on a folding screen for a sadistic lord, visualized the macabre aestheticism of Ryūnosuke Akutagawa.

To the degree that Toyoda's work manifested any thematic consistency, it was in expressing the recurrent concerns of Japanese fiction. *Young People, Wild Geese, Snow Country, Evening Calm* (*Yūnagi*, 1957), and *Sweet Sweat* (*Amai ase*, 1964) all focused on the sufferings of women—some unhappily in love, some torn between duty and personal fulfilment or between modernity and tradition. The last-mentioned of these films, "the story of the rise and fall of an utterly commercial woman" (Donald Richie's phrase), was one of Toyoda's finest, and was not an adaptation: evidence that the quality of his best work was not merely a reflection of the excellence of his sources, but also a consequence of his sensitivity and good taste. Nor were his virtues purely literary. *Wild Geese*, in particular, expressed the suppressed emotions of its trapped heroine through an almost mathematically precise use of interior geography, the distances between actors, the patterns of light on faces, and the dividing lines of *shōji*, slatted windows, sliding doors, and mosquito nets. Much of the power of *Snow Country*, too, can be ascribed to Toyoda's grasp of the emotional resonances of interior and exterior spaces.

Other films, such as the *bildungsroman Pilgrimage at Night* (*An'ya kōro*, 1959), based on Naoya Shiga's semi-autobiographical novel, were more conventionally realized, but Toyoda's work nevertheless displayed a consistent care and professionalism. The director himself stressed the importance of structure, continuity, and particularly casting, and his films were given depth by the superb acting he elicited from performers such as Ryō Ikebe, Hideko Takamine, Keiko Kishi, Machiko Kyō, Hisaya Morishige, and Chikage Awashima. The last two of these, acting together, made *Marital Relations* one of the screen's most mature and compelling depictions of sexual love. Toyoda's work was also distinguished by its exact atmosphere of time and place: in *Wild Geese*, the Meiji period; in *The Grass Whistle* (*Mugibue*,

1955), a melancholy story of a teenage love triangle, the Taisho period; the suburbs of prewar Osaka in *Marital Relations*; and Tokyo's decaying *shitamachi* area in *Twilight Story*. Often authenticity was achieved by location shooting: among the dazzling snowscapes of mountainous Niigata Prefecture for *Snow Country*; in Okinawa for *Oyake Akahachi* (1937), about a historical rebel who campaigned against the ill-treatment of the peasantry; and in the Inland Sea for *Spring on a Small Island* (*Kojima no haru*, 1940), where picturesque island backdrops offset the sombre story of a doctor's efforts to combat leprosy among the local population.

Though most of Toyoda's films were quality productions, he was sometimes assigned to commercial potboilers. *Legend of the White Serpent* (*Byakufujin no yōren*, 1956) was a special-effects-laden blockbuster, based on a Chinese legend about a man's love for a demonic woman; *Illusion of Blood* (*Yotsuya kaidan*, 1965) was a violent rendition of the old Kabuki standby, *The Yotsuya Ghost Story*; and *The Hotelman's Holiday* (*Kigeki: Ekimae ryokan*, 1958), a raucous account of events in an inn beside Ueno station, initiated a popular series of broad comedies to which Toyoda later contributed two further installments. His inability to transcend second-rate material exposed the limitations of his self-effacing approach, but his best films displayed a delicacy and discretion which remain wholly admirable.

1929 **Irodorareru kuchibiru** / Painted Lips

**Tokai o oyogu onna** / The Woman Who Swims in the City

1930 **Yūai kekkon** / Companionate Marriage

**Kokoro ogoreru onna** / The Heart of a Proud Woman

1935 **Sannin no josei** / Three Women

1936 **Tōkyō-Ōsaka tokudane ōrai** / Tokyo-Osaka Scoop

**Ōbantō kobantō** / Senior Clerk and Junior Clerk

**Kamata Ōfuna sutajio no haru** / Kamata and the Springtime of Ofuna Studios (*short*)

1937 **Minato wa uwakikaze** / Harbor of Fickle Winds

**Oyake Akahachi**

**Wakai hito** / Young People

**Jūji hōka** / Crossfire

1938 **Nakimushi kozō** / Crybaby Apprentice

**Fuyu no yado** / Winter Lodging

**Uguisu** / The Bush Warbler / Nightingale

1940 **Okumura Ioko** / Ioko Okumura

**Kojima no haru** / Spring on a Small Island / Spring on Leper's Island

**Ōhinata mura** / Ohinata Village

1941 **Waga ai no ki** / The Story of Our Love

1943 **Wakaki sugata** / Young Figure

1946 **Hinoki butai** / The Limelight / Cypress Boards (lit.)

1947 **Yottsu no koi no monogatari** / Four Love Stories (*co-director*)

1948 **Waga ai wa yama no kanata ni** / My Love Is Beyond the Mountains

1949 **Hakuchō wa kanashikarazuya** / The Swan Is Not Sad

1950 **Onna no shiki** / The Four Seasons of Women

1951 **Eriko to tomo ni (Daiichibu; Dainibu)** / With Eriko (Parts 1 and 2)

**Sekirei no kyoku** / The Wagtail's Song

1952 **Kaze futatabi** / The Wind Blows Twice

**Haru no sasayaki** / Whisper of Spring

1953 **Gan** / Wild Geese / The Mistress

1954 **Aru onna** / A Certain Woman

1955 **Mugibue** / The Grass Whistle / The Wheat Whistle / Love Never Fails

**Meoto zenzai** / Marital Relations / Love Is Like Shared Sweets

1956 **Byakufujin no yōren** / Legend of the White Serpent / The Bewitching Love of Madame Pai / Madame White Snake

**Neko to Shōzō to futari no onna** / A Cat, Shozo and Two Women

1957 **Yukiguni** / Snow Country

**Yūnagi** / Evening Calm / The Veil of Sin

1958 **Makeraremasen katsu made wa** / We Can't Lose Until We Win

**Kigeki: Ekimae ryokan** / The Hotelman's Holiday / The Inn in Front of the Train Station (lit.)

1959 **Hana noren** / Flower Shop Curtain

**Dansei shiiku hō** / Bringing Up Husbands

**An'ya kōro** / Pilgrimage at Night / A Dark Night's Passing

1960 **Chinpindō shujin** / The Curio Master

**Bokutō kidan** / Twilight Story / A Strange Story of East of the Sumida River

1961 **Tōkyō yawa** / The Diplomat's Mansion (lit. Tokyo Night Story)

1962 **Ashita aru kagiri** / Till Tomorrow Comes (lit. As Long as There Is Tomorrow)

**Ikanaru hoshi no moto ni** / Under Any Star

1963 **Yūshū heiya** / Madame Aki (lit. Plain of Melancholy)

**Daidokoro Taiheiki** / The Maid's Story (lit. The Kitchen Taiheiki)

**Shin meoto zenzai** / Marital Relations, New Version

1964 **Kigeki: Yōkina mibōjin** / The Merry Widow

**Amai ase** / Sweet Sweat

1965 **Namikage** / Shadow of the Waves

**Yotsuya kaidan** / Illusion of Blood / The Yotsuya Ghost Story (lit.)

**Daiku Taiheiki** / Tale of a Carpenter (lit. The Carpenter's Taiheiki)

1967 **Chikumagawa zesshō** / River of Forever

**Kigeki: Ekimae hyakunen** / A Hundred Years in Front of the Station

1968 **Kigeki: Ekimae kaiun** / Better Days in Front of the Station

1969 **Jigoku hen** / Portrait of Hell

1973 **Kōkotsu no hito** / Twilight Years (lit. Senile Person)

1976 **Tsuma to onna no aida** / Between Women and Wives

## TOYODA Toshiaki
(b. March 10, 1969)
豊田利晃

Toyoda's early work has proved representative of a vein of stylish nihilism prominent in twenty-first-century Japanese film. He worked initially as an assistant and screenwriter to Junji Sakamoto, whose boxing film *Knock Out* (*Dotsuitarunen*, 1989) had first inspired him to follow a career in cinema; his own documentary, *Unchain* (2001), focused on a boxer who has lost every bout he has ever fought. However, his first two fiction features, *Pornostar* (1998) and *Blue Spring* (*Aoi haru*, 2002), seemed indebted less to Sakamoto than to the elegant presentation of ultra-violence in the work of such contemporary figures as Shinji Aoyama, Takeshi Miike, and Takeshi Kitano. *Pornostar*, about a taciturn youth slaughtering yakuza in Tokyo, seemed almost a pastiche of Aoyama's early crime movies. *Blue Spring* was perhaps a response to *Battle Royale* (*Batoru Rowaiaru*, 2000): while in Kinji Fukasaku's film anarchic violence breaks out at the command of an adult

Kūchū teien / The Hanging Garden *(2005): This funny and chilling satire suggests its director may yet create outstanding work.*

authority, here violent power structures are seen to be internalized by the kids themselves. Both films, *Blue Spring* in particular, were visually remarkable, but the succession of startling camera angles often seemed bludgeoning, and hints of social commentary were belied by the artificiality of the premises, not to mention the gusto with which Toyoda filmed scenes of violence.

*9 Souls* (2003), about a prison breakout by a group of convicts, attempted to achieve greater depth, incorporating certain complexities of characterization and a few reflective moments. Nevertheless, thanks to Toyoda's penchant for stylistic pyrotechnics and creative bloodletting, it was still rather more style than substance. The Hanging Garden (*Kūchū*

*teien*, 2005), however, marked a departure from his previous subject matter, starting from the Buñuel-like premise of a family that insists on total honesty in all discussion. Set suggestively in one of the soulless conurbations which have sprung up around Japan's major cities, this alternately funny and chilling satire was Toyoda's most successful film, critically and commercially, in Japan. Though still stylistically uneven, it was certainly an advance, and suggested that the director may yet produce outstanding work if he can develop the stylistic maturity to control his undeniable talent.

1998   **Pornostar** / Pornostar / Tokyo
        Rampage
2001   **Unchain**

2002 **Aoi haru** / Blue Spring
2003 **9 Souls**
2005 **Kūchū teien** / The Hanging Garden

## TSUCHIMOTO Noriaki
## (December 11, 1928 - June 24, 2008)
## 土本典昭

A onetime student activist, Tsuchimoto sustained a long career making documentary films on progressive themes. He worked initially alongside such talented filmmakers as Kazuo Kuroki and Susumu Hani at Iwanami Productions before raising funds independently to make his first personal film, *Chua Swee Lin, Exchange Student* (*Ryūgakusei Chua Sui Rin*, 1965), about the prejudice faced by a Malaysian Chinese student at a Japanese university. Another film with a university setting was *Prehistory of the Partisans* (*Paruchizan zenshi*, 1969), a portrait of student extremists at Kyoto University, made for fellow documentarist Shinsuke Ogawa's production company. Tsuchimoto's most extensive project was the sequence of documentaries initiated by *Minamata: The Victims and Their World* (*Minamata: Kanja-san to sono sekai*, 1971), a haunting record of the sufferings of villagers afflicted by Minamata Disease, a form of poisoning caused by industrial mercury pollution in the seas around the Kyushu town of Minamata. Tsuchimoto juxtaposed footage of the victims and their campaign for compensation with depictions of the traditional lifestyles threatened by industrialization. Thereafter, Minamata became the dominant concern of Tsuchimoto's cinema: in an extensive series of films, made over the course of decades, he depicted the victims and their families and charted their

continuing struggle for compensation. *Shiranui Sea* (*Shiranui umi*, 1975), made after their court victory, followed the victims as they continue to deal with the effects of the disease.

Tsuchimoto first broached a concern with Japan's reliance on nuclear energy in *Nuclear Power Scrapbook* (*Genpatsu kirinukichō*, 1982), a short documentary consisting entirely of newpaper clippings on that subject. Nuclear energy was also the theme of his next feature-length project, which, like the Minamata documentaries, focused on a traditional community threatened by progress. *Robbing of the Sea: Shimokita Peninsula* (*Umitori: Shimokita hantō: Hamasekine*, 1984) detailed the reactions of villagers to a decision to construct a port for a nuclear-powered ship on the northerly Shimokita Peninsula; Tsuchimoto exposed the indifference of government and big business to local feelings. Subsequently, while continuing to focus on the sufferings of those exploited by established authority, Tsuchimoto widened his focus to the international arena. Working in collaboration with his compatriot Hiroko Kumagai and Afghan filmmaker Abdul Latif, he made *Afghan Spring* (*Yomigaere karēzu*, 1989), an examination of society and politics in Afghanistan at the time of the Soviet withdrawal, which now serves as a valuable record of a culture soon after partially obliterated by the Taliban regime.

Although Tsuchimoto's films were invariably partisan, he acknowledged the dangers of such partisanship, calling the "violent, compulsory power" of close ups a potentially fascistic device, and emphasizing the usefulness of long shots in establishing "a critical point of view." His frequent staging of interviews in long shot where he himself appeared on screen may be taken as an acknowledgment of his own subjectivity and a refusal to present his position as an uncomplicated truth.

1963 **Aru kikan joshi** / An Engineer's Assistant

1964 **Dokumento: Rojō** / Document: On the Road

1965 **Ryūgakusei Chua Sui Rin** / Chua Swee Lin, Exchange Student

1968 **Shiberiya-jin no sekai** / The World of the People of Siberia

1969 **Paruchizan zenshi** / Prehistory of the Partisans / Pre-Partisans

1971 **Minamata: Kanja-san to sono sekai** / Minamata: The Victims and Their World

1973 **Minamata repōto 1: Jitsuroku kōchōi** / Minamata Document: The Central Pollution Board

**Minamata ikki: Isshō o tou hitobito** / Riot at Minamata: A People's Quest for Life

1975 **Igaku toshite no Minamatabyō: Daiichibu: Shiryō shōgen hen** / Minamata Disease: Progress of Research

**Igaku toshite no Minamatabyō: Dainibu: Byōri byōma hen** / Minamata Disease: Pathology and Symptoms

**Igaku toshite no Minamatabyō: Daisanbu: Rinshō ekigaku hen** / Minamata Disease: Clinical Field Studies

**Shiranui umi** / Shiranui Sea

1976 **Message from Minamata to the World**

**Minamatabyō: Sono nijūnen** / Minamata Disease: 20 Years On

1977 **Shibarareta te no inori** / Prayer with Tied Hands

1978 **Waga machi waga seishun: Ishikawa Sayuri Minamata nesshō** / Our Town, Our Youth: Sayuri Ishikawa's Heartfelt Song of Minamata

1979 **Nihon no wakamono wa ima** / Japan's Young People Now

**Shinobu: Nakano Shigeharu** / Remembering Shigeharu Nakano

1981 **Minamata no zu: Monogatari** / Map of Minamata: A Tale

**Umi to otsukisamatachi** / The Sea and Moons

1982 **Genpatsu kirinukichō** / Nuclear Power Scrapbook

1984 **Umitori: Shimokita hantō: Hamasekine** / Robbing of the Sea: Shimokita Peninsula

**Hajike hōsenka : Waga Chikuhō waga Chōsen** / Balsam, Disperse Your Seeds: Our Chikuho, Our Korea

1987 **Minamatabyō: Sono sanjūnen** / Minamata Disease: 30 Years On

1989 **Yomigaere karēzu** / Afghan Spring (*co-director*)

1999 **Kaisō: Kawamoto Terao: Minamata: Ido o hotta hito** / Reminiscence: Terao Kawamoto: The Man Who Dug the Well at Minamata

2003 **Aishihi no Kāburu hakubutsukan: 1988-nen** / Traces: The Kabul Museum 1988

**Mō hitotsu no Afuganisutan: Kāburu nikki 1985-nen** / Another Afghanistan: Kabul Diary 1985

2005 **Hiroshima no Pika** / Pika from Hiroshima (*co-director*)

## TSUKAMOTO Shin'ya
### (b. January 1, 1960)
塚本晋也

Influenced by and often compared with David Lynch and David Cronenberg, Tsukamoto made 8mm amateur films as a teenager and directed advertisements before making his professional debut with *Tetsuo: The Iron Man* (*Tetsuo*, 1989). This low-budget, virtually plotless film about a man's inadvertent transformation into a cyborg earned an

©Kaijyu Theater/Tsukamoto Shin'ya

Tetsuo / Tetsuo: The Iron Man *(1989): This is the low-budget, virtually plotless film that inaugurated Tsukamoto's David Lynch–like vision.*

inexplicable cult reputation which enabled Tsukamoto to obtain funding for a sequel-cum-remake, *Tetsuo II: Body Hammer* (1992), and a more generic horror film, *Hiruko the Goblin* (*Hiruko: Yōkai hantā*, 1991). An interest in fantasy was still apparent in *Gemini* (*Sōseiji*, 1999), a visually opulent rendition of an Edogawa Ranpo story about a doctor and his vengeful twin, and, with its Meiji-era setting, Tsukamoto's only historical film. However, most of his mature films have rejected more obviously fantastic elements to focus on alienation in a modern urban environment. Tsukamoto's theme, in Tom Mes's words, is "the rediscovery of the feelings that were numbed by the drudging routine of urban life," and his most interesting films, like Lynch's, have explored instincts and desires usually kept suppressed. Thus, he has dwelt upon the

way in which routine existence is shattered by a crisis: in *Bullet Ballet* (*Baretto barē*, 1998) and *Vital* (*Vaitāru*, 2004), by death; in *Tokyo Fist* (*Tōkyō fisuto*, 1995) and *A Snake of June* (*Rokugatsu no hebi*, 2002), by sexual transgression.

A focus on sexual perversion has proved a consistent feature of Tsukamoto's work. The theme of *Tokyo Fist* was sado-masochism, expressed both in the overt sexuality of the heroine and the sublimated sexuality, in the boxing ring, of the male rivals for her affection. The bored housewife of *A Snake of June* is blackmailed into performing sex acts in public, while *Vital* hinted at themes of necrophilia in its story of a medical student dissecting the body of the girl who died after they were involved together in a car crash. Though superficially subversive, these films were nonetheless somewhat reactionary in implication:

the body horror of *Tetsuo* was rooted in homophobia and in fear of female sexuality. Such traits were also visible in *Tokyo Fist*, where female sexuality was the root cause of the crisis, and the liberation of the instincts was seen to result in brutal violence. Similarly, in *A Snake of June*, the harmless sexual transgression of masturbation initiates the heroine's ordeal at the blackmailer's hands. *Gemini* was politically more interesting in that its horror derived from class conflicts rather than sexuality; here, the vengeful brother represented the urban poor despised and neglected by their "civilized" wealthy neighbors.

Tsukamoto's style, as much as his themes, has been influenced by David Lynch: his films unfold in everyday settings "made strange" by thrusting camera angles, extreme close ups and fast motion. In his early work the effect was often grotesque: the pyrotechnics of *Tokyo Fist* dwelt so insistently on physical violence that the psychological complexity of the situation was sidelined. Tsukamoto's work in the twenty-first century, however, has used the same stylistic idiosyncrasies with a greater discipline: the blue-tinted, rainswept Tokyo of *A Snake of June* was an appropriately unsettling backdrop to its story of troubling emotions, while in *Vital*, Tsukamoto's tenderest film, the self-conscious compositions effectively reflected the dislocated outlook of its protagonist, a recovering amnesiac.

From the evidence of Tsukamoto's most recent work, the future direction of his career remains uncertain. With *Haze* (2005), a compact allegory about a man trapped in a labyrinth, he returned to the limited means and claustrophobic settings of *Tetsuo*. *Nightmare Detective* (*Akuma tantei*, 2006), on the other hand, was arguably his most commercial project to date: a glossy horror thriller with echoes of *A Nightmare on Elm Street* (1984, Wes Craven) in its story of victims induced to commit suicide in their sleep. Here, Tsukamoto's fruitful concern with the emotional consequences of physical frailty was underdeveloped; the spectacular bloodletting generated superficial shocks rather than piercing insights. The fact that he is working on a sequel to this film at the time of writing is not a wholly auspicious development. Nevertheless, it is unlikely that Tsukamoto will abandon the more experimental aspects of his work. If he has been overpraised in some quarters—even his best films are flawed by stylistic overstatement and dubious sexual politics—he has nevertheless proved himself an intransigent and individual talent, and it is likely that he will continue to surprise his audiences.

**1974 Genshi-san** / Mr. Primitive (*8mm short*)
**1975 Kyodai gokiburi monogatari** / Story of a Giant Cockroach (*8mm*)
**Tsubasa** / Wing (*8mm short*)
**1976 Donten** / Cloudy Sky (*8mm*)
**1977 Jigokumachi shōben geshuku nite tonda yo** / Flying in a Hell Town Piss Lodge (*8mm*)
**1978 Shin tsubasa** / Wing 2 (*8mm short*)
**1979 Hasu no hana tobe** / Lotus Flower, Fly! (*8mm*)
**1986 Futsū saizu no kaijin** / The Phantom of Regular Size (*8mm*)
**1987 Denchū Kozō no bōken** / The Adventure of Denchu Kozo (*8mm*)
**1989 Tetsuo** / Tetsuo: The Iron Man
**1991 Hiruko: Yōkai hantā** / Hiruko the Goblin
**1992 Tetsuo II: Body Hammer**
**1995 Tōkyō fisuto** / Tokyo Fist
**1998 Baretto barē** / Bullet Ballet
**1999 Sōseiji** / Gemini

## UCHIDA Tomu
### (April 26, 1898–August 7, 1970)
### 内田吐夢

Nearly four decades after his death, Uchida has only just begun to acquire an international reputation. Earlier appreciation may have been hindered by his status as a genre filmmaker when foreign audiences looked to the Japanese cinema for high art, but in fact, Uchida resembled such American directors as Anthony Mann who evolved personal resonances and ideological complexities from generic plots. In addition to their visual flair and intelligent social criticism, his films displayed a trenchant psychological insight, particularly in the recurrent focus on antagonists perversely bound together by their mutual hatred, a theme which formed the heart of *A Hole of My Own Making* (*Jibun no ana no naka de*, 1955), *The Outsiders* (*Mori to mizuumi no matsuri*, 1958), and *Straits of Hunger* (*Kiga kaikyō*, 1965).

Though most famous as a maker of samurai films, Uchida attached himself initially to the progressive *keikō-eiga* genre. His most admired contribution to this species of socially conscious filmmaking was *A Living Doll* (*Ikeru ningyō*, 1929), about a man who uses unscrupulous means to advance in society. Sadly this is now lost, as is *Champion of Revenge* (*Adauchi senshu*, 1931), in which Uchida's talent as a satirist was transferred to a period setting and trained on the codes of bushidō. However, the extant *Sweat* (*Ase*, 1930), another sharp satire about a millionaire playboy reduced by accidental circumstances to working as a laborer, visibly anticipated the sceptical attitude to class distinctions of his later work. A more conservative outlook was discernible in another surviving silent, the stylish and gripping thriller *Police* (*Keisatsukan*, 1933), which preached a message of social responsibility through its story of childhood friends on opposite sides of the law.

Later in the thirties, at Nikkatsu, Uchida became associated with the *junbungaku* ("pure literature") movement of prestigious literary adaptations: films such as *Theater of Life* (*Jinsei gekijō*, 1936) and *The Naked Town* (*Hadaka no machi*, 1937) are said to have been significant in introducing a novelistic realism into Japanese cinema. However, *Unending Advance* (*Kagiri naki zenshin*, 1937), from an Ozu script about a salaryman contemplating an insecure future after he is forced into early retirement, combined realistic observation with the extravagant fantasy of the sequences dramatizing the protagonist's unfulfilled dreams. Uchida's most famous prewar film, *Earth* (*Tsuchi*, 1939), was a humanist account of peasant life, shot on location in northern Japan over the course of a year. Again, its dramatic realism was offset by a rhetorical style patterned on German and Soviet models.

During the war, Uchida went to work in Manchuria and was not repatriated until the fifties. After returning to Japan, he directed mainly at Toei, specializing in samurai films. *Bloody Spear at Mount Fuji* (*Chiyari Fuji*, 1955), a picaresque account of the relationship between a foolish lord, his shrewd servant, and his spear carrier, revived the spirit of prewar directors such as Daisuke Itō (its co-writer) and Mansaku Itami with its well-judged blend of comedy and violence and its criticism of feudal values. These qualities were also visible in Uchida's other eccentric *jidai-geki*. *The Master Spearman* (*Sake to onna to yari*, 1960) was a wry black comedy which turned its account of a samurai refusing to fight into a sly satire on an audience eager for scenes of bloodshed. *The Horse Boy* (*Abarenbō kaidō*, 1957), one of Uchida's most underrated films, was an engaging and moving tragicomedy about a rogueish child raised as an orphan after his mother is forced to abandon him. Here Uchida contrasted the oppressive strictures of the court with the spontaneity and humanity of village life, and crafted a startlingly intense climax.

Meanwhile, his critical eye focused on modern Japan in *A Hole of My Own Making*, about a young woman whose life is ruined by her intransigence, and in *Twilight Saloon* (*Tasogare sakaba*, 1955), one of his more formally experimental works, which depicted the customers and staff at a Tokyo bar over the course of one evening as a microcosm of postwar Japanese society. At times Uchida tackled controversial subject matter: *Twilight Saloon* touched on Japanese war guilt, while *A Hole of My Own Making* was in part a critique of the country's postwar status as an unofficial colony of the United States. *The Outsiders*, rather reminiscent in style and themes of a Hollywood Western, was an intelligent study of the plight of the Ainu minority in the country's northernmost island of Hokkaido, set against the stunning 'Scope backdrops of its lakes, mountains and plains.

During the later years of his career, Uchida also helmed two epic serials based on popular narratives: the

©Toei Company Ltd.

Abarenbō kaidō / The Horse Boy *(1957): One of Uchida's most underrated films, it is an engaging tragicomedy that sharply condemned feudal values.*

first version in color of *Daibosatsu Pass* (*Daibosatsu Tōge*, 1957–9), in three episodes, and a five-part *Musashi Miyamoto* (*Miyamoto Musashi*, 1961–5). By the sixties, his classical style seemed old-fashioned, but he nevertheless realized one of his finest achievements in *Killing in Yoshiwara* (*Yōtō monogatari: Hana no Yoshiwara hyakuningiri*, 1960), a taut and chilling Edo-period melodrama with echoes of Jacobean tragedy in its story of a disfigured merchant ruined by love for a heartless woman. Arguably Uchida's gravest film, this built to a truly shattering conclusion—one of the single most brilliant scenes in Japanese cinema.

Surprisingly, a modernist aesthetic was apparent in some of Uchida's later work. *Chikamatsu's Love in Osaka* (*Naniwa no koi no monogatari*, 1959) and *The Mad Fox* (*Koi ya koi nasuna koi*, 1962) drew on the imagery of Bunraku and Kabuki to produce strikingly stylized versions of traditional stories: the former imaginatively situated playwright Chikamatsu as a character within a narrative derived from his own work, at first observing and taking inspiration from events, later trying to influence them. *Straits of Hunger*, filmed along New Wave lines in grainy monochrome, was a convoluted story of crime and punishment which spanned two decades and a geographical area stretching from Tokyo to Hokkaido. With its themes of guilt and obsession and its intimations of political allegory, it bettered Imamura as a study of the dark underbelly of postwar society, and confirmed that Uchida's talent was not limited to the creative reworking of genre.

1922  **Ā Konishi junsa** / Ah, Constable Konishi (*co-director*)
1925  **Sensō** / War (*co-director*)
      **Giketsu** / Dutiful Blood
      **Kyoei wa jigoku** / Vanity Is Hell
1927  **Kyōsō mikkakan** / Three Days of Competition
      **Kutsu** / Shoe
      **Mirai no shusse** / Rising in the World
      **Sōteiō** / The Rowing King
      **Tōyō bukyōdan** / Chivalrous Company of the Orient
      **Namakemono** / The Idler
      **Hōendan'u** / Cannon Smoke and Rain of Shells
1928  **Nomisuke kinshu sōdō** / Trials of a Tippler's Temperance
      **Chikyū wa mawaru: Daisanbu: Kūsō hen** / The World Turns: Part 3: Fantasy Chapter
      **Kechinbo chōja** / The Miserly Millionaire

**Hikari** / A Ray
1929  **Shaba no kaze** / The Wind of the Outside World
      **Ikeru ningyō** / A Living Doll
      **Nikkatsu kōshinkyoku** / Nikkatsu March (*co-director*)
      **Taiyōji defune no minato** / The Sea-Loving Son Sails Away
1930  **Ase** / Sweat
      **Rensenrenshō** / Successive Victories
      **Tengoku sono higaeri** / Return to Heaven
1931  **Jan Barujan (Zenpen; Kōhen)** / Jean Valjean (Parts 1 and 2)
      **Misu Nippon** / Miss Nippon
      **Sanmen kiji** / Stories of Human Interest
      **Adauchi senshu** / Champion of Revenge / The Revenge Champion
1932  **Daichi ni tatsu (Zenpen; Kōhen)** / Standing on the Earth (Parts 1 and 2)
      **Ai wa doko made mo** / Love Through Thick and Thin
1933  **Sakebu Ajia** / Asia Cries Out
      **Keisatsukan** / Police / Policeman / Police Officer
1934  **Kawa no ue no taiyō** / Sun over the River
      **Neppū** / Hot Wind
1935  **Hakugin no ōza (Zenpen; Kōhen)** / The Silver Throne (Parts 1 and 2)
1936  **Jinsei gekijō** / Theater of Life
      **Inochi no kanmuri** / Crown of Life
1937  **Hadaka no machi** / The Naked Town
      **Kagiri naki zenshin** / Unending Advance
1938  **Tōkyō sen'ichiya** / A Thousand and One Nights in Tokyo
1939  **Tsuchi** / Earth
1940  **Rekishi: Daiichibu: Dōran Boshin** / History: Part 1: Upheaval during the Boshin War
      **Rekishi (Dainibu: Shōdo kensetsu; Daisanbu: Reimei Nihon)** / History (Part 2: Scorched

Earth and Construction; Part 3: Dawn in Japan)

**1942 Torii Suneemon** / Suneemon Torii

**1955 Chiyari Fuji** / Bloody Spear at Mount Fuji

**Tasogare sakaba** / Twilight Saloon / Twilight Beer Hall

**Jibun no ana no naka de** / A Hole of My Own Making / In My Own Hole

**1956 Kuroda sōdō** / The Kuroda Affair / Disorder by the Kuroda Clan

**Gyakushū gokumon toride** / Counterattack at the Prison Gate Fortress

**1957 Abarenbō kaidō** / The Horse Boy (lit. The Hooligan's Highway)

**Daibosatsu Tōge** / Daibosatsu Pass / Sword in the Moonlight

**Dotanba** / The Scaffold / The Eleventh Hour / They Are Buried Alive

**1958 Senryō jishi** / The 1000-ryo Lion / The Thief Is Shogun's Kin

**Daibosatsu Tōge: Dainibu** / Daibosatsu Pass 2 / Sword in the Moonlight 2

**Mori to mizuumi no matsuri** / The Outsiders (lit. Festival of Lakes and Forests)

**1959 Daibosatsu tōge Kanketsu hen** / Daibosatsu Pass 3 / Sword in the Moonlight 3

**Daihyōga o yuku** / Crossing the Great Glacier

**Naniwa no koi no monogatari** / Chikamatsu's Love in Osaka / Their Own World

**1960 Sake to onna to yari** / The Master Spearman / The Drunken Spearman / Men's Ambition (lit. Wine, Women, and a Spear)

**Yōtō monogatari: Hana no Yoshiwara hyakuningiri** / Killing in Yoshiwara / Yoshiwara the Pleasure Quarter

**1961 Miyamoto Musashi** / Musashi Miyamoto

**1962 Koi ya koi nasuna koi** / The Mad Fox / To Love Again / Love, Thy Name Be Sorrow

**Miyamoto Musashi: Hannyazaka no kettō** / Musashi Miyamoto 2: Showdown at Hannyazaka Height

**1963 Miyamoto Musashi: Nitōryū kaigan** / Musashi Miyamoto 3: Duel against Yagyu

**1964 Miyamoto Musashi: Ichijō-ji no kettō** / Musashi Miyamoto 4: Duel at Ichijoji Temple

**1965 Kiga kaikyō** / Straits of Hunger / A Fugitive from the Past

**Miyamoto Musashi: Ganryūjima no kettō** / Musashi Miyamoto 5: Musashi vs. Kojiro

**1968 Jinsei Gekijō: Hishakaku to Kiratsune** / Hishakaku and Kiratsune: A Tale of Two Yakuza / Theater of Life: Hishakaku and Kiratsune (lit.)

**1971 Shinken shōbu** / Swords of Death

## URAYAMA Kirio
**(December 14, 1930–October 20, 1985)**
浦山桐郎

Perhaps because he made so few films, Urayama is barely known in the West. He is often bracketed with Imamura, having served as assistant director on all his early films from *Stolen Desire* (*Nusumareta yokujō*, 1958) to *Pigs and Battleships* (*Buta to gunkan*, 1961). Imamura in turn collaborated on the script of Urayama's directorial debut, *Street with a Cupola* (*Kyūpora no aru machi*, 1962), but this richly detailed, delicately acted film—an account of the lives of families and especially children in a working class community west of Tokyo—displayed a warmth and humanity far removed from Imamura's clinical approach. Urayama's next film, *Bad Girl* (*Hikō shōjo*, 1963), also focused

Kyūpora no aru machi / Street with a Cupola *(1962): Urayama's debut, a richly detailed, delicately acted account of working-class life, deserves greater fame in the West.*

on the young, charting the relationship between a delinquent girl and an unemployed boy. Rather bleaker in tone, with an intense emotional climax, it made effective use of the landscapes around Kanazawa, desolate in stark black and white. Less realist in style, with its fantasy sequences, flashbacks, and switches from monochrome to color rather reminiscent of the New Wave, was *The Girl I Abandoned (Watashi ga suteta onna,* 1969), based on a Shūsaku Endō novel. This powerful film followed the course of an ambitious businessman's relations with a rejected ex-lover after he marries a woman he does not love to advance his career. All these films examined the iniquities of the Japanese class system and the problems of the poor. Yet Urayama found hope in the strength of personal relationships: the affections between

family members and childhood friends in *Street with a Cupola,* the love of the teenage couple in *Bad Girl,* the wife's belated realization of her rival's humanity in *The Girl I Abandoned.*

Urayama returned to direction after a gap of several years, and the last decade of his career included some uncharacteristic work. *Taro, the Dragon Boy (Tatsu no ko Tarō,* 1979) was an animated film about a young boy's quest to save his mother, who has been turned into a dragon. *The Dark Room (Anshitsu,* 1983), made to mark the 70th anniversary of Nikkatsu studios, was a big-budget Roman Porno feature, based on the autobiography of writer Junnosuke Yoshiyuki, and chronicling his various affairs after the suicide of his wife. Elsewhere, however, Urayama continued to work in a broadly social realist vein.

*Gate of Youth* (*Seishun no mon*, 1975–7), in two parts, followed the life of a boy from the death of his father, through a period spent living with his stepmother, to his years as a student at Waseda University. *Children of the Sun* (*Taiyō no ko: Tedanofua*, 1980), about a married couple running a diner in Kobe, touched on the poverty of those emigrating from Okinawa to mainland Japan and also included elements reflecting Urayama's own life, such as the suicide of the father (the director's own father had killed himself when his son was a schoolboy). Urayama's final film, *Yumechiyo* (*Yumechiyo nikki*, 1985), recounted the last love affair of a geisha dying from leukemia after exposure to the atomic bomb.

Though several of Urayama's films ranked in the annual Kinema Junpō Best Ten listing, his reputation at home has sadly never translated into international appreciation. *Street with a Cupola* and *The Girl I Abandoned*, in particular, were considerable achievements, and his skill in directing actors, choreographing movement, and capturing the atmosphere of places merit wider appreciation.

1962 **Kyūpora no aru machi** / Street with a Cupola / Cupola / Cupola, Where the Furnaces Glow / Foundry Town
1963 **Hikō shōjo** / Bad Girl / Delinquent Girl / Each Day I Cry
1969 **Watashi ga suteta onna** / The Girl I Abandoned
1975 **Seishun no mon** / Gate of Youth
1977 **Seishun no mon: Jiritsu hen** / Gate of Youth: Independence Chapter
1979 **Tatsu no ko Tarō** / Taro the Dragon Boy (*animation*)
1980 **Taiyō no ko: Tedanofua** / Children of the Sun
1983 **Anshitsu** / The Dark Room
1985 **Yumechiyo nikki** / Yumechiyo / Yumechiyo's Diary (lit.)

# USHIHARA Kiyohiko
## (August 22, 1897–May 20, 1985)
牛原虚彦

Though few of his films are extant, Ushihara ranked among Shochiku's leading directors during the twenties. After scripting the studio's seminal *Souls on the Road* (*Rojō no reikon*, 1921), for Minoru Murata, he directed its next production, *The Mountains Grow Dark* (*Yama kururu*, 1921), and the first episode of a two-part 1923 adaptation of *Les Misérables* which transposed Hugo's story to ancient China.

Ushihara's admiration for the American cinema took him to Hollywood for nine months during 1926; there, he studied filmmaking technique under Charlie Chaplin. He achieved a major hit with the first film he made after returning to Japan, *Suffering Women* (*Junange*, 1926). A melodrama about the romantic travails of three high school classmates after graduation, this initiated a sequence of weepies which earned the director the nickname of "Sentimental Ushihara." Its athletic leading man Denmei Suzuki would become Ushihara's regular star in such works as the sports film *A King on Land* (*Riku no ōja*, 1928) and the youth movie *He and Tokyo* (*Kare to Tōkyō*, 1928), about the romantic and professional trials of a recent graduate in the big city. In the sequels to the latter film and several others, Suzuki was paired with Kinuyo Tanaka, then a demure leading lady. Their most notable joint vehicle was *Marching On* (*Shingun*, 1930), which combined romantic melodrama with action on the battlefield. Though echoes of Hollywood war films such as *The Big Parade* (1925, King Vidor) and *Wings* (1927, William Wellman) were noticeable, Ushihara's technique also displayed touches of individuality: for instance, the frequent use of dissolves within scenes.

Later that year, Ushihara again traveled abroad, to Europe and America, to familiarize himself with sound film techniques. His sound films are not generally highly regarded, though *The Ghost Cat and the Mysterious Shamisen* (*Kaibyō nazo no shamisen*, 1938), a ghost story with elements of the surreal, has a good reputation. Ushihara's postwar output included some films recalling his earlier enthusiasm for Hollywood: *A Popular Man in Town* (*Machi no ninkimono*, 1946) was a pro-democracy drama patterned on Frank Capra's *Meet John Doe* (1941), while *Until Forever* (*Itsu itsu made mo*, 1952) was a U.S.-Japan co-production about the love of a G.I. for a Japanese girl. Though Ushihara's best-regarded films are mostly lost, he seems to have been a distinctive talent.

1921 **Yama kururu** / The Mountains Grow Dark
**Dangai** / The Cliff
**Noroi no kinkō** / The Cursed Gold Mine
**Seizon no tameni** / To Survive
**Yama e kaeru** / Back to the Mountains
**Kenbu no musume** / The Sword Dance Girl
**Kurueru kengi** / Uncontrolled Swordsmanship

1922 **Haha izuko** / Where Is Mother?
**Kō no kagayaki** / The Glory of Filial Duty
**Futatsu no tamashii** / Two Souls
**Nijūseiki Hizakurige** / Twentieth Century Shank's Mare
**Tachibana daitaichō** / Battalion Leader Tachibana
**Kōjo Yoshiko** / Filial Daughter Yoshiko
**Wakaki hitobito** / Young People

**Nagare no hate** / Beyond the Current
**Omoide no uta** / Remembered Song
**Shimai** / Sisters
**Atarashiki sei e** / To New Life
**Seirei shirei** / Living Soul, Dead Soul
**Itameru kotori** / The Injured Little Bird
**Kowareta su** / The Broken Nest

1923 **Ōkami no mure** / The Wolf Pack
**Ā mujō: Daiippen: Hōrō no maki** / Les Misérables: Part 1: Wanderer's Reel (lit. Ah, Merciless: Part 1: Wanderer's Reel)
**Jinsei no ai** / Love of Life
**Dai Tōkyō no ushimitsudoki** / The Small Hours in Greater Tokyo (*co-director*)
**Daichi wa okoru** / The Earth Is Angry
**Rakujitsu no minato** / A Harbor at Sunset
**Minami no gyoson** / A Southern Fishing Village
**Yoru no warai** / Night Laughter
**Natsukashi no hana** / Dear Old Flower

1924 **Kodomo no sekai** / World of Children
**Ichijiku** / The Fig
**Kanji no yoi eigashū** / Films That Make You Feel Good (*co-director*)
**Kurokawa-hakase** / Dr. Kurokawa
**Shijin to undōka** / The Poet and the Athlete
**Futari no haha** / Two Mothers
**Bōya no fukushū** / A Boy's Revenge
**Ushi wa ushizure** / Birds of a Feather (lit. Cow with Cow)
**Koutashū: Daiippen: Suzuran** / Collection of Short Songs: Part 1: Lily of the Valley
**Seki no gohonmatsu** / Five Pines at the Barrier

Hyōhaku no biwashi / The Wandering Lute Player

Yubiwa / The Ring

1925 Natsukashi no Kamata (Zenpen; Kōhen) / Dear Old Kamata (Parts 1 and 2)

Daichi wa hohoemu (Zenpen; Chūhen; Kōhen) / The Earth Smiles (Parts 1, 2, and 3) (*co-director*)

Koi no senshu / Love's Athlete

Koi no eikan / Love's Victory

Zōge no tō / The Ivory Tower

Hōjōka / Song of Rich Love

Sensuiō / The Diving King

Seifukusha / The Conqueror

Nogi taishō / General Nogi

1926 Junange / Suffering Women

1927 Shōwa jidai / Showa Period

Mura no ninkimono / A Popular Man in the Village

Kaihin no joō / Queen of the Beach

Ojōsan / Young Miss

1928 Kindai musha shugyō / Modern Warriors' Training

Kangeki jidai / Age of Emotions

Kare to Tōkyō / He and Tokyo

Kare to den'en / He and the Countryside

Riku no ōja / A King on Land

1929 Kare to jinsei / He and Life

Daitokai: Rōdō hen / The Great Metropolis: Labor Chapter / The Life of Workers in the Big City

Yama no gaika / Victory Song of the Mountains

1930 Shingun / Marching On / The March / The Army Advances

Daitokai: Bakuhatsu hen / The Great Metropolis: Explosion Chapter

Wakamono yo naze naku ka / Why Do You Cry, Young People?

1933 Miraibana / Flower of the Future

Daigaku no uta / Song of University

Tōkyō matsuri / Tokyo Festival

1934 Kokoro no taiyō / The Heart's Sun

1935 Otoko sanjū mae / A Man Approaching Thirty

Kyūkō ressha / Express Train

1936 Furusato no uta / Song of Home

Machi no enkashi / The Town Troubadour

Gogo no haru / Several Springs

Suri no ie / House of a Pickpocket

Ani no tanjōbi / Older Brother's Birthday

Bōfū / Strong Wind

1937 Minamikaze Satsuma uta / Song of the South Wind in Satsuma

Hatamoto denpo: Ryū no maki / The Ostentatious Vassal: Dragon Reel

Hatamoto denpō: Tora no maki / The Ostentatious Vassal: Tiger Reel

1938 Sakebu nobushi / Cry of the Wild Warrior

Kaibyō nazo no shamisen / The Ghost Cat and the Mysterious Shamisen

1939 Yamanouchi Kazutoyo no tsuma / The Wife of Kazutoyo Yamanouchi

Nagadosu Danjūrō / Danjuro of the Long Sword

1940 Hataoka junsa / Hataoka the Constable

Hare kosode / Bright Short-Sleeved Kimono

1941 Hibari wa sora ni / Skylark in the Sky

Otoko no hibana: Shinmon Tatsugorō / A Man's Spark: Tatsugoro Shinmon

1942 Ishin no kyoku / Melody of Restoration / A Chronicle of the Restoration

1943 Chingisu Kan / Genghis Khan (*co-director*)

1944 Kenpū renpeikan / Sword-Wind Training Hall

1946 Machi no ninkimono / A Popular Man in Town

1947 Itsu no hi ka hana sakan / Some Day Flowers Will Bloom

1948 Dare ni koisen / Who Will You Love?

1949  **Niji otoko** / The Rainbow Man
1952  **Itsu itsu made mo** / Until Forever
      (*co-director*)

## WAKAMATSU Kōji
## (b. April 1, 1936)
## 若松孝二

Considered among the most important "pink" films, Wakamatsu's early independent productions, made for his own company, struck a precarious balance between unashamed exploitation and political commentary. His most famous and most notorious work, *Violated Angels* (*Okasareta hakui*, 1967), was based on Richard Speck's massacre of student nurses in Chicago. Concentrating less on the murderer's personality than on the various tactics employed by the women in dealing with him, it was, despite sensationalist elements, genuinely harrowing. Among Wakamatsu's other more outrageous films were *The Embryo Hunts in Secret* (*Taiji ga mitsuryō suru toki*, 1966), about a man torturing his lover, and *Go, Go, Second Time Virgin* (*Yuke yuke nidome no shojo*, 1969), chronicling the brief encounter between a suicidal victim of gang rape and a boy who has killed his family after being forced to participate in an orgy. Not all of Wakamatsu's work exhibited this kind of deliberate excess. *Secret Acts within Four Walls* (*Kabe no naka no himegoto*, 1965) was a relatively restrained, telling chronicle of youthful disillusionment, focusing on an unsuccessful student spying on his neighbors. The bleakly compassionate *Chronicle of an Affair* (*Jōji no rirekisho*, 1965) told the life story of a fallen woman falsely accused of murder.

Wakamatsu's films of this period displayed a deliberate theatricality: in *Violated Angels*, *The Embryo Hunts in Secret*, and *Go, Go, Second Time Virgin*, he strictly respected the classical unities and mounted scenes of violence as stylized tableaux, the artificiality of which was emphasized by sudden switches from monochrome to color. These techniques have earned comparisons with Brecht, though a more direct influence, doubtless encouraged by Wakamatsu's then regular screenwriter Masao Adachi (a sometime associate of Nagisa Ōshima), was the alienation effects of late sixties Godard. At its most effective, the resulting tension between involvement and distance provoked the viewer into questioning his own responses to onscreen violence.

Wakamatsu's work was often political in the broader sense of being concerned with power relations, whether between lovers or in society. These concerns were sometimes overwhelmed by the exploitation format: the Freudian themes of *The Embryo Hunts in Secret* served largely to make its sadism intellectually respectable, and the juxtaposition in *Violated Angels* of the arrest of the psychopath with the repression of a student demonstration was glib and irresponsible. *Secret Acts within Four Walls*, however, intelligently integrated a story of domestic violence with intimations of wider conflicts in Vietnam and elsewhere; the image of a man scarred from the Hiroshima bomb making love in front of a picture of Stalin evoked the iconoclastic humor of Dusan Makavejev. Wakamatsu could also use location expressively: evocative photography of urban wastelands suggested his characters' alienation in *Shinjuku Mad* (*Shinjuku maddo*, 1970) and *Go, Go Second Time Virgin*.

Political in the narrower sense of

Okasareta hakui / Violated Angels *(1967): This iconic image from Wakamatsu's best-known film chillingly illustrates his abiding theme: the link between sex and violence.*

advocating a specific cause were *Sex Jack (Sekkusu Jakku*, 1970) and *Ecstasy of the Angels (Tenshi no kōkotsu*, 1972). Charting the activities of leftist groups, these again testified to the influence of the Marxist Adachi. *Sex Jack* began with documentary footage of a student demonstration being put down by the police, but the sympathy of these films for their activist protagonists was generally qualified by their astringent portrayal of disunity and mistrust among radical groups, Wakamatsu hinting that revolution will fail because of human frailties. Related to this was a consistent emphasis on physical vulnerability. A recurrent image was the graphic depiction of the effect of violence on a naked body: in *Violated Angels*, the surviving nurse

cradles the killer among the blood-stained corpses of his victims; in *Violent Virgin (Shojo geba geba*, 1969), the hero embraces his crucified lover; murderers smear the blood of their victim on a naked girl in *Shinjuku Mad*; and victims of torture make love in *Ecstasy of the Angels*.

From the late seventies, Wakamatsu interspersed independent productions with studio filmmaking. Alongside such relatively conventional genre pieces as the yakuza movie *Street with No Tomorrow (Asu naki machikado*, 1997), he made more personal projects like *Ready to Shoot (Ware ni utsu yōi ari*, 1990), in which gangster movie conventions were used as a basis for an examination of the attitudes of former student radicals whose ideals have faded in middle age. Also personal in resonance was *Endless Waltz* (*Endoresu warutsu*, 1995), which recounted the self-destructive love affair of jazz musician Kaoru Abe and writer Izumi Suzuki, two former friends of Wakamatsu who committed suicide in the seventies. Wakamatsu has remained true to his idiosyncratic concerns: with *Scenery of Seventeen: What Did the Boy See?* (*17-sai no fūkei: Shōnen wa nani o mita no ka*, 2005), about a boy fleeing northward on a bicycle after murdering his mother, the director reaffirmed his commitment to formal experimentation and his interest in the extremes of youthful alienation. *United Red Army* (*Jitsuroku: Rengō Sekigun: Asama Sansō e no michinori*, 2007), meanwhile, used the 1972 Asama Sansō incident, in which Red Army members holed up in a mountain lodge in the aftermath of a violent purge, as a cue for a wide-ranging examination of the history of the postwar radical left.

1963  **Amai wana** / Sweet Trap
**Hageshii onnatachi** / Savage Women
**Oiroke sakusen: Purēgāru** / Erotic Strategies: Playgirl
1964  **Aku no modae** / Evil Agony
**Furin no tsugunai** / Illicit Reward
**Mesuinu no kake** / Game of Bitches
**Akai hankō** / Red Crime
**Namari no bohyō** / Lead Gravestone
**Kawaita hada** / Dry Skin
**Gyakujō** / Contrary Desires
**Ami no naka no onna** / Woman in the Net
**Shiroi hada no dasshutsu** / Escape of White Flesh
**Osorubeki isan: Hadaka no kage** / Dreadful Inheritance: The Naked Shadow

1965  **Rikon'ya kaigyōchū** / Divorce Business
**Jōji no rirekisho** / Chronicle of an Affair / Career of Lust / History of Sexual Liaisons
**Taiyō no heso** / The Sun's Navel
**Kabe no naka no himegoto** / Secret Acts within Four Walls
**Bōtoku no wana** / Profane Trap
**Yuganda kankei** / Perverse Liaisons / Warped Relations
**Yokubō no chi ga shitataru** / Craving in the Blood
**Odenwa chōdai: Ai no dezain** / Model for Love / The Love Robots
1966  **Chi wa taiyō yori mo akai** / Blood Is Redder than the Sun
**Hikisakareta jōji** / Ripped-Up Desire
**Taiji ga mitsuryō suru toki** / The Embryo Hunts in Secret
**Shiro no jinzō bijo** / White Man-Made Beauty
1967  **Jōyoku no kurosuisen** / Black Narcissus of Lust
**Ami no naka no bōkō** / Net of Violence / Rape Trap
**Okasareta hakui** / Violated Angels / Violated Women in White
**Aru mittsū** / A Certain Adultery (*co-director*)
**Nihon bōkō ankoku shi: Ijōsha no chi** / Dark History of Japanese Violence: Blood of an Abnormal Man
**Sei no hōrō** / Sexual Vagabond / Sex Beast
**Zoku Nihon bōkō ankoku shi: Bōgyakuma** / Dark History of Japanese Violence 2: Tyrant
**Sei hanzai** / Sex Crimes
**Rangyō** / Debauchery
1968  **Haragashi onna** / Womb to Let
**Nikutai no yokkyū** / Desires of the Flesh
**Kin Pei Bai** / The Notorious Concubines / Chin Ping-Mei (lit.)
1969  **Shin Nihon bōkō ankoku shi:**

**Fukushūki** / New Dark History of Japanese Violence: Vengeance Demon

**Shojo geba geba** / Violent Virgin

**Tōrima no kokuhaku: Gendai sei hanzai ankoku hen** / Confessions of a Killer: Modern Underground Sex Crime Story

**Kyōsō jōshikō** / Crazy Love Suicides / Death of a Madman / Running in Madness, Dying in Love

**Yuke yuke nidome no shojo** / Go, Go, Second Time Virgin

**Yawa hada mushuku: Otokogoroshi onnagoroshi** / Soft Skin: Man Killer, Woman Killer

**Otokogoroshi onnagoroshi: Hadaka no jūdan** / Man Killer, Woman Killer: Naked Bullet

**Gendai kōshoku hen: Teroru no kisetsu** / Tale of Modern Lovers: Season of Terror

1970 **Riyū naki bōkō: Gendai sei hanzai zekkyō hen** / Assault without Motive: Modern Sex Crimes

**Ai no tekunikku: Kāma Sūtora** / Love Techniques: The Kama Sutra

**Mahiru no bōkōgeki** / Violent Dramas in Broad Daylight

**Shinjuku maddo** / Shinjuku Mad

**Sekkusu Jakku** / Sex Jack

**Nihon bōkō ankoku shi: Enjū** / Dark History of Japanese Violence: Raging Beast

1971 **Zoku ai no tekkunikku: Ai no kōi** / Love Techniques 2: Act of Love

**Sekura makura: Shinitai onna** / Sex Cycle: The Woman Who Wants to Die

**Hika** / Secret Flower

**Watashi wa nureteiru** / I Am Wet

**Sekigun–PFLP–Sekai sensō sengen** / Red Army–PFLP–Declaration of World War (*co-director*)

**Sei kazoku** / Sex Family

1972 **Tenshi no kōkotsu** / Ecstasy of the Angels / Angelic Orgasm

**Gendai Nihon bōkō ankoku shi** / Modern Dark History of Japanese Violence

**Maruhi joshi kōsei: Kōkotsu no arubaito** / Confidential High School Girl: Part-Time Ecstasy Work / Young Girls Who Die for Love: Ecstasy Apprentice

**Kuroi jūyoku** / Black Beast of Lust

1973 **Maruhi joshi kōsei: Kagai sākuru** / Confidential High School Girl: Circle of Oppression / Young Girls Who Die for Love 2: Circle of Oppression

1974 **Nureta sai no me** / The Wet Flower's Budding Eye

**In'yoku rinjū** / Obscene Passion: Bestiality Collective

1975 **Deruta no okite** / Law of the Delta

**Baishunfu Maria** / Maria the Whore

**Gōmon hyakunen shi** / One Hundred Year Torture History

**Shinkon daihyakka** / The Big Encyclopedia of Honeymoons

**Gōkan ka wakan ka? Damashite bōkō** / Consent or Rape?: Trick Rape

**Poruno jikenbo: Sei no ankoku** / Pornographic Casebook: The Darkness of Sex

**Jitsuroku: Jokōsei shūdan baishun** / True Account of Young Schoolgirl Prostitutes

1976 **Gendai seigōmon** / Modern Sex Torture

**Zannin onna ankoku shi** / Dark History of Sadistic Women

1977 **Jokei gokinsei hyakunen** / One Hundred Years of Sex Prohibition and Female Punishment

**Seibo kannon daibosatsu** / The Holy Mother Avalokitesvara / Eros Eterna

**Nihon gokinsei: Nyonin baibai** / Sex Prohibition in Japan: Trade in Women

1978 **Bōgyaku onna gōmon** / Cruel Torture of Women

**Jūsannin renzoku bōkōma** / Serial
Rape / Thirteen Serial Assaults (lit.)
**Zannin renzoku gōkanma** / Cruel
Serial Rape Fiend
1979 **Gendai sei hanzai: Bōkō kankin**
/ Modern Sex Crimes: Violence,
Imprisonment
**Ejiki** / The Prey
**Gendai sei hanzai: Zen'in satsugai**
/ Modern Sex Crimes: Murdering
Everyone
1980 **Sei shōjo gōmon** / Torture of the
Holy Girl
1981 **Misshitsu renzoku bōkō** / Serial
Rape in a Secret Room
1982 **Mizu no nai pūru** / Pool without
Water
1984 **Sukurappu sutōrī: Aru ai no
monogatari** / Scrap of a Story:
Story of Secret Love
1986 **Matsui Kazuyo no shōgeki** /
Shocking Kazuyo Matsui
1989 **Kisu yori kantan** / Easily
Embarrassed / Easier than Kissing
(lit.)
1990 **Pantsu no ana: Mukesode
mukenai ichigotachi** / Hole in the
Pants (*co-director*)
**Ware ni utsu yōi ari** / Ready to
Shoot
1991 **Kisu yori kantan 2: Hyōryū hen**
/ Easily Embarrassed 2: Adrift /
Easier Than Kissing 2: Adrift
1992 **Netorare Sōsuke** / Sosuke's Stolen
Sleep
**Erotikkuna kankei** / Erotic
Liaisons
1993 **Shingapōru suringu** / Singapore
Sling
1995 **Endoresu warutsu** / Endless Waltz
1997 **Asu naki machikado** / Street with
No Tomorrow
1999 **Each Little Thing Wind
Fairground**
**Tobu wa tengoku, moguru ga
jigoku** / Flying Is Heaven, Diving Is
Hell
2004 **Kanzen naru shiiku: Akai satsui**

/ Complete Breeding: Intentions of
Murder
2005 **17-sai no fūkei: Shōnen wa nani o
mita no ka** / Scenery of Seventeen:
What Did the Boy See?
2007 **Jitsuroku: Rengō Sekigun: Asama
Sansō e no michinori** / United Red
Army (lit. True Record: United Red
Army: The Way to Asama Lodge)

**WATANABE Fumiki**
**(b. January 10, 1953)**
渡辺文樹

Like certain other contemporary independent filmmakers such as Naomi
Kawase and Nobuhiro Suwa, Watanabe
has endeavored to blur the line between
fiction and documentary. His earliest
films were made on 8mm and 16mm
formats while he attended university
and subsequently worked as a private
tutor. During this time he had an affair
with the mother of one of his students,
an incident which became the subject
of his feature debut, *The Tutor* (*Katei
kyōshi*, 1987). Watanabe reconstructed
the sequence of events and played himself; however, the other participants
acted, not their own roles, but each others', perhaps hinting that even the closest reconstruction of reality is inevitably
fictionalized. In his next film, *Homemade Movie* (*Shimaguni konjō*, 1990),
Watanabe again basically played himself
in a dramatization of the family life of a
tutor and filmmaker in his native city of
Fukushima. The title (literally "Insularity") hinted at a wider political context.
A political implication was also suggested by *Zazambo* (*Zazanbo*, 1992), in
which Watanabe investigated a real-life
case involving the suspicious death of a
child. Donald Richie has commented
that the scene in which Watanabe

exhumes the body "becomes a startling metaphor for amnesiac Japan forced to remember its own problematical past." *Bari-Zogon* (*Bari zōgon*, 1996), a more explicitly political film, was another investigation into a suspicious death: that of a young employee of a nuclear power station, also a political campaigner, who had planned to blow the whistle on electoral corruption and a safety cover-up at the plant. The film interspersed re-enactments of the events leading up to the murder with interviews with those involved, from whom Watanabe attempted to elicit confessions. He continued to court controversy with *Body Clock* (*Hara hara tokei*, 1999), which took its title from a book about a famous terrorist attack and earned the anger of rightist groups through its description of a plan to assassinate the Emperor. Later, *Mount Osutaka* (*Osutakayama*, 2005) examined conspiracy theories surrounding the notorious 1985 crash of a Japan Airlines jet in Gunma Prefecture.

1971  **Genin** / Lower-Class Ninja (*8mm short*)
1972  **Shimooshi** (*8mm*)
      **Fubo no ichinichi** / A Day in the Life of My Parents (*8mm short*)
1973  **Fundo no kawa** / River of Anger (*8mm*)
1974  **Ōshū zankyō** / Remnants of Chivalry in Oshu (*8mm*)
1975  **Nishijin** (*8mm*)
      **N-shi no yūgana seikatsu** / The Elegant Life of Mr. N (*8mm short*)
1977  **Mayakugai** / Drug Row (*16mm*)
1978  **Dokyumento: Jigoku no mushi** / Document: The Worms of Hell (*16mm short*)
1979  **Kaerazaru hashi** / Bridge of No Return (*16mm*)
1980  **Fukushima kenchō oshoku** / Corruption at the Fukushima Prefectural Office (*16mm*)
1981  **Sogekisha** / Sniper (*16mm short*)

1987  **Katei kyōshi** / The Tutor
1990  **Shimaguni konjō** / Homemade Movie (lit. Insularity)
1992  **Zazanbo** / Zazambo
1996  **Bari zōgon** / Bari-Zogon (lit. All Manner of Abuse)
1999  **Hara hara tokei** / Body Clock
2005  **Osutakayama** / Mount Osutaka
2007  **Nomonhan**

## WATANABE Kunio
### (June 3, 1899–November 5, 1981)
渡辺邦男

A prolific, versatile director of genre films, Watanabe worked mainly at Nikkatsu, Toho, and Toei. Among his early films, *Beyond Swords* (*Ken o koete*, 1930), a *jidai-geki* set at the time of the Shogunate's downfall, marked the debut of a 13-year-old Isuzu Yamada. By the mid-thirties, he had earned a reputation within the industry for proficiency and reliability. The lost *Draft Notice* (*Shōshūrei*, 1935) focused on a young man's heroic war service in China and spoke for the increasingly right-wing attitudes which later made Watanabe an ideal choice to helm several famous films on nationalistic themes. *Striking at the North China Skies* (*Hokushi no sora o tsuku*, 1937) was an account of a war correspondent whose patriotism leads him from reporting to active participation in the war effort. *Song of the White Orchid* (*Byakuran no uta*, 1939) and *Vow in the Desert* (*Nessa no chikai*, 1940) were both about the love of Japanese men for Chinese women, a theme which was used to promote pan-Asian sentiments; the heroine in both films was played by popular singer Ri Koran (Yoshiko Yamaguchi), born to Japanese parents in China. *Towards the Decisive Battle in the Sky* (*Kessen no ōzora e*, 1943) had Setsuko Hara as the woman inspiring her younger brother to overcome poor health and join the cadets.

Hara also appeared in Watanabe's first two postwar films, of which *The Belle* (*Reijin*, 1946) was a romantic drama about a woman who marries for money, only to fall in love with another man. However, in his later work the director still tended towards patriotic material. *Foreign Hills* (*Ikoku no oka*, 1949) focused on the family life of those Japanese servicemen lately repatriated from Soviet territory, and Watanabe also supervised the similarly themed *Repatriation* (*Damoi*, 1949), directed by Takeshi Satō. He subsequently made *The Emperor Meiji and the Great Russo-Japanese War* (*Meiji tennō to Nichiro daisensō*, 1957), a reverential biopic, and *The Kamikaze: Suicide Soldiers* (*Minami Taiheiyō namitakashi*, 1962), a celebration of the military spirit. Among his other later films were many *jidai-geki*, but he also handled some interesting Hollywood-style melodramas: *365 Nights* (*Sanbyakurokujūgoya*, 1962) was an intelligent comment on the hypocrisy of traditional sexual mores, while *Hibari's Tale of Pathos* (*Hibari no Sado jōwa*, 1962), set on Sado Island, examined the modernization of Japan's remoter regions as tourism became widespread. His last work was a remake of Akira Kurosawa's debut, the martial arts film *Sanshiro Sugata* (*Sugata Sanshirō*, 1970).

Watanabe does not command an especially high reputation, partly because of a directorial style which, in Peter High's words, "emphasized speed of production over careful coaching of his actors," and partly because of his enthusiastic commitment to the war effort. The historical importance of those war films, however, remains considerable, and he was certainly a competent journeyman filmmaker.

**1928**  **Kenran no mori** / Forest of Swordfighting

**1929**  **Tōyamazakura Kinsan bugyō** / Magistrate Kinsan: Cherry-Blossom Tattoo

**Atari kuji ijō** / More than a Lottery Win

**Gyakuten** / Reversal

**Nikkatsu kōshinkyoku** / Nikkatsu March (*co-director*)

**Daitōjin** / The Big Fight

**Tatsumaki nagaya** / Tornado Tenement

**Maken kago tsurube** / Mysterious Sword, Basket and Well Bucket

**Yamamoto Kansuke** / Kansuke Yamamoto

**1930**  **Ken o koete** / Beyond Swords

**Ude ippon** / Self-Reliance (lit. One Arm)

**Kyōen koi gassen** / Beauty Competition, Battle of Love

**Koiguruma: Zenpen** / Cart of Love: Part 1

**Namida no dōkeshi** / A Clown in Tears

**Chizome no kyara (Zenpen; Kōhen)** / Blood-Stained Aloe (Parts 1 and 2)

**1931**  **Rōnin to ahen** / The Ronin and Opium

**Maboroshi no hanayome** / The Phantom Bride

**Hadaka ikkan** / Without Any Means

**Rōnin no mure** / The Group of Ronin

**Higo no komageta** / The Wooden Clogs of Higo

**Kokoro no chikemuri** / Spattered Heart's Blood

**Korui Sakashita gomon** / Red Tears at the Sakashita Gate

**1932**  **Ishin no setsuna** / Moment of Restoration

**Tsuetate sōdō** / The Tsuetate Affair

**Izō no Yokichi** / Yokichi of Izo

**Rōnin shiguregasa** / A Ronin's Hat for Light Rain

**Bonnō hibunsho: Ryūsei hen** / Secret Story of Earthly Desires: Shooting Star

**Bonnō hibunsho: Kenkō hen** / Secret Story of Earthly Desires: Fighting Light

1933 **Bonnō hibunsho: Gedatsu hen** / Secret Story of Earthly Desires: Souls' Deliverance

**Daitō Jinnai sakkichō** / The Misfortunes of Great Thief Jinnai

**Furansu Omasa** / Omasa of France

**Shiranami renji kōshi** / White Waves and Latticework

**Ittōryū tōshijin** / School of One Sword: Fighting Camp

**Nuregarasu** / The Wet Crow

1934 **Haha no hohoemi** / A Mother's Smile

**Sakura ondo** / Sakura Dance

**Zensen butai** / Frontline Troops

**Hanayome nikki** / A Bride's Diary

**Onna ichidai** / A Woman's Life

1935 **Shōshūrei** / Draft Notice

**Uramachi no kōkyōkyoku** / Symphony of the Back Streets

**Otoko no namida** / A Man's Tears

**Abare andon** / Violent Lantern

**Jazu no machikado** / The Jazz Corner

1936 **Hirotta teisō** / Picked-Up Chastity

**Jihishinchō** / The Cuckoo

**Tamashii** / The Soul

**Takahashi Korekiyo jiden (Zenpen; Kōhen)** / The Autobiography of Korekiyo Takahashi

**Tange Sazen: Nikkō no maki** / Sazen Tange: Nikko Reel

1937 **Kenji to sono imōto** / The Prosecutor and His Younger Sister

**Tange Sazen: Aizō maken hen** / Sazen Tange: Love, Hate, and the Mysterious Sword

**Tange Sazen: Kanketsu: Hōkō hen** / Sazen Tange: Conclusion: Howl

**Otoko wa dokyō** / A Man Must Be Brave

**Hokushi no sora o tsuku** / Striking at the North China Skies

**Ishin hiwa: Tatakai no kyoku** / Secret Story of the Restoration: Melody of Battle

**Ketsuro** / The Way Out

**Minamoto Kurō Yoshitsune** / Kuro Yoshitsune Minamoto

1938 **Tetsuwan toshi** / The Strong-Armed City

**Seishun sumō nikki** / Diary of a Young Sumo Wrestler

**Aijō ichiro** / One Road of Love

**Shōgun no mago** / The Shogun's Grandchild

**Enoken no Tairiku tosshin: Zenpen: Hikan mata hikan no maki** / Enoken's Continental Charge: Pessimism

**Enoken no Tairiku tosshin: Kōhen: Yakushin mata yakushin no maki** / Enoken's Continental Charge: Leaps and Bounds

**Shinpen Tange Sazen: Yōtō hen** / Sazen Tange: The Bewitched °Sword

1939 **Wasurarenu hitomi** / Unforgettable Eyes

**Hadaka no kyōkasho** / The Naked Textbook

**Puropera oyaji** / Propellor Dad

**Seishun yakyū nikki** / Diary of Youth and Baseball

**Tetsu no kyōdai** / Brothers of Steel

**Echigo jishi matsuri** / Festival of the Lion of Echigo

**Byakuran no uta (Zenpen; Kōhen)** / Song of the White Orchid (Parts 1 and 2)

1940 **Kumotsuki no kudan no haha** / Kumotsuki's Merciful Mother

**Haru yo izuko** / Where Is Spring?

**Niizuma kagami (Zenpen;**

Kōhen) / Mirror for New Wives
(Parts 1 and 2)

**Nessa no chikai (Zenpen; Kōhen)** / Vow in the Desert (Parts 1 and 2)

1941 **Shinpen: Botchan** / Botchan, New Version

**Ishin zen'ya** / The Eve of the Restoration

1942 **Musashibō Benkei** / Benkei Musashibo

**Kuon no egao** / Eternal Smiling Face

1943 **Ongaku daishingun** / Music of the Army's Advance

**Otoko** / A Man

**Kessen no ōzora e** / Towards the Decisive Battle in the Sky

1944 **Inochi no minato** / Harbor of Life

1945 **Ato ni tsuzuku o shinzu** / I Believe It Will Go On

1946 **Midori no kokyō** / Green Home Country

**Reijin** / The Belle

**Ai no sensho** / Declaration of Love

1947 **Sakura ondo: Kyō wa odotte** / Sakura Dance: Today We Dance

**Dare ka yume naki (Zenpen; Kōhen)** / Who Is without Dreams? (Parts 1 and 2)

1948 **Aijō shindansho** / Prescription for Love

**Ano yume kono uta** / That Dream and This Song

**Enoken no Hōmuran-ō** / Enoken's Home Run King

**Mukō sangen ryōdonari: Shirayuki no maki** / Near Neighbors on Both Sides: White Lily Reel

**Mukō sangen ryōdonari: Sukotara jinsei no maki** / Near Neighbors on Both Sides: Easy Life Reel

**Utau Enoken torimonochō** / Casebooks of Singing Enoken

1949 **Enoken no Kentōkyō ichidaiki** / Enoken's Record of a Fistfight-Crazy Generation

**Ikoku no oka** / Foreign Hills

**Enoken Ōkōchi no Tabisugata ninki otoko** / Enoken and Ōkōchi: Popular Men Dressed for Travel

**Nabeshima kaibyōden** / Legend of the Nabeshima Ghost Cat

**Enoken Kasagi no Osome Hisamatsu** / Enoken and Kasagi: Osome and Hisamatsu

1950 **Kappore ondo** / Kappore Dance

**Irezumi hankan: Sakurahana ranbu no maki** / The Tattooed Judge: Cherry Blossom Dance

**Irezumi hankan: Rakka taiketsu no maki** / The Tattooed Judge: Showdown of Falling Flowers

**Enoken no Sokonuke daihōsō** / Enoken's Hilarious Broadcast

**Onna Sanshirō** / A Female Sanshiro

**Tenpō ninki otoko: Tsumakoizaka no kettō** / A Popular Man of the Tenpo Era: Duel at Tsumakoizaka

**Moyuru rōgoku** / Burning Prison

**Hadaka onna no urei** / A Naked Woman's Anguish

**Enoken no Happyakuya tanuki** / Enoken's Edo Raccoon Dog

**Enoken no Ten'ichibō** / Enoken's Ten'ichibo

1951 **Izu monogatari** / Story of Izu

**Mokka ren'aichū** / At the Moment, We're in Love

**Utau yakyū kozō** / Singing Baseball Kid

**Haha wa nagekazu** / Mother Doesn't Mourn

**Nodo jiman sanbagarasu** / Three Crows' Singing Contest

**Kaiketsu tetsukamen** / The Extraordinary Iron Mask

**Gokuraku rokkasen** / Collection of Heavenly Verses

**Nagurareta Ishimatsu** / Beaten Ishimatsu

1952 **Rakka no mai** / Dance of the Fallen Flower

**Mito Kōmon man'yūki:**

**Daiichibu: Jigoku no gōzoku /** Mito Komon's Pleasure Trip: Part 1: Clan of Hell

**Mito Kōmon man'yūki: Dainibu: Fushima-den no yōzoku /** Mito Komon's Pleasure Trip: Part 2: The Mysterious Clan of Fushima Palace

**Chakkari fujin to ukkari fujin /** Shrewd Wife and Absent-Minded Wife

**Ōatari ōgonkyō jidai /** Age of Bonanza: Gold-Crazy

**Hadaka daimyō (Zenpen; Kōhen) /** The Naked Daimyo (Parts 1 and 2)

**Zoku chakkari fujin to ukkari fujin: Sokonuke abekku sandan tobi /** Shrewd Wife and Absent-Minded Wife 2: Together Forever: Three Layers' Vault

**Kessen Takadanobaba /** Decisive Battle at Takadanobaba

**Geisha warutsu /** The Geisha Waltz

**Tobitcho hankan /** The Flying Judge

**Utamatsuri Shimizu minato /** Singing Festival at Shimizu Harbor

**Hanafubuki otoko matsuri /** Falling Blossoms at a Man's Festival

**1953 Oyabaka hanagassen /** Doting Competition

**Gozen reiji /** Midnight

**Jonan kaidō /** The Road of Woman Trouble

**Daibosatsu tōge: Kōgen ittōryū no maki /** Daibosatsu Pass: Swordsmanship

**Daibosatsu tōge: Dainibu: Mibu to Shimabara no maki; Miwa no kansugi no maki /** Daibosatsu Pass: Part 2: Mibu and Shimabara; Sacred Cedar of Miwa

**Daibosatsu tōge: Daisanbu: Ryūjin no maki; Sanrin kamitsugi no maki /** Daibosatsu Pass: Part 3: The Dragon God; The Mountain Between

**Teishu no saiten /** Husbands' Festival

**Sasurai no kohan /** Wandering by the Lakeside

**Shinpen abaregasa (Zenpen; Kōhen) /** The Extraordinary Hat (Parts 1 and 2)

**Nichirin /** The Sun

**Beranmē shishi /** The Damned Lion

**Nangoku Taiheiki /** South-Country Taiheiki

**1954 Zoku nangoku Taiheiki: Satsunan no arashi /** South-Country Taiheiki 2: A Storm in Southern Satsuma

**Kōsetsu Araki Mataemon: Akatsuki no sanjūhachiningiri /** An Intimate Story of Mataemon Araki: The Killing of Thirty-Eight at Dawn

**Naruto hichō (Zenpen; Kōhen) /** Secret Story of Naruto (Parts 1 and 2)

**Shigemori-kun: Jōkyōsu /** Shigemori Goes to the Capital

**Bakushō tengoku: Tonchi kyōshitsu /** Heaven of Laughter: Witty Classroom

**Inugami-ke no nazo: Akuma wa odoru /** The Mystery of the Inugami Family: The Devil Dances

**Obōzu tengu (Zenpen; Kōhen) /** Monk Goblin (Parts 1 and 2)

**Hatamoto taikutsu otoko: Nazo no kaijin yashiki /** The Boring Retainer: Mysterious Ghost Mansion

**Iwami Jūtarō: Kessen Amanohashidate /** Jutaro Iwami: Decisive Battle at Amanohashidate

**1955 Yancha musume gyōjōki /** Conduct Report on a Tomboy

**Koi tengu /** Goblin in Love

**Hanayome rikkōhō /** The Bride Announces Her Candidacy

**Onmitsu wakashū /** Young Spies

**Morishige no Shinnyū shain /** Morishige the New Employee

**Nonki saiban /** Carefree Trials / Comedy Court

Morishige no Yarikuri shain /
Morishige the Employee Making
the Budget Balance

Waga na wa petenshi / My Name
Is Con Artist

Morishige no demakase shinshi /
Morishige's Fibbing Gentleman

Seki no Yatappe / Yatappe from
Seki

1956 Abare andon / Violent Lantern

Hokkai no hanran / Revolt in the
North Sea

Morishige no Shinkonryokō /
Morishige's Honeymoon

Bikkuri torimonochō: Onna
irezumi hyakumanryō / Surprising
Casebooks: A Woman, a Tattoo and
a Million Ryo

Onmitsu shichishōki: Ken'un
Usui tōge ranjin / Spy Chronicle of
Seven Lives: Sword Cloud Battle at
Usui Pass

Zoku onmitsu shichishōki:
Ryūjōkohaku no kessen / Spy
Chronicle of Seven Lives 2: Decisive
Battle of Fierce Fighting

Kingorō no Heitai-san / Kingoro
the Soldier

Onryō Sakura daisōdō / Grudging
Ghost: Great Trouble at Sakura

Harikiri shachō / Good-Spirited
Boss

Kinnō? Sabaku? Nyonin mandara
/ Emperor? Shogunate? Female
Mandala

Zoku Kinnō? Sabaku? Nyonin
mandara / Emperor? Shogunate?
Female Mandala 2

Onihime kyōen roku / Record
of the Devil Princess' Beauty
Competition

Yōun Satomi kaikyoden / Satomi
of the Ominous Cloud: Story of
Success

1957 Yōun Satomi kaikyoden: Kaiketsu
hen / Satomi of the Ominous
Cloud: Story of Success: Conclusion

Meiji tennō to Nichiro daisensō
/ The Emperor Meiji and the Great
Russo-Japanese War

Shura hakkō: Satsuta tōge
no kenjin / The Pains of Hell:
Swordsman at Satsuta Pass

Shura hakkō: Mōshū Fushima-
den / The Pains of Hell: Furious
Attack on Fushima Palace

Hibari no san'yaku: Kyōen
Yukinojō henge (Zenpen; Kōhen)
/ Hibari's Three Roles: Beauty
Contest of the Avenging Ghost
(Parts 1 and 2)

1958 Ankōru Watto monogatari:
Utsukushiki aishū / Story of
Ankhor Wat: Beautiful Sorrow

Chūshingura / Vendetta of the
Loyal 47 Ronin

Tenryū shibukigasa / Splattered
Hat at Tenryu River

Tenpō Suikoden / Bloody River
(lit. Tenpo-Era Water Margin)

Onna zamurai tadaima sanjō /
Female Samurai: Just Arrived

Okon no hatsukoi: Hanayome
shichihenge / Okon's First Love:
Seven Changes of the Bride

Nichiren to Mōko daishūrai /
Nichiren and the Great Mongolian
Invasion / Nichiren: A Man of Many
Miracles

Iga no suigetsu / Ambush at Iga
Pass (lit. Rainy Season in Iga)

Ōabare Tōkaidō / Great Violence
on the Tokaido

1959 Hebihimesama / The Snake
Princess

Onna no kyōshitsu / Women's
Class

Kinokuniya Bunzaemon:
Araumi ni idomu otoko ippiki
/ Kinokuniya, the Dauntless
Merchant (lit. Bunzaemon
Kinokuniya: One Man Who
Challenges the Violent Seas)

Ōabare happyakuyachō / Great
Violence across Edo

Bōfūken / Typhoon Zone

Fūrai monogatari: Ninkyō hen /
Story of a Tramp: Chivalry

Haresugata seizoroi: Kenkyō

gonin otoko / All Well Dressed:
Five Chivalrous Swordsman

1960 **Futari no Musashi** / Two Musashis

**Osai Gonzō: Moyuru koigusa** /
Osai and Gonzo: Burning Love-
Grass

**Gentarō bune** / Gentaro's Boat

**Fūrai monogatari: Abarehisha** /
Story of a Tramp: The Violent Rook

**Kenkyaku harusamegasa** / The
Swordsman's Hat for Spring Rain

**Tenka gomen** / Under Official
License

1961 **Zenigata Heiji torimonobikae:
Yoru no enma chō** / The
Casebooks of Heiji Zenigata: Notes
on the Hell King of Night

**Kenka Fuji** / Quarrel at Fuji

**Shindō no shachō shirīzu: Zoku
Jirochō shachō to Ishimatsu shain**
/ Shindo's Boss Series: Jirocho the
Boss and Ishimatsu the Employee
2

**Mito Kōmon umi o wataru** / Mito
Komon Crosses the Sea

**Hibari min'yō no tabi: Beranmē
geisha Sado e iku** / Hibari's Folk
Song Travel: The Damn Fool
Geisha Goes to Sado

**Akuma no temariuta** / The Devil's
Bouncing-Ball Song

1962 **Minami Taiheiyō namitakashi** /
The Kamikaze: Suicide Soldiers /
High Waves in the South Pacific
(lit.)

**Beranmē geisha to Ōsaka
musume** / The Damn Fool Geisha
and the Osaka Girl

**Yukaina nakama** / Cheerful
Company

**Min'yō no tabi: Sakurajima
Otemoyan** / Folk Song Travel:
Otemoyan at Sakurajima

**Nagadosu Chūshingura** / 47
Ronin with Long Swords

**Sanbyakujūgoya** / 365 Nights

**Hibari no Sado jōwa** / Hibari's Tale
of Pathos (lit. Hibari's Sado Love
Story)

1963 **Beranmē geisha to detchi shachō**
/ The Damn Fool Geisha and the
Assistant-Turned-Boss

**Min'yō no tabi: Akita obako** /
Akita Folk Song

**Zoku Nippon chinshōbai** / Rare
Trade in Japan 2

1965 **Meiji no fūsetsu: Yawara senpū**
/ Meiji Snowstorm: The Gentle
Whirlwind / Judo Duel

1970 **Sugata Sanshirō** / Sanshiro Sugata
/ Dawn of Judo

## YAGUCHI Shinobu
**(b. May 30, 1967)**
矢口史靖

A proficient director of mainstream comedies, Yaguchi won the PIA Film Festival Grand Prize for his 2-part 8mm film *Rain Woman* (*Ame onna*, 1990), about two young female thieves. His first theatrical feature, made with PIA scholarship funding, was *Barefoot Picnic* (*Hadashi no pikunikku*, 1993), which dramatized the disastrous chain of events which ensnares a high school girl after she is caught without a ticket by an inspector on a train. It earned Yaguchi praise for his pacy, rhythmic cutting. His next feature, *The Secret Garden* (*Himitsu no hanazono*, 1997), was another rather dark-toned comedy, about a money-fixated young woman's obsessive search for a cash-filled suitcase lost in a failed bank heist. The decision to focus on such an unlikeable protagonist was rather brave, and Yaguchi avoided any sentimental final redemption. A similar tone of mild amorality was visible in *Adrenalin Drive* (*Adorenarin doraibu*, 1999), about a driver and a nurse who, after another improbable chain of events, find themselves in possession of a box of yakuza takings. The implication

Suwingu gāruzu / Swing Girls *(2004): The predictability of Yaguchi's crowd-pleasing comedies is their charm.*

that the hero and heroine deserve the cash merely because they are nicer than the gangsters was dubious, but the film was well-paced and entertaining.

The heroine of *The Secret Garden* takes up swimming and rock climbing to further her quest for the money, and the theme of characters who excel in surprising hobbies was at the heart of Yaguchi's most popular comedies, *Waterboys* (*Wōtābōizu*, 2001) and *Swing Girls* (*Suwingu gāruzu*, 2004). In both films, a group of high school kids unwillingly take up an activity (synchronized swimming in the former, jazz in the latter), and proceed to make a success of it. The sharper edges of Yaguchi's earlier films had been smoothed away in these crowd-pleasing stories celebrating teamwork and self-respect; both were slightly pat in development and broad in characterization, and *Waterboys* espe-

cially was a little over-reliant on physical gags. But they were inventively shot and engagingly acted, and their predictability was their charm.

1987 **Furasutureitā** / Frustrator (*8mm short*)

1988 **Kaikisen** / Tropic (*8mm short*)

1990 **Asaki yumemishi** / Life in a Dream (*8mm short*)

 **Suisen terebi** / Tap and Television (*8mm short*)

 **Ame onna** / Rain Woman (*8mm*)

1993 **Hadashi no pikkunikku** / Barefoot Picnic / Down the Drain (*16mm*)

1996 **Bādo uotchingu** / Birdwatching (*16mm short*)

1997 **Himitsu no hanazono** / The Secret Garden / My Secret Cache / My Secret Place

1999 **Adorenarin doraibu** / Adrenaline Drive

 **Wan pīsu** / One Piece (*co-director*)

2001 **Wōtābōizu** / Waterboys
2002 **Paruko fikushon** / Parco Fiction
(*co-director*)
2004 **Suwingu gāruzu** / Swing Girls
2007 **Kayōkyoku da yo, jinsei wa**
/ Tokyo Rhapsody (lit. Life's a
Popular Song) (*co-director*)

## YAMADA Yōji
(b. September 13, 1931)
山田洋次

Yamada has almost single-handedly
sustained the bittersweet "Ōfuna flavor" of Shochiku's classic comedies
and melodramas through more cynical
times. Having written scripts for Shochiku stalwart Yoshitarō Nomura, who
recommended his promotion to the
director's chair, he made his debut with
a comedy, *Stranger on the Second Floor*
(*Nikai no tanin*, 1961). In the sixties, he
also made occasional serious films such
as *Flag in the Mist* (*Kiri no hata*, 1965),
a thriller based on a Seichō Matsumoto
novel, and *Sunshine in the Old Neighborhood* (*Shitamachi no taiyō*, 1963), a politically progressive story about a young
woman rejecting a salaryman's proposal
in order to avoid a conventional married
life. This marked his first collaboration
with actress Chieko Baishō, who was to
become a regular in his films.

His specialty, however, was heartwarming comedy. The roguish protagonists of such films as *Honest Fool*
(*Baka marudashi*, 1964) and *The Love-
able Tramp* (*Natsukashii fūraibō*, 1966)
became the prototypes of Yamada's
most famous character, Tora-san, a
rough-edged, irresponsible, yet sincere,
enterprising, and basically decent fellow
who, with the long-suffering family of
which he is the black sheep, personified

the spirit of the old Tokyo *shitamachi*
quarter. Played with impeccable comic
timing and a well-judged balance of
tough and tender by Kiyoshi Atsumi,
Tora-san appeared in 48 episodes under
the umbrella title "It's Tough Being a
Man" *(Otoko wa tsurai yo)* between 1969
and 1995, Yamada directing all but two.
Basically salutes to the close-knit urban
communities that had been eroded by
war and development, the films were
nostalgic from the start and somewhat
formulaic (Tora-san inevitably meeting, falling for, and losing the girl).
Nevertheless, their gentle warmth and
cozy charm made them tremendously
popular, and they kept Shochiku solvent through the seventies and eighties.
After Atsumi's death in 1996, Yamada
paid tribute with *The Man Who Caught
the Rainbow* (*Niji o tsukamu otoko*, 1996),
a Tora-san-like sentimental comedy
about a cinema manager in Tokushima
Prefecture, and a toast to the film medium itself. Yamada's cinephilia had also
expressed itself in another of his non-
Tora-san films, *Final Take* (*Kinema no
tenchi*, 1986), a loving, if somewhat inconsequential, recreation of moviemaking at Shochiku in the thirties.

Yamada has achieved critical success with a number of other non-
Tora-san films. Displaying similar
virtues—sureness of touch, human
warmth, performances of spontaneity
and vitality—these have been set in less
idealized, more realistic communities.
*Where Spring Comes Late* (*Kazoku*, 1970)
followed a family's move from Kyushu
to northerly Hokkaido; Donald Richie
commented that "it had emotional honesty, humor, and concern for ordinary
feelings that many thought had deserted Japanese cinema forever." *Home
from the Sea* (*Kokyō*, 1972) was a drama
about life in the island communities of

*Otoko wa tsurai yo: Bōkyō hen /
Tora-san's Runaway (1970): With the
character of Tora-san (Kiyoshi Atsumi),
Yamada brought more pleasure to more
people than any other Japanese director of
his generation.*

the Inland Sea; Yamada focused with
subtle poignancy on the problems of
poverty, depopulation, and unemployment. *The Village* (*Harakara*, 1975) was
a sunnier treatment of country life, following the efforts of a local community
to mount a stage musical; it was largely
saved from sentimentality by engaging
performances.

These serious films revealed Yamada's liberal attitudes and his respect
for flawed people, qualities also visible
in *The Yellow Handkerchief* (*Shiawase
no kiiroi hankachi*, 1977) and *A Distant
Cry from Spring* (*Haruka naru yama
no yobigoe*, 1980), two dramas about
criminals seeking to make new lives
for themselves. An interest in socially
marginalized characters was sustained
during the nineties in the *School* (*Gakkō*)
series about teachers working in difficult circumstances. Of these, the first
focused on a night school educating students who failed to graduate from high
school, including several also marginalized by their immigrant status. The second touchingly examined the problems
involved in caring for mentally disabled
children. Perhaps Yamada's best film,
however, was *My Sons* (*Musuko*, 1991),
which evoked the spirit of Ozu. Indeed,
with its story of the distant relationship
between a father in the countryside and
his sons in Tokyo after the death of the
mother, it could almost have been conceived as a sequel to *Tokyo Story* (*Tōkyō
monogatari*, 1953). In recent years,
Yamada has widened his range with
three well-crafted period films: *The
Twilight Samurai* (*Tasogare seibei*, 2002),
*The Hidden Blade* (*Kakushi ken oni no
tsume*, 2004), and *Love and Honor* (*Bushi
no ichibun*, 2006). Though atypical in
setting, they focused characteristically
on ordinary or marginalized people: the
protagonists of the first two films were
low-ranking samurai, while the hero
of *Love and Honor*, employed as a food
taster for a local aristocrat, goes blind
after sampling a poisoned dish. *The
Hidden Blade*, in particular, was a moving account of an ordinary man striving
to act decently in turbulent times.

Despite his liberal politics, Yamada
has sometimes been criticized for stylistic conservatism. Certainly, his films lack
the formal innovation of his New Wave
contemporaries, but he is an undoubted
*auteur*, always scripting his own films,
and his sensitivity as a director of actors
is undeniable. He has also displayed a
nearly postmodern sophistication in
casting; in the seventies, for instance,
the regular Tora-san actors appeared
in non-Tora-san films so that, as with
Ozu's work, a surface realism was dis-
rupted by the viewer's consciousness of
the stars' established personae. Though
Yamada, unlike Ozu, has sometimes let

tenderness slip into sentimentality, he has probably brought more pleasure to more people than any other Japanese director of his generation.

1961 **Nikai no tanin** / Stranger on the Second Floor / The Stranger Upstairs

1963 **Shitamachi no taiyō** / Sunshine in the Old Neighborhood / The Sunshine Girl

1964 **Baka marudashi** / Honest Fool

**Iikagen baka** / The Irresponsible Fool

**Baka ga tanku de yatte kuru** / The Fool Comes on a Tank

1965 **Kiri no hata** / Flag in the Mist / The Trap

1966 **Un ga yokerya** / Gambler's Luck

**Natsukashii fūraibō** / The Lovable Tramp

1967 **Kyūchan no dekkai yume** / Let's Have a Dream (lit. Kyu-chan's Huge Dream)

**Ai no sanka** / Song of Love

**Kigeki: Ippatsu shōbu** / The Greatest Challenge of All

1968 **Hana Hajime no ippatsu daibōken** / The Million Dollar Pursuit

**Fukeba tobu yona otoko da ga** / The Shy Deceiver

1969 **Kigeki: Ippatsu daihisshō** / Vagabond Schemer

**Otoko wa tsurai yo** / Tora-san, Our Lovable Tramp / It's Tough Being a Man (lit.)

**Zoku otoko wa tsurai yo** / Tora-san's Cherished Mother / Tora-san 2

1970 **Otoko wa tsurai yo: Bōkyō hen** / Tora-San's Runaway / Tora-san 5

**Kazoku** / Where Spring Comes Late / The Family (lit.)

1971 **Otoko wa tsurai yo: Junjō hen** / Tora-san's Shattered Romance / Tora-san 6

**Otoko wa tsurai yo: Funtō hen** / Tora-san, the Good Samaritan / Tora-san 7

**Otoko wa tsurai yo: Torajirō koiuta** / Tora-san's Love Call / Tora-san 8

1972 **Otoko wa tsurai yo: Shibamata bojō** / Tora-san's Dear Old Home / Tora-san 9

**Kokyō** / Home from the Sea / Homecoming / Native Place (lit.)

**Otoko wa tsurai yo: Torajirō yumemakura** / Tora-san's Dream Come True / Tora-san 10

1973 **Otoko wa tsurai yo: Torajirō wasurenagusa** / Tora-san's Forget Me Not / Tora-san 11

**Otoko wa tsurai yo: Watashi no Tora-san** / Tora-san Loves an Artist / Tora-san 12

1974 **Otoko wa tsurai yo: Torajirō koiyatsure** / Tora-san's Lovesick / Tora-san 13

**Otoko wa tsurai yo: Torajirō komoriuta** / Tora-san's Lullaby / Tora-san 14

1975 **Otoko wa tsurai yo: Torajirō aiaigasa** / Tora-san's Rise and Fall / Tora-san Meets the Songstress Again / Tora-san: Love under One Umbrella / Tora-san 15

**Harakara** / The Village

**Otoko wa tsurai yo: Katsushika risshi hen** / Tora-san the Intellectual / Tora-san 16

1976 **Otoko wa tsurai yo: Torajirō yūyake koyake** / Tora-san's Sunrise and Sunset / Tora-san 17

**Otoko wa tsurai yo: Torajirō junjōshishū** / Tora-san's Pure Love / Tora-san 18

1977 **Otoko wa tsurai yo: Torajirō to tonosama** / Tora-san Meets His Lordship / Tora-san 19

**Shiawase no kiiroi hankachi** / The Yellow Handkerchief / The Yellow Handkerchief of Happiness (lit.)

**Otoko wa tsurai yo: Torajirō ganbare** / Tora-san Plays Cupid / Tora-san 20

1978 **Otoko wa tsurai yo: Torajirō waga michi o yuku** / Stage-Struck Tora-san / Tora-san 21

Otoko wa tsurai yo: Uwasa no
Torajirō / Talk of the Town Tora-
san / Tora-san 22

1979 Otoko wa tsurai yo: Tonderu
Torajirō / Tora-san, the
Matchmaker / Tora-san 23

Otoko wa tsurai yo: Torajirō haru
no yume / Tora-san's Dream of
Spring / Tora-san 24

1980 Haruka naru yama no yobigoe / A
Distant Cry from Spring / A Distant
Cry from the Mountains (lit.)

Otoko wa tsurai yo: Torajirō
haibisukasu no hana / Tora-san's
Tropical Fever / Tora-san 25

Otoko wa tsurai yo: Torajirō
kamome uta / Foster Daddy, Tora /
Tora-san 26

1981 Otoko wa tsurai yo: Naniwa no
koi no Torajirō / Tora-san's Love
in Osaka / Tora-san 27

Otoko wa tsurai yo: Torajirō
kamifūsen / Tora-san's Promise /
Tora-san 28

1982 Otoko wa tsurai yo: Torajirō
ajisai no koi / Hearts and Flowers
for Tora-san / Tora-san 29

Otoko wa tsurai yo: Hana mo
arashi mo Torajirō / Tora-san the
Expert / Tora-san 30

1983 Otoko wa tsurai yo: Tabi to onna
to Torajirō / Tora-san's Song of
Love / Tora-san 31

Otoko wa tsurai yo: Kuchibue
o fuku Torajirō / Tora-san Goes
Religious? / Tora-san 32

1984 Otoko wa tsurai yo: Yogiri ni
musebu Torajirō / Marriage
Counselor Tora-san / Tora-san 33

Otoko wa tsurai yo: Torajirō
shinjitsu ichiro / Tora-san's
Forbidden Love / Tora-san 34

1985 Otoko wa tsurai yo: Torajirō
ren'ai juku / Tora-san the Go-
Between / Tora-san 35

Otoko wa tsurai yo: Shibamata
yori ai o komete / Tora-san's Island
Encounter / Tora-san 36

1986 Kinema no tenchi / Final Take (lit.
The World of Cinema)

Otoko wa tsurai yo: Shiawase
no aoi tori / Tora-san's Bluebird
Fantasy / Tora-san 37

1987 Otoko wa tsurai yo: Shiretoko
bojō / Tora-san Goes North / Tora-
san 38

Otoko wa tsurai yo: Torajiro
monogatari / Tora-san Plays Daddy
/ Tora-san 39

1988 Dauntaun hīrōzu / Downtown
Heroes / Hope and Pain

Otoko wa tsurai yo: Torajirō
sarada kinenbi / Tora-san's Salad-
Day Memorial / Tora-san 40

1989 Otoko wa tsurai yo: Torajirō
kokoro no tabi / Tora-san Goes to
Vienna / Tora-san 41

Otoko wa tsurai yo: Boku no
ojisan / Tora-san, My Uncle / Tora-
san 42

1990 Otoko wa tsurai yo: Torajirō no
kyūjitsu / Tora-san Takes a Vacation
/ Tora-san 43

1991 Musuko / My Sons

Otoko wa tsurai yo: Torajirō no
kokuhaku / Tora-san's Confession /
Tora-san 44

1992 Otoko wa tsurai yo: Torajirō no
seishun / Tora-san Makes Excuses /
Tora-san 45

1993 Gakkō / A Class to Remember (lit.
School)

Otoko wa tsurai yo: Torajirō no
endan / Tora-san's Matchmaker
/ Tora-san's Marriage Proposal /
Tora-san 46

1994 Otoko wa tsurai yo: Haikei
Kuruma Torajirō-sama / Tora-
san's Easy Advice / Tora-san 47

1995 Otoko wa tsurai yo: Torajirō
kurenai no hana / Tora-san to the
Rescue / Tora-san 48

1996 Gakkō II / The Learning Circle / A
Class to Remember 2 (lit. School 2)

Niji o tsukamu otoko / The Man
Who Caught the Rainbow / The
Rainbow Seeker

1997 Niji o tsukamu otoko: Nangoku
funtō hen / The Man Who Caught

the Rainbow: Invigorating Fight in the South Country

1998 **Gakkō III** / The New Voyage (lit. School 3)

2000 **15-sai: Gakkō IV** / Fifteen / A Class to Remember 4: Fifteen (lit. Fifteen: School 4)

2002 **Tasogare Seibei** / The Twilight Samurai

2004 **Kakushi ken oni no tsume** / The Hidden Blade

2006 **Bushi no ichibun** / Love and Honor


# YAMAMOTO Kajirō
## (March 15, 1902–September 21, 1974)
山本嘉次郎

Yamamoto is remembered today largely as mentor to Akira Kurosawa, who assisted him on *Horse* (*Uma*, 1941), *Composition Class* (*Tsuzurikata kyōshitsu*, 1938), and *The Loves of Tojuro* (*Tōjūrō no koi*, 1938). At his best, however, he was a distinguished filmmaker in his own right. Having directed a handful of films in the mid twenties, he served from 1926 to 1932 as scenarist for Kenji Mizoguchi, Tomu Uchida, and Tomotaka Tasaka. Subsequently he joined P.C.L. (later Toho), a company specializing in literary adaptations; his two versions of novels by Sōseki Natsume, *Botchan* (1935) and *I Am a Cat* (*Wagahai wa neko de aru*, 1936), were somewhat academic in style, but revealed a talent for light comedy and social satire. A rather broader comic touch was evident in the many star vehicles he directed for comedian Enoken, who essayed parodic impersonations of famous samurai heroes. Of these films, *Pickpocket Kinta* (*Enoken no Chakkiri Kinta*, 1937) is considered the best.

Among Yamamoto's other prewar films, *The Loves of Tojuro* was an Edo-period drama with interesting metatheatrical elements, its actor hero finding inspiration for his role in memories of a youthful love affair. Best known today among his films of the era, however, are two realist accounts of life in northern Japan, both starring the young Hideko Takamine. *Composition Class* was a fascinating account of a teenage writer whose honesty offends her community. *Horse* was a touching story of a girl raising a colt; the drama was anchored in a semi-documentary portrait of a Tohoku farming community through four seasons. Yamamoto's rightist attitudes were implicit in the resolutions of these films: the heroine of *Composition Class* learns, in Peter High's words, "to dissemble in the face of intimidation," while in *Horse* the colt is finally sold to the army.

His pro-militarist sympathies and realist approach made Yamamoto a logical choice to direct *The War at Sea from Hawaii to Malaya* (*Hawai-Marē oki kaisen*, 1942), a big-budget, meticulously detailed reconstruction of the attack on Pearl Harbor, released on its first anniversary. He followed this with *Kato's Falcon Fighters* (*Katō hayabusa sentōtai*, 1944), a biopic of an ace pilot who had died in combat in 1942, and *Torpedo Squadrons Move Out* (*Raigekitai shutsudō*, 1944), a glorification of kamikaze pilots. After the war, Yamamoto was a co-founder of Motion Picture Art Association, the company that produced Kurosawa's *Stray Dog* (*Nora inu*, 1949). His own postwar work spanned various genres. He directed several gangster pictures, for instance, *Underworld* (*Ankokugai*, 1956) and *A Man among Men* (*Dansei No. 1*, 1955), and realized *The Adventures of Sun Wu Kung* (*Songokū*, 1959), a fantasy about the Buddhist monkey of Chinese folklore. But he continued to specialize primarily in comedy, making the popular film about salarymen, *Mr. Hope* (*Hōpu-san: Sararīman tora no maki*, 1951), and Toho's first color production, *Girls among the Flowers* (*Hana no naka no musumetachi*, 1953). His later films, however, lacked the distinction of his best prewar work.

1924 **Nekka no jūjiro** / Hot Fire at the Crossroads
**Kagonotori** / Caged Bird
**Dan'un** / Scattered Clouds
**Renbō kouta (Shōdoshima jōwa)** / Short Song of Love (Love Story of Shodoshima)
**Yama no shinpi** / Secret of the Mountain
**Kōfuku jidai** / Time of Happiness
1925 **Mori no asa** / Morning in the Forest
**Hito o kutta hanashi** / The Story That Mocked a Man
**Bakudanji** / Bomber Kid
**Kagayakeru tobira** / Gateway to Glory
1926 **Danji no ichidaku** / The Boy's Agreement
**Matsuda eiga shōhinshū** / Matsuda Collection of Short Films (*co-director*)
**Haha ni chikaite** / Vow to Mother
**Tōsan no urimono** / Father's Goods
1932 **Sai-kun shinsenjutsu** / Wife's New Tactic
**Junanka** / Passion Flower / Ordeal
**Hohoemu Nikkatsu** / Smiling Nikkatsu
1933 **Sōkyū no mon** / Gate to the Blue Sky
**Momoiro no musume** / The Pink Girl
**Ren'ai hijōji** / Love Crisis
**Nyōbō seifuku** / Conquest of a Wife
1934 **Furusato harete** / Brightening Hometown

**Ren'ai sukījutsu** / Love and the Art of Skiing
**Enoken no Seishun Suikoden** / Enoken's Youthful Liquor Margin
**Arupusu taishō** / General of the Alps / Alpine Victory
1935 **Botchan**
**Sumire musume** / The Violet Girl
**Itazura kozō** / Tricks of an Errand Boy
**Enoken no Kondō Isami** / Enoken Plays Isami Kondo
1936 **Enoken no Donguri Tonbei** / Enoken's Tombei of the Acorns
**Wagahai wa neko de aru** / I Am a Cat
**Enoken no Senman chōja** / Enoken the Billionaire
**Zoku Enoken no Senman chōja** / Enoken the Billionaire 2
**Shinkon ura omote** / Two Sides of a New Marriage
1937 **Otto no teisō: Zenpen: Haru kureba** / A Husband's Chastity: Part 1: When Spring Comes
**Otto no teisō: Kōhen: Aki futatabi** / A Husband's Chastity: Part 2: Autumn Once More
**Nihon josei dokuhon** / Japanese Women's Textbook
**Enoken no Chakkiri Kinta (Zenpen; Kōhen)** / Pickpocket Kinta (lit. Enoken's Kinta the Pickpocket) (Parts 1 and 2)
**Utsukushiki taka** / Beautiful Hawk
1938 **Tōjūrō no koi** / The Loves of Tojuro / Loves of a Kabuki Actor
**Tsuzurikata kyōshitsu** / Composition Class
**Enoken no Bikkuri jinsei** / Enoken: Life Is a Surprise
1939 **Enoken no Gatchiri jidai** / Enoken's Time of Shrewdness
**Chūshingura (Zenpen; Kōhen)** / The Loyal 47 Ronin (Parts 1 and 2)
**Nonki yokochō** / Easy Alley
1940 **Roppa no Shinkonryokō** / Roppa's Honeymoon

Enoken no Zangiri Kinta / Enoken's Slashing Kinta / Enoken's Cropped Hair

Songokū (Zenpen; Kōhen) / The Monkey King (Parts 1 and 2) / Monkey Sun

1941 Uma / Horse

Chimata ni ame no furu gotoku / Like Rain in the Neighborhood

1942 Kibō no seishun / Hopeful Youth

Hawai-Marē oki kaisen / The War at Sea From Hawaii to Malaya

1944 Katō hayabusa sentōtai / Kato's Falcon Fighters

Raigekitai shutsudō / Torpedo Squadrons Move Out

1945 Amerika yōrō / Straight to the Americans (*uncompleted*)

1946 Asu o tsukuru hitobito / Those Who Make Tomorrow (*co-director*)

1947 Yottsu no koi no monogatari / Four Love Stories (*co-director*)

Shin baka jidai (Zenpen; Kōhen) / The New Age of Fools / These Foolish Times (Parts 1 and 2)

Haru no kyōen / Spring Banquet

1949 Kaze no ko / Child of the Wind / Children of the Wind

Haru no tawamure / Spring Flirtation

1950 Datsugoku / Escape from Prison

Shinju fujin: Shojo no maki / Mrs. Pearl: Virgin Reel

Shinju fujin: Hitozuma no maki / Mrs. Pearl: Wife Reel

1951 Erejī / Elegy

Hōpu-san: Sararīman tora no maki / Mr. Hope (lit. Mr. Hope: Primer for the Salaryman)

Onnagokoro dare ga shiru / Who Knows a Woman's Heart?

1952 Nanairo no machi / Town of Seven Colors

1953 Koi no fūunji / Lucky Adventures of Love

Hana no naka no musumetachi / Girls among the Flowers / Girls in the Orchard

Yūgatō / Light Trap

1954 Botchan shain / Mr. Valiant (lit. The Young Master as Company Man)

Zoku botchan shain / Mr. Valiant Rides Again (lit. The Young Master as Company Man 2)

Doyōbi no tenshi / Saturday's Angel

1955 Dansei No. 1 / A Man among Men / No. 1 Man (lit.)

Ore mo otoko sa / I'm a Man Too!

Muttsuri Umon torimonochō / The Casebooks of Sullen Umon

Ai no rekishi / History of Love

1956 Ankokugai / Underworld

Ojōsan tōjō / A Young Lady on Her Way

Manasuru ni tatsu: Hyōkō 8125-mēta / Standing on Manaslu: 8125 Meters above Sea Level

1957 "Dōbutsuen monogatari" yori: Zō / From "Zoo Story": Elephant

Zenta to Sanpei monogatari: Kaze no naka no kodomo / The Tale of Zenta and Sanpei: Children in the Wind

Zenta to Sanpei monogatari: Obake no sekai / The Tale of Zenta and Sanpei: World of Monsters

1958 Jazu musume ni eikō are / Glory to the Jazz Girls

Tōkyō no kyūjitsu / A Holiday in Tokyo

1959 Songokū / The Adventures of Sun Wu Kung / Monkey Sun / The Monkey King

1960 Ginza taikutsu musume / Ginza Tomboy (lit. Bored Girl in Ginza)

1964 Tensai sagishi monogatari: Tanuki no hanamichi / Story of a Genius Swindler: A Raccoon Dog's Path to Success

Hana no Ōedo no musekinin / Flowers of Edo

1965 Tanuki no taishō / General Raccoon Dog / Samurai Joker

**1966** Tanuki no ōsama / King Raccoon
Dog / Thief on the Run
**Tanuki no kyūjitsu** / The Raccoon
Dog's Day Off / Swindler Meets
Swindler

## YAMAMOTO Satsuo
**(July 15, 1910–August 11, 1983)**
山本薩夫

An avowed social critic and polemicist long affiliated with the Japanese Communist Party, Yamamoto spent the prewar years at the progressive, Western-oriented studio P.C.L. (subsequently Toho), then something of a refuge for left-wingers. Several of his early films betrayed the influence of Western models: thus, *Pastoral Symphony* (*Den'en kōkyōkyoku*, 1938) adapted André Gide's novel about a pastor's love for a blind girl, while *Mother's Song* (*Haha no kyoku*, 1937) was a *haha-mono* inspired by the classic American melodrama of suffering motherhood *Stella Dallas*. Even in the early postwar period, *Who Turned Me into This Kind of Woman?* (*Konna onna ni dare ga shita*, 1949) continued to draw on foreign literature, relocating Thomas Hardy's *Tess of the D'Urbervilles* to a wartime field hospital.

Like most directors of his generation, Yamamoto was unable to avoid making patriotic films during the war, but his contributions were not especially propagandist in nature. In the Kurosawa-scripted *Winged Victory* (*Tsubasa no gaika*, 1942), about the relationship between two aviators who had been raised as brothers, "the old didacticism is almost overwhelmed by the film's real theme of love" (Peter High's words). Soon after the war, he collaborated with documentarist Fumio Kamei

on *War and Peace* (*Sensō to heiwa*, 1947). A powerful drama about a woman who remarries after being informed that her soldier husband has died, only for him to return alive, this was sometimes over-rhetorical in style, but inescapably moving.

Since the major studios refused to support his explicitly political projects, Yamamoto became a pioneer of independent production. *Street of Violence* (*Pen itsuwarazu: Bōryokugai no machi*, 1950), based on a true story, depicted a crusading journalist's campaign against organized crime; *The Sunless Street* (*Taiyō no nai machi*, 1954) charted a strike at a printing factory; *Vacuum Zone* (*Shinkū chitai*, 1952) was a savage indictment of the brutality of the Japanese army; and *Storm Clouds Over Hakone* (*Hakone fūun roku*, 1952) was a historical epic about peasants building a canal in defiance of the local aristocracy. These films were all visually striking: location shooting in the town where the original events had occurred gave *Street of Violence* an effective quality of documentary realism, while *Storm Clouds Over Hakone* evoked the montage and compositional techniques of Soviet silent film. However, their polemical intention stripped them of subtlety; the use of heavy close ups and hectoring camera angles, especially in *Vacuum Zone*, was less hard-hitting than bludgeoning. Donald Richie has complained that Yamamoto "uses an axe where he should use a scalpel"; certainly, his polarization of humanity into a heroic proletariat and villainous militarists, capitalists, and aristocrats was a little simplistic.

In fact, Yamamoto's political commentary was most effective when indirect. The independently produced *Ballad of a Cart* (*Niguruma no uta*, 1959) and the Daiei-made *The Public Benefactor*

©Dokuritsu Pro

Niguruma no uta / Ballad of a Cart *(1959): This dynamic scene of a farmers' riot tellingly illustrates Yamamoto's political commitment.*

(*Kizudarake no sanga*, 1964) had an untypical depth of characterization, thanks to intelligent scripts by distinguished screenwriters (Yoshikata Yoda and Kaneto Shindō, respectively). These films allowed their social critiques to emerge naturally from the drama. The former, chronicling an unhappy marriage from the Meiji period to the end of the war, detailed the oppression of Japanese women in exceptionally moving fashion, and was probably Yamamoto's masterpiece. The latter criticized big business largely through its depiction of a selfish tycoon's destructive effect on those around him. Also interesting was *Trouble about a Typhoon* (*Taifū sōdōki*, 1956), a witty and revealing satire about small-scale political corruption, in which a typhoon-hit village deliberately demolishes its unharmed school in order

to claim extra compensation. The film now seems to foreshadow the growing collusion in Japan between government and the construction industry, a concern which Yamamoto would later explore in *Total Eclipse* (*Kinkanshoku*, 1975), a thinly fictionalized assault on the leading politicians of the seventies.

Working mainly under contract at Daiei during the sixties, Yamamoto made several more socially aware comedies. *Red Water* (*Akai mizu*, 1963) was another sharp satire on small-town politics, about the machinations of councillors and the local priest seeking to capitalize on a possible hot spring development. *The Burglar Story* (*Nippon dorobō monogatari*, 1965), a wry account of a thief attempting to go straight, touched on a notorious act of sabotage which Yamamoto had treated more seriously in *The Matsukawa Derailment Incident* (*Matsukawa jiken*, 1961). It also formed something of a pair with *The Bogus Detective* (*Nise keiji*, 1967): although the protagonists of the two works (superbly played by Rentarō Mikuni and Shintarō Katsu, respectively) were on opposite sides of the law, both were naive men bewildered by the complexities and corruption of the world. Mikuni also played the arrogant surgeon antihero of *The Ivory Tower* (*Shiroi kyotō*, 1966), a slickly made but overlong indictment of Japanese medical ethics and of the machinations surrounding an election to a professorship in a university hospital.

Yamamoto's political commitment was sustained in several more generic films. *Band of Assassins* (*Shinobi no mono*, 1962), although essentially a conventional *jidai-geki* vehicle for popular star Raizō Ichikawa, preserved the director's customary sympathy for little people exploited by the powerful, while *Blood End* (*Tengutō*, 1969) showed how a group of warriors initially dedicated to the cause of liberating the farming and merchant classes disintegrated through mutual mistrust and the corruption of egalitarian ideals. More psychological in emphasis was *Freezing Point* (*Hyōten*, 1966), a melodrama probing issues of personal guilt and responsibility through a couple's reactions to their daughter's murder.

Though somewhat less personal than his independent work, Yamamoto's studio productions were more elegant: witness the flair of the opening crane shot over the battlefield in *Band of Assassins*, the shadowy figures emerging onto the railway tracks in *The Burglar Story*, and the eerie nighttime festival scene in the otherwise ordinary ghost story, *The Bride from Hades* (*Botan dōrō*,

1968). Yamamoto continued to work until his death: the two *Nomugi Pass* films (*Ā, Nomugi Tōge*, 1979 and 1982) were scathing accounts of the ill-treatment of Meiji-era silk workers by their employers. Though he has long been championed by Tadao Satō, Yamamoto's approach is currently unfashionable. Still, if his films lacked the complexity with which Kei Kumai examined similar issues, his limitations should not obscure the power of his best work.

1937 **Ojōsan** / The Young Miss
**Haha no kyoku (Zenpen; Kōhen)** / Mother's Song (Parts 1 and 2)
1938 **Den'en kōkyōkyoku** / Pastoral Symphony
**Katei nikki (Zenpen; Kōhen)** / Family Diary (Parts 1 and 2)
1939 **Shinpen Tange Sazen: Hayate hen** / Sazen Tange, New Version: Hayate Chapter
**Uruwashiki shuppatsu** / Beautiful Departure
**Machi** / The Street
**Ribon o musubu fujin** / A Lady with a Ribbon
1940 **Soyokaze chichi to tomo ni** / In the Breeze, with Father
**Kyōdai no yakusoku** / Sisters' Promise
1941 **Utaeba tengoku** / Heaven When I Sing
1942 **Tsubasa no gaika** / Winged Victory
1943 **Neppū** / Hot Winds / Searing Wind
1947 **Sensō to heiwa** / War and Peace / Between War and Peace (*co-director*)
1949 **Konna onna ni dare ga shita** / Who Turned Me into This Kind of Woman?
1950 **Pen itsuwarazu: Bōryoku no machi** / Street of Violence (lit. The Pen Does Not Lie: Street of Violence)
1952 **Hakone fūun roku** / Storm Clouds Over Hakone

Shinkū chitai / Vacuum Zone

1954 Hi no hate / To the End of the Sun

Taiyō no nai machi / The Sunless Street

1955 Ai sureba koso / Because I Love / If You Love Me (*co-director*)

Ukigusa nikki / Duckweed Story

1956 Nadare / Avalanche

Taifū sōdōki / Trouble about a Typhoon

1958 Akai jinbaori / The Scarlet Cloak

1959 Niguruma no uta / Ballad of a Cart / Song of the Cart / A Song of the Wagon

Ningen no kabe / The Human Wall

1960 Buki naki tatakai / Battle without Arms

1961 Matsukawa jiken / The Matsukawa Derailment Incident

1962 Chibusa o idaku musumetachi / The Girls Who Embrace Udders

Shinobi no mono / Band of Assassins / The Ninja

1963 Akai mizu / Red Water / The Red Tattoo

Zoku shinobi no mono / Band of Assassins 2 / The Ninja Part 2

1964 Kizudarake no sanga / The Public Benefactor / The Tycoon / Scarred Nature (lit.)

1965 Nippon dorobō monogatari / The Burglar Story

Shōnin no isu / The Witness Chair

Supai / The Spy

1966 Hyōten / Freezing Point

Shiroi kyotō / The Ivory Tower / The Great White Tower

1967 Nise keiji / The Bogus Detective

Zatōichi rōyaburi / Zatoichi the Outlaw / Zatoichi Breaks Jail (lit.)

1968 Dorei kōjō / Slave Factory

Botan dōrō / The Bride from Hades / A Tale of the Peony Lantern

1969 Betonamu / Vietnam

Tengutō / Blood End (lit. Party of Goblins)

1970 Sensō to ningen: Daiichibu: Unmei no jokyoku / Men and War: Part 1: Fate's Overture

1971 Sensō to ningen: Dainibu: Ai to kanashimi no sanga / Men and War: Part 2: Landscapes of Love and Sadness

1973 Sensō to ningen: Daisanbu: Kanketsu hen / Men and War: Part 3: Conclusion

1974 Karei naru ichizoku / The Family (lit. The Glorious Family)

1975 Kinkanshoku / Total Eclipse

1976 Fumō chitai / Barren Zone / The Marginal Land

Tenpō Suikoden: Ōhara Yūgaku / Tenpo-era Water Margin: Yugaku Ohara

1978 Kōtei no inai hachigatsu / August without an Emperor

1979 Ā, Nomugi tōge / Nomugi Pass

1981 Asshiitachi no machi / Town of Lovestruck Boys

1982 Ā, Nomugi tōge: Shinryoku hen / Nomugi Pass: Fresh Pastures

## YAMAMURA Sō
### (February 24, 1910–May 26, 2000)
### 山村聡

A distinguished actor with a long career in cinema, Yamamura also directed several creditable films, the best-known being his independently made debut, *The Crab-Canning Ship* (*Kanikōsen*, 1953), which described the ill-treatment and abortive mutiny of the workers on a factory ship off Northern Japan. Set in the 1920s, it was derivative in style of Soviet silent-film techniques; however, the homage was skillful, and though the characterizations tended to slip into caricature, it achieved a considerable force. A less partisan social conscience was visible in Yamamura's second film,

*The Black Tide* (*Kuroi ushio*, 1954), about a reporter's quest to uncover the truth, obscured by slanted editorial approaches, about the death of a Japanese National Railways president. His next work, *Sal Flower Pass* (*Sara no hana no tōge*, 1955), focused on the problems of farmers in a remote village.

Yamamura later directed three films at Toei. *Mother-and-Child Grass* (*Hahakogusa*, 1959) was a remake of a wartime film by Tomotaka Tasaka about a sacrificing mother. *Maidens of the Kashima Sea* (*Kashimanada no onna*, 1959) was another film about life among farmers, set in the countryside of Chiba Prefecture east of Tokyo. Yamamura's last film, *Deep River Melody* (*Fūryū Fukagawa uta*, 1960) was an engaging Taisho-period drama about the problems affecting a planned marriage between the daughter of a restaurant owner and his chef. Displaying a heartwarming optimism and humanity in its treatment of potentially bleak subject matter, this was also directed with something of the tenderness and stylistic invention of Heinosuke Gosho, confirming that Yamamura, despite the brevity of his directorial career, had a genuine talent as a filmmaker.

1953  **Kanikōsen** / The Crab-Canning Ship
1954  **Kuroi ushio** / The Black Tide
1955  **Sara no hana no tōge** / Sal Flower Pass
1959  **Hahakogusa** / Mother and Her Children / Mother-and-Child Grass (lit. Cottonweed)
      **Kashimanada no onna** / Maidens of the Kashima Sea
1960  **Fūryū Fukagawa uta** / Deep River Melody / The Song of Fukagawa (lit. Elegant Song of Fukagawa)

**YAMANAKA Sadao**
**(November 7, 1909–September 17, 1938)**
山中貞雄

Yamanaka's brief career, precocious talent, and premature death have earned him a reputation comparable to that of Jean Vigo in the French cinema. Becoming a director at the age of 22, he made nearly two dozen films in less than six years, of which just three are preserved complete. Of his silent films, only fragments from the action sequences survive; these display his skill in choreographing combat, but are doubtless unrepresentative of the tone of the original films, since the distinction of Yamanaka's work was in shifting the focus of the *jidai-geki* from action to character. His directorial debut, *Sleeping with a Long Sword* (*Iso no Genta: Dakine no nagadosu*, 1932), was admired for eschewing scenes of swordplay completely, while his second film, *Money Trickles Down* (*Koban shigure*, 1932), which won praise for its rhythmic montage techniques, narrated a distinctly unheroic plot about a ronin working in an Edo restaurant. Similarly, *The Elegant Swordsman* (*Fūryū katsujinken*, 1934) told the story of a ronin's search for his parents, but was primarily a group portrait of life in a Tokugawa-era tenement. Among Yamanaka's lost sound films, *The Village Tatooed Man* (*Machi no irezumimono*, 1935) followed a criminal's experiences after his release from prison, while *Ishimatsu of the Forest* (*Mori no Ishimatsu*, 1937) recounted the tragedy of a young outlaw.

In the still extant *Kochiyama Soshun* (*Kōchiyama Sōshun*, 1936) and *Humanity and Paper Balloons* (*Ninjō kamifūsen*, 1937) Yamanaka essayed anti-heroic reworkings of Kabuki narratives, bringing realism to stylized plots and deglamoriz-

Machi no irezumimono / The Village Tattooed Man *(1935): Yamanaka's work eschewed swordplay for realism of setting and characterization. Sadly, most of his films, including this one, are lost.*

ing flamboyant characterizations. Both films expressed an ironic attitude to human aspiration: in *Kochiyama Soshun*, the most resourceful character sacrifices his life for the most worthless, while the tenement dwellers in *Humanity and Paper Balloons* attempt to improve their lot by seeking patronage or by turning to crime, all to no result. Nevertheless, the excellence of the acting and precision of observation turned the films into celebrations of human vitality, ingenuity, and the capacity to endure, so that their desolate endings seemed incongruous. Less realistic in tone was *The Pot Worth a Million Ryo (Tange Sazen yowa: Hyakumanryō no tsubo*, 1935) the other Yamanaka film to be preserved today. This breezy farce also satirized aspiration as the whole of Edo embarks on a fruit-

less search for a lost pot which contains a map pointing to a priceless treasure. Again, Yamanaka subverted stereotypes in his portrayal of one-eyed, one-armed samurai Sazen Tange as a soft-hearted layabout, while also finding hope in the affections of the surrogate family established when he and his lover adopt an orphaned child.

Yamanaka's skill was in the creation of plausible communities, a talent furthered by his ability to dovetail numerous plot strands, and by the imaginative use of staging in depth which ensured that his characters were seen in the context of their environment. Though he worked exclusively in *jidai-geki*, his friend and fellow director Yasujirō Ozu suggested that he would have turned to contemporary subject matter had he lived. Kimitoshi Satō has observed that "We find people in his films to be just as our neighbors are in this modern world," and certainly, Yamanaka's recreations of the social milieux of old Edo were almost as rich in realistic detail as Ozu's depictions of contemporary Tokyo. He found his protagonists among the lower classes—the Edo-period equivalent of the *shomin*—with samurai and daimyo playing second fiddle to petty criminals, quack doctors, barbers, and pawnbrokers. Yamanaka was not a moralist; his films did not judge people, but explored the reasons for their actions. Yet his philosophy was not one of social determinism; rather, his concern was with society as constituted by the intricate interaction of individuals subject to various pressures, yet with their own intentions, motives, and desires.

Yamanaka's death in China after his conscription made him seem a martyr for Japanese liberalism. His last scenario, *The Night Before* (*Sono zen'ya*), was realized in 1939 by Ryō Hagiwara; set against the background of the Shogunate's downfall, it included a scathing portrayal of the Shinsengumi elite force of samurai. In the era of militarism, this had its contemporary relevance, just as his earlier films, with their precise depiction of the rigid class system of Edo-period Japan, expressed what Keiko McDonald terms "the sentimental realist's view of the underdog's life under an autocratic political regime." However, Yamanaka's social criticism was usually indirect. His primary concern was with the portrayal of people in their environment, and his abiding influence on the postwar *jidai-geki* lies in the meticulous atmosphere and behavioral realism which directors such as Kurosawa, Mizoguchi, and Kobayashi brought to their portrayals of the past.

**1932 Iso no Genta: Dakine no nagadosu** / Sleeping with a Long Sword (lit. The Genta Coast: Sleeping with a Long Sword)

**Koban shigure** / Money Trickles Down

**Ogasawara Iki no kami** / Ogasawara, the Governor of Iki

**Kuchibue o fuku bushi** / The Whistling Samurai

**Umon torimonochō: Sanjūban tegara: Obitoke buppō** / From the 30 Casebooks of Detective Umon: Sexual Salvation

**Tengu kaijō: Zenpen** / Tengu's Circulating Letter: Part 1

**1933 Satsuma hikyaku: Kōhen: Kenkō aiyoku hen** / The Satsuma Courier: Part 2: The Passionate Sword

**Bangaku no isshō** / The Life of Bangaku

**Nezumi kozō Jirokichi: Edo no maki** / Jirokichi the Ratkid: Edo Reel

**Nezumi kozō Jirokichi: Dōchū no maki** / Jirokichi the Ratkid: Journey Reel

**Nezumi kozō Jirokichi: Futatabi Edo no maki** / Jirokichi the Ratkid: Another Edo Reel

**1934 Fūryū katsujinken** / The Elegant Swordsman

**Ashigaru shussedan** / A Footman's Success Story

**Gantarō kaidō** / Gantaro's Travels

**1935 Kunisada Chūji** / Chuji Kunisada

**Tange Sazen yowa: Hyakuman-ryō no tsubo** / The Pot Worth a Million Ryo / Sazen Tange and the Pot Worth a Million Ryo (lit.)

**Seki no Yatappe** / Yatappe from Seki (*co-director*)

**Machi no irezumimono** / The Village Tattooed Man

**Daibosatsu tōge: Daiippen: Kogen ittōryū no maki** / Daibosatsu Pass: Part 1: Fencing School Reel / The Great

Bodhisattva Pass: Part 1: Fencing
School Reel (*co-director*)
**Kaitō shirozukin: Zenpen** / The
White-Hooded Burglar: Part 1
1936 **Kaitō shirozukin: Kōhen** / The
White-Hooded Burglar: Part 2
**Kōchiyama Sōshun** / Kochiyama
Soshun / Priest of Darkness
**Uminari kaidō** / Seacoast Highway
1937 **Mori no Ishimatsu** / Ishimatsu of
the Forest
**Ninjō kamifūsen** / Humanity and
Paper Balloons

## YAMASHITA Kōsaku
**(January 10, 1930–December 6, 1998)**
山下耕作

A Toei stalwart, Yamashita directed at
the studio from the sixties to the nineties, switching genres with changes in
studio policy. His earliest films were
*jidai-geki*, and he achieved critical notice with *Yatappe of Seki* (*Seki no Yatappe*,
1963), an adaptation of a Shin Hasegawa
novel about an Edo-era professional
gambler who acts as benefactor to the
orphan child whose pickpocket father
he saw killed. Particularly in the climactic scenes, this admirably displayed
Yamashita's ability to elicit emotionally
intense performances from his actors,
to draw out the pathos of situations,
and to pay attention to female emotions
as well as to combat between men. An
interest in the situation of women in a
man's world was sustained in some of
his later yakuza movies: thus, *Samurai
Geisha* (*Nihon jokyōden: Kyōkaku geisha*,
1969) intelligently dealt with the situation of geisha whose lives touch the underworld of Meiji-era Kumamoto and
dramatized a geisha strike in protest

against the crimes of a wicked local boss.
Yamashita was appropriately assigned to
direct the first in the popular series *Red
Peony Gambler* (*Hibotan bakuto*), starring Junko Fuji as a female professional
gambler capable of transforming in an
instant from delicate manners to feroc-
ity. Among his later films, *The Night
Train* (*Yogisha*, 1987) melded the genres
of yakuza thriller and woman's picture,
while he also made two contributions to
another female-centered crime series:
*Yakuza Wives* (*Gokudō no onnatachi*).

More masculine in focus was the
long-running *The Fast Liver* (*Gokudō*)
series, of which Yamashita directed numerous installments during the late sixties and early seventies. These focused
on a gangster seeking to rise up the
Osaka racket; the early episodes were
played straight, while the later ones
moved towards comedy. By this time
Toei's yakuza movies had shifted from
the romanticized *ninkyō-eiga* approach
to the grittier *jitsuroku-eiga*; in the latter mode, Yamashita achieved a hit with
*The Yamaguchi Group: The Third Gener-
ation* (*Yamaguchi-gumi sandaime*, 1973).
In later years, he interspersed crime
thrillers with *jidai-geki* such as *The Man
Who Killed Ryoma* (*Ryōma o kitta otoko*,
1987), which described the assassination of pro-democracy advocate Ryōma
Sakamoto from the point of view of the
man assigned to kill him.

Yamashita did not develop a visual
style as distinctive as the low-angle set-
ups of his Toei colleague Tai Katō or
the overt stylization achieved by Seijun
Suzuki at Nikkatsu. Nevertheless, the
unobtrusive *mise-en-scène* of his sixties
pictures displayed the classical virtues
of efficiency and narrative drive, and he
was capable of turning out well-crafted
and gripping entertainments.

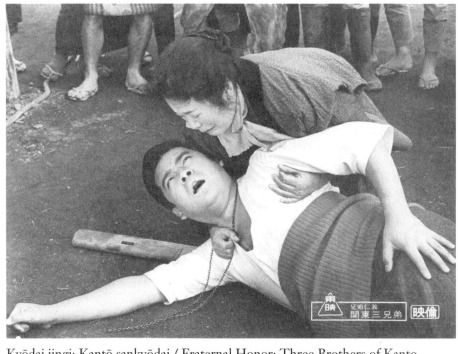

Kyōdai jingi: Kantō sankyōdai / Fraternal Honor: Three Brothers of Kanto
*(1966): Yamashita worked successfully in the popular* ninkyō-eiga *genre about the
chivalrous yakuza of the past.*

1961 **Wakadono senryōhada** / The
Young Master's 1000-ryo Skin

**Shin ogon kujaku-jō: Shichinin
no kishi** / New Golden Peacock
Castle: Seven Knights

1963 **Seki no Yatappe** / Yatappe of Seki /
Samurai and Orphan

1964 **Edo hanzaichō: Kuroi tsume** /
Notebooks on Crime in Edo: Black
Nails

**Ōgenka** / The Big Quarrel

1965 **Hana to ryū** / Flower and Dragon

**Onmitsu samurai kiki ippatsu** /
Samurai Spy: Moment of Crisis

1966 **Zoku hana to ryū: Dōkai-wan no
kettō** / Flower and Dragon 2: Duel
at Dokai Gulf

**Kyōdai jingi** / Fraternal Honor /
Family Obligations

**Tairiku nagaremono** / Girl

Vagrants of Tokyo (lit. Drifters on
the Continent)

**Zoku kyōdai jingi** / Fraternal
Honor 2

**Kyōdai jingi: Kantō sankyōdai** /
Fraternal Honor: Three Brothers of
Kanto

1967 **Isshin Tasuke: Edokko matsuri** /
Tasuke Isshin: Edoites' Festival

**Kyōdai jingi: Zoku Kantō
sankyōdai** / Fraternal Honor:
Three Brothers of Kanto 2

**Otoko namida no hamonjō** / A
Man's Tears: Letter of Expulsion

**Kyōdai jingi: Kantō inochi
shirazu** / Fraternal Honor:
Daredevil in Kanto

**Otoko no shōbu: Kantō arashi** / A
Man's Match: Storm in Kanto

1968 **Bakuchiuchi: Sōchō tobaku** /
Big Time Gambling Boss / Big

Gambling Ceremony (lit. Gamblers:
The Boss' Gamble)

**Otoko no shōbu: Byakko no
Tetsu** / A Man's Match: Tetsu of the
White Tigers

**Gokudō** / The Fast Liver

**Zenkamono** / The Ex-Convict

**Kaette kita gokudō** / The Fast
Liver Returns

**Hibotan bakuto** / Red Peony
Gambler

**Ōoku emaki** / Vanity of the
Shogun's Mistresses (lit. Picture
Scroll of the Inner Palace)

1969 **Matteita gokudō** / The Fast Liver
Was Waiting

**Sengo saidai no tobaku** / The
Largest Gambling Den in the
Postwar Era

**Onna shikyaku manji** / Female
Assassin Gammadion

**Nihon jokyōden: Kyōkaku geisha**
/ Samurai Geisha (lit. Chronicle
of Chivalrous Women of Japan:
Chivalrous Geisha)

**Hibotan bakuto: Tekkaba
retsuden** / Red Peony Gambler:
Biographies from the Gambling
Den

**Shōwa zankyōden: Hitokiri
karajishi** / Tales of Showa Era
Chivalry: Killer Lion

1970 **Gokudō Kamagasaki ni kaeru**
/ The Fast Liver Returns to
Kamagasaki

**Bakuchiuchi: Nagaremono** / The
Drifting Gambler

**Nihon kyōkakuden: Tekka geisha**
/ Chivalrous Chronicles of Japan:
Gambler Geisha

**Gokudō kyōjō tabi** / The Fast
Liver's Criminal Journey

**Noboriryū** / The Rising Dragon

1971 **Bakuchiuchi: Inochi fuda** /
Gambler: Card of Life

**Nihon jokyōden: Kettō
midarebana** / Chronicle of
Chivalrous Women of Japan: Bloody
Duel, Flower of Chaos

**Onna toseinin: Otanomōshimasu**
/ Woman Gambler: I Beseech You

**Ninkyō retsuden: Otoko** /
Biographies of the Chivalrous: A
Man

1972 **Zorome no sankyōdai** / Three
Brothers with Matching Dice

**Otoko no kaemon** / A Man's
Second Crest

**Bakuchiuchi gaiden** / Gamblers'
Supplementary Biography

**Hikagemono** / The Outcast

1973 **Mamushi no kyōdai: Musho
gurashi yonenhan** / Viper Brothers:
Four and a Half Years in the Clink

**Kamagasaki gokudō** / The Fast
Liver in Kamagasaki

**Yamaguchi-gumi sandaime** /
The Yamaguchi Group: The Third
Generation

**Kaigun Yokosuka keimusho** /
Naval Prison at Yokosuka

1974 **Yamaguchi-gumi gaiden: Kyūshū
shinkō sakusen** / Tattooed Hit
Man (lit. Supplementary Biography
of the Yamaguchi Group: Strategy
for Attacking Kyushu)

**Ā kessen kōkūtai** / Ah, Decisive
Battle in the Air

**Gokudō vs furyō banchō** / The
Fast Liver vs. the Delinquent Boss

1975 **Nihon ninkyōdō: Gekitotsu hen** /
The Japanese Way of Chivalry: The
Clash

**Nihon bōryoku rettō: Keihanshin
koroshi no gundan** / Japan's
Violent Archipelago: Kyoto-Osaka-
Kobe Killer's Gang

**Gōtō hōka satsujinshū** / Robber,
Arsonist, and Murderer in Prison

1976 **Yukaina gokudō** / The Cheerful
Fast Liver

**Dassō yūgi** / Game of Escape

**Yoake no hata: Matsumoto
Jiichirō den** / Flag at Dawn:
Chronicle of Jiichiro Matsumoto

1977 **Pirania gundan: Daboshatsu no
ten** / The Piranha Gang: Ten in a
Big Shirt

1980  Tokugawa ichizoku no hōkai /
      The Fall of the Tokugawa House
      **Kaigenrei no yoru** / Night of
      Martial Law

1984  **Shura no mure** / Herd of Hell

1985  **Saigo no bakuto** / The Last
      Gambler

1987  **Yogisha** / The Night Train
      **Ryōma o kitta otoko** / The Man
      Who Killed Ryoma

1988  **Anazā wei** / Another Way

1990  **Gokudō no onnatachi: Saigo no
      tatakai** / Yakuza Wives: The Last
      Struggle

1993  **Shin gokudō no onnatachi:
      Kakugo shiiya** / New Yakuza
      Wives: Be Prepared

1995  **Haruka: Sugao no 19-sai** / Haruka:
      Naked Face of a 19-year-old

1996  **Naite waratte namidashite:
      Poco a poco** / Crying, Laughing,
      Shedding Tears: Bit by Bit

1997  **Danjiri bayashi** / Danjiri Festival
      Music
      **Wakariaeru kisetsu** / Season for
      Mutual Understanding

## YAMASHITA Nobuhiro
(b. August 29, 1976)
山下敦弘

One of the most imaginative and individual of the youngest generation
of Japanese directors, Yamashita has
earned comparisons with Jim Jarmusch
and Aki Kaurismäki for his deadpan accounts of the directionless post-bubble
generation. Having trained at the Osaka
University of Arts, he made two features
focusing on young entrepreneurs working outside the margins of respectable
society. *Hazy Life* (*Donten seikatsu*, 1999)
was a study of two slackers dubbing
homemade pornographic videos, while
*No One's Ark* (*Baka no hakobune*, 2002)

detailed the attempts of a young couple
to sell their unpalatable "health drink"
in a small country town. A wry portrait
of provincial life and a response to the
collapse of the bubble economy, it was
justly praised by Tony Rayns as "more
droll and better observed than any major studio picture" on that subject. The
director's next feature, *Ramblers* (*Riarizumu no yado*, 2003), about a pair of aspiring filmmakers wandering aimlessly
around the countryside while waiting to
meet their lead actor, was a particularly
well-observed work in which an inconsequential story allowed Yamashita to
concentrate on revealing nuances of behavior and characterization.

These films were typified by a distinctive minimalist style, in which long
takes, with a generally static camera and
occasional simple tracking shots, merely
observed the movements and gestures
of the actors. Yamashita has commented
that a simple visual style is suited to
"films about people who move through
life at a kind of languid pace." Though
well received in foreign festivals,
Yamashita's work remained a niche interest in Japan until *Linda, Linda, Linda*
(*Rinda Rinda Rinda*, 2005), a lightweight
but still engaging film in which his stylistic peculiarities were fastened to a
more mainstream plot about a group of
high school rock singers practicing for
a festival. This subject matter, and the
presence of popular Korean actress Bae
Du-Na, earned Yamashita the commercial success that had previously eluded
him. His next film, *The Matsugane
Potshot Affair* (*Matsugane ransha jiken*,
2006), proved arguably his best work to
date. Tracing the bleak consequences of
a hit-and-run accident, Yamashita again
realized a film of beguiling humor distinguished by surprising shifts in tone
and the rich atmosphere of provincial

Riarisumu no yado / Ramblers *(2003): The film is one of this promising director's most engaging portraits of directionless youth.*

Japan, while also achieving a new depth in his portrait of the troubled relations between a strait-laced policeman and his mildly delinquent twin brother. He would seem to have a bright future ahead of him.

1997 **Kusaru onna** / The Rotten Woman (*16mm short*)

1999 **Donten seikatsu** / Hazy Life (*16mm*)

2002 **Baka no hakobune** / No One's Ark

2003 **Mottomo kikenna deka matsuri** / The Most Dangerous Cop Festival (*co-director*)

**Sono otoko, kyōbō ni tsuki** / Violent Stick (lit. That Man Pokes with a Crazy Stick) (*short*)

**Yotchan** (*short*)

**Riarizumu no yado** / Ramblers (lit. Realism Lodging)

2004 **Kurīmu remon** / Cream Lemon

2005 **Rinda Rinda Rinda** / Linda Linda Linda

2006 **Matsugane ransha jiken** / The Matsugane Potshot Affair

**Yume jūya** / Ten Nights of Dreams (*co-director*)

2007 **Tennen kokekkō** / A Gentle Breeze in the Village

## YANAGIMACHI Mitsuo
**(b. November 2, 1945)**
柳町光男

An outsider like his protagonists, Yanagimachi has worked infrequently, seeking independent funding for his austere, non-judgmental studies of the socially marginalized. His first film, *God Speed You, Black Emperor* (*Goddo supīdo yū! Black Emperor*, 1976), was a documentary account of Tokyo biker gangs; it suggested the influence both of Hollywood biker movies and of Kazuo Hara's early documentaries, although it lacked Hara's formal precision and political complexity. Here, Yanagimachi studied a close-knit alternative community, separate from conventional society, with its own distinct rules and codes of conduct. Subsequently, he shifted his focus to alienated individuals. *A Nineteen-Year-Old's Map* (*Jūkyūsai no chizu*, 1979) was a grim depiction of a disenchanted teenage newspaper boy who plans to bomb the houses of his customers. The anticipated violence was ultimately withheld, the film ending with the protagonist's realization that he lacks even the courage to destroy.

Yanagimachi's films of the eighties broadened their scope to make the emotional dislocation of individuals a microcosm of the general alienation of modern Japanese from nature and from their cultural traditions. *Farewell to the Land* (*Saraba itoshiki daichi*, 1982) used the death of two brothers in a boating accident, and their father's subsequent descent into infidelity, drug addiction, and violence, as a metaphor for the disintegration of traditional rural family structures. Yanagimachi's best film, *Fire Festival* (*Himatsuri*, 1985), similarly focused on the clash of traditional lifestyles, exemplified by the fishing and forestry industries and the animist beliefs of the woodcutter protagonist, with the new economies of construction and tourism. The film's setting, a tiny coastal settlement, seemed overshadowed by the imposing imagery of rain, sea, and mountains, suggesting the fragility of a civilization threatened by natural forces and primitive impulses.

During the nineties, Yanagimachi became interested in the culture and experiences of Chinese living outside the People's Republic. *Shadow of China*

(*Chaina shadō*, 1990), filmed in Hong Kong, focused on a former Red Guard member who becomes a successful businessman after illegally entering the colony. *The Wandering Peddlers* (*Tabisuru Pao Jian Fū*, 1995) was a documentary about itinerants selling traditional medicine in Taiwan. *About Love, Tokyo* (*Ai ni tsuite, Tōkyō*, 1993), more direct as social criticism than Yanagimachi's earlier work, was a bitter account of the experiences of Chinese immigrants in Japan; it courted accusations of racism, but in fact its theme was the way in which widespread prejudice and discrimination could encourage criminality. The relative failure of these films led to a decade-long hiatus in the director's career; he returned to work with *Who's Camus Anyway?* (*Camyū nante shiranai*, 2005), a self-referential account of a group of student filmmakers preparing to film a Yanagimachi-esque story of an apparently motiveless murder. Characterized by a looser, freer camera style than his earlier films, and by a streak of dark humor which saved its postmodern aspects from accusations of pretension, this was arguably his most humanly engaging work to date.

Yanagimachi, who has acknowledged an affinity with Robert Bresson, is not a conventional dramatist; his characters, like Bresson's, tend to lack psychological detail, so that their motives remain opaque. This fact, coupled with a detached visual style, has enabled his depictions of crime and violence to avoid both facile sociological explanations and simplistic notions of inherent human evil. Posing questions rather than offering answers, his work is both probing and disquieting.

**1976 Goddo supīdo yū! Black Emperor**
/ God Speed You, Black Emperor

1979  **Jūkyūsai no chizu** / A Nineteen-
      Year-Old's Map
1982  **Saraba itoshiki daichi** / Farewell to
      the Land
1985  **Himatsuri** / Fire Festival
1990  **Chaina shadō** / Shadow of China
      (*Japan / U.S.A.; filmed in Hong
      Kong*)
1993  **Ai ni tsuite, Tōkyō** / About Love,
      Tokyo
1995  **Tabisuru Pao Jian Fū** / The
      Wandering Peddlers (*Taiwan*)
2005  **Camyū nante shiranai** / Who's
      Camus Anyway?

## YOSHIDA Yoshishige
(b. February 16, 1933)
吉田喜重

Internationally the least famous of the major Japanese New Wave directors, Yoshida (latterly known as Kijū Yoshida) was one of the movement's most distinguished representatives and arguably its most technically adept filmmaker. Like Nagisa Ōshima and Masahiro Shinoda, he worked initially under contract at Shochiku, where he had served as assistant to Keisuke Kinoshita. His first films, *Good-for-Nothing* (*Rokudenashi*, 1960) and *Blood Runs Dry* (*Chi wa kawaiteiru*, 1960), were crime movies cast in a similar mould to Ōshima's early work. *Escape from Japan* (*Nihon dasshutsu*, 1964), another crime film, was distinctly overblown in style and plotting; like Seijun Suzuki, Yoshida used exaggeration to topple the codes of the genre into pastiche.

Perhaps the best of Yoshida's studio films was *18 Who Cause a Storm* (*Arashi o yobu jūhachinin*, 1963), a broadly neo-realist account of temporary workers employed in the shipbuilding industry in Western Japan. This revealed its director's talent for capturing the atmosphere of a place and for orchestrating fluent, complex camera movements. *Akitsu Spa* (*Akitsu Onsen*, 1962), was a melodramatic account of an affair unfolding over two decades at a spa town; as in his thrillers, Yoshida made exaggerated use of generic staples and conventional symbolism (falling cherry blossoms as harbingers of death) to shift the film towards pastiche. But in using melodramatic conventions as a vehicle for commenting obliquely on Japanese society and history, the film anticipated Yoshida's later work. It also marked his first collaboration with actress Mariko Okada, who would become his wife and star in all his films between 1965 and 1971.

Her presence enabled Yoshida to find financial backing for a remarkable series of independent films that narrated melodramatic stories in *avant-garde* fashion and dealt imaginatively with themes of transgressive sexuality and the situation of independent women in a conservative society. The atmospheric use of location—a decaying northern town and its environs in *A Story Written with Water* (*Mizu de kakareta monogatari*, 1965), the prosperous Shōnan coast in *The Affair* (*Jōen*, 1967)—contributed to a precise recreation of social milieux, but Yoshida's primary concern, in contrast to the more direct social criticism of Ōshima and Shinoda, was with the depiction of individual psychology. His characters often suffer because they have internalized social taboos; thus, the disapproval expressed by the heroine of *The Affair* when her widowed mother takes a lover is really a way to disavow her own sexual feelings for the man. In *A Story Written with Water*, a young man's repressed incestuous desires for his mother surface, with fatal consequences, when he discovers that his employer and father-

Erosu + gyakusatsu / Eros Plus Massacre *(1970): Yoshida's most formally radical film distilled complex political implications from its juxtaposition of events in two eras.*

in-law is her lover. Incest was also the metaphorical subject of the later *Heroic Purgatory* (*Rengoku Eroika*, 1970), about a girl who masquerades as a scientist's daughter only to become his seducer.

Yoshida's analysis of sexual mores achieved perhaps its most complex expression in *Impasse* (*Honoo to onna*, 1967), which charted the gradual disintegration of a marriage due to the husband's sterility. The wife, having resorted to artificial insemination to bear a son, seeks to exclude the husband from the upbringing of "her" child. Here as elsewhere, Yoshida's attitude was implicitly conservative; the technological advance that allows a sterile man to have a son cannot overcome an instinctive belief in the importance of biological fatherhood. The clearest example of this conservatism was, ironically, Yoshida's most formally radical film, *Eros Plus Massacre* (*Erosu + gyakusatsu*, 1970), which jux-

taposed the Taisho-period story of the relationship between a famous anarchist and a radical feminist with an account of life among the liberated, politicized youth of 1970. Here, Yoshida explicitly argued that the achievement of liberation will not lead to happiness, and that attempts to reform society are likely to founder on the impossibility of changing human nature. It may be significant that his only film to deal directly with power politics, *Martial Law* (*Kaigenrei*, 1973), was an account of a revolution that failed: the militarist uprising of February 26, 1936.

While Ōshima has been called the Japanese Godard, Yoshida has earned comparisons with Antonioni, whose work he acknowledged as an influence. Nevertheless, the two directors were distinct in tone and style: while Antonioni charted the enervation and emotional sterility of the wealthy classes,

Yoshida's concern was with bourgeois women possessed by feelings of destructive intensity. Indeed, Yoshida rejected Antonioni's measured, meditative camera movements in favor of fragmented editing and rapid, wheeling tracks and pans, which served to reflect the inner turmoil of his heroines.

Like others of his generation, Yoshida found it difficult to sustain regular film production in the more commercially motivated environment of the seventies onwards. Instead, he made documentaries, worked in television, and wrote a book on Ozu. Of his few later feature films, *A Promise* (*Ningen no yakusoku*, 1986) was an examination of old age and euthanasia, told in flashback after the death of an elderly woman brings her entire family under suspicion of murder, while the strikingly stylized *Onimaru* (*Arashigaoka*, 1988) borrowed techniques from Noh theater in order to transpose *Wuthering Heights* (another story with incestuous connotations) to Japan. After more than a decade, Yoshida made *Women in the Mirror* (*Kagami no onnatachi*, 2002), obliquely linking the painful relations between three generations of Japanese women to the experience of the Hiroshima atomic bomb and subtly suggesting the power of past traumas to shape human lives.

1960 **Rokudenashi** / Good-for-Nothing
**Chi wa kawaiteiru** / Blood Runs Dry

1961 **Amai yoru no hate** / The End of a Sweet Night

1962 **Akitsu Onsen** / Akitsu Spa / An Affair at Akitsu

1963 **Arashi o yobu jūhachinin** / 18 Who Cause a Storm / 18 Roughs

1964 **Nihon dasshutsu** / Escape from Japan

1965 **Mizu de kakareta monogatari** / A Story Written with Water

1966 **Onna no mizuumi** / Lake of Women / The Lake

1967 **Jōen** / The Affair
**Honoo to onna** / Impasse / Flames and a Woman (lit.)

1968 **Juhyō no yoromeki** / Affair in the Snow
**Saraba natsu no hikari** / Farewell to the Summer Light

1970 **Erosu + gyakusatsu** / Eros Plus Massacre
**Rengoku eroica** / Heroic Purgatory

1971 **Kokuhakuteki joyūron** / Confessions among Actresses

1973 **Kaigenrei** / Martial Law / Coup d'Etat

1977 **BIG-1 monogatari: Ō Sadaharu** / Baseball's Big One: Sadaharu O

1985 **Kyōgenshi: Miyake Tōkurō** / Kyogen Actor: Tokuro Miyake (*16mm short*)

1986 **Ningen no yakusoku** / A Promise / A Human Promise (lit.)

1988 **Arashigaoka** / Onimaru / Wuthering Heights (lit.)

1995 **Lumière et Compagnie** (*co-director*)

2002 **Kagami no onnatachi** / Women in the Mirror

2004 **Bem-Vindo a São Paolo** / Welcome to São Paolo (*co-director*)

## YOSHIMURA Kōzaburō
(September 9, 1911–November 7, 2000)
吉村公三郎

Though his style and subject matter were more varied than those of the other Japanese masters, Yoshimura was a distinguished artist who engaged throughout his career with the changing social and cultural circumstances of his country. Working at Shochiku from the thirties, he achieved a major commercial success in 1939 with *Warm Current*

Itsuwareru seisō / Clothes of Deception *(1951): Yoshimura's chronicle of the geisha system in decline initiated his masterly sequence of films set in a changing postwar Kyoto.*

(*Danryū*), a low-key melodrama about the romantic and professional travails of a young hospital superintendent. His next work, *The Story of Tank Commander Nishizumi* (*Nishizumi senshachōden*, 1940) has a reputation as a humanist war film, but during the war years Yoshimura also made several purely propagandistic films about espionage, such as *The Spy Isn't Dead Yet* (*Kanchō imada shisezu*, 1942). His mature style was only properly formed after the war, when his films achieved a new complexity of theme and structural precision, thanks in part to the collaboration of screenwriter Kaneto Shindō, later a director in his own right.

Among their collaborations, *Ishimatsu of the Forest* (*Mori no Ishimatsu*, 1949) was an innovative *jidai-geki* which, in Kyoko Hirano's words, "denounced in a satirical comedic style the useless vanity of yakuza loyalty," while *The Beauty and the Dragon* (*Kabuki jūhachiban Narukami: Bijo to kairyū*, 1955) was an experimental Kabuki adaptation, compared by Anderson and Richie to Laurence Olivier's *Henry V* (1944) for the way in which it shifted partway through from theatrical to cinematic techniques. Both these films used historical narratives to comment indirectly on the present and recent past. *On This Earth* (*Chijō*, 1957) and *Cape Ashizuri* (*Ashizuri misaki*, 1954), meanwhile, were more direct accounts of Japan's recent history: the former was a Taisho-period story about a schoolboy aspiring to be a reformist politician, while the latter was a claustrophobic study of the impotence of liberal students in the prewar era of militarist domination.

Yoshimura's most typical films, however, were dramas of contemporary life. *The Ball at the Anjo House* (*Anjō-ke no butōkai*, 1947), was an imaginatively shot melodrama about an aristocratic family in straitened circumstances forced to sell their mansion. Superbly acted by an excellent ensemble cast including Setsuko Hara and Masayuki Mori, this inaugurated the director's intelligent examination of social changes in postwar Japan. He pursued this theme in films such as *Waltz at Noon* (*Mahiru no enbukyoku*, 1949), another study of the decline of the prewar aristocracy, and it reached its most distinguished expression in a sequence of films set in Kyoto, all focusing on women working in traditional professions in the old capital. In *Clothes of Deception* (*Itsuwareru seisō*, 1951) the topic was the geisha system, in *Sisters of Nishijin* (*Nishijin no shimai*, 1952) and *Night River* (*Yoru no kawa*, 1956), kimono design and production, and in *A Woman's Uphill Slope* (*Onna no saka*, 1960), the making of Japanese confectionery. Meanwhile, *The Naked Face of Night* (*Yoru no sugao*, 1958) focused on another traditional female occupation, classical dance, in the more modern milieu of Tokyo. Each of these films was an affecting account of the situation of independent women in an era when conservative values persisted despite technological development; taken together, they constituted one of the Japanese cinema's most complex accounts of the country's social and cultural transformation in the early postwar years. Yoshimura suggested that change involves both gain and loss, but is inevitable; *Sisters of Nishijin* and *Clothes of Deception* expressed this theme with particular eloquence through their depiction of the changing appearance of Kyoto itself, at a time when its old streets were beginning to be demolished in favor of modernity. At the same time, these films were exceptionally poignant character studies dealing with fully rounded individuals: the heroine of *Clothes of Deception* combined a corrosive selfishness with the admirable qualities of practicality, resourcefulness and inner strength, while *Night River* was a precisely judged account of a woman's ambivalent feelings over the course of a destructive love affair.

Yoshimura's sympathetic portrayal of female characters earned comparisons with Mizoguchi, and these were sustained by *Night Butterflies* (*Yoru no chō*, 1957), a story of nightclub hostesses in Tokyo's Ginza district, and *Osaka Story* (*Ōsaka monogatari*, 1957), a satire on capitalist values in Japan's most commercial city and a project inherited from Mizoguchi on his death. However, Yoshimura's more direct attempts to echo Mizoguchi's aesthetic, such as his prestigious adaptation of Lady Murasaki's classic Heian-period saga, *The Tale of Genji* (*Genji monogatari*, 1951), achieved only a superficial prettiness. With *The Ball at the Anjo House* he worked effectively in an unusually baroque idiom, but at its best, his style was restrained, functional, and classical, and his films derived their strength less from their visual flair than from their meticulous creation of atmosphere and sensitive direction of actors. As his interest in female experience would lead one to expect, Yoshimura elicited particularly fine performances from women: Setsuko Hara, Fujiko Yamamoto, Mariko Okada, Ayako Wakao, and, above all, his regular collaborator Machiko Kyō, who starred in *Clothes of Deception*, *The Tale of Genji*, *Night Butterflies*, *The Naked Face of Night*, and *A Design for Dying* (*Onna no kunshō*, 1961).

Yoshimura continued to work through the sixties and into the seventies, with occasional successes such as *Bamboo Doll of Echizen* (*Echizen takeningyō*, 1963), a stylish melodrama about the love affair between a craftsman and a fallen woman, which revealed intriguing Freudian undertones, but lacked the social context of his finest films. A social concern was again apparent in his last film, the privately financed *The Tattered Banner* (*Ranru no hata*, 1974), about the poisoning of land by runoff from the Ashio copper mine. Nevertheless, Yoshimura was clearly happiest working within the traditional studio system and after its collapse his output was relatively undistinguished. His best films in the forties and fifties, however, rank among the outstanding products of the classical Japanese cinema, and he merits proper retrospectives.

1934 **Nukiashi sashiashi** / Sneaking
1938 **Gunkoku no haru** / Spring of the Militarist Nation
1939 **Onna koso ie o mamore** / Women, Defend the Home!

**Yōkina uramachi** / Cheerful Alley

**Ashita no odoriko** / Tomorrow's Dancers

**Gonin no kyōdai** / Five Brothers and Sisters

**Danryū: Zenpen: Keiko no maki** / Warm Current: Part 1: Keiko's Reel

**Danryū: Kōhen: Gin no maki** / Warm Current: Part 2: Gin's Reel

1940 **Nishizumi senshachōden** / The Story of Tank Commander Nishizumi
1941 **Hana** / Blossom
1942 **Kanchō imada shisezu** / The Spy Isn't Dead Yet

**Minami no kaze** / South Wind

**Zoku minami no kaze** / South Wind 2

1943 **Kaisen no zen'ya** / On the Eve of War

**Tekki kūshū** / Enemy Air Raid (*co-director*)
1944 **Kessen** / Decisive Battle (*co-director*)
1947 **Zō o kutta renchū** / The Fellows Who Ate the Elephant

**Anjō-ke no butōkai** / The Ball at the Anjo House

1948 **Yūwaku** / Temptation

**Waga shōgai no kagayakeru hi** / The Day Our Lives Shine / The Brightest Days of My Life

1949 **Shitto** / Jealousy

**Mori no Ishimatsu** / Ishimatsu of the Forest

**Mahiru no enbukyoku** / Waltz at Noon

1950 **Shunsetsu** / Spring Snow

**Senka no hate** / Beyond the Battlefield

1951 **Itsuwareru seisō** / Clothes of Deception / Under Silk Garments / The Disguise

**Jiyū gakkō** / School of Freedom

**Genji monogatari** / The Tale of Genji

1952 **Nishijin no shimai** / Sisters of Nishijin

**Bōryoku** / Violence

1953 **Senbazuru** / A Thousand Cranes

**Yokubō** / Desires

**Yoake mae** / Before Dawn

1954 **Ashizuri misaki** / Cape Ashizuri

**Wakai hitotachi** / Young People

1955 **Ai sureba koso** / Because I Love / If You Love Me (*co-director*)

**Ginza no onna** / Women of the Ginza

**Kabuki jūhachiban Narukami: Bijo to kairyū** / The Beauty and the Dragon

1956 **Totsugu hi** / Day of Marriage

**Yoru no kawa** / Night River / Undercurrent

**Yonjūhassai no teikō** / 48-Year-Old Rebel

1957 **Ōsaka monogatari** / Osaka Story

**Yoru no chō** / Night Butterflies

**Chijō** / On This Earth

1958 **Hitotsubu no mugi** / A Grain of
Wheat

**Yoru no sugao** / The Naked Face
of Night / The Ladder of Success

1959 **Denwa wa yūgata ni naru** / The
Telephone Rings in the Evening

**Kizoku no kaidan** / The
Aristocrat's Stairs

1960 **Jokyō** / A Woman's Testament (*co-director*)

**Onna no saka** / A Woman's Uphill
Slope / Women of Kyoto

1961 **Konki** / Marriageable Age /
Marriage Time

**Onna no kunshō** / A Design for
Dying (lit. A Woman's Medal)

1962 **Katei no jijō** / Their Legacy (lit.
Family Situation)

**Sono yo wa wasurenai** / A Night to
Remember / Hiroshima Heartache /
I Won't Forget That Night (lit.)

1963 **Uso** / Lies / When Women Lie (*co-director*)

**Echizen takeningyō** / Bamboo
Doll of Echizen

1966 **Kokoro no sanmyaku** / The Heart
of the Mountains

1967 **Daraku suru onna** / A Fallen
Woman

1968 **Nemureru bijo** / House of the
Sleeping Virgins (lit. The Sleeping
Beauties)

1971 **Amai himitsu** / Sweet Secret

1973 **Konketsuji Rika: Hamagure
komoriuta** / Rika the Mixed-Blood
Girl: Juvenile Lullaby

1974 **Ranru no hata** / The Tattered
Banner

## YUKISADA Isao

**(b. August 3, 1968)**

行定勲

One of the most fashionable, and bankable, of younger Japanese directors, Yukisada worked initially as assistant to youth film specialist Shunji Iwai. His own early films, such as *Open House* (1998) and *Luxurious Bone* (*Zeitakuna hone*, 2001), were not unlike Iwai's, with a similar, dreamlike visual style, a focus primarily on the young, and a talent for exploring the intensely private mental worlds inhabited by his characters. Popular success, however, came with *Go* (*Gō*, 2001), an atypically social realist drama examining the troubled life of a resident Korean teenager in Japan. Though marred, especially in its early scenes, by pop video editing techniques and camera rhetoric, the film contained many telling moments, such as the hero's encounter with a bemused policeman unaware of his status as a "foreigner."

Yukisada's next films continued to focus on contemporary youth. *A Day on the Planet* (*Kyō no dekigoto*, 2004) was a perceptive mosaic of student life, revolving around a house party where the fears, desires, and insecurities of its characters are gradually revealed. Subplots about a trapped workman and a beached whale offset the theme of people metaphorically hemmed in by their own self-perceptions and psychological quirks; with its multi-layered characterizations and complex attitudes towards people, this was perhaps its director's best film.

Yukisada's biggest commercial success, however, was *Crying Out Love, in the Center of the World* (*Sekai no chūshin de, ai o sakebu*, 2004), a well-crafted melodrama about a thirty-something man remembering his youth and coming to terms with the death of his girlfriend from leukemia. Though emotionally overblown, the film made atmospheric use of the contrasts between the mellow sunlight of the romantic scenes, the cold, artificial glare of the hospital wards, and the cloudy, disenchanted present.

The popularity of this film earned

Yukisada the budgets he needed to mount two period epics: *Year One in the North* (*Kita no zeronen*, 2005), the story of a samurai's wife trying to settle in the wilderness of nineteenth-century Hokkaido, and *Spring Snow* (*Haru no yuki*, 2005), a sumptuously designed Taisho-period tale of *amour fou*, derived from the first novel in Yukio Mishima's *Sea of Fertility* tetralogy. These films, too, achieved considerable box-office success, and led Mark Schilling to declare that Yukisada had become "Japan's David Lean: a maker of big-budget, big-scale dramas set in a romanticized, sanitized past, that celebrate the purest of pure love." His subsequent work has been characterized by a similar blend of immaculate production values, sentimental themes and excessive length. *Closed Note* (*Kurōzudo nōto*, 2007) was a drama about a trainee teacher impelled to make changes in her own life when she finds and reads the diary of a former tenant of her flat. *Into the Faraway Sky* (*Tōku no sora ni kieta*, 2007) was a children's drama about the friendship between a Hokkaido farm boy and the son of a civil servant sent to the northern island to buy up land for the construction of a new airport. This storyline suggested at least a partial return to the social awareness of *Go*, but Yukisada's films now generally seem more style than substance.

1998 **Open House**
2000 **Himawari** / Sunflower
**Tojiru hi** / A Closing Day / Enclosed Pain
2001 **Engawa no inu** / The Dog on the Veranda
**Zeitakuna hone** / Luxurious Bone
**Gō** / Go
2002 **Rokkun rōru mishin** / Rock' n' Roll Mishin / Rock 'n' Roll Sewing Machine (lit.)

**Tsuki ni shizumu** / Sinking the Moon (*short*)
**Jam Films** (*co-director*)
2003 **Kanon** (*short*)
**Sebunsu anibāsarī** / Seventh Anniversary
2004 **Kyō no dekigoto** / A Day on the Planet
**Sekai no chūshin de, ai o sakebu** / Crying Out Love, in the Center of the World
2005 **Kita no zeronen** / Year One in the North
**Haru no yuki** / Spring Snow / Snowy Love Fall in Spring
2006 **Yubisaki kara sekai o** / Yubisaki (lit. From the Fingertips toward the World)
2007 **Tōku no sora ni kieta** / Into the Faraway Sky
**Kurōzudo nōto** / Closed Note
**Shokora o mita sekai** / The World that Saw Chocolate

## ZEZE Takahisa
(b. May 24, 1960)
瀬々敬久

Zeze first achieved notice as one of the *Shitennō* ("Four Devils"), a group of directors who attempted to transcend the exploitation format of "pink" cinema through formal experimentation and political engagement. His feature debut, *Good Luck Japan* (*Kagai jugyō: Bōkō*, 1989), focused on Taiwanese gangsters and Asian prostitutes living near Tokyo's Haneda Airport, while *No Man's Land* (*Waisetsu bōsō shūdan: Kedamono*, 1991) set its story of urban alienation against the backdrop of constant media coverage of the Gulf War. Co-scripted by Shinji Aoyama, Zeze's best-known "pink" film, *The Dream of Garuda* (*Kōkyū sōpu tekunikku 4: Monzetsu higi*,

Kuroi shitagi no onna: Raigyo / *Raigyo (1997): Zeze's work has balanced art and exploitation, shocking violence and political commentary.*

1994), about a paroled criminal's obsessive quest to find the woman he once raped, interspersed sex scenes with stylized dream sequences. Despite success in mainstream filmmaking, Zeze has not abandoned "pink," considering it more amenable to experimentation. *Tokyo X Erotica* (*Tōkyō X erotika*, 2001) was a sensational story of a perverse love affair, while *Gap in the Skin* (*Hada no sukima*, 2005) charted a violent relationship between two criminals on the run. Zeze's oblique narratives and overt symbolism were far from the "pink" norm, but the depth of his political engagement is questionable: the references in *Tokyo X Erotica* to major historical events (the Tiananmen Square massacre, the Aum Shinrikyo terrorist attack) barely related to the drama, seeming pretentious in the absence of more detailed analysis.

*Raigyo* (*Kuroi shitagi no onna: Raigyo,* 1997), perhaps Zeze's finest achievement, was based, like many of his films, on a real crime: the murder of a man by a woman he met through a telephone dating service. It was again sexually explicit, but art movie techniques won out over exploitation, immaculate long-shot compositions bringing conviction to the portrayal of a desolate environment where the only meaningful contact is violent. Another transitional work was the austere *Dirty Maria* (*Kegareta Maria: Haitoku no hibi*, 1998), about a taxi driver investigating his wife's disappearance helped by the woman he does not know to be her murderer. By this time, Zeze had made his first true mainstream film, *Kokkuri* (*Kokkuri-san*, 1997), a conventional if agreeably understated horror film about schoolgirls using a ouija board. He has worked subsequently in a wide variety of genres: *Dog Star* (*Doggu sutā*, 2002) was a fantasy about a dog re-incarnated in human form, while *Rush!* (2001) was an action comedy about a kidnapping.

Zeze's mainstream works have intermittently attempted social criticism, his science fiction films touching, like *Good Luck Japan*, on the situation of immigrants in Japan and Japan's relationship with its Asian neighbors. The parodic *SF Whip Cream* (*SF hoippu kurīmu*, 2002) interpreted the term "illegal alien" literally, detailing the experiences of an extra-terrestial deported to his home planet after being raised in Japan. *Moon Child* (2003), about a young gangster's relationship with an immortal vampire, was set in a dystopian future in which a financial crash has led Japanese economic migrants to emigrate to China. Though incoherently plotted, it was eyecatchingly designed and slickly handled, and interestingly drew out the homoerotic undertones of the vampire myth. Having directed these eccentric takes on popular genres, Zeze made *Sisei 2* (*Shisei: Ochita jorōgumo*, 2007), another study of perverse sexuality, based on a Jun'ichirō Tanizaki story.

Zeze has proved an eclectic stylist, moving from the extreme austerity of *Raigyo* to the bizarre blend of artifice and pseudo-documentary in *Secret Journey* (*Yuda*, 2004). His method of narration is also experimental: *Tokyo X Erotica* unfolded in non-chronological order, while *Rush!*, according to Mark Schilling, "scrambled narrative logic to the point of total confusion." This experimentation betrays a wide range of influences; Zeze admired radical documentarists Kazuo Hara and Shinsuke Ogawa and acknowledged the influence on *SF Whip Cream* of an obscure Russian science fiction comedy, *Kin Dza-*

*Dza* (1986, Georgi Daneliya). Such surprising influences have resulted in a body of work which is undeniably offbeat, but budgetary limitations have often restricted Zeze's technique, and it is debatable whether he has ever made a completely satisfactory film. His intransigence remains commendable.

*NB: The commercial titles assigned to most of Zeze's films on release in Japan differ from the director's preferred titles, used when his films are shown at international festivals. I supply both where relevant, with the commercial title preceding the director's title.*

**1977** **Boku wa dare desu ka** / Who Am I? (*8mm short*)

**1978** **Harō guddobai** / Hello, Goodbye (*8mm short*)

**1980** **Semete kon'ya wa nemuritai** / At Least Tonight I Want to Sleep (*8mm short*)

**1981** **Mai pēsu yua pēsu** / My Pace, Your Pace (*8mm short*)

**1982** **Shōnenhan shibojō: Kunisada, Kyōto, Hinota** / Private Longings: Boy's Version: Kunisada, Kyoto, Hinota (*8mm*)

**1983** **Saka no ue no kazoku shashin** / Family Photograph at the Top of the Slope (*8mm*)

**1985** **Gyangu yo: Mukō wa hareteiru ka** / Gangster! Is It Brightening Over There? (*16mm short*)

**1989** **Kagai jugyō: Bōkō / Haneda ni itte mo soko ni wa kaizoku ni natta gakidomo ga ima ya to shuppatsu o matteiru** / Extra-curricular Lesson: Assault / Go to Haneda and You Will See Kids Dressed Like Pirates Waiting to Depart / Good Luck Japan

**Jūyokuma: Rangyō / Aozora** / Demon of Lust: Debauchery / Blue Sky

**1990** **Chikan densha: Rie no fundoshi / Coconut Crush** / Molestor Train: Rie's Loincloth / Coconut Crush

Harenchi zetsugi tekunikku / **Tsuki no sabaku** / Tongue Show Technique / Moon over the Desert

1991 **Waisetsu bōsō shūdan: Kedamono / No Man's Land /** Obscene Runaway Gang: Beast / No Man's Land

1992 **Kindan no sono: Za seifuku rezu / Watashi to iu genshō wa kateisareta yuki koru dentō no hitotsu no aoi shōmei desu** / Amazon Garden: Uniformed Lesbians / My Existence is a Phenomenon Based on the Hypothesis of Blue Light Generated by Organic Currency

**Chikan densha: Ikenai tsumatachi / Watakushi no kasha wa kita e hashitteiru hazuna no ni koko de wa minami e kaketeiru** / Molestor Train: Michievous Wives / My Train Is Supposed to Be Going North But It's Going South

1993 **Mibōjin: Shonanuka no modae / Bōsan ga hekoita** / The Widow: Anguish at the Seventh-Day Memorial Service / The Monk Farted

**Mibōjin: Mofuku no modae** / The Widow: Anguish in Mourning Dress

1994 **Kōkyū sōpu tekunikku 4: Monzetsu higi / Karura no yume** / High Class Bathhouse Sex Technique: Blissful Secret Acts / The Dream of Garuda

**Honban rezu: Hazukashii taii / Kugatsu no datenshi** / Genuine Lesbian: Shy Posture / Fallen Angels in September

1995 **Sukebe tenkomori / End of the World** / Full of Lechery / End of the World

**Owaranai sekkusu / Yoru naku semi** / Endless Sex / A Cicada Chirping in the Night

1996 **Akai jōji / Kurubeki kōkei** / Red Liaison / The Expected Scene

**Mesukusai: Torokeru kashin** / Scent of a Female : Melting Clitoris

1997 **Kokkuri-san** / Kokkuri

**Kuroi shitagi no onna: Raigyo /** Raigyo / Snake-Headed Fish (lit. Woman in the Black Underwear: The Snakehead Mullet)

1998 **Kegareta Maria: Haitoku no hibi** / Dirty Maria

**Reiketsu no wana** / The Cold-Blooded Trap

1999 **Anākī in Japansuke: Mirarete iku onna** / Anarchy in Japan

2000 **Hysteric**

2001 **Rush!**

**Tōkyō X erotika** / Tokyo X Erotica

2002 **Doggu sutā** / Dog Star

**SF hoippu kurīmu** / SF Whip Cream

2003 **Kaette kita deka matsuri** / Cop Festival Returns (*co-director*)

**Moon Child**

2004 **Yuda** / Secret Journey

2005 **Hada no sukima** / Gap in the Skin

2006 **Sankuchuari** / Sanctuary (Mrs.)

2007 **Shisei: Ochita jorōgumo** / Si-Sei 2 (lit. The Tattoo: Fallen Spider)

# Appendixes

# Glossary

**Anime:** Short for "animation"; animated film.

**Benshi:** In the silent era, a narrator who commented on the film, explaining the story and supplying voices for the characters.

**Bunraku:** A form of classical Japanese theater performed by large puppets, each manipulated by three actors.

**Burakumin:** Literally, "village people"; an underclass, often associated with trades considered unclean, such as leather-working or butchery. Historically and still, to a degree, today, they were victims of prejudice and ill-treatment.

**Bushidō:** "The way of the warrior"; the code of conduct and morality espoused by samurai.

**Chanbara** (sometimes transliterated "chambara"): Swordplay film. Refers to samurai films with a primary stress on scenes of combat and action. The term is sometimes used derogatively, but is generally merely descriptive.

**Daimyō:** A feudal lord or clan leader.

**Dōjō:** A training hall for a martial art.

**Enjo kōsai:** Literally, "compensation dating"; less euphemistically, teenage prostitution.

**Enka:** Type of popular song on melodramatic themes, which blends Western and Japanese musical influences.

**Gendai-geki:** Film about contemporary life: cf. *jidai-geki*.

**Gō:** The Japanese term for the Buddhist concept of *karma*: the concept that good or bad human actions lead to consequences in this life or the next.

**Haha-mono:** Film about a mother; a popular genre of the classical Japanese cinema.

**Hibakusha:** A surviving victim of the atomic bombings of Hiroshima or Nagasaki.

**Iemoto:** The head of a school teaching a traditional art form.

**Ikebana:** Literally, "living flowers"; flower arrangement, a respected art form in Japan.

**J-horror:** Term used to refer to the distinctive horror films made in the 1990s by such directors as Hideo Nakata and Kiyoshi Kurosawa, generally notable for a lack of gore and cheap shocks.

**Jidai-geki:** Period film, as opposed to the *gendai-geki* about contemporary life. Technically, a film set before the Meiji Restoration of 1868.

**Jishu-eiga:** Literally, "self-made film"; a film made, often by aspiring filmmakers, with private funding and not intended for mainstream exhibition. Often shot on 8mm or 16mm formats.

**Jitsuroku-eiga:** Literally, "true record film"; subgenre of the yakuza film, popular in the 1970s, characterized by extreme violence and pseudo-documentary techniques.

**Junbungaku:** "Pure literature"; refers to films based on respected novels; an important movement in the 1930s.

**Kabuki:** A form of classical Japanese drama, less stately and more dramatic than the older Noh.

**Kaidan** (sometimes transliterated "Kwaidan"): Ghost story.

**Kaijū-eiga:** "Monster movie"; science fiction genre produced particularly at Toho during the 1950s and 1960s.

**Karayuki-san:** Term referring to Japanese women sold into prostitution elsewhere in Asia during the Meiji and Taisho periods.

**Keikō-eiga:** Literally, "tendency film"; a genre of left-wing films which flourished during the late 1920s and early 1930s.

**Kendō:** Literally, "The Way of the Sword"; martial art using bamboo staves.

**Kinema Junpō:** Influential Japanese magazine of film criticism, established in 1917. Since 1926, it has published an annual Critics' Top Ten of Japanese films.

**Kōdan:** A form of popular oral storytelling based on legend or history, with a didactic purpose.

**Kuchidate:** In the silent era, the technique essayed by pioneer Shōzō Makino of reciting lines to his actors while filming.

**Manga:** Japanese comics and cartoons.

**Manzai:** A form of stand-up comedy, popular in Osaka, performed by a two-person team of straight man/woman (*tsukkomi*) and comic (*boke*).

**Matatabi-eiga:** Literally, "wanderer-film"; film about yakuza and vagabond gamblers, often set in the Edo period. A popular genre in the 1960s.

**Meiji-mono:** Film set during the Meiji period (1868–1912).

**"Nakanai" realism:** Realism "without tears." A form of drama characterized by an unsentimental approach; a term applied by Japanese critics to the films of Tadashi Imai, in contrast to the more melodramatic approach of, say, Keisuke Kinoshita.

**Nansensu-eiga:** Literally, "nonsense film"; comic subgenre, popular in the late 1920s and early 1930s, characterized by incoherent plots consisting of absurd happenings.

**Ninkyō-eiga:** Literally, "chivalry film"; subgenre of the yakuza film with a romanticized approach; generally set in the Meiji, Taisho, or early Showa periods (1868 to the 1930s).

**Noh:** The oldest extant form of Japanese classical drama: a slow, stately form of dance drama.

**Nūberu bāgu:** Transliterated form of *Nouvelle Vague* or New Wave; used in the 1960s to refer to Japanese filmmakers whose approach paralleled that of the French New Wave.

**"Ōfuna flavor":** A term used to describe the bittersweet, subtly sentimental tone of Shochiku productions from the 1930s to the 1950s. Named after the location of Shochiku's studios outside Tokyo.

**Onnagata:** See *oyama*.

**Otaku:** Nerd or obsessive.

**Oyama** (sometimes *onnagata*): A female impersonator, used on the Japanese stage, and carried over to silent Japanese films. Obsolete by the mid-1920s.

**PIA Film Festival:** A festival dedicated to promoting new talent in Japanese cinema, which awards scholarships to winning amateur filmmakers.

**"Pillow shots":** Term used in English-language criticism to describe cuts away from the drama to surrounding objects or scenery; particularly common in films by Yasujirō Ozu.

**"Pink" film:** *Pinku-eiga* in Japanese; softcore pornographic film, made on a low budget, produced and distributed outside the studio system.

**Rakugo:** A form of comic stage monologue especially popular in the early Showa period.

**Rōnin:** Masterless samurai.

**Roman Porno:** *Roman Poruno* in Japanese: softcore pornographic film in which Nikkatsu specialized during the 1970s and 1980s; distinct from "pink" film in being produced by a major studio.

**Seppuku:** Literally, "belly-cutting," informally known as *hara-kiri*; the traditional Japanese form of ritual suicide.

**Shakai-mono:** Film on socially conscious themes.

**Shingeki:** Literally, "New Drama"; Western-style realist theater, as contrasted with the Japanese/Western hybrid form of *shinpa*. An important influence on early Japanese cinema.

**Shinpa** (also transliterated *shimpa*): Literally, "New School"; a form of theater combining Western and Japanese elements, often characterized by intensely melodramatic plots. An important influence on early Japanese films, particularly during the Taisho period.

**Shinsengumi:** An elite corps of warriors who defended the Shogunate in the last years before the Meiji Restoration of 1868.

**Shitamachi:** Literally, "downtown"; refers particularly to the older, more working-class districts of Tokyo.

**Shōji:** A sliding screen of wood and translucent paper that divides spaces in a traditional Japanese house.

**Shomin-geki:** Film about the lower middle classes or *shomin*; a particular specialty of Shochiku and such directors as Yasujirō Ozu, Heinosuke Gosho, and Yasujirō Shimazu.

**Surechigai:** Literally, "brushing past each other"; term used to describe a melodramatic subgenre in which lovers repeatedly come close to meeting, but miss each other by meters or moments.

**Taishō-mono:** Film set during the Taisho period (1912–26).

**Taiyōzoku-eiga:** "Sun Tribe" film: a genre of films about rebellious and delinquent youth, fashionable in the 1950s.

**Tatami:** Rectangular woven straw mats (c. 6ft by 3ft; 2m by 1m), used as a floor covering in traditional Japanese homes.

**Tsuma-mono:** Film about a wife; a popular genre in the classical Japanese cinema.

**Ukiyo-e:** Literally, "Pictures of the Floating World"; woodblock prints on everyday themes, especially during the Edo period.

**Yakuza:** A gangster; collectively, the Japanese Mafia.

**Zankoku-eiga:** Literally, "cruelty film"; a subgenre at Toei during the late 1960s and 1970s, characterized by the imaginative recreation of explicit violence.

# Notes on Major Japanese Production Companies

## Nikkatsu *(日活)*

Japan's oldest operating film studio was founded as a trust in 1909 and renamed Nippon Katsudō Shashin (Nikkatsu being its shortened form) in 1912. During the 1910s the studio produced *shinpa*-style melodramas in Tokyo and Kabuki-influenced costume dramas in Kyoto. The latter, particularly those directed by Shōzō Makino and starring Matsunosuke Onoe, gained Nikkatsu commercial success. In the 1920s, after more realistic films such as Eizō Tanaka's *The Kyoya Collar Shop* (*Kyōya erimise*, 1922) won critical acclaim, the studio earned a reputation for stories detailing the daily lives of the lower classes: among the directors noted for their contributions to this genre were Kenji Mizoguchi and Minoru Murata. Also during the twenties, Nikkatsu produced the sophisticated comedies of Yutaka Abe and the flamboyant period films of Daisuke Itō.

After an awkward transition to sound, Nikkatsu returned to form in the mid-1930s with its contribution to the *junbungaku* movement of films adapted from prestigious literary sources. Directors specializing in this realist genre included Tomu Uchida and Tomotaka Tasaka; the latter was also responsible for two of Nikkatsu's most famous war films. Meanwhile, Sadao Yamanaka and Hiroshi Inagaki made some excellent *jidai-geki* at the studio. During the war, however, as part of a government policy to consolidate the film industry, Nikkatsu's production facilities were absorbed into the newly founded Daiei, leaving it a theater-owning company only.

Resuming production in 1954, Nikkatsu gravitated gradually towards pictures aimed at a youthful audience, such as Kō Nakahira's seminal *taiyōzoku* ("sun tribe") film *Crazed Fruit* (*Kurutta kajitsu*, 1956). Many of these were action pictures, and by the 1960s "Nikkatsu Action" had become a trademark. Among directors specializing in this genre were Seijun Suzuki, Toshio Masuda, and Yasuharu Hasebe. Nikkatsu also made a contribution to the Japanese New Wave by producing Shōhei Imamura's early films. However, growing financial problems in the early 1970s led to a decision to switch to the production of low-budget softcore pornography, known as Roman Porno. Among the more notable directors in this subgenre, which Nikkatsu continued to produce through the 1980s, were Noboru Tanaka and Tatsumi Kumashiro. Nikkatsu filed for bankruptcy in 1993 but was eventually able to resume production and has continued to produce films, albeit less individual in style and subject matter, to the present day.

## Shochiku (Shōchiku, 松竹)

Initially a theatrical concern, Shochiku entered the film industry in 1920, aiming to realize pictures utilizing Western techniques—a brief certainly fulfilled with one of its earliest productions, Minoru Murata's *Souls on the Road* (*Rojō no reikon*, 1921). After the Great Earthquake of 1923, however, directors such as Hōtei Nomura and Yasujirō Shimazu began to perfect what would become Shochiku's specialty, the realist *shomin-geki* genre, which by the early 1930s had found its most distinguished exponent in Yasujirō Ozu. In this period, the company's Kamata studios in Tokyo tended to produce sophisticated and cosmopolitan stories of urban life, such as the flamboyant early melodramas of Mikio Naruse and Hiroshi Shimizu.

Shochiku's house style, however, was fully formed after its move to the new Ōfuna studios, and the term "Ōfuna flavor" quickly became synonymous with a style of subdued melodrama, typified by domestic subject matter and a subtle blend of pathos, humor, and realistic observation. Shimazu, Shimizu, Ozu, and Heinosuke Gosho all contributed to the development of this style in the thirties, and it was sustained with aesthetic distinction and rewarded with commercial success in the postwar period. Among its practitioners in the postwar era were Ozu, such younger directors as Minoru Shibuya and Keisuke Kinoshita, and lesser talents such as Hideo Ōba and Noboru Nakamura.

In the early 1960s Shochiku was substantially responsible for the birth of the Japanese New Wave, giving young directors such as Nagisa Ōshima, Masahiro Shinoda, and Yoshishige Yoshida the opportunity for formal experimentation. Although the relative commercial failure of these films led the studio away from such innovation, it had provided an impetus to several notable careers. During the sixties, Shochiku also made some interesting period films, including the early work of Hideo Gosha and Masaki Kobayashi's *Hara-Kiri* (*Seppuku*, 1962).

In the 1970s and 1980s, directors such as Yoshitarō Nomura made some distinguished thrillers at Shochiku, but its biggest commercial success of the era was Yōji Yamada's *Tora-san* (*Otoko wa tsurai yo*) series, a nostalgic recapitulation of the charm, wit, and pathos which had typified the "Ōfuna flavor." Although that flavor has grown less distinctive in recent years, Shochiku has continued to specialize primarily in comedy and melodrama to the present day.

## Toho (Tōhō, 東宝)

The precursor of Toho, PCL (Photo Chemical Laboratories) began production in 1933 with the specific intention of capitalizing on new sound technology. During the 1930s, the work of directors such as Mikio Naruse and Sotoji Kimura earned the studio a reputation for sophisticated subject matter and stylistic innovation. Toho itself was formed from the amalgamation of PCL with a smaller company, J.O., and a number of other independent production houses, and quickly became the most financially successful of the studios. During the war, Kajirō Yamamoto and others realized some noteworthy nationalist films at Toho. The wartime period also saw the debut of its most acclaimed talent, Akira Kurosawa.

Industrial action and the temporary departure of several of the studio's most important staff to form an independent company led to a crisis in the immediate postwar years, but in the 1950s, Toho balanced prestige projects with more populist fare. Among the former were Kurosawa's serious samurai films and Naruse's understated domestic dramas; among the latter were a series of comedies about white collar workers and, most famously, the *kaijū-eiga* featuring monsters such as Godzilla and mostly realized by Kurosawa's friend Ishirō Honda. These artists were joined in the 1960s by younger talents such as Kihachi Okamoto, who directed stylish action pictures.

In the 1970s, Toho co-produced the old-fashioned literary adaptations of Katsumi Nishikawa and some of Kei Kumai's best social conscience pictures, while continuing to sustain the Godzilla franchise, as, indeed, the studio has done to this day. In more recent years, the company has tended to finance expensive blockbusters, such as those directed by Isao Yukisada. Toho has also often provided distribution for independent productions, including films by *anime* outfit Studio Ghibli.

## Daiei *(大映)*

Established in 1942 from three smaller companies (Nikkatsu, Shinkō, and Daito) as part of a wartime scheme to consolidate the industry, Daiei made a handful of notable films during the war, such as Hiroshi Inagaki's *The Life of Matsu the Untamed* (*Muhō Matsu no isshō*, 1943). In the postwar period, the studio was responsible for some of the first Japanese films to achieve widespread foreign distribution, including Akira Kurosawa's *Rashomon* (*Rashōmon*, 1950) and Teinosuke Kinugasa's *Gate of Hell* (*Jigokumon*, 1953). The 1950s was Daiei's Golden Age, when directors such as Kenji Mizoguchi and Kōzaburō Yoshimura realized subtle, beautifully made human dramas, often focused on female characters, and Kon Ichikawa directed his sharp satires on social and sexual mores. Yasuzō Masumura sustained this satirical tradition at Daiei through the 1960s, and the studio also produced the socially conscious genre films of Satsuo Yamamoto during that decade. Increasingly, however, Daiei concentrated on well-crafted *chanbara*, among the best of which were the work of Kenji Misumi and Issei Mori.

In 1971, Daiei filed for bankruptcy and ceased production. The business was eventually sold to publisher Haruki Kadokawa, who had established his own company in the 1970s, producing popular big-budget entertainments helmed by such directors as Nobuhiko Ōbayashi. Kadokawa briefly preserved the old name in the combined moniker of Kadokawa Daiei Pictures Incorporated, but the company is now referred to simply as Kadokawa Pictures (Kadokawa Eiga).

## ShinToho *(ShinTōhō,* 新東宝*)*

The shortest-lived of the postwar majors, ShinToho, as its name ("New Toho") suggests, started life as an offshoot of Toho; the new company broke away from the original studio in 1947, though the parent initially continued to finance ShinToho productions. The studio's first films included some of Kon Ichikawa's early works, and it was involved in the production of notable works by such distinguished figures as Mikio Naruse and Heinosuke Gosho. Yet it had few major talents actually under contract, and soon ran into financial difficulties. These led to a change in studio policy towards more populist subject matter, and by the mid-1950s ShinToho had begun to specialize in exploitation pictures, including *chanbara*, gang films, nationalistic war movies, and horror. Among the more distinctive productions in this mode were the eerie ghost stories of Nobuo Nakagawa and the sensationalist thrillers of Teruo Ishii. The studio finally went bankrupt and ceased production in 1961. A later company, active from the 1970s in the production of pornographic films, used the same name, but was unrelated to the original ShinToho.

## Toei *(Tōei,* 東映*)*

Formed in 1951 from the merger of several small companies, Toei specialized initially in low-budget *jidai-geki*. The studio's ability to produce enough films to fill a double bill each week, its popular stars, and the crowd-pleasing appeal of its blend of action, pathos, and humor brought the company huge commercial success, and by 1957 it had become a pioneer of widescreen production. Certain distinguished directors, such as veterans Masahiro Makino, Tomu Uchida, and Tadashi Imai, made films at Toei during the late fifties and early sixties, the latter two being responsible for some of the studio's rare prestige pictures.

Gradually during the 1960s, however, Toei shifted towards yakuza films, initially of the chivalrous *ninkyō-eiga* subgenre set in the Edo, Meiji, or early Showa periods. Contributors to this school included Makino and Tai Katō. The 1970s saw a shift towards grittier yakuza pictures characterized by a hyperrealist style; the most notable exponent of these films was Kinji Fukasaku. Alongside these, the studio also produced the violent horror films and *zankoku-eiga* of Teruo Ishii. Of all the surviving studios, Toei has perhaps proved the most faithful to its original manner, continuing to produce popular films in mainly masculine genres through the 1980s and 1990s, and into the twenty-first century.

## Art Theater Guild (ATG)

Founded in 1961 as a distributor for imported foreign films and Japanese films produced outside the studio system, ATG began to fund the production of independent films in the late 1960s. Partially funded by Toho, the company was aesthetically more the child of husband-and-wife team Nagamasa and Kashiko Kawakita, who encouraged innovation in form and content. The first film produced by ATG was Nagisa Ōshima's *Death by Hanging* (*Kōshikei*, 1968), and this was followed by several more of Ōshima's best films and other distinguished works by Japanese New Wave directors, such as Yoshishige Yoshida, Susumu Hani, and Masahiro Shinoda. Experimental filmmakers Shūji Terayama and Toshio Matsumoto made important features at ATG in the early 1970s, while the company's most regular directors, each making several films there during that decade, were Akio Jissōji and Kazuo Kuroki. The relative artistic freedom offered by ATG (although with the handicap of low budgets) enticed several established studio directors, such as Kon Ichikawa, Kihachi Okamoto, and Kōichi Saitō, to make occasional art films there.

Later in the seventies, ATG increasingly began to offer opportunities to young filmmakers attempting to establish careers in cinema. Among these were Kazuhiko Hasegawa, Sōgo Ishii, Kazuki Ōmori, and Yoshimitsu Morita. The latter moved from "pink" film to the mainstream via ATG; other notable directors who had already worked in pornography but who made their first non-erotic films for ATG included Kazayuki Izutsu and Kichitarō Negishi. Thus, although the company ceased production in the mid-1980s, it shaped the careers of many prominent figures still active in modern Japanese film.

# Periods of Japanese History

Some of the following are approximate, as different historians offer slightly different dates for the different periods depending on which events are perceived to mark the transition. The earliest periods are excluded as they have not been dramatized in many films and hence are not referred to in the text.

## Nara Period (710–94)

Named after the capital established at Heijō-kyō (present-day Nara) in 710. The era was characterized by the strong influence of China, including the spread of Buddhism and use of Chinese characters in writing. The Nara period is noted for its flourishing literary culture, including seminal early works of poetry and narrative history, and for its monumental architecture.

## Heian Period (794–1185)

Named after the new capital established at Heian-kyō (present-day Kyoto) in 794. The Emperor was head of state, but real power was wielded by the Fujiwara clan, members of which served as regents. During the Heian period, Japanese culture began to evolve away from Chinese models, developing native scripts which led in turn to the creation of a sophisticated prose literature. The era also saw the establishment of influential new Buddhist sects such as those of Tendai and Shingon. A period of relative peace and stability, it is often considered the Golden Age of Japanese art and culture.

## Kamakura Period (1185–1333)

Named after the political capital of Kamakura in Eastern Japan, where Shogun Yoritomo, of the Minamoto (Genji) clan, established his *bakufu* ("tent government"). The Emperor remained a figurehead in the imperial capital of Kyoto. An age of military rule, the period was marked by violence and instability, both internally due to factional infighting, and as a consequence of two attempted Mongol invasions, both repelled. New Buddhist sects such as Zen, Jōdoshū ("Pure Land"), and Nichiren took root in Japan during this era, helping the religion to spread across all social classes. Artistically, the Kamakura period produced outstanding sculpture and distinguished works of prose.

## Muromachi Period (1333–1573)

Named after the area of Kyoto that Shogun Takauji Ashikaga made his base after the defeat of the Kamakura Shogunate and the failure of an attempt by the Emperor to regain political power. Politically, the era saw the delegation of authority to provincial lords known as *daimyō*, but Japan continued to be plagued by instability and civil war, most catastrophically, the Ōnin Wars of 1467–77, in which Kyoto was razed to the ground. Indeed, the portion of the Muromachi period from 1467 onwards, combined with the Momoyama period which succeeded it, is often referred to as the **Sengoku** (literally, "Warring States") period. Nevertheless, the Muromachi period was a time of great importance in the development of the nation's culture, witnessing the birth or refinement of such quintessentially Japanese art forms as Noh theater, tea ceremony, *ikebana*, and garden design. The austere style favored for art and architecture in this period has left its mark on Japanese aesthetics to this day.

## Momoyama Period (1573–1603)

Properly the "Azuchi-Momoyama period," named after the respective seats of power of Japan's then rulers, Nobunaga Oda and Hideyoshi Toyotomi. It was Hideyoshi who, after Oda's death, ultimately reunited Japan, defeating the rival Hōjō clan in 1590. Hideyoshi initiated trading missions abroad, but his attempts to found a foreign empire by conquering Korea were unsuccessful. The Momoyama period was characterized by a remarkable degree of foreign influence, partly due to the presence of Europeans—mainly Dutch traders and Portuguese missionaries—in Japan. This left its mark on the arts of the period, which displayed a new opulence and elaboration clearly influenced by the West.

## Edo Period (1603–1868)

Named after the new political capital of Edo (present-day Tokyo), where Shogun Ieyasu Tokugawa took up residence on becoming ruler of Japan. The era is alternatively known as the **Tokugawa** period, after the family name of Ieyasu and his successors. Having defeated his rivals at the Battle of Sekigahara in 1600, Ieyasu presided over a unified, stable, and peaceful Japan, sustained under subsequent Tokugawa Shoguns. Order was assured by regulations governing the conduct of provincial *daimyō*, and a rigid social structure developed, guided by Confucian principles. A growing isolationism led to the period of *sakoku* (literally "closed country"), whereby Japanese were forbidden to travel abroad, and, with the exception of a few merchants and traders, foreigners were prohibited from entering Japan. Christianity was banned, and many of its practitioners martyred. The urban population grew rapidly and the merchant class became larger and more socially significant. The era saw the development of new art forms such as the Kabuki and Bunraku theater, and the prints known as *ukiyo-e*, which depicted the daily life of Japanese townspeople. In the last years of the Tokugawa Shogunate, the country was destabilized by the arrival of an American government mission determined to establish trade links with Japan. Differences of opinion regarding how to deal with this foreign incursion precipitated a civil war, ultimately won by forces loyal to the Emperor.

## Meiji Period (1868–1912)

Named after the formal appellation of the reigning Emperor (literally translating as "Enlightened Rule"). In 1868 the Meiji Restoration led to the abolition of the Shogunate and returned full power to the Emperor. The Imperial capital was moved from Kyoto to Edo, which was renamed Tokyo. Drawing on Western technology, Meiji-period Japan underwent a rapid process of industrialization. There was also some cultural Westernization; a parliamentary government was established, and the new constitution was strongly influenced by that of Prussia. At the same time, nationalist ideals were encouraged, and the native Shinto faith was favored over the imported religion of Buddhism. Abroad, Japan initiated a policy of imperialism, annexing the Ryūkyū Kingdom (present-day Okinawa), Formosa (Taiwan), and ultimately Korea, achieving substantial economic concessions in China, and defeating Russia in the Russo-Japanese War of 1904–5. The arts of the Meiji period were notable for a creative fusion of Japanese and Western influences. The cinema reached Japan late in the era, and the earliest Japanese fiction films, mostly inspired by Kabuki narratives, were produced.

## Taisho (Taishō) Period (1912–26)

Named after the formal appellation of the reigning Emperor (literally "Great Righteousness"). This brief period was characterized by efforts to introduce democratic reforms and a fashionable Westernization among the bourgeoisie, which left its mark on the period's Hollywood-influenced silent cinema. Less fortunate aspects of the era included unrest among farmers and industrial workers, and the 1923 Great Kantō Earthquake, which devastated Tokyo and Yokohama.

## Showa (Shōwa) Period (1926–89)

Named after the formal appellation of the reigning Emperor (literally "Enduring Peace"). Early in the era, the Great Depression led to an increase in nationalist sentiments, and the military was able to consolidate its power over a weakened civilian government. In 1931 Japanese troops invaded Manchuria and in the following year established the puppet state of Manchukuo. In 1937, an all-out attack on China was launched, bringing much of the eastern part of the country, including Beijing and Shanghai, under Japanese control. An oil embargo imposed in response by the United States persuaded Japanese leaders to order a surprise attack on the U.S. naval base of Pearl Harbor in December 1941, bringing Japan into World War II (the "Pacific War," in Japanese terminology) on the Axis side. Intensive bombing of Japanese cities, including the dropping of atomic bombs on Hiroshima and Nagasaki, led eventually to Japan's surrender, and American troops occupied the country until 1952. During this time a new liberal constitution was drafted, guaranteeing human rights and renouncing war. After the Occupation ended, close ties with the U.S. were sustained by the ruling conservative Liberal Democratic Party, which has governed almost uninterrupted since 1955. The efficiency of its manufacturing industries allowed postwar Japan to experience a sustained period of economic growth, transforming itself from an underdeveloped country to one of the world's most prosperous nations. The 1980s was the era of the bubble economy, when spiraling land prices fed an unprecedented, but temporary, economic boom.

The dominant art forms of the Showa period were prose literature and cinema. Jun'ichirō Tanizaki, Yasunari Kawabata, and Yukio Mishima wrote outstanding novels, while directors such as Kenji Mizoguchi, Yasujirō Ozu, and Akira Kurosawa made the 1930s and 1950s the two acknowledged Golden Ages of Japanese film. The 1960s saw the finest products of the

Japanese New Wave, but the distinction of the country's cinema faded in the last two decades of the era.

## Heisei Period (1989–present)

Named after the formal appellation of the reigning Emperor (literally "Achieving Peace"). In the early 1990s the bubble economy of the late Showa period collapsed and Japan entered a prolonged economic slump, from which, despite attempts at economic liberalization, it has yet fully to emerge. Traditional guarantees of lifetime employment began to be eroded, and a new class of low-paid temporary workers ("freeters") emerged. A subtle resurgence of nationalism was apparent during the five-year premiership of Jun'ichirō Koizumi. In the cinema, the Heisei period has seen the rise of independent filmmakers and the international success of Japanese horror films.

# Select Bibliography

This Bibliography is not intended as an absolutely complete list of everything I have read about Japanese cinema while writing this book. It lists all of my main and most of my tangential sources of information and critical commentary, but its primary function is as a reading list for those interested in exploring what has been written about Japanese film in greater depth. Accordingly, being aware that most of my readers will not read Japanese, I have concentrated on English-language books. However, the major Japanese-language film histories are as follows:

Satō, Tadao: *Nihon eiga shi* (*A History of Japanese Film*), 4 vols., 1995, Iwanami Shoten, Tokyo.

Tanaka, Jun'ichirō: *Nihon eiga hattatsu shi* (*A History of the Developments of Japanese Film*), 3 vols., 1957, Chūō Kōron, Tokyo; updated with vol. 4 in 1967 and vol. 5 in 1980.

Yamada, Kazuo: *Nihon eiga no hachijūnen* (*Eighty Years of the Japanese Film*), 1976, Issei-sha, Tokyo.

Yomota, Inuhiko: *Nihon eigashi no hyakunen* (*One-Hundred-Year History of the Japanese Film*), 2000, Shūeisha, Tokyo.

Indispensable as a source of factual information, and vital in the production of the filmographies, has been *Nihon eiga jinmei jiten: Kantoku hen* (*Illustrated Who's Who of Japanese Cinema: Directors*, Kinema Junpōsha, Tokyo, 1997). This has been my main source for the titles of films made before 1997. In all cases I have also compared the online filmographies of the Japanese Movie Database (www.jmdb.ne.jp), which includes films made up to 2004. I have verified the titles of the most recent films from official websites, the annual UniJapan magazines, newspaper reviews, and, where no other source is available, the Japanese-language edition of the internet encyclopedia *Wikipedia* (www.wikipedia.org). Where sources differ, I have referred to original issues of *Kinema Junpō*.

Where a film is preserved in the archive of the Film Center in Tokyo, I have checked the *National Film Center Film Catalog 2000: Japanese Feature Films* (Tōkyō kokuritsu kindai bijutsukan, Tokyo, 2001), which gives reliable readings in kana script for included titles. Another book that supplies kana readings for many films is *PIA Shinemakurabu: Nihon eiga hen: 2006–7* (PIA, Tokyo, 2006). For documentary directors, the filmographies in *Documentary Box* (the journal of the Yamagata International Documentary Film Festival, reproduced online at www.yiddf.jp) have often proved the most comprehensive (this journal has also been a useful source for discussion of Japanese documentary films). Although they have already been thanked in the Acknowledgments, I should finally mention again here the assistance of Roland Domenig, Atsuko Fukuda, Aaron Gerow, Hiroshi Komatsu, and Michael McCaskey in verifying certain awkward titles where neither the available sources nor my Japanese-language skills were sufficient.

In English, I have made use of general reference works for transliterations and translations: these are Stephen Cremin: *The Asian Film Library Reference to Japanese Film* (Asian Film Library, London, 1998) and Stuart Galbraith IV: *The Japanese Filmography* (see reference below). Also useful, both for supplying readings of film titles and for providing brief plot summaries, have been the annual UniJapan publications: *Japanese Films* (1958–75) and *Selected Japanese Feature Films* (1975–present). For directors active during the silent era, I have used the filmographies included in the CD-ROM *Masterpieces of Japanese Silent Cinema* (2000, Urban Connections), compiled from the Matsuda Film Library. I have also consulted many other published filmographies, including those in books devoted to particular directors listed in the English-language bibliography below. Online, I have checked the filmographies on the Internet Movie Database (www.imdb.com), which I have used as a source for translations where others do not exist. However, I have not relied solely on English-language sources for my transliterations: I have always confirmed readings with Japanese sources and/or native speakers.

The list of English-language materials below is confined to books; there are, of course, many short articles in English on Japanese cinema, which for practical purposes it has not been possible to list here. I have also drawn some factual information and quoted critical commentary from festival catalogues and retrospective programs at both Western and Japanese cinemas, and have occasionally quoted from sleeve notes of DVD releases of Japanese films. Again, I do not have space to list all these individually, but where necessary credit has been given to the relevant authors in the text.

Internet resources have proliferated in recent years, but sadly many are inaccurate and poorly written. It is, however, worth mentioning the best of them. The major webzine in English devoted to Japanese cinema is *Midnight Eye* (www.midnighteye.com), a useful source of reviews, interviews, and articles, focusing primarily but not exclusively on modern films. Various medium-length articles on Japanese directors, including some of my own, are online at *Senses of Cinema* (www.sensesofcinema.com). *Japan Film News: Ryuganji* (www.ryuganji. net) and *Twitch* (www.twitchfilm.net) are often useful for up-to-date information about new releases and other news. In Japanese, *Goo* (http://movie.goo.ne.jp) has helpful plot summaries and factual information.

The following is a list of notable English-language books about Japanese film. It is not exhaustive but includes all those I have quoted or consulted in writing this book. For those relatively new to Japanese cinema and wondering where to start, I have marked about twenty favorite books in bold, with brief descriptions. I admit to a bias towards books that occupy a middle ground between journalism and academia, and most of my recommendations fall into that category (as, I hope, does this book).

## List of English-language Books on Japanese Film

Anderson, Joseph, and Donald Richie: *The Japanese Film: Art and Industry*, 1982, Princeton University Press, Princeton, NJ.

> *Although it focuses primarily on Japanese cinema up to its original publication date of 1959, this text—the first account of its subject in English—remains indispensable for any fan or student.*

Barrett, Gregory: *Archetypes in Japanese Film: The Sociopolitical and Religious Signifiers of the Principal Heroes and Heroines*, 1989, Susquehanna University Press/London Associated University Presses, Selinsgrove.

Bernardi, Joanne: *Writing in Light: The Silent Scenario and the Japanese Pure Film Movement*, 2001, Wayne State University Press, Detroit.

> *Thoroughly researched and detailed study of an important movement in Japanese silent film: provides much useful information about films which sadly no longer survive.*

Bock, Audie: *Japanese Film Directors*, 1978, Kodansha International for the Japan Society and Phaidon, Tokyo; New York and Oxford.

*Somewhat outdated but informative and critically perceptive extended introductory essays on ten major Japanese filmmakers.*

Broderick, Mick (ed.): *Hibakusha cinema: Hiroshima, Nagasaki, and the Nuclear Image in Japanese Film*, 1996, Paul International, London.

Buehrer, Beverley Bare: *Japanese Films: A Filmography and Commentary, 1921–1989*, 1990, St. James Press, London.

Burch, Noel: *To the Distant Observer: Form and Meaning in the Japanese Cinema*, 1979, Scolar Press, London.

*Tendentious but important study of Japanese films, focusing on their deviation from the stylistic norms of Western cinema; infuriating and fascinating in equal measure, with useful chapters on such overlooked directors as Hiroshi Shimizu and Tamizō Ishida.*

Buruma, Ian: *Behind the Mask: On Sexual Demons, Sacred Mothers, Transvestites, Gangsters, Drifters and Other Japanese Cultural Heroes*, 1984, Pantheon Books, New York.

Buruma, Ian: *A Japanese Mirror: Heroes and Villains of Japanese Culture*, 1985, Penguin, Harmondsworth.

Cazdyn, Eric: *The Flash of Capital: Film and Geopolitics in Japan*, 2002, Duke University Press, Durham, NC.

Davis, Darrell William: *Picturing Japaneseness: Monumental Style National Identity, Japanese Film*, 1996, Columbia University Press, New York.

D(esjardins), Chris: *Outlaw Masters of Japanese Film*, 2005, I. B. Tauris, London and New York.

Desser, David: *Eros plus Massacre: An Introduction to the Japanese New Wave Cinema*, 1988, Indiana University Press, Bloomington.

Friends of the Silent Films Association (ed.): *Recalling the Treasures of Japanese Cinema*, 2003, Urban Connections, Tokyo.

Galbraith, Stuart, IV: *The Japanese Filmography: A Complete Reference Guide to 200 Filmmakers and over 1,250 Films Released in the United States, 1900 through 1994*, 1996, McFarland, Jefferson, NC; London.

Galbraith, Stuart, IV: *Japanese Science Fiction, Fantasy and Horror Films: A Critical Analysis of 103 Features Released in the United States, 1950–1992*, 1994, McFarland, Jefferson, NC; London.

Galloway, Patrick: *Stray Dogs and Lone Wolves: The Samurai Film Handbook*, 2005, Stone Bridge Press, Berkeley, CA.

High, Peter B.: *The Imperial Screen: Japanese Film Culture in the Fifteen Years' War, 1931–1945*, 2003, University of Wisconsin Press, Madison, WI.

*Superb academic study of prewar and wartime cinema in the context of the rise and fall of Japanese militarism: likely to remain the definitive word on its subject.*

Hirano, Kyoko: *Mr. Smith Goes to Tokyo: The Japanese Cinema under the American Occupation, 1945–1952*, 1992, Smithsonian Institute, Washington, DC.

*Fascinating account of the difficulties of filmmaking during the postwar Occupation: focus on historical context rather than critical analysis.*

Macias, Patrick: *Tokyoscope: The Japanese Cult Film Companion*, 2001, Cadence Books, San Francisco.

McDonald, Keiko I.: *Cinema East: A Critical Study of Major Japanese Films*, 1983, University Presses, East Brunswick, NJ.

McDonald, Keiko I.: *Japanese Classical Theater in Films*, 1994, Dickinson University Press, Associated University Presses, Rutherford; London.

McDonald, Keiko I.: *Reading a Japanese Film: Cinema in Context*, 2006, University of Hawai'i Press, Honolulu.

Mellen, Joan: *Voices from the Japanese Cinema*, 1975, Liveright, New York.

> *Important collection of interviews with major figures of the Japanese cinema up to the seventies; contains much material not otherwise available in English.*

Mellen, Joan: *The Waves at Genji's Door: Japan through Its Cinema*, 1976, Pantheon, New York.

> *Wide-ranging examination of Japanese culture through its cinema, from a left-wing, feminist perspective. There are a few too many factual errors, and ideology sometimes overpowers analysis, but a fascinating book, nevertheless.*

Mes, Tom, and Jasper Sharp: *The Midnight Eye Guide to New Japanese Film*, 2005, Stone Bridge Press, Berkeley.

> *Profiles of twenty major modern filmmakers, with much useful material taken from interviews with the directors concerned; style is enthusiastic to the point of breathlessness, but this is the most comprehensive treatment of its subject in English.*

Nolletti, Jr., Arthur, and David Desser (eds.): *Reframing Japanese Cinema: Authorship, Genre, History*, 1992, Indiana University Press, Bloomington and Indianapolis.

Nornes, Abe Markus: *Japanese Documentary Film: The Meiji Era through Hiroshima*, 2003, University of Minnesota Press, Minneapolis; London.

Oshima, Nagisa: *Cinema, Censorship and the State: The Writings of Oshima Nagisa* (trans. Dawn Lawson), 1992, MIT Press, Cambridge, MA.

> *Collection of Ōshima's writings on film and politics: important to an understanding of this most political of filmmakers.*

Phillips, Alastair, and Julian Stringer (ed.): *Japanese Cinema: Texts and Contexts*, 2007, Routledge, Abingdon and New York.

> *Stimulating collection of academic essays analyzing individual films in depth; contributors include many eminent names in Japanese film criticism, along with the author of the present work.*

Richie, Donald: *Japanese Cinema: Film Style and National Character*, 1972, Secker and Warburg, London.

Richie, Donald: *The Japanese Movie*, 1982, Kodansha International, Tokyo.

Richie, Donald: *Japanese Cinema: An Introduction*, 1990, Oxford University Press, Hong Kong and Oxford.

Richie, Donald: *A Hundred Years of Japanese Film*, 2005, Kodansha International, Tokyo.

> *The most recent of Richie's several histories. Should be used in tandem with* The Japanese Film: Art and Industry, *which treats the early years in greater detail; this brings the story up to date.*

Sato, Tadao: *Currents in Japanese Cinema: Essays* (trans. Gregory Barrett), 1982, Kodansha International, Tokyo.

> *Perceptive essays by Japan's most respected film critic: an opportunity, still too rare, for non-Japanese speakers to approach the Japanese film from a local perspective.*

Schilling, Mark: *Contemporary Japanese Film*, 1999, Weatherhill, New York.

> *Collection of essays and reviews from the regular critic of the* Japan Times; *contains much information about directors neglected in the West. Schilling's more recent writings on film can be consulted on the* Japan Times *website.*

Schilling, Mark: *The Yakuza Movie Book: A Guide to Japanese Gangster Films*, 2003, Stone Bridge Press, Berkeley.

Silver, Alain: *The Samurai Film*, 1983, Overlook, Woodstock, New York.

Standish, Isolde: *Myths and Masculinity in the Japanese Cinema: Towards a Political Reading of the "Tragic Hero,"* 2000, Curzon, Richmond, Surrey.

Standish, Isolde: *A New History of Japanese Cinema: A Century of Narrative Film*, 2005, Continuum, London.

Svensson, Arne: *Japan*, 1971, Zwemmer/Barnes, New York.

Thornton, S. A.: *The Japanese Period Film: A Critical Analysis*, 2007, McFarland, Jefferson, NC.

Tucker, Richard N.: *Japan, Film Image*, 1973, Studio Vista, London.

Washburn, Dennis, and Carole Cavanaugh (eds.): *Word and Image in Japanese Cinema*, 2001, Cambridge University Press, Cambridge.

Weisser, Thomas, and Yuko Mihara Weisser: *Japanese Cinema Encyclopedia: The Sex Films*, 1998, Vital Books, Miami.

Weisser, Thomas, and Yuko Mihara Weisser: *Japanese Cinema: Essential Handbook*, 1998 (Revised Edition), Vital Books, Miami.

## Books about Individual Directors

Allyn, John: *Kon Ichikawa: A Guide to References and Resources*, 1985, G. K. Hall, Boston.

Andrew, Dudley, and Carole Cavanaugh: *Sansho Dayu*, 2000, BFI, London. (*on Mizoguchi*)

Andrew, Dudley, and Paul Andrew: *Kenji Mizoguchi: A Guide to References and Resources*, 1981, G. K. Hall, Boston.

Bock, Audie: *Naruse: A Master of the Japanese Cinema*, 1984, Art University of Chicago, Chicago.

Bordwell, David: *Ozu and the Poetics of Cinema*, 1988, BFI Publishing, Princeton University Press, London and Princeton, NJ.

> *Detailed account of Ozu's films, from a formalist perspective; more descriptive than analytical, but vital to an understanding of the director.*

Breakwell, Ian: *An Actor's Revenge (Yukinojo Henge)*, 1994, BFI Publishing, London. (*on Kon Ichikawa*)

Desser, David: *The Samurai Films of Akira Kurosawa*, 1983, UMI Research, Ann Arbor.

Ellen, Patricia: *Akira Kurosawa: A Guide to References and Resources*, 1979, G. K. Hall, Boston.

Freiburg, Freda: *Women in Mizoguchi's Films*, 1981, Japanese Studies Centre, Melbourne.

Galbraith, Stuart, IV: *The Emperor and the Wolf: The Lives and Films of Akira Kurosawa and Toshiro Mifune*, 2002, Faber and Faber, New York and London.

> *Exceptionally well-written and informative joint biography of Kurosawa and his regular star.*

Gerow, Aaron: *Kitano Takeshi*, 2007, British Film Institute, London.

*Excellent study of one of the Japanese cinema's most important modern filmmakers, by a knowledgeable and meticulous writer.*

Goodwin, James: *Akira Kurosawa and Intertextual Cinema*, 1994, Hopkins University Press, Baltimore.

Goodwin, James (ed.): *Perspectives on Akira Kurosawa*, 1994, G. K. Hall, New York.

Jacobs, Brian (ed.), *"Beat" Takeshi Kitano*, 1999, Tadao, RM Europe, Edgeware.

Kirihara, Donald: *Patterns of Time: Mizoguchi and the 1930s*, 1992, University of Wisconsin Press, Madison, WI.

Kurosawa, Akira: *Something Like an Autobiography* (trans. Audie Bock), 1982, Knopf, New York.

*The autobiography of Japan's most internationally renowned filmmaker: a crucial text for any Kurosawa fan.*

Le Fanu, Mark: *Mizoguchi and Japan*, 2005, British Film Institute, London.

*Passionate and beautifully written critical study of perhaps Japan's greatest director, from a liberal humanist perspective.*

McDonald, Keiko I.: *Mizoguchi*, 1984, Twayne Publishers, Boston.

Mellen, Joan: *Seven Samurai*, 2002, BFI Publishing, London.

Mes, Tom: *Iron Man: The Cinema of Shinya Tsukamoto*, 2005, FAB Press, London.

Mes, Tom: *Agitator: The Cinema of Takashi Miike*, 2006, FAB Press, London.

Nolletti, Jr., Arthur: *The Cinema of Gosho Heinosuke: Laughter Through Tears*, 2005, Indiana University Press, Bloomington.

*Intelligent and engaging study of the work of a major filmmaker still neglected in the West. A model for academic writing on film.*

Nornes, Abe Mark: *Forest of Pressure: Ogawa Shinsuke and Postwar Japanese Documentary*, 2007, University of Minnesota Press, Minneapolis; London.

*Splendid account of the life and work of Japan's most important documentary filmmaker, by a collaborator and personal friend; informative and impassioned.*

O'Grady, Gerald (ed.): *Mizoguchi the Master*, 1996, Cinematheque Ontario, Toronto.

*Collection of articles and interviews produced to accompany a major Mizoguchi retrospective; vital reading for any admirer of this great director.*

Prince, Stephen: *The Warrior's Camera: The Cinema of Akira Kurosawa*, 1999, Princeton University Press, Princeton, NJ.

Quandt, James (ed.): *Shohei Imamura*, 1997, Toronto International Film Festival Group, Toronto.

Quandt, James (ed.): *Kon Ichikawa*, 2001, Cinematheque Ontario, Toronto.

Richie, Donald: *The Films of Akira Kurosawa*, 1999, University of California Press, Berkeley.

Richie, Donald: *Ozu: His Life and Films*, 1977, University of California Press, Berkeley.

Schrader, Paul: *Transcendental Style in Film: Ozu, Bresson, Dreyer*, 1972, University of California Press, Berkeley; London.

Turim, Maureen: *The Films of Nagisa Oshima: Images of a Japanese Iconoclast*, 1998, University of California Press, Berkeley.

Yoshida, Kiju (Yoshishige): *Ozu's Anti-Cinema* (trans. Kyoko Hirano and Miyao Daisuke), 2003, University of Michigan Center for Japanese Studies, Ann Arbor.

*Study of a classical filmmaker by a New Wave director; supplies a useful Japanese perspective on an outstanding artist.*

Yoshimoto, Mitsuhiro: *Kurosawa: Film Studies and Japanese Cinema*, 2000, Duke University Press, Durham, NC.

# Index of Names

*This is an index of names only. Due to the sheer number of films listed and referred to in this guide, it has not been practical to supply an index of film titles. In addition to the directors who have full entries in the text, all other film personnel mentioned in the text are referenced here, as are authors of original novels and so forth. I also include historical or mythical figures who have been depicted in films, if they are themselves mentioned in the text. However, they are not indexed if their names have merely been used as film titles. Similarly, critics quoted in the text are indexed, but where their books are merely listed in the Bibliography, I have excluded them from the Index.*